Theory and Practice of the European Convention on Human Rights

by

P. van Dijk
G.J.H. van Hoof

Second Edition

Kluwer Law and Taxation Publishers
Deventer - Boston

Kluwer Law and Taxation Publishers
P.O. Box 23   Tel.: 31-5700-47261
7400 GA Deventer   Telex: 49295
The Netherlands   Fax: 31-5700-22244

ISBN: 90 6544 319 3

to P.J.G. Kapteyn
who introduced us into principles
of international law and humanity

FROM THE PREFACE TO THE FIRST EDITION

.....

The present book is designed to serve a twofold purpose: it is meant to be a general textbook for university courses as well as a guide to practising lawyers.

As a textbook it may be used both as reading material and as a basis for discussion within the framework of courses and seminars on, *inter alia*, public international law, the law of international organizations, European law, constitutional law, national and international criminal law, and, of course, special courses and seminars on the international law of human rights. The book has been set up in such a way that it can be assigned for reading as a whole - for instance, when a teacher does not intend to cover all issues of the European Convention on Human Rights, but still wants the students to prepare for discussing any of these issues - or in part, when only one or a number of the provisions contained in the Convention are relevant to the subject matter of a particular course or seminar.

With regard to both students and practising lawyers, the book provides them first of all with a general survey of the history, the structure, and the functioning of the Convention. Its main part, however, is devoted to an elaborate description of the Convention's supervisory procedures and an extensive analysis of the rights and freedoms contained therein, based mainly upon the "Strasbourg" case-law, *i.e.* the decisions on admissibility and the reports of the European Commission of Human Rights, the judgments of the European Court of Human Rights and - to a lesser extent - the resolutions of the Committee of Ministers of the Council of Europe. Extensive references to this case-law are included in the footnotes particularly for the benefit of practising lawyers, although they may prove useful also to students, for instance, as an aid in writing a comprehensive paper on a specific issue.

An analysis of the national case-law of the Contracting States related to the Convention has not been undertaken, because this would not only have exceeded the scope of the present book, but also the expertise of its authors.

Reference to the literature has been confined to cases where this offers additional authority or an additional explanation and therefore furthers a better understanding of the issue concerned.

.....

The theory and practice of the European Convention on Human Rights are important first and foremost to law-students and legal practitioners in Member

States of the Council of Europe. Nevertheless, the Convention's relevance may go beyond this now that the International Covenant on Civil and Political Rights and, more recently, the American Convention on Human Rights have entered into force. Both these latter instruments contain a larger number of provisions which are very similar to those contained in the Convention. It may therefor be expected that the theory and practice of the European Convention will gain the interest of an increasing number of students and practioners from outside the Council of Europe countries. This book is intended to guide them in that interest.

.....

February 1984
P. van Dijk
Bilthoven, the Netherlands

G.J.H. van Hoof
IJsselstein, the Netherlands

PREFACE TO THE SECOND EDITION

It is a cause for great satisfaction to the authors that, together with the third edition of the Dutch version of the book, this second edition of the English version is now published. Developments under the European Convention on Human Rights, in particular of its case-law, have been so fast and numerous, that a revision of the book was overdue. Its publication would seem to be right in time for the many governmental and private persons in Central and Eastern Europe, who have a great interest in the Convention and its case-law in view of a possible accession of their respective States to the Convention.

From the start the book was set up as a survey and analysis of the Strasbourg case-law. Due to the further elaboration of that case-law by the Commission and the Court, there was even less necessity for complementary references to literature, which, moreover, would have made the notes even longer and more numerous than they are now.

Both for teaching purposes and for legal practice the book may well be used in combination with the "Digest of Strasbourg Case-Law relating to the European Convention on Human Rights", which has been prepared under the supervision of the authors by Mr. Leo Zwaak of the Netherlands Institute of Human Rights (S.I.M.) in cooperation with the Division of Human Rights of the Council of Europe. At the present moment six volumes of the Digest and three loose-leave updates have been published by Carl Heymanns Verlag, while additional updates will follow.

This second edition would have been impossible without the extensive research assistance of Mr. Leo Zwaak and Ms. Els Tange, who for their part were assisted by other persons at times. The authors fully acknowledge their valuable contribution. Moreover, as in the case of the first edition, Miss Cary Dikshoorn was of great help in checking the English terminology and reading proofs. Mrs. Marcella van Beusekom-Kiel and Carla Groenestein typed and retyped the whole manuscript with their usual, but not less admirable care and patience, while Jacqueline Smith, the editor of the Netherlands Institute for Social and Economic law Research (NISER), transformed the manuscript into camera-ready pages. To all of them the authors wish to express their sincere gratitude.

Any comments, observations and suggestions from the users of the book will be welcomed by the authors.

July 1990
P. van Dijk
Bilthoven, the Netherlands

G.J.H. van Hoof
IJsselstein, the Netherlands

TABLE OF CONTENTS

CHAPTER III
THE EXAMINATION OF A CASE BY THE EUROPEAN
COURT OF HUMAN RIGHTS   133

CHAPTER VII
PROVISIONS CONCERNING ENJOYMENT OF THE RIGHTS
AND FREEDOMS AND CONCERNING RESTRICTION OF
THESE RIGHTS AND FREEDOMS

LIST OF ABBREVATIONS

A.J.I.L.	American Journal of International Law
B.Y.I.L.	British Yearbook of International Law
Bulletin E.C.	Bulletin of the European Communities
Coll.	Collection of Decisions of the European Commission of Human Rights
Cons.Ass.	Consultative Assembly of the Council of Europe
D & R	Decisions and Reports of the European Commission of Human Rights
E.C.	European Communities
EuGRZ	Europäische Grundrechte Zeitschrift
HRLJ	Human Rights Law Journal
I.C.J. Reports	International Court of Justice, Reports of Judgments, Advisory Opinions and Orders
ILC	International Law Commission
ILM	International Legal Materials
ILO	International Labour Organization
Jur.	Case-Law of the Court of Justice of the European Communities
Parl.Ass.	Parliamentary Assembly of the Council of Europe
P.C.I.J., Series A	Permanent Court of International Justice, Collection of Judgments
Publ. E.C.H.R., Series A	Publications of the European Court of Human Rights; Judgments and Decisions
Publ. E.C.H.R., Series B	Publications of the European Court of Human Rights; Pleadings, Oral Arguments and Documents
R.C.A.D.I.	Recueil des Cours de l'Académie de Droit International de la Haye
R.D.H.	Revue des Droits de l'Homme
Res.	Resolution
U.N. Doc.	United Nations Documents
U.N.T.S.	United Nations Treaty Series
Yearbook	Yearbook of the European Convention on Human Rights

American Journal of International Law
British Yearbook of International Law
Bulletin of the European Economic Community
Collection of Decisions of the European Commission
of Human Rights
Consultative Assembly of the Council of Europe
Decisions and Reports of the European Commission
of Human Rights
European Commission
Europäische Grundrechte Zeitschrift
Human Rights Law Journal
International Court of Justice, Reports of Judgments,
Advisory Opinions and Orders
Inter-American Law Commission
International Law Commission
International Law Reports
Classeur of the Court of Justice of the European
Communities
Parliamentary Assembly of the Council of Europe
Permanent Court of International Justice, Collection
of Judgments
Publications of the European Court of Human
Rights, Series A and Series B
Publication of Documents and Materials of the
Legal Proceedings Instruments
Recueil des Arrêts, Français... 1968
Internationale de la Haye
Revue du Droit de l'Homme
Resolution
United Nations Documents
United Nations Treaty Series
Yearbook of the European Convention on Human
Rights

CHAPTER I

GENERAL SURVEY OF THE EUROPEAN CONVENTION

§ 1. THE GENESIS OF THE CONVENTION[1]

1. The European Convention for the Protection of Human Rights and Fundamental Freedoms is a product of the period shortly after the Second World War, when the issue of international protection of human rights attracted a great deal of attention. These rights had been crushed by the atrocities of National Socialism, and the guarantee of their protection at the national level had proved completely inadequate.

2. As early as 1941 Churchill and Roosevelt, in the Atlantic Charter, launched their four freedoms: freedom of life, freedom of religion, freedom from want and freedom from fear. After the Second World War the promotion of respect for human rights and fundamental freedoms became one of the aims of the United Nations. Within that framework the Universal Declaration of Human Rights, which was adopted on 10 December 1948 by the General Assembly of the United Nations, became a significant milestone.

3. Meanwhile, preliminary steps were also taken at the European level. In May 1948 the International Committee of the Movements for European Unity organized a "Congress of Europe" in The Hague. This initiative gave the decisive impetus to the foundation of the Council of Europe in 1949. At the Congress a resolution was adopted, the introductory part of which reads as follows:

> The Congress
> Considers that the resultant union or federation should be open to all European nations democratically governed and which undertake to respect a Charter of Human Rights;
> Resolves that a Commission should be set up to undertake immediately the double task of drafting such a Charter and of laying down standards to which a State must conform if it is to deserve the name of democracy.

These matters formed the subject of a discussion during the first session of the Consultative Assembly (at present called the Parliamentary Assembly) of the Council of Europe in August 1949. The Assembly charged its Committee on Legal and Administrative Questions to consider in more detail the matter of a collective guarantee of human rights.

---

1. Council of Europe, *Manual of the Council of Europe*, London 1970, pp. 3-7, 261-264; G.L. Weil, *The European Convention on Human Rights, European Aspects*, Series C, no. 12, Leyden 1963, pp. 21-40.

4. From that moment onwards the Convention was drafted in a relatively short time. In September of the same year the Assembly adopted the Committee's report, in which ten rights were included that were to be the subjects of a collective guarantee, and the establishment of a European Commission of Human Rights and a European Court of Justice was proposed. In November of that year the Committee of Ministers of the Council of Europe decided to appoint a Committee of Government Experts, which was entrusted with the task of preparing a draft text on the basis of this report.

This Committee completed its work in the spring of 1950. It had made considerable headway, but it failed to find a solution to a number of political problems. The subsequently appointed Committee of Senior Officials was also forced to leave the ultimate decision on a number of matters to the Committee of Ministers, even though it reached agreement about the greater part of the text of the Committee of Experts.

On 7 August 1950 the Committee of Ministers approved a revised draft text, which went considerably less far than the original proposals on a number of points. For example, the system of individual applications and the jurisdiction of the Court were made optional. This draft text was not substantially altered afterwards.

5. On 4 November 1950 the Convention, which according to its preamble was framed "to take the first steps for collective enforcement of certain rights stated in the Universal Declaration", was signed in Rome.[2] It entered into force on 3 September 1953 and at the moment has been ratified by twenty-two Member States of the Council of Europe: Austria, Belgium, Cyprus, Denmark, the Federal Republic of Germany, France, Greece,[3] Iceland, Ireland, Italy, Liechtenstein, Luxembourg, Malta, the Netherlands, Norway, Portugal, San Marino, Spain, Sweden, Switzerland, Turkey and the United Kingdom. Finland has become a member of the Council of Europe on 5 May 1989, has also signed the Convention, but at present (January 1990) not yet ratified. Meanwhile Hungary and Poland have shown their desire to become Members of the Council of Europe and as a consequence thereof to become parties to the Convention.

Up to the present, eight Protocols have been added to the Convention,[4]

---

2.   213 *U.N.T.S.*, p. 221, no. 2889; Council of Europe, European Treaty Series, 4 November 1950, no. 5; Council of Europe, *Collected Texts*, Strasbourg 1987, pp. 3-21.
3.   Greece withdrew from the Council of Europe in 1969, but in 1974 became a member again and re-ratified the Convention.
4.   Protocol no. 1 of 20 March 1952 entered into force on 18 May 1954; Council of Europe, *European Treaty Series*, 20 March 1952, no. 9; Protocols nos 2 and 3 of 6 May 1963 entered into force on 21 September 1970; *ibidem*, 6 May 1963, nos 44 and 45; Protocol no. 4 of 16 September 1963 entered into force on 2 May 1968; *ibidem*, 16 September 1963, no. 46; Protocol no. 5 of 20 January 1966 entered into force on 20 December 1971; *ibidem*, 20 January 1966, no. 55. Protocol no. 6 of 28 April 1983 entered into force on 1 March 1983; *ibidem*, 28 April 1983, no. 114; Protocol no. 7 of 22 November 1984 entered into force on 1 November 1988; *ibidem*, 22 November 1984, no. 117; Protocol no. 8 of 19 March 1985 entered into force on 1 January 1990; *ibidem*, 19 March 1985, no. 118. The English text of all Protocols is included in Council of Europe, *Collected Texts*, Strasbourg 1987,
                                                                                          (continued...)

but not all of them have been ratified by all the contracting States.[5]

§ 2. THE STRUCTURE OF THE CONVENTION

1. Under Article 1 of the Convention the contracting States are bound to secure to everyone within their jurisdiction the rights and freedoms set forth in Section I of the Convention. To the extent that a State has ratified the First, Fourth, Sixth, or Seventh Protocol, this obligation also applies to the rights and freedoms laid down in these Protocols, since the latter are considered as supplementary articles of the Convention, to which all the provisions of the Convention apply in a similar way.[6]

As stated above, the contracting States must secure these rights and freedoms to "everyone within their jurisdiction". These words of Article 1 do not imply any limitation as to nationality. Even those who are not nationals either of the State concerned or of any one of the other contracting States may claim this guarantee when they are in some respect subject to the jurisdiction of the State from which they claim that guarantee.[7] Furthermore it is irrelevant whether they have their residence inside or outside the territory of that State.[8]

4.(...continued)
pp. 23-65. Protocols nos 3, 5 and 8 have been incorporated as amendments into the text of the Convention.
5. Protocol no. 1 has not been ratified by Liechtenstein, Spain and Switzerland. Protocols nos 2 and 3 have been ratified by all the contracting States. Protocol no. 4 has not been signed by Greece, Liechtenstein, Malta, Switzerland and Turkey, and has been signed, but not yet ratified by Spain and the United Kingdom. Protocol no. 5 has been ratified by all the contracting States. Protocol no. 6 has not been signed by Cyprus, Ireland, Liechtenstein, Malta, Turkey and the United Kingdom, and signed, but not yet ratified, by Belgium and Greece. Protocol no. 7 has not been signed by Belgium, Cyprus, Liechtenstein, Malta and the United Kingdom, and signed, but not yet ratified, by the Federal Republic of Germany, Ireland, Italy, the Netherlands, Portugal, Spain and Turkey. Protocol no. 8 has been ratified by all member States. See *Chart showing Signatures and Ratifications of Conventions and Agreements concluded within the Council of Europe*, Strasbourg.
6. See Art. 5 of the First Protocol, Art. 6(1) of the Fourth Protocol, Art. 6 of the Sixth Protocol and Art. 7(1) of the Seventh Protocol.
7. See, e.g., Appl. 788/60, *Austria v. Italy, Yearbook* IV (1961), p. 116 (138) and (140): "Whereas, therefore, in becoming a Party to the Convention, a State undertakes, vis-à-vis the other High Contracting Parties, to secure the rights and freedoms defined in Section I to every person within its jurisdiction, regardless of their nationality or status; whereas, in short, it undertakes to secure these rights and freedoms not only to its own nationals and those of other High Contracting Parties, but also to nationals of States not parties to the Convention and to stateless persons".
8. The Consultative Assembly had proposed in the draft for the Convention the words "all persons residing within the territories of the signatory States", but these were changed by the Committee of Experts in the sense mentioned. See Report of the Committee of Experts to the Committee of Ministers, Council of Europe, *Collected Edition of the "Travaux Préparatoires" of the European Convention on Human Rights*, vol. IV, The Hague 1977, p. 20: "It was felt that there were good grounds for extending the benefits of the Convention to all persons in the territories of the signatory States, even those who could not be considered as residing there in the legal sense of the word". An even broader interpretation is given by H. Golsong, "Implementation of International Protection of Human Rights", *R.C.A.D.I.* 110 (1963-III), pp. 1-151 (61). See also Appl. 1611/62, *X v. Federal Republic of Germany, Yearbook* VIII (1965), p. 158 (168), where the Commission held: "in certain respects the nationals of a Contracting State are within its jurisdiction even

(continued...)

3

2. Section I of the Convention contains the following rights and freedoms:
Article 2: right to life;
Article 3: freedom from torture and inhuman or degrading treatment;
Article 4: freedom from slavery and forced or compulsory labour;
Article 5: right to liberty and security of person;
Article 6: right to a fair and public trial within a reasonable time;
Article 7: freedom from retrospective effect of penal legislation;
Article 8: right to respect for private and family life, home and correspondence;
Article 9: freedom of thought, conscience and religion;
Article 10: freedom of expression;
Article 11: freedom of assembly and association;
Article 12: right to marry and found a family.

The First Protocol has added the following rights:
Article 1: right to peaceful enjoyment of possessions;
Article 2: right to education and free choice of education;
Article 3: right to free elections by secret ballot.

In the Fourth Protocol the following rights and freedoms have been included:
Article 1: prohibition of deprivation of liberty on the ground of inability to fulfil a contractual obligation;
Article 2: freedom to move within and freedom to choose residence in a country;
Article 3: prohibition of expulsion of nationals and right of nationals to enter the territory of the State of which they are nationals;
Article 4: prohibition of collective expulsion of aliens.

The Sixth Protocol has added the prohibition of the condemnation to and execution of the death penalty (Article 1).

The Seventh Protocol contains the following rights and freedoms:
Article 1: procedural guarantees in case of expulsion of aliens lawfully resident in the territory of a State;
Article 2: right of review by a higher tribunal in criminal cases;
Article 3: right to compensation to a person convicted of a criminal offence, on the ground that a new or newly discovered fact shows that there has been a miscarriage of justice;
Article 4: prohibition of new criminal proceedings for offences for which one has already been finally acquitted or convicted (*ne bis in idem*);
Article 5: equality of rights and responsibilities between spouses.

8.(...continued)
    when domiciled or resident abroad". In the same sense Appl. 7289/75 and 7349/76, *X and Y v. Switzerland*, Yearbook XX (1977), p. 372 (402). See also *infra* pp. 7-9.

3. The other articles of Section I of the Convention contain general provisions concerning the enjoyment, the protection and the limitation of the rights and freedoms mentioned above. Article 13 stipulates that everyone whose rights and freedoms mentioned in the Convention are violated shall have an effective remedy before national authorities, notwithstanding the fact that the violation has been committed by persons acting in an official capacity. Article 14 requires the contracting States to secure the rights and freedoms without discrimination on any ground whatsoever. Article 15 allows States to derogate from a number of provisions of the Convention in time of war or any other public emergency threatening the life of the nation. Under Article 16 States are allowed to impose limitations on political activities of aliens notwithstanding Articles 10, 11 and 14 of the Convention, while Article 17 provides that nothing in the Convention may justify activities aimed at the destruction of any of the rights and freedoms set forth in the Convention or their limitation to a greater extent than is provided for in the Convention. Finally, Article 18 implies a prohibition of misuse of power (*détournement de pouvoir*) as to the right of contracting States to impose restrictions on the rights and freedoms guaranteed by the Convention.

4. Besides these substantive provisions, the European Convention also contains a number of provisions to ensure the observance by the contracting States of their obligations under the Convention. In this connection it should be noted that the supervision of the implementation of the Convention rests primarily with the national authorities, in particular the national courts[9] (at least in States where the Convention is directly applicable). This is also implied in Article 13. With regard to those cases where a national procedure is not available or does not provide for an adequate remedy, or in the last resort has not produced a satisfactory result in the opinion of the prejudiced party or of a contracting State, the Convention itself provides for a supervisory procedure. This system consists of two phases, *viz.* the procedure before the European Commission of Human Rights (Section III) and subsequently the procedure before the European Court of Human Rights (Section IV) or before the Committee of Ministers of the Council of Europe (Articles 30 and 31). In addition, the Secretary General of the Council of Europe also takes part in the supervision of the observance of the Convention (Article 57).

5. Section V contains, *inter alia*, the final provisions of the Convention (Articles 60 to 66 inclusive). Article 63, concerning the territorial scope, and Article 65, which deals with denunciation of the Convention, will be discussed hereafter in another context.[10] Article 64, concerning reservations, will be dealt with separately in Chapter VII.[11]

---

9. On this, *infra* pp. 11-15 and 81-98.
10. See *infra* pp. 7-9 and 11.
11. See Chapter VII, Section 9, *infra* pp. 606-613.

6. Article 60 embodies what has become a general rule of international human rights law, *viz.* that the agreement implying a more far-reaching protection takes priority over any other, less far-reaching instrument. The article provides that nothing in the Convention may be construed as limiting or derogating from any of the human rights and fundamental freedoms as they may be ensured under the national laws of any contracting State or under any other international agreement to which the latter is a party.

7. Article 61 stipulates that the Convention shall not prejudice the powers conferred on the Committee of Ministers by the Statute of the Council of Europe.

8. Article 62 is aimed at leaving the supervision of the observance of the Convention at the international level exclusively in the hands of the organs designated by the Convention itself. The article provides that the contracting States, except by special agreement, will not try to settle their disputes on the interpretation and application of the Convention by other means. In those instances where the Convention is expressly invoked, such an exclusive competence is obvious. With respect to disputes where this is not the case, but where a right that is also protected by the Convention is nevertheless in issue, the rationale for such a regulation is much less self-evident. In our opinion the text of Article 62 does not necessarily dictate the exclusivity of the procedure provided for in the Convention as far as those latter cases are concerned. There is, however, some difference of opinion as to the exact content of the obligation of the contracting States under Article 62. At any rate, in a resolution of 1970 the Committee of Ministers took a position different from the one taken here, although it recognized at the same time that the interpretation of Article 62 raises some problems. In the resolution the Committee:

> Declares that, as long as the problem of interpretation of Article 62 of the European Convention is not resolved, States Parties to the Convention which ratify or accede to the U.N. Covenant on Civil and Political Rights and make a declaration under Article 41 of the Covenant should normally utilize only the procedure established by the European Convention in respect of complaints against another Contracting Party of the European Convention relating to an alleged violation of a right which in substance is covered both (by) the European Convention (or its protocols) and by the U.N. Covenant on Civil and Political Rights, it being understood that the U.N. procedure may be invoked in relation to rights not guaranteed in the European Convention (or its protocols) or in relation to States which are not Parties to the European Convention.[12]

In practice, no problems have arisen yet in this respect. Since the entry-into-force of the Covenant in 1976, only two inter-State complaints have been dealt with in the context of the European Convention: Cyprus v. Turkey[13] and Denmark, France, the Netherlands, Norway and Sweden v. Turkey.[14] Since Turkey has not ratified the Covenant and Cyprus and France have not

---

12.   Res. (70)17 of 15 May 1970, Council of Europe, *Collected Texts*, Strasbourg 1987, p. 208.
13.   Appl. 8007/77, *Yearbook* XX (1977), p. 98; *D & R* 13 (1979), p. 85.
14.   Appl. 9940-9944/82, *D & R* 35 (1984), p. 143.

recognized the competence of the Human Rights Committee to receive inter-State complaints, there was no other possibility than to submit the case to the European Commission.

9. Finally, Article 66 contains a number of self-explanatory provisions about the ratification and the entry-into-force of the Convention.

§ 3. THE TERRITORIAL SCOPE OF THE CONVENTION

1. Article 63 imposes a limitation on the principle of Article 1 according to which the Convention is applicable to everyone within the jurisdiction of one of the contracting States. According to general international law a convention is applicable to the whole territory of a contracting State, including those territories for whose international relations the State in question is responsible.[15] This is different only when a reservation has been made for one or more of those territories in the treaty itself, or at the time of its ratification. Under Article 63(1), however, the European Convention extends to the latter territories only when the contracting State concerned has agreed to this via a declaration to that effect addressed to the Secretary General of the Council of Europe. Such declarations were made in the course of time by Denmark with respect to Greenland,[16] by the Netherlands with respect to Surinam[17] and the Netherlands Antilles and by the United Kingdom with respect to most of the non-self-governing territories belonging to the Commonwealth.[18] The question of what has to be understood by the words "territory for whose international relations a State is responsible" was raised in a case concerning the former Belgian Congo. The applicants submitted that at the time to which their complaint related this area formed part of the national territory of Belgium, and that accordingly the Convention, including the Belgian declaration under Article 25, was applicable to the Belgian Congo even though Belgium had not made any declaration as referred to in Article 63 with reference thereto. The Commission, however, came to the conclusion that the Belgian Congo had to be regarded as a territory for whose international relations a contracting State was responsible in the sense of Article 63, and that the complaint was not admissible *ratione loci*, since Belgium had not made any declaration under Article 63 with reference to this territory.[19]

---

15. See Art. 29 of the Vienna Convention on the Law of Treaties of 1969, *I.L.M.* 8 (1969), p. 679.
16. Since 1953 Greenland forms an integral part of Denmark.
17. Surinam became independent in 1975.
18. See Council of Europe, *Collected Texts*, Strasbourg 1987, p. 75. The reservation which was made by the Netherlands at the time with respect to the Netherlands Antilles with reference to Art. 6(3)(c) has meanwhile been withdrawn; see Council of Europe, *Information Bulletin on Legal Activities*, November 1981, vol. 10, p. 1.
19. Appl. 1065/61, *X v. Belgium*, Yearbook IV (1961), p. 260 (266-268).

7

In accordance with paragraph 3 the provisions of the Convention are applied to the territories referred to in Article 63 with due regard to local requirements. In the *Tyrer* Case the British Government submitted in this context that corporal punishment in the Isle of Man was justified as a preventive measure, based on public opinion in the island. The Court, however, held that

> for the application of Article 63(3), more would be needed: there would have to be positive and conclusive proof of a requirement, and the Court could not regard beliefs and local "public" opinion on their own as constituting such proof.[20]

When territories become independent, the declaration of Article 63 automatically ceases to exist, because the contracting State which has made it is no longer responsible for the international relations of the new State.[21] This new State does not automatically become a party to the Convention. In the majority of cases[22] it will not even be able to become a party, since Article 66(1) makes signature possible only for Member States of the Council of Europe and membership of the latter organization is open only to *European* States.[23]

2. The fact that the Convention is applicable only to the territory of the contracting States, with the qualification of Article 63, does not imply that a contracting State cannot be responsible under the Convention for acts of its organs that have been committed outside its territory. Thus the Commission decided that in principle the acts of functionaries of the German embassy in Morocco might involve the responsibility of the Federal Republic of Germany,[24] and Turkey was held responsible for the acts of its invasion forces in Cyprus.[25] Similarly, Switzerland was deemed responsible for acts committed under a treaty of 1923 concerning the incorporation of Liechtenstein into the Swiss customs area. The Commission held that acts of Swiss authorities having effect in Liechtenstein place all those to whom these acts are applicable,

---

20. Judgment of 25 April 1978, A.26 (1978), pp. 17-19 (18), from which it likewise appears that, even apart from the correctness of public opinion, the Court does not wish to regard the corporal punishment itself, intended as a preventive measure, as a local requirement in the sense of Art. 63(3), which would have to be taken into account in the application of Art. 3. See also Appl. 7456/76, *P. Wiggins v. United Kingdom*, D & R 13 (1979), p. 40 (48).
21. See, *e.g.*, Appl. 7230/75, *X v. the Netherlands*, D & R 7 (1977), p. 109 (110-111).
22. This was different in the cases of Cyprus and Malta only, which after their independence actually became members of the Council of Europe and parties to the Convention.
23. Art. 4 of the Statute of the Council of Europe.
24. Appl. 1611/62, *X v. Federal Republic of Germany*, Yearbook VIII (1965), p. 158 (163).
25. Appls 6780/74 and 6950/75, *Cyprus v. Turkey*, Yearbook XVIII (1975), p. 82 (118-120). See in general on this matter Appl. 8007/77, *Cyprus v. Turkey*, D & R 13 (1979), p. 85 (148-149). In this case the Commission held "that these armed forces are authorised agents of Turkey and that they bring any other person or property in Cyprus within the jurisdiction of Turkey, in the sense of Article 1 of the Convention". The Commission also declared that Art. 63 may not be interpreted "as limiting the scope of the term 'jurisdiction' in Article 1". According to the Commission the purpose of Art. 63 is "not only the territorial expansion of the Convention but its adaptation to the territories and to the cultural and social differences in such territories; Article 63(3) confirms this interpretation. This does not mean that the territories to which Article 63 applies are not within the 'jurisdiction' within the meaning of Article 1".

under Swiss jurisdiction in the sense of Article 1 of the Convention.[26] On the other hand, a contracting State is responsible for acts committed on its territory only to the extent that they have been committed by its own organs.[27]

§ 4. THE TEMPORAL EFFECT OF THE CONVENTION

1. By virtue of a generally accepted principle of international law a treaty is not applicable to acts or facts that have occurred, or to situations that have ceased to exist, before the treaty entered into force and was ratified by the State in question.[28] This applies also to the European Convention.[29] In the *Pfunders* Case the Commission inferred from the nature of the obligations under the Convention that the fact that the respondent State (in this case Italy) was a party to the Convention at the time of the alleged violation was decisive, without it being necessary that at that moment the applicant State (in this case Austria) had ratified the Convention.[30]

2. In this context it is worth-while to mention the case-law of the Commission concerning complaints which relate to a continuing situation, *i.e.* to violations of the Convention which are caused by an act committed at a given moment, but which continue owing to the consequences of the original act. Such a case occurred when a Belgian national lodged a complaint on account of a conviction by a Belgian court for treason during the Second World War. The verdict had been pronounced before Belgium had ratified the Convention, but the situation complained about - the punishment in the form of, *inter alia*, a limitation of the right of free expression - continued after the Convention had become binding upon Belgium. According to the Commission the latter fact was decisive, and the complaint accordingly was declared

---

26. Appls 7289/75 and 7349/76, *X and Y v. Switzerland, D & R* 9 (1978), p. 57 (73). In this context see also Appl. 6231/73, *Ilse Hess v. United Kingdom, Yearbook* XVIII (1975), p. 146 (174-176), in which the British Government was not held responsible, in the terms of the Convention, with respect to alleged violations in Spandau Prison, because the Commission concluded that the responsibility for the prison was exercised on a Four-Power basis and that the United Kingdom acted only as a partner in the joint responsibility. Since decisions could only be taken unanimously, the prison was not under the jurisdiction of the United Kingdom in the sense of Art. 1.

27. See Appl. 2095/63, *X v. Sweden, Federal Republic of Germany and other States, Yearbook* VIII (1965), p. 272 (282), where it was decided that the alleged violations of the Convention by the Supreme Restitution Court could not be held against the Federal Republic of Germany, even though this tribunal had its sessions on West German territory. It was to be considered as an international tribunal, in respect of which Germany had neither legislative nor supervisory powers. See also Appl. 235/56, *X v. Federal Republic of Germany, Yearbook* II (1958/59), p. 256 (304), where the Commission reached the same conclusion with respect to the American Court of Restitution Appeals in Germany.

28. See Art. 28 of the Vienna Convention on the Law of Treaties, *supra* note 15, p. 679.

29. Appl. 343/57, *Schouw Nielsen v. Denmark, Yearbook* II (1958/59), p. 412 (454); Appl. 7742/76, *A.B. & Company A.S. v. Federal Republic of Germany, D & R* 14 (1979), p. 146 (167).

30. Appl. 788/60, *Austria v. Italy, Yearbook* IV (1961), p. 116 (142).

admissible.[31]

3. A declaration of a contracting State as referred to in Article 25, in which the competence of the Commission to receive applications from individuals is recognized, in principle has retrospective effect to the moment of the ratification of the Convention.[32] As a consequence of this approach an individual may therefore draw the Commission's attention to an alleged violation of the Convention via an application, even if this violation took place prior to the moment at which the respondent State made the declaration under Article 25, provided that at the moment in question the Convention was binding upon that State. When making the said declaration, a State may, however, indicate that it applies to the future only.[33]

A special situation occurred when several complaints concerning criminal procedures in Italy were lodged. In its declaration under Article 25 this country had established that it was to apply as from 1 August 1973. The procedure in the first instance against the applicant had ended in 1969. On appeal, the verdict had been pronounced on 11 February 1976. To the extent that the complaint concerned the first-mentioned procedure it was rejected by the Commission *ratione temporis*, while with respect to the appeal procedure the application was declared admissible. The Commission used as the only criterion the question of whether the proceedings had terminated prior to or after the date indicated by Italy in its declaration under Article 25, taking that date also as the starting-point for the six-month rule.[34] However, the Commission has in the meantime reversed its case-law on this point and now strictly adheres to the point of departure that the six-month time-limit is to be calculated as from the final domestic decision.[35]

Declarations under Article 46, through which the jurisdiction of the Court is recognized, have in principle retrospective effect as will be pointed out below.[36]

The competence of the Commission to receive applications from States under Article 24 arises automatically from the fact that the Convention has become binding, so that the problem of the retrospective effect does not play a part in this respect, unless in the form discussed under 2 of an application which relates to a moment at which the applicant State had not yet ratified

---

31. Appl. 214/56, *De Becker v. Belgium, Yearbook* II (1958/59), p. 214 (244). See also Appl. 7031/75, *X v. Switzerland, D & R* 6 (1977), p. 124; Appl. 7202/75, *X v. United Kingdom, D & R* 7 (1977), p. 102; and Appl. 8701/79, *X v. Belgium, D & R* 18 (1980), p. 250 (251) concerning disfranchise. See, however, the negative decision of the Commission in the joined Appls 8560/79 and 8613/79, *X and Y v. Portugal, D & R* 16 (1979), p. 209 (211-212), in which two servicemen complained that their transfer had taken place in contravention of Art. 6.
32. Appl. 9587/81, *X v. France, D & R* 29 (1982), pp. 238-239; Appl. 9559/81, *De Varga-Hirsch v. France, D & R* 33 (1983), pp. 209-210; Appl. 9990/82, *Bozano v. France, D & R* 39 (1984), p. 143.
33. See, e.g., the declaration of the United Kingdom; *Yearbook* IX (1966), p. 8; see also Appl. 6323/73, *X v. Italy, D & R* 3 (1976), p. 80 (82).
34. Appl. 8261/78, *X v. Italy, D & R* 18 (1980), p. 150 (151).
35. See *infra* p. 102.
36. See *infra* p. 141.

the Convention.

4. Finally, as to the temporal scope of the Convention, it has to be observed that, even after a State has denounced the Convention in accordance with Article 65(1), it remains fully applicable to that State for another six months (Art. 65(2)). A complaint submitted between the date of denunciation of the Convention and that on which that denunciation becomes effective thus falls within the scope of the Convention *ratione temporis*. This occurred in the case of the second complaint, of April 1970, by Denmark, Norway and Sweden against Greece. On 12 December 1969 Greece had denounced the Convention. This denunciation was therefore to become effective on 13 June 1970. The Commission therefore decided that on the ground of Article 65(2) Greece was still bound, at the time of the complaint, to comply with the obligations ensuing from the Convention, and that accordingly the Commission could consider the complaint.[37]

§ 5. THE EFFECT OF THE CONVENTION WITHIN THE NATIONAL LEGAL SYSTEM

1. As has been said above, it is primarily the task of the national authorities of the contracting States to secure the rights and freedoms set forth in the Convention. To what extent the national courts can play a part in this, by reviewing the acts and omissions of those national authorities, depends mainly on the question of whether the provisions of the Convention are directly applicable in proceedings before those national courts. The answer to this question depends in turn on the effect of international law within the national legal system.

In this respect there are two contrasting views. In the so-called *dualistic* view the international and the national legal system form two separate legal spheres, and international law has effect within the national legal system only after it has been "transformed" within the latter into national law via the required procedure. The legal subjects depend on this transformation for their protection; their rights and duties exist only under national law. In the so-called *monistic* view, on the other hand, the various legal systems are viewed as elements of the all-embracing international legal system, in which the national authorities are bound by international law in their relations with individuals as well, regardless of whether or not the rules of international law have been transformed into national law. In this view the individual derives

---

37. Appl. 4448/70, *Denmark, Norway and Sweden v. Greece*, Yearbook XIII (1970), p. 108 (120). After the admissibility declaration the Commission desisted from further examination. However, on 18 November 1974 Greece became a party again to the Convention, and the Commission then resumed its examination of the complaint. Finally, on 4 October 1976, after both the applicant States and the defendant State had intimated that they were no longer interested in proceeding with the case, the Commission struck the case from the list; *D & R* 6 (1977), p. 6 (8).

rights and duties directly from international law, so that in the national procedure he may directly invoke rules of international law, which must be applied by the national courts and to which the latter must give priority over any national law conflicting with it.

In the prevailing opinion the system resulting from the monistic view is not prescribed by international law at its present stage of development. In other words, international law leaves the States free to decide for themselves in what way they will fulfil their international obligations and implement the pertinent international rules within their national legal system; they are internationally responsible only for the ultimate result of this implementation.[38] This is true of the European Convention. The consequence is that in some contracting States no internal effect is assigned to the Convention, while in others it is so assigned.[39]

In States in which international law has internal effect one must ascertain for each provision of international law separately whether it is directly applicable - is self-executing -, so that individuals may directly invoke such a provision before the national courts. The self-executing character of a provision of international law may generally be presumed when the content of such a provision can be applied in a concrete case without there being a need for supplementary measures on the part of the national authorities.

All this means that in its present form international law still presumes separate legal spheres. In fact, even if the constitutional law of a State assigns internal effect and priority to international law, international law has this status by virtue of that constitutional law, not by virtue of its own nature.

2. The Court of Justice of the European Communities, however, has taken a different position with respect to the relation between Community law and the law of the member States.[40] According to the Court, directly applicable provisions in the Community Treaties and in the decisions of the Community institutions do have internal effect within the legal systems of the member

---

38. See the judgment of 6 February 1976, *Swedish Engine Drivers' Union*, A.20 (1976), p. 18, in which the Court held that "neither Article 13 nor the Convention in general lays down for the Contracting States any given manner for ensuring within their internal law the effective implementation of any of the provisions of the Convention". In the same sense the judgment of 23 July 1968, *Belgian Linguistic Case*, A.6 (1968), p. 35 and the judgment of 27 October 1975, *National Union of Belgian Police*, A.19 (1975), p. 20. See also the dissenting opinion of the Commission members Sperduti and Opsahl in the Report of the Commission in Ireland v. United Kingdom, B.23-I (1976-1978), pp. 503-505. On this problem in general, see M. Sørensen, "Obligations of a State Party to a treaty as regards its municipal law", in: A.H. Robertson (ed.), *Human Rights in National and International Law*, Manchester 1968, pp. 11-31 (22-27); J.H.W. Verzijl, *International Law in Historical Perspective*, Vol. I, Leyden 1968, pp. 33-35; P.J.G. Kapteyn and P. VerLoren van Themaat, *Introduction to the Law of the European Communities*, Deventer (Second edition) 1989, pp. 36-99.
39. See Lars Adam Rehof and Claus Gulmann (eds), *Human Rights in Domestic Law and Development Assistance Policies in the Nordic Countries*, Dordrecht etc. 1989, pp. 125-209. For detailed information on the status of the Convention in the legal systems of the contracting States, see A.Z. Drzemczewski, *European Human Rights Convention in Domestic Law; A Comparative Study*, Oxford 1983.
40. On this, see Kapteyn and VerLoren van Themaat, *supra* note 38, p. 39 and the case-law cited there.

States, regardless of what each particular national legal system provides in that respect. Moreover, in the view of the Court, the provisions with a self-executing character have priority over provisions of national law, even over those of the national Constitution. The Court infers this from the character of Community law and bases its position on the principle of effectiveness (*l'effet utile*). Without priority, those rules that form the core of Community law would become devoid of sense, or at least could not be applied in a reasonable and useful way. The theoretical premise on which the Court bases this view is that the member States have renounced their sovereign rights in favour of the legal system of the Community in the areas coming under the Community Treaties.

The Court of Justice can disclose its view concerning the internal effect and the priority of Community law directly to the national court via the preliminary rulings which the national court may, and in the last resort even must, request if in the national procedure it is confronted with the question of the relation of national law to, and its compatibility with, Community law. For ordinary treaties, however, among which in this respect the European Convention must also be reckoned, the question concerning internal effect and priority is decided exclusively by the national courts. The relation between the European Court of Human Rights and the national courts is much less direct than that between the Court of Justice of the European Communities and the national courts. It is not, therefore, to be expected that a development comparable to Community law will be initiated by the Strasbourg Court with respect to the Convention, because it lacks the requisite instruments for this. Nevertheless, it would appear to us that in view of its character the European Convention contains the germs for a gradual development into a common legal system for the contracting States, to which their national law must be subordinate. The subject-matter regulated by the Convention - the protection of civil and political rights - lends itself eminently to direct effect. In fact, it concers precisely the recognition of rights of individuals which can be exercised without further measures being taken by the national authorities; that is, rights which by their nature are directly applicable.[41] In our opinion the priority of the Convention over provisions of national law conflicting therewith may very well be defended, on the one hand on the ground of the fundamental - one might say constitutional - character of the rights and freedoms protected in the Convention, on the other hand on the basis of the aim of the Council of Europe as set forth in the Preamble of the Convention, *viz.* the achievement of greater unity between the member States; a unity which is also intended by the supervisory system provided for in the Convention.

As has been said above, the Court in Strasbourg is not able to set such a development in motion. Any initiative in this direction will therefore have

41.   In the contracting States where the Convention has internal effect almost all the provisions of Section I of the Convention are considered as self-executing.

to be taken either by the Council of Europe or by the national authorities, including the courts in those States where internal effect is assigned to the Convention. The construction of renunciation of part of the sovereignty, used by the Court of Justice of the European Communities, might also be utilized by the national courts with respect to the effect of the Convention within the national legal system. The national courts will not be able to do this if in their view constitutional law is expressly opposed to it. The constitutions of various contracting States, however, contain provisions which make it possible in so many words to transfer sovereign rights to inter-governmental institutions.[42] In those cases the courts have a possibility for assigning internal effect and priority to the Convention within their national legal system.

3. In the present legal climate, however, the chances that a development in the direction outlined above may materialize would not appear very great. In general national courts are hardly inclined to allow provisions of international law to prevail over their own national law. This applies to an even greater extent to rules concerning human rights, which may indeed have a far-reaching impact upon the national legal system, so that the national courts will shrink from being guided by rules which are relatively alien to that national legal system, so long as those rules are not based on a solid constitutional foundation as well.[43]

Moreover, within the European Communities too, precisely in the matter of human rights, the willingness of some national tribunals to give unconditional priority to Community law has given rise to serious difficulties in the past, as may be seen from decisions of the highest constitutional courts in the Federal Republic of Germany and Italy.[44] This was based on the argument that these courts consider the Community system for the protection of fundamental rights and its (lack of a) democratic basis to constitute as yet too weak a foundation for subordinating thereto the national constitutional guarantees. It is true that the Court of Justice of the European Communities has taken the position that Community law includes also general principles of the law of human rights, and for these principles has sought to base itself on the constitutional principles of the member States as well as on the European Convention,[45] but this was evidently considered too weak a constitutional foundation by the tribunals referred to above. In the meantime, the Court of Justice has strengthened this foundation. Both the *Bundesverfassungsgericht* in the Federal Republic of Germany and the Italian *Corte Constituzionale* have

---

42. See, *e.g.*, Art. 24 of the German, Arts 53 and 54 of the French and Art. 20 of the Danish Constitution. The constitutions of the contracting States are to be found in: A.J. Peaslee, *Constitutions of Nations*, third revised edition, vol. III: Europe, The Hague 1968.
43. See, however, for the Netherlands P. van Dijk, "Domestic Status of Human-Rights Treaties and the Attitude of the Judiciary; The Dutch Case", in: M. Nowak et al. (eds), *Progress in the Spirit of Human Rights; Festschrift für Felix Ermacora*, Kehl etc. 1988, pp. 631-650.
44. See W.R. Edeson and F. Wooldridge, "European Community Law and Fundamental Human Rights; some recent decisions of the European Court and National Courts", *Legal Issues of European Integration* (1976/1), pp. 1-55.
45. See *ibidem*.

reviewed their opinions, by holding that fundamental rights are sufficiently guaranteed in the Community's legal order, and that therefore their reservations with regard to the priority of Community law over national law could be lifted.[46]

§ 6. "DRITTWIRKUNG" (EFFECT ON RELATIONS BETWEEN PRIVATE PARTIES)

1. *Drittwirkung* is a complicated phenomenon about which there are widely divergent views. At this place only those general aspects which are directly connected with the Convention will be dealt with. Hereafter, in the discussion of the separate rights and freedoms, certain aspects of *Drittwirkung* will be discussed in so far as the case-law of Court and Commission calls for it. For a detailed treatment of *Drittwirkung*, in particular also as to its recognition and effect under national law, reference may be made to the literature.[47]

2. What does the term *Drittwirkung* mean? Two views in particular must be distinguished. According to the first view it means that the provisions concerning human rights also *apply* in mutual legal relations between private individuals, and not only in legal relations between an individual and the public authorities. According to the second view, *Drittwirkung* is defined as the possibility for an individual to *enforce* his fundamental rights against another individual. Advocates of the latter view therefore consider that *Drittwirkung* of human rights is present only if an individual in his legal relations with other individuals is able to enforce the observance of the law concerning human rights via some procedure or other.

As to the latter view, it may at once be submitted that no *Drittwirkung* of the rights and freedoms set forth in the Convention can be directly effectuated via the procedure set up by the Convention. In fact, in Strasbourg it is possible to lodge complaints only about violations of the Convention by one of the contracting States; a complaint directed against an individual is inadmissible by reason of incompatibility with the Convention *ratione personae*.[48] This follows from Articles 19, 24, 25, 31, 32 and 50 of the

---

46. See the comments on these judgments by Gaja, *Common Market Law Review* (1984), pp. 756-772 and Frowein, *idem*, 1988, pp. 201-206.
47. See E.A. Alkema, "The third-party applicability or 'Drittwirkung' of the ECHR", in: *Protecting Human Rights; The European Dimension*, Köln 1988, pp. 33-45; A. Drzemczewski, "The domestic status of the European Convention on Human Rights; new dimensions", *Legal Issues of European Integration* (1977/1), pp. 1-85; M.A. Eissen, "La convention et les devoirs des individus", in: *La protection des droits de l'homme dans le cadre européen*, Paris 1961, pp. 167-194; H. Guradze, "Die Schutzrichtung der Grundrechtsnormen in der Europäischen Menschenrechtskonvention", *Festschrift Nipperdy*, vol. II, 1965, pp. 759-769; M.M. Hahne, *Das Drittwirkungsproblem in der Europäischen Konvention zum Schutz der Menschenrechte und Grundfreiheiten*, Heidelberg 1973; D.H.M. Meuwissen, *De Europese Conventie en het Nederlandse Recht* (The European Convention and Dutch Law), Leyden 1968, pp. 201-211.
48. See *infra* p. 77.

Convention, and has also been confirmed by the case-law of the Commission.[49] An individual cannot therefore bring up an alleged violation of his fundamental rights and freedoms by other individuals in Strasbourg. This can only be done indirectly, *viz.* when a contracting State can be held responsible for it in one way or another.[50] In that case the investigation in the Strasbourg procedure concerns that responsibility of the State and not the private actor.

The fact that in Strasbourg no complaints can be lodged against individuals need not, however, bar the recognition of *Drittwirkung* of the Convention, not even in the second sense referred to above. The possibility of enforcement which in this view is required does not necessarily have to be enforcement under international law, but may also arise from national law.[51] In that context two situations must be distinguished. In the first place there are States where those rights and freedoms included in the Convention, which are self-executing, can be directly applied by the national courts.[52] In these States the relevant provisions of the Convention can be directly invoked by individuals against other individuals in so far as their *Drittwirkung* is recognized by the national courts. Judgments of these national courts which conflict with the Convention, for which indeed the contracting State concerned is responsible under the Convention, may then be submitted to the Strasbourg organs via the procedure under Article 25 (provided that the individual right of complaint has been recognized by the State in question) or via the procedure under Article 24. In addition there are those States in whose national legal systems the provisions of the Convention are not directly applicable. These States, too, are obliged under the general guarantee clause of Article 1 of the Convention to protect the rights and freedoms set forth in the Convention via the national legal system. If one starts from the principle of *Drittwirkung*, such States also have to secure to individuals protection against violations of their fundamental rights by other individuals by means of national provisions of penal and civil law. If the competent national authorities default in this respect or if the said provisions of national law are not enforced, responsibility arises for the State concerned, a responsibility which may be brought up via the procedure under Article 25, or Article 24, of the Convention.[53]

From the above it follows in our opinion that the supervisory system of the Convention in itself does not bar the recognition of *Drittwirkung*, not even in the second sense described above, in which such *Drittwirkung* is made dependent upon the possibility of enforcing the relevant rights. On the other hand, the existence of such a supervisory system does not in itself imply *Drittwirkung* either. If in a given State individuals may directly invoke the Convention before the courts, this does not yet mean that the Convention is

49. See *infra* p. 77, note 74.
50. As a rule a State is not internationally responsible for the acts and omissions of its nationals or of individuals within its jurisdiction; on this, see *infra* pp. 77-78.
51. See Hahne, *supra* note 47, pp. 81-94.
52. That this so-called "internal effect" of the Convention does not follow imperatively from international law according to its present state has been explained *supra* pp. 11-15.
53. For the above, see Hahne, *supra* note 47, pp. 89-90.

also applicable to legal relations between individuals. And the nature, too, of the obligation arising from Article 1 of the Convention for those States in whose legal system the Convention is not directly applicable, is in itself not connected with the question about that *Drittwirkung*. In fact, one cannot deduce from Article 1 whether the contracting States are obliged to secure the rights and freedoms only in relation to the public authorities or also in relation to other individuals. For a possible *Drittwirkung*, therefore, other arguments have to be put forward.

3. What arguments can be inferred for *Drittwirkung* from the Convention itself? It is beyond doubt that the problem of *Drittwirkung* was not taken into account when the Convention was drafted, if it played any part at all in the discussions. One can infer from the formulation of various provisions that they were not written with a view to relations between individuals. On the other hand, the subject-matter regulated by the Convention - the fundamental rights and freedoms - lends itself eminently to *Drittwirkung*. Precisely on account of the fundamental character of these rights it is difficult to appreciate why they should deserve protection in relation to the public authorities, but not in relation to private individuals. We therefore submit that it is irrelevant whether the drafters of the Convention had in mind *Drittwirkung*. A question of greater importance is what conclusions must be drawn for the present situation from the principles set forth in the Convention, and specifically also in its Preamble. In the Preamble the drafters of the Convention gave evidence of the great value which they attached to general respect for the fundamental rights and freedoms.[54] From this emphasis on general respect an argument *pro* rather than *contra Drittwirkung* can be inferred. But, as has been said above, the drafters have not pronounced on this.

Neither do the separate provisions of the Convention constitute any clear arguments for or against *Drittwirkung*. Article 1 has already been discussed above.[55] Article 13 is also mentioned in this context. From the last words of this article, *viz.* "notwithstanding that the violation has been committed by persons in their official capacity", it is inferred by some that the Convention evidently also intends to provide a remedy against violations by individuals,[56] whereas others assert that those words merely indicate that the State is responsible for violations committed by its officials,[57] or that Article 13 at all events does not afford an independent argument for *Drittwirkung*.[58] From

---

54. It is there stated, among other things, that the Universal Declaration, of which the Convention is an elaboration, "aims at securing universal and effective recognition and observance of the rights therein declared" and the contracting States affirm "their profound belief in those Fundamental Freedoms which are the foundation of justice and peace in the world".
55. See *supra* at this page.
56. See Eissen, *supra* note 47, pp. 177 *et seq.*
57. See Guradze, *supra* note 47, p. 764.
58. See Meuwissen, *supra* note 47, p. 210.

Article 17, too, it is sometimes inferred that the Convention has *Drittwirkung*. It is, however, doubtful whether such a general conclusion may be drawn from Article 17.[59] That provision forbids not only the public authorities, but also individuals, to invoke the Convention for the justification of an act aimed at the destruction of fundamental rights of other persons. Such a prohibition of abuse of the Convention is quite another matter than a general obligation for individuals to respect the fundamental rights of other persons in their private legal relations.

Summarizing one may conclude that *Drittwirkung* does not ensue imperatively from the Convention. On the other hand, nothing in the Convention prevents the States from conferring *Drittwirkung* upon the fundamental rights and freedoms within their national legal systems in so far as they lend themselves to it. In some States *Drittwirkung* of the rights and freedoms guaranteed by the Convention is already recognized, whilst in other States this *Drittwirkung* at least is not excluded in principle.[60] A view in conformity with this tendency is that it may be inferred from the changing social circumstances and opinions that the purport of the Convention *is going to be* to secure a certain minimum guarantee to the individual also in his relations with other persons.[61] It would seem that in the spirit of the Convention a good deal may be said for this view, although in the case of such a subsequent interpretation one must ask oneself whether one does not thus assign to the Convention an effect which is unacceptable to (a number of) the contracting States,[62] and consequently is insufficiently supported by their implied mutual consent.

Meanwhile it will also depend in particular on the nature and the formulation of each separate right embodied in the Convention whether *Drittwirkung* can be assigned to it at all. In this context Alkema warns us that the nature of the legal relations between individuals may be widely divergent, and that consequently *Drittwirkung* is a pluriform phenomenon, about which general statements are hardly possible.[63]

4. The case-law of the Commission does not afford much clarity concerning *Drittwirkung*. This is not surprising because, as stated above, in Strasbourg complaints may only be lodged against States.[64] Most of the Commission's decisions quoted on this subject in the literature accordingly concern dismissals of complaints directed against individuals.[65] A decision of the Commission which curiously appears to point in the direction of *Drittwirkung*,

---

59. *Ibidem.*
60. See A. Drzemczewski, *supra* note 47, p. 63 *et seq.*
61. See Meuwissen, *supra* note 47, p. 211.
62. See H. Guradze, *Die Europäische Menschenrechtskonvention*, Berlin 1968, p. 21.
63. See E.A. Alkema, *supra* note 47, pp. 254-255.
64. See *supra* pp. 15-16.
65. See, *e.g.*, Appl. 33/55, *X v. Sweden, Yearbook* I (1955-57), pp. 154-155 and Appl. 1816/63, *X v. Austria, Yearbook* VII (1964), p. 204 (210). For the other statements of the Commission which contain aspects of *Drittwirkung,* but from which no clear conclusion of the Commission concerning *Drittwirkung* can be inferred, reference may be made here to the literature mentioned in note 47.

although the Commission does not refer to that issue specifically, should be mentioned separately. A German lawyer had been assigned to an individual as a free legal aid counsel. After having rendered his services for a considerable time, he requested the German authorities an advance on his fee. His request was refused. He lodged a complaint about this with the Commission, referring to Article 4(2): freedom from forced or compulsory labour. In connection with *Drittwirkung* the following passage in the Commission's decision is of interest:

> The Convention itself recognises the necessity of providing for free legal assistance (see Art. 6(3)(c)). It is clear therefore that the obligation of practising lawyers to perform duties as legal aid counsel for which they receive reasonable remuneration can never be considered as constituting forced or compulsory labour in the sense of Article 4(2) of the Convention.[66]

The claim of the German lawyer based on Article 4(2) was rejected by the Commission on the ground of the existence of a right to free legal aid. This decision creates the impression that from this right an obligation also for individuals may arise, in this case for lawyers. This would imply that *Drittwirkung* would have to be assigned to Article 6(3)(c). It is, however, highly questionable whether this provision admits of such an interpretation. Article 6(3)(c) grants individuals a right which in our opinion applies typically in their relations with the public authorities and which can hardly be conceived also to create rights directly with respect to individuals. Perhaps the argument of the Commission will therefore have to be understood in the sense that the drafters of the Convention wished to create for the authorities an obligation to provide free legal aid in the case referred to in Article 6(3)(c), so that their intention cannot have been that the authorities, by imperatively imposing a legal aid obligation upon lawyers, should come into conflict with Article 4(2). If so, the Commission ought to have investigated whether in the challenged arrangement the German authorities had taken into account the rights and interests of lawyers to such an extent as is reasonably required.[67]

5. In three successive judgments the Court has interpreted the freedom to form and join trade unions (Article 11) in a way which appears to point in the direction of the assignment of *Drittwirkung* to that provision. In these judgments the Court held:

> What the Convention requires is that under national law trade unions should be enabled, in conditions not at variance with Article 11, to strive for the protection of their members' interests.[68]

---

66. Appl. 7641/76, *X and Y v. Federal Republic of Germany, D & R* 10 (1978), p. 224 (230).
67. A presumption of *Drittwirkung* can also be inferred from Appl. 4125/69, *X v. Ireland, Yearbook* XIV (1971), p. 198 (218-224).
68. Judgment of 27 October 1975, *National Union of Belgian Police,* A.19 (1975), p. 18; judgment of 6 February 1976, *Swedish Engine Drivers' Union,* A.20 (1976), pp. 15-16; and in almost the same formulation the judgment of 6 February 1976, *Schmidt and Dahlström,* A.21 (1976), p. 16.

In the first two cases the Court inferred from this a right for trade unions to be heard, while the State was granted discretion with regard to the way in which that right is regulated.[69] In the last case, too, the Court left this discretion to the State.[70] With regard to the right to strike it added:

> The grant of a right to strike represents without any doubt one of the most important of these means, but there are others.[71]

From a provision of the Convention the Court here infers rights for individuals, which, via an obligation of the contracting States to take measures in order to make their exercise possible, must also be enforced with respect to third persons. From the viewpoint of the Convention, however, this may at most be called "indirect *Drittwirkung*", since it is put into effect *via* an obligation of the State.[72]

§ 7. THE EUROPEAN COMMISSION OF HUMAN RIGHTS

1. The European Commission of Human Rights (hereafter: the Commission), like the European Court of Human Rights (hereafter: the Court) to be discussed later on, has been specially set up to ensure the observance of the engagements undertaken by the contracting States in the Convention (Art. 19).

At present the Commission consists of twenty-one members. In fact, Article 20 provides that the number of members of the Commission shall be equal to the number of the parties to the European Convention. However, at this moment (January 1990) for San Marino no candidates for Commission membership have been proposed yet. The same article also provides that no two members of the Commission may be nationals of the same State. It is theoretically not impossible that a national of a State which is not a party to the Convention, or even is not a member of the Council of Europe, may be a member of the Commission. In practice, however, so far one national of each of the contracting States has always sat on the Commission. As a rule, with a view to the powers which the Commission has under the Convention in the matter of the protection of human rights, each of the contracting States will wish to be assured that one of its nationals is a member of the Commission.[73] However, that this does not have to remain a general practice is shown by Liechtenstein in relation to the Court; the judge appointed in the Court for that country is a non-national.[74]

The members of the Commission cannot be considered as government representatives. Article 23 provides expressly that they sit in their individual

---

69. The first two cases mentioned in the preceding note, *ibidem*.
70. The last case mentioned in note 68, *ibidem*.
71. *Ibidem*.
72. See also Alkema, *supra* note 47, p. 33.
73. Thus also F. Monconduit, *La Commission Européenne des Droits de l'Homme*, Leyden 1965, p. 54.
74. See *infra* p. 26.

capacity. The independent position of the members of the Commission in relation to the national governments also appears from the oath or the declaration which they have to make before taking up their duties (Rule 2 of the Rules of the Commission[75]). This requirement of independence has the consequence that government functionaries should not be elected as members of the Commission.[76]

Although, until 1990, the criterion of Article 23 was the only one to be found in the Convention for the eligibility of the members of the Commission, in practice the additional requirement was made that candidates should be of high moral integrity, should be competent in matters concerning human rights, and should have substantial legal experience.[77] The candidates were not, however, always strictly confined to the circle of jurists. However, in Protocol no. 8, in addition to the requirements of independence and impartiality, and high moral character the requirement has been expressly laid down that the candidates "must either possess the qualifications required for appointment to high judicial office or be persons of recognised competence in national or international law".[78] As a consequence of this Protocol these requirements have become part of the Convention, in the form of amendments to Article 21 and Article 23 respectively.

Article 59 confers on the members of the Commission, during the discharge of their functions, the privileges and immunities provided for in Article 40 of the Statute of the Council of Europe and in the agreements made thereunder.[79]

2. The procedure for the election of the members of the Commission is regulated in Article 21. Each national group of parliamentary representatives of the contracting States in the Parliamentary Assembly[80] of the Council of Europe puts forward three candidates, of whom at least two must be nationals of that particular State. The Bureau of the Parliamentary Assembly[81] draws up a list of these names, from which the members of the Commission are elected by an absolute majority of votes by the Committee of Ministers.

---

75. The Rules are included in *Collected Texts*, Strasbourg 1987, pp. 118-139.
76. When a vacancy arises, the President of the Parliamentary Assembly addresses himself to the chairman of the national delegation concerned, using the following words: "National delegations of course have entire freedom of choice when preparing their lists of candidates. In the view of the Bureau of the Assembly, however, it is desirable when the choice comes to be made that the following qualities - essential for any member of the Commission who is to fulfil his duty - be taken into consideration: (a) high moral integrity; (b) recognised competence in matters concerned with human rights; (c) substantial legal or judicial experience. The Bureau has further asked me to call your attention to the difficulties in which a member of the Commission might find himself if he were at the same time a member of a national public service, and to the doubts which might arise in such circumstances as to the impartiality of the Commission".
77. See note 76.
78. Articles 2 and 3 of Protocol no. 8.
79. See Second Protocol to the General Agreement on Privileges and Immunities of the Council of Europe, 261 *U.N.T.S.* 1957, p. 410.
80. In 1974 the name Consultative Assembly was changed into Parliamentary Assembly.
81. The Bureau consists of the President and the Vice-Presidents of the Parliamentary Assembly.

The same procedure is followed when a vacancy arises, either because a new State becomes a party to the Convention or when a sitting member of the Commission resigns (Art. 21(2)) or dies. In such a case only the group of parliamentary representatives of that State for whose nationality the post in question is predestined, is invited to put forward candidates.[82]

The members of the Commission are elected for a period of six years. They may be re-elected (Art. 22(1)). In the case of interim replacement of a member of the Commission by another person, the latter holds office for the remainder of his predecessor's term (Art. 22(5)). Members of the Commission hold office until replaced. After their replacement they continue to deal with such cases as they already had under consideration (Art. 22(6)).[83] The consequence of the last sentence of Article 22(1) is that not all the members of the Commission resign at the same time, but every three years one half of them, as far as possible, so that a certain continuity in the activities of the Commission is ensured.

3. The seat of the Commission is in Strasbourg, but, if desired, it may also perform its activities elsewhere (Rule 14 of the Rules). The Commission does not sit permanently. It decides every year, how many sessions will be held. In 1988, the Commission held nine sessions which consisted of five sessions of two weeks and four sessions of one week.[84] The Commission meets at the order of its President or at the request of one third of its members, so that extraordinary sessions are also possible. Because the Commission meets only a few times annually, the members usually also have other functions.[85] This in turn has the consequence that the members of the Commission do not have all their time available for the work in the Commission. In view of the considerable backlog in the examination of the applications submitted and the lengthy nature of the procedure, therefore, the question would seem justified whether it is not advisable to give the session of the Commission a permanent character and make membership full-time. However, in that case the link with the national legal environment which several Commission members have at the moment would partly be lost.

This drawback is not involved in the construction introduced by Protocol no. 8 in 1990, whereby Chambers may be set up, which shall exercise all the powers of the plenary Commission relating to individual complaints which can be dealt with on the basis of established case law or which raise no serious questions affecting the interpretation or application of the Convention. Each Chamber will be composed of at least seven members. The first Article of the Protocol in addition opens the possibility to set up Committees, each composed of at least three members, with the power to unanimously declare

---

82. See Monconduit, *supra* note 73, pp. 60-61.
83. On the meaning of "cases" in Art. 22(6), see Monconduit, *supra* note 73, pp. 67 *et seq.*
84. Council of Europe, *Survey of Activities and Statistics 1988*, p. 3.
85. The President of the Commission, however, is expected to be available on a more regular basis in order to deal with urgent cases.

inadmissible or strike from its list of cases an application submitted under Article 25 when such a decision can be taken without further examination. A Chamber or Committee may at any time relinquish jurisdiction in favour of the plenary Commission.

This last mentioned option could, in practice, greatly reduce the effect of this provision if a situation would arise whereby the more complicated cases, which demand a lot of time, would still have to be dealt with by the plenary Commission. At present (January 1990), the system of three-person Committees has been put into effect. However, the system of Chambers still awaits the appointment of the necessary staff for the Secretariat.[86]

An additional solution has been sought in increasing the amount of time available to the members of the Commission for dealing with cases. Originally, the Commission generally held five sessions a year in Strasbourg, with a total duration of ten weeks. In 1989 the Commission met for fourteen weeks. In addition several weeks of preparatory work are required, and about twelve days are spent for travelling. Acting as a Commission's delegate in proceedings before the Court takes up additional time. Both the Steering Committee for Human Rights, which reports to the Committee of Ministers, and the Commission itself reached the conclusion that membership of the Commission could not be combined with a full-time other function any longer. Commencing in 1990, members of the Commission will be expected to be available for 16 weeks of Commission meetings in Strasbourg, as well as to spend an additional 16 weeks on preparatory work. The system of remuneration has been adjusted accordingly. In practice, this has made the Commission a semi-permanent organ.[87] Its membership has now become the main occupation of its members, still allowing them to engage in a part-time profession in their home country and thus to keep in touch with the domestic legal environment and legal practice.

4. Because of the non-permanent character of the Commission, its Secretariat plays an important part as a permanent factor in the whole system. The Secretariat of the Commission is provided by the Secretary General of the Council of Europe (Art. 37). Besides the Secretary, a number of other qualified jurists from contracting States make up this Secretariat. They are in the full employ of the Council of Europe and are assisted by a record department and an administrative staff. In 1988, the staff of the Secretariat totaled 50 persons: 32 lawyers and 18 administrative assistants.[88] Among the most important duties of the Secretariat are: conducting correspondence with persons filing applications and with governments; preparing cases for

---

86. Especially Deputy-Secretaries to make it possible that two or three Chambers meet at the same time.
87. See "Towards a Semi-Permanent European Commission of Human Rights", Report No. 8 of the Netherlands Advisory Committee on Human Rights and Foreign Policy, April 1989.
88. See Council of Europe, *European Commission of Human Rights, Survey of Activities and Statistics* 1988, p. 1.

examination; submitting reports to the Commission on matters of national law and the law of the European Convention; and assisting the members of the Commission in drafting decisions and reports (*cf.* Rule 12 of the Rules).

5. The hearings and other meetings of the Commission are held *in camera* (Art. 33). The deliberations of the Commission are confidential (Rule 17 of the Rules). Even parties appearing before the Commission are not allowed to divulge information about the course of the proceedings. In certain cases transgression of this rule might even lead to dismissal of the application on the ground of abuse of the right of petition.[89] The most important decisions of the Commission on admissibility as well as the great majority of its reports, however, are published.[90]

The confidential character of the examination of applications by the Commission has advantages as well as disadvantages for the effective protection of the rights guaranteed in the Convention. Owing to this secrecy not all details of the supervisory system of the Convention become public, which may bar confidence in the system and does not stimulate the filing of applications. Moreover, publicity in itself would already form an element of sanction, because States would thus be exposed to the criticism of other States and of public opinion. Finally, public examination of a complaint against a given State might have a preventive effect on the behaviour of the other States. On the other hand, States will be more readily prepared to accept international supervision if this is kept out of publicity, particularly in the initial phase. The highly reserved attitude of States with respect to international supervision is quite evident from the fact that, even under the present confidential procedure, it took years, up to 1988, before all contracting States proved prepared to accept the individual right of complaint. For a proper discharge of the task with which the Commission has been entrusted in Article 28(1)(b), *i.e.* trying to secure a friendly settlement, secrecy would even seem to be an essential condition. In that case certain concessions will in general have to be made by the States concerned. This will become very difficult if they have previously committed themselves in public to a fixed position and will have to conduct the deliberations under the pressure of public opinion.

---

89. In the same sense F.G. Jacobs, *The European Convention on Human Rights*, Oxford 1985, p. 246.
90. The publication system of the Commission is rather confusing and therefore requires some elucidation. Not all decisions of the Commission are published, especially not those taken after summary proceedings. A number of the decisions concerning admissibility are to be found in the *Yearbook* of the European Convention on Human Rights and in the *Collection of Decisions*, continued after 1975 as *Decisions and Reports*. The Reports of the Commission are published separately; in addition they are sometimes included in the *Yearbooks* and in the *Decisions and Reports*. Sometimes a decision is included in the *Yearbooks* but not in the *Collection of Decisions/Decisions and Reports* and *vice versa*. In the "Digest of Strasbourg case-law relating to the European Convention on Human Rights", the complete case-law of the Commission and the Court has been incorporated. As far as cases have been referred to the Court, the main parts of the reports of the Commission are since 1985 also published as an Annex to the judgment of the Court (Series A), while before 1985 they were included in the materials published in Series B.

6. Members of the Commission cannot take part in the examination of a case in which they have any personal interest or if they have participated in any decision on the facts on which the application is based, as an adviser to any of the parties, in public service or as a member of any tribunal or body of enquiry (Rule 21(1) of the Rules). If the President of the Commission considers that a member should not take part in the examination of a given case, because there are circumstances which might affect his impartiality, the Commission decides on the matter. The member in question, too, may submit the matter to the Commission (Rule 21(2) of the Rules). He may also decide for other reasons, after consultation with the President, not to take part in the examination of a given case. If no agreement about this is reached between them, the Commission decides (Rule 22 of the Rules). The President relinquishes his function during the examination of a case involving a State of which he is a national, or which has presented him as a candidate for membership of the Commission (Rule 9 of the Rules).

7. The quorum of the Commission is ten members. For the examination of an application by an individual, however, seven members constitute the quorum when a decision according to Rule 42(2) of the Rules is to be made (Rule 16 of the Rules). According to this provision the Commission, on account of the report of the rapporteur, may decide to invite the individual applicant or the applicant State to submit relevant information, or may give notice of the application to the respondent State and invite it to submit observations on its admissibility. Seven members also constitute a quorum if the Commission declares the application inadmissible or decides to strike it off its list, provided that no notice of the application has been given to the State concerned (Rule 16(2)(b) of the Rules).

8. The Commission decides by a majority of votes (Art. 34). If the voting is equal, the President has a casting vote (Art. 18(3) of the Rules).
 Unlike the procedure for reports of the Commission on the merits (Art. 31),[91] in the case of decisions on admissibility the members of the Commission cannot add their individual opinion. They may, however, have a statement inserted in the records of the deliberations (Rule 19(1) of the Rules), but the minutes will be published only when the President considers this useful (Rule 20 of the Rules).

§ 8. THE EUROPEAN COURT OF HUMAN RIGHTS

1. The European Court of Human Rights has also been specially set up to supervise the observance by the contracting States of their engagements arising from the Convention.

---

91.   See *infra* p. 114.

Unlike the Commission, the number of members of the Court is not related to the number of the contracting States, but to the number of member States of the Council of Europe. At present the Court consists of twenty-two members.[92] This composition, which now makes the Court the largest international tribunal, has been opted for at the insistence of the minor States, which feared a monopoly position of the greater States in proposing candidates for the Court.[93] Just as in the case of the Commission, the Convention provides for the Court, in Article 38, that no two members may be nationals of the same State. And here again the possibility is left open that a national of a State which is not a member of the Council of Europe may be a member of the Court. This occurred for the first time in 1980, when the Canadian Professor MacDonald was elected in the Court after being nominated by Liechtenstein.[94]

2. For the election of the judges every member of the Council of Europe nominates three candidates, of whom two at least must be its nationals. From the list thus produced the Parliamentary Assembly elects the members of the Court by a majority of the votes cast (Art. 39(1)). In practice this provision has been interpreted in the sense that in the first ballot an absolute majority is required, while in the second ballot a simple majority suffices.[95]

Article 39(2) provides that the same procedure must be followed when new members are admitted to the Council of Europe, and in filling interim vacancies. In the former case only the new member State puts forward candidates, in the latter case this is done by the State which had nominated the candidate to whose resignation or death the vacancy is due.[96]

The members of the Court are elected for a period of nine years and may be re-elected. A member of the Court elected to replace a member whose term of office had not expired holds office for the remainder of his predecessor's term (Art. 40(5)). The members of the Court hold office until replaced. After having been replaced, they continue to deal with such cases as they already had under consideration (Art. 40(6)).

The end of the terms of the members of the Court is staggered in the sense that, to the extent possible, every three years one third of them resigns (Arts 40(1) and 40(3)).

3. The Convention lays down certain qualifications for members of the Court. The candidates must be of high moral character and must either possess the qualifications required for appointment to high judicial office or be jurisconsults of recognized competence (Art. 39(3)). Originally, the Convention did

---

92. San Marino, which became a member of the Council of Europe on 16 November 1988, has not yet (January 1990) proposed a candidate for membership of the Court.
93. See K. Vasak, *La Convention Européenne des Droits de l'Homme*, Paris 1964, p. 150.
94. Council of Europe, *The Protection of Human Rights in Europe*, Strasbourg 1981, p. 7.
95. See Vasak, *supra* note 93, p. 152.
96. See *Yearbook* IV (1961), p. 88.

not mention the independence of the judges at all. On this point Article 40 has been supplemented by Protocol no. 8.[97] According to Rule 3 of the Rules of Court[98] the members, therefore, before taking up their duties, must take an oath or make a declaration to the effect that they will exercise their function independently and impartially. Similarly, a judge may not exercise his function when he is a member of a government or holds a post or exercises a profession which is incompatible with his independence and impartiality (Rule 4 of the Rules). Moreover, the Parliamentary Assembly has adopted a resolution concerning the qualifications to be satisfied by candidate-members of the Court. This resolution reads as follows:

The Assembly,
1. Referring to Recommendation 809(1977) on the qualification of candidates for the European Court of Human Rights;
2. Recalling that judges of the Court are elected for a term of nine years;
3. Requests its members not to vote for candidates:
   i. who have not given a formal undertaking to retire from the office of judge during the year in which they reach the age of 75;
   ii. who, by nature of their functions, are dependent on government and who have not given a formal undertaking to resign the said functions upon their election to the European Court of Human Rights;
4. Considers that a list which includes more than one candidate in the situation indicated under paragraphs 3(i) or (ii) above should not be put to the vote, since in this case effective choice would be vitiated.[99]

Finally, Article 59 also provides that the members of the Court are entitled to the privileges and immunities provided for in Article 40 of the Statute of the Council of Europe and in the agreements made thereunder,[100] which furthers the independent exercise of their function.

4. The seat of the Court is in Strasbourg, but if it considers it expedient, the Court may also exercise its functions elsewhere in the territories of the member States of the Council of Europe (Rule 15 of the Rules).

5. The sessions of the Court are even less frequent than those of the Commission. Rule 16 of the Rules of Court provides that the President convenes the Court at least once annually in a plenary session and also at the request of at least one third of the members. Further, he convenes the Court whenever the exercise of its functions so requires. In 1989 the Court held during twenty-one days public hearings. The quorum for the sessions of the plenary Court is twelve judges (Rule 17 of the Rules).

For the consideration of a case a Chamber composed of seven judges is constituted from the Court (Art. 43). This provision meets the drawbacks of

---

97. See Article 9 of the Eighth Protocol.
98. The Rules of Court are included in *Collected Texts,* Strasbourg 1987, pp. 151 *et seq.* The Rules of Court have been amended on 26 January 1980. This revised text exists as a separate publication.
99. Resolution 655 (1977) "On the qualification of candidates for the European Court of Human Rights", Council of Europe, Parl. Ass., Twenty-Ninth Ordinary Session, First Part, 25-29 April 1977, *Texts adopted.*
100. See *supra* p. 21, note 79.

the large number of members of the Court. Persons sitting as *ex officio* members of the Chambers are those judges who are nationals of the States parties to the case or, if such a judge is not available, a person of the choice of the State in question, who must then satisfy the requirements of Article 39(3) of the Convention (Rules 21-23 of the Rules). This has the advantage that at least one person who is familiar with the legal system of the State involved in the case is a member of the Chamber. The President or the Vice-President, too, sits as an *ex officio* member of the Chamber. The other members of the Chamber are chosen by lot (Rule 21 of the Rules).

As a consequence the composition of the Court may vary considerably from case to case. This is even more so due to the fact that under Rule 24(5) of the Rules a judge who has been a member of a Chamber in one or more recent cases may, at his request, be exempted from sitting on a new case.

To prevent disintegration in the case-law, in its Rules the Court has assigned to the Chambers the right to relinquish jurisdiction in favour of the plenary Court when a case pending before a Chamber raises serious questions affecting the interpretation of the Convention. A Chamber is even obliged to do so where the resolution of such questions might have a result inconsistent with a judgment previously delivered by a Chamber or by the plenary Court (Rule 51 of the Rules).[101] Moreover, if the President of the Court finds that two cases concern the same party or parties and raise similar issues, he may refer the second case to the Chamber already constituted, or constitute a Chamber to consider both cases (Rule 21(6) of the Rules). Finally, the fact that the President or the Vice-President sits as an *ex officio* member also ensures some sort of continuity.

6. Just as is the case with the members of the Commission, the judges of the Court may not take part in the consideration of any case in which they have a personal interest or in which they have previously acted as the agent, advocate, or adviser of a party or of a person having an interest in the case, or as a member of a tribunal or commission of enquiry, or in any other capacity. If a judge considers that he should not take part in the consideration of a particular case, he informs the President, who shall exempt him from sitting. The initiative may also be taken by the President, when the latter considers that such a withdrawal is desirable. In case of disagreement the Court decides (Rule 24(2), (3) and (4) of the Rules).

7. The hearings of the Court are public, unless the Court decides otherwise in exceptional circumstances (Rule 18 of the Rules). This publicity is a logical implication of the judicial character of the procedure. Moreover, at this stage of the procedure there is less reason for secrecy to protect the defendant

---

101. See for an overview of judgments, in which Art. 50 of the Rules has been applied: appendix III.

State against needlessly harmful publicity than in the procedure before the Commission. Indeed, no case can be brought before the Court unless it has been dealt with by the Commission, where an application has been examined for its admissibility by reference to a number of stringent requirements. Any deceptive or obviously ill-founded applications will not therefore reach the Court, since they have already been eliminated.

The deliberations, on the other hand, are in private (Rule 19 of the Rules).

8. The Court takes its decisions by a majority of votes of the judges present. If the voting is equal, the President has a casting vote (Rule 20 of the Rules).

All the judgments of the Court are published, as are also the documents relating to the proceedings, including the report of the Commission, but excluding any document which the President considers unnecessary to publish (Rule 56(1) of the Rules).[102]

§ 9. THE COMMITTEE OF MINISTERS

1. Unlike the Commission and the Court, the Committee of Ministers has not been set up by the Convention, but here a function has been entrusted to an already existing body of the Council of Europe. Accordingly, the composition, organization, and general functions and powers of the Committee of Ministers are not regulated in the Convention, but in the Statute of the Council of Europe.[103]

2. The function assigned to the Committee of Ministers in the Convention is the result of a compromise. On the one hand, during the drafting of the Convention there was a body of opinion which in addition to the Commission wished to institute a Court with compulsory jurisdiction. Others, however, held that it was preferable to entrust supervision, apart from the Commission, only to the Committee of Ministers. In that case the Committee was to decide on whether or not the opinion of the Commission should be published, and to take, in the light of the Commission's report, those measures which it deemed necessary for the protection of human rights. Ultimately the two alternatives were combined by, on the one hand, making the jurisdiction of the Court optional and, on the other, granting the Committee the power to decide, in

---

102. The judgments and decisions of the Court are published in: *Publications of the European Court of Human Rights*, Series A. The documents of the case, including the report of the Commission, are published in: *Publications of the European Court of Human Rights*, Series B. Since 1985, the main parts of reports of the Commission are also published as an annex in the Series A. In addition a summary is published in the *Yearbook* of the European Convention on Human Rights. Shortly after the judgment of the Court a provisional publication in mimeographed form is available.
103. See Arts 13-21 of the Statute of the Council of Europe.

those cases that are not, or cannot be, submitted to the Court, on the question of whether there has been a violation of the Convention.[104]

3. The Committee of Ministers consists of one representative of each member State of the Council of Europe, as a rule the Minister for Foreign Affairs. In case of the latter's inability to be present, or if other circumstances make it desirable, an alternate may be nominated, who shall, whenever possible, be a member of the government (Art. 14 of the Statute). The Committee in practice has sessions only twice annually (see Art. 21(c) of the Statute). In the intervening periods its duties are discharged by the so-called "Committee of the Ministers' Deputies", consisting of high officials who generally are the permanent representatives of their governments with the Council of Europe. Every representative on the Committee of Ministers appoints a deputy (Rule 14 of the Rules of the Committee of Ministers).

Under its Rules of Procedure the Committee of Deputies is undoubtedly competent to take a decision as provided for in Article 32 of the European Convention.[105] Whether in practice the matter is settled by the Committee of Ministers itself will depend on the circumstances of the case, since the Deputies are not competent to make decisions about matters which in the opinion of one or more of them have important political consequences (Rule 2(3) of the Rules).[106]

4. The sessions of the Committee of Ministers are not public, unless the Committee itself decides otherwise (Art. 21(a) of the Statute). In principle the other rules of procedure, too, which apply to the Committee as executive organ of the Council of Europe, are applicable to its functions within the context of the European Convention. An exception is constituted by Article 32(1) of the Convention. It says that the Committee decides by a majority of two-thirds of the members entitled to sit on the Committee whether there has been a violation of the Convention, whereas under Article 20(a) of the Statute resolutions concerning important matters require the unanimous votes of the representatives casting a vote, and a majority of the representatives entitled to sit on the Committee. This departure from the voting procedure was necessary to give the Committee real powers of decision. Indeed, if the rule of Article 20(a) of the Statute had been declared applicable here as well, a State involved in a given dispute would actually have a right of veto with regard to the examination of that dispute, so that in practice the Committee

---

104. On this, among others, Vasak, *supra* note 93, pp. 198-199.
105. Art. 2 of the Rules of Procedure for meetings of the Ministers' Deputies provides that "the Ministers' Deputies are competent to discuss all matters within the competence of the Committee of Ministers. Decisions taken by the Deputies in virtue of the authority given to them by the Ministers by whom they are appointed are considered as taken on behalf of the Committee of Ministers and have the same force and effect as decisions of the Committee". See the Manual, mentioned *supra* in note 1, p. 20.
106. For decisions of the Committee it is always mentioned in the *Yearbooks* whether the matter has in fact been dealt with by the Committee of Deputies.

in all probability would never be able to decide that there had been a violation of the Convention.

5. As an addition to the provisions in the Convention the Committee has adopted a number of rules for the application of Article 32 of the European Convention,[107] which will be discussed in more detail below.[108] Here it suffices to mention the principal points dealt with in these rules. Article 32(2) of the Convention enables the Committee to give opinions to the State concerned or to make recommendations that are related to the violation of the Convention.[109] Such opinions or recommendations are not binding on the States concerned, since they do not constitute decisions in the sense of Article 32(4) of the Convention (Rule no. 5). It appears from Rule no. 6 that the Committee considers that the Commission is not entitled to make proposals as referred to in Article 31(3) of the Convention when the Commission holds that there has not been a violation of the Convention. Rule no. 10 declares the voting rules of Article 20 of the Statute to be generally applicable.[110] This means in particular that States parties to the dispute, too, have the right to vote. The opinions and recommendations referred to in Rule no. 5 require, in accordance with Rule no. 10, a two-thirds majority of the representatives casting a vote and a majority of the representatives entitled to sit on the Committee. Certain questions of procedure, however, may be determined by a simple majority of the representatives entitled to sit on the Committee. On the procedure, Rules nos 8 and 9 give some very general provisions. The Chairman of the Committee obtains the opinion of the State(s) involved in the dispute in regard to the procedure to be followed. The Committee specifies in what order and within what time-limits the required documents are to be deposited. During the examination of the case the Committee may request information on particular points in the report of the Commission.

§ 10. THE SECRETARY GENERAL OF THE COUNCIL OF EUROPE

1. Besides the Committee of Ministers yet another organ of the Council of Europe plays a part in the Convention, viz. the Secretary General. The Secretary General is the highest official of the Council of Europe and is elected for a period of five years by the Parliamentary Assembly from a list of candidates which is drawn up by the Committee of Ministers (see Art. 36 of the Statute of the Council of Europe).

2. The Secretary General is concerned with the Convention in various ways,

---

107. See *Collected Texts*, Strasbourg 1987, pp. 192-196.
108. See *infra* pp. 192-204.
109. See, *e.g.*, the Resolution of the Committee of Ministers in the Greek Case, *Yearbook* XII; *The Greek Case* (1969), pp. 511 *et seq.*
110. See, however, the voting requirement of Art. 32 of the Convention mentioned on p. 30.

viz. on the one hand by reason of his administrative functions as they result from the Statute of the Council of Europe, and on the other hand in connection with a specific supervisory duty created by the Convention.

In the first place, ratifications of the Convention must be deposited with the Secretary General (Art. 66(1)) and he has to notify the Members of the Council of Europe of the entry-into-force of the Convention and to keep them informed of the names of the States that have become parties to the Convention (Art. 66(4)).[111] A denunciation of the Convention must also be notified to the Secretary General, who informs the other contracting States (Art. 65). In addition, the various declarations which the contracting States may make under the Convention must also be deposited with him. This applies, for instance, to the declaration in which a State recognizes the individual right of complaint. The Secretary General further provides for the publication of such a declaration and transmits a copy of it to the other contracting States (Art. 25(3)). Deposition with the Secretary General is also required for the declaration in which a State recognizes the jurisdiction of the Court as compulsory (Art. 46(3)), and for the notification by a State in which the Convention is declared to extend to a territory for whose international relations it is responsible (Art. 63(1)).

Moreover, any applications to be submitted to the Commission must be filed with the Secretary General (Arts 24 and 25(1)).

Finally, the Secretary General fulfils an important administrative function under Article 15(3) of the Convention. Any State availing itself under Article 15 of the right to derogate, in time of war or another emergency threatening the life of the nation, from one or more provisions of the Convention, must keep the Secretary General fully informed of the measures taken in that context. It must also inform him when such measures have ceased to operate.

3. The most important function assigned to the Secretary General in the Convention, however, is of quite a different nature. Under Article 57 he has the duty to supervise the effective implementation by the contracting States of the provisions of the Convention. This supervisory duty of the Secretary General will be dealt with in a separate chapter (Chapter V).

§ 11. THE RIGHT OF COMPLAINT

What is called here the "right of complaint" under the Convention is in fact the right to take the initiative for the supervisory procedure provided for in the Convention on the ground that the Convention has allegedly been violated by one of the contracting States. The Convention differentiates between the right of complaint for States on the one hand and that for individuals on the other hand. These two forms will be discussed here successively.

---

111. The same applies for all Protocols to the Convention.

11.1. Inter-State applications (Art. 24)

1. When the Convention enters into force for a State, that State acquires the right to lodge, through the Secretary General, an application with the European Commission of Human Rights on the ground of an alleged violation of one or more provisions of the Convention by one of the other contracting States. The right of complaint for States under the European Convention constitutes an important divergence from the traditional principles of international law concerning inter-State action.

According to these principles a State can bring an international action against another State only when a right of the former is at stake because of the alleged violation of international law, or when that State takes up the case of one of its nationals whom it considers to have been treated by the other State in a way contrary to the rules of international law; the so-called "diplomatic protection".[112]

Under the European Convention a State may also lodge a complaint about violations committed against persons who are not its nationals or against persons who are not nationals of any of the contracting States, or are stateless, and even about violations against nationals of the respondent State. States may equally lodge a complaint about the incompatibility with the Convention of the national legislation or of an administrative practice of another State without having to allege a violation against any specified person: the so-called "abstract applications". Thus the right of complaint for States assumes the character of an *actio popularis*: any contracting State has the right to lodge a complaint about an alleged violation of the Convention, regardless of whether there is a special relation between the rights and interests of the applicant State and the alleged violation.[113]

In the *Pfunders* Case between Austria and Italy the Commission stressed that a State which brings an application under Article 24

> is not to be regarded as exercising a right of action for the purpose of enforcing its own rights, but rather as bringing before the Commission an alleged violation of the public order of Europe.[114]

The supervisory procedure provided for in the Convention, therefore, has an objective character; its aim is to protect the fundamental rights of the individual against violations by the contracting States, rather than to implement mutual rights and obligations between those States.

This objective character of the procedure is also clearly stressed in other decisions of the Commission. Thus the Commission has adopted the view that on the ground of the general function assigned to it in Article 19 "to ensure

---

112. On this diplomatic protection, see P. van Dijk, *Judicial Review of Governmental Action and the Requirement of an Interest to Sue*, The Hague 1980, pp. 399-427.
113. On the *actio popularis* in international law: Van Dijk, *supra* note 112, pp. 19-20.
114. Appl. 788/60, *Austria v. Italy, Yearbook* VI (1961), p. 116 (140). See also Appls 9940/82-9944/82, *France, Norway, Denmark, Sweden and the Netherlands v. Turkey, D & R* 35 (1984), p. 143 (169).

33

the observance of the engagements undertaken by the High Contracting Parties in the present Convention", it is competent to examine *ex officio*, also in case of an application by an individual, whether there has been a violation. It need not confine itself to an examination of the violations expressly alleged by the applicant.[115] Another implication of this objective character has been put forward by the Commission's view that, when an applicant withdraws his application or no longer shows any interest in the case, the procedure does not necessarily come to an end, but may be pursued in the public interest. Thus, in its decision on Appl. 2294/64 the Commission expressly held

> that the interests served by the protection of human rights and fundamental freedoms guaranteed by the Convention extend beyond the individual interests of the persons concerned; ... whereas, consequently, the withdrawal of an application and the respondent Government's agreement thereto cannot deprive the Commission of the competence to pursue its examination of the case.[116]

In the case of an inter-State application this objective character also follows from the fact that the procedure is based on a system of *collective* guarantees by the contracting States of the rights and freedoms set forth in the Convention, one or more contracting States taking the initiative on behalf of the collective. Clear examples of this are the applications of Denmark, Norway, Sweden and the Netherlands of September 1967 and the joint application of the three Scandinavian countries of April 1970 against Greece,[117] and the application of the Scandinavian countries, France and the Netherlands of July 1982 against Turkey.[118] The complaints against Greece were in fact lodged at the instance of the Parliamentary Assembly, which considered it the duty of the contracting States to lodge an application under Article 24 in the case of an alleged serious violation.[119]

2. The Convention of course at the same time protects the personal interests of the contracting States when they claim that the rights set forth in the Convention must be secured to their nationals coming under the jurisdiction of another contracting State. And even though States have the right to initiate a procedure in which they have no special interest, in practice they will more readily be inclined to bring an application when there has been a violation against persons who are their nationals or with whom they have some special link.

---

115. See, *e.g.*, Appl. 202/56, *X v. Belgium, Yearbook* I (1955-57), p. 190 (192) and the joined Appls 7604/76, 7719/76 and 7781/77, *Foti, Lentini and Cenerini v. Italy, D & R* 14 (1979), p. 133 (143).
116. Appl. 2294/64, *Gericke v. Federal Republic of Germany, Yearbook* VIII (1965), p. 314 (320); see also Appl. 2686/65, *Heinz Kornmann v. Federal Republic of Germany, Yearbook* IX (1966), p. 494 (506-508).
117. Appls 3321-3323 and 3344/67, *Denmark, Norway, Sweden and the Netherlands v. Greece, Yearbook* XI (1968), p. 690, and Appl. 4448/70, *Denmark, Norway and Sweden v. Greece, Yearbook* XIII (1970), p. 108.
118. Appls 9940-9944/82, *France, Norway, Denmark, Sweden and the Netherlands v. Turkey, D & R* 35 (1984), p. 143.
119. Resolution 346 (1967), "On the situation in Greece", Council of Europe, Cons. Ass., Nineteenth Ordinary Session, Second Part, 25-28 September 1967, *Texts Adopted.*

A case in which the applicant State's own nationals were involved occurred for the first time when Cyprus brought applications against Turkey concerning the treatment of the Cypriotic nationals during the Turkish invasion of Cyprus.[120] In total, three applications emanated from this dispute.[121] Examples of applications concerning persons with whom the applicant State had a special relation other than the link of nationality are the applications of Greece against the United Kingdom, which concerned the treatment of Cypriots of Greek origin.[122] Further, Austria lodged a complaint in the above-mentioned *Pfunders* Case in connection with the prosecution of six young men by Italy for the murder of an Italian customs officer in the boundary region of Alto Adige (Upper Tyrol) disputed by both States.[123] The applications of Ireland against the United Kingdom, finally, concerned the treatment of and the legislation concerning the Roman Catholics of Northern Ireland, who aspire for union with the Irish Republic.[124]

3. In order for State complaints to be admissible hardly any evidence is required. In fact the Commission has deduced from the English text ("alleged breach") and from the French wording ("qu'elle croira pouvoir être imputé") that the allegation of such a breach is, in principle, sufficient under this provision (Article 24).[125] According to the Commission State complaints do not even require *prima facie* evidence at the admissibility stage. The Commission bases this point of view on the fact that the provisions of Article 27(2) - empowering it to declare inadmissible any petition submitted under Article 25, which it considers either incompatible with the provisions of the Convention or manifestly ill-founded - apply, according to their express terms, to individual applications under Article 25 only, and that, consequently, any examination of the merits of State complaints must be entirely reserved for the post-admissibility stage.[126] On the other hand the Commission is of the opinion that Article 27 does not exclude the application of a general rule according to which an application under Article 24 may be declared inadmissible if it is clear from the outset that it is wholly unsubstantiated, or otherwise lacking the requirements of a genuine allegation in the sense of Article 24 of the Convention.[127]

4. Up to the present moment, a total of 18 applications by States have been lodged. This total, which is already low, moreover gives a distorted picture. In fact, only six situations in different States have been put forward in

120. Appls 6780/74 and 6950/75, *Cyprus v. Turkey*, Yearbook XVIII (1975), p. 82.
121. See also: Appl. 8007/77, *Cyprus v. Turkey*, Yearbook XX (1977), p. 98.
122. Appls 176/56 and 299/57, *Greece v. United Kingdom*, Yearbook II (1958/59), pp. 182 and 186 respectively.
123. Appl. 788/60, *Austria v. Italy*, Yearbook IV (1961), p. 116.
124. Appls 5310/71 and 5451/72, *Ireland v. United Kingdom*, Yearbook XV (1972), p. 76.
125. Appls 9940/82-9944/82, *France, Norway, Denmark, Sweden and the Netherlands v. Turkey*, D & R 35 (1984), p. 143 (161).
126. *Ibidem.*
127. *Ibidem*, p. 162.

Strasbourg by means of an inter-State application. In the fifties, Greece complained twice about the conduct of the United Kingdom in Cyprus, Austria filed a complaint in 1960 about the course of events during proceedings against South Tyrolean activists in Italy, the five applications of the Scandinavian countries and the Netherlands concerned the situation in Greece during the military regime, Ireland lodged two applications against the United Kingdom about the activities of the military and the police in Ulster, all three applications of Cyprus were connected with the Turkish invasion of that island, while the five applications of 1982 all relate to the situation of Turkey under the military regime.

Given the number of violations that have occurred during the almost forty years that the Convention is in force, it is evident that the right of complaint of States has proved not to be very effective. The idea contained in the preamble, as it was also formulated by the Commission in the above-mentioned *Pfunders* Case, *viz.* that the contracting States were to guarantee the protection of the rights and freedoms collectively, has hardly materialized. Save for two exceptional cases,[128] the contracting States have not been willing to lodge complaints about situations in other States if no interest of their own was involved. Such a step generally runs counter to their own interest in that a charge of violation of the Convention is bound to be considered an unfriendly act by the other party, with all the political consequences that may be involved.[129] On the other hand, an application by a State which does have an interest of its own may equally create negative effects. As Polak, a one-time member of the Commission, stated, lodging such an application acts as a weapon which often will not contribute to the solution of the underlying political dispute.[130] In comparison with inter-State applications, individual complaints have the advantage that in general political considerations will not play so important a part in them, although there, too, political motives may sometimes constitute the real incentive for an application. For this reason as well it is highly desirable that individual complaints can be lodged against all contracting States. At the time when some contracting States had not recognized the individual right of complaint, the inter-State procedure - apart from the remedy of Article 57, which so far has not been very satisfactory - was the only, though not very effective, expedient for supervising the observance by all contracting States of their obligations under the Convention.

---

128. The applications of the Scandinavian countries and the Netherlands against Greece in 1967 and 1970 and the applications of France, the Netherlands and the Scandinavian countries against Turkey in 1982.
129. For this reason, if an individual complaint and a complaint by a State are filed on the same subject, Alkema wants to regard the former in comparison with the latter as a domestic remedy in the sense of Art. 26, which would first have to be exhausted: Alkema, *supra* note 47, pp. 6-7.
130. C.H.F. Polak, "Het Europees verdrag tot bescherming van de rechten van de mens en de fundamentele vrijheden" (The European Convention for the protection of human rights and fundamental freedoms), in: P. van Dijk (ed.), *Rechten van de mens in mundiaal en Europees perspectief* (Human rights in worldwide and European perspective), 2nd ed., Utrecht 1980, pp. 58-76 (61).

11.2. Individual applications (Art. 25)

1. Article 25(1) of the Convention provides:

> The Commission may receive petitions addressed to the Secretary General of the Council of Europe from any person, non-governmental organisation or group of individuals claiming to be the victim of a violation by one of the High Contracting Parties of the rights set forth in this Convention, provided that the High Contracting Party against which the complaint has been lodged has declared that it recognizes the competence of the Commission to receive such petitions. Those of the High Contracting Parties who have made such a declaration undertake not to hinder in any way the effective exercise of this right.

The individual right of complaint was not accepted without dispute during the drafting of the Convention. Initially there were great differences of opinion between the Consultative Assembly and the Committee of Ministers. The Assembly wanted an individual right of complaint which could be exercised in all cases, whereas in the view of the Ministers such a right ought to be exercised only under the supervision and with the consent of the government concerned. Some less far-reaching constructions were also found to be unacceptable to the Committee of Ministers. It was proposed, for instance, to incorporate the individual right of complaint into the Convention on the condition that a State might veto the examination by the Commission of particular applications. This right of veto in turn would have to be subject to the collective supervision of the other States in order to prevent its abuse. The Consultative Assembly also proposed the formula according to which the individual right of complaint was to be incorporated into the Convention, but the States could exclude this right with respect to applications directed against them.[131] Finally, agreement was reached on the compromise as now laid down in the Convention: the Commission may receive an application from an individual only if the State against which such an application has been lodged has expressly recognized the competence of the Commission to receive such applications. States which, via the so-called "colonial clause", have declared the Convention to be applicable to one or more of the territories under their responsibility may recognize also for those territories the competence of the Commission to receive applications of individuals (art. 63(4)).

2. The Commission has had the competence to receive applications of individuals since 5 July 1955. At that date the condition of Article 25(4) was satisfied that at least six contracting States must have made a declaration as referred to in Article 25(1). Since 1987 an individual may lodge an application against all twenty-two contracting States.

3. Article 25 undoubtedly constitutes the most progressive provision of the European Convention. It removes the principal limitation by which the position of the individual in international law is generally characterized.

---

131. For a more detailed discussion, see Monconduit, *supra* note 73, pp. 177 *et seq.*

Elsewhere attention has already been drawn to the deficiencies of the institute of diplomatic protection as an instrument for effective protection of human rights.[132] One improvement in that respect is the elimination of the condition of the link of nationality in the case of a complaint by a State. Especially, however, the individual right of complaint, despite its limitations, constitutes a considerable improvement over the classic system. Precisely because States are generally reluctant to submit an application against another State, the individual right of complaint constitutes a necessary expedient for achieving the aim of the Convention to secure the rights and freedoms of individuals against the States.

The English version of Article 25 speaks of "petition". In the practice of the Commission this term has been replaced by "application", a term which comes nearer to the French "requête". Indeed, the meaning of the term "petition" in continental and international legal usage is somewhat different from its meaning within the common-law systems. In the former meaning, the aim of the right of petition is mainly to inform the relevant authorities of a certain problem or situation, and does not lead automatically to subsequent proceedings. The application of an individual under the European Convention, on the contrary, means the start of proceedings. In fact, the Commission is bound, after receipt of an application, to examine the latter for its admissibility, and subsequently, if it is declared admissible, to pursue the procedure, i.e. to attempt to bring about a friendly settlement and, if no friendly settlement is reached, to draw up a report on the facts of the case, which is then transmitted to the Committee of Ministers. Throughout this procedure before the Commission the individual applicant may be regarded as a party, a position which, under international law, a petitioner does not have during the examination of his petition.

4. When a State has made the declaration under Article 25(1), anyone who is in some respect subject to the jurisdiction of that State may lodge an application against the State in question. As appears from Article 1 the nationality of the applicant is irrelevant. This means that the right of complaint is conferred not only on the nationals of the State concerned, but also on those of other contracting States - regardless of whether the latter themselves have made the declaration of Article 25(1) -, on the nationals of States which are not parties to the Convention, and on stateless persons, so long as they satisfy the condition referred to in Article 1, viz. that they come under the jurisdiction of the respondent State.

Besides individuals, also non-governmental organizations and groups of persons may lodge an application. With respect to the last-mentioned category the Commission decided during its first session that these must be groups which have been established in a regular way according to the law of one of the contracting States. If that is not the case, the application must have been

132.   See p. 33 and note 112.

signed by all the persons belonging to the group.[133] As to the category of non-governmental organizations, the Commission decided that they must be *private* organizations, and that municipalities, for instance, cannot be considered as such.[134]

5. Unlike what applies to States, for individuals a special relation to the violation complained of is required. Whereas States may complain about "any alleged breach of the provisions of the Convention by another High Contracting Party" (Art. 24), and consequently also about national legislation or administrative practices *in abstracto*,[135] individuals must claim "to be the victim of a violation by one of the High Contracting Parties of the rights set forth in this Convention" (Art. 25). The special relation required is therefore that the individual applicant himself is the victim of the alleged violation.[136] He may not bring an *actio popularis*, that is to say that he may not submit to the Commission abstract complaints or complaints relating exclusively to other individuals.[137]

The Commission has, however, declared admissible individual applications which had a *partly* abstract character. Thus, a number of Northern Irishmen complained on the one hand about torture to which they had allegedly been subjected by the British during their detention, while further they claimed that this treatment formed part of "a systematic administrative pattern which permits and encourages brutality". They requested the Commission, *inter alia*, for "a full investigation of the allegations made in the present application as well as of the system of interrogation currently employed by security forces under the control of the United Kingdom in Northern Ireland, for the purpose of determining whether or not such specific acts and administrative practices are incompatible with the European Convention for the Protection of Human Rights and Fundamental Freedoms".[138] The British Government submitted that the second part of the application was not admissible and referred to the case-law of the Commission with respect to abstract complaints. The Commission held, however, that

> neither Article 25, nor any other provisions in the Convention, *inter alia* Article 27(1)(b), prevent an individual applicant from raising before the Commission a complaint in respect of an alleged administrative practice in breach of the Convention provided that he brings

---

133. See the report of the session in question; DH(54)3, p. 8.
134. See, *e.g.*, the joined Appls 5767/72, 5922/72, 5929-5931/72, 5953-5957/72, 5984-5988/73 and 6011/73, *Austrian municipalities v. Austria, Yearbook* XVII (1974), p. 338 (352).
135. See *supra* p. 33.
136. This question remains relevant throughout the examination of the application: Appl. 9320/81, *D v. Federal Republic of Germany, D & R* 36 (1984), p. 24 (30-31).
137. Thus the Commission in, *e.g.*, Appl. 6481/74, *X v. Italy, D & R* 1 (1975), p. 79; Appl. 6742/74, *X v. Federal Republic of Germany, D & R* 3 (1976), p. 98; Appl. 8612/79, *Alliances des Belges de la Communauté Européenne v. Belgium, D & R* 15 (1979), p. 259 (262-263); Appl. 9297/81, *X Association v. Sweden, D & R* 28 (1982), p. 204 (206); Appl. 9900/82, *X Union v. France, D & R* 32 (1983), p. 261 (265); Appl. 9777/82, *T. v. Belgium, D & R* 34 (1983), p. 158 (169). See also the judgment of 13 June 1979, Marckx, A.31 (1979), p. 13.
138. Appls 5577-5583/72, *Donnelly v. United Kingdom, Yearbook* XVI (1973), p. 212 (216).

prima facie evidence of such a practice and of his being a victim of it.[139]

An individual application may therefore be concerned not only with the personal interest of the applicant, but also with the public interest, and thus the procedure that originates from an individual complaint may in some respects also assume an objective character.[140]

6. The requirement of "victim" implies that the violation of the Convention must have affected the applicant in some way. According to the Court's well-established case-law "The word 'victim' in Article 25 refers to the person directly affected by the act or omission at issue".[141] To this the Court usually adds a phrase of the sort that "the existence of a violation is conceivable even in the absence of prejudice, prejudice being relevant for the purposes of Article 50".[142]

In the cases of *Van den Brink* and those of *Zuiderveld and Klappe* the respondent government contended before the Court that the applicants could not claim to be victims of a breach of Article 5(3) as the time each one spent in custody on remand was deducted in its entirety from the sentence ultimately imposed on them. According to the Court the relevant deduction from sentence does not *per se* deprive the individual concerned of his status as an alleged victim within the meaning of Article 25 of a breach of Article 5(3). The Court added: "The position might be otherwise if the deduction from sentence had been based upon an acknowledgement by the national courts of a violation of the Convention".[143]

Similarly, in the *Inze* Case the fact that a judicial settlement, concluded between the private parties on their own, had possibly mitigated the disadvantage suffered by the applicant, was considered insufficient reason to deprive him of his status as victim. Here again the Court added that

The position might have been otherwise if, for instance, the national authorities had acknowledged either expressly or in substance, and then afforded redress for, the alleged breach of the Convention.[144]

The requirement that the applicant be *personally* affected by the alleged violation has also been stressed by the Commission right from the beginning. Thus, an application in which it was submitted that the Norwegian legislation concerning *abortus provocatus* conflicted with Article 2(1) of the Convention, was declared inadmissible because of the fact that the applicant had not

---

139. *Ibidem*, p. 260. However, in the second instance, via application of Art. 29, the said complaints have after all been declared inadmissible, because of non-exhaustion of domestic remedies; *Yearbook* XIX (1976), p. 82 (252-254).
140. See *supra* pp. 33-35.
141. Most recently the judgment of 28 October 1987, *Inze*, A.126 (1988), p. 16. See also the judgment of 10 December 1982, *Corigliano*, A.57 (1983), p. 12; the judgment of 22 May 1984, *De Jong, Baljet and Van den Brink*, A.77 (1984), p. 20; the judgment of 22 May 1984, *Van der Sluys, Zuiderveld and Klappe*, A.78 (1984), p. 16; and the judgment of 18 December 1986, *Johnston and others*, A.112 (1987), p. 21.
142. *Idem.*
143. A.77 (1984), p. 20 and A.78 (1984), p. 16 respectively.
144. A.126 (1988), p. 16.

alleged that he himself was the victim of this legislation. Indeed, he had lodged his application "on behalf of parents who without their own consent or knowledge ... have or will have their offspring taken away by abortus provocatus, and on behalf of those taken away by such operations - all unfit or unable to plead on their own behalf".[145]

In an almost identical case an Austrian applicant submitted that the abortion legislation of his country conflicted with Articles 2 and 8 of the Convention. His application was also not admitted, because the Commission, as it stated, "is not competent to examine *in abstracto* its [the disputed legislation's] compatibility with the Convention". According to the Commission the applicant had meant to bring an *actio popularis*. He had submitted that the legislation in question actually concerned every Austrian citizen "because of its effects for the future of the nation and for the moral and legal standard of the nation", and had declared himself willing "to be nominated curator to act on behalf of the unborn in general".[146]

A somewhat divergent view was taken in some other decisions of the Commission concerning cases in which abortion legislation was involved. A German Act of 1974, which removed penalties for abortion, had been declared by the *Bundesverfassungsgericht* to conflict with the German Constitution. A regulation concerning abortion was subsequently enacted which met the requirement, laid down in this judicial decision, and was then incorporated into a new Act of 1976. With respect to the judgment of the *Bundesverfassungsgericht* and its consequences an application was lodged on the ground of alleged violation of Article 8 of the Convention by an organization, a man and two women. The application of the organization was declared inadmissible by the Commission, fully in line with its decision in the above-mentioned Norwegian case, because it did not concern a physical person, but a legal person;[147] the abortion legislation could not be applicable to the organization, and the latter could not therefore be considered the victim.[148] The same also applied to the application of the man; the law had

---

145. Appl. 867/60, *X v. Norway*, Yearbook IV (1961), p. 270 (276).
146. Appl. 7045/75, *X v. Austria*, D & R 7 (1977), p. 87 (88). See also Appl. 7806/77, *Webster v. United Kingdom*, D & R 12 (1978), p. 168 (174).
147. See Annex II to the report of 12 July 1977, *Brüggemann and Scheuten*, D & R 10 (1978), p. 100 (121).
148. In other cases, too, it was stressed that some of the rights and freedoms included in the Convention apply only to natural persons. See, *e.g.*, Appl. 9900/82, *X Union v. France*, D & R 32 (1983), p. 261 (264), where the Commission stated: "In the present case, the applicant union as a legal person does not itself claim to be the victim of an infringement of the right to free choice of residence guaranteed by Article 2 of Protocol no. 4, since the legislative restrictions in question are only applicable to natural persons. ... It might however be considered that the application really emanates from the members of the union, which is empowered ... to initiate proceedings on behalf of its members. ... However, it is noted in this context that the petition does not mention any specific case of one or more teachers alleged to be subjected to a measure constituting an infringement." Obviously, other rights or freedoms are clearly applicable to legal persons as well; see Appl. 9905/82, *A. Association and H. v. Austria*, D & R 36 (1984), p. 187 (192-193), lodged by a political party and its chairman/legal representative alleging violation of Article 11 because of the prohibition of a meeting: "As the right invoked ... can be exercised by both the organisor of a meeting, even if it should be a legal person as in the present case, and
(continued...)

not been applied to him and according to the Commission he had not proved at all that the bare existence of the law had injured him to such an extent that he could claim to be the victim of a violation of the Convention.[149] However, the Commission here seems to leave open the possibility that the bare existence of abortion legislation also injures a man to such an extent that he must be considered its victim. This impression is corroborated by the decision of the Commission with respect to the two women. Indeed, according to their submissions they themselves were not pregnant, nor had an interruption of pregnancy been refused to them, and they had not been prosecuted for illegal abortion either. However, they considered that the Convention had been violated *vis-à-vis* them because in consequence of the legislation in question they were obliged to abstain from sexual relations, or to use contraceptives, of which they disapproved for several reasons, including health, or to become pregnant against their will. The Commission recognized that both women were victims in the sense of Article 25 on the following ground:

> The Commission considers that pregnancy and the interruption of pregnancy are part of private life, and also in certain circumstances of family life. It further considers that respect for private life comprises also, to a certain degree, the right to establish and develop relationships with other human beings, especially in the emotional field, for the development and fulfilment of one's own personality ... and that therefore sexual life is also part of private life; and in particular that legal regulation of abortion is an intervention in private life which may or may not be justified under Article 8(2).[150]

The Commission therefore takes the position that a legal regulation of abortion constitutes an interference with private life, and under certain circumstances with family life as well, which may or may not be justified on the ground of Article 8(2). Women may allege to be the victims of that regulation even if it has not actually been enforced against them. The consideration quoted above is formulated in very general terms and leaves scope for the interpretation that in certain cases even men may be considered victims of the bare existence of abortion legislation. As stated, in the case concerned the man was not admitted, because the victim-requirement was not satisfied. However, he had lodged his application in his capacity as chairman of the above-mentioned organization. The decision, therefore, does not exclude that a man's application be declared admissible if he complains before the Commission about abortion legislation in his capacity as a husband or a partner in an extramarital relationship. In a case of 1980 the Commission confirmed this interpretation. There the applicant challenged the English legislation under which his wife had undergone *abortus provocatus*. According to the Commission the requirement of Article 25 had been satisfied on the simple consideration that "the applicant, as potential father, was so closely

---

148.(...continued)
    by individual participants, the Commission accepts that both applicants are entitled to be victims of a violation of their rights under Article 11." With regard to non-governmental organizations, see also pp. 404-405.
149. *D & R* 10 (1978), p. 121.
150. Appl. 6959/75, *Brüggemann and Scheuten v. Federal Republic of Germany, D & R* 5 (1976), p. 103 (115).

affected by the termination of his wife's pregnancy that he may claim to be a victim".[151]

In a case where a journalist and two newspapers alleged violation of their right to receive and impart information as a result of a ruling by the House of Lords that a lawyer had acted in contempt of court because she had allowed inspection of confidential documents by the journalist after these had been read out in the course of a public hearing, the Commission took a more restrictive position. It declared the application inadmissible because it did

> not consider that the concept of "victim" in Article 25(1) may be interpreted so broadly, in the present case, as to encompass every newspaper or journalist in the United Kingdom who might conceivably be affected by the decision of the House of Lords. The form of detriment required must be of a less indirect and remote nature.[152]

This decision would seem to deviate from the Commission's above-mentioned case-law as the ruling by the House of Lords clearly implied a restraint for the applicants. Furthermore, the reasoning upon which it is based is, in our opinion, not very convincing. The argument that the applicants remained free to publish articles on the disputed subject overlooks that not only the right to impart but also that to receive information was invoked. Similarly, the fact that the decision of the House of Lords was, according to the Commission "one which affected every interested journalist in the United Kingdom", does not justify the conclusion that therefore the applicants cannot be considered victims within the meaning of Article 25(1).[153]

In another case the Commission as well as the Court accepted as victims in the sense of Article 25 a category of persons who could not be ascertained with certainty to have suffered an injury. The reason of this acceptance consisted in the fact that the applicants could not know whether the challenged legislation had or had not been applied to them. This matter came up in the *Klass* Case.[154] In this case three lawyers, a judge and a public prosecutor alleged the violation of the secrecy of mail and telecommunications by the authorities. The measures concerned were secret in so far that the persons in question were not informed of them in all cases, and if so, only afterwards. The Commission settled the matter of the victim-requirement in a brief consideration, stressing the secret character of the measures and concluding as follows: "In view of this particularity of the case the applicants have to be considered as victims for purposes of Article 25".[155] The Court dealt with the matter much more in detail. It stated at the outset that according to Article 25 individuals in principle may neither bring an *actio popularis* nor complain about legislation *in abstracto*.[156] The principle of effectiveness (*l'effet utile*), however, according to the Court calls for exceptions to this rule. This principle implies that the procedural provisions of the

---

151. Appl. 8416/78, *X v. United Kingdom*, D & R 19 (1980), p. 244 (248).
152. Appl. 10039/82, *Leigh and others v. United Kingdom*, D & R 38 (1984), p. 74 (78).
153. *Ibidem*.
154. For the examination of the merits, see *infra* pp. 597-600.
155. Appl. 5029/71, *Klass v. Federal Republic of Germany*, Yearbook XVII (1974), p. 178 (208).
156. Judgment of 6 September 1978, A.28 (1979), pp. 17-18.

Convention are to be applied in such a way as to contribute to the effectiveness of the system of individual applications. All this induced the Court to conclude that

an individual may, *under certain conditions*, claim to be the victim of a violation occasioned by the mere existence of secret measures or of legislation permitting secret measures, without having to allege that such measures were in fact applied to him.[157]

Such conditions were satisfied in the case under consideration, since

the contested legislation institutes a system of surveillance under which all persons in the Federal Republic of Germany can potentially have their mail, post and telecommunications monitored, without their even knowing this unless there has been either some indiscretion or subsequent notification.[158]

This may be summarized to imply that in case of the existence of secret measures (whether based on legislation or not) the victim-requirement under Article 25 may already be satisfied when the applicant is a *potential* victim. A comparable line of reasoning was followed by the Commission in the *Malone* Case, in which it found that the

applicant is directly affected by the law and practice in England and Wales ... under which the secret surveillance of postal and telephone communications on behalf of the police is permitted and takes place. His communication has at all relevant times been liable to such surveillance without his being able to obtain knowledge of it. Accordingly ... he is entitled to claim ... to be a victim ... irrespective of whether or to what extent he is able to show that it has actually been applied to him.[159]

The reasoning of the Court in the *Klass* Case quoted above was relied upon by two mothers, who submitted, on behalf of their children, violation of Article 3 of the Convention on the ground of the existence of a system of corporal punishment at the schools in Scotland attended by their children. According to the Commission there was no direct analogy with the *Klass* Case, but it did refer to the criterion of effectiveness relied upon by the Court in that case, and it held subsequently:

that in order to be accepted as victims under Article 25 of the Convention, individuals must satisfy the Commission that they run the risk of being directly affected by the particular matter which they wish to bring before it.[160]

Thus, here again the mere fact of running a risk was deemed sufficient to be considered as "victims". According to the Commission it would be too restrictive an interpretation of Article 25 to require that the children had in actual fact been subjected to corporal punishment. It therefore considered the children as victims because they "may be affected by the existence of physical violence around them and by the threat of a potential use on themselves of corporal punishment".[161]

---

157. *Ibidem*, p. 18.
158. *Ibidem*, pp. 19-20.
159. Report of 17 December 1982, *Malone*, A.82 (1984), p. 52. So also Appl. 10799/84, *Radio X, S, W & A v. Switzerland*, D & R 37 (1984), p. 236 (239).
160. Report of 16 May 1980, *Campbell and Cosans*, B.42 (1985), p. 36.
161. *Ibidem*, pp. 36-37. The Court in its judgment of 25 February 1982 did not deal with this question, as it had concluded that Article 3 of the Convention had not been violated, A.48 (1982), p. 14.

Shortly afterwards, in the *Marckx* Case, the Court reached the same decision by express reference to the *Klass* Case. In the *Marckx* Case it had been advanced that the Belgian legislation concerning illegitimate children conflicted with the Convention. Before the Court the Belgian Government submitted that this was in reality an abstract complaint, since the challenged legislation had not been applied to the applicant. The Court held:

> Article 25 of the Convention entitles individuals to contend that a law violates their rights by itself, in the absence of an individual measure of implementation, if they run the risk of being directly affected by it.[162]

This was considered to be the case here. According to the Court the question of whether the applicant has actually been placed in an unfavourable position is not a criterion of the victim-requirement:

> the question of prejudice is not a matter for Article 25 which, in its use of the word "victim", denotes "the person directly affected by the act or omission which is in issue".[163]

The question of whether applicants having a *future* interest may also be considered victims in the sense of Article 25 was avoided by the Commission in a case concerning Article 2 of the First Protocol. In this case forty mothers claimed that, in consequence of an Act on pre-school education promulgated in Sweden on 21 December 1973, they had been deprived of the right to send their children to the school of their choice. As to the admissibility of their application, the Commission divided the mothers into three groups. The mothers from the first group could not be regarded as victims, because their children were already past pre-school age at the moment of the Act's effective date. The second group consisted of mothers whose children had not yet reached pre-school age at that moment. With respect to this group the Commission held as follows:

> The Commission understands that these applicants consider themselves to be victims of a violation of the Convention in that the Act on Pre-School Activities may affect them in the future. The Commission notes that the children of these applicants in some cases might have reached pre-school age in the course of proceedings before the Commission. However, having regard to the fact that the applicants in Group 3 [the mothers of children that had pre-school age at the moment referred to] can be considered to be victims within the meaning of Article 25 of the Convention for the purpose of the present application, the Commission can abstain from examining as to whether the applicants in Group 2 also can be so considered.[164]

Here the Commission therefore did not go into the issue of whether a person satisfies the victim-requirement according to Article 25 when he complains about an alleged violation of the Convention which may injure him in the future. From an earlier decision of the Commission in a similar case, however, one can infer implicitly that the Commission is indeed prepared to recognize

---

162. Judgment of 13 June 1979, *Marckx*, A.31 (1979), pp. 12-14.
163. *Ibidem*. See also the judgment of 22 October 1981, *Dudgeon*, A.45 (1982), p. 18, where the Court held: "In the personal circumstances of the applicant, the very existence of this legislation continuously and directly affects his private life". See also the Commission in: Appl. 8307/78, *De Klerck v. Belgium*, D & R 21 (1981), p. 116 (124); Appl. 8811/79, *Seven individuals v. Sweden*, D & R 29 (1982), p. 104 (109); Appl. 9697/82, *J. and others v. Ireland*, D & R 34 (1983), p. 131 (137).
164. Appl. 6853/74, *40 Mothers v. Sweden*, Yearbook XX (1977), p. 214 (236).

a future interest in certain cases. In that case two parents complained about legal and administrative measures concerning sexual instruction at primary schools, which, however, were not yet applicable to their school-age daughter. Nevertheless, the Commission admitted their application. Curiously enough, however, it did not mention the victim-requirement at all.[165] All the same, in our opinion the admissibility may very well be justified as follows: in cases like this one the consideration that the alleged violation - in this case the application of the said measures to the child - will at all events take place in the near future is of greater weight than the fact that this is not yet the case at the moment of the examination of the complaint. Certainly in cases where otherwise the interests of the applicant would be irreparably prejudiced, this view ensues imperatively from the nature of the legal protection envisaged by the Convention.

In the *Kirkwood* Case such a situation was at stake. This case concerned a man complaining that his envisaged extradition from the United Kingdom to California would amount to inhuman and degrading treatment contrary to Article 3 of the Convention since, if extradited, he would be tried for two accusations of murder and one of attempt to murder, and would very probably be sentenced to death. He argued that the circumstances surrounding the implementation of such a death penalty, and in particular the "death row" phenomenon of excessive delay during a prolonged appeal procedure lasting several years, during which he would be gripped with uncertainty as to the outcome of his appeal and therefore as to his fate, would constitute inhuman and degrading treatment. The Commission held as follows with respect to the victim-requirement:

> In these circumstances, faced with an imminent act of the executive, the consequences of which for the applicant will allegedly expose him to Article 3 treatment, the Commission finds that the applicant is able to claim to be a victim of an alleged violation of Article 3.[166]

On the other hand, if an alleged future prejudice cannot yet be foreseen at all, the Commission declares the application inadmissible.[167]

The construction of the so-called *indirect* victim has become firmly established in the case-law of the Commission: it is conceivable that an individual may experience a personal injury owing to a violation of the Convention against another. Under certain circumstances the Commission therefore confers on an individual the right to lodge an application on his own account about a violation of the Convention against another, *i.e.* without the applicant himself having directly suffered a violation of one of his rights or freedoms. In such a case the applicant must have so close a link with the direct victim of the violation of the Convention that he himself is also to be considered a victim and accordingly has suffered a personal injury. On that basis the Commission has developed in its case-law the concept of "indirect

---

165. Appl. 5095/71, *V and A Kjeldsen v. Denmark, Yearbook* XV (1972), pp. 482-502.
166. Appl. 10479/83, *Kirkwood v. United Kingdom, D & R* 37 (1984), p. 158 (182).
167. Appl. 2358/64, *X v. Sweden, Coll.* 23 (1967), p. 147 (151).

victim", meaning that a near relative of the victim or any other third party can refer the matter to the Commission on his own initiative in so far as the violation concerned is (also) prejudicial to him or in so far as he has a valid personal interest in the termination of that violation.[168] Thus, a woman was considered a victim in view of the fact that she had suffered financial and moral injury in consequence of a violation of the Convention committed against her husband.[169] That a purely non-material interest, too, is sufficient for the admissibility of the action of an applicant as the indirect victim becomes evident, for example, from the decision by the Commission that a complaint of a mother about the treatment of her detained son was admissible.[170] On the other hand, an applicant was not admitted who submitted that his sisters had wrongfully failed to receive compensation for their sufferings during the Nazi regime, and who now claimed this as yet in his own name. This compensation could relate only to the sufferings of the sisters, not to those of the applicant, so that the latter could not be considered as the victim.[171]

Finally, it should be mentioned here that in certain cases the Commission qualifies shareholders as victims of alleged violations of rights and freedoms against the company. It appears from its case-law that the Commission does not, however, regard shareholders in such cases as indirect but as direct victims.[172] It should be stressed, however, that in the cases referred to the individual concerned held a majority shareholding in the company. Conversely, according to the Commission in the *Yarrow* Case, a minority shareholder of Company A cannot claim to be a victim of an interference with property rights of Company B, all the securities in which are owned by Company A, because the nationalization measure did not involve him personally. In the view of the Commission, it was only open to Company A to lodge a complaint under the Convention.[173]

---

168. Appl. 100/55, *X v. Federal Republic of Germany, Yearbook* I (1955-57), p. 162 (162-163).
169. Appl. 1478/62, *Y v. Belgium, Yearbook* VI (1963), p. 590 (620). See also Appl. 7467/76, *X v. Belgium, D & R* 8 (1978), p. 220 (221), where an applicant was regarded as an indirect victim because he had submitted that his twin brother had wrongfully been detained in a State institution, in which he had died later. And see Appls 9214/80, 9473/81 and 9474/81, *X, Cabales & Balkandali, D & R* 29 (1982), p. 176 (182): "When the alleged violation concerns a refusal of a leave to remain or an entry clearance, the spouse of the individual concerned can claim to be a victim, even if the individual concerned is in fact staying with her, but unlawfully and under constant threat of deportation".
170. Appl. 898/60, *Y v. Austria, Coll.* 8 (1962), p. 136. See also Appl. 7011/75, *Becker v. Denmark, Yearbook* XIX (1976), p. 416 (450), where a German journalist challenged the repatriation of 199 Vietnamese children, proposed by the Danish Government, as contrary to Art. 3 of the Convention. And Appl. 9320/81, *D v. Federal Republic of Germany, D & R* 36 (1984), p. 24 (31): "The answer to this question (whether an applicant can claim to be a victim) depends largely on the legal interest which the applicant has in a determination of his allegations of Convention breaches. In assessing this interest, any material or immaterial damage suffered ... as a result of the alleged violation must be taken into account." See also Appl. 9348/81, *W v. United Kingdom, D & R* 32 (1983), p. 190 (198-200) and Appl. 9360/81, *W v. Ireland, D & R* 32 (1983), p. 211 (212-216).
171. Appl. 113/55, *X v. Federal Republic of Germany, Yearbook* I (1955-57), p. 161 (162). See also Appl. 9639/82, *B, R and J v. Federal Republic of Germany, D & R* 36 (1984), p. 139.
172. Appl. 1706/62, *X v. Austria, Yearbook* XI (1966), p. 112 (130) and the report of 17 July 1980, *Kaplan, D & R* 21 (1981), p. 5 (23-24).
173. Appl. 9266/81, *Yarrow and others v. United Kingdom, D & R* 30 (1983), p. 155 (184-185).

Cases may occur in which the violation complained of has meanwhile been terminated, or at least no longer exists at the moment the Commission examines the case. The applicant will then not be admitted, because he can no longer allege that he is a victim; the alleged violation, therefore, must still exist at the moment the case is examined by the Commission.[174]

7. The requirement that the violation of the Convention must have caused the applicant a personal injury does not, of course, prevent an application from being lodged by his representative.[175] Furthermore, if the victim himself is not, or not very well, able to undertake an action - for example a detained person, a patient in a mental clinic, a very young person - then a close relative, a guardian, a curator, or another person may act on his behalf. In that case, however, the name of the victim must be made known and the latter, if possible, must have given his consent for lodging the application.[176] In case of decease of the victim, his heir may lodge an application or uphold a previously lodged application, only if the allegedly violated right forms part of the estate or if on other grounds he himself is to be considered the (direct or indirect) victim.[177]

In the *Kofler* Case the Commission stated clearly: "the heirs of a deceased applicant cannot claim a general right that the examination of the application introduced by the *de cujus* be continued by the Commission". The nature of the complaint (the application concerned the duration of the proceedings which resulted in applicant's conviction and sentence) did not allow that complaint to be considered as transferable: the complaint was closely linked with the late applicant personally and his heirs "cannot now claim ... to have

---

174. See, *e.g.*, Appl. 7826/77, *X v. United Kingdom, D & R* 14 (1978), p. 197 (197-198). On the other hand there is a case such as Appl. 8290/78, *X and others v. Federal Republic of Germany, D & R* 18 (1979), p. 176 (180), in which the applicants submitted that the authorities' recording of their telephone conversations with counsels was contrary to the Convention. The records, however, had meanwhile been destroyed, and in view of this the German Government advanced that the alleged violation had become moot. The Commission, however, decided that since the destruction had not taken place in response to a request of the applicants and the latter had not received reparation otherwise, "the applicants still have to be considered as victims although the records in question no longer exist". See also the report of 15 October 1980, *Foti and others v. Italy,* B.48 (1986), p. 30; the report of 6 July 1983, *Dores and Silveira v. Portugal,* pp. 19-20; Appl. 9267/81, *Moureaux and others v. Belgium, D & R* 33 (1983), p. 97 (127-128); Appl. 10103/82, *Faragut v. France, D & R* 39 (1984), p. 186 (207). If somehow there has been a recognition of a violation of the Convention and the applicant has got sufficient redress, he can no longer claim to be a victim of that violation. See Appl. 8865/80, *Verband Deutscher Flugleiter and others v. Federal Republic of Germany, D & R* 25 (1982), p. 252 (254-255); Appl. 10092/82, *Baraona v. Portugal, D & R* 40 (1985), p. 118 (137); Appl. 10259/83, *Anca and others v. Belgium, D & R* 40 (1985), p. 170 (177-178), and as regards "reasonable time": Appl. 8858/80, *G. v. Federal Republic of Germany, D & R* 33 (1983), p. 5 (6-7).
175. Appl. 282/57, *X v. Federal Republic of Germany,* Yearbook I (1955-57), p. 164 (166).
176. See, *e.g.*, Appl. 155/56, *X v. Federal Republic of Germany,* Yearbook I (1955-57), p. 163; Appl. 5076/71, *X v. United Kingdom, Coll.* 40 (1972), p. 64 (66).
177. See on the one hand Appl. 282/57, *X v. Federal Republic of Germany,* Yearbook I (1955-57), p. 164 (166), on the other hand Appl. 1706/62, *X v. Austria,* Yearbook IX (1966), p. 112 (124). See also Appls 7572/76, 7586/76 and 7587/76, *Ensslin, Baader and Raspe v. Federal Republic of Germany,* Yearbook XXI (1978), p. 418 (452). See, however, Appl. 6166/73, *Baader, Meins, Meinhoff, Grundmann v. Federal Republic of Germany,* Yearbook XVIII (1975), p. 132 (142).

themselves a sufficient legal interest to justify the further examination of the application on their behalf". The Commission considered next whether any question of general interest would justify a further examination of the application and stated: "Such a situation can arise in particular where an application in fact concerns ... the legislation or a legal system or practice of the defendent State". The Commission concluded that in this case such a general interest did not exist.[178] However, if the death of the direct victim is the result of the alleged violation, *e.g.* in the case of torture, his relatives will as a rule qualify as indirect victims.

8. For admissibility the applicant is not required to *prove* that he is the victim of the alleged violation. Article 25(1) only provides that the applicant must be a person "claiming to be the victim" (*"qui se prétend victime"*).[179] However, this does not mean that the mere submission of the applicant that he is a victim, is in itself sufficient. The Commission examines whether, assuming that the alleged violation has taken place, it is to be deemed plausible that the applicant is a victim, on the basis of the facts submitted by the applicant and the facts, if any, advanced against them by the defendant State. If in the Commission's opinion this is not the case, it declares the application "incompatible with the provisions of the present Convention" and, on the ground of Article 27(2), pronounces its inadmissibility.[180] On the other hand, even if the applicant does not expressly submit that he is the victim of the challenged act or omission, the Commission is nevertheless prepared to examine this point and to declare the application admissible if there appears to be sufficient ground for this.[181]

9. According to the last sentence of Article 25 those contracting States which have made the declaration referred to in that article, undertake not to interfere in any way with the exercise of the individual right of complaint. In the Commission's view this provision does not create a right like those incorporated into Section I of the Convention. Correspondence with the Commission about the right of complaint itself is not therefore considered by

---

178. Report of 9 October 1982, *Kofler, D & R* 30 (1983), p. 5 (9-10). See also the report of 7 March 1984, *Altun, D & R* 36 (1984), p. 236 (259-260) and the judgment of 25 August 1987, *Nölkenbockhoff,* A.123 (1987), pp. 77-78.
179. An amendment to replace these words by "which has been the victim", tabled at the Consultative Assembly, was withdrawn after discussion, because it was recognized that this was a "right to complain from the point of view of procedure" and not a "substantial right of action"; Council of Europe, Cons. Ass., First Session, Fourth Part, *Reports* 1949, pp. 1272-1274.
180. See, *e.g.,* Appl. 1983/63, *X v. the Netherlands, Yearbook* IX (1966), p. 286 (304). In a few cases the Commission declared the application "manifestly ill-founded" because in its view the applicant could not be regarded as a victim; see, *e.g.,* Appl. 2291/64, *X v. Austria, Coll.* 24 (1967), p. 20 (33 and 35); and Appl. 4653/70, *X v. Federal Republic of Germany, Yearbook* XVII (1974), p. 148 (178). This also leads to a declaration of inadmissibility, but the ground was indicated wrongly here, since the question of whether the application is well-founded depends on whether there has been a violation of the Convention, not on the question of the effect of such a violation, if any, for the applicant.
181. See, *e.g.,* Appl. 99/55, *X v. Federal Republic of Germany, Yearbook* I (1955-57), p. 160 (161).

it as an "application" or "requête" to which the rules of admissibility are applicable. In general the case will be settled between the Commission and the contracting State concerned on an administrative basis, the applicant being permitted to react to any observations which a State may make. However, if along with another complaint there is also one on interference with the exercise of the right of complaint, the Commission appears to be prepared to examine this together with the first complaint.[182]

In practice difficulties arise in this area particularly with respect to persons who have been deprived of their liberty in one way or another. The Commission does not regard every form of monitoring of the mail of detained persons addressed to it as unlawful, although it considers it more in conformity with the spirit of the Convention that the letters should be forwarded unopened.[183] According to the Commission there is a conflict with Article 25 only when an applicant cannot submit his grievances to the Commission in a complete and detailed way.[184]

In connection with this case-law of the Commission, Mikaelson has raised the question of whether an alleged violation of the last sentence of Article 25, notwithstanding its slightly different, more procedural character, would not have to be examined and dealt with by the Commission in the same way as the substantive provisions of Section I. In the present situation the Commission usually decides, even in cases where interference with the exercise of the right of complaint has been found, that no further steps are necessary ("to take no further action") as long as the applicant has been able to submit his grievances in an adequate manner.[185] But precisely in view of the existence of such interference it is at least doubtful whether the Commission is really able to form an opinion as to whether the application could be submitted adequately. On the basis of a number of arguments which appear convincing to us, Mikaelson therefore concludes that it would be desirable for the Commission to change its approach in this matter. In our view the most relevant argument is that Article 25 forms the corner-stone on which the whole system of the Convention depends. Indeed, if and in so far as the exercise of the individual right of complaint is restricted, the Strasbourg organs are also deprived of the principal instrument for assessing the situation as to the protection of the other rights and freedoms guaranteed in the Convention. Moreover, besides the legal protection of individuals, an element of "European public order" is also involved.[186] If the Commission should

---

182. See, e.g., Appl. 1593/62, *X v. Austria*, Yearbook VII (1964), p. 162 (166-168) and Appl. 1753/63, *X v. Austria*, Yearbook VIII (1965), p. 174 (188).
183. Appl. 1593/62, *X v. Austria*, Yearbook VII (1964), p. 162 (166-168).
184. See, e.g., Appl. 892/60, *X v. Federal Republic of Germany*, Yearbook IV (1961), p. 240 (258) and Appl. 5265/71, *X v. United Kingdom*, D & R 3 (1976), p. 5 (7).
185. The case-law of the Commission, however, also discloses cases where complaints concerning interference with the exercise of the right of complaint are dealt with via the normal procedure, although in connection with complaints about one or more of the provisions of Section I; see Appl. 369/58, *X v. Belgium*, Yearbook II (1958-59), p. 376 (380-381) and the joined Appls 5351/72 and 6579/74, *X v. the Netherlands*, Coll. 46 (1974), p. 85 (86-87).
186. L. Mikaelson, *European Protection of Human Rights*, Alphen aan de Rijn 1980, pp. 27-33.

decide to follow the course suggested here, the question as to the violation of the "right" set forth in the last sentence of Article 25 will be subjected to an independent examination, although a complaint about this can, of course, be submitted only in combination with the alleged violation of one of the "genuine" rights and freedoms. In that case the former complaint would no longer depend for its fate on the admissibility or well-foundedness of the latter.

In this context the *European Agreement relating to persons participating in proceedings before the European Commission and the European Court of Human Rights* is also of interest.[187] In Article 3(2) of this Agreement States undertake to guarantee also to detained persons the right to free correspondence with the Commission and the Court.[188] This means that, if their correspondence is at all examined by the competent authorities, this may not entail undue delay or alteration of the correspondence.[189] Nor may detained persons be subjected to disciplinary measures on account of any correspondence with the Commission or the Court.[190] Finally they have a right to speak, out of hearing of other persons, with their lawyer concerning their application to the Commission and any subsequent proceedings, provided that the lawyer is qualified to appear as a barrister before the courts of the State concerned. With respect to these provisions the authorities may impose limitations only in so far as they are in accordance with the law and are necessary in a democratic society in the interests of national security, for the detection and prosecution of a crime, and for the protection of health. Despite the fact that individuals cannot rely directly on this Agreement, still it is of importance for the promotion of an undisturbed exercise of the individual right of complaint, because the Commission can take its provisions into account in connection with Article 25. The scope of the State's obligation under Article 25, however, is not necessarily confined to the provisions of this Agreement.

Finally, it deserves attention that neither the Convention nor the above-mentioned *European Agreement* imposes an obligation on the contracting States of *Rechtsmittelbelehrung*, i.e. an obligation to inform private parties of the possibility to file an application with the Commission after they have exhausted the domestic remedies. At any rate, according to the Commission such an obligation cannot be inferred from the words "not to hinder in any way the effective exercise of this right" of Article 25:

> it cannot be inferred that the Convention has conferred upon the Contracting Parties an obligation to inform persons, whose proceedings before the national courts have resulted

---

187. This Agreement entered into force on 17 April 1971 and has not been ratified by Greece, Iceland, Spain and Turkey. For the text of the Convention see: Council of Europe, *European Treaty Series*, 6 May 1969, no. 67.
188. See, *e.g.*, Appl. 4351/70, *X v. Federal Republic of Germany*, Yearbook XIII (1970), p. 914 (924).
189. Appl. 530/59, *X v. Federal Republic of Germany*, Yearbook III (1960), p. 184 (194-196) and Appl. 2137/64, *X v. Federal Republic of Germany*, Yearbook VII (1964), p. 310 (312-314).
190. Appl. 3702/68, *X v. Belgium*, 4 October 1968 (not published) and joined Appls 7126/75 and 7573/76, *X and Y v. United Kingdom*, 9 March 1977 (not published).

in a final decision, of their possibility of lodging Applications with the Commission in accordance with Article 25 of the Convention.[191]

Considering the text of Article 25 this interpretation is not incomprehensible. Still, it would be in keeping with the spirit of the Convention if, in appropriate cases, after the domestic remedies have been exhausted, the attention of individuals were drawn to the possibility of lodging a complaint with the Commission. After all, a State which recognizes the right of complaint according to Article 25 may be expected to assure the effective exercise of this right by giving as much publicity as possible to the existence of the right of complaint. It would therefore be desirable if an obligation to that effect on the part of the contracting States were laid down in a future amendment.

10. The importance of the individual right of complaint for the supervisory system under the European Convention might appear from the large number of individual applications that are submitted to the Commission. On 31 December 1989 a total of 15,911 applications had been registered at the Secretariat of the Commission, and the Commission had taken a decision with respect to admissibility in 14,241 cases. However, it should be borne in mind that a great many cases (12,272) were at once declared inadmissible. Of the remaining cases the majority (1,299) were declared inadmissible after having been transmitted to the government concerned for its observations. In the course of the examination of the merits another eight cases were afterwards rejected in accordance with Article 29 for inadmissibility.[192] Only a total of 670 cases were therefore ultimately declared admissible.[193] These include many cases which concern approximately the same legal issues.[194]

§ 12. EXCURSUS: BRIEF COMPARISON OF THE SYSTEM OF IMPLEMENTATION OF THE EUROPEAN CONVENTION WITH THAT OF THE U.N. COVENANT ON CIVIL AND POLITICAL RIGHTS

1. On 26 March 1976, within the framework of the United Nations, the International Covenant on Civil and Political Rights and the Optional Protocol annexed thereto entered into force. Several contracting States of the European Convention have also become parties to the Covenant, and some of them also

---

191. See, e.g., Appl. 1877/63, *X v. Austria*, 22 July 1963 (not published).
192. On this, see *infra* pp. 107-108.
193. See Council of Europe, *European Commission of Human Rights, Survey of Activities and Statistics* 1989, p. 16.
194. See Council of Europe, *Stock-Taking on the European Convention on Human Rights*, Strasbourg 1986, p. 126.

to the Optional Protocol.[195] Those States are thus bound not only by the European Convention, but also by a world-wide treaty in which a great many civil and political rights are guaranteed.

In the discussion of the substantive provisions of the Convention in Chapter VI, a brief comparison with the corresponding provisions of the Covenant will be included. The provisions on the supervisory system do not lend themselves very well to such an article-by-article comparison. Still, also with respect to the supervisory system of the Convention, the entry-into-force of Covenant and Protocol is of importance. In fact, for those contracting States which have recognized the optional procedure of inter-State communications contained in Article 41 of the Covenant,[196] and for those individuals who are subjected to the jurisdiction of a contracting State which has ratified the Optional Protocol,[197] a new possibility is thus created for submitting alleged violations of human rights to an international body. On the other hand, co-existence of the two procedures may also lead to rejection of the application. It is thus important to compare briefly at this point the supervisory mechanism of the Convention and that of the Covenant, the emphasis being on the differences between the two and on questions arising in connection with their co-existence.[198]

2. Both for supervision under the Convention and for that in relation to the Covenant, three procedures have been provided, to wit: reporting by the contracting States, the complaint procedure on the initiative of a contracting State and the complaint procedure initiated by an individual. The reporting system is regulated in both treaties in one article. Article 40 of the Covenant, however, is considerably more elaborate and detailed than the rather obscure Article 57 of the Convention.[199] The expectation pronounced in the first Dutch edition of this book, *viz.* that the reporting procedure would play a more important part within the supervisory mechanism of the Covenant than Article 57 has done so far within the system of the Convention, has fully

---

195. On 1 January 1990 the following contracting States had ratified the Covenant: Austria, Belgium, Cyprus, Denmark, the Federal Republic of Germany, France, Iceland, Ireland, Italy, Luxembourg, the Netherlands, Norway, Portugal, San Marino, Spain, Sweden and the United Kingdom; the Optional Protocol had been ratified by the following contracting States: Austria, Denmark, France, Iceland, Ireland, Italy, Luxembourg, the Netherlands, Norway, Portugal, San Marino, Spain and Sweden.
196. On 1 January 1990 these were the following contracting States: Austria, Belgium, Denmark, the Federal Republic of Germany, Iceland, Ireland, Italy, Luxembourg, the Netherlands, Norway, Spain, Sweden and the United Kingdom.
197. See note 195.
198. For the last-mentioned problems, see J. de Meyer, "International Control Machinery", in: *The European Convention on Human Rights in Relation to other International Instruments for the Protection of Human Rights*, Colloquy on Human Rights, Athens, 21-22 September 1978, Strasbourg 1978, *H/Coll.*(78)5, pp. 45-58; M.A. Eissen, "The European Convention on Human Rights and the United Nations Covenant on Civil and Political Rights: Problems of Co-existence", *Buffalo Law Review* (1972), pp. 181 et seq.; T. Opsahl, "Ten years co-existence Strasbourg-Geneva", in: *Protecting Human Rights; The European Dimension*, Köln 1988, pp. 431-439.
199. On Art. 57, see *infra* pp. 207-212.

come true. As will be set forth below,[200] the Secretary General of the Council of Europe has made use only sporadically of the powers conferred on him in Article 57. In spite of the fact that the reporting system of the Covenant has functioned for only a comparatively short time, the approach of the Human Rights Committee[201] may be called promising, and in certain respects even surprising.[202] Certainly when viewed against the background of the political context in which the Committee has to perform its work, the present state of affairs is striking, although this very political context has given rise to a number of problems which have their impact on the functioning of supervision.[203] In comparison with Article 57 the reporting procedure within the context of the Covenant plays a far more important role, especially because there the complaint procedure is considerably "weaker" than under the Convention.

3. In the case of the Covenant, the complaint procedure is less effective, especially as far as the right of complaint of the States is concerned. In actual fact this right is hardly a right of complaint. Article 41 therefore speaks of "communications". Moreover, unlike in the case of the Convention, this right of complaint of States is optional, which means that it can be exercised only if both the applicant State and the respondent State have recognized in a declaration the possibility of complaints being lodged by States against them. According to paragraph 2, such declarations must have been received from at least ten contracting States. On 1 March 1979, this condition was fulfilled.[204] However, the right of complaint has not been used up to the present by any State.

The most essential difference between the complaint procedure by States under the Covenant and that under the Convention, however, is that the

---

200. See *infra* pp. 210-211.
201. For this Committee, see Arts 28-39 of the Covenant.
202. On the functioning of the reporting procedure within the framework of the Covenant, see M. Nowak, "The Effectiveness of the International Covenant on Civil and Political Rights - Stocktaking after the first eleven sessions of the UN-Human Rights Committee", in: *HRLJ* (1980), pp. 136-170 (146-151). See also: M. Nowak, "Survey of decisions of the Human Rights Committee", in: *HRLJ* (1982), parts 1-4, pp. 207-220, *HRLJ* (1984), parts 2-4, pp. 199-219, *HRLJ* (1986), parts 2-4, pp. 287-307. B. Graefrath, *Menschenrechte und internationale Kooperation; 10 Jahre Praxis des Internationalen Mensenrechtskomitees*, Berlin 1988; M. Nowak, *CCPR-Kommentar zum UNO-Pakt über bürgerliche und politische Rechte und zum Fakultativprotokoll*, Kehl am Rhein 1988.
203. This applies in particular to the powers of the Committee concerning the way in which the reports of States have to be examined. The differences of opinion between East and West have traditionally played a main part in this. In this respect the Western members of the Committee advocated a much less lenient form than colleagues from the East. Meanwhile agreement has been reached within the Committee about a number of rules concerning its procedure, which have been laid down in a general comment on Article 40 (UN Doc. CCPR/C/SR.260). The compromise contained in this document no doubt constitutes an important step towards greater effectiveness of the reporting procedure. However, in particular the Western members of the Committee intimated in their comments that they wished to regard this as a first step. See also the Provisional Rules of Procedure, Rules 66-71 (A/32/44 (1977), pp. 48-66).
204. Apart from the States mentioned above in note 196, as per 1 January 1990, the declaration had also been made by Algeria, Argentina, Australia, Canada, Congo, Ecuador, Gambia, Hongary, New Zealand, Peru, Philippines, Senegal and Sri Lanka.

former has the character of a conciliation procedure in which especially the parties to the dispute are involved, rather than, as in the case of the European Convention, an objective procedure in which the ultimate decision is in the hands of a third organ. If a State considers that another State does not fulfil its obligations under the Covenant, it must first bring the matter to the notice of that other State (Article 41(1)(a)). If after this stage of bilateral negotiations, which are not prescribed in the European Convention, the matter has not been adjusted to the satisfaction of the States concerned, both States may request the good offices of the Human Rights Committee (Article 41(1)(b) to (e) inclusive). The Committee may only pursue a friendly settlement of the matter (which in the case of the European Commission is not its only task and, certainly in practice, not the most important one). Unlike the European Commission, the Committee cannot give its opinion on the question of whether the facts of the case disclose a violation of the Covenant. In case of failure to reach a friendly settlement, its report must be confined to a brief statement of the facts and a record of the written and oral submissions of the parties.[205] Considering its more limited task, it is not surprising that the powers of the Committee *vis-à-vis* the contracting States are more limited than those of the European Commission. It appears from Article 41(1)(f) that the Committee may "call upon the States Parties concerned ... to supply any relevant information". The text of Article 28 of the Convention on the one hand has a wider scope and on the other hand is more imperative. It states that the Commission has competence to undertake "an investigation, for the effective conduct of which the States concerned shall furnish all necessary facilities, after an exchange of views with the Commission".

The procedure under the Covenant further provides for a third stage, which is not found in the European Convention. With the consent of the States concerned, an *ad hoc* Conciliation Commission may be appointed, whose duties and powers, however, hardly differ from those of the Committee (Art. 42). If its attempts at conciliation fail, the report of this *ad hoc* Commission may also include its views on the possibilities of a friendly settlement (Art. 42(7)(c)). With the report of the Commission the procedure under the Covenant comes to an end. Even if no friendly settlement has been reached, no further steps are provided for. It is here that this procedure differs markedly from that under the European Convention. In the latter case, if no friendly settlement is reached, ultimately a binding decision is always taken, either by the Court or by the Committee of Ministers (Arts 32, 48 and 53).

As to the co-existence of the two procedures, in the above discussion of Article 62 it has already been set out that the contracting States of the European Convention have to use the procedure provided for there, to the exclusion of any other procedures, in the case of disputes arising between

---

205. *Cf.* Art. 4(1)(e) and (h) of the Covenant and Arts 28 and 31 of the Convention.

them concerning the interpretation and/or application of the Convention.[206] As has been said, the Committee of Ministers has interpreted this provision broadly. If the regulation of the matter in the Covenant had been approximately identical, contracting States to the Convention could not have recognized the optional right of complaint for States under the Covenant unconditionally without placing themselves in a difficult position. The situation is considerably simpler now that Article 62 of the Convention and Article 44 of the Covenant are each other's mirror image. In fact, the last-mentioned Article provides that:

> The provisions for the implementation of the present Covenant ... shall not prevent the States Parties to the present Covenant from having recourse to other procedures for settling a dispute in accordance with general or special international agreements in force between them.

4. The individual right of complaint is optional in both cases. In the European Convention this is regulated in Article 25, for the Covenant in the Optional Protocol belonging thereto.[207] A State which becomes a party to the Protocol

> recognizes the competence of the Committee to receive and consider communications from individuals subject to its jurisdiction who claim to be victims of a violation by that State Party of any of the rights set forth in the Covenant (Art. 1).

From the entry-into-force of the Protocol to the middle of 1989 a total of 371 communications have reached the Committee.[208] With respect to such communications of individuals the following admissibility conditions apply: the domestic remedies must have been exhausted (Art. 2), the communications must not be anonymous, must not constitute an abuse, and must not be incompatible with the provisions of the Covenant (Art. 3). Finally, the Protocol lays down the condition to be discussed in more detail below, *viz.* that a communication must not concern the same matter that is being examined under another procedure of international investigation or settlement (Art. 5(2)(a)). The European Convention also contains all these conditions, but in addition requires that the application must have been lodged within a period of six months from the date at which the final national decision was taken (Art. 26) and must not be manifestly ill-founded (Art. 27(2)).

A communication is brought by the Committee to the notice of the respondent State. Within a period of six months the latter may submit written explanations or statements elucidating the case and any measures that may have been taken (Art. 4). These explanations or statements are transmitted to the author of the communication for comments. The Committee subsequently considers the case "in the light of all written information" (Art. 5(1)). Finally, the Committee forwards its view of the matter to the respondent State and

---

206. See *supra* pp. 6-7.
207. For the contracting States to the Convention which have also ratified the Optional Protocol, see supra note 195.
208. See *Report of the Human Rights Committee* of 1989 (A/44/40), p. 138.

the individual concerned.[209] Article 6 of the Protocol provides that in the annual report of the Committee shall be included a summary of its activities concerning communications of individuals. In practice, however, the Committee has so far published all its "decisions" in full.[210]

From the above survey it appears that the individual right of complaint under the Covenant, in spite of the broad interpretation which the Committee gives to its powers, is weaker than that of the Convention. Whereas according to the former at best political pressure may be brought to bear on the defaulting State, according to the latter, if the complaint is admissible and a friendly settlement cannot be reached, the matter ends with a binding decision either of the Committee of Ministers or of the European Court.

5. The co-existence of two possibilities of an individual right of complaint under the Covenant and the European Convention raises in particular two questions. Is an individual, when he considers that one or more of his rights and freedoms, laid down in both treaties, has been violated, allowed to choose which action to institute? And may he also bring both actions for the same matter, either simultaneously or successively?

In our opinion the first question may at once be answered in the affirmative. An individual who regards himself as the victim of a violation of one of the rights and freedoms which are guaranteed in the Convention as well as in the Covenant must be considered free to use the procedure which he regards as the most favourable for his case, since neither of the two treaties prohibits this choice.[211]

With respect to the second question three situations may arise: (1) identical applications are lodged at the same time with both organs; (2) the applicant tries first the procedure of the Covenant and then that of the Convention; (3) the applicant applies first to the European Commission and subsequently to the Human Rights Committee.

In the first case the applicant incurs the risk of being received by neither the Commission nor the Committee. In fact, according to Article 27(1)(b) the European Commission cannot consider an application which

> is substantially the same as a matter which has already been submitted to another procedure of international investigation or settlement and if it contains no relevant new information.[212]

On its part, Article 5(2) of the Optional Protocol provides:

---

209. The practice of the Committee induces us to speak, instead of "view", of "decision on the merits"; see C. Tomuschat, "Evolving Procedural Rules: The U.N. Human Rights Committee's First Two Years of Dealing with Individual Communications", *HRLJ*, Vol. I (1980), pp. 249-257 (255-256).
210. Besides by the UN themselves, the decisions (or abstracts of them) have also been published thus far in the *Human Rights Law Journal* (HRLJ). See: Nowak, *supra* note 202.
211. See: *Secretariat Memorandum prepared by the Directorate of Human Rights on the effects of the various international human rights instruments providing a mechanism for individual communications on the machinery of protection established by the European Convention on Human Rights*, H(85)3, no. 23, p. 9.
212. On this, see *infra* pp. 71-75.

The Committee shall not consider any communication from an individual unless it has ascertained that: (a) the same matter is not being examined under another procedure of international investigation or settlement.[213]

From these provisions it appears that there is a real possibility that the application may be rejected by both organs. Such a highly unsatisfactory situation may be avoided if the Commission and the Committee pursue a flexible policy on this point. They might postpone consideration so as to enable the applicant to withdraw one of the two complaints. However, the situation where two applications are lodged at precisely the same moment is likely to occur only rarely.

It is more conceivable that applications in Geneva and Strasbourg are lodged successively. If, as in the case mentioned above sub (2), the second application is lodged in Strasbourg, this leads to its being declared inadmissible under Article 27(1)(b), unless relevant new information is put forward. In the opposite case, that sub (3), such a conclusion does not follow imperatively from the text of Article 5(2)(a) of the Protocol. This provides for inadmissibility of a matter which is "being examined under another procedure". It is thus only the fact that the matter *is being* examined elsewhere which bars its admissibility, not the fact that the matter *has been* examined elsewhere. The Human Rights Committee therefore has actually taken the view that no complaint submitted to it is inadmissible merely on account of the fact that this case has already been examined in another procedure.[214]

It is questionable whether it is desirable that cases considered in Strasbourg may afterwards be brought up before the Committee again. An argument against this is that such a form of "appeal" against decisions of the Strasbourg organs is contrary to the intention of the drafters of the European Convention that the outcome of the procedure provided there were to be final. This intention may be inferred from Articles 26, 27, 32 and 52 of the Convention. Moreover, reasons of procedural economy may be advanced against renewed consideration by the Human Rights Committee. In general it takes a number of years before a case has passed through the Strasbourg procedure and the preceding national procedures. One may ask oneself whether after such a long procedure the case should be re-opened again by the filing of another application.

At all events the Committee of Ministers of the Council of Europe has answered that question in the negative. In 1970 it urged those contracting States of the Convention, which were to ratify the Optional Protocol, to attach to their ratification a declaration denying the competence of the Human Rights Committee to receive communications from individuals concerning matters which have already been or are being examined in a procedure under the European Convention, unless rights or freedoms not set forth in the

213. On the interpretation of this provision by the Committee, see C. Tomuschat, *supra* note 209, p. 251.
214. See *Report of the Human Rights Committee* of 1978, General Assembly Official Records, (A/33/40), p. 100.

European Convention are invoked in such communications.[215] Most of the contracting States which are also parties to the Protocol, have followed up this suggestion by making a declaration or a reservation.[216] The Netherlands, however, have refrained from making such a declaration or reservation. According to the Explanatory Memorandum, in the opinion of the Dutch Government there are indeed some practical objections to possible double procedures about the same matter, but they constitute an insufficient argument for preventing individuals from applying to the Human Rights Committee after having done so to the European Commission. Moreover, the Dutch Government submits that the Committee and the Commission have different powers in a number of respects. Finally, according to the Explanatory Memorandum, the making of declarations as suggested by the Committee of Ministers might be imitated in other regional arrangements, which might be detrimental to the world-wide system for the protection of human rights.[217] For individuals subject to the jurisdiction of the Netherlands, therefore, it is possible to initiate, after the Strasbourg procedure, the procedure provided for in the Optional Protocol to the Covenant.

As regards the relevant practice of the two bodies concerned the following may be said. On 1 January 1990 no single application had been rejected by the European Commission under Article 27(1)(b) of the European Convention. The Secretariat usually prevents this by advising an applicant, who lodges a complaint already brought before the Committee, of the content of Article 27(1)(b). The Committee, on its part, has in a number of cases dealt with the problems referred to above. In the Case of *Fanali v. Italy* the Committee held that the concept of "the same matter" within the meaning of Article 5(2)(a) of the Optional Protocol had to be understood as including the same claim concerning the same individual, submitted by him or someone else who has the standing to act on his behalf before the other international body. Consequently, as Mr. Fanali had not submitted his specific case to the European Commission, his communication was not considered inadmissible under the Optional Protocol.[218]

An interesting issue came up in the Case of *A.N. v. Denmark*. Denmark had made a reservation, with reference to Article 5(2)(a) of the Optional Protocol, in respect of the competence of the Committee to consider a communication from an individual if the matter has already been considered under other procedures of international investigation. The author of the communication had already filed an application concerning the same matter with the European Commission, which had been declared inadmissible as manifestly ill-founded. On the basis of these facts but without any further argument the Committee concluded that it was not competent to consider the

215. See *Yearbook* XIII (1970), pp. 74-76.
216. These States are Denmark, France, Iceland, Italy, Luxembourg, Norway, Spain and Sweden; United Nations, *Status of International Instruments*, 1987, pp. 90-93.
217. Second Chamber, Session 1975-1976, 13 932 (R 1037), nos 1-6, p. 42.
218. *Report of the Human Rights Committee* of 1983, (A/38/40), p. 163.

communication. It thus implicitly dismissed the position taken by one of its members in his individual opinion. There it was argued that an application that has been declared inadmissible has not, in the meaning of the Danish reservation, been "considered" in such a way that the Human Rights Committee is precluded from it. According to this point of view, the reservation aims at preventing a review of cases but does not seek to limit the competence of the Human Rights Committee merely on the ground that the rights of the Covenant allegedly violated may also be covered by the European Convention and its procedural requirements since it concerns a separate and independent international instrument.[219]

---

219. *Report of the Human Rights Committee* of 1982, (A/37/40), p. 213, and the individual opinion of the East German expert, Mr. Graefrath, appended to this decision, p. 214.

CHAPTER II

THE PROCEDURE BEFORE THE EUROPEAN COMMISSION OF HUMAN RIGHTS

§ 1. INTRODUCTION

The Commission has several duties. First it considers the admissibility of the submitted applications, by reference to the admissibility conditions set forth in the Convention (Arts 26 and 27). When it accepts an application, it undertakes together with the representatives of the parties an examination of the application in order to ascertain the facts. During this examination the Commission also places itself at the disposal of the parties with a view to securing a friendly settlement (Art. 28(1)(b)). If such a settlement is secured, the Commission draws up a report with a brief statement of the facts and the solution reached, and sends it to the States concerned, to the Committee of Ministers and, for publication, to the Secretary General of the Council of Europe (Art. 28(2)). If a solution is not reached, the Commission draws up a report on the facts and states its opinion as to whether these facts disclose a violation of the Convention. This report is transmitted to the Committee of Ministers and to the parties concerned; in doing so, the Commission may make such proposals as it thinks fit (Art. 31).

§ 2. THE EXAMINATION OF THE ADMISSIBILITY

1. When the Convention was drawn up, the main task of the Commission was considered to be that of functioning as a kind of screen for the large number of applications to be expected. The examination of the admissibility was therefore regarded as the core of the procedure before the Commission. It still forms the most important function of the Commission.

In the first instance a complaint usually reaches the Secretariat of the Commission by way of a letter. Such letters as a rule have the character of a provisional first contact and not of a formal application. In that case, therefore, they do not (yet) lend themselves to official registration. The Secretariat of the Commission makes a provisional file for each case, in order to obtain in the earliest possible stage as complete a picture as possible of any complaint. The applicant also receives a form for him to fill out. However, he may also submit other documents in addition to or instead of this form. The application, which must bear his signature, must contain: the name, age, occupation and address of the applicant; the name, occupation and address of his representative, if any; the name of the contracting State against which the application is made; as far as possible, the object of the application and the provision of the Convention alleged to have been violated; a statement of the facts and arguments on which the application is based; and finally any relevant documents, and in particular any judgment or other act relating to the object of the application.[1] Moreover, in his application the applicant must provide information showing that the conditions laid down in Article 26 concerning the exhaustion of the domestic remedies and the six-month time-limit for filing the application have been complied with.[2] In general, however, as an international tribunal the Commission does not treat procedural rules with the same stringency as national courts are accustomed to do.[3]

If the above-mentioned requirements are satisfied and the complaint on the face of it discloses a violation of the Convention, it will in general be entered in the official register of the Commission. Registration has no other meaning than that the complaint is pending before the Commission; no indications as to the question of its admissibility may be inferred from it.

According to the Secretary of the Commission, registration of a complaint in principle is not refused if the party submitting it insists on registration.[4] In practice, nevertheless, only part of all cases received is actually registered.[5] The other cases are withdrawn during the phase of the first correspondence of applicants with the Secretariat of the Commission, for the Secretariat has been instructed to draw the attention of potential applicants to the possibility of rejection of the complaint in cases where the case-law of the Commission points in that direction. The Secretariat does so by means of standard letters.

It is mainly because of the formulation of these letters that Mikaelson considers this practice as contrary to the Convention. In his view the Secretariat thus in fact makes a decision on admissibility and by doing so performs a task which the Convention has reserved exclusively to the Commission.[6] Formally, this is not correct: prior to the moment of registration there is not yet an application in the sense of the Convention, and accordingly no decision of the Commission is required. On the other hand, the present practice may very well create the impression "that the Secretariat's first aim - at least in some cases - is to discourage or perhaps even frustrate the individual, in the hope that he will give up before the application is formally filed".[7] Although one need not doubt the commonly known accuracy and caution with which the Secretariat performs its task, it may be acknowledged that for the layman it may be difficult to infer from the standard letters that

---

1. Rule 38(1) of the Rules of Procedure of the European Commission of Human Rights, *Collected Texts*, Strasbourg 1987, pp. 117-138 (hereafter: Rules of Procedure). See E. Fribergh, "The Commission Secretariat's handling of provisional files", in: F. Matscher, H. Petzold (eds), *Protecting Human Rights: The European Dimension*, Köln 1988, pp. 181-191.
2. Rule 38(2) of the Rules of Procedure.
3. See Appl. 332/57, *Lawless v. Ireland*, *Yearbook* II (1958-59), p. 308 (326).
4. H. Krüger, "The European Commission of Human Rights", *HRLJ* Vol. 1 (1980), pp. 66-87.
5. L. Mikaelson, *European Protection of Human Rights*, Alphen a/d Rijn 1980, p. 40. In 1988, the Secretariat of the Commission received 4108 communications, 1009 of which were registered; European Commission, *Survey of Activities and Statistics*, 1988, p. 2.
6. Mikaelson, *supra* note 5, pp. 40-42.
7. *Ibidem*, p. 40.

they contain *information* supplied by the Secretariat rather than a *decision* of the Commission. In our opinion, therefore, it is advisable to change this practice. The nature of the individual right of complaint - confirmed by the Commission and the Court - as the corner-stone of legal protection under the Convention entails that the whole of the Strasbourg procedure should be as "kind to the applicant" as possible and it is the Secretariat's task to assist, not to discourage the potential applicant. In particular the sometimes advanced efficiency grounds, derived from the limited capacity of the Commission in relation to the (large) number of applications, should not be decisive in this respect. Although all in all it is understandable, and also defensible, that the desire exists to exclude patently inadmissible complaints, it would seem preferable to us that any information in this respect be supplied by an independent organ[8] or by the Directorate of Human Rights, and not by the Secretariat, which tends to be identified so easily with the Commission. Any view within the Commission on whether the (potential) application is manifestly inadmissible or ill-founded should rest with the Commission itself or with one or more of its members.

2. The official languages for the Commission are English and French, but the President may permit the members of the Commission and the parties to use another language.[9] In practice this means that the parties may also use any of the other languages of the contracting States which have recognized the individual right of complaint, and that the correspondence may also be conducted in those languages.

States are represented before the Commission by their Agents, who may be assisted by (legal) advisers.[10] Individuals, non-governmental organizations, or groups of individuals may present and conduct applications before the Commission on their own behalf, but may also be represented or assisted by a lawyer or any other person residing in a contracting State, unless the Commission at any stage decides otherwise.[11] The representative must give evidence that he/she has been authorized by the applicant to act as such.

3. The procedure before the Commission is free of charge for the parties; the expenses are accounted for by the Council of Europe.[12] The expenses of witnesses, experts and other persons whom the Commission hears at the request of an individual applicant may in the Commission's discretion be borne by the Council of Europe.[13] The same holds true for the costs of obtaining written expert opinions and evidence.[14] Finally, in every stage of the procedure, after the written observations of the respondent government

8. As a kind of a European Human Rights Commissioner.
9. Rule 24 of the Rules of Procedure.
10. Rule 25 of the Rules of Procedure.
11. Rule 26(2) of the Rules of Procedure.
12. Art. 58 of the Convention.
13. Rule 35 bis (1) of the Rules of Procedure.
14. Rule 35 bis (3) and (4) of the Rules of Procedure.

concerning the admissibility have been received or the time-limit for this has expired, or after an application has been declared admissible, the Commission may grant the applicant free legal aid if it deems this necessary for the proper discharge of its duties and the applicant does not have sufficient means.[15]

The Commission will conclude that free legal aid is necessary for the proper discharge of its duties when it is evident that the applicant has had no legal training, or when it appears from the written documents submitted by him that he is unable to defend his case adequately before the Commission. In order to establish that he does not have sufficient means, the applicant must submit a declaration to that effect, certified by the appropriate domestic authorities. If the latter requirement creates difficulties for one reason or another, the Commission is satisfied when the applicant is able to prove by declaration that he would be eligible for free legal aid under the national legal system concerned. In a number of cases the Commission has refused free legal aid because it held that the income of the applicant in combination with that of his/her spouse was sufficient to defray the costs of the suit.[16]

The free legal aid may comprise not only lawyer's fees but also the travelling and subsistence expenses and any other necessary expenses of both the applicant and his lawyer.[17]

4. After an application has been received by the Secretary General of the Council of Europe, it is transmitted to the President of the Commission. If the application is brought by a State, the President gives notice of the application to the State against which the claim is made and invites the latter to submit written observations on the admissibility.[18]

In the case of an individual complaint this does not take place automatically. Since the amendment of the Rules of Procedure of the Commission in 1973[19] the procedure with respect to individual complaints has been as follows: the President appoints one member of the Commission as rapporteur, who is to submit a report on admissibility. This rapporteur may request relevant further information on the complaint from the applicant and/or the State concerned, upon which he communicates any information obtained from the State to the applicant for comments.[20] Upon receipt of the report of the rapporteur the Commission may at once declare the application inadmissible. This method is known as the "summary procedure". Protocol no. 8, which entered into force on 1 January 1990, has again introduced a new element: a committee of three members of the Commission, by unanimous vote, may

---

15. See the Addendum to the Rules, *Collected Texts*, Strasbourg 1987, pp. 138-139.
16. H. Krüger, *supra* note 4, pp. 85-86.
17. See Art. 4 of the Addendum to the Rules of Procedure, *supra* note 15, p. 139.
18. Rule 39 of the Rules of Procedure.
19. This amendment became necessary as a result of the entry-into-force of the Third Protocol to the Convention, which is incorporated in Arts 29, 30 and 34 of the Convention.
20. Rule 40(2) of the Rules of Procedure.

declare an application inadmissible or strike it from the list, when such a decision can be taken without further examination.[21]

If the complaint gives cause for it, the Commission may request relevant information from the applicant or the State concerned and/or give notice of the application to the State and invite it to present written observations on the admissibility of the application. The latter will take place in any case, if the Commission does not decide to declare the case inadmissible or to strike it off the list. The information and/or observations of the State are communicated to the applicant, so that the latter may comment on it. After receipt of the observations of the State against which the application is brought, the application is examined by the rapporteur. Before deciding upon his report on the admissibility, the Commission may invite the parties to submit further observations in writing or orally.[22] If the Commission decides to hold a hearing in this phase, the parties are invited to plead also on the merits. Such a combined procedure is intended to save time.[23]

The above-mentioned difference in treatment between individual applications and applications by States would seem to be justified. A State may be assumed not to lodge an application lightly, on account of the political complications which such a step may involve. In the case of individual applications the chances for this to happen are greater. It would therefore not be right to communicate for comments to the governments concerned also those numerous applications which *prima facie* fail to satisfy the admissibility conditions. Nor does it appear to be objectionable that among individual applications a first selection should be made via a simplified procedure, provided that the legal position of the applicant in such a procedure is not affected. It is therefore of the greatest importance that the rapporteur be obliged to transmit any information he obtains from a government to the applicant, upon which the latter may comment. Thus the equality of the parties is properly secured.

5. A number of interrelated provisions from the Commission's Rules of Procedure on urgent cases and interim measures should be mentioned separately here. In contrast with the Rules of Court, the Commission's Rules originally did not contain any provision for such actions, although the latter organ would appear to be much more suitable than the former to take interim measures. Meanwhile this situation has changed, a number of provisions having been included in the Rules of Procedure. Even before that time the Commission had already proved prepared to urge the contracting States to take such interim measures as it deemed necessary. This was the case in particular where the applicants were in danger of being expelled

---

21. Art. 20(3) of the Convention. Art. 20(2) enables the Commission to set up Chambers of seven members to examen applications. This provision has not been put into effect yet (April 1990). See *infra* p. 113.
22. Rule 42(1), (2) and (3) of the Rules of Procedure.
23. On the proceedings on admissibility, see also H. Krüger, *supra* note 4, pp. 72-80.

before the Commission could consider their case.[24] This practice has now been formalized in the Rules of Procedure.

Under Rules 27 and 28 of the Rules of Procedure, in urgent cases the Commission may give precedence to a particular complaint, thus derogating from its normal procedure, according to which complaints are considered in the order in which they become ready for examination. According to Article 41 the Secretary of the Commission then informs the respondent State of the introduction of the application and adds a summary of its contents. The purpose of this provision is of course not to spring a surprise on the contracting State concerned if afterwards any interim measures should be desirable. The latter measures are regulated in Rule 36 of the Rules of Procedure:

> The Commission or, where it is not in session, the President may indicate to the parties any interim measure the adoption of which seems desirable in the interest of the parties or the proper conduct of the proceedings before it.

From this formulation it becomes apparent that this amounts to recommendations of the Commission which involve no legal obligations for the contracting States. This is due to the fact that the Convention does not confer on the Commission any power to impose interim measures with binding force. Nevertheless, in practice the suggestions made by the Commission in this respect are taken very seriously by the national authorities. In fact, it is only in cases of extreme urgency that the Commission proceeds to recommend interim measures: the facts must *prima facie* point to a violation of the Convention, and the omission to take the proposed measures must result in irreparable injury to certain interests of the parties or to the progress of the examination.[25] In our opinion, in certain cases the provision of Article 25 of the Convention that those contracting States which have accepted the right of individual applications undertake not to hinder in any way the effective exercise of this right, may imply the obligation to take the measures as indicated by the Commission.

6. As already mentioned in the preceding chapter, the consideration of the case by the Commission takes place *in camera* and the Commission decides by a majority of the representatives casting a vote.[26] The decision of the Commission on the admissibility must be accompanied or followed by the reasons on which it is based. No appeal lies against this decision. A declaration of *inadmissibility* is final. A declaration of *admissibility*, however, can still be reversed in a later stage. Under Article 29 of the Convention, in the course of the examination of the merits, *i.e.* after the application has been accepted, the Commission may nevertheless decide *ex officio* and with a two-third majority of its members to reject the application if it becomes

---

24. See also *infra* p. 116.
25. See H. Krüger, *supra* note 4, pp. 73-75.
26. See *supra* pp. 24-25.

evident that it does not after all satisfy all the admissibility conditions.[27] Moreover, as will be explained later,[28] the Court considers itself competent to decide for its part on the admissibility of an application submitted to it.

2.1. The admissibility conditions

1. Two of the admissibility conditions set forth in the Convention hold for applications submitted by States as well as for those submitted by individuals. These are the condition that all remedies within the legal system of the respondent State must have been exhausted before the case is submitted to the Commission, and the condition that the application must have been submitted within a period of six months from the date on which the final national decision was taken (Art. 26). For the admissibility of an individual application additional requirements are that the application is not anonymous; that it is not substantially the same as a matter which has already been examined by the Commission or has already been submitted to another procedure of international investigation or settlement and contains no relevant new information; that the application is not incompatible with the provisions of the Convention; that it is not manifestly ill-founded; and that it does not constitute an abuse of the right to file an application (Art. 27(1) and (2)).

Strictly speaking, one ought to differentiate between applications which are inadmissible and applications falling outside the competence of the Commission, even though the admissibility grounds which are expressly mentioned do not provide a clear basis for such a distinction. Applications by States, for instance, may only be rejected on the grounds mentioned in Article 26, and not on the ground of incompatibility with the Convention mentioned in Article 27(2), a ground on which the Commission sometimes rejects individual applications with respect to which it has no competence.[29] All the same, it is evident that applications by States may also fall outside the competence of the Commission, for instance when the application relates to a period in which the Convention was not yet binding upon the respondent State. The Commission will have to reject such an application, but in this case, properly speaking, on account of incompetence, not on account of inadmissibility, the grounds for which are enumerated exhaustively in the Convention. The practice concerning individual applications, however, shows that the Commission usually rejects applications outside its competence *ratione personae, ratione materiae, ratione loci,* or *ratione temporis* on account of inadmissibility. That is why problems which relate to the competence of the Commission will here be discussed under the heading of admissibility conditions.

---

27. Since the entry-into-force of Protocol no. 8 the original requirement of unanimity has been changed into a two-third majority.
28. See *infra* pp. 142-146.
29. See, *e.g.,* Appl. 473/59, *X v. Austria, Yearbook* II (1958-59), p. 400 (406) and Appl. 1452/62, *X v. Austria, Yearbook* VI (1963), p. 268 (276).

2. In practice the Commission applies a particular sequence in the admissibility conditions by reference to which an application is examined. This sequence is based partly on logical, partly on practical grounds.[30] But on the very ground of practical considerations the case-law of the Commission diverges from this sequence on numerous occasions. Especially the use of the so-called "global formula" is striking.[31] The Commission uses this formula for rejecting an application which contains various separate complaints, as a whole on account of its manifestly ill-founded character, although the separate complaints may be inadmissible on different grounds. The Commission bases this approach on the fact that it does not consider it necessary in such a case to make a detailed examination of the separate elements of the application.

Here follows a discussion of the separate admissibility conditions in the sequence referred to above.

2.2. The application must not be anonymous (Art. 27(1)(a))

This condition makes it possible to bar applications which have been lodged for purely political or propagandistic reasons, although of course cases are also conceivable in which a serious individual applicant wishes to remain anonymous for fear of repercussions.

In practice, however, this condition does not play an important part. The large majority of applications contains the name of the applicant and the other information which has to be supplied according to the Rules of the Commission. Moreover, the Commission takes a flexible attitude as regards the identity of the applicant. Thus, although it declared inadmissible an application that was signed "lover of tranquillity", it did so only because the documents filed did not contain a single clue as to the identity of the applicant.[32] The Commission's flexible attitude appears, for instance, from a case in which a number of complaints had been submitted by an association. The Commission considered both the association and its individual members as applicants. With respect to the individual members the Commission held that their identity had been insufficiently established and that accordingly their application, properly speaking, was inadmissible under Article 27(1)(a). Nevertheless, the Commission pursued the examination of the case, on the presumption that this procedural defect would subsequently be redressed. Later, however, the application was declared inadmissible after all on other grounds.[33]

---

30. See also H. Krüger, *supra* note 4, pp. 75-78, and L. Mikaelson, *supra* note 5, pp. 67-68.
31. This is often formulated by the Commission as follows: "An examination by the Commission of this complaint as it has been submitted does not disclose any appearance of a violation of the rights and freedoms set out in the Convention".
32. Appl. 361/58, *X v. Ireland, Case-Law Topics*, No. 3, Bringing an application before the European Commission of Human Rights, Strasbourg 1972, p. 10.
33. Appl. 3798/68, *Church of X v. United Kingdom, Yearbook* XII (1969), p. 306 (318).

2.3. The application must not constitute an abuse of the right of complaint (Art. 27(2))

1. On this ground, too, in practice very few applications are declared inadmissible. This may probably be accounted for by the fact that it is very difficult to establish such an abuse, since the applicant's motives cannot easily be ascertained and distinguished, certainly not in so early a stage of the examination.

The prudence of the Commission in this respect appears from the meaning it has given to the term "abuse". Thus, the fact that the applicant is inspired by motives of publicity and political propaganda does not necessarily have to imply that the application constitutes an abuse of the right of complaint.[34] In such a case it is only possible to speak of an abuse if an applicant unduly stresses the political aspects of the case.[35] The Commission has also left open the question of whether an abuse is involved on the mere ground that no practical effects are envisaged with the application.[36]

2. An abuse may consist primarily in the object one wishes to attain with the application. A clear example of such an abuse of the right of complaint constitutes the Case of *Ilse Koch*. This wife of the former commandant of the Buchenwald concentration camp had been convicted for violation of the most elementary human rights. She submitted that she was innocent and claimed her release, without invoking a specific provision of the Convention. In her application she voiced a number of accusations and complaints which were not supported in any way by the Convention. The Commission declared her application inadmissible, because her sole aim evidently was to escape the consequences of her conviction, so that her application constituted a "clear and manifest abuse".[37]

The condition that an application must not constitute an abuse is for the Commission also a (defective) expedient for holding querulous applicants at bay. A German in the course of time had lodged a great many applications which had been rejected without exception, either because they were manifestly ill-founded or because of non-exhaustion of the local remedies. When - together with his wife - he once again lodged several applications, which were moreover substantially the same as previous cases submitted by him, the Commission declared them inadmissible on account of abuse, and gave the applicant to understand:

---

34. Appl. 332/57, *Lawless v. Ireland*, Yearbook II (1958-59), p. 308 (338). See also Appl. 8317/78, *McFeely v. United Kingdom*, D & R 20 (1981), p. 44 (70-71).
35. Appl. 1468/62, *Iversen v. Norway*, Yearbook VI (1963), p. 278 (326).
36. Appls 7289/75 and 7349/76, *X and Y v. Switzerland*, Yearbook XX (1977), p. 372 (406): "even assuming that the concept of abuse within the meaning of Art. 27(2) in fine may be understood as including the case of an application serving no practical purpose".
37. Appl. 1270/61, *Ilse Koch v. Federal Republic of Germany*, Yearbook V (1962), p. 126 (134-136). See also Appl. 5207/71, *Raupp v. Federal Republic of Germany*, Coll. 42 (1973), p. 85 (90).

It cannot be the task of the Commission, a body which was set up under the Convention "to ensure the observance of the engagements undertaken by the High Contracting Parties in the present Convention", to deal with a succession of ill-founded and querulous complaints, creating unnecessary work which is incompatible with its real functions, and which hinders it in carrying them out.[38]

3. Not only the aim pursued in lodging an application, but also the applicant's conduct during the procedure may lead to a declaration of inadmissibility on account of abuse. Thus, applications have been rejected because the applicant had deliberately made false declarations in an attempt to mislead the Commission,[39] or because the applicant failed to furnish the necessary information even after repeated requests,[40] or because the applicant had broken bail and had fled,[41] or because he had used threatening or insulting language before the Commission or the respondent government.[42] It is to be doubted, however, whether the use of threatening or insulting language in itself should ever be considered to constitute sufficient ground for a declaration of inadmissibility on account of abuse, when it is plausible that the applicant indeed has lodged his application with a view to the establishment of a violation of the Convention, committed against him.[43]

4. Finally, the fact that an applicant gives publicity to certain elements from the examination of his case, contrary to Article 33 of the Convention, may also induce the Commission to declare the application inadmissible on account of abuse.[44]

5. As has already been observed, the present admissibility condition does not apply to applications by States. Nevertheless, the case-law of the Commission would appear not to exclude the possibility that an application by a State may likewise be rejected on account of abuse. This would not be done on the ground of the admissibility condition mentioned in Article 27(2), but on the ground of the general legal principle that the right to bring an action before an international organ must not be abused. Referring to its decision in the first *Greek* Case,[45] the Commission stated in the case of *Cyprus v. Turkey* that,

> even assuming that it is empowered on general principle to make such a finding, [the Commission] considers that the applicant Government have, at this stage of the proceedings, provided sufficient particularised information of alleged breaches of the

38. Appls 5070, 5171, 5186/71, *X v. Federal Republic of Germany*, Yearbook XV (1972), p. 474 (482); Appls 5145/71, 5246/71, 5333/72, 5586/72, 5587/72 and 5332/72, *Michael and Margarethe Ringeisen v. Austria*, Coll. 43 (1973), p. 152 (153).
39. Appls 2364/64, 2584/65, 2662/65 and 2748/66, *X v. Federal Republic of Germany*, Coll. 22 (1967), p. 103 (109) and Appl. 6029/73, *X v. Austria*, Coll. 44 (1973), p. 134.
40. Appl. 244/57, *X v. Federal Republic of Germany*, Yearbook I (1955-57), p. 196 (197) and Appl. 1297/61, *X v. Federal Republic of Germany*, Coll. 10 (1963), p. 47 (48).
41. Appl. 9742/82, *X v. Ireland*, D & R 32 (1983), p. 251 (253).
42. Appl. 2625/65, *X v. Federal Republic of Germany*, Coll. 28 (1969), p. 26 (41-42) and Appl. 5267/71, *X v. Federal Republic of Germany*, Coll. 43 (1973), p. 154.
43. See P. van Dijk, *Judicial Review of Governmental Action and the Requirement of an Interest to Sue*, Alphen a/d Rijn 1980, p. 333.
44. Council of Europe, *Press Release* C(78)42, 11 October 1978.
45. Appls 3321-3323/67 and 3344/67, *Norway, Sweden, Denmark and the Netherlands v. Greece*, Yearbook XI (1968), p. 690 (764).

Convention for the purpose of Article 24.[46]

In our view the Commission thus leaves open the possibility that applications by States are rejected on account of violation of the general prohibition of abuse of right, even though it is not to be assumed that in practice it will lightly reach such a conclusion.[47]

2.4. The application must not be substantially the same as a matter which has already been examined by the Commission or has already been submitted to another procedure of international investigation or settlement unless it contains relevant new information (Art. 27(1)(b))

1. So far no decision of the Commission has been published in which an application was declared inadmissible on the ground of the fact that a matter had already been submitted to another international body for investigation or settlement. In view of the small number of international organs charged with the protection of human rights this is not astonishing. This admissibility condition, however, may become more and more important in connection with the Covenant on Civil and Political Rights of the United Nations and the Optional Protocol accompanying it.[48] In fact, this Protocol confers on individuals the right to submit an application to the Human Rights Committee,[49] so that a case like that referred to in Article 27(1)(b) is quite conceivable.[50]

2. Such a case might also occur in connection with a matter which has been submitted to the Court of Justice of the European Communities. Indeed, as appears from its case-law, this Court is prepared to review the acts and omissions of the Member States of the Communities and of the Community Institutions for their conformity with fundamental human rights on the ground that they form part of the general principles of Community law.[51] The chances of such a coincidence, however, are not very great. Indeed, if, in connection with the same factual situation, a case were to be brought before the Courts both in Strasbourg and in Luxembourg, in the two procedures different legal

---

46. Appls 6780/74 and 6950/75, *Cyprus v. Turkey, Yearbook* XVIII (1975), p. 82 (124).
47. See Van Dijk, *supra* note 43, pp. 331-332.
48. The Covenant on Civil and Political Rights and the Optional Protocol belonging thereto entered into force on 26 March 1976. For the procedure provided for, see *supra* pp. 53-60.
49. See *supra* pp. 56-57.
50. See *supra* pp. 57-60.
51. On this case-law, see W.R. Edeson and F. Wooldridge, "European Community Law and Fundamental Human Rights: some recent decisions of the European Court and National Courts", in: *Legal Issues of European Integration*, 1976/1, pp. 1-54. See in general about the relationship between the European Convention and the protection of human rights within the European Communities L. Betten, *The Incorporation of Fundamental Rights in the Legal Order of the European Communities*, The Hague 1985.

issues will probably be involved.[52] Moreover, even if the two cases are identical, the fact that a case has already been submitted to another judicial organ does not bar its admissibility under the European Convention if relevant information that is new to the Commission is put forward which is not or has not been examined by that other organ.

3. In practice declarations of inadmissibility on the ground of the identical character of two or more cases submitted to the Commission do not occur frequently.[53] However, according to the Commission any preceding procedures before the Court should also be taken into consideration.[54] In Appl. 10243/83, *Times Newspapers Ltd.*, the applicants referred to their earlier application 6538/74 and alleged the failure of the United Kingdom Government to implement the judgment of the Court in that case.[55] With respect to this part of the application the Commission first pointed out that the supervision of judgments of the Court under Article 54 is entrusted to the Committee of Ministers and subsequently decided that it "cannot now examine these new developments in relation to the facts of the former case No. 6538/74, as it is barred from doing so by Article 27 para. 1(b) of the Convention".[56]

For an answer to the question of whether a concrete case concerns a matter which is substantially the same as a matter which has already been examined by the Commission, it is decisive to know whether new facts have been put forward in the application. These facts must be of such a nature that they cause a change in the legal and/or factual data on which the

52. An example of this is Appl. 6452/74, *Sacchi v. Italy*, *D & R* 5 (1976), p. 42, the core of which was also discussed at the Court of Justice in Luxembourg, of which the Court of Biella had requested a preliminary ruling in Case 155/73, *Sacchi, Jur.* 1974, p. 409. Mr. Sacchi, operator of a cable television firm (Telebiella) without a licence, refused to pay the contribution for the TV receiving sets, which was punishable according to Italian law. Upon this, he was convicted. A request for a licence for transmission via a cable system was refused. A presidential decree of 29 March 1973 assimilated cable TV equipment to radio and TV equipment, thus making it subject to the RAI/TV monopoly. Sacchi lodged a complaint with the Commission in Strasbourg about violation of Art. 10(1) of the Convention. Questions were submitted to the Court in Luxembourg, *inter alia* about free movement of goods and services, competition and national monopolies of a commercial nature. For the consideration of the merits, see *infra* p. 419.
53. Some of the rare published cases in which this aspect came up for discussion are the Appls 5145/71, 5246/71, 5333/72, 5586/72, 5587/72 and 5332/72, *Michael and Margarethe Ringeisen v. Austria, Coll.* 43 (1973), p. 152 (153); the Appls 5070, 5171 and 5186/71, *X v. Federal Republic of Germany*, Yearbook XV (1972), p. 474 (482); and the Appls 7572/76, 7586/72 and 7587/76, *Ensslin, Baader and Raspe v. Federal Republic of Germany*, Yearbook XXI (1978), p. 418 (452). In Appl. 3479/68, *X v. Austria and the Federal Republic of Germany, Coll.* 28 (1969), p. 132 (138), the Commission took into account a previously lodged complaint, "even if it cannot strictly be said to be substantially the same".
54. See Appl. 6832/74, *X v. Sweden* (not published): "It is true that the Court is not mentioned in Art. 27(1)(b). The article distinguishes between a previous examination by the Commission and another procedure of international investigation or settlement. It follows, however, from a comparison with Art. 62 that the latter type of procedure is another than that provided for in the Convention. This does not therefore exclude the Commission from having regard, under Art. 27(1)(b), to proceedings before the Court".
55. Judgment of 26 April 1979, A.30 (1979).
56. Appl. 10243/83, *Times Newspapers Ltd. and others v. United Kingdom, D & R* 41 (1985), p. 123 (129). It is incomprehensible why the Commission without any explanation adds: "This part of the application is therefore incompatible ratione materiae with the provisions of the Convention and must be rejected under Article 27 para. 2."

Commission based its earlier decision. The mere submission of one or more new legal arguments is therefore insufficient, if the facts on which the application is based are the same.[57]

A new fact is indeed involved when an applicant whose earlier application has been declared inadmissible on account of non-exhaustion of the local remedies has afterwards obtained a decision in the last resort in the national legal system. The Commission's flexibility in this respect is evident from the following example. An applicant had submitted in a previous application that the final decision in his case had been taken by the Court of Appeal at Liège. On that basis, his application was declared inadmissible because he was assumed not to have exhausted the local remedies. In a new application he proved that he had made a mistake, since the decision in question had in reality been taken by the Court of Cassation, from whose decisions no appeal lay. The Commission considered this as relevant new information in the sense of Article 27(1)(b).[58] Obviously, a subsequent appeal in the last resort does not avail an applicant if his earlier application has been declared inadmissible on *another* ground *as well*.

A new fact is of course also involved when new obligations arise from the Convention for the contracting State in question. An example is the case where a detained person complained about the refusal of the German authorities to permit him to leave Germany and live in Poland. His application was declared inadmissible on account of incompatibility with the provisions of the Convention, because the right to leave the country was not guaranteed in the Convention. In his new application, however, he invoked the Fourth Protocol - which had meanwhile become binding on Germany -, Article 2(2) of which confers on everyone the right to leave a country, including that of which he is a national. As a result, the application was admissible under Article 27(1)(b). However, it was now rejected as being manifestly ill-founded, because paragraph 3 of Article 2 of the Fourth Protocol was held to permit an exception with respect to detained persons.[59] The information put forward was indeed new, but was not deemed applicable to the applicant.

Those cases in which the requirement of "a fair and public hearing within a reasonable time" of Article 6 is at issue[60] may present a somewhat special feature, as is shown by the following decision of the Commission. In his first complaint the applicant alleged a violation of the Convention, because a bankruptcy procedure had been pending against him for the past three years. This application was declared manifestly ill-founded. At the moment the Commission had to give its opinion on his second - identical - complaint, the

---

57. See Appl. 202/56, *X v. Belgium*, Yearbook I (1955-57), p. 190 (191) and Appl. 8206/78, *X v. United Kingdom*, D & R 25 (1982), p. 147 (150).
58. Appl. 3780/68, *X v. Belgium*, Coll. 37 (1971), p. 6 (8). See also on the one hand Appl. 4517/70, *Huber v. Austria*, Yearbook XIV (1971), p. 548, on the other hand Appl. 6821/74, *Huber v. Austria*, D & R 6 (1977), p. 65.
59. Appl. 4256/69, *X v. Federal Republic of Germany*, Coll. 37 (1971), p. 67 (68-69).
60. See on this *infra* pp. 328-335.

period had meanwhile increased to four years and eight months. This time the applicant was not dismissed by the Commission, on the ground that "the time aspect constitutes in itself the relevant new information in the sense of Article 27(1)(b)".[61]

4. From the formulation of Article 27(1)(b) it might be inferred that substantially the same matter is also concerned when an application that is otherwise identical is lodged by another applicant. In our view this provision should, however, be interpreted in the sense that it is only directed against identical applications by *the same* applicant. It would not be in conformity with the emphasis which the Convention puts on the individual legal protection, if an application from X, who considers himself to be the victim of a violation of the Convention, would not be admitted on the ground of the fact that an identical violation in relation to Y is already being examined or has already been examined. As appears from its case-law, the Commission, too, does not object to identical applications from *different* applicants, although it will then join such cases, if possible.[62] If an application, both in its facts and in law, is (almost) identical to the case which has already been dealt with by the Commission, it is of course not possible to join it with the previous case, but it would be advisable to deal with it in a summary procedure.

Article 27(1)(b) may, however, bar applications from different applicants which concern the same violation against the same person, as in the case where in connection with one and the same violation both the direct and the indirect victim lodge an application. In its earlier case-law, the Commission opined that a new examination of the case is justified only if in each individual case a new fact is involved.[63] In a more recent case, however, the Commission was less strict. This case concerned the execution of an expulsion order from the Federal Republic of Germany to Yugoslavia. At first instance, the fiancée of the person to be expelled lodged a complaint with the Commission, several years later followed by a complaint of the person himself. With respect to the latter application, the Commission decided that it could not be rejected under Article 27(1)(b) as being substantially the same as the first application, because "this applicant has a specific personal interest in bringing an application before the Commission".[64] Here, the criterion was not the identity of the case, but of the interests of the applicants involved. Since

61. Appl. 8233/78, *X v. United Kingdom, D & R* 17 (1980), p. 122 (130). *Cf.* also Appl. 9621/81, *Vallon v. Italy, D & R* 33 (1983), p. 217 (239), in which the continuing detention on remand constituted the relevant new information.
62. See, *e.g.*, the successive Appls 6878/75, *Le Compte v. Belgium, D & R* 6 (1977), p. 79 and 7238/75, *Van Leuven and De Meyere v. Belgium, D & R* 8 (1977), p. 140. In its decision in the last-mentioned case the Commission held (p. 160): "In view of all the similarities between the two applications it is desirable that they should be examined together". The same conclusion can also be drawn from the opinion of the Commission in the Appls 5577/72-5583/72, *Donnelly et al. v. United Kingdom,* Yearbook XVI (1973), p. 212 (266) that "apart from the fact that the applicants are different in each case ... this complaint could still not be rejected under Article 27(1)(b) of the Convention".
63. Appl. 499/59, *X v. Federal Republic of Germany,* Yearbook II (1958-59), p. 397 (399).
64. Appl. 9028/80, *X v. Federal Republic of Germany, D & R* 22 (1981), p. 236 (237).

the second application was lodged by the direct victim, the Commission could of course hardly have decided otherwise.

The question of identical complaints may also arise in connection with the lodging of a complaint by a State as well as by an individual. Thus, in the applications of a number of Northern Irishmen, matters were denounced which had already formed the subject of the application of the Irish Government against the United Kingdom. This application had meanwhile been declared admissible, but the examination of the merits was still pending. The Commission did not decide on the question of whether the individual applications were now to be rejected on account of their having the same character as the application by a State, because "The relevant part of the inter-State case has ... not yet been examined within the meaning of Article 27(1)(b) of the Convention".[65] This result in itself may be welcomed, but the reasoning on which it is based is less satisfactory. Indeed, the argument followed by the Commission leaves wide open the possibility that similar cases, where the examination has already been completed, may be decided differently. On the ground of the above-mentioned emphasis which the Convention puts on individual legal protection this is to be regretted since it would discourage individual applicants. Moreover, the complaint of a State and an individual complaint are distinctly different in character. The latter specially concerns the personal interests of the individual applicant, while the former is aimed much more at denouncing a general situation concerning "European public order". It is therefore questionable whether in the case of a succession of two applications of so different a character it is still possible to speak of "a matter which is substantially the same".

2.5. The application must not be incompatible with the provisions of the Convention (Art. 27(2))

1. Incompatibility with the Convention is assumed in the case-law of the Commission: (1) if the application falls outside the scope of the Convention *ratione personae, ratione materiae, ratione loci*, or *ratione temporis*; (2) if the individual applicant does not satisfy the condition of Article 25(1); and (3) if the applicant, contrary to Article 17, aims at the destruction of one of the rights and freedoms guaranteed in the Convention.

2. As regards the cases referred to sub (1), it has already been observed above that the Commission does not differentiate clearly between its competence and the admissibility of the application.[66]

---

65. Appls 5577-5583/72, *Donnelly et al. v. United Kingdom, Yearbook* XVI (1973), p. 212 (266).
66. See *supra* pp. 67-68. See also K. Vasak, *La Convention Européenne des Droits de l'Homme*, Paris 1964, p. 133 and Mikaelson, *supra* note 5, p. 64.

Whether an application falls within the scope of the Convention *ratione personae* is determined by the answer to the question who may submit the application to the Commission (active legitimation) and against whom such an application may be lodged (passive legitimation). This question has already been answered *passim* above. An application may be lodged by the contracting States as well as by those natural persons, non-governmental organizations and groups of individuals who come under the jurisdiction of the State against which the complaint is directed.[67] With respect to applications by States it is also to be noted that they must be lodged by a national authority competent to act on behalf of the State in international relations. In principle this competence should ensue directly from the national constitution. It may be necessary, however, to take the constitutional practice into account in that context as well.[68]

An application by a State may be directed against any other contracting State, an individual application only against those contracting States which have recognized the competence of the Commission to receive such applications. This means that the Commission cannot receive applications directed against a State which is not a party to the Convention[69] or, as the case may be, to one of the Protocols added thereto,[70] or, in the case of an individual application, against a State which is a party to the Convention, but which has not made the declaration referred to in Article 25.[71]

Furthermore, an application will be declared inadmissible *ratione personae* if the alleged violation does not fall under the responsibility of the respondent State. In general a State is internationally responsible for the acts of its legislative, its executive, and its judicial branch of government. The question, however, may arise as to whether a particular organ or person can really be considered to belong to these government organs within the framework of the European Convention. The case has already been mentioned of a foreign or international organ which is active in the territory of a contracting State, but does not fall under its responsibility.[72] Furthermore, the situation may arise where a State is responsible for the international relations of a given territory, but without the possibility that an application may be lodged against it on account of the acts of the authorities in those territories. Indeed, the Convention is only applicable to those territories if the State in question has made a declaration as referred to in Article 63(1).[73]

---

67. See *supra* pp. 33 and 39.
68. Appls 6780/74 and 6950/75, *Cyprus v. Turkey, Yearbook* XVIII (1975), p. 82 (112-116).
69. For some of the numerous examples, see Appl. 262/57, *X v. Czechoslovakia, Yearbook* I (1955-57), p. 170; and Appl. 8030/77, *Confédération Française Démocratique du Travail v. European Communities, Yearbook* XXI (1978), p. 530 (536-538).
70. See, *e.g.*, the Appls 5351/71 and 6579/74, *X v. Belgium, Coll.* 46 (1974), p. 71 (80-81).
71. See Appl. 62/55, *X v. Federal Republic of Germany, Yearbook* I (1955-57), p. 180; Appl. 88/55, *X v. Federal Republic of Germany, Yearbook* I (1955-57), p. 180 (181); Appl. 150/56, *X v. Federal Republic of Germany, Yearbook* I (1955-57), p. 181 (182).
72. See *supra* p. 9, note 27. For the special position of the British Judicial Committee of the Privy Council, see Appl. 3813/68, *X v. United Kingdom, Yearbook* XIII (1970), p. 586 (598-600).
73. On this, see pp. 7-8.

Applications may be directed only against *States*, and consequently not against individuals or groups of individuals. Applications against individuals are therefore declared inadmissible *ratione personae*.[74] In practice a comparatively large number of complaints are directed against the most widely varied categories of individuals and organizations, such as judges and lawyers in their personal capacity, employers, private radio and TV stations and banks. For the rejection of such complaints the Commission generally invokes Article 19, under which it has to ensure the observance of the engagements which the *contracting States* have undertaken, and also Article 25, which permits the Commission to consider applications if the applicant claims to be the victim of a violation of the Convention by a *contracting State*.[75] It appears from its case-law that the Commission does, however, investigate whether a violation of the Convention by an individual may involve the responsibility of a State. According to the principles of international law a State is responsible for acts of individuals to the extent that the State has urged the individuals to commit the acts in question, or has given its consent to them, or in violation of its international obligations has neglected to prevent those acts, to punish the perpetrators, or to impose the obligation to redress the injury caused.[76] These principles also apply within the framework of the European Convention,[77] on the understanding that Article 1 creates that responsibility with respect to the treatment of "everyone within their jurisdiction", and not only of foreigners.

The starting-point for State responsibility under the Convention is that it applies to all organs of the State, even those which under national law are independent of the government, such as the judiciary.[78] However, it is not cristal clear in all cases whether a particular institution must be considered, with respect to the Convention, as an organ of the State concerned, so that the latter is responsible for it. It is hardly possible to provide general answers to this question; a good deal depends, in each concrete case, on the precise position of the said institution under national law.[79] With respect to so-called public industries and enterprises, for instance, the case-law of the Commission is still comparatively casuistic. In a number of cases it did not reach a decision on responsibility.[80] In one case the Commission described public transport companies as "*entreprises para-étatiques*", for which the government was not responsible.[81] Two later decisions, however, point in the other direction. In both cases the applicants had been discharged by British Rail, because they had refused to join a trade union (the so-called "closed-shop system"). The Commission reached the conclusion that, as a public industry,

---

74. See Appl. 6956/75, *X v. United Kingdom, D & R* 8 (1978), p. 103 (104).
75. See, *e.g.*, Appl. 2413/65, *X v. Federal Republic of Germany, Coll.* 23 (1967), p. 1 (7).
76. See M.N. Shaw, *International Law*, Cambridge 1986, pp. 412-414.
77. See Appl. 852/60, *X v. Federal Republic of Germany, Yearbook* IV (1961), p. 346 (350-352).
78. See, *e.g.*, Appl. 7743/76, *J.Y. Cosans v. United Kingdom, D & R* 12 (1978), p. 140 (149).
79. See, *e.g.*, Appl. 1706/62, *X v. Austria, Yearbook* IX (1966), p. 112 (162-164).
80. Appl. 3059/67, *X v. United Kingdom, Coll.* 28 (1969), p. 89 (93) and Appl. 4515/70, *X and the Association of Z v. United Kingdom, Yearbook* XIV (1971), p. 538 (544).
81. Appl. 3789/68, *X v. Belgium, Coll.* 33 (1970), p. 1 (3-4).

British Rail came under the responsibility of the United Kingdom, and that accordingly the applications were admissible *ratione personae*.[82]

Does the responsibility of the contracting States under the Convention extend still further, in the sense that it also covers cases where there is no question of a direct responsibility for the acts or omissions of governmental organs or of negligence with respect to the acts of individuals? One decision of the Commission seems to point in that direction. The issue was whether the Irish Government was responsible for certain acts of an institution which had been called into existence by law, but which otherwise was largely independent of the State. The Commission came to the conclusion that the acts concerned in this case (alleged violation of Article 11) did not fall under the direct responsibility of the Irish Government. However, the Commission subsequently accepted the submission that, despite this, the Irish Government would have violated the Convention if it were to be established that the national law does not protect one of the rights or freedoms guaranteed by the Convention, the violation of which is alleged before the Commission, or at least does not provide a remedy for enforcing such protection.[83] However, rather than a matter of State responsibility for acts of individuals this is a case of the possible violation by the State of a special obligation resulting from the Convention, *viz.* under Article 13.[84] All in all the exact scope under the Convention of State responsibility for private acts or omissions has not yet been clearly defined.

3. In order to answer the question of whether an application falls within the scope of the Convention *ratione materiae*,[85] it is necessary to differentiate between State applications and individual applications.[86]

Article 24, which permits the contracting States to lodge applications on "any alleged breach of the provisions of the Convention by another High Contracting Party", leaves open the possibility for States to submit applications which relate to provisions of the Convention other than the articles of Section I. Articles that might be considered as such, for instance, are Article 1 concerning the obligation for a contracting State to secure to everyone within its jurisdiction the rights and freedoms of Section I of the Convention,[87] and Article 25(1) in case of interference with the exercise of the individual right of complaint. The same applies to Articles 32(4) and 53 in case of refusal to give effect to a decision of the Committee of Ministers or the Court

---

82. Appl. 7601/76, *Young and James v. United Kingdom*, Yearbook XX (1977), p. 520 (560-562) and Appl. 7806/77, *Webster v. United Kingdom*, D & R 12 (1978), p. 168 (173-175).
83. Appl. 4125/69, *X v. Ireland*, Yearbook XIV (1971), p. 198 (218-224).
84. On this, see *infra* pp. 520-532.
85. For the relationship between this admissibility condition and the requirement that the complaint must not be manifestly ill-founded, see *infra* pp. 105-106.
86. Strictly speaking, inter-State applications cannot be rejected on this ground. As already indicated above (p. 67), inter-State applications also may fall outside the competence of the Commission, and that point is in general dealt with by the Commission as an admissibility problem.
87. On this, see *infra* pp. 519-520.

respectively, and Article 57 in case of refusal to furnish the requested information to the Secretary General of the Council of Europe concerning the implementation of the provisions of the Convention. In practice so far the contracting States have not availed themselves of this wider remedy, except where Article 1 is concerned.

The right of complaint of individuals has a somewhat more limited character. It appears from Article 25 that individuals may lodge complaints only about "the rights set forth in this Convention", which implies that their complaints may relate only to the articles of Section I.[88] The question does arise whether an exception must be made for Article 25; in other words, whether the right of complaint itself, the exercise of which the contracting States have undertaken not to hinder, may be considered a "right". As a rule the Commission deals with such a complaint in another way than with a complaint concerning one of the rights or freedoms of Section I, in that it consults directly with the government concerned.[89]

The Commission cannot, of course, deal with complaints about rights or freedoms not set forth in the Convention. Complaints concerning such rights and freedoms are declared inadmissible by the Commission as being incompatible with the Convention. In practice a great many complaints concern the most widely varied "rights and freedoms". From the very colourful case-law of the Commission the following examples of incompatibility *ratione materiae* may be cited: right to a university degree, right to asylum, right to start a business, right to diplomatic protection, right to divorce, right to a driving licence, a general right to free legal aid, right to free medical aid, right to adequate housing, right to a nationality, right to a passport, right to a pension, right to a promotion and the right to be recognized as a scholar. In this context it should, however, be borne in mind that a right which is not set forth in the Convention may find protection *indirectly* via one of the provisions of the Convention. Thus it is conceivable that, although the right to admission to a country of which one is not a national has not been included in the Convention, under certain circumstances a person cannot be denied admission to a country if his right to respect for his family life (Art. 8) would be violated. Similarly, although the Convention does not recognize a right to a pension, violation of an existing right to a pension may be contrary to Article 1 of the First Protocol, in which the right to the enjoyment of possessions is protected.[90]

Complaints to be equated with those concerning rights not protected in the Convention are complaints concerning rights which are indeed incorporated in the Convention, but with respect to which the respondent State has made a reservation.[91] Complaints relating to such rights are also declared inadmis-

---

88. For the question of whether individuals may bring an independent complaint concerning Art. 1, see *infra* p. 591.
89. See *supra* pp. 49-52.
90. For these examples, see *infra* pp. 387-389 and p. 455.
91. See *infra* pp. 606-613.

sible by the Commission on account of incompatibility with the Convention.[92]

For all this it is important that the Commission does not require the applicant to indicate accurately in his application the rights set forth in the Convention which in his opinion have been violated. The Commission has proved prepared to investigate *ex officio*, by reference to the submissions of the applicant, whether there has been a violation of one or more of the provisions of Section I. This approach of the Commission is in conformity with the above-mentioned objective character of the European Convention.[93] Nevertheless it remains advisable for an applicant and his counsel to raise all important points of fact and law already during the examination of admissibility. The possible consequences if this is not done are apparent from the *Winterwerp* Case. When the question arose whether Article 6(1), too, was applicable in that case, the Commission submitted:

> This question, which was raised by the applicant's counsel in the course of the examination of the merits, relates to facts distinct from those originally presented to the Commission, which has not received any detailed submissions thereon.
> The Commission therefore considers that it ought not, in the present case, to express an opinion on this important new point.[94]

In this case, however, in our opinion neither the applicant nor his counsel was to be blamed for not having raised the issue of Article 6, which, moreover, was much more closely related to the subject-matter of the original complaint than the Commission suggested. In addition, one may wonder why the Commission had not invited the parties to elaborate on the issue if the submissions received were not detailed enough. Anyhow, the Court held that there was an evident connection between the issue of Article 6 and the initial complaints. This, in combination with the fact that the Netherlands Government had not raised a preliminary objection on the point, induced the Court to take the alleged violation of Article 6 into consideration.[95]

4. The territorial and the temporal effect of the Convention have already been discussed above.[96]

5. The second of the above-mentioned categories of cases in which the application is not compatible with the provisions of the Convention - those cases where the applicant does not satisfy the condition of Article 25 - in fact

92. See, *e.g.*, Appl. 1452/62, *X v. Austria*, Yearbook VI (1963), p. 268 (276).
93. See *supra* pp. 33-35. This was confirmed expressly by the Court in its judgment of 6 November 1980, *Guzzardi*, A.39 (1981), pp. 21-23. In that case the Commission had - wrongly, according to the Italian Government - also considered the complaint in the light of Art. 5, whereas the applicant had not expressly referred to it. On the basis of a detailed motivation the Court held as follows: "The Commission and the Court have to examine in the light of the Convention as a whole the situation impugned by an applicant. In the performance of this task, they are, notably, free to give to the facts of the case, as found to be established by the material before them ..., a characterisation in law different from that given to them by the applicant" (p. 23).
94. Report of 15 December 1977, B.31 (1983), p. 45.
95. Judgment of 24 October 1979, A.33 (1980), pp. 27-28.
96. See *supra* pp. 7-11.

concerns the condition that has already been discussed at length, *viz.* that an individual applicant must be able to furnish *prima facie* evidence that he is personally the victim of the violation of the Convention alleged by him, or at least has well-founded reasons for considering himself to be the victim. If he merely puts forward a violation *in abstracto*, or a violation which has done a wrong only to other persons, his application is incompatible with the provisions of the Convention.[97]

6. The most obvious case of incompatibility with the provisions of the Convention is the third of the above-mentioned categories. This concerns applications which are directed at the destruction or limitation of one of the rights or freedoms guaranteed in the Convention, and as such conflict with Article 17, which will hereafter be discussed in greater detail.[98] Even if Article 17 had not been written, such applications of course would still be inadmissible, *viz.* on account of abuse of the right of complaint in the sense of Article 27(2).

2.6. The domestic remedies must have been exhausted (Arts 26 and 27(3))

1. Article 26 provides:

> The Commission may only deal with the matter after all domestic remedies have been exhausted, according to the generally recognised rules of international law.

This is the so-called rule of the "exhaustion of local remedies" (*épuisement des voies de recours internes*), which is to be regarded as a general rule of international procedural law.[99]

Article 26 refers expressly to the general rules of international law in the matter, and in its case-law the Commission is indeed frequently guided by international judicial and arbitral decisions with respect to this rule, which will hereafter be called the "local remedies rule". The Commission referred expressly, for instance, to the judgment of the International Court of Justice in the *Interhandel* Case concerning the rationale of the local remedies rule.[100] In the *Nielsen* Case the Commission formulated this rationale as follows:

> The Respondent State must first have an opportunity to redress by its own means within the framework of its own domestic legal system the wrong alleged to have been done to the individual.[101]

2. The requirement of the prior exhaustion of the local remedies holds in principle for applications by States as well as for individual applications. This

---

97. See *supra* pp. 39-49.
98. See pp. 562-567.
99. For a detailed discussion of the nature, substance and rationale of this rule, see Van Dijk, *supra* note 43, pp. 381-391, and the case-law and literature there mentioned.
100. *I.C.J. Reports* 1959, p. 6 (27).
101. Appl. 343/57, *Schouw Nielsen v. Denmark, Yearbook* II (1958-59), p. 412 (438). See also Appl. 5964/72, *X v. Federal Republic of Germany, D & R* 3 (1976), p. 57 (60).

is implied in the wording of Article 27(1) and (2) on the one hand, and Articles 26 and 27(3) on the other. In fact, the first two paragraphs of Article 27 expressly declare the admissibility conditions mentioned therein to be applicable only to applications lodged under Article 25, while the third paragraph of Article 27, which refers to Article 26, where the local remedies rule is laid down, refers quite generally to "any petition" and is therefore also applicable to applications by States. The same conclusion follows from the fact that the local remedies rule is a general rule of international procedural law.

While in the case of an individual application the local remedies must have been exhausted by the applicant himself, the local remedies rule with respect to applications by States implies that the local remedies must have been exhausted by those individuals in respect to whom, according to the allegation of the applicant State, the Convention has been violated.[102]

In the *Pfunders* Case Austria submitted that, since the right of complaint of States is based on the principle of the collective guarantee and the public interest, and since an applicant State need not prove that an injury has been sustained, the local remedies rule does not hold for States.[103] The Commission, however, rejected this line of reasoning by referring to the terms of Articles 26 and 27, and held that the principle on which the local remedies rule is based should be applied *a fortiori* in an international system which affords protection not only to the applicant State's own nationals, but to everyone who is in one way or another subject to the jurisdiction of the respondent State.[104] By this statement the Commission confirmed its earlier case-law of the second *Cyprus* Case.[105]

3. The local remedies rule is not an admissibility condition with an *absolute* content. On the basis of the reference in Article 26 to the "generally recognized rules of international law" this rule is applied with flexibility by the Commission. The Commission's point of departure is that each concrete case should be judged "in the light of its particular facts".[106]

It may be mentioned at the outset that the local remedies rule does not apply at all to proceedings for affording satisfaction under Article 50 of the Convention.[107] In fact, such proceedings do not ensue from a new application, but constitute a continuation of the original application after a violation has been found by the Court. Questions of admissibility are not involved there at

---

102. The condition applies in international law only when the action of a State is concerned with the treatment of individuals. If a State in instituting an action puts forward its own legal position, the condition is not applied, since as a rule a State cannot be subjected against its will to the jurisdiction of another State. On this, see Ch. de Visscher, "Le déni de justice en droit international", *R.C.A.D.I.* 52 (1935-II), pp. 364-442 (425).
103. Appl. 788/60, *Austria v. Italy, Yearbook* IV (1961), p. 116 (146-148).
104. *Ibidem*, pp. 148-152. See also Appls 6780/74 and 6950/75, *Cyprus v. Turkey, Yearbook* XVIII (1975), p. 82 (100).
105. Appl. 299/57, *Greece v. United Kingdom, Yearbook* II (1958-59), p. 186 (190-196).
106. Appl. 343/57, *Schouw Nielsen v. Denmark, Yearbook* II (1958-59), p. 412 (442-444).
107. On this, see *infra* pp. 171-185.

all.[108] Furthermore, it is obvious that the rule does not apply when a State brings up the legislation or administrative practice of another State without the complaint being related to one or more concrete persons as victims of this legislation or administrative practice (the so-called "abstract" complaints). In fact, in such a case there are no individuals who ought to have exhausted the local remedies, while the applicant State itself cannot be expected to institute proceedings before the national authorities of the respondent State. An example is the first *Cyprus* Case, where Greece submitted that a number of emergency acts which were in force in Cyprus at that time conflicted with the provisions of the Convention. In this case the Commission decided that

> the provision of Article 26 concerning the exhaustion of domestic remedies ... does not apply to the present application, the scope of which is to determine the compatibility with the Convention of legislative measures and administrative practices in Cyprus.[109]

Later case-law of the Commission also shows that the local remedies rule is not applied if the application does not relate to individual decisions or acts of the authorities and to the concrete persons who are the victims of them, but is rather designed to national legislation and/or an administrative practice examined for their compatibility with the Convention.[110] According to the Commission, an administrative practice comprises two elements: repetition of acts and official tolerance. The first element is defined as

> an accumulation of identical or analogous breaches which are sufficiently numerous and interconnected to amount not merely to isolated incidents or exceptions but to a pattern or system.[111]

By official tolerance is meant that,

> though acts of torture or ill-treatment are plainly illegal, they are tolerated in the sense that the superiors of those immediately responsible, though cognisant of such acts, take no action to punish them or to prevent their repetition; or that a higher authority, in face of numerous allegations, manifests indifference by refusing any adequate investigation of their truth or falsity, or that in judicial proceedings a fair hearing of such complaints is denied.[112]

In the case of *France, Norway, Denmark, Sweden and the Netherlands against Turkey*, the Commission added that

> any action taken by the higher authority must be on a scale which is sufficient to put an end to the repetition of acts or to interrupt the pattern or system.[113]

A condition is always that the applicant State should give "substantial evidence" of the existence of the national legislation or administrative practice concerned. This requirement of "substantial evidence" may take on a different

---

108. Judgment of 10 March 1972, *De Wilde, Ooms and Versyp* ("*Vagrancy*"-cases) A.14 (1972), p. 8.
109. Appl. 176/56, *Greece v. United Kingdom*, Yearbook II (1958-59), p. 182 (184).
110. See, *e.g.*, Appl. 5310/71, *Ireland v. United Kingdom*, Yearbook XV (1972), p. 76 (242); Second Greek Case, Yearbook XIII (1970), p. 108 (134-136); and Appls 9940-9944/82, *France, Norway, Denmark, Sweden and the Netherlands v. Turkey*, D & R 35 (1984), p. 143 (162 et seq.).
111. Judgment of 18 January 1978, *Ireland v. United Kingdom*, A.25 (1978), p. 64.
112. Report of 5 November 1969, *Greek Case*, Yearbook XII (1969), p. 196.
113. Appl. 9940-9944/82, *France, Norway, Denmark, Sweden and the Netherlands v. Turkey*, D & R 35, p. 143 (164).

meaning depending on whether the admissibility stage or the examination of the merits is concerned. According to the Commission:

> The question whether the existence of an administrative practice is established or not can only be determined after an examination of the merits. At the stage of admissibility *prima facie* evidence, while required, must also be considered as sufficient. ... There is *prima facie* evidence of an alleged administrative practice where the allegations concerning individual cases are sufficiently substantiated, considered as a whole and in the light of the submissions of the applicant and the respondent Party. It is in this sense that the term "substantial evidence" is to be understood.[114]

If the State does not succeed in doing so, the local remedies rule is applicable. In the case of individual applicants there can be no question of a completely abstract complaint; indeed, the applicant must submit that he is the victim of the alleged violation, so that he is at the same time the person who must have exhausted all available local remedies.

When an applicant submitted that no local remedy had been available to him, because his complaint concerned the compatibility of the Belgian divorce legislation with the Convention, the Commission decided that nothing had prevented him from submitting this question to the Belgian Court of Cassation.[115] And in the case of an application against the Netherlands concerning the fiscal legislation relating to married women the Commission pointed out that the applicant could have submitted the question of the compatibility of the challenged provisions with the Convention, under the then Article 66 of the Dutch Constitution, to the Dutch courts.[116] Both applications were declared inadmissible under Article 26.[117] It may be assumed that the Commission will take a similar position when in the case of an application by a State certain legislation or an administrative practice is submitted for review, but the complaint at the same time concerns concrete persons to whom an effective and adequate local remedy is available.

As has been mentioned above, in an individual application an administrative practice may indeed be challenged, provided that the applicant proves satisfactorily that he himself is the victim of it. That administrative practice may be of such a nature as to justify the presumption that the remedies of the State in question offer no prospects of effective redress. Thus, for example, in the Case of *G v. Belgium*, the Commission concluded that "as far as Article 5(4) is concerned, the question of exhaustion of domestic remedies does not arise". The reason, according to the Commission, was "that Belgian law does not provide for a judicial remedy which would make it possible to take a speedy decision as to the lawfulness of the detention of a person placed at the Government's disposal". The procedures referred to by the

---

114. *Ibidem*, pp. 164-165.
115. Appl. 1488/62, *X v. Belgium*, *Coll.* 13 (1964), p. 93 (96).
116. Appl. 2780/66, *X v. the Netherlands* (not published).
117. The two applications mentioned were rejected on the ground of Art. 26, but might also have been declared inadmissible on the ground of Art. 27(2). In both cases the applicants had not submitted that they were victims of the alleged violation, so that these cases concerned in reality completely abstract complaints, which the Commission usually rejects on account of incompatibility with the provisions of the Convention.

Belgian Government did not fulfil the requirement of effectiveness.[118]

The Commission has recognized that ineffectiveness of remedies might particularly occur in the case of practices of torture and inhuman treatment. On that ground in the *Donnelly* Case it took the view that in such a situation the local remedies rule is not applicable, provided that the applicant gives *prima facie* evidence that such a practice has occurred and that he is the victim of it.[119] Unlike in the above-mentioned inter-State applications, here the rule is not inapplicable because the application is assumed to have an abstract character, but as a result of the principle, also recognized in general international law, that remedies which in advance are certain not to be effective or adequate need not be exhausted.[120] This became quite clear when in the next stage of the same *Donnelly* Case the Commission, quite unexpectedly, on the basis of its examination of the facts concluded that effective possibilities of redress were indeed present, and on that ground, by applying Article 29, declared the application inadmissible because the local remedies rule had not been complied with.[121] A given administrative practice may therefore give rise to the presumption that the local remedies are not effective, but the Commission reserves the right to inquire into this.[122]

4. In connection with the local remedies rule it is, of course, in the first place important to know what remedies are available. That question is to be answered on the basis of national law and is therefore decided by the competent national authorities.

A question, which for a long time has been left undecided in the case-law is what an applicant should do when different remedies are open to him. Must he pursue them all or may he confine himself to bringing the action which in his view is most likely to be successful? The text of Article 26 appears to suggest the former, for it refers to "all domestic remedies". The Commission in a 1974 decision seemed to take a less stringent approach. It held that:

> where there is a single remedy it should be pursued up to the highest level. The position is not so certain where the domestic law provides a number of different remedies. In such cases the Commission tends to admit that Article 26 has been complied with if the applicant exhausts only the remedy or remedies which are reasonably likely to prove

---

118. Appl. 9107/80, *D & R* 33 (1983), p. 76 (79).
119. Appls 5577-5583/72, *Yearbook* XVI (1973), p. 212 (262). See also the report of the Commission of 5 November 1969 in the *Greek Case*, *Yearbook* XII; *The Greek Case* (1969), p. 194. Cf. Appls 9911/82 and 9945/82, *R, S, A and C v. Portugal, D & R* 36 (1984), p. 200 (207), in which the Commission stated that the applicant must provide detailed allegations, if the remedy is to be considered ineffective.
120. For this principle, see with respect to inter-State applications Appl. 299/57, *Greece v. United Kingdom, Yearbook* II (1958-59), p. 186 (192-194), and with respect to individual applications Appl. 5493/72, *Handyside v. United Kingdom, Yearbook* XVII (1974), p. 228 (288-290).
121. *Yearbook* XIX (1976), p. 84 (248-254).
122. Cf. also Appl. 9471/81, *X and Y v. United Kingdom, D & R* 36 (1984), p. 49 (61). Here the Commission simply concluded that, since there is no dispute between the parties where the compliance with Art. 26 is concerned, it is not necessary to go into the question whether Article 26 is inapplicable in the present case because of the existence of a State practice.

effective.[123]

In a later case the Commission added:

> Where ... there is a choice of remedies open to the applicant to redress an alleged violation of the Convention, Article 26 of the Convention must be applied to reflect the practical realities of the applicant's position in order to ensure the effective protection of the rights and freedoms guaranteed by the Convention.[124]

It is up to the applicant in those cases to indicate which remedy he has chosen and for what reasons. These grounds have to be objective and reasonable.[125]

With respect to the way in which and the time-limits within which proceedings must be instituted, national law is equally decisive. That question is therefore also decided by the competent national authorities. If in his appeal to a national court an applicant has failed to observe the procedural requirements or the time-limits, and his case accordingly has been rejected, the condition of exhaustion of the local remedies has not been complied with and his application is declared inadmissible by the Commission.[126] It may also be necessary for a correct exhaustion of the local remedies that the applicant calls in the assistance of a counsel in the action in question, if national law requires this.[127]

The interpretation and the application of the relevant provisions of national law in principle belong to the competence of the national authorities concerned. The Commission, on the other hand, is competent to judge whether, as a result of such an interpretation or application, the applicant would become the victim of a denial of justice.[128]

Moreover the local remedies rule is considered to be complied with only if the points on which an application is lodged with the Commission have also been put forward in national proceedings.[129] That the Commission takes a stringent attitude in this respect becomes clear from the case where a complaint was lodged against Norway on account of the refusal of a Norwegian judicial organ to publish the reasons for its judgment. Since this point had not been put forward before the highest court in Norway, in the opinion of the Commission the local remedies rule had not been complied with, although a number of other objections against the judgment in question had indeed been raised in those proceedings.[130] This decision of the Commission shows at the same time that the injured person cannot rely on

---

123. Appl. 5874/72, *Monika Berberich v. Federal Republic of Germany*, Yearbook XVII (1974), p. 386 (418).
124. Appl. 9118/80, *Allgemeine Gold- und Silberscheideanstalt A.G. v. United Kingdom*, D & R 32 (1983), p. 159 (165).
125. *Ibidem.*
126. See, e.g., Appl. 2854/66, *X and Y v. Austria*, Coll. 26 (1968), p. 46 (53-54).
127. Appl. 6878/75, *Le Compte v. Belgium*, Yearbook XX (1977), p. 254 (274).
128. Appl. 1191/61, *X v. Federal Republic of Germany*, Yearbook VIII (1965), p. 106 (154-156).
129. See, e.g., Appl. 5574/72, *X v. United Kingdom*, D & R 3 (1976), p. 10 (15); Appls 5573/72 and 5670/72, *Adler v. Federal Republic of Germany*, Yearbook XX (1977), p. 102 (128); Appl. 7238/75, *Van Leuven and De Meyere v. Belgium*, D & R 8 (1977), p. 140 (158).
130. Appl. 2002/63, *X v. Norway*, Yearbook VII (1964), p. 262 (266).

an alleged obligation of the national court to supplement the legal grounds *ex officio*.[131] This was expressly confirmed by the Court:

> The fact that the Belgian Courts might have been able, or even obliged, to examine the case of their own motion under the Convention cannot be regarded as having dispensed the applicant from pleading before them the Convention or arguments to the same or like effect.[132]

In the case of *Kröcher and Möller v. Switzerland* the applicants alleged violation of Article 3 because of the conditions imposed on them both during the period of their detention on remand and during their preventive detention and while serving their sentences. As far as the first-mentioned period was concerned it was not disputed that the applicants properly exhausted the domestic remedies available. The final national decision, however, referred solely to the conditions of detention on remand. With respect to the last-mentioned period the Commission considered whether the fact or conditions complained of subsequently constituted a mere extension of those complained of at the outset. It concluded that this was not the case and declared the applicants inadmissible for not having properly exhausted the domestic remedies, since the last-mentioned period had not been expressly at issue in the national proceedings.[133] The formula used in the case-law requires that the point concerned must have been submitted "in substance" to the national organs.[134] The precise implications of this requirement will depend on the concrete circumstances of the case. In general the applicant will not be required to have explicitly indicated the relevant articles of the Convention in the national action.[135] Express reference to provisions of the Convention may, however, be required in certain cases:

> In certain circumstances it may nonetheless happen that express reliance on the Convention before the national authorities constitutes the sole appropriate manner of raising before those authorities first, as is required by Article 26, an issue intended, if need be, to be brought subsequently before the European review bodies.[136]

In other words, express reference to the provisions of the Convention is necessary if there is no other possibility of submitting the case in the appropriate way to the national organs.[137]

---

131. See Appl. 2322/64, *X v. Belgium, Coll.* 24 (1967), p. 36 (42).
132. Judgment of 6 November 1980, *Van Oosterwijck*, A.40 (1981), p. 19.
133. Appl. 8463/78, *Kröcher and Möller v. Switzerland*, *D & R* 26 (1982), p. 24 (48-52).
134. See, *e.g.*, Appl. 9186/80, *De Cubber v. Belgium*, *D & R* 28 (1982), p. 172 (175); and Judgment of 28 August 1986, *Glasenapp*, A.104 (1986), p. 28.
135. See the words of the Court in the *Van Oosterwijck*-judgment (note 132). Thus also the Commission in Appl. 1661/62, *X and Y v. Belgium*, *Yearbook* VI (1965), p. 360 (366): "whereas an application against a State where the Convention is an integral part of municipal law ... may thus prove to be inadmissible if the victim of the alleged violation has not given his judges an opportunity to remedy that violation because the Convention was not invoked or no other arguments to the same effect were raised". See also: Appl. 9228/80, *X v. Federal Republic of Germany*, *D & R* 30 (1983), pp. 132 (141-142).
136. Thus the Court in its judgment of 6 November 1980, *Van Oosterwijck*, A.40 (1981), p. 17.
137. See the Court's judgment of the same date, *Guzzardi*, A.39 (1981), p. 27, where it was held: "However, a more specific reference was not essential in the circumstances since it did not constitute the sole means of achieving the aim pursued ... . He [the applicant] ... derived from the Italian legislation pleas equivalent, in the Court's view, to an allegation of a breach of the right guaranteed by Article 5 of the Convention". See also the
(continued...)

The above statement holds true for those contracting States where the Convention has internal effect. Things are different, of course, in contracting States where the Convention has no internal effect. Indeed, in such a case it is impossible to directly invoke the Convention before the national authorities. Consequently the Commission decided in a case against the United Kingdom:

> Before lodging this application the applicant lodged an appeal against her conviction and sentence. Although in the appeal proceedings she did not invoke the rights guaranteed in Articles 5, 9 and 10, she has to be considered to have exhausted domestic remedies because the Convention which guarantees the said rights is not binding law for the British courts and it is doubtful whether the rights and liberties in question constitute general principles which could successfully be invoked by the defence in criminal proceedings before the British courts.[138]

Here again, however, it may be required that the applicant has invoked legal rules or principles of domestic law which are "in substance" the same as the relevant provisions of the Convention.

5. The most important question in connection with Article 26 is what legal remedies must have been pursued. Here, too, a good deal depends on the relevant national law, and the answer to this question can only be given on a case-by-case basis.[139] From the very voluminous and rather casuistic case-law of the Commission the following trends may be inferred.

No definition of the term "remedy" is to be found in the case-law of the Commission. In various places it does give some indications as to its meaning. The concept of "remedy" at all events does not cover those procedures in which one does not claim a right, but attempts to obtain a favour. Examples are the action for rehabilitation in Belgium[140] and the so-called "petition to the Queen" in England.[141] The right of petition under Article 5 of the Dutch Constitution is another example.[142] In the *Nielsen* Case the Commission submitted quite generally that

> the rules governing the exhaustion of the local remedies, as they are generally recognized today, in principle require that recourse should be had to all legal remedies available under the local law which are in principle capable of providing an effective and sufficient means of redressing the wrongs for which, on the international plane, the Respondent State is alleged to be responsible.[143]

137.(...continued)
    Commission in Appl. 8130/78, *Hans and Marianne Eckle v. Federal Republic of Germany*, *D & R* 16 (1979), p. 120 (127-128).
138. Appl. 7050/75, *Arrowsmith v. United Kingdom*, *Yearbook* XX (1977), p. 316 (334-336). See Appl. 6871/75, *Caprino v. United Kingdom*, *Yearbook* XXI (1978), p. 284 (286-288).
139. This standpoint was already taken expressly by the Commission at a very early date: see Appl. 343/57, *Schouw Nielsen v. Denmark*, *Yearbook* II (1958-59), p. 412 (442-444): "the competence which the Commission has in every case to appreciate in the light of its particular facts whether any given remedy at any given date appeared to offer the Applicant the possibility of an effective and sufficient remedy".
140. Appl. 214/56, *De Becker v. Belgium*, *Yearbook* II (1958-59), p. 214 (236-238).
141. Appl. 299/57, *Greece v. United Kingdom*, *Yearbook* II (1958-59), p. 187 (192).
142. See the report of the Budget Committee for Foreign Affairs of the Dutch Parliament, *Yearbook* II (1958-59), p. 566.
143. Appl. 343/57, *Yearbook* II (1958-59), p. 412 (440). See also Appl. 10092/82, *Baraona v. Portugal*, *D & R* 40 (1985), p. 118 (136), where the Commission held that "the crucial point is ... whether an appeal might have secured redress in the form of direct, rather than indirect, protection of the rights laid down in ... the Convention".

In fact this is the core of the Commission's case-law concerning the local remedies rule. An individual is therefore dispensed from the obligation to exhaust certain local remedies if in the circumstances of his case these remedies are ineffective or inadequate.[144] In the same vein the answer to the question of whether non-judicial procedures belong to the local remedies that have to be exhausted depends on whether those procedures are provided with sufficient guarantees to ensure an effective legal protection against the authorities.[145]

For a given local remedy to be considered adequate and effective it is, of course, not required that the claim in question had actually been recognized by the national court. In this stage of the examination by the Commission the question of whether the application is well-founded is not considered; the only point at issue is the question of whether, assuming that the complaint is well-founded, this particular remedy would have provided the applicant the possibility of redress.[146] In this context it must be noted that the applicant's personal view of the effectiveness or ineffectiveness of a given remedy in itself is not decisive.[147]

The Commission has built up a voluminous case-law concerning what may be regarded as an effective and adequate remedy. From this case-law, the following elements emerge as the most important. In the first place an applicant must have used the remedies provided for up to the highest level only if and in so far as the appeal to a higher tribunal can still substantially affect the decision on the merits.[148] An applicant may of course refrain from such an appeal if the tribunal in question is not competent in the matter of

144. See, e.g., Appl. 7011/75, *Hennig Becker v. Denmark*, D & R 4 (1976), p. 215 (232-233); Appl. 7465/76, *X v. Denmark*, D & R 7 (1977), p. 153 (154). A special case is Appl. 7397/76, *Peyer v. Switzerland*, D & R 11 (1978), p. 58 (75-76), in which in the opinion of the Commission the applicant did not need to appeal, since he could not rely on the Convention before the national court, as it had not yet entered into force with respect to Switzerland, while in addition there was no legal ground on which such an appeal could be based. See also joint Appls 8805/79 and 8806/79, *De Jong and Baljet v. the Netherlands*, D & R 24 (1981), p. 144 (150), in which the action for damages of Art. 1401 of the Netherlands Civil Code was not considered effective to question the detention, which was in conformity with domestic law. Similarly, in the case of *Z v. the Netherlands*, the appeal before the Judicial Division of the Council of State against the Deputy Minister of Justice was considered not effective because such proceedings do not suspend the execution of the decision to deport the applicant. Appl. 10400/83, D & R 38 (1984), p. 145 (150). See also: Appl. 10078/82, *M v. France*, D & R 41 (1985), p. 103 (119).
145. See, e.g., Appl. 155/56, *X v. Federal Republic of Germany*, Yearbook I (1955-57), p. 412 (420).
146. Appl. 1474/62, *Twenty-three inhabitants of Alsemberg and Beersel v. Belgium*, Coll. 12 (1964), p. 18 (27).
147. Appl. 289/57, *X v. Federal Republic of Germany*, Yearbook I (1955-57), p. 148 (149). See also Appl. 6271/73, *X v. Federal Republic of Germany*, D & R 6 (1976), p. 62 (64), and Appl. 7317/75, *Lynas v. Switzerland*, Yearbook XX (1977), p. 412 (442). Appl. 10148/82, *Garcia v. Switzerland*, D & R 42 (1985), p. 98 (122).
148. Appl. 788/60, *Austria v. Italy*, Yearbook IV (1961), p. 116 (172) and Appl. 2690/65, *Televizier v. the Netherlands*, Yearbook IX (1966), p. 512 (548). See also Appl. 6289/73, *Airey v. Ireland*, Yearbook XX (1977), p. 180 (200); Appl. 6870/75, *Y v. United Kingdom*, D & R 10 (1978), p. 37 (67); and Appls 9362/81, 9363/81 and 9387/81, *Van der Sluijs, Zuiderveld and Klappe v. the Netherlands*, D & R 28 (1982), p. 212 (219).

his claim.[149] In some legal systems, for instance, a higher or the highest court has jurisdiction only with respect to legal questions and cannot pronounce on the facts. If the application submitted to the Commission precisely concerns facts, the applicant need not previously have applied to such a court.[150] The same holds good with respect to the possibility of appeal to a constitutional court from a decision of another court, such as it is provided for in the German Federal Republic, Italy and Austria, for instance. Such an appeal belongs to the remedies that must have been exhausted if and in so far as the decision of the constitutional court may have any influence on the situation about which a complaint is lodged with the Commission.[151] In some legal systems, such as the Italian one, individuals have no direct appeal to the constitutional court; they are dependent on a decision of the ordinary court to refer the issue of constitutionality of a specific law to the constitutional court. In such a case, according to the Commission, the individual applicant is required to have raised the question of that constitutionality in the proceedings before the ordinary court. If he has not done so, he cannot claim that he had no access to the constitutional court.[152] In Ireland the granting of leave for appeal to the Supreme Court lies at the discretion of the Attorney-General, and in Denmark it is the Minister of Justice who has a wide discretion in granting leave for appeal. In both legal systems, moreover, such a leave is granted only exceptionally. With respect to both cases the Commission has decided that the appeal to the Supreme Court does not constitute an effective remedy in the sense of Article 26.[153]

It is not only the *judicial* procedures which must be instituted, but every remedy available under national law which may lead to a decision that is binding on the authorities[154] - including the possibility of appeal to administrative bodies - provided that it is adequate and effective. In a case concerning the nationalization of Yarrow Shipbuilders under the British Aircraft and Shipbuilding Industries Act 1977 the Commission faced the question of whether the reference of a dispute on compensation to an arbitration tribunal provided for in the 1977 Act constituted an effective remedy to be exhausted. According to the Commission the tribunal had jurisdiction to determine the amount of compensation under the statutory formula, but did not sit as a tribunal of appeal pronouncing on the adequacy of the offers made in the negotiations by the Secretary of State. It thus represented an alternative means of assessing the compensation due under the statutory formula, if

---

149. See, *e.g.*, Appl. 7598/76, *Kaplan v. United Kingdom*, D & R 15 (1979), p. 120 (122). Thus also the judgment of 6 November 1980, *Guzzardi*, A.39 (1981), pp. 21-22.
150. See, *e.g.*, Appl. 1437/62 (not published) and Appl. 10741/84, *S v. United Kingdom*, D & R 41 (1985), p. 226 (231).
151. See, *e.g.*, Appl. 1086/61, *X v. Federal Republic of Germany*, Yearbook V (1962), p. 149 (154). See also Appls 5573 and 5670/72, *Adler v. Federal Republic of Germany*, Yearbook XX (1977), p. 102 (132).
152. See Appl. 6452/74, *Sacchi v. Italy*, D & R 5 (1976), p. 43 (51).
153. Appl. 9136/80, *X v. Ireland*, D & R 26 (1982), p. 242 (244) and Appl. 8395/78, *X v. Denmark*, D & R 27 (1982), p. 50 (52). *Cf.* also Appl. 8950/80, *H v. Belgium*, D & R 37 (1984), p. 5 (13).
154. Appl. 332/57, *Lawless v. Ireland*, Yearbook II (1958-59), p. 308 (322-324).

agreement as to the appropriate amount could not be reached. As the substance of the applicant company's complaint was not that it received less than the Act entitled it to but that the very nature of the statutory compensation formula was such that it inevitably failed to reflect the company's proper value, the Commission held that resort to arbitration would not have constituted an effective and sufficient remedy.[155]

The question of whether extraordinary remedies must also have been used cannot be answered in a general way. In the *Nielsen* Case the Commission required such exhaustion, in so far as it can be expected to produce an effective and adequate result. It must be decided for each individual case whether the remedy is effective and adequate. In the *Nielsen* Case the Commission considered an application to the Special Court of Revision as a remedy that should be exhausted.[156] In the later case-law, however, applications for reopening of the proceedings were not regarded as "domestic remedies" in the sense of Article 26 of the Convention.[157]

An appeal is ineffective and does not therefore have to be instituted if it is certain that, considering the well-established case-law, it does not offer any chances of success.[158] In that case, however, the applicant must give some evidence of the existence of such case-law.[159] That the Commission is not inclined to accept an argument to that effect easily, if the case-law proves not to be as well-established as was alleged, appears from its decision in the *Retimag* Case. Retimag was a Swiss company, but it was actually controlled by the German Communist Party. The latter was declared unconstitutional by the German court, and consequently the property of Retimag was confiscated. The company invoked before the Commission the right to the peaceful enjoyment of possessions. Article 19 of the German Constitution declares the provisions on fundamental rights to be applicable to *internal* legal persons. On this ground Retimag argued that it had not been able to appeal to the *Bundesverfassungsgericht* because it was a Swiss company, and accordingly not an internal legal person. However, after Retimag had lodged its application with the Commission, the *Bundesverfassungsgericht* decided that Article 19 was not to be interpreted *a contrario* and did not exclude an appeal by external legal persons. On this basis the Commission decided that Retimag had not exhausted the local remedies and it declared the application inadmissible

155. Appl. 9266/81, *Yarrow P.L.C. and others v. United Kingdom*, D & R 30 (1983), p. 155 (188-190).
156. Appl. 343/57, *Yearbook* II (1958-59), p. 412 (438-442).
157. See, *e.g.*, Appl. 2385/64, *X v. Norway*, *Coll.* 22 (1967), p. 85 (88). Moreover, in a case which was practically identical with the *Nielsen* Case, for the future the Commission expressly left open the question of whether a petition to the Danish Special Court of Revision constitutes an effective remedy: Appl. 4311/69, *X v. Denmark*, *Yearbook* XIV (1971), p. 280 (316-320).
158. Appl. 27/55, *X v. Federal Republic of Germany*, *Yearbook* I (1955-57), p. 138 (139). See also Appl. 7705/76, *X v. Federal Republic of Germany*, D & R 9 (1978), p. 196 (203); Appls 9362/81, 9363/81 and 9387/81, *Van der Sluijs, Zuiderveld and Klappe v. the Netherlands*, D & R 28 (1982), p. 212 (219); and Appl. 10103/82, *Farragut v. France*, D & R 39 (1984), p. 186 (205).
159. See, *e.g.*, Appl. 788/60, *Austria v. Italy*, *Yearbook* IV (1961), p. 116 (168).

under Article 26.[160] A comparable situation occurred in the case of *De Varga-Hirsch v. France*, in which *inter alia* a violation of the requirement of "reasonable time" of Article 5(3) was alleged. The applicant had been held in detention on remand for almost five years. Although he repeatedly applied to the courts for release on bail, he did not appeal to the Court of Cassation, except in two cases. In these two cases, however, he did not rely on the Convention or on comparable provisions of domestic law. The applicant contended that, because of its limited jurisdiction, the Court of Cassation could not be considered as an effective remedy. The Commission rejected this argument by referring to case-law of the Court of Cassation with regard to detention on remand, dating from after the applicant's detention on remand had ended. It held that the appeal to the Court of Cassation was neither a new remedy nor an appeal likely to be dismissed as inadmissible. The Commission added that

> if there is any doubt as to whether a given remedy is or is not intrinsically able to offer a real chance of success, that is a point which must be submitted to the domestic courts themselves, before any appeal can be made to the international court.[161]

It thus appears to be hazardous for an applicant to rely simply on a particular interpretation if the latter is not supported by clear and constant national case-law.[162] Moreover, an applicant cannot rely on case-law if the legal provisions on which that case-law is based have meanwhile been altered. Indeed, in such a case there is no certainty that the decision in his case would have been identical with previous decisions, so that the relevant remedy cannot in advance be qualified as ineffective and inadequate.[163]

For purposes of comparison, reference may be made to the decision of the Commission in the so-called *Vagrancy* Case, where three Belgians claimed that they had been unlawfuly detained for vagrancy.[164] Up to the moment at which the applications were lodged it had been established in the case-law of the Belgian Council of State that the latter had no jurisdiction with respect to an appeal against such detention. After the applications had been declared admissible, the Council of State reversed its approach. According to the Commission, however, this was no reason for declaring the applications as yet inadmissible because of non-exhaustion of an effective local remedy.[165] In the case of *X v. Belgium*, the question was raised whether a change in the case-law concerning the condition of access to a court of appeal, introduced

160. Appl. 712/60, *Yearbook* IV (1961), p. 384 (404-406).
161. Appl. 9559/81, *D & R* 33 (1983), p. 158 (211-212).
162. See also Appl. 10789/84, *K, F and P v. United Kingdom*, *D & R* 40 (1985), p. 298 (299).
163. See Appl. 8408/78, *X v. Federal Republic of Germany* (not published), where the Commission also attached importance to the fact that the case-law had been formed before the Commission itself had shown in a decision that it took a different view. In other words, the Commission assumes that the relevant national tribunal will take the Commission's view in a new case into consideration, and consequently will reach a different decision.
164. Appls 2832, 2835 and 2899/66, *De Wilde, Ooms and Versyp v. Belgium*, *Yearbook* X (1967), p. 420.
165. Report of 19 July 1969, *De Wilde, Ooms and Versyp* ("Vagrancy"-cases), B.10 (1969-71), p. 94. See also Appl. 8544/79, *Öztürk v. Federal Republic of Germany*, *D & R* 26 (1982), p. 55 (69).

only a few days before the applicant brought her own application, could be held against her. Unfortunately, the Commission did not pursue this question as it declared the application inadmissible on other grounds.[166]

The personal appearance of the applicant before the court taking the decision may constitute so substantial an element of the procedure that the rejection of a request to that effect renders the procedure ineffective.[167] That effectiveness is also considered to be lacking when the procedure is exceptionally protracted.[168] It appears that ineffectiveness is concerned here only if a given procedure is structurally protracted, *i.e.* in all cases. The fact that a given procedure is very lengthy in a concrete case does not in itself set aside the condition of the Convention that such a procedure must be instituted. In fact, in that case the applicant will first of all have to protest against that long duration within the national legal system concerned. It is perhaps mainly for this reason that the Commission arrived at the rejection of an application filed by a Belgian at a moment at which the Court of Appeal had not yet pronounced a verdict, although the applicant had filed his appeal more than six years previously. Curiously enough the Commission held:

> It is true that the Commission finds that the length of the procedure before Belgian jurisdiction cannot be held against either the applicant or his lawyer. However, the Commission considers that it should put an end to a procedure pending before it for five years.[169]

More sense makes the Commission's decision with respect to a complaint concerning the length of criminal proceedings, where the question arose whether the accused should have instituted a procedure designed to accelerate proceedings but which could not have led to any other effect. In the Commission's opinon such a procedure cannot be considered an effective and sufficient remedy whose use is required by Article 26.[170]

Furthermore the Commission considers the prior exhaustion of local remedies not to be required if the competent court is not completely independent, so that the necessary guarantees for a fair trial are not present. The latter occurred in the first *Greek* Case, where Denmark, Norway, Sweden and the Netherlands complained about the torture of political prisoners in Greece. They alleged the existence of an administrative practice and that accordingly the local remedies rule was not applicable. In the Commission's opinion, however, the applicant States had not given "substantial evidence" for the existence of such a practice. Nevertheless, their complaints were not rejected under Article 26. In fact, the Greek Government had discharged

---

166. Appl. 9097/80, *D & R* 30 (1983), p. 119 (130).
167. Appl. 434/58, *X v. Sweden, Yearbook* II (1958-59), p. 354 (374-376).
168. See, *e.g.,* Appl. 222/56, *X v. Federal Republic of Germany, Yearbook* II (1958-59), p. 344 (350-351) and Appl. 7161/75, *X v. United Kingdom, D & R* 7 (1977), p. 100 (101).
169. Appl. 5024/71, *X v. Belgium, D & R* 7 (1977), p. 5 (7). See, however, Appl. 6699/74, *X v. Federal Republic of Germany, D & R* 11 (1978), p. 16 (23-24), where the Commission found differently, even despite the fact that the applicant had consented to postponement of the national procedure. In this case the Commission evidently reached an "equity" standpoint in view of the emergency in which the applicant found herself.
170. Appl. 8435/78, *X v. United Kingdom, D & R* 26 (1982), p. 18 (20).

several judges for political reasons, and under those circumstances the Commission found that there was insufficient independence of the judiciary. It concluded that the judicial procedures provided for under Greek law no longer constituted an effective remedy which should have been exhausted.[171]

A comparable situation arose as a result of the Turkish military action in Cyprus. According to the Commission the action had "deeply and seriously affected the life of the population in Cyprus and, in particular, that of the Greek Cypriots".[172] The circumstances were such that the existing remedies "available in domestic courts in Turkey or before Turkish military courts in Cyprus" could be considered as effective remedies which had to be exhausted according to Article 26 with respect to complaints of inhabitants of Cyprus only "if it were shown that such remedies are both practicable and normally functioning in such cases".[173] This had not been proved by the Turkish Government.[174]

The Commission has accepted the possibility that according to the generally recognized rules of international law there may be special circumstances in which even effective and adequate remedies may be left unutilized.[175] The following examples of special circumstances have been dealt with in the Commission's case-law: doubt as to the effectiveness of the relevant remedy;[176] lack of knowledge on the part of the applicant as to (the existence of) a particular remedy;[177] the poor health of the applicant;[178] the advanced age of the applicant;[179] the poor financial position of the applicant or the high costs of the procedure;[180] lack of free legal aid;[181] fear of repercussions;[182] errors or wrong advice by a counsel or by the authorities;[183] two applicants filing the same complaint, while only one applicant has exhausted the domestic remedies.[184] So far, the existence of such special circumstances has been recognized by the Commission only in a few cases.

171. Appls 3321-3323 and 3344/67, *Denmark, Norway, Sweden and the Netherlands v. Greece*, Yearbook XI (1968), p. 730 (774).
172. Appls 6780/74 and 6950/75, *Cyprus v. Turkey*, *D & R* 2 (1975), p. 125 (137).
173. *Ibidem*, pp. 137-138.
174. *Ibidem*.
175. Appl. 2257/64, *Soltikow v. Federal Republic of Germany*, Yearbook XI (1968), p. 180 (224). See also Appl. 6861/75, *X v. United Kingdom*, *D & R* 3 (1976), p. 147 (152).
176. Appl. 3651/68, *X v. United Kingdom*, Yearbook XIII (1970), p. 476 (510-514).
177. Appl. 5006/71, *X v. United Kingdom*, *Coll.* 39 (1972), p. 91 (95).
178. Appl. 3788/68, *X v. Sweden*, Yearbook XIII (1970), p. 548 (580-582).
179. Appl. 568/59, *X v. Federal Republic of Germany*, *Coll.* 2 (1960), p. 1 (3).
180. Appl. 181/56, *X v. Federal Republic of Germany*, Yearbook I (1955-57), p. 139 (140-141).
181. Appl. 1295/61, *X v. Federal Republic of Germany* (not published).
182. Appl. 2257/64, *Soltikow v. Federal Republic of Germany*, Yearbook XI (1968), p. 180 (228).
183. Appl. 818/60, *X v. Belgium* (not published). See, however, the Court's judgment of 13 May 1980, *Artico*, A.37 (1980), p. 18. In Appl. 10000/82, *H. v. United Kingdom*, *D & R* 33 (1983), p. 247 (253), the Commission accepted that all domestic remedies were exhausted, since the applicant had received counsel's advice that a domestic remedy would have no prospects of success.
184. Appl. 9905/82, *A. Association and H. v. Austria*, *D & R* 36 (1984), p. 187 (192) where the Commission considered also the second applicant to be admissible.

The case-law of the Commission presents a great many instances which can hardly be fitted into the broad categories outlined above.[185] And in certain cases, the issue of the exhaustion of the local remedies may coincide with the question of whether or not the Convention has been violated. In the case of *X v. the United Kingdom*, for example, the Commission decided that

> Having regard to the fact that the applicant has included in his application a complaint under Article 13 of the Convention concerning the absence of an effective remedy, ... the Commission considers that it cannot reject all or part of the application as being inadmissible for failure to comply with the requirements as to the exhaustion of domestic remedies.[186]

Finally, it deserves to be mentioned that the appplicant deprives himself of the possibility to exhaust the local remedies when he consents to a settlement of his claim with the national authorities. If that is the case, his complaint under the Convention is declared inadmissible in Strasbourg on account of non-exhaustion.[187]

6. The Commission investigates *ex officio* whether the local remedies rule has been complied with. In many cases of individual applications this is the way in which the application is declared inadmissible under this rule, because such applications are not transmitted at once to the State against which the application is directed. If the application is transmitted to the State concerned - and with inter-State applications this is always the case (Rule 39 of the Rules of Procedure) -, the burden of proof with respect to the local remedies rule is divided as follows: the respondent State which relies on the rule must prove that certain effective and adequate remedies exist under its system of law;[188] subsequently it is for the applicant to prove that those remedies have been exhausted, or that they are not effective or adequate.[189]

The Court does take cognisance of preliminary objections concerning the exhaustion of local remedies only in so far as the respondent State has raised them before the Commission, in principle at the stage of the initial examina-

---

185. See, *e.g.*, the following cases: Appls 3435-3438/67, *W, X, Y and Z v. United Kingdom*, *Yearbook* XI (1968), p. 562: purely internal measures within the military hierarchy do not constitute remedies in the sense of Art. 26; Appl. 6701/74, *X v. Austria, D & R 5* (1976), p. 69 (78): the institution of a disciplinary action against judges is not in general an effective remedy; Appl. 1936/63, *Neumeister v. Austria, Yearbook* VII (1964), p. 224 (242): remedies which are available need not be used again if this has been done shortly before without success; Appl. 5613/72, *Hilton v. United Kingdom, Yearbook* XIX (1976), p. 256 (274): the use of a remedy may be superfluous in certain circumstances; and Appl. 9816/82, *Poiss v. Austria, D & R* 36 (1984), p. 170 (178): the issue involved, the length of the proceedings and the continuous damage, could not be effectively raised before the competent domestic authorities.
186. Appl. 7990/77, *X v. United Kingdom, D & R* 24 (1981), p. 57 (60).
187. See, *e.g.*, Appl. 7704/76, *X v. Federal Republic of Germany* (not published).
188. Thus the judgment of 18 November 1970, *De Wilde, Ooms and Versyp* ("*Vagrancy*"-cases), A.12 (1971), p. 33; judgment of 27 February 1980, *De Weer*, A.35 (1980), p. 15; and judgment of 18 December 1986, *Bozano*, A.111 (1987), p. 19. In the last-mentioned case the Court stated that the Government has to indicate sufficiently clearly the remedies that are open to the applicant: "it is not for the Convention bodies to cure of their own motion any want of precision or shortcomings in respondent States' arguments".
189. See, *e.g.*, Appl. 788/60, *Austria v. Italy, Yearbook* IV (1961), p. 116 (168), and Appl. 4649/70, *X v. Federal Republic of Germany, Coll.* 46 (1974), p. 1 (17).

tion of admissibility, if their character and the circumstances permitted the State to do so at that moment.[190] This latter qualification was at issue in the case of *Campbell and Fell*. Here the Government raised the plea of non-exhaustion in its observations on the merits after the Commission had declared the complaints admissible, because new developments had taken place in the relevant English case-law only a few days before the Government had submitted its observations on the admissibility. According to the Court, the Government could not reasonably have been expected to raise the plea of non-exhaustion at an earlier stage. There was, therefore, no estoppel. On the other hand, the Court held that it would be unjust now to find these complaints inadmissible for failure to exhaust domestic remedies, because after the Government had raised the issue the Commission had decided on the basis of Article 29 not to reject the application on this ground. Consequently, the applicant was justified in relying on the Commission's decision by pursuing his case under the Convention instead of applying to the domestic courts.[191]

In general the Commission is well informed about the remedies available under the different national systems of law and, in dubious cases, may ascertain their existence via its Secretariat. In cases where the complaint is not transmitted at once to the respondent State, the Commission will usually have established for itself which remedies exist under national law. There again it is for the applicant to prove that these remedies have been exhausted or that they are not effective or adequate.

The question may be raised as to whether the Commission should institute *ex officio* an inquiry into the compliance with the local remedies rule after the case has been transmitted to the State and if the respondent Government has not raised an exception as to the admissibility under Article 26. The Commission does not institute an inquiry into the admissibility of the complaint under Article 26 if the respondent State expressly waives or has waived its right to rely on the local remedies rule.[192] The position is different, however, if the State has not expressly waived this right. The case-law of the Commission discloses examples of declarations of inadmissibility without the respondent State having raised an exception to that effect.[193] Despite the general wording of Article 26, one might ask whether the Commission ought not to take a somewhat more passive attitude in this matter. It should be

---

190. See, *inter alia*, judgment of 13 May 1980, *Artico*, A.37 (1980), pp. 12-14; judgment of 6 November 1980, *Guzzardi*, A.39 (1981), p. 24; and judgment of 10 December 1982, *Foti and others*, A.56 (1983), p. 16.
191. Judgment of 28 June 1984, *Campbell and Fell*, A.80 (1984), pp. 31-33.
192. See, *e.g.*, Appl. 1727/62, *X v. Belgium*, Yearbook VI (1963), p. 370 (396); Appl. 1994/63, *Fifty-seven inhabitants of Leuven and environs v. Belgium*, Yearbook VII (1964), p. 252 (258-260); and Appl. 8919/80, *Van der Mussele v. Belgium*, D & R 23 (1981), p. 244 (257). This is different with regard to the six-month rule. There the Commission holds that, "in view of the importance of this rule in the Convention system, the Contracting States cannot on their own authority waive compliance with it"; Appl. 9587/81, *X v. France*, D & R 29 (1982), p. 228 (240) and Appl. 10416/83, *K. v. Ireland*, D & R 38 (1984), p. 158 (160).
193. See Appl. 2547/65, *X v. Austria*, Coll. 20 (1966), p. 79 (83), and Appl. 5207/71, *X v. Federal Republic of Germany*, Yearbook XIV (1971), p. 698 (708-710).

borne in mind that the local remedies rule is intended primarily to protect the interest of the respondent State, and that the fact that the latter has failed to rely on that protection may indicate that it does not consider such reliance to be in its interest. After all, the rejection of an application after a thorough investigation will often be more convincing, and consequently more satisfactory for the respondent State than a declaration of inadmissibility on formal grounds.[194]

7. Finally it must be mentioned that the Commission takes a flexible attitude with respect to the moment at which the local remedies must have been exhausted. It considers it sufficient if the decision of the highest national court has been given at the moment when it decides on the admissibility of the application.[195] However, the Commission's flexible attitude in this respect may also cause problems for the applicant. The Commission has, for instance, decided that a remedy which was not open to the applicant at the time of the lodging of his application, but became available only afterwards as a result of a change in the case-law of the national court concerned, has nevertheless to be exhausted in order to satisfy the requirements flowing from the local remedies rule.[196]

8. The effect of a declaration of inadmissibility on account of non-exhaustion of the local remedies is generally of a *dilatory* character. The applicant may submit his case again to the Commission after having obtained a decision by the highest national court. In fact, such a decision is considered as relevant new information by the Commission, so that the application will not be rejected as being substantially the same as a matter already examined by the Commission in the sense of Article 27(1)(b).[197] The question of whether the local remedies rule must also be applied if meanwhile the national time-limits for appeal have expired, so that in fact local remedies are no longer available, will have to be decided on a case-by-case basis. Application of the rule in such a case has *peremptory* effect, since both the national and the international procedure are then barred. Such a consequence appears justified only when the individual in question is to be blamed for having allowed the time-limit to expire. A cut-and-dried answer to this as well as other questions concerning the application of the local remedies rule cannot be given *in abstracto*. For guidance, use may be made of the general starting-point that what can be demanded of the individual is not "what is impossible or ineffective, but only what is required by common sense, namely 'the diligence

---

194. The decision on Appl. 9120/80, *Unterpertinger v. Austria, D & R* 33 (1983), p. 80 (83), seems to go into this direction.
195. Appl. 2614/65, *Ringeisen v. Austria, Yearbook* XI (1968), p. 268 (306). See also the judgment of 16 July 1971, *Ringeisen*, A.13 (1971), p. 38 and Appl. 9019/80, *Luberti, D & R* 27 (1982), p. 181 (193).
196. Appl. 7878/77, *Fell v. United Kingdom, D & R* 23 (1981), p. 102 (112).
197. See *supra* p. 73.

of a bonus pater familias'".[198]

2.7. The application must have been submitted within a period of six months from the date on which the final national decision was taken (Art. 26)

1. The six-month time-limit set in Article 26 serves to prevent that the compatibility of a national decision, action or omission with the Convention might still be brought up after a considerable time by the submission of an application to the European Commission.

This again is an admissibility condition which holds good for applications by States as well as individuals. As is the case for the condition of the prior exhaustion of the local remedies, this follows from the text of Article 26 and Article 27(3) as compared with that of Article 27(1) and (2).[199]

2. There is a close relation between these two admissibility conditions: from the grammatical construction of Article 26, in which the two conditions are mentioned, the Commission inferred that

> the term "final decision", therefore, in Article 26 refers exclusively to the final decision concerned in the exhaustion of all local remedies according to the generally recognized rules of international law, so that the six-month period is operative only in this context.[200]

From this the Commission has later concluded that if no local remedy is available, the challenged act or decision itself must be considered as the "final decision".[201]

In the case of *Christians against Racism and Facism v. the United Kingdom* the applicant association complained about a regulation prohibiting all public processions other than those of a religious, educational, festive or ceremonial character during the period of 24 February to 23 April 1978, no additional administrative measures being required for its application. No remedy was available to challenge the ensuing measures or their application to the association's planned procession on 22 April 1978. With respect to the six-month period the Commission decided:

> This period must normally be calculated from the final domestic decision, but where, as in the present case, no domestic decision is required for the application of a general measure to the particular case, the relevant date is the time when the applicant was actually affected by that measure. In the present case, this was the date of the procession planned by the applicant association, *i.e.* 22 April 1978.[202]

---

198. Thus Judge Tanaka in his separate opinion in the *Barcelona Traction* Case, *I.C.J. Reports* (1970), p. 148. See also M. Bourquin, *Annuaire de l'Institut de Droit International* (1954-I), p. 61: "La règle doit être comprise d'une manière raisonnable, en tenant compte de ce que ferait un plaideur normal, ayant le souci de défendre ses intérêts, mais sans se croire obligé cependant de mettre en action toutes les procédures imaginables, quels que soient les retards et les frais qui peuvent en résulter".
199. See *supra* p. 82.
200. Appl. 214/56, *De Becker v. Belgium*, Yearbook II (1958-59), p. 214 (242).
201. See, *e.g.*, Appl. 7379/76, *X v. United Kingdom*, D & R 8 (1977), p. 211 (212-213).
202. Appl. 8440/78, *D & R* 21 (1981), p. 138 (147).

In the same vein the Commission treated an applicant complaining that he had not been entitled to have the lawfulness of his detention determined by a court contrary to Article 5(4). As the right guaranteed in Article 5(4) is applicable only to persons deprived of their liberty the Commission decided that a person alleging a breach of that provision must, in the absence of a particular constitutional remedy or other similar remedies which could redress an alleged breach of Article 5(4), submit such a complaint to the Commission within six months from the date of his release.[203]

In the meantime the Commission has further specified its point of view as follows:

> In the Commission's opinion Article 26 cannot be interpreted so as to require an applicant to seize the Commission at any time before his position in connection with the matter complained of has been finally determined or settled on the domestic level.[204]

In the concrete case this meant that when an application concerns the level of compensation after nationalization of an industry, the six-month period does not run from the date of the Act on nationalization but from the date on which the amount of compensation for shareholders is fixed.

The above-mentioned link between the two admissibility conditions laid down in Article 26 has the further consequence that the criteria used by the Commission in answering the question of whether a given local remedy must or must not be used[205] are also relevant for the question of whether the time-limit has been observed. Indeed, this time-limit starts after the last national decision in the chain of local remedies that had to be exhausted. This means that remedies which the applicant did not have to pursue, for instance because they are not effective and adequate, cannot be taken into account as the starting-point of the time-limit. An applicant cannot therefore defer the time-limit, for instance by lodging a request for pardon, applying to an incompetent organ, or asking for reopening of his case. Decisions on such requests are not regarded as final national decisions in the sense of Article 26.[206]

A curious decision of the Commission in this connection is the *Nielsen* Case, discussed above. Although Nielsen's application had been lodged more than six months after the decision of the highest Danish court, still the Commission did not declare it inadmissible on that account. In fact, in the meantime Nielsen had addressed a request to the Special Court of Revision,

---

203. Appl. 10230/82, *X v. Sweden, D & R* 32 (1983), p. 303 (304-305).
204. Appl. 9266/81, *Yarrow P.L.C. and others v. United Kingdom, D & R* 30 (1983), p. 155 (187). Similarly, in Appls 8588/79 and 8589/79, *Bramelid and Malmström v. Sweden, D & R* 29 (1982), p. 64 (84), the Commission decided that in proceedings concerning the right to purchase company shares leading to two subsequent decisions, one on the right to purchase and the other on the price, the six-month time-limit runs from the second decision to the extent that the individuals concerned complain in particular about the price.
205. See, e.g., Appl. 5759/72, *X v. Austria, D & R* 6 (1977), p. 15 (16); Appl. 7379/76, *X v. United Kingdom, D & R* 8 (1977), p. 211 (212); Appl. 7805/77, *X and Church of Scientology v. Sweden, D & R* 16 (1979), p. 68 (71).
206. See, for example, with regard to a request to re-open the case Appl. 10431/83, *G. v. Federal Republic of Germany, D & R* 35 (1984), p. 241 (243) and Appl. 10308/83, *Altun v. Federal Republic of Germany, D & R* 36 (1984), p. 209 (231).

and the Commission took the date of the decision of that Court as the starting-point of the time-limit for appeal.[207] As has been said, later case-law indicates that the Commission's position with respect to this has changed.[208]

The close relation between the two admissibility conditions of Article 26 may place the applicant in a difficult situation if he is not sure whether a particular remedy must or must not be pursued. If he first institutes that particular procedure, he incurs the risk of not being subsequently received by the Commission on account of exceeding the time-limit of six months, if the remedy in question need not have been sought in the Commission's opinion. If, however, he does not apply for that local remedy, he incurs the risk of not being received on the ground of non-exhaustion of the local remedies. In such a case an applicant is well-advised to lodge an application with the Commission and at the same time to institute the national procedure. If later the Commission concludes that he need not have instituted the national procedure, at any rate the time-limit has been complied with. And if the Commission decides otherwise, the final national decision as a rule will still be in time, since the local remedies have to be exhausted only at the moment at which the Commission decides on the admissibility.[209] If the national decision is not in time, the applicant may in any case again lodge an application with the Commission, the final national decision meanwhile pronounced serving as a new fact.[210] In matters like these the Commission again takes a flexible attitude. An Italian applicant contacted the Commission for the first time on 21 July 1978 setting out in his letter the substance of his complaints. Subsequently he sought reopening of proceedings in Italy, possibly as a result of the information provided by the Commission's Secretariat. The applicant did not contact the Commission again until 17 February 1981, at the end of the reopening procedure. The Commission nevertheless considered his application to have been introduced on 21 July 1978 and therefore in time.[211]

3. Although the six-month time-limit formally starts running at the moment at which the final national decision is taken, the Commission has adopted the date on which the decision has been notified to the applicant as the relevant moment, provided that the applicant was previously ignorant of the decision.[212] If a judgment is not delivered at a public hearing, the six-month period starts at the moment it was served on the applicant concerned.[213] Depending on the nature of the case concerned, notification of the operative part of the judgment might be insufficient. For the six-month period to start running the

207. Appl. 343/57, *Yearbook* II (1958-59), p. 412 (434-444).
208. See *supra* p. 91, note 157.
209. See *supra* p. 97.
210. See *supra* p. 73.
211. Appls 9024/80 and 9317/81, *Colozza and Rubinat v. Italy*, D & R 28 (1982), p. 138 (158).
212. Appl. 899/60, *X v. Federal Republic of Germany*, *Yearbook* V (1962), p. 136 (144-146). For a case in which the final decision was known to counsel of the applicant, see Appl. 5759/72, *X v. Austria*, D & R 6 (1977), p. 15 (16). Cf. Appl. 9991/82, *Bozano v. Italy*, D & R 39 (1984), p. 147 (155).
213. Appl. 9908/82, *X v. France*, D & R 32 (1983), p. 266 (272).

subsequent notification of the full text giving the reasons for the judgment may be decisive.[214] However, if the applicant knew that the decision was taken, but has made no further efforts to become acquainted with its contents, the date of the decision is considered the starting-point of the time-limit.[215]

Unlike the case of the *local remedies* rule, where the moment at which the Commission decides on admissibility is decisive, for the time-limit for filing an application with the Commission the date of receipt of the application counts. In the case of the *local remedies* rule the Commission evidently relies on the English version of Article 26, which speaks of "may only deal with the matter", while for its view concerning the time-limit for bringing the application it finds support in the French text, which speaks of *"ne peut être saisie que"*. In the *Iversen* Case the Norwegian Government submitted that the date of registration of the application with the Secretariat was considered as the decisive date (see Rule 13 of the Rules of Procedure). The Commission, however, decided that for the question of whether an application has or has not been lodged in due time the relevant date is "at the latest the date of its acknowledged arrival in the Secretariat-General".[216] In practice the Commission takes as the decisive moment the date of the applicant's first letter, in which he states that he wishes to lodge an application and gives some indication of the nature of the complaint.[217] The mere submission of certain documents is not enough. The Commission holds that the "related complaint must be raised in express terms or at least implicitly as a claim before the Commission within six months from the final domestic decision".[218] In the case of *19 Chilean nationals and the S. Association v. Sweden*, the Commission was confronted with the question how to treat the declaration of 18 Chileans that they adhered to an application already lodged by another Chilean with the Commission. The Commission took as the date of application for the 18 persons their declaration, and not the date of the filing of the first application.[219]

Applications about violations of the Convention which took place before the Convention became binding upon the respondent State are inadmissible *ratione temporis*. In such a case the six-month rule is therefore not at issue at all. However, as said above, a declaration as referred to in Article 25 concerning the recognition of the right of complaint for individuals has retrospective effect in so far as an individual application may also concern a violation which took place between the entry-into-force of the Convention for

214. Appl. 9299/81, *P. v. Switzerland, D & R* 36 (1984), p. 20 (22).
215. Appl. 458/59, *X v. Belgium, Yearbook* III (1960), p. 222 (234).
216. Appl. 1468/62, *Iversen v. Norway, Yearbook* VI (1963), p. 278 (322).
217. Appl. 4429/70, *X v. Federal Republic of Germany, Coll.* 37 (1971), p. 109 (110). See also Case-Law Topics, *supra* note 32, pp. 16-17 and Appl. 8299/78, *X and Y v. Ireland, D & R* 22 (1981), p. 51 (72).
218. Appl. 9314/81, *N. v. Federal Republic of Germany, D & R* 31 (1983), p. 200 (201).
219. Appls 9959/82 and 10357/83, *19 Chilean nationals and the S. Association v. Sweden, D & R* 37 (1984), p. 87 (89).

the respondent State and the date of the said declaration by that State, provided that the declaration does not restrict the scope of the competence of the Commission in time.[220]

Can an individual still lodge an application if the final national decision dates back more than six months but was taken prior to the date on which the declaration under Article 25 was made? The Commission has originally decided that in such a case the time-limit does not start at the moment of the final national decision, but at the time of the declaration under Article 25, because the applicant did not have an earlier opportunity to apply to the Commission.[221] This approach has the disadvantage that, if the declaration has been made a long time after the entry-into-force of the Convention in a particular country, the outcome may stand in the way of the legal certainty and stability aimed at by the time-limit. This seems to be the reason that in its more recent case-law the Commission has left the above-mentioned approach and now feels itself obliged to calculate the six-month time-limit as from the final national decision. The argument used is that the Commission considers the six-month rule "an element of legal stability".[222] This rule, according to the Commission,

> would not be observed, particularly in the case of States having ratified the Convention but not yet having recognized the right of individual petition, if the six-month time-limit were only to rule from the date of deposit of the declaration made in accordance with Article 25 of the Convention. The Commission considers consequently that the Contracting States cannot on their own authority put aside the rule of compliance with the six-month time-limit.[223]

The latter consideration is remarkable: recognition of the right of individual complaint on the part of contracting States obviously is not aimed at putting aside compliance with the six-month rule. Nevertheless, the substance of the Commission's decision would seem to make sense.

The rigidity with which the Commission adheres to its new approach becomes clear from a more recent decision in a case against Ireland. The applicant had submitted that there were special circumstances in his case which ought to be regarded as interrupting or suspending the running of the six-month period. The respondent Government replied that it had decided not to contest the facts alleged in support of the existence of special circumstances. The Commission pointed out that the six-month rule serves the interest not only of the respondent Government but also of legal certainty as a value in itself. On that basis it decided

> that the decision of the respondent Government not to contest the facts alleged in support of the existence of special circumstances cannot operate as a form of waiver or be determinative of the issue and it falls to the Commission to make its own assessment of the matter in the light of the circumstances of the case.[224]

---

220. See *supra* p. 10 and Appl. 9587/81, *X v. France, D & R* 29 (1982), p. 228 (238).
221. Appl. 214/56, *De Becker v. Belgium, Yearbook* II (1958-59), p. 214 (243), and Appl. 846/60, *X v. the Netherlands, Coll.* 6 (1961), p. 63 (64-65).
222. Appl. 9587/81, *X v. France, D & R* 29 (1982), p. 228 (240).
223. *Ibidem.*
224. Appl. 10416/83, *K. v. Ireland, D & R* 38 (1984), pp. 159-160.

A special starting date for the time-limit applies to the cases, discussed above,[225] of a so-called continuing situation, where the violation is not constituted by an act performed or a decision taken at a given moment, but by its consequences, which continue and thus repeat the violation day by day. As long as that situation exists, the time-limit does not commence, since it serves to make acts and decisions *from the past* unassailable after a given period. A clear example from the case-law is the *De Becker* Case. De Becker had been sentenced to death in 1946 for treason during the second world war. This sentence was later converted into imprisonment, and in 1961 he was released under certain conditions. Under Belgian criminal law, such a sentence resulted in the limitation of certain rights - including the right to freedom of expression - which also continued to apply after the release. The Commission held that this was a continuing situation and considered the complaint admissible *ratione temporis*. It considered that the six-month rule was not applicable here, because the question was whether, by the application to De Becker of the Belgian legislation in question, the Convention was still being violated.[226]

The Commission disagreed, however, with an applicant who alleged the existence of a continuing violation of Article 13 in so far as no domestic remedy was available to him in respect of a deprivation of his possession, based on a British Act of 1968. According to the Commission

Where domestic law gives no remedy against such a measure, it is inevitable that unless the law changes that situation will continue indefinitely. However the person affected suffers no additional prejudice beyond that which arose directly and immediately from the initial measure. His position is not therefore to be compared to that of a person subject to a continuing restriction on his substantive Convention rights.[227]

In the above-mentioned *De Becker* Case the continuing situation had been called into existence by a legal provision. In those cases where the continuing situation was due to a judicial decision or a decision of the executive, the Commission applied the time-limit in the usual way.[228] In this context the Commission apparently takes the view that legal measures on the one hand and judicial judgments and decisions of the executive on the other cannot be equated with one another. In fact, with respect to those judgments and decisions, it states in the cases referred to that they are pronounced at a clearly defined moment and that the resulting consequences may be of a temporary nature. Nevertheless, it is difficult to understand why a continuing situation could not thus be called into existence as well. Legislative measures, too, are of course taken at a clearly defined moment, and the legal consequences envisaged therewith may also be of a temporary nature. The

---

225. *Supra* p. 9.
226. Appl. 214/56, *De Becker v. Belgium, Yearbook* II (1958-59), p. 214 (230-234). See also Appl. 4859/71, *X v. Belgium, Coll.* 44 (1973), p. 1 (18), and Appls 7572, 7586 and 7587/76, *Ensslin, Baader and Raspe v. Federal Republic of Germany, D & R* 14 (1979), p. 66 (113).
227. Appl. 8206/78, *X v. United Kingdom, D & R* 25 (1982), p. 147 (151).
228. See, *e.g.*, Appl. 1038/61, *X v. Belgium, Yearbook* IV (1961), p. 324 (334), and Appls 8560 and 8613/79, *X v. Portugal* (not published).

distinction made by the Commission would therefore appear to be not very well-reasoned.

4. With respect to the six-month rule, too, the Commission admits that special circumstances may occur in which the applicant need not satisfy this requirement. The case-law of the Commission on this point is almost identical with that regarding special circumstances in connection with the local remedies rule.[229]

2.8. The application must not be manifestly ill-founded (Art. 27(2))

1. For understandable reasons this admissibility condition applies only to individual applications; in the case of an inter-State application, which will have been prepared by expert legal advisers of the Government, it is hardly to be expected that it will be manifestly ill-founded. Nevertheless, while reiterating that the wording of Article 27(1) and (2) makes reference only to Article 25, the Commission

> does not exclude the application of a general rule providing for the possibility of declaring an application under Article 24 inadmissible, if it is clear from the outset that it is wholly unsubstantiated or otherwise lacking the requirements of a genuine allegation in the sense of Article 24 of the Convention.[230]

Until now this has not occurred in practice. On the other hand a great many individual applications are declared inadmissible by the Commission on the ground of being manifestly ill-founded.

2. From a strictly formal viewpoint the competence of the Commission to declare an application inadmissible on account of manifest ill-foundedness does not fit in very well with the division of power laid down in the Convention. The Commission is competent only to pronounce on the *admissibility* of the application, while a decision on the *merits* is reserved to the Committee of Ministers or the Court, as the case may be. However, when the Commission declares an application to be manifestly ill-founded, in actual fact it pronounces on the merits, on the ground of a *prima facie* opinion on the alleged facts and the legal grounds put forward. On the other hand, the drafters of the Convention have indeed intended to entrust the Commission with the task of acting as a screen for the great number of applications to be expected.[231] The competence of the Commission to exclude manifestly ill-founded applications from the further procedure would seem to fit in with this aim of procedural economy.

---

229. See *supra* pp. 94-95.
230. Appls 9940-9944/82, *France, Norway, Denmark, Sweden and the Netherlands v. Turkey, D & R* 35 (1984), pp. 143 (161-162).
231. See *supra* p. 61.

3. When declaring an application manifestly ill-founded, unlike a declaration of inadmissibility on the ground of one of the previously discussed admissibility conditions, the Commission itself makes a *final* decision on the interpretation and application of one or more of the provisions of Section I of the Convention. Therefore, the meaning which the Commission gives in its case-law to the term "manifestly ill-founded" is of great importance. In fact, it bars the possibility for the Court - or the Committee of Ministers - to deal with the case.

In several decisions the Commission has indicated what it understands by "manifestly ill-founded". In the *De Becker* Case, for instance, the Commission held that it can declare an application manifestly ill-founded only if the examination of the complaint does not disclose any *prima facie* violation of the Convention.[232] The same view appears from the Commission's decision in the *Pataki* Case:

> whereas it follows that at the present stage of the proceedings the task of the Commission is not to determine whether an examination of the case submitted by the Applicant discloses the actual existence of a violation of one of the rights and freedoms guaranteed by the Convention but only to determine whether it includes any possibility of the existence of such a violation.[233]

In practice applications are declared manifestly ill-founded in particular if the facts about which a complaint is lodged evidently do not constitute a violation of the Convention, or if those facts have not been proved or are manifestly incorrect. As to the latter, the Commission requires the applicant to give *prima facie* evidence of the facts put forward by him.[234] As regards the former ground, it is not always possible to differentiate sharply between manifest ill-foundedness and incompatibility with the Convention. There is incompatibility *ratione materiae* if an application concerns the violation of a right not protected by the Convention.[235] In that case the application falls entirely outside the scope of the Convention and no examination of the merits is possible. An application is manifestly ill-founded if it does indeed concern a right protected by the Convention, but a *prima facie* examination discloses that the facts put forward cannot by any means justify the claim, so that an examination of the merits is superfluous.

The case-law of the Commission in this matter has not always been constant and consistent. An obvious example is the case-law with respect to Article 14. According to this article the enjoyment of the rights and freedoms set forth in the Convention must be guaranteed without discrimination on any ground. Applications containing complaints about discrimination with respect to rights or freedoms which the Convention does not protect have sometimes been declared to be manifestly ill-founded and sometimes incompatible with

---

232. Appl. 214/56, *Yearbook* II (1958-59), p. 214 (254).
233. Appl. 596/59, *Yearbook* III (1960), p. 356 (368). In the same sense, Appl. 7640/76, *Geerk v. Switzerland*, *Yearbook* XXI (1978), p. 470 (474-476).
234. See, *e.g.*, Appl. 556/59, *X v. Austria*, *Yearbook* III (1960), p. 288.
235. See *supra* pp. 78-80.

the Convention.[236] In general the Commission takes the position that applications leading to the interpretation of one or more articles of Section I of the Convention should not be rejected as being incompatible with the Convention *ratione materiae*. It is, however, doubtful whether this criterion is adequate in all cases. If the right invoked is actually set forth in the Convention, but it is quite obvious from the alleged facts that there has been no violation, an interpretation of the article of the Convention invoked by the applicant will hardly be needed, if at all, while on the other hand the Commission may conclude that the application is incompatible with the Convention precisely on the ground of the interpretation of one or more of the provisions of Section I. Indeed, its very task is to examine whether the right invoked by the applicant can be brought under those provisions, and for this in most cases an interpretation will be necessary.

4. The degree of interpretation required before a decision can be taken also plays a part in the case of the declaration of manifest ill-foundedness as such. It has been stated above that the competence of the Commission to declare an application manifestly ill-founded fits into the framework of the screening function which the drafters of the Convention intended the Commission to perform. For a proper discharge of that function, however, no more is needed than the competence to reject those applications the ill-founded character of which is actually *manifest*. In several cases, however, the Commission has used this competence in a way which clearly went beyond this.

A familiar example is the *Iversen* Case, in which the applicant complained about the possibility existing in Norway that dentists who have recently completed their studies can be obliged to work for some time in the public service. The complaint was declared "manifestly ill-founded" by the Commission,[237] while it raised such complicated questions concerning Article 4 that in our view a more detailed examination of the merits appeared decidedly justified. Equally, an application on account of violation of the freedom of expression was declared manifestly ill-founded by the Commission on the basis of the finding that the prohibition against a Buddhist prisoner's sending a manuscript to the publisher of a Buddhist journal constituted a reasonable application of the prison rule concerned, and that this rule itself "is necessary in a democratic society for the prevention of disorder or crime within the meaning of Article 10(2)".[238] There again, to put it mildly, it was doubtful whether this was so obvious an interpretation of the said provision of the Convention that no difference of opinion was possible among reasonable persons. Since such decisions bar the possibility that the Court - or the Committee of Ministers - may give its opinion on the interpretation and

---

236. For a declaration of manifest ill-foundedness, see, *e.g.*, Appl. 1452/62, *X v. Austria*, Yearbook VI (1963), p. 268 (278), and for a declaration of incompatibility, *e.g.*, Appl. 2333/64, *Inhabitants of Leeuw-St. Pierre v. Belgium*, Yearbook VIII (1965), p. 338 (360-362).
237. Appl. 1468/62, Yearbook VI (1963), p. 278 (326-330).
238. Appl. 5442/72, *X v. United Kingdom*, D & R 1 (1975), p. 41 (42).

application of such important provisions, this case-law of the Commission gives rise to serious objections, in the sense that it is contrary to the division of power such as it is laid down in the Convention. The Commission may declare an application to be manifestly ill-founded only if its ill-founded character is actually evident at first sight, or if the Commission bases its decision on the constant case-law of the Court.[239]

Doubt about the practice of the Commission also arises in those cases where the Commission is obviously divided internally about the question of whether an application is or is not manifestly ill-founded, as occurred, for instance, in the *Iversen* Case. Of course the Commission cannot derogate from the rules concerning the voting procedure and require unanimity for such decisions, but if only a bare majority can be obtained for a declaration of manifest ill-foundedness, this in itself makes it evident that the ill-foundedness is not very manifest.

§ 3. THE PROCEDURE AFTER AN APPLICATION HAS BEEN DECLARED ADMISSIBLE

1. After the Commission has declared an application admissible, on the basis of Article 28(1)(a) it subjects the complaint contained therein to an examination of the merits. Under Article 28(1)(b) the Commission further places itself at the disposal of the parties "with a view to securing a friendly settlement of the matter on the basis of respect for Human Rights as defined in this Convention".

2. Before these two functions of the Commission are discussed in greater detail, the reader may be reminded once more that during this examination an application may still be declared inadmissible under Article 29 if on the basis of that examination the Commission yet reaches the conclusion that not all the conditions of Article 27 have been complied with. Such a decision of the Commission requires a two-third majority of its members and must state the reasons on which it is based. It is communicated to the parties. Article 29 thus enables the Commission, if an individual application that was originally accepted is later found not to satisfy all the admissibility conditions, to stop the procedure, thus preventing the Court or the Committee of Ministers from having to deal with the case.[240]

From the text of Article 29 one cannot infer that this provision may be applied only if *new* facts have become known to the Commission. In our opinion, however, the principle of legal security demands that application shall

---

239. See Van Dijk, *supra* note 43, p. 322.
240. See Committee of Experts, *Explanatory Report on the Second to Fifth Protocols to the European Convention for the Protection of Human Rights and Fundamental Freedoms*, H(71)11, Strasbourg 1971, p. 27.

be confined to such cases.[241] Nevertheless, it appears from the case-law that the Commission takes the view that Article 29 may also be applied on the basis of facts which were already known or might have been known to the Commission during the admissibility examination.[242]

From the *Schiesser* Case one might even conclude that the Court is prepared to interpret Article 29 in a still "more flexible" way.[243] In that case the applicant had submitted violation of Article 5(4), after his complaint concerning Article 5(3) had already been declared admissible by the Commission. In its report the Commission stated that, as regards Article 5(4), the requirement of previous exhaustion of the local remedies had not been complied with. When the Swiss Government subsequently requested the Court to declare the complaint incompatible with the requirements of Article 26, the latter took the position that it had no competence to deal with the issue, holding among other things:

> The Court takes the view that, on the point now being considered, the Commission's report amounts, in substance, to an implicit decision of inadmissibility, although it does not expressly refer to Article 29(1) or even to Article 27(3).[244]

However, there cannot possibly be a question of an implicit decision on the basis of Article 29, since the decision of the Commission had been taken with eleven votes in favour, one against and two abstentions. Since Article 29 (old) explicitly required unanimity, it must be assumed that in this case there was an error on the part of the Court.[245]

3.1. The examination of the merits (Art. 28(1)(a))

1. A proper understanding of all the aspects of the case helps the Commission in securing a friendly settlement (Art. 28(1)(b)) and further enables it to form an opinion on whether there has been a violation of the Convention (Art. 31(1)). In this context it is not sufficient for the Commission to examine the facts and circumstances of the case; it must also concern itself with the legal issues.

---

241. A new fact was concerned, for example, when the Commission found during the examination of the merits that the applicant had used the procedure before the Commission to evade her obligations of payments *vis-à-vis* her creditor and thus had abused her right of complaint in the sense of Art. 27(2) of the Convention; Appl. 5207/71, *Raupp v. Federal Republic of Germany, Coll.* 42 (1973), p. 85 (89-90).
242. See Appls 5577-5583/72, *Donnelly v. United Kingdom, Yearbook* XIX (1976), p. 85 (252-254). See also the decision of the Commission on the Appls 5100/71, 5354/72 and 5370/72, *Engel, Dona and Schul v. the Netherlands*, B.20 (1974-76), pp. 134-140, and the decision under Article 29 of 29 May 1973 on Appl. 4771/71, *Kamma v. the Netherlands* (not published). An application of Art. 29 in those cases did not lead to rejection of the complaints, because the Commission held that all the conditions of admissibility had been satisfied. However, it may be inferred from the decisions that the Commission would have rejected them if the said conditions had not been satisfied, even if this could have been known during the examination of the admissibility.
243. Judgment of 4 December 1979, A.34 (1980), pp. 16-17.
244. *Ibidem*, p. 17.
245. This would also seem to ensue from the reference to the *Schiesser* Case in the Court's judgment of 13 May 1980, *Artico*, A.37 (1980), p. 13.

2. The procedure concerning the merits has a contradictory[246] and quasi-judicial character. However, like the procedure concerning admissibility, the examination of the merits also takes place *in camera*.

3. Since the entry-into-force of the Third Protocol on 20 September 1970 the examination is no longer conducted in the first instance by a Sub-Commission. The application is now initially examined by one or more rapporteurs whom the Commission appoints from among its members (Rule 46 of the Rules of Procedure). The powers of the rapporteur may be very wide. In accordance with Rule 28(2) of its Rules of Procedure the Commission may delegate one or more of its members, and consequently also the rapporteur, to take any action in its name which it considers expedient or necessary for the proper performance of its duties under the Convention, in particular the hearing of witnesses or experts, the examination of documents, or the visit to any locality. In every stage of the consideration of an application under Article 25 the rapporteur may decide to invite the parties to submit further written evidence or observations. The rapporteur is obliged to draft memoranda if the Commission asks him to do so in connection with its consideration of the case concerned (Rule 46(3)(a) of the Rules of Procedure). Finally, under Rule 46(3)(b), the rapporteur must draft a report for the Commission in accordance with Rule 50 (in case a friendly settlement has been reached), Rule 53 (if no friendly settlement has been reached), or Rule 54 (when a case that has already been accepted is struck off the list).

4. The procedure before the Commission is generally characterized by great freedom to conduct the examination of the case as the Commission sees fit and to adapt it to the special circumstances of each case. Normally the parties are first invited to make written observations and subsequently to submit oral arguments at one or more hearings. Usually these will be supplementary observations, because the more fundamental legal arguments concerning the merits have already been put forward during the admissibility examination. At such a hearing any member of the Commission may, with the consent of the President, put questions to the parties and request them to elucidate particular points in addition to their written observations and/or oral arguments (Rule 31 of the Rules of Procedure).

5. Under Rule 28(1) and (2) of its Rules of Procedure the Commission may delegate one or more of its members to take any action which it considers expedient or necessary for the proper performance of its duties under the Convention. The Commission used this wide power of delegation which already existed under Rule 51(1) of its old Rules of Procedure (but there only in connection with its duties under Article 28) for instance by leaving the

---

246. This does not necessarily imply direct contact between the parties; see Appl. 8007/77, *Cyprus v. Turkey, D & R* 13 (1979), p. 85 (147).

hearing of evidence in the examination of the complaint of Ireland against the United Kingdom to three of its members.[247]

6. If the Commission considers it necessary, it may, under Article 28(a) of the Convention in conjunction with Rule 14(2) of the Rules of Procedure, make an inquiry on the spot or order such an inquiry to be made. If it does so, it invites, through the intermediary of the Secretary General of the Council of Europe, the contracting State in question to furnish all necessary facilities. Under the Convention the contracting States are obliged to furnish these facilities (Art. 28(a)).

The Commission availed itself of this power for the first time in connection with the first complaint of Greece against the United Kingdom.[248] On that occasion an inquiry was made in Cyprus into the existence of certain practices of torture, and additionally into whether the threat to public order was such that the measures taken by the British were justified.[249] In September 1975 the Commission again went to Cyprus, this time, *inter alia*, for a visit to two refugee camps in connection with complaints of Cyprus against Turkey.[250] In the *Greek* Case, too, the Commission made use of the power in question. The Greek Government, however, refused to admit members of the Commission to the Averoff prison in Athens and a number of prison camps in the island of Leros.[251] In the *Northern Ireland* Case the cooperation was not refused, but the Court expressed its disapproval of the fact that, as the Commission had hinted in its report, the British Government had not always afforded the desirable assistance. In its judgment the Court emphasized the importance of the obligation of contracting States set forth in Article 28(a), the present Article 28(1)(a).[252] In connection with the five applications which were lodged against Turkey, the Commission decided to send a delegation to this country in order to continue its efforts to reach a friendly settlement in this case. The delegation had discussions with, *inter alia*, the Minister of Justice, members of the Grand National Assembly and members of the Military Court of Cassation. The delegation also met with journalists, academics and trade unionists, and it visited Military Detention Centres, where it was able to talk in private with prisoners.[253]

In the case of individual complaints, too, sometimes witnesses are heard or evidence is collected in some other way on the spot, as happened in the

---

247. Appl. 5310/71, *Ireland v. United Kingdom*, Yearbook XV (1972), p. 76. See Council of Europe, *Stock-Taking on the European Convention on Human Rights*, Strasbourg 1981, pp. 21-22.
248. Appl. 176/56, *Greece v. United Kingdom*, Yearbook II (1958-59), p. 182.
249. On this, see in greater detail F. Monconduit, *La Commission Européenne des Droits de l'Homme*, Leyden 1965, pp. 278 *et seq.*
250. Appls 6780/74 and 6950/74, *Cyprus v. Turkey*, Yearbook XVIII (1975), p. 82. See Stock-Taking, *supra* note 247, p. 25.
251. See Stock-Taking, *supra* note 247, p. 16.
252. Judgment of 18 January 1978, *Ireland v. United Kingdom*, A.25 (1978), p. 60.
253. Report of 7 December 1985, *France, Norway, Denmark, Sweden and the Netherlands v. Turkey*, D & R 44 (1985), p. 31 (36-37).

case of the IRA prisoner Bobby Sands.[254]

The Convention does not provide for enforcement of the cooperation of a contracting State. Nor do the present Rules of Procedure of the Commission contain any provision to that effect. One of the old Rules contained the rather ineffective provision that the Commission formally took note of the refusal of a contracting State to cooperate in measures which the Commission had taken to perform its duties under Article 28 of the Convention (Rule 50(2) of those Rules of Procedure). In the *Greek* Case the consequences of the refusal were not too great, because the Commission was able by other means to obtain sufficient information to form an opinion on the application. In a case in which in the Commission's opinion an inquiry on the spot is absolutely necessary it would appear to be in conformity with the spirit of the Convention to appeal to the Committee of Ministers in case of a refusal. Via a resolution the latter organ might bring pressure to bear on the recalcitrant State to comply with its obligations and to cooperate in making an investigation on its territory possible. Although in practice this is not very likely to occur, in such a case, as a possible reaction to non-compliance with the resolution of the Committee of Ministers, another contracting State might lodge an application against the recalcitrant State for alleged violation of Article 28. As was stated above Article 24 permits the contracting States to complain about "any alleged breach of the provisions of the Convention by another High Contracting Party", so that they need not confine themselves to the rights and freedoms of Section I of the Convention, but may also bring up an article such as Article 28.[255]

7. Under Rule 28(1)(a) of its Rules of Procedure the Commission may, at the request of each of the parties or on its own initiative, take any action which it considers expedient or necessary for the proper performance of its duties under the Convention. It appears from the second paragraph of this provision that this also covers the hearing of witnesses. This provision was already formulated so widely in its old Rules of Procedure that the Commission could hear anyone it wanted. In the *Lawless* Case, for instance, it ordered the applicant himself and the police officer who had arrested him to appear as witnesses.[256] The present Rule 32 is formulated even more widely and refers to "any individual applicant, expert or other person whom the Commission decides to hear as a witness". Witnesses and experts, at their own choice, take the oath or make the declaration mentioned in Rule 33 of the Rules of Procedure.

Apart from the expenses of witnesses, experts and other persons whom the Commission decides to hear on its own initiative, which expenses in any case have to be borne by the Council of Europe (Rule 35 bis(2)), the Commission

---

254. See Council of Europe, *Press Release* C(81)16, 24 April 1981.
255. See *supra* pp. 78-79.
256. See report of 19 December 1959, B.1 (1960-61), p. 53.

may decide, with regard to expenses of witnesses, experts and other persons whom the Commission hears at the request of one of the parties, that these expenses shall also be borne by the Council of Europe (Rule 35 bis(1)).

With the permission of the President or the delegate of the Commission under Rule 28(2), witnesses, experts and other persons may be asked questions at the session by any member of the Commission or any of the parties (Rule 34). The same Rule 14 which authorizes the Commission to carry out an inquiry on the spot[257] also empowers it to hear witnesses elsewhere than in Strasbourg. In *Ireland v. United Kingdom*,[258] for instance, three sessions for the hearing of witnesses were held, for security reasons, at an airport at Stavanger, Norway.[259]

The Commission does not have any means of its own for compelling a witness, expert or other person to appear before it. Unlike the old Rules, the present Rules of Procedure no longer contain any provision about this. Rule 57 of the old Rules provided that, if the persons in question, after having been summoned by the Commission, failed to appear, refused to bear witness, or violated the oath or declaration which they were obliged to take, the Secretary General of the Council of Europe was to communicate this, at the request of the President of the Commission, to the contracting State to whose jurisdiction the person in question was subject. Even without an express provision in the Rules of Procedure it would seem possible for such a communication to be addressed to the contracting State concerned. This State will then have to take any appropriate measures to ensure that the persons in question will cooperate. In fact, the contracting States are obliged to give the Commission the necessary assistance in the performance of its duties. This appears by analogy from Article 28(1)(a) of the Convention, which provides that, if the Commission decides to carry out an inquiry on the spot, "the States concerned shall furnish all necessary facilities".

Cancellation of Rule 57 of the old Rules of Procedure is probably due to the fact that the communication in question to the contracting State is not very effective, if the latter has not incorporated into its national legislation any rules making it possible to compel recalcitrant persons to bear witness before the Commission.

8. The examination of the merits usually takes a good deal of time; apart from exceptional cases, about two years. In some cases this is inevitable, *viz.* if it is very difficult to ascertain the facts, or if the attempts to reach a friendly settlement take a long time. On the whole, however, the necessity to cut short the procedure is evident, especially if it is borne in mind that the time which elapses between the moment at which an application is submitted and the date of the decision on admissibility is also rather long in many

---

257. See *supra* p. 110.
258. Appl. 5310/71, *Yearbook* XV (1972), p. 76.
259. See Stock-Taking, *supra* note 247, p. 22.

cases. Moreover, there is the chance that the application must still pass through the procedure before the Court. Furthermore, in most cases all this has been preceded by a lengthy national procedure. As a measure for speeding up the procedure, since 1970 and 1973 respectively the possibility exists that a rapporteur be appointed in the procedure concerning the merits and that concerning admissibility. This replaced the system in which the examination of the merits in the first instance was carried out in a more laborious way by a sub-commission, and that of admissibility in the first instance by a commission of three members.[260] In addition the Commission may apply an accelerated procedure for urgent cases (Rule 41). Especially, however, the puting of Protocol no. 8 into practice may be expected to speed up proceedings. According to Article 1 of this Protocol the Commission may set up Chambers of at least seven members, which may examine individual petitions that can be dealt with on the basis of established case-law or which raise no serious questions, affecting the interpretation or application of the Convention. Furthermore, the Commission may set up committees of at least three members which can unanimously declare an application inadmissible or strike it from its list of cases when such a decision can be taken without further examination. In addition, the new Protocol enables the Commission to strike a petition from the list of cases if the applicant does not intend to pursue his petition, if the matter has been resolved, or if "for any other reason established by the Commission, it is no longer justified to continue the examination of the petition".[261] Although this Protocol has entered into force on 1 January 1990, at that moment it was not possible to introduce the system of Chambers because the facilities required for that in the Secretariat of the Commission were still lacking. However, commencing in 1990 the length of the sessions of the Commission has been extended to sixteen weeks, while in addition the members of the Commission have sixteen weeks available for preparatory work.[262]

9. After conclusion of the examination the Commission may deliberate with a view to reaching a provisional opinion on the merits of the case (Rule 47).

At this stage of the proceedings, too, *i.e.* after an application has been declared admissible, the Commission may decide to strike a case off the list.

However, it will not make such a decision if it holds that any reason of a general character affecting the observance of the Convention justifies further examination of the application (Rule 49(1) in conjunction with Rule 44(1)). In the case of an inter-State application a condition for striking the case off the list is that the applicant State has declared that it wishes to withdraw its application. When the application has been submitted by an individual, it must have become evident in one way or another that the individual applicant does

---

260. See Rules 40 and 46 of the Rules of Procedure.
261. Article 6(1)(a)-(c) of Protocol no. 8.
262. See also *supra* p. 65.

not intend to pursue his application. If a case is struck off the list, the Commission drafts a report which must satisfy the requirements set forth in Rule 54.[263] Applications which have been declared admissible, however, cannot be struck off the list without consultation of the respondent State (Rule 49(2)).

10. The rapporteur draws up a draft Report on the basis of the provisional opinion reached by the Commission under Rule 47 (Rule 51). If the Commission was divided in its provisional opinion, this is stated in the draft Report (Rule 51). After consideration of the draft Report the Commission draws up its Report referred to in Article 31 of the Convention. For this, it proceeds as follows. First those parts of the Report are adopted in which the facts are established and the submissions of the parties are set out (Rule 52(1)). The Commission then deliberates and votes on whether the facts found disclose any violation by the State concerned of its obligations under the Convention (Rule 52(2)). Unless the Commission decides otherwise, only those members who have participated in the last-mentioned deliberations and vote are entitled to express their separate opinion in the Report (Rule 52(3)).[264]

The Report is sent, through the Secretary General of the Council of Europe, to the Committee of Ministers and those States which are involved in the case.[265] The latter would seem to include in any case the respondent State and the State of which the alleged victim is a national or, in case of an inter-State application, the applicant State(s). These States may not publish the contents of the Report.[266]

The Convention is silent on the question of whether in case of an individual application the Report must or may also be sent to the individual applicant. Rule 61 of the old Rules of Procedure of the Commission provided that, if in such a case the application was submitted to the Court, the Report was sent to the individual applicant, unless the Commission decided otherwise. In the present Rules of Procedure, this provision is, for unclear reasons, omitted. However, in that case Rule 29(3) of the Rules of Court applies, providing that, unless the President of the Court decides otherwise, the Report shall be made available to the public through the Registrar as soon as possible after the case has been brought before the Court. If an individual application is not submitted to the Court and consequently is settled by the Committee of Ministers, point 3(b) of the Appendix to the "Rules" which the Committee of Ministers has adopted with respect to its examination of cases[267] provides that communication to an individual applicant of the complete text

263. See *infra* pp. 129-130.
264. The fact that the above-mentioned finding of the facts and the opinion of the Commission on the question of whether the facts found disclose a violation of the Convention have to be incorporated into the Report follows from Art. 31(1) of the Convention. For what the Report further has to contain, see Rule 53 of the Rules of Procedure.
265. Art. 31(2) of the Convention in conjunction with Rule 53(2) of the Rules of Procedure.
266. See Art. 31(2) of the Convention.
267. See *Collected Texts, supra* note 1, pp. 500-504.

or extracts from the Report of the Commission should take place only as an exceptional measure, and then only on a strictly confidential basis and with the consent of the State against which the application was lodged. The Committee of Ministers therefore considers in each individual case whether there is occasion for sending the Report to the individual applicant, for instance with a view to obtaining his observations on the Report.

It is rather strange indeed that the very person who has taken the initiative for the procedure and may therefore be deemed to be vitally concerned in it is not kept informed of the contents of an extremely important document in that procedure. When the Convention was drafted, this was a point of discussion. A body of opinion in the Consultative Assembly considered the publication of the Report as a form of redress for an individual applicant after the lodging of an application with the Commission.[268] An argument against publication was that this might endanger any attempt of the Committee of Ministers to secure a friendly settlement.[269] One could indeed imagine that there is such an objection with regard to publication of the Report on an unlimited scale (in the press, for instance), but on the other hand it must be borne in mind that so far only a very small number of procedures before the Committee of Ministers have been broken off because the parties had reached some sort of settlement.[270] The latter would seem to indicate that the best chances of securing a friendly settlement exist during the procedure before the Commission, not after it. However this may be, the above objection cannot be maintained with respect to the sending of the Report to the individual applicant on the condition that the complete Report or extracts from it may not be communicated to others. In our opinion any disadvantages that might result from this in a small number of cases are outweighed by the advantages from the viewpoint of the legal interests of the original applicant.

Under Article 32(3) the Report is published when the Committee of Ministers decides by a two-third majority of the members entitled to sit on the Committee that the contracting State in question has violated the Convention (Art. 32(1)) and has not taken the measures required by the Committee under Article 32(2) within the prescribed time-limit. The publication of the Report thus assumes the form of a sanction for the non-compliance by the contracting State with a decision of the Committee of Ministers. Unless there is good reason to do otherwise, the Report is generally published at once when the Committee has decided that there has been no violation of the Convention; in that case publication has the character of furnishing information, and of course constitutes a form of redress for the respondent State. Furthermore, as said before, the Report is published by the Registrar of the Court in cases where the application is brought before the

---

268. See also *infra* pp. 203-204.
269. See Council of Europe, *Collected Edition of the "Travaux Préparatoires" of the European Convention on Human Rights*, vol. III, The Hague 1977, p. 272.
270. See *infra* pp. 198-200.

Court under Article 48 of the Convention.[271] Originally the Consultative Assembly had proposed to confer the power to do so on the Commission.[272] This power ultimately was not incorporated into the Convention, in order to enable the Committee of Ministers to play also a part with respect to the friendly settlement. Via a provision in its old Rules, however, the Commission - as said above - had authorized itself to send its Report for written observations to the individual applicant when the case had been referred to the Court.[273] More generally the Commission has stated as its opinion:

> that in entrusting special responsibilities and functions to the Commission the High Contracting Parties intended the Commission to possess all the powers necessary for the effective discharge of those responsibilities and functions, including the power, if it thinks fit, to publish or communicate its Report to any person.[274]

In the *Lawless* Case, for instance, the Commission had reached the conclusion that there had been no violation of the Convention, and nevertheless decided to refer the case to the Court. Indeed, it held that important legal problems were concerned. Because it feared that this might give rise to all sorts of speculations, it deemed it necessary for a proper application of the Convention to publish the conclusions of its Report.[275] The Court did not pronounce on this point in its subsequent decision in this case. On the basis of this silence it may be assumed that the Court does not regard such a procedure of the Commission as contrary to the Convention, because it would no doubt have pointed this out to the Commission, since the Court considers it as its duty "to ensure that the Convention is respected and, if need be, to point to any irregularities".[276]

11. Under Article 31(3) of the Convention the Commission, in transmitting its Report to the Committee of Ministers, may add such proposals as it thinks fit. In practice such proposals are addressed to the Committee of Ministers as well as to the respondent State. An example of the former is to be found in the *Pataki* Case and the *Durnshirn* Case.[277] During the procedure before the Commission the legal regulations complained about were abolished by means of an amendment of the law. In reaction the Commission proposed

> that the Committee of Ministers take note of this report, express its appreciation of the legislative measures adopted in Austria with a view to giving full effect to the Convention of Human Rights, and decide that no further action should be taken in the present cases.[278]

In the *Greek* Case the Commission made a great many proposals to the

---

271. See Rule 29(3) of the Rules of Procedure of the Court.
272. Council of Europe, Cons.Ass., Recommendation No. 38, 8 September 1949, Document 108, pp. 261-264.
273. See Rule 61 of the old Rules of Procedure.
274. Report of 19 December 1959, *Lawless*, B.1 (1960-61), p. 248.
275. *Ibidem*, p. 252.
276. Judgment of 14 November 1960, *Lawless*, A.1, (1960-61), p. 12.
277. Appl. 596/59, *Pataki v. Austria*, Yearbook III (1960), p. 357; Appl. 789/60, *Durnshirn v. Austria*, Yearbook IV (1961), p. 187.
278. See *Yearbook* VI (1963), p. 734.

Greek Government aimed at altering the situation in Greece on those points which were contrary to the Convention.[279] Another communication of the Commission was addressed to the respondent Government in the *Pfunders* Case,[280] recommending that

the Commission considered it desirable for humanitarian reasons, among which may be counted the youth of the prisoners, that measures of clemency be taken in their favour.[281]

The peculiar aspect of this case was that in its Report the Commission had reached the conclusion that Italy had not violated the Convention.

In Rule 6 of the "Rules" adopted by the Committee of Ministers the latter has expressed its view that the Commission is not entitled to make proposals under Article 31(3) in cases where it considers that there has not been a violation of the Convention.[282] Such a provision is not binding upon the Commission, but it is clear that a proposal of the Commission addressed to the Committee of Ministers, when it considers that there has been no violation of the Convention, will not be effective if the Committee abides by its interpretation in this matter. Against the competence of the Commission to make proposals in such a case it may be argued that Article 19 of the Convention defines the duties of the Commission as "to ensure the observance of the engagements undertaken by the High Contracting Parties", which could be said to imply that it can make proposals under Article 31(3) only in cases where it has actually reached the conclusion that this "observance" is at stake. On the other hand, Article 31(3) provides that the Commission may make such proposals "as it thinks fit", without any further qualification. This appears to imply complete freedom for the Commission. Moreover, a proposal of the Commission, even if it has not reached the conclusion that there has been a violation of the Convention, may have a preventive effect because it may induce the respondent State to take certain measures in the spirit of the Convention. As such, the competence of the Commission to make proposals fits in with its duty "to ensure the observance of the engagements undertaken by the High Contracting Parties in the present Convention". Italy, for instance, actually granted a pardon to the youngest of the prisoners in the *Pfunders* Case after the above-mentioned proposal of the Commission.

12. The Report of the Commission is not a legally binding decision.[283] The final decision is made either by the Court or by the Committee of Ministers. These two organs are not bound by the views set forth in the Report of the Commission, even though that Report constitutes the most important document in the proceedings before the two other organs. As to the question whether the Commission itself is bound by the conclusions in its Reports in

---

279. See *Yearbook* XII; *The Greek Case* (1969), pp. 514-515.
280. Appl. 788/60, *Austria v. Italy*, *Yearbook* IV (1961), p. 117.
281. See *Yearbook* VI (1963), p. 800.
282. See *Collected Texts, supra* note 1, p. 193.
283. Thus also expressly the then President of the Commission in the *Lawless* Case, B.1 (1960-61), pp. 264-268.

other cases, the Commission takes the view that in principle it is free to reach different conclusions in two cases of the same character. In practice, however, the case-law of the Commission is fairly constant, both as to admissibility and with respect to the interpretation of the rights and freedoms set forth in the Convention.

13. Apart from the ordinary reports, with respect to which the Convention expressly contains provisions (Arts 28(2) and 31), in practice two special kinds of reports have developed. This is so because in special cases the Commission follows a slightly different procedure. Below the so-called summary reports will be discussed, which the Commission transmits to the Committee of Ministers when at the request of the parties the case is struck off the list as a result of a non-official settlement.[284] Another special kind is the so-called provisional report, which the Commission draws up when at a given moment, for one reason or another, the examination of a case must be stopped prematurely. In the *Second Greek* Case, for example, in which, because the Greek Government did not put up a defence, the Commission, with a view to the "special and unprecedented circumstances described in its subsequent report, also reached the conclusion that it could not, in the present situation, continue its function adequately in the case with a view to the eventual adoption of a report under Article 30 and 31 of the Convention".[285] After the application had been declared admissible, the Commission refrained from dealing with the case. After Greece had become a party to the Convention again on 18 November 1974, the Commission resumed its examination of the application. However, after both the applicant States and the respondent State had stated that they were no longer interested in continuance of the case, the Commission struck the case off the list on 4 October 1976.[286]

3.2. The friendly settlement (Art. 28(1)(b))

1. From the terms of Article 28 it is clear that the drafters of the Convention intended the attempts to reach a friendly settlement to take place simultaneously with the examination of the merits. This is quite natural. In fact, on the one hand a complete examination of the merits is superfluous if a friendly settlement is reached. On the other hand the Commission cannot mediate in an effective way with a view to reaching such a settlement until it has gained some insight into the question of whether or not the application is well-founded. Moreover, the provisional views within the Commission on the latter question may put pressure on (one of) the parties to cooperate with reaching a settlement.

---

284. See *infra* pp. 128-130.
285. Report of 4 October 1976, *D & R* 6 (1977), p. 5 (6).
286. *D & R* 6 (1977), p. 5 (8).

2. The friendly settlement is one of the two methods provided for in the Convention for resolving a dispute concerning the human rights set forth in the Convention. The other is the settlement of the dispute by a decision of the European Court of Human Rights or the Committee of Ministers.

The friendly settlement is a form of *conciliation*, one of the traditional methods of peaceful settlement of international disputes. The term "conciliation", which refers particularly to inter-State disputes, has been replaced in the European Convention by "friendly settlement" because disputes between States and individuals may also be concerned.[287] With the method of the friendly settlement a non-legal element has been introduced into the procedure. Indeed, this method is not necessarily based on exclusively legal considerations; other factors may also play a part in it. In consequence, the entire settlement procedure has a flexible and informal character.

3. The Commission has great discretion with respect to the way in which it may try to secure a friendly settlement. Its Rules of Procedure contain only one general provision: Rule 45 provides that the Commission, with a view to securing a friendly settlement, shall decide on the procedure to be followed. The Convention, too, does not impose any limitations on the Commission in this matter, with the exception of the requirement to be discussed below that the settlement reached must be based on respect for human rights as defined in the Convention.

This flexible and informal character of the procedure makes it possible to create an atmosphere in which it is easier for the parties to reach a compromise. In this context the fact that the consideration of the application by the Commission takes place *in camera* plays an important part. Furthermore, the fact that it will often be attractive for the respondent State to avoid continuation of the procedure, which may involve a thorough examination of the facts and public condemnation if the Commission, or a majority of its members, believes that there has been a violation of the Convention, helps create a situation in which States are more willing to accept a compromise. The individual applicant may also benefit from the compromise by having certainty about the issue of the dispute, and reparation, if any, of the damages incurred, at the earliest possible moment. He will generally also wish to avoid lengthy proceedings before the Court, involving the risk of an unfavourable judgment. All this makes the friendly settlement an instrument by means of which disputes about situations concerned with human rights may be resolved relatively promptly, if the parties are prepared to reach such a settlement.

On the other hand the construction of the friendly settlement involves the drawbacks attached to a non-public procedure for the protection of human rights. Owing to the fact that it is a compromise the friendly settlement,

---

287. See *Collected Edition of the "Travaux Préparatoires" of the European Convention on Human Rights*, vol. III, The Hague 1977, pp. 271-272.

without further qualifications, would involve the risk that ultimately an agreement may be reached which does not satisfy the standards with respect to human rights set by the Convention. However, the concluding words of Article 28(1)(b) require the settlement to be reached "on the basis of respect for Human Rights as defined in this Convention". It is the duty of the Commission to see to this. Besides the parties concerned, the Commission must agree to the content of the settlement. In some cases, for instance, it is not unlikely that the victim of a violation is ready to accept a given sum of money with which the government concerned might as it were wish to buy off the violation, while the cause of the violation, for instance in the form of a legal provision or an administrative practice conflicting with the Convention, would continue to exist.[288] In such a case the Commission will have to demand that the government concerned, in addition to giving compensation to the victim, shall take measures to alter the law or administrative practice in question. In its attempts to secure a friendly settlement, too, the Commission therefore has a duty with respect to the public interest, which constitutes a further indication of the "objective" character of the procedure provided for in the Convention.[289]

Besides the public interest in the maintenance of the legal order created by the Convention, that of the *Rechtsfrieden* (peace through justice) also plays a part here. Indeed, if the Commission did not see to it that the existing violation be ended, there would be considerable risk that repeated applications might be submitted about the same situation conflicting with the Convention in a given contracting State.

Up to the present the Commission has not refused a proposed settlement for the reason that it had not been reached "on the basis of respect for Human Rights as defined in this Convention".[290]

4. About the actual course of the attempts to reach a friendly settlement and the role of the Commission in them only a few general remarks can be made, precisely because the procedure takes place *in camera* and data about it are therefore scanty.[291]

Article 28 states that the Commission places itself at the disposal of the parties.[292] Immediately after a complaint has been declared admissible, the

---

288. The fact that the Court, too, is not prepared to strike the case off the list when the parties have reached some sort of settlement, but the essence of the case has not yet been resolved, appears from its judgment of 25 April 1978, *Tyrer*, A.26 (1978), pp. 12-14.
289. See *supra* pp. 33-34.
290. See H. Krüger and C.A. Nørgaard, "Reflections concerning friendly settlement under the European Convention on Human Rights", in: F. Matscher & H. Petzold (eds), *Protecting Human Rights: The European Dimension*, Cologne 1988, pp. 329-334 (332).
291. On this, see a somewhat more detailed discussion in the publication mentioned in the preceding note.
292. Since the entry-into-force of the Third Protocol on 20 September 1970 the functions referred to in Art. 28 are performed by the Commission itself, and no longer by a sub-commission as provided for in the original Art. 29. However, the preparatory negotiations will as a rule be attended by the Secretary of the Commission and, where needed, its President.

Secretary of the Commission invites the parties to state whether they wish to make proposals for a possible settlement. In this early phase this will usually not be the case. In a later phase, when the Commission is informed of all the elements of the merits, it may be important for it to avail itself of the power, conferred on it in Rule 47 of its Rules of Procedure, to give a provisional opinion on the merits. Such a provisional opinion, which is notified orally and confidentially to the parties, may of course stimulate the willingness of the parties to reach a settlement. Further, it will depend on the circumstances of each individual case whether the Commission confines itself to such a passive role, or takes steps to start the negotiations. The Commission must also be deemed capable to do the latter, because it is well informed of the facts of the case concerned and is in a position to contact the parties in an informal way. Sometimes the Commission will first examine the possibilities for a friendly settlement in discussions with one or both of the parties separately. In other cases it will at once bring the parties into contact with each other because it considers that there are possibilities for a settlement.

The role of the Commission will also have to be more or less active depending on whether an inter-State application or an individual application is concerned. In the first case the parties are more or less on equal terms, so that the Commission may confine itself to a more passive role. In case of an individual application, on the contrary, it may be true that the parties are formally on equal terms, but the respondent State is obviously better equipped to conduct the negotiations within the framework of a friendly settlement than is an individual applicant. It is therefore obvious that the latter, in taking a decision on whether or not to agree to a given settlement, will be guided largely by the attitude of the Commission. The Commission, owing to its expertise and experience, will often be better able to evaluate the content of the settlement, and by playing an active role it may to some extent neutralize a factual inequality of the parties to the negotiations. However, since the notion of a settlement implies that the two parties are in agreement on the content of the settlement reached, the role of the Commission may not dominate to such an extent that it is actually the Commission which determines the terms of the settlement and imposes it more or less upon the individual applicant. Up to the present, however, there have been no indications of such a situation.

5. If a friendly settlement in the sense of Article 28 is reached, the Commission draws up a Report in accordance with Article 28(2) containing a brief statement of the facts and the substance of the solution reached.[293] The Report is transmitted to the States concerned, to the Committee of Ministers and for publication to the Secretary General of the Council of Europe. In case of an individual application the Report is also transmitted to the individual applicant.

---

293. For the further points which the report has to contain, see Rule 50 of the Rules.

6. Up to the end of 1989, as far as may be ascertained, eighty-four friendly settlements had been reached.[294]

The first settlement concerned a special case. In the *Boeckmans* Case the applicant complained about remarks made by a judge during his trial, which were alleged to be incompatible with the rights of accused persons under Article 6 of the Convention. The Belgian Government, while upholding the validity of the judgment in question, agreed to pay to Boeckmans a compensation of 65,000 Belgian francs, because the remarks were such "as to disturb the serenity of the atmosphere during the proceedings in a manner contrary to the Convention and may have caused the applicant a moral injury".[295]

An Irish woman received an *ex gratia* payment after her husband was shot and killed by British soliders in Northern Ireland. The British Government granted the compensation considering that the death of the applicant's husband was an unfortunate mistake, and acting on compassionate grounds without implying any admission of a violation of the Convention or any reproach against the soldiers.[296]

In a number of other cases, too, the substance of the settlement consisted merely in that the government concerned paid compensation and/or redressed the consequences of the violation for the victim as much as possible.[297] A special case belonging to this category was one in which, according to the Commission, a threatening deportation of a South African who had gone into exile, allegedly for political reasons, raised questions in connection with the prohibition of degrading and inhuman treatment set forth in Article 3 of the Convention. This case was ultimately resolved because the Belgian authorities

294. See *European Commission of Human Rights: Survey of Activities and Statistics*, Council of Europe, Strasbourg, 1989, p. 16.
295. Report of 17 February 1965, *Yearbook* VIII (1965), p. 410 (422).
296. Report of 2 October 1984, *Farrell v. United Kingdom*, D & R 38 (1984), p. 44 (47-48).
297. See, *e.g.*, Report of 13 December 1966, *Poerschke v. Federal Republic of Germany*, *Yearbook* IX (1966), p. 632 (640); Report of 24 March 1972, *Sepp v. Federal Republic of Germany*, Stock-Taking on the European Convention on Human Rights (1954-1984), Strasbourg 1984, p. 118; Report of 12 December 1973, *Mellin v. Federal Republic of Germany*, *ibidem*, p. 121, in which the Commission accepted the view of the German Government that considerations based on the public interest could not justify continuance of the procedure, since Germany had meanwhile introduced such amendments of the law that the conflict with the Convention had been removed, and, moreover, it pointed out that the same matter was concerned in two other cases pending before it; Report of 19 July 1974, *Amekrane v. United Kingdom*, *ibidem*, p. 122; Report of 2 May 1978, *Nagel v. Federal Republic of Germany*, D & R 12 (1978), pp. 97-102, in which the applicant was granted a pardon; Report of 8 March 1979, *Peyer v. Switzerland*, D & R 15 (1979), pp. 105-119; Report of 4 May 1979, *Geerk v. Switzerland*, D & R 16 (1979), pp. 56-67; Report of 9 July 1980, *Uppal v. United Kingdom*, D & R 20 (1980), pp. 29-39, in which the deportation order issued against the applicant was withdrawn. In the Report of 7 October 1986, *Widmaier v. the Netherlands*, Stock-Taking on the European Convention on Human Rights, Strasbourg 1986, p. 45, the applicant had been convicted for drug trafficking without being allowed to appear in person at the hearing. Under the terms of the settlement the Netherlands Government declared to be prepared not to enforce the judgment, to remove the applicant's name from the list of wanted persons and to pay him compensation. In two other cases the settlement was confined to awarding financial compensation: Report of 15 May 1986, *Conroy v. the United Kingdom*, where the applicant was dismissed as a result of his expulsion from his trade union, *ibidem*, p. 42; and Report of 11 May 1985, *Naldi v. Italy*, D & R 42 (1985), p. 63 (71-72), where the applicant had been detained in contravention of Article 5(4).

provided the applicant with the documents required for emigration to Senegal as desired by him, and paid his travelling expenses.[298] Complaints concerning inhuman treatment and a breach of the right to respect for family life were raised in a similar case against Sweden by a 12-year-old Lebanese boy whose deportation was at issue. The application originally was filed also on behalf of his two elder brothers who were already deported from Sweden. Under the terms of the friendly settlement eventually arrived at the Swedish Government agreed to grant permission to the applicant's brothers to reside and work in Sweden, their travel expenses being paid by the Government, to make an *ex gratia* payment as well as a payment for legal expenses, and to revise the relevant regulations concerning expulsion.[299]

In some cases considerations of public interest also play a part. In the *Alam* Case, in which a complaint was lodged, *inter alia*, about Article 6(1), the Commission included in its considerations the fact that the British Government had introduced bills in which aliens were granted the right to appeal against decisions of immigration officers.[300] Again, in a case against Austria concerning Article 6(1) the principal element of the settlement reached was constituted by the fact that the Government had proposed an amendment of the law as a result of which detained persons henceforth could also be present at hearings where an appeal lodged to their detriment is dealt with.[301] In the *Knechtl* Case, which also concerned Article 6(1), the Commission agreed to the friendly settlement after having taken note of a White Paper of the British Government in which it was suggested "that further consideration should be given to the arrangements which are followed in considering applications by prisoners to seek legal advice where negligence by officers of the Home Office is alleged" and of the assurance by that Government that this suggestion had been followed.[302]

In two further cases the friendly settlement included the readiness on the part of the United Kingdom Government to amend prison administrative practices in order to inform a prisoner's relatives in due time of his imminent transfer to another prison[303] and to better safeguard the prisoners' right to respect for their correspondence.[304]

According to the Commission a friendly settlement in the case of a complaint against Austria about inhuman and degrading treatment contrary to Article 3 satisfied the requirement of respect for human rights in the sense of Article 28, since the Austrian Minister of Justice in a directive had ordered the authorities concerned to see to it that sick or wounded prisoners

---

298. Report of 17 July 1980, *Giama v. Belgium, D & R* 21 (1981), p. 73.
299. Report of 8 December 1984, *Bulus v. Sweden, D & R* 39 (1984), p. 75 (78-79).
300. Report of 17 December 1968, *Mohammed Alam v. United Kingdom, Yearbook* X (1967), p. 478.
301. Report of 13 October 1981, *Peschke v. Austria, D & R* 25 (1982), p. 182.
302. Report of 24 March 1972, *Knechtl v. United Kingdom, Yearbook* XIII (1970), p. 730.
303. Report of 15 May 1986, *Seale v. the United Kingdom, Stock-Taking on the European Convention on Human Rights*, Strasbourg 1986, pp. 38-39.
304. Report of 15 May 1986, *McComb v. the United Kingdom, ibidem*, pp. 40-41.

were not subjected in an indirect way to "inhuman or degrading treatment or punishment" while they were tended in public hospitals.[305] A more or less identical case concerned an action against the United Kingdom. There again a complaint was lodged about inhuman and degrading treatment contrary to Article 3, this time in connection with solitary confinement of a detained person in a clinic for mental patients. Here a settlement could be reached because the British Government showed its willingness not only to award damages to the applicant, but also to supply information on the directives concerning the treatment of patients in the clinic in question, and promised to review regularly the directives for possible improvements in the future.[306] And in the case of *Reed*, also against the United Kingdom, the British Government was willing to pay an *ex gratia* payment to Mr. Reed as well as a payment for his lawyer's fees and disbursements, and to change the rules regarding the right of prisoners to complain about prison treatment.[307] In the case of *Schuurs v. the Netherlands*, the Government admitted that Article 5(1)(e) has been violated and that it "will, in so far as possible under national constitutional law, promote the adoption by the Upper House of Parliament of the Bill concerning particular detentions in psychiatric hospitals".[308]

In the *Gussenbauer* Case against Austria the settlement resulted in radical changes in the Austrian system of counsels assigned to prisoners.[309] Furthermore, in the case of *Zimmermann*, the Austrian Government was willing to propose to the Federal President to quash, by an act of grace, the conditional prison sentence of seven months imposed on Zimmermann by the Vienna Regional Court. In this case financial compensation was also offered.[310]

In the *Harman* Case the United Kingdom Government, apart from paying all the applicant's legal costs and expenses, undertook to change the law so that it would no longer be a contempt of court to render public material that is contained in documents which are compulsorily disclosed in civil proceedings, once those documents have been read out in open court.[311]

Two comparable complaints against the Federal Republic of Germany in fact both concerned the *presumptio innocentiae*. In the first of these cases the applicant had at first been convicted for fraud, but on appeal the action conducted against him was discontinued. The court took its decision on the ground of the insignificance of the case (*Geringfügigkeit*). The applicant, however, had to pay his own costs of the suit, because according to the court of appeal "the outcome of the investigation and the findings of the first judge appeared to have justified the conviction".[312] For this reason the applicant

---

305. Report of 19 December 1972, *Simon-Herold v. Austria, Yearbook* XIV (1971), p. 352.
306. Report of 16 July 1980, *A. v. United Kingdom, D & R* 20 (1980), pp. 5-18.
307. Report of 12 December 1981, *Reed v. United Kingdom, D & R* 25 (1982), p. 5 (9).
308. Report of 7 March 1985, *J. Schuurs v. the Netherlands, D & R* 41 (1985), p. 186 (189).
309. Report of 8 October 1974, *Gussenbauer v. Austria, Yearbook* XV (1972), p. 558.
310. Report of 6 July 1982, *Zimmermann v. Austria, D & R* 30 (1983), p. 15 (20).
311. Report of 15 May 1986, *Stock-Taking on the European Convention on Human Rights,* Strasbourg 1986, pp. 43-44.
312. Report of 9 March 1977, *Neubecker v. Federal Republic of Germany, D & R* 8 (1977), p. 30 (32).

applied to the Commission, submitting violation of Article 6(1) and (2). However, he was afterwards found willing to withdraw his complaint, after the German Government had declared, as part of the friendly settlement, that

pursuant to the discontinuance of proceedings by the Berlin Regional Court ... the judgment given against the applicant on 6 May 1968 by the Tiergarten District Court in Berlin ... is devoid of any effect. No opinion concerning the applicant's guilt may accordingly be inferred from the judgment or from the aforementioned decision of the Berlin Regional Court.[313]

In the other case the action was discontinued on the ground of a legal provision permitting the court to abandon further prosecution if the penalty which might ensue is negligible in comparison with a penalty which has already been imposed on the accused in connection with another punishable offence. Here, too, the applicant had to pay his own costs, and here, too, the complaint submitted in Strasbourg concerning violation of Article 6(2) ended with a friendly settlement, the principal part of which was formed by a declaration of the German Government to the effect that

the Oldenburg District Court's decision on 15 August 1973 to discontinue proceedings ... closed the criminal proceedings opened against the applicant. This decision is final. Consequently, no appreciation of the applicant's guilt can be deduced from the decision relating to court fees taken on 22 April 1974 by the Juvenile Chamber of the Oldenburg Regional Court.[314]

A friendly settlement was also reached when the Austrian Government, as lessee, came into conflict with one of its subjects, as lessor. The latter wished to increase the rent of a garage block in a way which according to the Government was contrary to the relevant legal regulations. The lessor thereupon wished to terminate the lease, but after a procedure taking more than eight years this was ultimately refused by the highest domestic court. During the Strasbourg proceedings concerning the alleged violation of the reasonable-time requirement of Article 6, however, a solution was reached because the Austrian Government agreed to termination of the contract.[315]

Two further cases concerned property rights under Article 1 of the First Protocol. In a complaint against the United Kingdom the applicant in addition alleged violation of his right to respect for family life and home as a result of noise and vibration nuisance affecting his property located a quarter of a mile from Heathrow Airport. The matter was settled by an *ex gratia* payment by the Government.[316] A settlement on the basis of compensation was also reached in a case against Belgium. The applicant had alleged violation of her right to peaceful enjoyment of her possessions because of the failure of the Belgian State to abide by a court judgment awarding the applicant compensation for damages suffered as a result of a refusal of a building permission. During the Strasbourg proceedings, however, the Government proved prepared

---

313. *Ibidem*, p. 34.
314. Report of 11 May 1978, *Liebig v. Federal Republic of Germany*, D & R 17 (1980), p. 5 (18).
315. Report of 4 May 1979, *Karrer v. Austria*, D & R 16 (1979), p. 42 (49).
316. Report of 8 July 1987, *Baggs v. the United Kingdom*, *Stock-Taking on the European Convention on Human Rights*, Strasbourg 1987, p. 25.

to do so after all.[317]

The problem of transsexuals was at issue in a case in which the applicant had undergone a change of sex through a medical operation and had subsequently requested the German authorities for a change of her name and adaptation of the register of births. This was considered not to be possible in the case of sex changes, since the German legislation did not contain any provisions about it and a similar application was still pending before the *Bundesverfassungsgericht*. The Commission declared the complaint concerning Articles 5(1) and 6(1) admissible, but the matter was settled in a friendly way when during the proceedings the German Government declared that the following decision had been taken:

> By decision of the District Court in B. dated 17 January 1979, concerning entry No. ...
> in the birth register at the Registrar's Office in B., the relevant entry has been corrected
> by adding the following remark: "By reason of a change of sex the child here designated
> is of female sex with effect from the date of this entry and bears the Christian name
> Gunde".[318]

More recently a number of cases concerning alleged violations of Article 6 have been settled by way of compensation provided by the Government. In five of these cases the length of the relevant proceedings was at stake,[319] in four other cases a violation was alleged of respectively the requirement of an independent and impartial tribunal,[320] of access to court[321] and of a fair and public hearing.[322]

In a number of other cases matters of family law were at issue. In two of these cases against Sweden the applicants complained about the taking into public care of their respective children. As in both cases the children had in the meantime returned to their mothers, both cases could be settled on the basis of compensation paid by the Government.[323] Two other cases dealt with proceedings concerning custody over children. In a case against Denmark the settlement was confined to an offer of compensation by the Government, acceptance by the applicant and subsequent approval by the Commission.[324] In a comparable case against the Federal Republic of Germany the settlement

---

317. Report of 13 November 1987, *Leemans-Ceuremans v. Belgium, ibidem*, p. 30.
318. Report of 11 October 1979, *X v. Federal Republic of Germany, D & R* 17 (1980), p. 21 (26). Moreover the German Government afforded the prospect that legal measures in this matter were to be taken, and offered the applicant compensation *(ibidem*, p. 26).
319. Report of 11 October 1984, *Versos v. Portugal, D & R* 38 (1984), p. 137 (143); Report of 12 July 1985, *Sacca v. Italy, D & R* 42 (1985), p. 5 (13); Report of 12 July 1985, *Russo v. Italy, D & R* 42 (1985), p. 14 (22; Report of 6 July 1985, *Farragut v. France, D & R* 42 (1985), p. 77 (83); and Report of 3 March 1987, *Smidt v. Denmark, Stock-Taking on the European Convention on Human Rights*, Strasbourg 1987, p. 33.
320. Report of 18 October 1985, *Stevens v. Belgium, D & R* 44 (1985), p. 5 (12) and Report of 8 July 1987, *Nyssen v. Belgium, Stock-Taking on the European Convention on Human Rights*, Strasbourg 1987, p. 32.
321. Report of 9 March 1987, *Van Hal v. the Netherlands, Stock-Taking on the European Convention on Human Rights*, Strasbourg 1987, p. 35.
322. Report of 8 October 1987, *Von Sydow v. Sweden, ibidem*, p. 36.
323. Report of 10 October 1986, *Aminoff v. Sweden, Stock-Taking on the European Convention on Human Rights*, Strasbourg 1986, p. 46, and Report of 10 October 1986, *Widén v. Sweden, ibidem*, p. 47.
324. Report of 9 March 1984, *Pedersen v. Denmark, D & R* 37 (1984), p. 66 (70).

consisted in the continuation of arrangements already made, providing the applicant with access to her son as well as with the opportunity to make telephone calls every fortnight.[325] Two cases against Belgium and one against Ireland ended in a settlement which, apart from financial compensation for the applicants, included (proposed) legislative amendments in order to undo (formerly) existing discrimination against children born out of wedlock and out of an adulterous relationship.[326]

A final category of settlements is in fact based on judgments of the Court in cases which rose identical issues. In a case against the United Kingdom six applicants complained about their dismissal from employment after refusal to join a trade union. After the Court's judgment in the *Young, James and Webster* Case the Government settled the case by offering the applicants compensation for material loss in respect of loss of earnings, pension rights and other employment benefits.[327] Similarly, in the *Geniets v. Belgium* Case the admitted part of the application was similar to the *Van Droogenbroeck* Case where the Court found a breach of Article 5(4) because of the absence of an effective and accessible judicial remedy which satisfied the requirements of that provision. As a result the Belgian Government showed itself prepared to pay compensation to Geniets.[328] With respect to two complaints regarding corporal punishment of children at school the way to a settlement was paved by the Court's judgment in the *Campbell and Cosans* Case as a result of which the United Kingdom Government changed the relevant legislation and in addition made *ex gratia* payments to the applicants concerned.[329]

Finally mention should be made of the settlement in the case of *France, Norway, Denmark, Sweden and the Netherlands v. Turkey*, which was accepted by the Commission in 1985. The substantive parts of the settlement included the assurance by the Turkish Government to strictly observe its obligations under Article 3 of the Convention, a vague promise concerning the granting of amnesty and - as regards the derogations under Article 15 of the Convention - a reference to an even more vague declaration by the Turkish Prime Minister of 4 April 1985, stating that "I hope that we will be able to lift martial law from the remaining provinces within 18 months".[330] Particularly the acceptance by the applicant States of that part of the settlement is striking in view of the fact that when lodging their complaint the applicant States upheld that a public emergency threathening the life of the nation did not obtain in Turkey in 1982. It is also a disappointing fact that although

---

325. Report of 14 May 1987, *D v. the Federal Republic of Germany, Stock-Taking on the European Convention on Human Rights*, Strasbourg 1987, p. 29.
326. Report of 8 October 1987, *Lucile Marie de Mot and others v. Belgium, ibidem*, p. 27; Report of 8 October 1987, *Jolie and Lebrun v. Belgium, ibidem*, p. 28; and Report of 17 December 1987, *Stoutt v. Ireland, ibidem*, p. 34.
327. Report of 10 December 1984, *Eaton and others v. the United Kingdom, D & R* 39 (1984), p. 11 (15).
328. Report of 15 March 1985, *D & R* 41 (1985), p. 5 (12).
329. Report of 23 January 1987, *Durairq, Townend and Brent v. the United Kingdom, Stock-Taking on the European Convention on Human Rights*, Strasbourg 1987, p. 26; and Report of 16 July 1987, *A. Family v. the United Kingdom, ibidem*, p. 31.
330. Report of 7 December 1985, *D & R* 44 (1985), p. 31 (39).

the application, as declared admissible, also included alleged violations of the Articles 5, 6, 9, 10, 11 and 17, those provisions are not explicitly mentioned in the settlement.

Because of their lenient attitude the applicant Governments have manoeuvred the Commission into a very difficult position. It may even be argued that the Commission was left with no choice but to accept the settlement. Indeeed, in the alternative the case would have been decided by the Committee of Ministers - Turkey had not recognized the jurisdiction of the Court yet - in which organ the applicant States and Turkey would obviously have played a prominent if not decisive role. Convincing as this argument may be it does not turn the settlement into one which has been reached "on the basis of respect for Human Rights as defined in this Convention". It is, therefore, at least questionable whether the Commission has sufficiently upheld this requirement of Article 28(b).

In our view the Commission should at any rate have insisted on a stricter type of supervision over the observance by Turkey of its commitments under the settlement. With respect to Article 15 as well as to the granting of amnesty there was in fact no supervision at all: the Turkish Government undertook to keep the Commission informed of further developments. As far as Article 3 is concerned supervision was confined to a commitment by Turkey to submit three reports under Article 57 during 1986, a dialogue with the Commission on each of those reports, and a short final report on the implementation of the settlement to be prepared not later than 1 February 1987. All this, moreover, was to be conducted in a confidential manner.[331] As was to be expected, these supervisory arrangements have turned out to be inadequate. Although martial law was lifted in Turkey in the course of 1987, serious violations of human rights have continued being reported from that country.[332]

7. Apart from the friendly settlement referred to in Article 28(1)(b), the parties sometimes also reach a settlement of the dispute among themselves. In those cases the applicant withdraws his complaint after having come to some kind of arrangement with the government concerned.

A well-known example is the *Televizier* Case.[333] In this case the applicant complained about violation of its freedom of expression (Art. 10) and discriminatory treatment (Art. 14) in connection with a judgment of the Dutch Supreme Court, which was based on the Copyright Act and which was unfavourable to the applicant. The case concerned giving information and commenting on radio and television programmes, for which use had been

---

331. *Ibidem.*
332. See Amnesty International, *Turkey, Brutal and Systematic Abuse of Human Rights,* London 1989.
333. Report of 3 October 1968, *N.V. Televizier v. the Netherlands, Yearbook* IX (1966), p. 512. See also the Report of 4 October 1976, *Denmark, Norway and Sweden v. Greece, D & R* 6 (1977), p. 5, and Appl. 6242/73, *Brückmann v. Federal Republic of Germany, D & R* 6 (1977), p. 57.

made of summaries of programmes of the Central Broadcasting Bureau in the Netherlands. Some years after the application had been submitted the parties informed the Commission that they had arrived at an arrangement and that the applicant wished to withdraw its application. Televizier had meanwhile concluded an agreement with one of the broadcasting organizations about the publication of the latter's radio and TV guide.[334]

In the cases here mentioned, the Commission is also willing to accept the withdrawal of the application and to strike the case off the list only if considerations of public interest are not opposed to it. Thus, in the *Gericke* Case the Commission at first refused to agree to the withdrawal of the application on the ground that

> the present application raises problems of individual freedom involved in the application of Article 5, paragraph 3, of the Convention, which may extend beyond the interests of the particular applicants.[335]

After the adoption of the report in the *Wemhoff* Case,[336] in May 1966, the Commission stopped the procedure in the Case of Gericke, who had been condemned as an accomplice of Wemhoff, because it held that reasons of public interest no longer made it necessary to examine the case any further.[337] Similarly, a number of cases have been terminated because the issue(s) at stake had in the meantime been decided by the Court in comparable cases.[338] In some cases the main element of the informal settlement consisted of the amelioration of the legislation which was the cause of the alleged violation.[339]

With respect to these non-official settlements, before the entry into force of the new Rules of Procedure of the Commission on 13 December 1974 the question arose whether Article 30 (old), the present Article 28(2), or Article 31 of the Convention was applicable to such cases, or neither of the two. In the *Gericke* Case the Commission took the position that neither of the two articles could be applicable if the case were struck off the list at the request of the parties in consequence of a non-official settlement.[340] In such a case the Commission drew up a so-called summary report, which was transmitted for information and publication to the Committee of Ministers.[341] Rule 54 of the present Rules of Procedure provides for the drawing up of a Report

334. For other cases belonging to the same category, see: Council of Europe, *Stock-Taking on the European Convention on Human Rights* (1954-1984), Strasbourg 1984, pp. 143-162.
335. Report of 22 July 1966, *Gericke v. Federal Republic of Germany, Yearbook* VIII (1965), p. 314 (320).
336. Report of 1 April 1966, B.5 (1969).
337. See Council of Europe, *Stock-Taking on the European Convention on Human Rights* (1954-1984), Strasbourg 1984, p. 145.
338. Report of 9 May 1987, *Bozano v. Switzerland, Stock-Taking on the European Convention on Human Rights,* Strasbourg 1987, p. 87; the case was terminated after the Court's *Sanchez-Reisse* judgment, while the Case of *Scotts' of Greenock Ltd and Lithgow Ltd v. United Kindom,* Report of 5 March 1987, *ibidem,* p. 38, was withdrawn on the basis of the *Lithgow* judgment.
339. Appl. 10664/83, *Bowen v. Norway, Stock-Taking on the European Convention on Human Rights,* Strasbourg 1985, pp. 44-45; Report of 7 May 1986, *Prasser v. Austria, Stock-Taking on the European Convention on Human Rights,* Strasbourg 1986, pp. 48-49.
340. Appl. 2294/64, *Gericke v. Federal Republic of Germany, Yearbook* IX (1966), pp. 618-620.
341. See *Case-Law Topics,* No. 3, *supra* note 32, pp. 35-36.

when the Commission strikes a case, which it has declared admissible, off the list.[342] This report must contain, *inter alia*, a statement of the facts, an account of the procedure, and the terms of the decision to strike the case off the list, together with the reasons.

8. If no friendly settlement is reached, the Commission pursues its examination of the facts and, under Article 31, draws up a Report in which it gives its opinion on the question of whether these facts disclose a violation of the Convention. With this, the procedure before the Commission has come to an end, but its conciliatory task is not necessarily completed. Even during the proceedings before the Court or the Committee of Ministers the consideration of the case may be terminated on the basis of an arrangement made between the parties, and for this, too, the Commission may offer to mediate. This matter will be dealt with below in the discussion of the proceedings before the two other Strasbourg organs.

9. Should the case occur where the terms of a friendly settlement are not complied with by one of the States concerned, the Committee of Ministers, by analogy with Article 32(2) and (3) and Article 54, would seem to be the proper organ for taking suitable measures.[343] There is no express provision on this in the Convention. For such a case it would be natural that the Commission should be competent to bring the non-compliance before the Committee. It is self-evident that the Commission would have to investigate thoroughly whether the settlement really has not been complied with. The defaulting State would therefore first have to be given an opportunity to prove adequately that it *has* complied with the obligations ensuing from the settlement. If in the Commission's opinion it does not succeed in proving this, the latter organ must be able to undertake further steps in the matter. The Commission is the most suitable organ for this, because it has usually been involved very closely in the establishment of the settlement, its duty being the protection of the public interest. It would be highly inefficient to demand that an application should be lodged again, even apart from the question of whether the admissibility conditions set in the Convention could then again be complied with in all cases. Moreover, a premium would be put on non-compliance with the settlement if a State could thus defer its condemnation for a considerable time, because the whole procedure would have to be gone through again from the beginning.

The construction here proposed would, however, require an amendment of the Convention, since it does not give the Commission such power, and its

---

342. This competence of the Commission has also been provided for in Article 6 of Protocol no. 8.
343. In this context see also Rule 48(3) of the Rules of Court, which provides that the Chamber of the Court, when it decides to strike a case off the list, informs the Committee of Ministers in order to enable them to supervise "in accordance with Article 54 of the Convention" the execution of any undertakings which may be attached to striking a case off the list.

role as Public Prosecutor is not implied in the Commission's functions as regulated in the Convention. It would seem to be possible in the present circumstances that one of the contracting States may submit non-compliance with a friendly settlement to the Committee. In fact, as members of the Council of Europe the contracting States may take the initiative for the much more far-reaching procedure of expulsion of a member State from the organization under Article 8 of the Statute of the Council of Europe, when the latter member State has seriously violated its engagements concerning human rights and fundamental freedoms. The contracting States therefore must certainly also be considered authorized to submit non-compliance with a friendly settlement to the Committee of Ministers in order to try, through that organ, to induce the State in question to comply with its obligations under the settlement. In view thereof it would be advisable if in the settlement resolution, when stating that no further steps in the respective case are necessary, the Committee of Ministers were to reserve to itself the right to take appropriate measures at a later date if one of the two parties does not comply with its obligations.

In general the Commission has been much less closely involved in the above-mentioned non-official arrangements. In such circumstances the case may already be struck off the list before there is a decision on admissibility, or at a time when the examination of the merits has not yet advanced very far, so that there is as yet little clarity as to whether there has been a violation of the Convention. On the other hand, a non-official settlement may also be reached when the Commission's examination of the merits is quite complete, or almost so. It must therefore be determined for each individual case what is the best solution if such a settlement is not complied with by the contracting State in question. When a thorough examination of the merits has not yet taken place, it would seem to be most appropriate for the Commission to place the case on the list again when "the circumstances of the case as a whole justify such restoration".[344] The consequence of this is that the original application as a whole is resuscitated, so that no additional difficulties may arise in connection with the admissibility conditions. Here again, however, the Commission will first have to ascertain whether the settlement has really not been complied with, and it will therefore have to give the State concerned an opportunity to prove the contrary.

---

344. See *Case-Law Topics*, No. 3, *supra* note 32, pp. 31-32.

CHAPTER III

THE EXAMINATION OF A CASE BY THE EUROPEAN COURT OF HUMAN RIGHTS

§ 1. INTRODUCTION

After an application has been declared admissible by the Commission and attempts to reach a friendly settlement have failed, within a period of three months from the date on which the Commission has transmitted its report to the Committee of Ministers, the case may be referred to the European Court of Human Rights (Arts 32(1) and 47). The following may bring a case before the Court: (1) the Commission, (2) the contracting State of which the alleged victim is a national, (3) the contracting State which has brought the case before the Commission and (4) the contracting State against which the complaint is directed (Art. 48).

A case can be dealt with by the Court only if the State against which the complaint is directed has previously recognized in a declaration the jurisdiction of the Court as compulsory or accepts *ad hoc* the Court's jurisdiction (Art. 48 in conjunction with Art. 46).

The decision of the Court is binding on the parties (Art. 53) and no appeal lies against it (Art. 52). Under certain conditions the Court may afford just satisfaction to the injured original applicant, to be paid by the defaulting State (Art. 50).

The Committee of Ministers supervises the execution of the Court's decisions (Art. 54).

§ 2. QUESTIONS OF ADMISSIBILITY AND JURISDICTION IN THE PROCEEDINGS BEFORE THE COURT

1. As has already been observed with respect to admissibility conditions in the proceedings before the Commission, the distinction between admissibility and jurisdiction is not always strictly observed.[1] Among the authors on the subject and in the case-law there exist great differences of opinion as to when the non-observance of a procedural requirement must induce a court to consider that it has no jurisdiction, and when it should declare the application to be inadmissible.[2] In the following discussion of questions of admissibility and jurisdiction in the proceedings before the Court it should be borne in

1. See *supra* pp. 67-68.
2. See P. van Dijk, *Judicial Review of Governmental Action and the Requirement of an Interest to Sue*, Alphen a/d Rijn 1980, pp. 11-12.

mind that on some points there will not always be agreement on the question of whether a specific issue is a matter of jurisdiction or rather of admissibility.

2. The following procedural requirements may come up in the proceedings before the Court: (1) the case must have been brought before the Commission and must have been declared admissible; (2) the attempts of the Commission to reach a friendly settlement must have failed; (3) the case must have been referred to the Court within a period of three months from the date of the transmission of the Commission's report to the Committee of Ministers; (4) this must have been done by the Commission or by one of the States which are competent to do so under Article 48; and (5) the respondent State must have recognized the Court's jurisdiction as compulsory.

It is self-evident that no case could be submitted until the Court existed as such. Article 56(2) of the Convention states that no case can be brought before the Court before the first election of the members of the Court. The first paragraph of the same article provides that the first election of the members of the Court takes place after at least eight States have made the declaration concerning the recognition of the Court's jurisdiction. This condition was fulfilled on 3 September 1958, when Austria and Iceland as the seventh and the eighth State respectively made this declaration. In January 1959 the first election of the members took place and on 20 April 1959 the Court was inaugurated officially.

2.1. The case must have passed through the whole procedure before the Commission and must have been submitted to the Court within a period of three months from the date of the transmission of the report to the Committee of Ministers

1. A case cannot be submitted directly to the Court. From Articles 32(1) and 47 the intention of the drafters of the Convention is clear that an application must have passed through the whole procedure before the Commission before it can be dealt with by the Court. Article 47 provides expressly that the Court may only deal with a case after the Commission has acknowledged the failure of efforts to reach a friendly settlement, and impliedly that the Commission must first have submitted its report on the merits of the case. Applications that have been declared inadmissible by the Commission cannot be brought before the Court, for a declaration of inadmissibility by the Commission is final.[3]

2. The period of three months referred to in Articles 32 and 47 commences on the date of the transmission of the Commission's report to the Committee

---

3.   See *supra* p. 66.

of Ministers. In the *Lawless* Case the report had been adopted by the Commission on 19 December 1959, but it had been transmitted to the Committee, and also to the Irish Government, on 1 February 1960. In view of this delay, in a preliminary objection Ireland asked the Court to declare that it had no jurisdiction, since the Commission had not proved that during this delay it had not deliberated on referring the case to the Court. In consequence of this the Irish Government felt that it had been brought into an unfavourable position in relation to the Commission, which would be contrary to the principle of equality that ensues from the spirit of the Convention.[4]

The Commission took the view that not a single provision of the Convention obliges it to transmit the report immediately after adoption, and that, since Article 31(3) permits it, in transmitting the report, to make proposals to the Committee of Ministers, it may also deliberate for some time after adoption of the report.[5] The Irish Government later withdrew its objection and the Court therefore did not pronounce on this point.[6] The text of the Convention appears to confirm the Commission's view. On this point no further difficulties have arisen.

2.2. The jurisdiction of the Court *ratione personae*: active legitimation

1. The jurisdiction of the Court *ratione personae* is regulated by the previously mentioned Article 48 of the Convention. Between the competence to bring a case before the Court and the right to submit a complaint to the Commission there exist considerable differences. Although the former competence also differs considerably from traditional international law, in this respect the Convention goes much less far than in the regulation of the right of complaint in the first stage of the procedure. From Article 48 it appears in the first place that, unlike the situation with respect to the right to submit a complaint to the Commission, not every contracting State may bring an alleged violation of the Convention before the Court. A State bringing a case before the Court has to prove either that the alleged victim (the original applicant) is its national, or that it has submitted the case to the Commission, or that it is the State against which the complaint has been lodged. Secondly - and this difference is much more striking - an individual cannot bring a case before the Court. This appears not only from Article 48, but also expressly from Article 44: "Only the High Contracting Parties and the Commission shall have the right to bring a case before the Court".

---

4. Report of 19 December 1959, *Lawless*, B.1 (1960-61), pp. 212-214.
5. *Ibidem*, pp. 237-241.
6. Judgment of 14 November 1960, *Lawless*, A.1 (1960-61), p. 10.

2. When the Convention was drafted, the idea of also conferring *locus standi* before the European Court of Human Rights upon individuals was found not to be feasible. This is not very surprising, if one bears in mind that at that time the idea was rather revolutionary and that the jurisdiction of the Court would not be confined to matters of a mainly technical character, but might encroach on matters which are among the most essential interests of States.

One may ask oneself whether, considering the present state of affairs within the Council of Europe, the situation is still justifiable that the person the protection of whose rights is the very aim of the Convention - the individual - is not a party to this very important last stage of the proceedings provided for.[7] Conferment upon the individual of *locus standi* before the European Court of Human Rights would seem desirable from the viewpoint of effective protection of human rights.[8] This would, however, require an amendment of the Convention, and it appears from the discussion that the contracting States are not prepared to agree on such an amendment at the moment.[9] Even if such an amendment of the Convention could be realized, it would not improve the situation if conferment of *locus standi* were to have the consequence that some of the States which now recognize the jurisdiction of the Court would no longer be prepared to do so, because they fear submission to the Court of a number of applications which are directed against them and which in their opinion are ill-founded or have already been considered by the Court in other cases, and therefore should be dealt with by the Committee of Ministers. If that were the result, the present situation is preferable, where an alleged breach of the Convention by a contracting State may be submitted to the Court in the case of all twenty-two contracting States, albeit that the initiative for such a procedure cannot be taken by the alleged victim himself.

Moreover, the disadvantages for the legal protection of the individual attached to the present situation should not be dramatized, since besides the States concerned the Commission is also competent to submit the case to the Court. In practice, in almost all cases the Commission is found to be the organ which brings a case before the Court in the interest of an individual. Formally, according to Article 48, the contracting State which has submitted the case to the Commission and the contracting State of which the alleged victim is a national[10] are also competent to refer the case to the Court. With respect to the first-mentioned category of States it has already been observed above that States as a rule are inclined to file an application with the

---

7. On the position of the individual in the proceedings before the Court, see also *infra* pp. 164-171.
8. See *infra* pp. 164-166.
9. In May 1989 the Steering Committee for Human Rights decided to remove from its agenda the subject of conferment upon the individual of *locus standi* before the European Court of Human Rights until May 1990.
10. The latter situation occurred for the first time in the *Soering* Case; see the judgment of 7 July 1989, A.161 (1989), where the Federal Republic of Germany referred the case to the Court, after the respondent State had done so.

Commission only if it concerns a violation in relation to persons who are their nationals or with whom they have at least a special link.[11] Applications in which States speak up for specific persons who are not their nationals, and with whom they do not have any other special link, are therefore rare. Such a case has not yet been brought before the Court. As to the second category of States - States of which the alleged victims are nationals -, in practice the great majority of cases is precisely formed by complaints of individuals against the State of which they are a national. In all those cases the State of which the victim is a national and the respondent State are therefore the same. Of course the respondent State does not take into account the interests of the individual applicant when considering whether it is going to bring the case before the Court. So far only one inter-State case has been referred to the Court.[12] Consequently, the majority of cases dealt with by the Court have been submitted to the Court by the Commission.[13] When deciding on whether to refer the case to the Court the Commission will take into consideration also the interests of the original individual applicant.

3. When the Commission brings a case before the Court, it does so by virtue of its authority to represent the public interest.[14] Waldock, the then President of the Commission, stated in connection with the first case dealt with by the Court that the Commission brings a case before the Court

on behalf of the governments and peoples of all the member countries of the Council of Europe.[15]

This is implied in the definition of the duty of the Commission in Article 19 of the Convention: "To ensure the observance of the engagements undertaken by the High Contracting Parties in the present Convention." The special position of the Commission in the proceedings before the Court will be further elaborated on below.[16]

The Commission has full discretion whether to refer a case to the Court. The Convention does not contain a single provision about this. That the Commission itself also assumes full discretion in the matter is evident from the following words of its then President:

When we bring a case before the Court, we do so simply because we think that the appropriate tribunal for deciding the case is the Court rather than the Committee of Ministers.[17]

This shows that the criterion applied by the Commission is whether it believes that this particular case lends itself better for a decision by a judicial or by a political organ. The former will be the case in particular when an

---

11. See *supra* p. 35.
12. Appl. 5310/71, *Ireland v. United Kingdom*, *Yearbook* XV (1972), p. 76.
13. See *infra* Appendix III.
14. See Waldock, the then President of the Commission, *Lawless*, B.1 (1960-61), p. 245.
15. *Ibidem*, p. 207.
16. See *infra* pp. 161-164.
17. B.1 (1960-61), p. 266.

application raises questions of principle, which are of essential importance for the interpretation and the application of the Convention in general.

This was the situation, for instance, in the *Lawless* Case. There the question was, among other things, what circumstances justify derogation by a State from its engagements under the Convention, *i.e.* a question concerning the interpretation of Article 15. The Commission had been greatly divided on this issue. Despite the fact that a majority had come to the conclusion that there had been no violation of the Convention, it resolved to bring the case before the Court, the motivation being that

> the present case raises issues which are of fundamental importance in the application of the Convention.[18]

This is the most frequent reason why the Commission refers a case to the Court.[19] Another factor which sometimes plays a part is the fact that the Commission is greatly divided internally on the question of whether in the case concerned there has been a violation of the Convention.[20]

The Commission's policy has sometimes been criticized. It has been stated that the Commission makes too little use of its competence to refer cases to the Court.[21] However, as with the Commission's policy concerning admissibility, and probably for approximately the same reasons, with respect to its policy in this matter a significant change has taken place in the sense that gradually it has brought more cases before the Court. Thus, in the period from 1959 to 1968 the Court could give judgment in only two cases, although 49 applications had been declared admissible by the Commission in that period. From 1968 up to the end of 1988, 138 cases were decided by the Court, while 30 more cases are pending before the Court. Out of this total of 138 cases, 133 were (partly) referred to the Court either by the Commission alone or by the Commission together with a State.[22] This changing policy of the Commission has had the result that in a greater number of cases the final decision is taken in a way more satisfactory from the viewpoint of legal protection, *viz.* by an independent tribunal. Furthermore it enables the Court to elaborate in greater detail the often vague provisions of the Convention, a circumstance which promotes an effective implementation of the Convention.

In the *Axen* Case the Government of the Federal Republic of Germany

---

18. Report of 19 December 1959, B.1 (1960-61), p. 206.
19. See, *e.g.*, report of the Commission of 24 June 1965, *Belgian Linguistic Case*, B.3 (1965-67), p. 384; report of 1 April 1966, *Wemhoff*, B.5 (1969), pp. 207-208; report of 27 May 1974, *Swedish Engine Drivers' Union*, B.18 (1977), pp. 104-105; report of 17 July 1974, *Schmidt and Dahlström*, B.19 (1977), p. 95; report of 14 December 1976, *König*, B.25 (1982), p. 10; report of 9 March 1977, *Klass and others*, B.26 (1982), p. 74; report of 18 May 1977, *Times Newspapers Ltd. and others*, B.28 (1982), p. 305; report of 14 December 1979, *Le Compte, Van Leuven and De Meyere*, B.38 (1984), p. 97; report of 8 December 1982, *De Cubber*, B.69 (1988), p. 8. The Commission does not always explicitly give the reasons for referring a case to the Court.
20. See, *e.g.*, report of 24 June 1965, *Belgian Linguistic Case*, B.3 (1965-67), p. 384; report of 1 October 1968, *Delcourt*, B.9 (1970), p. 134.
21. See, *e.g.*, F.G. Jacobs, The European Convention on Human Rights, Oxford 1985, p. 262.
22. For this, see Appendix III. In these numbers the judgments of the Court ex Article 50 of the Convention are excluded.

138

contested the expediency of referring the present case to the Court. The Court considered

> that it is not part of its function to evaluate the expediency of the decision to bring a case before it. In this domain the Commission exercises an autonomous power conferred on it by Article 48, paragraph (a), of the Convention; the same is true, moreover, of the Contracting States listed in paragraphs (b), (c) and (d).[23]

2.3. The jurisdiction of the Court *ratione personae*: passive legitimation

1. Article 48 also regulates the jurisdiction of the Court *ratione personae* with respect to the respondent State. A case can be brought before the Court only on condition that the respondent State is subject to the compulsory jurisdiction of the Court or consents *ad hoc* to the case being brought before the Court.

A State may submit to the jurisdiction of the Court by depositing with the Secretary General of the Council of Europe a so-called "optional declaration", in which it recognizes as compulsory *ipso facto* and without special agreement the jurisdiction of the Court in all matters concerning the interpretation and application of the Convention (Art. 46(1)). At the present moment all twenty three contracting States have made such a declaration. Turkey has done so just before the end of 1989.[24]

2. The declaration of Article 46(1) may be made unconditionally or on condition of reciprocity on the part of all or certain of the other contracting States. It may be made for a specified period or for an indefinite time (Art. 46(2)). Most of the contracting States which have submitted to the jurisdiction of the Court have made the declaration on condition of reciprocity.[25]

The condition of reciprocity, which is customary in general international law and makes good sense there because the decisions concern disputes about legal rules which call reciprocal rights into existence for States, is not in keeping with the objective character of the European Convention and the resulting collective guarantee by the contracting States of the rights and freedoms set forth in the Convention.[26] From that viewpoint it would be preferable that the contracting States should no longer include this condition in their declaration under Article 46(1), or that the phrase in question should be cancelled from Article 46(2). This might, however, lead to a situation in which a contracting State might bring a supposed violation of the Convention by another contracting State before the Court, while its own acts could not be examined against its will by the Court for their conformity with the Convention because it has not in advance submitted to the jurisdiction of the Court. Such an unequal position would not be acceptable for most States. The

---

23. Judgment of 8 December 1983, A.72 (1984), p. 11.
24. See Council of Europe, *Collected Texts*, Strasbourg 1987, p. 74.
25. *Ibidem.*
26. See *supra* pp. 33-34.

139

objective character of the supervision as provided for in the Convention will therefore not be done full justice to until ratification of the Convention by a State shall at the same time imply recognition of the Court's jurisdiction.[27] The whole problem of the condition of reciprocity would thus be eliminated. Since most of the contracting States have up to now still tied their recognition of the jurisdiction of the Court to a specific time-limit, the feasibility of such a compulsory jurisdiction of the Court must be doubted at the moment. In fact, here again it must be said that the present imperfect situation is to be preferred to that in which the jurisdiction of the Court would indeed be compulsory, but in which the Convention would be denounced by some contracting States as a result.[28]

The condition of reciprocity of course cannot be invoked against the Commission when it refers a case to the Court. In fact, the Commission cannot make a declaration as referred to in Article 46, nor can it ever get into the position of a respondent party before the Court, so that there is no question of reciprocity. When Denmark - probably erroneously - disputed via a preliminary objection the right of the Commission to bring the case before the Court by invoking the condition of reciprocity,[29] this objection was hastily withdrawn again by the Danish Government at the instance of its own parliament.[30]

3. Most States make the declaration referred to in Article 46(1) for a period of five years at the most. So far only Ireland, the Netherlands and Switzerland have recognized the jurisdiction of the Court for an indefinite time.[31]

The declarations under Article 46(1) which were made for a specified period have so far invariably been renewed after the expiration of that period. In practice, therefore, the question has not yet arisen whether the Court has jurisdiction *ratione personae* when on the date of submission of the case the optional declaration is no longer in force, but still was on the date on which the original application was filed with the Commission. A grammatical interpretation of Article 48 might lead one to conclude that in such a case the date on which the case is brought before the Court must be considered as conclusive. However, considering the nature of the supervisory procedure, where the Commission and the Court do not act in two separate procedures, but in two successive stages of one and the same procedure, it would seem that a good deal may be said for regarding the date on which the application is filed with the Commission as decisive. In practice, non-renewal or withdrawal of the optional declaration for the purpose of making the submission of a given case to the Court impossible would be of little avail to

---

27. This would therefore be the same construction as that now laid down in Art. 24 with respect to the Commission.
28. Cf. *supra* p. 136.
29. See the Judgment of 7 December 1976, *Kjeldsen, Busk Madsen and Pedersen*, A.23 (1976), pp. 5-6.
30. *Ibidem*, p. 6.
31. See *Collected Texts, supra* note 24, p. 74.

a contracting State as even then a binding decision is taken in the case. Indeed, even if it is assumed that such a non-renewal or withdrawal would bar the jurisdiction of the Court, the case will then be decided by the Committee of Ministers. Denunciation of the Convention, too, cannot release a contracting State from the supervisory procedure of the Convention, because in that case Article 65 applies.[32]

As has already been said above,[33] a declaration as referred to in Article 46(1) has in principle retrospective effect to the moment of ratification of the Convention by the State concerned in the sense that a case which is brought before the Court after the declaration has been made may also refer to an alleged violation of the Convention that has taken place after the Convention came into force for the State in question, but before the date of its declaration under Article 46(1). This is not the case only when in the declaration the retrospective effect is expressly excluded. This may be looked upon as a general rule of international law, which has been expressed as follows by the Permanent Court of International Justice:

> The reservation made in many arbitration treaties regarding disputes arising out of events previous to the conclusion of the treaty seem to prove the necessity for an explicit limitation of jurisdiction.[34]

4. Instead of recognizing the Court's jurisdiction in advance for an indefinite number of cases by means of the so-called "optional declaration", a State may, according to Article 48, consent *ad hoc* to the consideration of a given case by the Court. This may be done explicitly by a unilateral declaration of the State in question. As an example of this, one may regard the declaration of the British Government in the *Tyrer* Case, where the latter consented to the consideration of that case by the Court after doubt had arisen as to whether the Court had jurisdiction on the ground of the optional declaration of the United Kingdom.[35]

Since Article 48 does not contain any further requirements of form as to the giving of such a consent, it must be assumed that this can also be inferred from the behaviour of a contracting State, such as the fact that it pleads its case on the merits without raising an objection as to the Court's jurisdiction on the ground that it had not given its consent. Such behaviour implies tacit recognition of the jurisdiction: the principle of *forum prorogatum*, which has also been recognized for the jurisdiction of the International Court of Justice.[36]

---

32. On this, see *supra* p. 11.
33. See *supra* p. 10.
34. *Mavrommatis Palestine Concessions* Case, *Publ. P.C.I.J.*, Series A, no. 2, p. 35.
35. Judgment of 25 April 1978, A.26 (1978), p. 12.
36. See S. Rosenne, *The Law and Practice of the International Court*, Leyden 1965, pp. 344-363.

2.4. The jurisdiction of the Court and the examination by the Commission of the compatibility of the application with the provisions of the Convention

1. In addition to the conditions discussed above, which are listed in the Convention specifically in relation to the procedure before the Court, may those procedural conditions on which the Commission has already decided explicitly or implicitly at an earlier stage of the procedure also be raised again before the Court?

The question as to the relation between the Commission's examination of admissibility and that of the procedural conditions applying to the procedure before the Court consists of two parts. In the first place the same questions of *jurisdiction* may arise in the two procedures, and in the second place the same questions of *admissibility* may come up. This latter case, which is to be dealt with in the next section, has occurred in the most pregnant way.

2. The case-law of the Court shows that problems may also arise in connection with a decision of the Commission concerning the compatibility of an individual application with the Convention *ratione materiae* and a judgment of the Court on its jurisdiction *ratione materiae*. It is true that the Commission formally does not make a distinction between questions concerning its competence and questions concerning the admissibility of the application, and that it puts its decision on whether a procedural condition has been fulfilled in the form of a pronouncement on admissibility.[37] It is evident, however, that the examination by the Commission and that by the Court deal with the same question, *viz.* whether the application concerns the violation of a right that is protected by one or more provisions of the Convention or the Protocols.

Thus, in the *Belgian Linguistic* Case,[38] Belgium asked the Court to declare that it had no jurisdiction *ratione materiae* on the ground that the right to receive education in one's own language, which had allegedly been violated according to the individual applicants, was not protected in the Convention and the Protocols.[39] The Commission requested the Court to reject the objection of Belgium concerning jurisdiction and submitted that when it has brought a case before the Court,

> the Court needs no more than a summary examination to enable it to verify that the complaints declared admissible by the Commission concern the interpretation or application of the Convention within the meaning of Article 45.[40]

With a reference to the provision of Article 49 of the Convention that "in the event of a dispute as to whether the Court has jurisdiction, the matter shall be settled by the decision of the Court", and on the ground of the consideration, taken from the text of Article 45, "that the basis of jurisdiction *ratione*

37. See *supra* pp. 67-68.
38. Judgment of 9 February 1967, A.6 (1967).
39. *Ibidem*, p. 13.
40. *Ibidem*, p. 17.

142

materiae of the Court is established once the case raises a question of the interpretation or application of the Convention", the Court concluded that it had jurisdiction *ratione materiae* in the case concerned.[41] What the Court actually did was no more than make, in the terms of the Commission, a "summary examination". However, this does not appear to have resulted from considerations inferred from the relationship between Commission and Court, which played an important part for the Commission, but rather from the fact that in this case matters were fairly simple. This is evident from the conclusion of the Court "that the jurisdiction *ratione materiae* of the Court is so evidently established in this case that it should be affirmed here and now".[42]

3. Here the Commission and the Court therefore reached the same conclusion concerning the compatibility *ratione materiae* and the jurisdiction *ratione materiae* respectively. However, what will the situation be if in one and the same case the two organs hold different views on the matter? In such a case an application might be rejected by the Court on a point on which the same application had been declared admissible by the Commission. In itself this is not a very felicitous situation in a procedure which must be regarded as forming a whole, and the Strasbourg organs should try to prevent such a situation.

However, in this context, too, one should keep in mind the above-mentioned distinction between questions of *jurisdiction* and of *admissibility*. Questions of admissibility in our opinion belong to the exclusive competence of the Commission, and the Court ought therefore to acquiesce in the decision of the Commission on such points.[43] The matter is, however, more difficult in the case of questions of jurisdiction, specifically the question of whether the application submitted actually concerns one of the rights and freedoms guaranteed in the Convention, *i.e.* the question as to the jurisdiction *ratione materiae*.[44] The possibilities for the Commission to prevent its decision and that of the Court from differing from it on this point are limited. In fact, it always takes its decision sooner than the Court. The Commission will of course take account as much as possible of judgments of the Court in preceding cases, but it is not obliged to do so. As regards the role of the Court, it would be conceivable for it not to consider questions concerning its jurisdiction *ratione materiae* on which the Commission has already pronounced explicitly or implicitly, thus bringing out the unity of the procedure and the connection between the organs involved. Reasons of expediency, which are very compelling in so lengthy a procedure as that of Strasbourg, would also

41. *Ibidem*, pp. 18-20.
42. *Ibidem*, p. 19.
43. See the next section.
44. As has been said, the Commission's decision on compatibility *ratione materiae* with the Convention in fact is a decision on competence, even though it is taken in the form of a decision on admissibility.

tell in favour of this.[45] On the other hand, it is asking a good deal of a judicial organ to give up the authority over its own jurisdiction *ratione materiae*. The Court can hardly be expected to acquiesce in a decision about this by a non-judicial organ, in this case the Commission. Moreover, the final result would still be invariably that the opinion of the Court on the matter prevails over that of the Commission. Indeed, even assuming that the Court should accept a decision of the Commission in which the latter considered an application as coming within the scope of the Convention, while in fact the Court itself takes the contrary position, in the examination of the merits the application will be dismissed on account of non-violation of the Convention, precisely because it refers to an alleged violation of a right which in the Court's view is not protected by the Convention or the Protocols.[46] The only difference would therefore be that the application is rejected in the one case for lack of jurisdiction and in the other on the merits.

As appears from the above-mentioned case-law, the Court indeed is not prepared to take a passive attitude *vis-à-vis* the Commission and itself decides on its jurisdiction *ratione materiae*.[47]

4. A similar all but passive attitude of the Court *vis-à-vis* the Commission becomes apparent in a question which greatly resembles that of the jurisdiction *ratione materiae*. This concerns the delimitation of the object of examination in the proceedings before the Court. In principle that object is formed by those elements of the original application which have been declared admissible by the Commission and have subsequently been brought before the Court.[48] In practice in a few cases doubt arose with respect to the decision of the Commission concerning the admissibility, as a result of which that decision required a further interpretation in order that the object of examination might be established with accuracy. In such a case, too, the Court acts fully independently and does not in advance consider the Commission's view of the matter as decisive, even though that view plays an important part in the determination of the Court's attitude.

The *Kjeldsen, Busk Madsen and Pedersen* Case, for instance, concerned the question of how the passage from the report of the Commission was to

45. See also R. Pelloux, "L'Arrêt de la Cour Européenne des Droits de l'Homme dans l'affaire Belge (Exception Préliminaire)", in *Annuaire Français de Droit International* (1967), pp. 205-216 (215).
46. See the finding of the Court in its judgment of 9 October 1979, *Airey*, A.32 (1980), p. 10: "the distinction between finding an allegation manifestly ill-founded and finding no violation is devoid of interest for the Court whose task is to hold in a final judgment that the State concerned has observed, or, on the contrary, has infringed the Convention".
47. See also, *e.g.*, the judgment of 28 August 1986, *Glasenapp*, A.104 (1986), p. 23; judgment of 28 August 1986, *Kosiek*, A.105 (1986), p. 19; judgment of 18 December 1986, *Bozano*, A.111 (1987), p. 18.
48. In this context see also the attitude of the Commission in the *Airey* Case, which, to say the least, is confusing: "In its report, the Commission expressed the opinion that, in view of its conclusion concerning Article 6(1), there was no need for it to consider the application under Article 8. However, during the oral hearing the Principal Delegate submitted that there had also been a breach of this Article"; A.32 (1980), p. 17. See also the judgment of 2 March 1987, *Weeks*, A.114 (1987), p. 21.

be understood according to which the point to be examined for conflict with the Convention was "the Danish legislation which provides for integrated sex education", not "the manner in which the instruction is given in different schools". A certain working document used in local schools, which the Commission had qualified as "legislation", according to the Court could not be regarded as such and therefore could only be taken into account "insofar as it contributes to an elucidation of the spirit of the legislation in dispute".[49]

Approximately the same case presented itself in the Case of *Ireland v. United Kingdom*.[50] The Commission had declared admissible the complaint that "the treatment of persons in custody ... constituted an administrative practice in breach of Article 3". The British Government submitted in the proceedings before the Court that a number of specific complaints did not concern a "practice", but were isolated cases and as such fell outside the object of the examination. The Court held that

> Article 49 of the Convention provides that the Court shall settle disputes concerning its jurisdiction. It follows that, in order to rule on this preliminary plea, the Court must itself interpret the above-mentioned decision [of the Commission] of 1 October 1972, in the particular light of the Commission's explanations.

The Court concluded that

> it has jurisdiction to take cognisance of the contested cases of violation of Article 3 if and to the extent that the applicant Government put them forward as establishing the existence of a practice.[51]

A decision tending more or less in the same direction as the cases just mentioned is the decision in the *Winterwerp* Case, where the Court held that the alleged violation of Article 6 fell under the object of the case submitted to it, in spite of the fact that at an earlier stage the Commission had decided that it should disregard the applicant's submissions about this, because they were assumed to form a separate complaint and, according to the Commission, had not been put forward until after the admissibility examination.[52]

In the *Barthold* Case[53] the Court considered that "this complaint falls outside the ambit of the case referred to the Court", because it concerned a complaint declared inadmissible by the Commission as being incompatible *ratione materiae* and did not merely amount to a supplementary legal submission or argument adduced in support of a claim already examined by the Court.

Also in the *Bozano* Case the Court declared that it had no jurisdiction, because "It is a separate complaint, and one which has been rejected in the decision setting out the limits of the dispute referred to the Court".[54]

---

49. Judgment of 7 December 1976, A.23 (1976), pp. 22-24.
50. Judgment of 18 January 1978, A.25 (1978).
51. *Ibidem*, pp. 61-64.
52. See *supra* p. 80. See also the judgment, there mentioned, of 6 November 1980, *Guzzardi*, A.39 (1980), pp. 21-23.
53. Judgment of 25 March 1985, A.90 (1985), p. 27.
54. Judgment of 18 December 1986, A.111 (1987), p. 27. Also: the judgments of 23 April 1987, *Erkner and Hofauer and Poiss*, A.117 (1987), p. 61 and p. 102.

In the *Bönisch* Case the applicant also contended a violation which had been declared inadmissible on the ground that it had not been put forward before the Commission at the start. The Court held that although the complaint in question was not mentioned in the applicant's written and oral arguments before the Commission, it had an evident connection with the complaints he did make; therefore the Court had jurisdiction.[55]

2.5. The examination by the Court in relation to the Commission's examination of admissibility

1. At first sight the relationship between the Commission and the Court as to admissibility issues seems to be clearer than is the case with respect to jurisdiction issues. In fact, the Convention itself seems to provide that the Commission is the organ competent to take decisions about admissibility. Nevertheless the Court considers itself competent to play an important part in this field as well. This approach of the Court was introduced in its decision in the *Vagrancy* Case and the *Ringeisen* Case.

In the *Vagrancy* Case the Belgian Government asked the Court to declare that it had jurisdiction to pronounce on the admissibility of the complaints to which the case related, and subsequently to declare these complaints inadmissible because they did not comply with the conditions mentioned in Article 26 of the Convention. The Commission's delegate submitted that the Court has no jurisdiction to pronounce on the decisions of the Commission concerning admissibility. On the ground of the wide formulation of Article 45, and with a reference to its judgment in the *Belgian Linguistic* Case mentioned above, however, the Court concluded that

> once a case is duly referred to it, ... the Court is endowed with full jurisdiction and may thus take cognisance of all questions of fact and of law which may arise in the course of the consideration of the case. It is therefore impossible to see how questions concerning the interpretation and application of Article 26 raised before the Court during the hearing of the case should fall outside its jurisdiction.[56]

This view of the Court would appear incorrect to us. In our opinion the Court in its judgment wrongly disregarded the fact that Article 45 cannot be viewed in isolation from the other provisions concerning the procedure in the European Convention.[57] Articles 24 to 27 are especially relevant in this context. In particular from Article 27 it seems to be evident that the Commission has exclusive competence with respect to questions of admis-

---

55. Judgment of 6 May 1985, *Bönisch*, A.92 (1985), p. 17; see also the judgment of 18 December 1986, *Johnston*, A.112 (1987), pp. 22-23.
56. Judgment of 18 June 1971, *De Wilde, Ooms and Versyp* ("*Vagrancy*" Case), A.12 (1971), pp. 29-30.
57. Art. 31(1) of the Vienna Treaty on the Law of Treaties provides as a general rule of interpretation: "A treaty shall be interpreted in good faith in accordance with the ordinary meaning to be given to the terms of the treaty in their context and in the light of its object and purpose". According to para. 2, "context" must be understood to include also the text of the treaty itself.

sibility.[58] This results from the fact that the drafters of the European Convention did not aim at a hierarchically organized division of competence between two organs, but juxtaposed the Commission and the Court, each of them with its own duties within the supervisory procedure, without one organ being subordinate to the other.[59] The Court, too, in its judgment held that decisions of the Commission "to reject applications which it considers to be inadmissible are without appeal as are, moreover, also those by which applications are accepted".[60] It is therefore all the more curious that immediately following this consideration the Court held that the decision of the Commission in which it declares an application admissible

> is not binding on the Court any more than the Court is bound by the opinion expressed by the Commission in its final report as to whether the facts found disclose a breach by the State concerned of its obligations under the Convention (Article 31).[61]

After reading the first quotation one would expect the Court to have reached the opposite conclusion.

The parallel here drawn by the Court between the *decision* of the Commission on admissibility and its *opinion* laid down in its report on the question of whether the facts disclose a violation of the Convention by the respondent State does not hold water in our opinion. The former has the character of a (quasi-)judicial decision, the latter serves only to inform the Court or the Committee of Ministers. They cannot therefore be equated as regards their legal effects.

Articles 28 to 31 inclusive would also seem to show that the Court has put too wide an interpretation on Article 45. In fact, it appears from the said articles that the case which, after having been declared admissible by the Commission, is brought before the Court or the Committee of Ministers, concerns only the question of whether the alleged violation of the Convention by the respondent State has taken place and whether compensation should be awarded.

Finally, the view taken by the Court leads to a dubious consequence from the viewpoint of the equality aimed at in the Convention, because the respondent State may now bring a positive decision on admissibility before the Court, but the State or the individual who has lodged the complaint may *not* do so with a negative decision on admissibility. Moreover, the answer to the question of whether the admissibility can again be considered now appears to depend on whether the case is submitted to the Court or is decided by the Committee of Ministers, because the latter organ deals exclusively with the

---

58. See K. Vasak, *La Convention Européenne des Droits de l'Homme*, Paris 1964, p. 160. See also the joint separate opinion of Judges Ross and Sigurjonsson in the *Case of De Wilde, Ooms and Versyp ("Vagrancy"* Case), A.12 (1971), p. 50, and the separate opinions of Judge Bilge *(ibidem*, p. 54) and of Judge Wold *(ibidem*, pp. 55-58).
59. Thus also the Commission itself by the words of its then President in the Case of *De Wilde, Ooms and Versyp ("Vagrancy"* Case), B.10 (1971), p. 209.
60. Judgment of 18 June 1971, *De Wilde, Ooms and Versyp ("Vagrancy"* Case), A.12 (1971), p. 30.
61. *Ibidem.*

merits and not with admissibility issues.[62] Equality would seem to require that the Convention should provide for the possibility of *appeal* to the Court from *all* decisions of the Commission or exclude reconsideration of admissibility issues altogether.

The above-mentioned viewpoint of the Court in the *Vagrancy* Case did not have any great consequences for that case. The Belgian Government submitted that the six-month rule of Article 26 had not been observed, but the Court concluded that Belgium had lost its right to raise this objection since it did so for the first time during the hearing before the Court, *i.e.* not in the procedure before the Commission or in the written proceedings before the Court.[63] The Court also held that the submission of the Belgian Government that local remedies had not been exhausted was ill-founded.[64] Ultimately, therefore, the Court reached the same result as the Commission.

This also happened in the *Ringeisen* Case. In that case, too, the Court considered that it was competent to subject an application admitted by the Commission to a renewed examination of admissibility, referring in so many words to its judgment in the *Vagrancy* Case.[65] Subsequently, however, the submission of the Austrian Government that Ringeisen had not yet exhausted all local remedies at the moment at which he filed his application, and that consequently, under Article 26, his application ought to have been declared inadmissible by the Commission, was dismissed by the Court in this case again.[66]

The viewpoint that it is competent to subject questions concerning admissibility to a renewed examination was once more confirmed by the Court in the *Klass* Case[67] and has since become constant case-law of the Court, as appears from a number of judgments which also contain decisions on matters of admissibility.[68]

Meanwhile the Commission has also contributed in a rather curious way to this development, which in our opinion is to be regretted. In the *Belgian Linguistic* Case the Commission had challenged the Court's jurisdiction in matters of admissibility. In the *Klass* Case, however, it took quite a different position. In that case the delegate of the Commission himself invited the Court to examine a particular admissibility condition by requesting the Court in his final submissions

---

62. See *infra* pp. 192-204.
63. Judgment of 18 June 1971, *De Wilde, Ooms and Versyp* ("*Vagrancy*" Case), A.12 (1971), p. 30.
64. *Ibidem*, pp. 33-35.
65. Judgment of 16 July 1971, A.13 (1971), pp. 35-36.
66. *Ibidem*, pp. 36-38.
67. Judgment of 6 September 1978, A.28 (1979), pp. 16-20.
68. See, *inter alia*, the judgment of 9 October 1979, *Airey*, A.32 (1980), pp. 10-11; judgment of 4 December 1979, *Schiesser*, A.34 (1980), pp. 16-17; judgment of 27 February 1980, *De Weer*, A.35 (1980), pp. 14-19; judgment of 22 May 1984, *De Jong, Baljet and Van den Brink*, A.77 (1984), pp. 17-20; judgment of 22 May 1984, *Duinhof and Duijf*, A.79 (1984), p. 14: in this case the Court, referring to the *De Weer* judgment, rejected the argument of the Government of the Netherlands "that the Commission was obliged to inquire *ex officio* into exhaustion of domestic remedies and that, consequently, the question should also be considered by the Court".

to say and judge
1. Whether, having regard to the circumstances of the case, the applicants could claim
to be "victims" of a violation of their rights guaranteed by the Convention.[69]

The Court accordingly found that the Commission concurred with the Court's jurisdiction in the matter.[70] The Commission thus reversed its previously taken position and apparently was prepared to share with the Court a competence which in our opinion, under the Convention, is exclusively that of the Commission. In this case again the consequences were not radical. In fact, with respect to the question of whether applicants could submit that they were victims of a violation of the Convention the Court came to the same affirmative answer as the Commission in an earlier stage of the procedure.

In the *Airey* Case the Commission, via a curious argument, tried to give a sound basis to the said change of position. In that case Ireland requested the Court to find that the Commission ought to have declared the application inadmissible on account of non-exhaustion of local remedies. The President of the Commission first of all submitted in his oral exposition during the proceedings before the Court that here no appeal against the decision of the Commission was involved, since the Convention does not provide for this, but that the Court "has full jurisdiction to determine all issues of fact and law that arise".[71] Subsequently he submitted that the local-remedies rule has two aspects, *viz.* a procedural aspect and an aspect concerning the merits. In the procedure in which the Commission decides on admissibility, in his opinion the local-remedies rule is a procedural rule. In the sequel to the procedure, and specifically in the proceedings before the Court, these facts assume a substantive character. To this he attached the following consequence:

were the Court, when examining all the facts of the case, to consider that, even with regard to the facts presented and arising before the decision on admissibility, there was still an indication of non-exhaustion of remedies, I submit that the Court would not then be saying "inadmissible because of non-exhaustion": it would be making a substantive decision that there were in fact remedies available at that time, and that therefore there would be no justification for proceeding further with the case. This would be a substantive decision that there was, at that stage, no breach of the Convention.[72]

According to this conception the question as to what is *the matter on which* the Court takes a decision is apparently subordinate to that about *the form in which* this is done. Indeed, in this view the Court in fact may take a decision on admissibility, provided that this decision is cast in the form of a judgment on the merits. In our opinion the local-remedies rule is not a question which also concerns the merits, *viz.* the question of whether there has been a violation of the Convention, but a mere admissibility condition, of which the rationale is that a State should not be subjected to an international procedure so long as not all possibilities for redress within its national legal

69. Judgment of 6 September 1978, A.28 (1979), p. 15.
70. *Ibidem,* pp. 16-17.
71. Council of Europe, *Cour/Misc.*(79)19, pp. 3-4.
72. *Ibidem,* pp. 6-7.

system have been put to the test.[73] If the application has been declared admissible by the Commission and if the latter, during its examination of the merits, has not found occasion to apply Article 29, the applicant party should be secure that the Court will consider the merits of his application and not the local-remedies rule or other admissibility questions. In this stage the respondent State can no longer ward off the complaint on violation of the Convention with the mere reference to a possible local remedy that has not been put to the test.[74]

In the *Schiesser* Case the Commission seems to have acquiesced completely in the line developed by the Court. In its report the Commission had stated that Schiesser's complaint concerning Article 5(2) ought to be rejected:

> because the Convention has been incorporated into Swiss law and takes precedence over Cantonal law, Mr. Schiesser should have raised this issue before the Federal Court. Having failed to do so, he had not ... exhausted domestic remedies in this respect.[75]

Nevertheless, the Commission requested the Court to decide:

> whether the applicant could nevertheless invoke Article 5(4),

and the Commission's delegate invited the Court

> on account of the failure to comply with Article 26, to decline jurisdiction to rule on the merits of the complaint relating to Article 5(4).[76]

2. The first instance in which the Court came to a different decision on admissibility from that taken by the Commission occurred in the *Van Oosterwijck* Case. This case concerned the complaint of a transsexual about the refusal of the Belgian authorities to adapt his civil status certificate to his change of sex. The admissibility issue concerned the question as to exhaustion of the local remedies. The Commission had found this requirement to be met and had declared the complaint admissible. The Court, however, decided that Van Oosterwijck had not applied for all the remedies existing in Belgium, or had not exhausted them in the right way. Consequently the Court decided that it could not deal with the merits.[77] Thus the Court, for the first time in the history of the Convention, passed a judgment that did not concern the merits. As said above, in our opinion the approach chosen by the Court is

---

73. For a detailed discussion of the rational and the procedural character of the local remedies rule, see Van Dijk, *supra* note 2, pp. 383-388.
74. That the delegate of the Commission did not distinguish correctly here between the admissibility and the merits is also disclosed, in our opinion, in his viewpoint in this same *Airey* Case with respect to Art. 29. From the fact that this provision speaks of "reject", and not of "declare it admissible", he inferred, *inter alia*, that "the approach which Article 29 is making for the Commission in respect of facts arising after the admissibility - indication of non-exhaustion, for example - is to treat this as a substantive matter for decision by the Commission when expressing its opinion, in effect, as to whether it should proceed with the application because there is no visible breach of the Convention"; Council of Europe, *Court/Misc.*(79)19, pp. 7-8. Considering the rationale of Art. 29, the fact that this provision refers expressly to the admissibility conditions of Art. 27, and the fact that in the system of the Convention the Commission does not have competence to decide on the merits, we believe this conclusion also to be wrong.
75. Judgment of 4 December 1979, A.34 (1980), pp. 16-17.
76. *Ibidem*, p. 17.
77. Judgment of 6 November 1980, A.40 (1981), p. 20.

150

not compatible with the Convention.[78] Apart from the arguments directly derived from the Convention, other factors also play a part in this context. In the first place, legal certainty requires that the individual applicant has clarity about the admissibility of his application in the Strasbourg procedure at a given moment. In our view this implies that admissibility ought not to be brought up again after the frequently prolonged procedure before the Commission, including a possible re-examination via the procedure of Article 29. Moreover, it can only be prejudicial to the confidence of the individual in the Strasbourg procedure, complex as it is already, if after a litigation of many years on the national as well as the international level he is informed by the highest international organ that the complaint must be rejected on the ground of an admissibility condition.

§ 3. THE PROCEEDINGS BEFORE THE COURT

1. The proceedings before the Court start with a request by the Commission or an application by a State having the right under Article 48 to bring a case before the Court. If there is doubt as to whether the applicant State falls under the terms of Article 48, the question is submitted by the President to the plenary Court for decision (Rule 34 of the Rules of Court).

The request or the application must contain the following data: the parties to the proceedings before the Commission; the date on which the Commission adopted its report; the date on which the report was transmitted to the Committee of Ministers; the object of the request or application (Rule 32(1) of the Rules of Court). By means of these data the Court is able to ascertain whether all the conditions for the filing of an application or request laid down in the Convention have been complied with. The requirement that the Commission, too, must state the object of its request was incorporated into the Rules of Court in 1972 and was intended specifically for the case in which the Commission has not concluded that there has been a violation of the Convention, but nevertheless brings the case before the Court. In such a case the respondent State ought to know what exactly the Commission aims at with its request, in order that the State may be able to prepare itself adequately for the proceedings before the Court.

When a State has brought the case before the Court, the name and the address of the person whom the State has appointed as its Agent in the sense of Rule 28 of the Rules of Court must also be mentioned (Rule 32(1) of the Rules of Court). This Agent may be assisted by counsel and advisers. The Commission delegates one or more of its members to take part in the consideration of the case before the Court; they may be assisted by other persons (Rule 29(1) of the Rules of Court). The Delegates are appointed by the Commission in a plenary session. They represent the whole Commission

---

78. See *supra* pp. 147-148.

and "shall act in accordance with such directives as they may receive from the Commission" (Rule 56(1) of the Rules of the Commission). In practice, therefore, it may happen that they are not prepared to decide on a given matter unless after previous consultation with the Commission.[79] The names and addresses of these Delegates must also be communicated to the Court (Rule 32(2) of the Rules of Court).

A copy of the application or request is transmitted to the members of the Court, to each of the States mentioned in Article 48 in so far as they themselves have not submitted the case to the Court, and to the person, non-governmental organization or group of individuals who lodged the complaint with the Commission under Article 25 of the Convention. The State against which the application is directed is invited to supply the Registrar with the name and address of its Agent. The other States here referred to are requested to inform the Registrar within two weeks whether they wish to appear as parties to the case brought before the Court. Thus also the person, non-governmental organization or group of individuals mentioned above are invited to notify whether he or it wishes to take part in the proceedings (Rule 33(3)(d) of the Rules of Court), and if so, the name and address of the person appointed in accordance with Rule 30. If the case has not been brought before the Court by the Commission, its members also receive a copy of the application (Rule 33(1)(c) of the Rules of Court).

After the request or the application has been filed and the constitution of a Chamber in the way described above has taken place,[80] the composition of the Chamber is communicated to the judges, the Agent of the respondent State, the Commission and the original applicant. It may be pointed out once more that the proceedings may also take place before the plenary Court, *viz.* if for the reasons stated above the Chamber relinquishes its jurisdiction in favour of the plenary Court.[81] The President of the Court or, if the Chamber has been constituted, the Chamber or its President may indicate interim measures to any Party and, where appropriate, the original applicant. This may be done at the request of a Party, the Commission, the original applicant or any other person concerned. The President, the Chamber or its President may also do so *proprio motu* (Rule 36(1) of the Rules of Court). As appears from the formulation of this provision, the Court may suggest interim measures but it cannot enforce them. The reason for the fact that the Court is empowered here only to make a recommendation, not to take a decision, is the circumstance that the Convention nowhere confers the right to order interim measures. As has been said, the same also applies to interim measures on the part of the Commission.[82] In fact, it would appear to be incumbent on the Commission rather than on the Court to recommend interim measures.

---

79. Verbatim Record of the public hearing by the Court, 5 October 1961, *De Becker*, B.2 (1962), p. 230.
80. See *supra* pp. 27-28.
81. See *ibidem.*
82. See *supra* p. 66.

The Commission is involved in the case at a much earlier stage. At that moment there is at least still some chance that imminent damage may be prevented or limited by the taking of interim measures. When the Court has ultimately been seised of the case, even more time has elapsed since the facts concerned have taken place. This probably accounts for the fact that the Court has not yet applied Rule 36 of its Rules. The amended Rule 36 provides that where the Commission pursuant to Rule 36 of its Rules of Procedure has indicated an interim measure, it shall remain recommended after the case has been brought before the Court, unless and until the President or Chamber decides otherwise or until paragraph 1 of Rule 36 is applied.

2. Like the Commission, the Court applies its rules in a flexible way. The Title in the Rules of Court dealing with the procedure indeed opens with the general rule that for the consideration of a particular case the Court may derogate from the provisions contained in this Title with the agreement of the Parties, and after having obtained the opinion of the Delegates of the Commission and the applicant (Rule 26 of the Rules of Court). In the provision relating to the use of the official languages before the Court the possibility of derogation is again mentioned in so many words. It is true that French and English are to be considered as the official languages, but the Court may authorize the parties, the applicant and any person assisting the Delegates of the Commission to use another language (Rule 27 of the Rules of Court).

3. In normal cases the examination of the case starts with written proceedings. The President of the Chamber consults the Agents of the parties and the Delegates or, if the latter have not yet been appointed, the President of the Commission and the original applicant, on whether they each consider a written procedure to be necessary. In the event of an affirmative answer by any of them, he lays down the time-limits within which memorials and other documents are to be filed (Rule 37(1) of the Rules of Court). Until the expiry of this time-limit the parties may file preliminary objections. The Chamber gives its decision on such objections after receipt of the replies or comments of every other party and of the Delegates of the Commission, or joins the objections to the merits (Rule 48 of the Rules of Court).

From the formulation of Rule 37(1) it appears to be possible that the proceedings before the Court may consist only of an oral stage. In the *Ringeisen* Case, for instance, the Court decided after consultation with the Agent of the Austrian Government and the Delegates of the Commission that no memorials need be filed.[83]

Memorials and other documents must, when they are submitted by a Party, by another State or by the Commission, be filed in forty copies. They are

83.   Judgment of 16 July 1971, A.13 (1971), p. 5.

153

transmitted by the Registrar to the judges, to the Agents of the Parties, to the Delegates of the Commission and to the applicant (Rule 37(4) of the Rules of Court). Subsequently the President of the Chamber, again after consultation with the parties concerned, fixes the date of the opening of the oral proceedings (Rule 38 of the Rules of Court).

4. The President of the Chamber directs the hearings. He also prescribes the order in which the Agents, counsel or advisers of the Parties, the Delegates of the Commission, any other persons assisting the delegates and the original applicant shall be called upon to speak (Rule 39 of the Rules of Court).

5. A Chamber may procure information in different ways for its examination of a case. The basis of the examination is undoubtedly the report of the Commission. Under Rule 29(2), whether a case is referred to the Court by a State or by the Commission, the Court will in any case take into consi-deration the report of the Commission. However, it is bound neither by the view of the Commission on whether there has been a violation of the Convention, nor by the facts as they have been ascertained by the Commission. But specifically as regards the latter aspect, the report constitutes an extremely important source of information, in view also of the way in which it was drawn up.

At the request of a Party, of the Delegates of the Commission, of the original applicant or of a third party invited or granted leave to submit written comments, or *proprio motu*, the Chamber may hear witnesses, experts or any persons in another capacity whose evidence or statements seem likely to be of assistance (Rule 41(1) of the Rules of Court). The expense of such persons is borne by the Party at whose request they have been heard, unless the Chamber decides otherwise. In other cases, the Chamber shall decide whether such costs are to be borne by the Council of Europe, or awarded against an applicant or a third party at whose request the person summoned appeared (Rule 42 of the Rules of Court). Such persons are summoned by the Registrar. In case of a communication, notification, or summons addressed to persons other than the Agents of the parties or the Delegates of the Commission, for which the assistance is deemed necessary of the government of the contracting State on whose territory such communication, notification or summons is to have effect, the President of the Court may, under Rule 31(1), apply directly to that government in order to obtain the necessary facilities. The Convention does not contain a provision requiring the contracting States to grant such facilities. Such an obligation may, however, be inferred from the spirit of the Convention. A contracting State may be expected to lend its assistance if the Court tries to arrive at as correct as possible an opinion on the case via normal judicial methods. The obligation to lend assistance results from the ratification of the Convention and the consequent recognition of the existence and the function of the Court.

In case of objections to a particular person as a witness or an expert, the Chamber decides. Persons who cannot in consequence be heard as witnesses may, however, be heard for the purpose of information (Rule 44 of the Rules of Court). Witnesses and experts must take the oath or make the declaration mentioned in Rules 43(1) and 43(2) respectively. Like other persons appearing before the Court, they may use their own language. At the session they may, subject to the control of the President, be examined by the Agents, counsel or advisers of the Parties, as well as by the Delegates of the Commission and those assisting them and by the original applicant (Rule 45(2) of the Rules of Court). The same applies of course to the judges, who may also address the Agents, advocates, or advisers of the Parties as well as the Delegates of the Commission and the original applicant and to any other persons appearing before them (Rule 45(1) of the Rules of Court). When, without good reason, witnesses or other persons, after having been duly summoned, fail to appear or refuse to give evidence, the contracting State to whose jurisdiction the respective person is subject may be informed. The same will apply when a witness or an expert has violated the oath taken or the declaration made by him (Rule 46 of the Rules of Court). As has been stated above with respect to the procedure before the Commission,[84] here again the effect of such a communication to the State in question will not be great if the national legislation does not provide for forcing such recalcitrant persons to appear before the Court and to give their evidence or make their deposition duly before the Court.

During the proceedings the Chamber may depute one or more of its members to conduct an investigation, to carry out an inquiry on the spot or to take evidence in some other manner (Rule 41(4) of the Rules of Court). For the assistance of a contracting State in such an investigation on the spot the President may apply to the respective government (Rule 31(2) of the Rules of Court). Here again the obligation of the contracting States to lend their assistance results from the mere fact that they have ratified the Convention.

Finally, the Chamber may ask any person or institution of its choice to obtain information, express an opinion or make a report upon any specific point (Rule 41(2) of the Rules of Court).

6. In most cases the proceedings before the Court conclude with a decision in the form of a judgment. Under Rule 53(1) of the Rules of Court the judgment must contain the following elements: the names of the President and the judges constituting the Chamber and the name of the Registrar; the dates on which the judgment was adopted and delivered; a description of the Party or Parties; the names of the Agents, counsel or advisers of the Party or Parties; the names of the Delegates of the Commission and of the persons assisting them; the name of the original applicant; an account of the

84. See *supra* p. 112.

procedure followed; the final submissions of the Party or Parties and, if any, of the Delegates of the Commission and of the original applicant; the facts of the case; the reasons in point of law; the operative provisions of the judgment; the decision, if any, in respect of costs; the number of judges constituting the majority; and, where appropriate, a statement as to which of the two texts, French or English, is authentic. Reasons must be given for the judgment of the Court (Art. 51(1) of the Convention). Any judge who has taken part in the consideration of the case is entitled to annex to the judgment either a separate opinion, concurring with or dissenting from that judgment, or a bare statement of dissent (Art. 51(2) of the Convention in conjunction with Rule 53(2) of the Rules of Court).

The judgment is signed by the President and the Registrar and is read out by the President or a delegated judge at a public hearing (Rule 55(1) and (2) of the Rules of Court). The text is submitted to the Committee of Ministers for the purpose of the supervision of its execution under Article 54 of the Convention (Rule 55(3) of the Rules of Court). Certified copies are sent to the Parties, to the Commission, to the original applicant, to the Secretary General of the Council of Europe, to the contracting States and to any persons who have submitted written comments, and to any other person directly concerned (Rule 54(4) of the Rules of Court). The latter category includes, *inter alia*, also any victim of the alleged violation specified in an application by a State.

Judgments of the Court are final (Art. 52 of the Convention). However, a request for interpretation or revision of a judgment may be addressed to the Court.[85]

Under Article 53 of the Convention parties have to abide by the decisions of the Court. They must therefore execute them. The Committee of Ministers supervises the execution (Art. 54 of the Convention). Especially with a view to its supervisory function under Article 54 the Committee adopted a number of rules in 1976.[86] In these rules it is laid down that, when the Court has decided that there has been a violation of the Convention and/or when it has afforded just satisfaction to the injured party, the Committee shall invite the State concerned to inform it of the measures it has taken in pursuance of the judgment of the Court (Rule 2). The Committee does not regard its function under Article 54 as having been exercised until it has taken note of the information supplied and, when just satisfaction has been afforded, until it has satisfied itself that this has actually been awarded.

If a State fails to execute a judgment of the Court, the Committee may decide on the measure to be taken by a two-third majority of the representatives casting a vote and a majority of the representatives entitled to sit on

---

85. See *infra* pp. 185-187.
86. See *Collected Texts, supra* note 24, pp. 196-197.

the Committee.[87] The Committee does not have the means to force a defaulting State to execute the judgment of the Court. In view of its position, however, the Committee, if it so desires, may bring considerable political pressure to bear on such a State, including suspension or even expulsion from the Council of Europe.[88]

7. Judgments and other decisions of the Court are published, as are the documents relating to the proceedings. With the exception of any document which the President considers unnecessary or inadvisable to publish, the reports of the Commission, too, are published, as well as the reports of the public hearings. Moreover, the President of the Court may order the publication of any other document which he considers useful. Documents which are not published may be inspected at the Registry, unless decided otherwise by the President of the Court either on his own initiative or at the request of a Party, the Commission, the original applicant or any person concerned. The publication of judgments, decisions, applications, petitions and the report of the Commission takes place in both official languages. The other documents are published only in the official language in which they occur in the proceedings (Rule 56(1) of the Rules of Court). In 1968 the Court decided that its judgments and decisions will be translated through the mediation of the Registrar in cases in which a State is directly concerned where English or French is not the national language or one of the national languages. In several cases this decision has been put into practice.

8. At the end of 1988, 147 cases had been dealt with by the Court. In these 147 cases the Court pronounced a total of 205 decisions, including decisions concerning preliminary objections, concerning the merits, concerning the interpretation of a judgment, and concerning just satisfaction under Article 50 of the Convention.[89] At the same date, 33 cases were still pending before the Court.

9. The Court may also pronounce a judgment by default. In fact, Rule 52 of the Rules of Court provides that where a party fails to appear or to present its case before the Court, a decision will nevertheless be taken. The case may therefore occur in which not a single party appears in the proceedings before the Court, but the Commission alone brings in arguments.[90] In practice, however, no such case has occurred as yet.

---

87. The Convention is silent on the voting procedure with respect to decisions under Art. 54. The Rules of Procedure of the Committee refer in general to Art. 20 of the Statute of the Council of Europe (Rule 10). It appears from Art. 20 that decisions concerning a number of expressly mentioned matters require unanimity or a simple majority. Decisions on all other matters, including therefore decisions under Art. 54 of the Convention, are taken with a two-third majority of the representatives casting a vote and a majority of the representatives entitled to sit on the Committee.
88. See Art. 8 of the Statute of the Council of Europe.
89. See the list of judgments of the Court at the end of this book, appendix III.
90. On the role of the Commission in proceedings before the Court, see *infra* pp. 161-164.

10. The procedure before the Court does not always conclude with a judgment properly speaking, *i.e.* with a decision on the merits. Like the procedure before the Commission,[91] that before the Court may be interrupted before a decision has been taken. Two different situations may cause such an interruption.

Rule 49(1) of the Rules of Court deals with the possibility of striking off the list a case which has been brought before the Court by a State, when that State notifies the Registrar of its intention not to proceed with the case and the other parties agree to this. In view of the formulation of Rule 49(1) it must be assumed that such a notification is possible at any moment during the proceedings and consequently even in the very last stage. No reason need be given. Usually, however, the wish not to proceed with the case may be due to the fact that the parties have reached some sort of a settlement.

And indeed Rule 49(2) of the Rules of Court provides that the Chamber may strike a case, brought before the Court by the Commission and/or a State, out of the list when the Chamber is informed that a friendly settlement, arrangement or some other solution of the matter has been reached.[92] After the notification by the State or the information about a friendly settlement the Chamber obtains the opinion of the Parties, the Commission and the original applicant on the matter and subsequently decides whether the discontinuance may be approved and the case may be struck off the list. If the Chamber agrees, it gives a reasoned decision. This is communicated to the Committee of Ministers in order to allow them to supervise the execution of any obligations which the parties may have undertaken in the settlement reached by them. This supervisory function of the Committee of Ministers runs parallel to that which is exercised under Article 54 of the Convention.

The Chamber, however, is not obliged to strike the case off the list in the above-mentioned circumstances. In fact, having regard to the responsibilities of the Court in pursuance of Article 19 of the Convention, the Chamber may decide that the consideration of the case should proceed (Rule 49(4) of the Rules of Court).

Rule 47(3) of its old Rules, which was almost identical with the present Rule 49(4), was applied by the Court in the *De Becker* Case. During the proceedings before the Court, Belgium made an amendment in its legislation on the point to which the complaint of De Becker related. By this, the Belgian Government argued, the complaint had been satisfied. The original applicant agreed. Belgium thereupon requested the Court to strike the case off the list, to which neither the Commission nor the original applicant objected. The Court held that under Article 19 it was competent to proceed

---

91. See *supra* pp. 128-130.
92. Three examples of cases which were struck off the list under Article 48(2) are: judgment of 3 June 1985, *Vallon*, A.95 (1985), p. 6; judgment of 30 September 1985, *Can*, A.96 (1985), pp. 6-7, where the Court indicated that the "case-law does already provide certain indications as to the answer to the question"; and the judgment of 27 November 1987, *Yaacoub*, A.127 (1988), pp. 8-9.

ex officio with the case in the interest of the maintenance of the Convention, but that in this case there was no ground for this, since the original difference of opinion underlying the case now only had historical importance.[93]

From the viewpoint of an effective maintenance of the Convention this decision of the Court was not very felicitous.[94] Although it was competent to stop the proceedings, the Court left out of consideration the fact that a declaratory decision may have a general preventive effect even if it concerns a situation that has meanwhile been changed. Moreover, the confidence in the remedy provided for in the Convention may be impaired if proceedings can be stopped in such an advanced stage on the ground of an eleventh-hour reaction of the respondent State, which in an earlier stage refused to agree to a settlement. In this way the Court might encourage the attitude that, during the negotiations about a friendly settlement in the procedure before the Commission, States will persist longer in their positions, because they know that they can always reconsider the matter in a later stage without any harmful consequences.[95]

In the *Skoogström* Case a friendly settlement between the applicant and the Swedisch Government was reached during the proceedings before the Court. The Swedish Commission for Revision of Certain Parts of the Code of Judicial Procedure had been asked to propose and work out the details for an amendment of the Code as required in order to put it beyond any doubt that it was in conformity with Article 5(3) of the Convention. In connection with this settlement the applicant was further paid a sum of SEK 5,000 for his legal costs. In the light of the settlement reached, the Swedish Government requested the Court to strike the case off its list. The Delegate of the Commission proposed that the Court should not strike the case off its list but should adjourn examination of the case "in order to ascertain what progress has been made in the work to amend the legislation, or alternatively to ascertain the timetable for the work which will lead to those amendments".[96] The Court, however, stated that it had no cause to believe that the settlement did not reflect the free will of the applicant. As far as the general interest was concerned, the court did not feel able to defer judgment nor did it see any reason of public policy sufficiently compelling to warrant its proceeding to consider the merits of the case and concluded that it would be appropriate to strike the case off the list.[97]

In a number of cases the Court refused to entertain the suggestion or the request to strike the case off the list. The situation in those cases differed to some extent from that in the *De Becker* Case. In the *Kjeldsen, Busk*

---

93. Judgment of 27 March 1962, A.4 (1962), pp. 23-27. See also the judgment of 26 October 1984, *Skoogström*, A.83 (1984), pp. 9-10.
94. On this, see also Van Dijk, *supra* note 2, pp. 351-352.
95. See in this respect Judge Ross in his dissenting opinion, A.4 (1962), pp. 28-33. And in the *Skoogström* Case the joint dissenting opinions of judges Wiarda, Ryssdal and Ganshof van der Meersch, A.83 (1984), p. 11.
96. Judgment of 26 October 1984, A.83 (1984), p. 9.
97. *Ibidem*, p. 10.

Madsen and Pedersen Case two of the original individual applicants (Mr and Mrs Kjeldsen) declared that they withdrew their complaint and further asked for a separate consideration of their case, but the Court refused to strike their case off the list. It held that it could not do so under Rule 47(1) (old) (the present Rule 49(1)), since that provision made it possible to strike a case off the list under certain circumstances after the intention not to proceed with the case was notified by a "Party which has brought the case before the Court, that is to say by an Applicant Contracting State in proceedings before the Court". In the Court's opinion the original individual applicants were not covered by this provision. Nor could a striking off the list be based on Rule 47(2) (now Rule 49(2)), which made this measure dependent upon the existence of a "friendly settlement, arrangement or other fact of a kind to provide a solution of the matter". The Court was of the opinion that this condition, too, had not been complied with in the case under consideration.[98]

On the same grounds the Court refused to strike the *Tyrer* Case out of the list after a declaration of the original applicant that he wished to withdraw his complaint. The Commission had opposed such a procedure, because in its view the wishes of the applicant in this case should yield to the public interest. A proposed amendment of the law which had been mentioned by the Attorney General of the Isle of Man did not, in the Court's view, constitute a "fact of a kind to provide a solution of the matter", specifically not because the situation conflicting with the Convention was not completely redressed.[99] For the refusal to strike the Case of Koç, in the *Belkacem and Koç* Case, off the list, the Court advanced almost the same arguments as in the *Kjeldsen* Case.[100]

In both the *De Weer* Case[101] and the *Guzzardi* Case[102] the respondent State submitted that the object of the complaint had ceased to exist. In the first-mentioned case the Belgian Government inferred this submission from the fact that the *Conseil d'Etat* had meanwhile nullified (a part of) the impugned legislation. In the other case the reason was the abolition of the measure which had given rise to the complaint (*viz.* enforced stay in the island of Asinara as part of a special supervision under which Guzzardi was placed). In both cases the Court considered, for practically the same reasons as in the cases just mentioned, that the conditions of Rule 47(2) (old) had not been satisfied, and for that reason it refused to strike the case off the list. In the *Guzzardi* judgment it was expressly added that "proceedings under the Convention frequently serve a declaratory purpose".[103]

In the *Bagetta* Case the Italian Government contended that the applicant could no longer claim to be a victim of a violation of the Convention owing

---

98. Judgment of 7 December 1976, A.23 (1976), pp. 21-22.
99. Judgment of 25 April 1978, A.26 (1978), pp. 12-14.
100. Judgment of 28 November 1978, A.29 (1979), pp. 13-16.
101. Judgment of 27 February 1980, A.35 (1980), pp. 19-20.
102. Judgment of 6 November 1980, A.39 (1981), pp. 30-31.
103. *Ibidem*, p. 31.

to two events that had occurred after the case was referred to the Court, namely the judgment of the Italian Court of Cassation holding that the applicant's prosecution was time-barred and the decision to recruit the applicant for a post on the railways, subject to a medical examination. The Court noted, however, that in the present case there had been neither a friendly settlement nor an arrangement. It considered that the two new facts brought to its notice were not of a kind to provide a solution of the matter and that a decision must accordingly be taken on the merits.[104]

§ 4. THE POSITION OF THE COMMISSION IN THE PROCEEDINGS BEFORE THE COURT

1. Of the various functions which the Commission exercises under the European Convention the description of the one which it fulfils in the proceedings before the Court is the most difficult. The reason for this is in the first place that the Convention does not make any reference to the fact that the Commission is involved in the proceedings before the Court.[105] The nature and the substance of the role played by the Commission during the proceedings before the Court have therefore become defined in particular in the Rules of Procedure of the Commission and the Rules of Court, and in the first cases brought before the Court. Secondly, a characterization of the function of the Commission after the case has been brought before the Court is problematic because on certain points this function differs rather considerably from the other tasks of the Commission, which *have* been laid down in the Convention.

2. In the stage of the proceedings here dealt with, the Commission does not take binding decisions, as in its *quasi*-judicial function during the examination of the admissibility or when it decides on the acceptability of the substance of a friendly settlement in connection with the requirements set by the Convention. Nor is its role in the proceedings before the Court comparable with its mediatory role in the attempts to reach a friendly settlement, its role in connection with the report referred to in Article 31(1) or the initiative it may take to refer a case to the Court.

The role of the Commission in the proceedings before the Court is best described as that of *amicus curiae*, an independent and impartial advisory organ with respect to the questions of fact and of law concerning a case before the Court. As stated above, the position of the Commission as an organ of the Convention entails that in the proceedings before the Court, even if it has itself referred the case to the Court, it does not appear as a

---

104. Judgment of 25 June 1987, A.119 (1987), p. 31.
105. The only provision in the Convention from which this might be inferred is that on the right conferred on the Commission in Art. 48 to submit a case to the Court.

party, but as a representative of the public interest.

At all events the Commission is not a party to the proceedings before the Court on the same footing as a contracting State may be. This is also reflected, for instance, in Rule 1 of the Rules of Court, in which the term "Parties" is defined as "those Contracting Parties which are the Applicant and Respondent Parties", and in the fact that a State brings a case before the Court by means of an application, while the Commission may do so by filing a request (Rule 32 of the Rules of Court). The role of the Commission in the proceedings before the Court has therefore been compared to that of an Attorney General.[106]

In this context it is to be noted that the Commission will play this part in a more or less active way depending on whether two States confront each other in the proceedings or States are involved as respondent parties only. In the first case there are two equivalent parties in the proceedings; these proceedings are therefore completely adversary. The Delegates of the Commission may keep somewhat in the background. If, however, the case is brought by the Commission or the respondent State before the Court for a decision and no other State presents itself afterwards as a party, an element is lacking for fully adversary proceedings, viz. a real applicant party, and the Commission will have to play a more pronounced role in order to restore the balance to some extent.[107] In the present text the last-mentioned situation will generally be assumed, because this occurs most frequently in practice.

3. Rule 56 of the Rules of Procedure of the Commission provides that the Commission "shall assist the European Court of Human Rights in any case brought before the Court". In addition, the provision that the Commission shall communicate to the Court, at its request, any memorials, evidence, documents or information concerning the case, with the exception of documents relating to the attempts to secure a friendly settlement, shows that the Commission is expected to assist the Court as much as possible (Rule 60 of the Rules of Procedure of the Commission). The Commission is of course eminently able to give such assistance. It has been very closely involved with the case during the entire procedure and at a given moment has been faced with the same task as that with which the Court is entrusted, viz. to give an answer to the question of whether there has been a violation of the Convention.

Despite the difference in character between the task of the Commission in the proceedings before the Court and that in the earlier stage of the procedure there is thus also an important element of continuity in it. The President of the Commission therefore declared in the Lawless Case:

> Our sole task remains that of ensuring the observance of the engagements of the High Contracting Parties undertaken in the Convention, which is also the task of the Court.[108]

---

106. Thus Waldock, the then President of the Commission; Lawless, B.1 (1960-1961), p. 360.
107. On this, see further infra pp. 163-164.
108. B.1 (1960-1961), p. 267.

The result, according to the President, is that

> Our function before the Court - as we see it - is therefore objectively to present to the Court the issues in the case, and all the relevant information which we, ourselves, have obtained concerning the case, and to assist the Court in its examination of the case.[109]

Before this, the President had already defined the Commission's task in the proceedings before the Court as

> to place before you all the elements of the case relevant for the determination of the case by the Court.[110]

From this definition of function is clearly appears that in the exercise of its function the Commission wishes to be objective and impartial. This was repeatedly emphasized by its then President in the *Lawless* Case, and in this respect again its functioning in the two stages of the procedure is marked by continuity. In fact, a different attitude would not be possible. If the Commission were to act as a party or as an advocate of one of the parties in the proceedings before the Court, this would seriously impair the confidence in the Commission of governments as well as individuals, in consequence of which it would not be able independently to perform its tasks in an earlier stage of the procedure, specifically those under Article 28 of the Convention.[111]

4. In practice the manner in which the Commission performs its function described above depends largely on the circumstances of each individual case. The Commission has assured itself a certain latitude in this respect. In his defence of the method chosen by the Commission in the *Lawless* Case, President Waldock submitted:

> I do not want to be understood to be laying down any general principle which might fetter or embarrass the Commission in formulating its submission in any other type of case.[112]

In the *Lawless* Case the Commission had made its submissions to the Court in the form of the following request: "May it please the Court ... to decide whether or not ...".[113] The Irish Government objected to this and submitted that the Commission ought to have confined itself to asking the Court to confirm the conclusions of its report (which in this case indeed were in favour of Ireland).[114] The Commission, however, relied on Articles 44 and 48 of the Convention, which it held did not imply any limitation with regard to the manner in which it lays its submissions before the Court. In addition the Commission explained that it had reached the conclusions in favour of Ireland by a bare majority, and submitted that

> in a case where the Commission has reached conclusions by a majority of eight votes to

---

109. *Ibidem.*
110. *Ibidem*, p. 262.
111. In this sense also Waldock, the then President of the Commission, *ibidem*, p. 234.
112. *Ibidem*, p. 266.
113. *Ibidem*, pp. 207-208.
114. *Ibidem*, pp. 220-221.

six, and where those conclusions are in favour of the Government, the appropriate form of the submission, in our view, is the form found in our Memorial.[115]

The difference of opinion within the Commission on whether or not there had been a violation of the Convention played still another part in the proceedings before the Court. According to the Irish Government the Commission was not authorized to draw the Court's notice to the minority opinions, but ought to have confined itself to the conclusion of the majority.[116] The Commission defended its action on the ground of the definition of its task under the Convention and submitted

> that we should be abdicating our responsibilities under Article 19 of the Convention if we were to ask the Court to consider only the opinions of the majority.[117]

It then added:

> As defenders of the public interest, we think it is our duty to place before you, with all objectivity and impartiality, all the elements of fact and law which appear to be relevant for you to take into consideration in reaching your decision upon the matters in this case.[118]

This objectivity and impartiality are essential to the role of the Commission before the Court, specifically also in connection with the position of the individual applicant in the proceedings before the Court, to which we now turn.

§ 5. THE POSITION OF THE INDIVIDUAL APPLICANT IN THE PROCEEDINGS BEFORE THE COURT

1. An individual who has applied to the Commission with a complaint about an alleged violation of the Convention cannot personally bring his case before the Court after his complaint has been declared admissible by the Commission and no friendly settlement has been reached.[119] For that he is entirely dependent on the Commission or the respondent State, or, in the rare cases where his complaint is not directed against the State whose national he is, on the latter State. And when his case is ultimately brought before the Court, the original applicant holds no initiative as to the presentation of his viewpoints concerning the case to the Court.

In 1982 the Rules of the Court have been changed in order to improve this unsatisfactory position of the individual as much as possible.[120]

2. Article 44 of the Convention provides expressly:

> Only the High Contracting Parties and the Commission shall have the right to bring a case before the Court.

115. *Ibidem*, pp. 265-266.
116. *Ibidem*, pp. 341-342.
117. *Ibidem*, p. 360.
118. *Ibidem*.
119. On this, see *supra* pp. 135-137.
120. See *infra* p. 165 and p. 170.

This English text of Article 44 has a somewhat less stringent formulation with regard to the role of the individual before the Court than the French version, which reads:

> Seuls les Hautes Parties Contractantes et la Commission ont qualité pour se représenter devant la Cour.

Relying on the French text, the Irish Government in the *Lawless* Case concluded that

> it was clearly intended that the individual would have no control of any kind, nor should he play any active part in the conduct of proceedings before the Court.[121]

The Commission, on the contrary, submitted that it is not possible

> to attribute to the authors of the Convention an intention to place an impenetrable curtain between the individual and an organ specifically set up as a judicial tribunal to make a judicial determination of his case.[122]

Article 44 furnishes little clarity about the exact position of an individual in the proceedings before the Court. It is, however, evident, specifically from the French text, that the individual has no *locus standi*; the *travaux préparatoires*, too, do not leave any doubt about this.[123] The text of Article 44, particularly the English version, does not, however, necessitate the conclusion that the individual cannot act in any way in the proceedings before the Court. And indeed, the Rules of Court contain several provisions pointing in a different direction, especially since their 1982 revision. Rule 30 is even specifically devoted to the representation of the original applicant in the proceedings before the Court. And under Rule 36 also the original individual applicant may request the Court to bring to the attention of the contracting State concerned any interim measures which seem advisable. Rule 41 includes the original applicant among the persons who may request the Court to obtain evidence. Under the same provision, he may be heard by the Court as a person capable of providing clarification of the facts of the case. Finally, he belongs to the category of persons and organs to which according to Rule 54(4) a certified copy of the judgment of the Court is sent and which may request the President of the Court not to make non-published documents accessible to the public (Rule 55(2)).

Besides the arguments inferred from the text of the Convention and of the Rules of Court (in its pre-1982 edition), it was particularly "general considerations of equity and justice" which induced the Commission to oppose the elimination of the individual from the proceedings before the Court, urged by the Irish Government in the *Lawless* Case.[124] According to the Commission a government may put forward new facts and arguments before the Court and is free to comment on and criticize the Commission's report. The Commission therefore found it difficult to imagine that in such a situation the original

---

121. B.1 (1960-1961), pp. 216-217 and 277.
122. *Ibidem*, p. 254.
123. Thus also the Commission in the *Lawless* Case, *ibidem*, p. 257.
124. *Ibidem*.

individual applicant should not have the right to inform the Court in one way or another of its viewpoint concerning new points of fact or law, or may not give his opinion on the statements and conclusions in the Commission's report:

> The Commission doubts very much whether the authors of the Convention can be understood to have intended to create such a marked degree of inequality in the presentation of two sides of a case to a judicial tribunal.[125]

In its judgment of 14 November 1960 the Court endorsed the view of the Commission. It defined the position of the original applicant as follows:

> Whereas, in the present case, G.R. Lawless, the Applicant, although he is not entitled to bring the case before the Court, to appear before the Court or even to make submissions through a representative appointed by him, is nevertheless directly concerned in the proceedings before the Court; whereas it must be borne in mind that the Applicant instituted the proceedings before the Commission and that, if the Court found that his complaints were justified, he would be directly affected by any decision, in accordance with Article 50 of the Convention, on the substance of the case.[126]

From this definition of the position of the individual the Court concluded that

> the Court must bear in mind its duty to safeguard the interests of the individual, who may not be a party to any Court proceedings, and whereas the whole of the proceedings in the Court, as laid down by the Convention and the Rules of the Court, are upon issues which concern the Applicant; whereas, accordingly, it is in the interests of the proper administration of justice that the Court should have knowledge of and, if need be, take into consideration, the Applicant's point of view.[127]

3. Since the individual cannot appear as a party to the proceedings before the Court and cannot therefore take the initiative to making submissions to the Court personally or through a representative, the question arose as to how the Court could then become informed of the views of the original individual applicant. The Court naturally knows the allegations of the original applicant with regard to the factual and legal aspects of the case as contained in the Commission's report. However, this does not yet mean that the original individual applicant - like the respondent State - has an opportunity to advance new factual or legal arguments before the Court or to notify his comments on or criticism of the Commission's report. The Court may hear the original applicant as a witness or as an expert under Rule 41 (Rule 38 old) of its Rules, but as a witness or as an expert one is not of course in a position in which one can notify and elucidate one's views with regard to all the aspects of the case.

The Commission, via its position in the proceedings before the Court, has tried to fill as effectively as possible the "gap" which arose in consequence of the absence of the original applicant as a party to the proceedings. Because of its conception of its task as "defender of the public interest", in view of which it considers that it must put forward all the relevant elements of the case,[128] it has made all efforts to do full justice also to the views of the

---

125. *Ibidem.*
126. Judgment of 14 November 1960, *Lawless*, A.1 (1961), p. 14.
127. *Ibidem*, p. 15.
128. See *supra* p. 163.

original applicant before the Court. To this end the Commission included in its Rules of Procedure the following provision:

> When a case brought before the Commission in pursuance of Article 25 of the Convention is subsequently referred to the Court, the Secretary of the Commission shall immediately notify the Applicant. Unless the Commission shall otherwise decide, the Secretary shall also in due course communicate to him the Commission's Report, informing him that he may, within a time-limit fixed by the President, submit to the Commission his written observations on the said Report. The Commission shall decide what action, if any, shall be taken in respect of these observations.

This old Rule 76[129] has been applied by the Commission for the first time in the *Lawless* Case. The Commission had sent its report to the original applicant and the latter had submitted his observations on it. Thereupon the Commission requested the Court's permission "to submit to the Court the Applicant's comments on the Commission's Report as one of the Commission's documents in the case".[130] The Irish Government disputed the lawfulness of the Commission's action. In the first place it inferred from Article 31(2) of the Convention that the report of the Commission should in principle remain secret. According to the Irish Government it is transmitted only to the Committee of Ministers, to the States concerned - which must not publish it - and, if the case is referred to the Court, also to the Court. Publication is possible only after a decision to that effect of the Committee or of the Court. In the opinion of the Irish Government the Commission therefore ought not to have sent the report to Lawless.[131] Furthermore the Irish Government submitted that in the proceedings before the Court the initiative for collecting new information is not to be taken by the Commission, but by the Court itself.[132] In particular it argued that an impartial organ such as the Commission cannot permit itself to receive the observations on its report from a party concerned in the case without impairing the confidence to be placed in it. The Irish Government raised the following question:

> How can that attitude of impartiality be maintained, particularly in the public mind, if there is any nexus between the Commission's own findings and the views or comments of the individual Applicant?[133]

From the submissions of the Commission and the preliminary objections raised by the Irish Government the Court deduced three questions about which a decision had to be taken. In the first place there was the question of whether Rule 76 of the Rules of Procedure of the Commission was generally compatible with the Convention. The Court held that it could not interpret the Convention in an abstract way,[134] and referred therefore to Articles 45, 47 and 53 of the Convention. Because of this, it did not consider itself competent to decide about the validity of a provision from the Rules of

---

129. This became later Article 61, and has, for unclear reasons, been taken out of the present Rules.
130. Judgment of 14 November 1960, A.1 (1961), p. 8.
131. B.1 (1960-1961), pp. 214-216.
132. *Ibidem*, p. 284.
133. *Ibidem*, pp. 289-290.
134. At that moment the Second Protocol was not yet in force.

Procedure of the Commission and came to the conclusion that it could not answer a question in so general a sense.

The situation was different for the second question, *viz.* whether the Commission had been permitted to send its report to Lawless or had acted contrary to the Convention in doing so. The Court first of all pointed out the public character of its proceedings in contrast with those before the Commission and the Committee of Ministers, which take place *in camera.* Indeed, the Court admitted, only the reports of the sessions and the judgment are published, and the publication of other documents requires the express consent of the Court. It is, however, necessary to distinguish between the publication of documents for which the consent of the Court is required, and the transmission of such documents to the individual applicant after the case has been referred to the Court, for which such consent is not required. As regards the latter aspect, in view of the importance of the proceedings before the Court for the original individual applicant, the Court concluded:

> that the Commission is enabled under the Convention to communicate to the Applicant, with the proviso that it must not be published, the whole or part of its Report or a summary thereof, whenever such communication seems appropriate; whereas, therefore, in the present case, the Commission, in communicating its Report to G.R. Lawless, the Applicant, did not exceed its powers.[135]

In addition to its own report, the Commission had also transmitted the observations of the Irish Government to the individual applicant.[136] The Irish Government had objected to this too.[137] However, in its judgment of 7 April 1961 the Court did not consider these acts as contrary to the Convention. It referred to its judgment of 14 November 1960, in which the Commission's right had been recognized "to take into account the Applicant's view on its own authority, as a proper way of enlightening the Court". The Court now further explained this and submitted that:

> this latitude enjoyed by the Commission extends to any other views the Commission may have obtained from the Applicant in the course of the proceedings before the Court.[138]

The third question concerned the request of the Commission for permission to submit the observations of the original applicant concerning its report to the Court. The Court observed that it was unable to decide on that request, since it had not yet been able to examine the merits. It therefore reserved to itself the right to do so in a later stage.[139] It actually did so in its judgment of 7 April 1961, when it decided:

> at the present stage the written observations of the Applicant, as reproduced in paragraphs 31 to 49 of the Commission's statement of 16th December 1960, are not to be considered as part of the proceedings in the case.

It added, however:

---

135. Judgment of 14 November 1960, *Lawless*, A.1 (1961), p. 14.
136. B.1 (1960-1961), pp. 348-351.
137. *Ibidem*, pp. 353-354.
138. Judgment of 7 April 1961, A.2 (1961), pp. 23-24.
139. Judgment of 14 November 1960, A.1 (1961), p. 16.

that the Commission has all latitude in the course of debates and in so far as it believes
they may be useful to enlighten the Court, to take into account the views of the
Applicant concerning either the Report or any other specific point which may have arisen
since the lodging of the Report.[140]

The Commission therefore keeps its own responsibility when it notifies the
Court of the views of the individual applicant.

Originally, this responsibility also existed when the question arose as to
whether a case could be struck off the list because some sort of settlement
had been reached. In relation to that question the Court used to take note
of the view of the original individual applicant in particular via the Commission. Problems could present themselves in such a case because the Commission on the one hand had to defend the public interest and on the other
hand did not want to lose sight of the interests of the individual applicant
and wanted to do justice to his view in the matter.[141] In the revised Rules of
Court Rule 49 provides that the Court, before deciding whether to strike a
case out of its list, consults also the original applicant directly.

4. Another method which the Commission has used to do justice to the views
of the original individual applicant in the proceedings before the Court
consists in inviting this individual to appoint a person who may be present
during the proceedings before the Court. This person should then put himself
at the disposal of the Delegates of the Commission in order to assist them
at their request. This method is based on Rule 29(1) of the Rules of Court
and was also defended for the first time by the Commission in the *Lawless*
Case.[142]

With regard to this again the discussion between the Irish Government and
the Commission was concentrated on the question of whether, when acting in
this way, the Commission could still be called impartial and objective. The
Irish Government thought not:

If the Commission should choose counsel for the individual Applicant as one of their
advisers to assist them in taking part in the deliberations of the Court, they would, in
the view of the Government, cease to command the respect that an impartial body such
as the Commission would be regarded as entitled to command.[143]

The Commission argued against this that it was precisely its impartiality and
objectivity and the interest of the administration of justice which demanded
this step from the Commission. Its President therefore declared that

we feel we should be failing in our duty if, when we think there are elements which it
is useful for the Court objectively to take into consideration in arriving at its judicial
determination, we do not take the appropriate initiative.[144]

On this point, too, the Court followed the Commission and found that

---

140. Judgment of 7 April 1961, A.2 (1961), p. 24.
141. An illustrative example is the action of the Commission in the *De Becker* Case, B.2 (1962),
pp. 212-216 and 270-280.
142. B.1 (1960-1961), p. 350.
143. *Ibidem*, p. 370.
144. *Ibidem*, pp. 365-366.

the Commission is entirely free to decide by what means it wishes to establish contact with the Applicant and give him an opportunity to make known his views to the Commission; whereas in particular it is free to ask the Applicant to nominate a person to be available to the Commission's delegates; whereas it does not follow that the person in question had any *locus standi in judicio*.[145]

In the *Vagrancy* Case the Court further developed its viewpoint as described above. In that case at a given moment the Commission intimated its intention to be assisted by the lawyer of the original individual applicants, in the sense that it wished this lawyer to give the Court a more detailed explanation of a number of points about which the Commission itself was insufficiently informed. The Belgian Government opposed the Commission's application of Rule 29(1) of the Rules of Court, arguing that Article 44 and the spirit of the Convention, which entail that individuals cannot appear before the Court, would thus be nullified. The Court, however, considered the intention of the Commission admissible:

Rule 29, paragraph 1, does not place any limit on the freedom of the Delegates in their choice of persons to assist them; and whereas, therefore, it does not preclude them, *inter alia*, from having assistance of the lawyer or former lawyer of an individual applicant.

It added to this:

the person assisting the Delegates must restrict himself in his statements to presenting to the Court explanation on points indicated to him by the Delegates, and this always subject to the control and responsibility of the Delegates. Whereas it is the duty of the Delegates to ensure the observance of this fundamental requirement by any person assisting them, in order to avoid any situation inconsistent with Article 44 of the Convention.[146]

In the *Golder* Case and the *National Union of Belgian Police* Case, too, the lawyer of the original individual applicants appeared as assistant of the Commission before the Court in the manner described above.[147] This method became constant practice. In the *Schmidt and Dahlström* Case Professor Schmidt himself, one of the two original applicants, elucidated as an expert some aspects of Swedish labour law before the Court at the invitation of the Commission.[148]

As stated above, the Rules of Court as revised in 1982 contain a separate Rule 30 regulating the representation of the original applicant. Under this Rule, therefore, the original applicant is in the position to present his own case or have it presented by his representative independently from the Commission. This independent position of the original applicant in the proceedings before the Court has been further elaborated in Rule 37 (written procedure), Rules 38 and 39 (oral proceedings) and Rule 41 (measures for taking evidence).

145. Judgment of 7 April 1961, A.2 (1961), p. 24.
146. Judgment of 18 November 1970, A.12 (1971), pp. 6-8.
147. *Golder*, B.16 (1973-1975), p. 233, and *National Union of Belgian Police*, B.17 (1973-1975), pp. 157-159 and 176-184.
148. See B.18 (1974-1975), pp. 122 and 126-136. On the foregoing, see also Council of Europe, *Human Rights Files; Outline of the position of the individual applicant before the European Court of Human Rights* (1), DH(78)3, Strasbourg, 28 March 1978.

5. From the above it appears that the main disadvantages attached to the system of the European Convention, according to which the individual applicant is not a party to the proceedings before the Court, have been eliminated in practice. This does not mean that the individual has fully assumed in those proceedings the place to which in our opinion he is entitled, considering the subject and the purpose of the Convention. In order for this to be achieved, the Convention itself would have to be amended on this point. The feasibility of this has been briefly discussed above.[149] The Court and the Commission seem to have gone as far into the direction of full participation of the applicant as the Convention allows.

§ 6. THE AWARD OF COMPENSATION UNDER ARTICLE 50 OF THE CONVENTION

1. When the Court finds that a violation of the Convention by a contracting State has taken place, under Article 50 it may afford just satisfaction to the injured party, provided that the consequences of the violation cannot fully be repaired according to the internal law of the State concerned.

The initiative for proceedings for the determination of just satisfaction lies with the original individual applicant as the person who may have been injured. Originally he had to address the Commission for this (or the Government of his national State, should it decide to refer his case to the Court), which then could present a proposal concerning just satisfaction to the Court in the document instituting proceedings or at any stage of the written or oral proceedings (Rule 47bis of the Rules of Court before the 1982 revision). However, since the 1982 revision of the Rules of Court, which introduced for the original applicant the possibility of making written and oral statements in the proceedings before the Court, he may submit such a proposal himself. Until the 1989 revision he could do so "at any stage of the written or oral procedure" (Rule 49 (old) of the Rules of Court). The revised first paragraph of Rule 50 provides:

> Any claims which the applicant may wish to make under Article 50 of the Convention shall, unless the President otherwise directs, be set out in his memorial or, if he does not submit a memorial, in a special document filed at least one month before the date fixed pursuant to Rule 38 for the opening of the oral proceedings.

The revised second sentence of the first paragraph of Rule 54 provides as follows:

> If, on the other hand, this question has not been raised under Rule 50, the Chamber may lay down a time-limit for the applicant to submit any claim for just satisfaction that he may have.

This revision makes it clear that in cases brought before the Court after 1 April 1989 it is only up to the original applicant to bring a claim for just

---

149. See *supra* p. 136.

satisfaction, and no longer to the Commission or the State which has referred the case to the Court. This seems also to imply that in inter-State applications no claim under Article 50 may be brought, since "applicant" in the Rules of Court refers to the applicant under Article 25 only (Rule 1(k) of the Rules of Court).

If the decision on the application of Article 50 is not taken in the judgment on the merits of the case, the Chamber reserves it in whole or in part and fixes the further procedure (Rule 54(1) of the Rules of Court). In that case, and also in the case that the claim by the applicant is brought after the judgment on the merits, the Chamber which rules on the application of Article 50 shall, as far as possible, be composed of those judges who sat to consider the merits of the case, even if one or more of them have ceased to be members of the Court (Rule 54(2) of the Rules of Court).

This is most appropriate from the viewpoint of procedural economy. These judges are best informed of the different aspects of the case, and for that reason seem to be the persons most competent to judge whether the application is well-founded and to determine the amount of the compensation to be awarded, if any.[150]

The same idea - viz. that the decision on compensation should be taken by the same body as the decision on the merits - was brought up explicitly in the *Ringeisen* Case. The Austrian Government submitted that the Court could consider an application for compensation only after it had been filed in the form of a new complaint under Article 25, subsequently examined by the Commission and finally submitted to the Court in accordance with Articles 47 and 48. For this, the Austrian Government also referred to Article 52 of the Convention, which provides that "the judgment of the Court shall be final". The Court held that the only purpose of Article 52 is "to make the Court's judgment not subject to any appeal to another authority"[151] and found that "in the interests of the proper administration of justice" it is preferable "that consideration of the reparation of damage following from a violation of the Convention should be entrusted to the judicial body which has found the violation in question".[152]

2. From the quotations given above, and also from the other case-law of the Court on this matter, it becomes quite clear that an application for compensation according to Article 50 is not considered as an independent procedure, but is dealt with as an element of a larger whole, of which the examination of the merits forms the first part. In the *Vagrancy* Case, the Court stated that the application for compensation is closely linked to the proceedings concerning the merits before the Court, and cannot therefore be regarded as

---

150. Rule 54(3) of the Rules of Court provides that the plenary Court may refer a case concerning Art. 50 to the Chamber which in the first instance had renounced jurisdiction in favour of the plenary Court.
151. Judgment of 22 June 1972, A.15 (1972), p. 7.
152. *Ibidem.*

a new complaint, to which Articles 25, 26 and 27 of the Convention apply. For that reason the original individual applicant did not need to exhaust once more the local remedies with respect to his application for compensation.[153]

In the *Neumeister* Case the Austrian Government argued that the Commission had committed an error by transmitting Neumeister's application for compensation directly to the Court, whereas it ought to have considered and examined it as a new complaint under Article 25. This complaint was assumed to concern the alleged violation of Article 5(5) of the Convention, in which it is provided that "Everyone who has been the victim of arrest or detention in contravention of the provisions of this Article shall have an enforceable right to compensation". The principal argument of the Court against this was as follows:

> the proceedings in the present case no longer fall within Section III of the Convention but are the final phase of proceedings brought before the Court under Section IV on the conclusion of those to which the original petition of Neumeister gave rise in 1963 before the Commission.[154]

3. Article 50 appears to imply that the decision on an award of compensation must be given together with the judgment on the merits. Rule 54 of the Rules of Court, however, leaves the moment of the decision on an award of compensation entirely open. If the Chamber of the Court which deals with the case finds that there is a violation of the Convention, the Chamber gives a decision on the application of Article 50 in the same judgment only if the question, after being raised under Rule 49, is ready for decision. As an example, reference could be made to the judgment in the *Golder* Case, in which the Court, after having found that there had been a violation of Article 6(1) and Article 8, decided unanimously "that the preceding findings amount in themselves to adequate just compensation under Article 50".[155] Decisions concerning Article 50 which were made simultaneously with the judgment on the merits are to be found also, *e.g.*, in the *De Weer* Case,[156] the *Artico* Case,[157] the *Guzzardi* Case,[158] the Case of *Schönenberger and Durmaz*[159] and the *Berrehab* Case.[160]

As has been said above, if the question of compensation has been raised, but is not yet ready for decision, the Chamber reserves it in whole or in part and fixes the further procedure. If the question of the compensation has not been raised, the Chamber lays down a time-limit within which this may be done by the original applicant (Rule 54(2) of the Rules of Court).[161] Owing to this very flexible arrangement the possibilities for raising the question of

---

153. Judgment of 10 March 1972, A.14 (1972), pp. 7-9. See also the judgment of 6 November 1980, *Guzzardi*, A.39 (1981), p. 41.
154. Judgment of 7 May 1974, A.17 (1974), pp. 13-14.
155. Judgment of 21 February 1975, A.18 (1975), p. 23.
156. Judgment of 27 February 1980, A.35 (1980), pp. 31-32.
157. Judgment of 13 May 1980, A.37 (1980), pp. 19-22.
158. Judgment of 6 November 1981, A.39 (1981), pp. 41-42.
159. Judgment of 20 June 1988, A.137 (1988), pp. 14-16.
160. Judgment of 21 June 1988, A.138 (1988), p. 17.
161. See, for example, the judgment of 28 June 1978, *König*, A.27 (1978), pp. 40-41.

compensation have been left as wide as possible. At the same time the interests of the respondent States are served in this way because, as the Court itself formulated it:

> they may be reluctant to argue the consequences of a violation the existence of which they dispute, and they may wish, in the event of a finding of a violation, to maintain the possibility of settling the issue of reparation directly with the injured party without the Court being further concerned.[162]

Even if an agreement is reached between the injured party and the State liable, the Court finds it is still involved in the matter. In fact, according to Rule 54(4) of its Rules the Court shall verify the equitable nature of such agreement and, when it finds the agreement to be equitable, strike the case off the list by means of a judgment. Such a supervision of the equitability of the agreement on compensation was exercised by the Court in, *e.g.*, the *Luedicke, Belkacem and Koç* Case,[163] in the *Airey* Case[164] and in the *Malone* Case.[165]

In the *Winterwerp* Case the judgment under Article 50 consisted in the unanimous decision of the Court to strike the case off the list. The reason for this was that meanwhile an arrangement had been made between the Netherlands and Winterwerp, which agreement was judged for its equitability by the Court. This arrangement in part even went beyond that originally suggested by Winterwerp's counsel. The principal elements of the arrangement were as follows:

> (1) The State shall promote that Mr. Winterwerp be placed as soon as possible in a hostel. The State Psychiatric Establishment at Eindhoven is and will remain prepared to give Mr. Winterwerp medical treatment whenever this might be necessary; (2) The State shall transfer a lump sum of f 10,000 (ten thousand guilders) to Mr. Winterwerp's new guardian to be used for the resocialisation of Mr. Winterwerp.[166]

Sometimes the agreement concerns only a part of the claim of the applicant and the Court has to decide about the rest of the claim: in the *Barthold* Case the settlement concerned the claims for fees and expenses and for loss of earnings.[167]

4. As to the merits of the procedure for compensation under Article 50, it is especially the passage "if the internal law of the said Party allows only partial reparation to be made for the consequences of this decision or measure" which has caused problems.

In the *Vagrancy* Case the Belgian Government submitted that the application for compensation was ill-founded, because under Belgian law

---

162. Judgment of 22 June 1972, *Ringeisen*, A.15 (1972), p. 7.
163. Judgment of 10 March 1980, A.36 (1980), p. 7.
164. Judgment of 6 February 1981, A.41 (1981), p. 8.
165. Judgment of 26 April 1985, A.95 (1985), p. 4. See also the judgments of 29 September 1987, *Erkner and Hofauer, and Poiss*, A.124 (1988), pp. 35 and 41 and the judgment of 27 June 1988, *Bouamar*, A.136, p. 48.
166. Judgment of 27 November 1981, A.47 (1982), p. 6.
167. Judgment of 31 January 1986, A.98 (1986), p. 7. See also the judgments of 9 June 1988, *O, H, W and R v. the United Kingdom*, A.136 (1988), pp. 7, 15, 23 and 40.

compensation can be obtained from the State for damage caused by an unlawful situation for which the State is responsible under national or international law. Those who claimed compensation before the Court therefore ought to have applied first to the national court.[168] The Court held that the treaties from which the text of Article 50 has been derived undoubtedly related in particular to cases in which, considering the nature of the damage, its consequences could be eliminated altogether, but in which under the internal law of the State concerned this is impossible. However, according to the Court this does not alter the fact that Article 50 is also applicable to cases in which such a *restitutio in integrum* is not possible precisely on account of the nature of the damage concerned. The Court added the following: "indeed, common sense suggests that this must be so *a fortiori*".[169] The Court distinguishes here between those cases in which *restitutio in integrum* is possible and those in which it is not, and considers it has jurisdiction in both cases; in the first case, however, only when such *restitutio in integrum* is excluded under national law. Thus, in the *Vagrancy* Case, which according to the Court belonged to the second category, the Court declared that it had jurisdiction to award compensation. It declared, however, that the applicants' claims for damages were not well-founded. Although in this case the decision not to grant compensation was taken unanimously, there were considerable differences of opinion within the Court on the argument described above.

In their joint separate opinion the Judges Holmback, Ross and Wold state that the argument followed by the Court is "unsound" and "completely alien to the text of Article 50" for those cases in which *restitutio in integrum* is impossible.[170] In the first place they submit with regard to the Court's argument:

> It presupposes that there is an absolute obligation on the State to restore to the applicants the liberty of which they have been deprived. But this cannot be so because of the maxim *impossibilium nulla est obligatio.*[171]

It is, however, more important in this context that they hold that in the two cases distinguished by the Court the jurisdiction of the Court should depend on the fact that "the internal law does not allow full reparation".[172] On the ground of Articles 5(5), 13, 53 and 54 they are of the opinion that the general rule underlying the Convention is that "a party claiming to be injured must seek redress before national courts and not before the European Court of Human Rights". The only exception to this is the jurisdiction conferred on the Court by Article 50 to award compensation in case the internal law in question does not make full reparation possible.[173] In their view the Court's conception leads

---

168. Judgment of 10 March 1972, A.14 (1972), p. 9.
169. *Ibidem*, pp. 9-10.
170. *Ibidem*, p. 14.
171. *Ibidem.*
172. *Ibidem.*
173. *Ibidem*, p. 15.

to the Court in fact assuming jurisdiction in respect to claims for reparation in all cases where *restitutio* is impossible, regardless of the state of internal law.[174]

The conclusion here drawn by the said judges from the Court's argument, in our opinion, goes too far, at least in the general formulation used. In its decision in the *Vagrancy* Case as well as in the subsequent *Ringeisen* Case the Court did take into account the fact that the Belgian and the Austrian Government respectively had refused compensation to the applicant.[175] But in the *Vagrancy* Case it immediately added:

> The mere fact that the applicants could have brought and could still bring their claims for damages before a Belgian Court does not therefore require the Court to dismiss their claims as being ill-founded any more than it raises an obstacle to their admissibility.[176]

In the *Ringeisen* Case the Court is even more explicit. The necessity to apply Article 50 exists

> once a respondent government refuses the applicant reparation to which he considers he is entitled.[177]

Between the view of the three above-mentioned judges and that of the Court here described, a considerable difference remains. According to the three judges the Court may award compensation only in one exceptional case, *viz.* when under internal law there is no possibility of obtaining full compensation. In the Court's view it is sufficient for the application of Article 50 that a government has refused the compensation claimed by the applicant. The view of the three judges resembles most closely the principle of general international law that a State must be enabled as much as possible to redress itself the consequences of any violation of its international obligations within the context of its own national legal system.[178] On the other hand, the Court has argued that, if for the consideration of an application under Article 50 it should be required again that the local remedies have first been exhausted, the total length of the procedure provided for in the Convention could hardly be considered compatible with the idea of effective protection of human rights.[179] Moreover, it might be argued that the consideration of applications under Article 50 and the examination of the merits should be regarded as one and indivisible,[180] so that the decision of the Commission that the local remedies have been exhausted, in combination with the finding of the Commission that a friendly settlement has not been reached and that the State has not been found willing to pay damages, must be considered a sufficient basis for the application of Article 50. The consequence of this

---

174. *Ibidem,* p. 14.
175. Judgment of 10 March 1972, A.14 (1972), p. 10, and judgment of 22 June 1972, A.15 (1972), p. 9 respectively.
176. A.14 (1972), p. 10.
177. A.15 (1972), p. 9.
178. Compare the corresponding principle of general international law underlying the local remedies rule, *supra* pp. 81-82.
179. Judgment of 10 March 1972, *De Wilde, Ooms and Versyp* ("*Vagrancy*" Case), A.14 (1972), p. 9.
180. See *supra* pp. 172-173.

latter idea is that, with respect to the decision on an application for compensation under Article 50 of the Convention, the internal law of the State concerned becomes irrelevant.

This is why the middle course suggested by Judge Verdross in his separate opinion would appear to us the most attractive. From the text of Article 50 he infers that the Court, when dealing with an application for compensation, should first of all ascertain whether the injured individual can obtain adequate compensation under the internal law. If that is the case, the respondent State should first be enabled to award compensation according to its own procedures, but with the Court remaining competent to assure itself that just satisfaction has indeed duly been given, and to fix a time within which this should take place.[181] In this construction the State concerned is given the opportunity to settle the matter within the context of its own legal system, while the Court is able to judge afterwards whether the compensation is equitable and at the same time to keep the total duration of the procedure within reasonable limits.

The viewpoint of the Court set forth above appears to have become constant case-law, however, since it has been confirmed explicitly or implicitly in a series of judgments.[182] Thus, in the *De Cubber* Case the Court notes that Article 50 is applicable, because the conditions of Article 50 are fulfilled:

> the proceedings in Belgium after 26 October 1984 ... have not redressed the violation found in its judgment of that date; they have not brought about a result as close to *restitutio in integrum* as was possible in the nature of things.[183]

5. As to the other elements of Article 50 there are fewer differences of opinion. Thus, the term "injured party" is fairly clear in the Court's view. "Injured party" is a synonym for "victim" in Article 25, and as such may be considered "the person directly affected by the failure to observe the Convention".[184] From this it follows, for instance, that counsel for the applicant cannot bring his fee directly under the claim for reparation pursuant to Article 50, although it may after all form part of the reparation awarded to the applicant. In the *Belkacem* Case the applicant had received free legal aid with respect to the Strasbourg proceedings and had not stated that he owed his counsel any additional amount. When the latter nevertheless claimed a supplementary fee, the Court decided that a lawyer "cannot rely on Article 50 to seek just satisfaction on his own account".[185]

---

181. A.14 (1972), p. 16.
182. Judgment of 10 March 1980, *König*, A.36 (1980) pp. 14-15; judgment of 13 May 1980, *Artico*, A.37 (1980), pp. 20-21; judgment of 6 November 1980, *Sunday Times*, A.38 (1981), pp. 8-9; and the judgment of 6 November 1980, *Guzzardi*, A.39 (1981), pp. 41-42.
183. Judgment of 14 September 1987, A.124/B (1988), pp. 17-18.
184. See the judgment of 6 February 1981, *Airey*, A.41 (1981), p. 7 and the judgment of 6 November 1980, *Sunday Times*, A.38 (1981), p. 8. See also the judgment of 14 September 1987, *Gillow*, A.124/C (1988), p. 29: "Since this case relates to events and their consequences which were experienced by Mr and Mrs Gillow together, the Court considers it equitable that all sums awarded in this judgment should be paid to the survivor of them, Mrs Gillow."
185. Judgment of 10 March 1980, A.36 (1980), p. 8. See also the judgment of 13 May 1980, *Artico*, A.37 (1980), p. 19.

In the *Pakelli* Case, counsel had not claimed an immediate payment of his fee because of the financial situation of his client. A reparation of these costs was awarded, because counsel had not waived his right to reparation of his costs (as the Government suggested). The Court noted that "in a human rights case a lawyer will be acting in the general interest if he agrees to represent or assist a litigant even if the latter is not in a position to pay him immediately"[186] and brought the payment under the reparation.

As to the term "satisfaction", the formulation of Article 50 makes it plain in the first place that the Court has a certain discretion in determining it:

> as is borne out by the adjective "just" and the phrase "if necessary", the Court enjoys a certain discretion in the exercise of the power conferred by Article 50.[187]

With this as a starting-point, the Court strictly upholds that the only element qualifying for satisfaction is the injury due to the previously found violation of the Convention. Injury which is connected therewith, but which in fact is due to other causes, does not qualify for satisfaction.[188] The Court therefore requires a causal link between the injury and the violation.[189]

In the Case of *Albert and Le Compte* the first claim concerned a request to the Court to direct the State to annul the disciplinary sanctions imposed on the applicants. The Court decided that, even when leaving aside the fact that the Court is not empowered to do this,[190]

> the disciplinary sanctions, which were the outcome of proceedings found by the Court not to have complied with one of the rules of Article 6 § 1 of the Convention, cannot on that account alone be regarded as the consequences of that breach. As for the criminal sentence, there is no connection whatsoever between them and the violation ... . As for the applicant's second series of claims ..., the Court considers it proper to distinguish here, as in the Case of *Le Compte, Van Leuven and De Meyere* ..., between damage caused by a violation of the Convention and the costs incurred by the applicant.[191]

As regards the last-mentioned category, a trend appears to develop in the case-law of the Court to the effect that injury pursuant to Article 50 can be made good as far as it was "incurred by the applicants in order to try to prevent the violation found by the Court or to obtain redress therefor" and only if it fulfils specifically three criteria: costs and expenses susceptible of

---

186. Judgment of 25 April 1983, A.64 (1983), p. 20.
187. Judgment of 6 November 1980, *Guzzardi*, A.39 (1981), p. 42.
188. See the judgment of 10 March 1980, *König*, A.36 (1980), p. 16: "The only heads of injury capable of giving rise to an award of just satisfaction are those which the applicant would not have sustained had the two actions come to a close within a reasonable time". See also the judgment of 6 February 1981, *Airey*, A.41 (1981), pp. 8-9: "Her decision to move appears to have been motivated not by the fact that she did not enjoy an effective right of access to the High Court for the purpose of petitioning for juridical separation but rather by her general situation underlying her wish to have such access and, in particular, by her fear of molestation by her husband".
189. Judgment of 23 October 1985, *Benthem*, A.97 (1986), p. 19; judgment of 2 June 1986, *Bönisch*, A.103 (1986), p. 8; judgment of 26 May 1988, *Pauwels*, A.135 (1988), p. 20 and judgment of 21 June 1988, *Berrehab*, A.138 (1988), p. 17.
190. See *infra* pp. 184-185.
191. Judgment of 24 October 1983, *Albert and Le Compte*, A.68 (1983), pp. 6-7. See on the said distinction also, *e.g.*, judgment of 6 November 1980, *Sunday Times*, A.38 (1981), p. 9; judgment of 18 October 1982, *Le Compte, Van Leuven and De Meyere*, A.54 (1983), p. 7; judgment of 25 April 1983, *Van Droogenbroeck*, A.63 (1983), p. 6.

satisfaction must have been (1) "actually incurred", (2) "necessarily incurred" and (3) "reasonable as to quantum".[192] These criteria apply to costs described as material damage as well as to costs referable to proceedings.[193]

6. The main purpose of the reparation under Article 50 is to place the applicant as far as possible in the position he would have been had the violation of the Convention not taken place.[194]

Whether and to what extent satisfaction will be awarded by the Court depends on the circumstances of the case. Thus, in the *Neumeister* Case[195] there had been a violation of Article 5(3) and the Court awarded the applicant a compensation, amounting to Austrian Sch. 30,000. An important factor in the determination of the amount was the degree to which the detention under remand had exceeded reasonable limits. In this case, however, there were a number of circumstances which induced the Court to decide that compensation for material injury was not necessary. In the first place the duration of the detention under remand counted towards the ultimately imposed imprisonment. For the remainder he had been granted a pardon. These factors also amply counterbalanced, in the Court's opinion, the moral injury which Neumeister had sustained. Even though this did not, according to the Court, constitute a genuine *restitutio in integrum*, it approached this very closely. The sum of money was therefore awarded to him as compensation for the damage he had incurred in the form of costs in the matter of legal assistance in his attempts to prevent the violation of the Convention, subsequently to request the Commission and the Court to establish this violation, and finally to obtain compensation.

In the *Engel* case, only a symbolical compensation of Dfl. 100 was awarded to Engel. Compensation was refused to De Wit, Dona and Schul, because the violation of the Convention in regard to them only consisted in the fact that the Supreme Military Court had dealt with their cases *in camera*. In its judgment on the merits the Court had already found that they did not seem to have suffered as a result, and they had not since then advanced any new arguments for their claims for damages. In awarding Dfl. 100 to Engel the Court took into account the very short duration of the detention and the fact that the injury caused by the violation of Article 5(1) had been largely compensated by the circumstance that Engel had not actually had to undergo his punishment.[196]

---

192. Judgment of 18 October 1982, *Le Compte, Van Leuven and De Meyere*, A.54 (1983), pp. 8-9; judgment of 24 February 1983, *Dudgeon*, A.59 (1983), p. 9; judgment of 30 November 1987, *H. v. Belgium*, A.127/B, p. 38.
193. See, *e.g.*, judgment of 6 November 1980, *Sunday Times*, A.38 (1981), pp. 13-18, judgment of 24 February 1983, *Dudgeon*, A.59 (1983), pp. 9-11 and judgment of 27 October 1987, *Bodèn*, A.125/B (1988), p. 43.
194. Judgment of 23 October 1984, *Piersack*, A.85 (1984), pp. 15-16.
195. Judgment of 7 May 1974, A.17 (1974), pp. 16-21.
196. Judgment of 23 November 1976, A.22 (1977), pp. 68-70.

On the other hand, in the *Guincho* Case[197] the Court found a violation of Article 6(1), the reasonable-time requirement, which stemmed from two periods of almost total inactivity on the part of the State. The resultant lapse of time, totalling more than two years, did not only "reduce the effectiveness of the action brought, but it also placed the applicant in a state of uncertainty which still persists and in such a position that even a final decision in his favour will not be able to provide compensation for the lost interest". Accordingly, the Court awarded the applicant a compensation of 150,000 Escudos.

Other factors can also play a part in the awarding of reparation of costs and expenses. In the *Airey* Case,[198] for instance, it seems to have been an important factor that the British Government had already declared itself prepared before the proceedings started to award a given amount. And in the *Pakelli* Case, although the applicant, because of his financial situation, did not have to pay the bill of his lawyer immediately, he could ask for the amount he needed to pay that bill.[199] On the other hand, no compensation is awarded if the fees were borne by an insurance company, since "there is no prejudice capable of being the subject of a claim for restitution".[200] The same argument applies, if the applicant has received free legal aid.[201]

In the *Eckle* Case[202] the Court extensively went into the matter of restitution of costs of proceedings. The Court first held that an applicant is entitled to an award of costs and expenses under Article 50, when these costs are incurred in order to seek, through the domestic legal order, prevention or redress of a violation, to have the same established by the Commission and later by the Court, or to obtain reparation therefor, and when they "were actually incurred, were necessarily incurred and were also reasonable as to quantum". Considering, however, the proceedings in which the costs were incurred in this case, the claim for restitution of costs and expenses incurred in the proceedings before the Koblenz Court of Appeal was rejected because

it should not be overlooked that the complaint in question was not aimed at securing a more expeditious conduct of the proceeding: the complaint was directed against the unreasonable length of the detention on remand and had as its sole object Mr. Eckle's release from custody. It could have been of relevance in relation to Article 5, para. 3 - if, ... the Commission had not declared the application inadmissible on that score - but not in relation to Article 6, para. 1.[203]

In relation to the claims for restitution of costs incurred in the "review" procedure before the Regional Court of Trier, the Court considered that "in

---

197. Judgment of 10 July 1984, *Guincho*, A.81 (1984), p. 18. See also, *inter alia*, the judgment of 22 March 1983, *Campbell and Cosans*, A.60 (1983), pp. 7-13 and the judgment of 14 September 1987, *Gillow*, A.124/C (1988), p. 26.
198. Judgment of 6 February 1981, A.41 (1981), pp. 7-9.
199. Judgment of 25 April 1983, *Pakelli*, A.64 (1983), p. 20.
200. Judgment of 23 October 1984, *Öztürk*, A.85 (1984), p. 9.
201. Judgment of 18 December 1986, *Johnston and others*, A.112 (1987), pp. 32-33; judgment of 25 June 1987, *Baggetta*, A.119 (1987), p. 34; judgment of 27 July 1987, *Feldbrugge*, A.124/A (1988), pp. 9-10; judgment of 2 December 1987, *Bozano*, A.124/F (1988), p. 48.
202. Judgment of 21 June 1983, A.65 (1983), pp. 11-20.
203. *Ibidem*, p. 13.

view of his not having raised the issue of 'reasonable time' himself the applicant cannot recover in full Mr. von Stackelberg's fees and disbursements".[204] Concerning the recovery of costs in relation to the procedure in Strasbourg, the Government expressed the view "that a deduction should be made in view of the applications having been unsuccessful in relation to three complaints declared inadmissible by the Commission". The Court did not agree with this, because

> in contrast to what occurred in the case of *Le Compte, Van Leuven and De Meyere*, to which the Government referred ..., the complaints in question failed at the admissibility stage. Furthermore the Commission did not reject them as being manifestly ill-founded, and hence after a preliminary inquiry into the merits, but for being out of time and for non-exhaustion of domestic remedies. ... As is apparent from the decision on admissibility, the examination of these two questions of admissibility ... was not of such complexity that its outcome could warrant the deduction called for by the Government.[205]

On the other hand, in the Case of *Campbell and Fell*[206] the restitution of costs and expenses was made conditional on the degree in which the complaints were successful.

What other kind of damage may be compensated next to direct costs of proceedings? In the *König* Case, according to the Court, the extent to which the "reasonable time" had been exceeded had left the applicant in prolonged uncertainty as to the possibilities of his career, which in the Court's opinion ought to be compensated in the form of DM 30,000 of damages.[207] In the *Goddi* Case the applicant maintained that if he had had an opportunity of having his defence adequately presented, he would certainly have received a lighter sentence. The Court did not accept so categorical an allegation. However, it held that the outcome might possibly have been different if the applicant had had the benefit of a practical and effective defence and that, therefore, such a loss of real opportunities warranted the award of just satisfaction.[208] A similar reasoning was followed by the Court in the *Colozza* Case, where it had found a violation of Article 6(1) of the Convention, since the applicant was never heard in his presence by a "tribunal" which was competent to determine all the aspects of the matter. The Court noted that an award of just satisfaction could only be based on the fact that the applicant did not have the benefit of the guarantees of Article 6 and awarded a just satisfaction to the applicant's widow for loss of real opportunities.[209] Reparation of loss of earnings is also possible,[210] as well as the repayment of

---

204. *Ibidem*, p. 14.
205. *Ibidem*, pp. 18-19.
206. Judgment of 28 June 1984, A.80 (1984), p. 56. See also the judgment of 18 December 1986, *Johnston and others*, A.112 (1987), p. 33.
207. Judgment of 10 March 1980, A.36 (1980), p. 16.
208. Judgment of 9 April 1984, A.76 (1984), pp. 13-14.
209. Judgment of 12 February 1985, A.89 (1985), p. 17. See also the judgment of 2 June 1986, *Bönisch*, A.103 (1986), p. 8, the judgment of 8 July 1986, *Lingens*, A.103 (1986), p. 29 and the judgment of 28 October 1987, *Inze*, A.126 (1988), p. 20.
210. For instance, the judgment of 24 November 1986, *Unterpertinger*, A.110 (1987), p. 16 and the judgment of 21 June 1988, *Berrehab*, A.138 (1988), p. 17, in which indeed no reparation of loss of earnings was awarded because of the lack of a causal link.

fines and costs unjustly awarded against applicant,[211] and reimbursement of the travel and subsistence expenses met by the applicant in attending the hearings before the Commission and the Court.[212] Reparation of immaterial damage can be awarded for suffered uncertainty, feeling of unequal treatment,[213] unjust imprisonment[214] and feeling of frustration.[215]

Several factors can also play a part in the determination of the amount of compensation. In the *Ringeisen* Case,[216] the Court had found that there had been a violation of Article 5(3). The Court awarded the applicant a compensation of DM 20,000, and in fixing the amount of this sum, took into account the following factors. Firstly, the fact that the detention under remand had exceeded reasonable limits by 22 months. Although the period of imprisonment to which he had ultimately been condemned was reduced by the duration of the detention under remand, he had always maintained that he was innocent, and on that account had undoubtedly felt so long a detention under remand as unjust. Secondly, the fact that his detention had been hard on him, since it had been impossible for him to undertake anything to avoid bankruptcy.

In the *Artico* Case,[217] the Court took three elements into consideration, *viz.* the imprisonment actually served, the additional imprisonment which the applicant had possibly incurred in consequence of the lack of effective legal aid, and the isolated position in which he had been placed as a result of this. The Court held that

> none of the above elements of damage lends itself to a process of calculation. Taking them together on an equitable basis, as is required by Article 50, the Court considers that Mr. Artico should be afforded satisfaction assessed at three million (3,000,000) Lire.[218]

In the *Sporrong and Lönnroth* Case the Court had found a violation of Article 1 of Protocol no. 1 of the Convention. In order to decide whether or not the applicants had been prejudiced, the Court had to determine during which periods the continuation of the measures complained of had been in violation of Protocol no. 1, and then which constituent elements of damage warranted examination. The Court found it reasonable that a municipality should, after obtaining an expropriation permit, require some time to undertake and

---

211. For instance, the judgment of 27 February 1980, *De Weer*, A.35 (1980), pp. 31-32; judgment of 8 July 1986, *Lingens*, A.103 (1986), p. 29.
212. For instance, the judgment of 10 December 1982, *Corigliano*, A.57 (1983), p. 17.
213. Judgment of 2 June 1986, *Bönisch*, A.103 (1986), p. 8; judgment of 23 April 1987, *Lechner and Hess*, A.118 (1987), p. 22; judgments of 25 June 1987, *Capuano, Baggetta and Milasi*, A.119 (1987), pp. 15, 34 and 48 and the judgment of 8 July 1987, *Baraona*, A.122 (1987), p. 22.
214. Judgment of 24 November 1986, *Unterpertinger*, A.110 (1987), p. 16.
215. The judgments of 9 June 1988, *O, H, W, B and R v. United Kingdom*, A.136/A-E (1988), pp. 9, 17, 25, 33 and 42-43.
216. Judgment of 22 June 1972, A.15 (1972), pp. 9-10. The Court did not exclude that a third factor - the deteriorated health due to the detention - could also have played a role, but Ringeisen had not advanced any evidence for that fact while from medical reports the contrary could be inferred.
217. Judgment of 13 May 1980, A.37 (1980), pp. 21-22. See further: judgment of 21 June 1983, *Eckle*, A.65 (1983), pp. 10-11 and particularly the judgment of 18 December 1984, *Spörrong and Lönnroth*, A.88 (1985), pp. 13-15.
218. Judgment of 13 May 1980, A.37 (1980), p. 22.

complete the planning needed to prepare the final decision on the expro-priation contemplated. Whilst a comparison between the beginning and the end of the periods of damage did not show that the applicants were prejudiced in financial terms, the Court nevertheless did not conclude that there was no loss within that period. There were, in fact, other factors which also warranted attention. Firstly, there were limitations on the utilization of the properties. In addition, during the periods of damage the value of the properties in question fell. Furthermore there were difficulties in obtaining loans, secured by way of mortgage. Above all, the applicants were left in prolonged uncertainty as they did not know what the fate of their properties would be. To these factors had to be added the non-pecuniary damage occasioned by the violation of Article 6(1) of the Convention: the applicants' case could not be heard by a tribunal competent to determine all the aspects of the matter. The applicants thus suffered damage for which reparation was not provided by the withdrawal of the expropriation permits.[219]

In the *Bozano* Case the applicant claimed just satisfaction for the violation of Article 5(1) of the Convention. The Court stated that the applicant's detention in France involved a serious breach of the Convention, which inevitably caused him substantial non-pecuniary damage. With regard to his subsequent detention in Switzerland and Italy the Court found that it had no jurisdiction to review the compatibility of that detention with the Convention, since the Commission had either declared the applicant's complaints against those two States inadmissible or else struck them off its list. Nonetheless, there was a need to have regard to the applicant's detention as it was prior to the enforcement of the deportation order. In the Court's view the real damage was that sustained as a consequence of the process of enforcing the deportation order and of the unlawful and arbitrary deprivation of liberty.[220]

When the damage or the costs do not lend themselves for a process of calculation or the calculation presented to the Court is unreasonable, the Court fixes them on an equitable basis.[221] In the *Young, James and Webster* Case there was no dispute that all three applicants had incurred pecuniary and non-pecuniary losses and also liability for legal costs and expenses referable to the Strasbourg proceedings, but certain claims exceeded as to the quantum sums offered by the British government during unsuccessful friendly settlement negotiations. The Court observed that

high costs of litigation may themselves constitute a serious impediment to the effective protection of human rights. It would be wrong for the Court to give encouragement to such a situation in its decisions awarding costs under Article 50. It is important that applicants should not encounter undue financial difficulties in bringing complaints under the Convention and the Court considers that it may expect that lawyers in Contracting

219. Judgment of 18 December 1984, A.88 (1985), pp. 12-13.
220. Judgment of 2 December 1987, A.124/F (1988), pp. 47-48.
221. Judgment of 13 May 1980, *Artico*, A.37 (1980), p. 22; judgment of 18 October 1982, *Young, James and Webster*, A.55 (1983), p. 7; judgment of 2 June 1986, *Bönisch*, A.103 (1986), p. 8 and the judgments of 9 June 1988, *O, H, W, B and R v. United Kingdom*, A.136/A-E (1988).

7. During the settlement negotiations, the British government offered to have the costs in question independently assessed or "taxed", by a Taxing Master. In the Opinion of the Court, this would have been a reasonable method of assessment. However, the applicants did not take up this offer. In these circumstances the Court accepted the figure of £ 65,000 offered by the government in respect of all legal costs and expenses.[223] A claim for compensation will be rejected, when there is nothing to suggest with reasonable certainty that without the violation the result would have been different.[224] Other possible reasons for rejection of reparation claims are: the Court's finding that, by holding that the violation has occurred, its judgment has already furnished sufficient satisfaction for the purposes of Article 50;[225] the conclusion that the applicants did not suffer any damage;[226] the fact that the domestic court has imposed a sentence identical to that given before the judgment of the Court, but now after a trial attended by all the guarantees laid down by the Convention;[227] the circumstance that the applicant has adduced insufficient evidence or information in support of his claim;[228] or the Court's holding that the "claims stem from matters in respect of which it has found no violation".[229]

Repeatedly the Court had to declare that it lacked jurisdiction to direct a State to take certain measures, for instance to abolish the violation found by the Court, to repair the costs, *etcetera*. The Court notes regularly that it is left to the State concerned to choose the means to be used in its domestic legal system to give effect to its obligations under Article 53.[230]

In the *Corigliano* Case the Court declared the claim inadmissible to order the State to make certain articles of the Penal Code inapplicable to "political and social trials". This "falls outside the scope of the case brought before the Court", according to the Court.[231]

In the *Bozano* Case, the applicant had requested the Court to recommend

---

222. Judgment of 18 October 1982, A.55 (1983), p. 8; see also the judgment of 2 June 1986, *Bönisch*, A.103 (1986), p. 9.
223. *Ibidem*, p. 8.
224. Judgment of 10 March 1972, *Vagrancy*, A.14 (1972), p. 11; judgment of 25 April 1983, *Van Droogenbroeck*, A.63 (1983), p. 6; judgment of 23 February 1984, *Luberti*, A.75 (1984), p. 18; and judgments of 9 June 1988, *O, H, W, B and R v. United Kingdom*, A.136 (1988).
225. Judgment of 18 October 1982, *Le Compte, Van Leuven and De Meyere*, A.54 (1983), p. 8; judgment of 10 December 1982, *Corigliano*, A.57 (1983), p. 17; judgment of 18 December 1987, *F v. Switzerland*, A.128 (1988), p. 20; and judgment of 20 June 1988, *Schönenberger and Durmaz*, A.137 (1988), p. 15.
226. Judgment of 23 November 1976, *Engel*, A.22 (1977), p. 69.
227. Judgment of 23 October 1984, *Piersack*, A.85 (1984), p. 17.
228. Judgment of 21 November 1983, *Foti and others*, A.69 (1983), p. 7; judgment of 29 May 1986, *Deumeland*, A.100 (1986), p. 31; judgment of 14 September 1987, *Gillow*, A.124/C (1988), pp. 26-27; and judgment of 20 June 1988, *Schönenberger and Durmaz*, A.137 (1988), p. 15.
229. Judgment of 18 December 1986, *Johnston and others*, A.112 (1987), p. 32.
230. Judgment of 25 April 1983, *Pakelli*, A.64 (1983), pp. 19-20; judgment of 24 October 1983, *Albert and Le Compte*, A.68 (1983), p. 6; judgment of 26 October 1984, *McGoff*, A.83 (1984), p. 28; judgment of 26 May 1985, *Pauwels*, A.135 (1988), p. 19 and the judgment of 9 June 1988, *B v. United Kingdom*, A.136/D (1988), p. 35.
231. Judgment of 10 December 1982, *Corigliano*, A.57 (1983), p. 17.

the French Government to approach the Italian authorities through diplomatic channels, with a view to securing either a "presidential pardon" - leading to his "rapid release" - or a reopening of the criminal proceedings taken against him in Italy from 1971 to 1976. The Government argued that the Court did not have power to take such a course of action. Furthermore, they maintained that it would in any case be unconnected with the subject-matter of the dispute, since it would amount to recommending France to intervene in the enforcement of final decisions of the Italian courts. The Court did not go into these arguments. It merely pointed out that Mr Bozano's complaints against Italy were not in issue before it, as the Commission had declared them inadmissible.[232] One cannot escape from the impression that the Court did not want to enter into the issue whether or not it had power to make a recommendation as requested by the applicant. It might be argued that in cases where *restitutio in integrum* is impossible, as in the present case, the Court had nothing left than to award just satisfaction. However, what Mr Bozano in addition requested from the Court was only a *recommendation* and such a recommendation should, in general, not be inappropriate, comparable as it would be more or less with the recommendation of provisional measures, for which there is also no express basis in the Convention.

§ 7. THE REQUEST FOR INTERPRETATION OF A JUDGMENT OF THE COURT

1. Rule 57 of the Rules of Court deals with the possibility to request the Court for the interpretation of a judgment.

According to paragraph 1 a Party or the Commission may request such an interpretation within three years following the delivery of the judgment. The request must state precisely the point or points in the operative provisions of the judgment on which interpretation is required (Rule 57(2) of the Rules of Court). After receipt, the request is communicated to any other Party, to the original applicant and, where the request has been submitted by a State, to the Commission, all of which are then invited to submit any written comments within a fixed time-limit (Rule 57(3) of the Rules of Court). In this procedure, too, the Court applies the principle that the request for interpretation shall be considered by the Chamber which gave the judgment and which, as far as possible, shall be composed of the same judges (Rule 57(4) of the Rules of Court).

2. The judgment of 23 June 1973 is the only example of a decision of the Court on a request for interpretation so far.

On 21 December 1972, on the basis of a letter from the original individual

---

232. Judgment of 18 December 1986, A.111 (1987), p. 28.

applicant, the Commission submitted to the Court a request for interpretation of the Court's second judgment in the *Ringeisen* Case of 22 June 1972. By this judgment Ringeisen had been awarded a compensation of DM 20,000. The question whether this amount would have to be paid directly to Ringeisen or whether it might be claimed by the trustee in the bankruptcy of Ringeisen, had been left by the Court to the discretion of the Austrian Government. In this connection, however, the Court had referred to the Austrian legislation concerning compensation on account of detention under remand, which implied that no attachment or seizure may be made against such compensation. The money was, however, sent by the Austrian authorities on consignment to a judicial tribunal. The latter decided that upon request of the persons entitled to it or after a final judicial decision the money was to be paid.

The Commission asked the Court what was meant by the order to pay compensation, in particular with respect to the currency and the place of the payment, and whether the term "compensation" was to be understood as an amount that was exempt from any judicial claims under Austrian law, or on the contrary was subject to such claims. The Court replied that the compensation was to be paid in German marks and was to be made payable in the Federal Republic of Germany. Further the Court ruled that the money was to be paid to Ringeisen personally, exempt from any claim or title to it. This ruling, therefore, implied disapproval of the position taken by the Austrian authorities.

Austria had called into question the competence of the Court in the matter, stating that

> the competence of the ... Court ... for interpretation of its judgments ... is based solely on the Rules of the Court. Therefore in the light of Article 52 of the ... Convention, the well-founded question may even be raised whether this legal institution is compatible at all with the Convention.

The Court pointed out that the sole purpose of Article 52 is to exclude appeal to another authority from decisions of the Court.[233] It submitted that there is no question of appeal when the Court deals with a request for interpretation. In such a case the Court exercises inherent jurisdiction, because such a request concerns only elucidation of the purport and scope of a preceding judgment. Furthermore the Court pointed out that Rule 56 (the present Rule 57) had been submitted to the contracting States at the time of its adoption and that no objections had been raised against it by those States.[234]

233. See *supra* p. 172.
234. Judgment of 23 June 1973, *Ringeisen*, A.16 (1973), pp. 4-9.

§ 8. THE REQUEST FOR REVISION OF A JUDGMENT

1. The competence of the Court to deal with requests for revision of its judgments is likewise not regulated by the Convention. Like the competence to give an interpretation of a judgment, the competence to revise a judgment may also be considered as inherent in the jurisdiction of the Court. The procedure to be followed in connection with a request for revision is also to be found in the Rules of Court, *viz.* in Rule 58.

A request for revision of a judgment may be submitted by a Party in the case in which that judgment has been delivered, or by the Commission. Revision may be requested in the event of the discovery of a fact which might by its nature have a decisive influence and which, when the judgment was delivered, was unknown both to the Court and to the Party or the Commission now requesting revision. The request must be filed within a period of six months after the fact became known to that Party or the Commission, as the case may be (Rule 58(1) of the Rules of Court).

2. Up to the moment at which the manuscript for this edition was finalized (January 1990) no requests for revision had reached the Court. This is not astonishing. In general, cases in which after the final judgment an originally unknown fact of decisive importance is discovered are very rare. It is even less likely that such a situation will occur after lengthy local proceedings and the elaborate proceedings before the Commission and the Court.

Should a request for revision reach the Court at some future time, this will be dealt with, according to Rule 58, in proceedings largely resembling the normal proceedings before the Court. The only difference is that a request for revision is first examined for its admissibility, by reference to the conditions mentioned in Rule 58(1), by a Chamber of the Court composed in the normal way, *i.e.* in accordance with Article 43 of the Convention. When the request is found to be admissible, the Chamber thus composed does not itself examine the merits of the request, but transmits it to the Chamber which gave the original judgment. It is only when the latter is not reasonably possible that the Chamber which has decided on the admissibility also takes a decision on the merits of the request (Rule 58(4)).

§ 9. EXCURSUS: ADVISORY JURISDICTION OF THE COURT

1. Since the entry-into-force of the Second Protocol on 21 September 1970 the Court has jurisdiction to give advisory opinions on legal questions concerning the interpretation of the Convention and the Protocols thereto (Art. 1(1) of the Second Protocol).

Properly speaking, this jurisdiction falls outside the scope of this chapter, since the latter deals with the consideration of complaints or requests connected with them. The matter is, nevertheless, discussed in this chapter, since it is entirely devoted to the Court.

2. The advisory jurisdiction of a court may be of great importance for a uniform interpretation and the further development of the law. With regard to international law, this is quite evident from the practice of the International Court of Justice and the Court of Justice of the European Communities. Via its advisory opinions the International Court of Justice has made an important contribution to the interpretation and the further development of particularly the law of the United Nations.[235] The advisory jurisdiction of the International Court of Justice is formulated very broadly, without any conditions being made as to the scope of such advisory opinions. According to Article 96 of the Charter of the United Nations in conjunction with Article 65 of the Court's Statute, the Court may give advisory opinions "on any legal question", so that the most varied issues of international law may be submitted to the Court. The jurisdiction of the Court of Justice of the European Communities is indeed very limited as to its scope, but still it comprises the field of the conclusion of treaties, which is of great importance for the Communities.[236]

The practical importance of the advisory jurisdiction of the European Court of Human Rights, on the other hand, has been reduced to a minimum from the outset because of the restrictions which are put on it in the said Protocol. In fact, Article 1(2) provides that advisory opinions of the European Court

> shall not deal with any question relating to the content or scope of the rights or freedoms defined in Section I of the Convention and in the Protocols thereto, or with any other question which the Commission, the Court, or the Committee of Ministers might have to consider in consequence of any such proceedings as could be instituted in accordance with the Convention.

It is obvious that a high degree of inventiveness is required for the formulation of a question of any importance which could stand the test of Article 1(2) and could therefore be submitted to the Court. So far, at any rate, this has not happened, and for the future one should not expect that the Court will receive many requests for an advisory opinion.

3. In our opinion it is regrettable that the advisory jurisdiction of the Court does not have a wider scope. Such advisory opinions might have the salutary effect that gaps still existing at the moment in the Court's case-law might be filled without the necessity of the previous submission to the Court of a complaint about an alleged violation of the Convention. This is all the more urgent since it appears in practice that, in comparison with the large number

---

235. In this context see in particular the advisory opinions of the Court in: "Injuries suffered in the service of the United Nations", *I.C.J. Reports* 1949, p. 174; "Certain Expenses of the United Nations", *I.C.J. Reports* 1962, p. 151; and "Legal Consequences for States of the Continued Presence of South Africa in Namibia notwithstanding Security Council Resolution 276 (1970)", *I.C.J. Reports* 1971, p. 6.
236. See Art. 228 of the EEC Treaty. See, *e.g.*, the important advisory opinion of the Court of Justice of the European Communities 1/76, *Jur.* 1977, p. 741, which partly laid the basis for the present conception of the external powers of the EEC.

of issues that may arise in connection with the Convention and the total of the complaints submitted to the Commission, the number of cases that is submitted to the Court is still rather limited.[237]

Widening of the scope of the Court's advisory jurisdiction would require amendment of the Second Protocol. In our opinion the subject-matter to which requests for an advisory opinion may relate should in the first place be extended to any legal question concerning the Convention and the Protocols, though on condition that the giving of an advisory opinion by the Court must not amount to a decision of the Court under Section IV of the Convention, while a certain discretion ought to be allowed to the Court with respect to the importance of the question submitted to it.

Secondly, more organs should be entitled to submit a request for an advisory opinion. Under the present circumstances only the Committee of Ministers may address a request for an advisory opinion to the Court (Art. 1(1) of the Second Protocol). However, in particular the Commission, in view of its general task of protector of the legal order created by the Convention, would seem to be eminently qualified to make such requests. In addition, the Parliamentary Assembly of the Council of Europe, and perhaps each of the individual contracting States, might be considered.

However, in this context too it may be said that such changes depend on the consent of the contracting States, and that so far there has been little evidence of willingness on their part to widen the scope of the advisory jurisdiction of the Court.

4. A request for an advisory opinion must indicate in precise terms the question on which the opinion of the Court is sought, and further the date on which the Committee of Ministers decided to request an advisory opinion, and the names and addresses of the person or persons appointed by the Committee to give the Court any explanations which it may require (Rule 60 of the Rules of Court). A copy of the request is transmitted to the members of the Court and to the Commission. For the rest the Commission is concerned in the proceedings only if the President of the Court takes the initiative to invite the Commission, by reason of the nature of the question, to submit written observations to the Court. Such an invitation is addressed at all events to the contracting States (Rule 61 of the Rules of Court).

The President lays down the time-limits for the filing of written comments or other documents (Rule 62 of the Rules of Court). He also decides whether after the closure of the written procedure an oral hearing is to be held (Rule 63 of the Rules of Court).

Advisory opinions are given by majority vote of the plenary Court. They shall mention the number of judges constituting the majority, while any judge may attach to the opinion of the Court either a separate opinion, concurring with or dissenting from the advisory opinion, or a bare statement of dissent

---

237. See *supra* p. 138.

(Rule 65 of the Rules of Court).

The advisory opinion is read out by the President or his delegate at a public hearing, and certified copies are sent to the Committee of Ministers, the contracting States, the Commission and the Secretary General of the Council of Europe (Rules 66 and 67 of the Rules of Court).

If the Court considers that the request for an advisory opinion is not within its consultative competence, it so declares in a reasoned decision (Rule 64 of the Rules of Court).

CHAPTER IV

THE EXAMINATION OF A CASE BY THE COMMITTEE OF MINISTERS

§ 1. INTRODUCTION

1. Unlike the Commission and the Court, the Committee of Ministers was not set up in connection with the adoption of the European Convention. It is the policy-making and executive organ of the Council of Europe.[1]

2. One of the tasks of the Committee of Ministers concerning human rights results directly from the Statute of the Council of Europe, *viz.* from Article 8. In virtue of this article the Committee supervises the observance of the obligation contained in Article 3 of the Statute, according to which every Member of the Council of Europe "must accept the principles of the rule of law and of the enjoyment by all persons within its jurisdiction of human rights and fundamental freedoms". The more specific tasks of the Committee of Ministers with regard to human rights, however, have been laid down in the Convention.

According to Article 21 of the Convention, the Committee of Ministers elects the members of the Commission.[2] In the election of the members of the Court, too, the Committee plays an important part. According to Article 39 of the Convention the judges are elected by the Consultative (read now: Parliamentary) Assembly of the Council of Europe from a list of persons nominated by the Members of the Council of Europe.[3] Since the Committee represents the Members within the Council of Europe, it is in fact this organ which draws up the list.

Apart from its function in these election procedures, the Committee of Ministers also performs a number of supervisory tasks under the European Convention. One of these, the supervision under Article 54 of the execution by the parties of the decisions of the Court, has been described above.[4]

3. The most important function of the Committee of Ministers, however, is that which results from Article 32. In those instances where, after a complaint has been declared admissible by the Commission and a report on the merits has been sent to the Committee, the case has not been referred to the Court within a period of three months, the Committee decides whether there has been a violation of the Convention. With respect to those cases the

---

1.   On the Committee, see also *supra* Chapter I, section 9.
2.   See *supra* p. 21.
3.   See *supra* p. 26.
4.   See *supra* pp. 156-157.

Committee has a task comparable to that of the Court, although the procedure followed by the two organs differs quite substantially. The decisions of both organs are binding: contracting States have undertaken to regard as binding on them the decision taken by the Committee of Ministers in the case concerned (Art. 32(4)). However, the State which is declared in default by the Committee of Ministers has a certain discretion in taking "satisfactory" measures within a prescribed period (Art. 32(3)), while a decision of the Court must be complied with directly (Art. 53).

All in all it may be said that the Committee performs a (quasi-)judicial function under Article 32 in the second phase of the supervisory procedure, just as does - alternatively - the Court. This in spite of the fact that, considering its composition,[5] procedure and functions under the Statute of the Council of Europe, the Committee has to be regarded as a political organ.

This situation, in which a judicial function is performed by a political organ, is the result of a compromise reached during the drafting of the Convention.[6] On the one hand it appeared impossible to find sufficient support for a Court with compulsory jurisdiction. On the other hand it was deemed desirable that the supervisory procedure should ultimately result, in all cases, in a binding decision on whether or not there had been a violation of the Convention. Ultimately the solution found was to entrust that decision to the Committee of Ministers of the Council of Europe for those cases where the Court did not have jurisdiction or the case was not brought before the Court.[7]

§ 2. THE EXAMINATION OF THE CASE BY THE COMMITTEE OF MINISTERS

1. After the Commission has completed its examination of the merits of a case, it draws up a report. This report is transmitted to the Committee of Ministers. This does not yet mean that the latter organ is competent to consider the case. Such competence arises only after a period of three months from the date of transmission of the report, provided that within that period the case has not been referred to the Court (Art. 32). If the respondent State is not subject to the compulsory jurisdiction of the Court, that State may give its consent to the case being brought before the Court (Art. 48).

The Convention does not contain any more provisions about the examination of a case by the Committee. The Committee itself has adopted a number of Rules in connection with the application of Article 32 of the

5.   See *supra* p. 30.
6.   See *supra* pp. 29-30.
7.   See *supra* pp. 29-30.

Convention.[8] From these Rules and a number of other points discussed by the Committee of Ministers[9] the following general lines may be inferred.

2. Rule 1 provides that, when exercising its functions under Article 32 of the Convention, the Committee is entitled to discuss the substance of any case on which the Commission has submitted a report, for example by considering written or oral statements of the parties and hearing of witnesses. The formulation of this rule does not appear quite accurate. Indeed, it refers to any case on which the Commission has submitted a report, while according to Article 32 of the Convention it ought to be added: "and which has not been referred to the Court within the prescribed period".

Evidently, in the view of the Committee, an examination of the case by the Committee itself should be the exception. Rule 4 states that the Committee must have all the necessary powers to reach a decision on the report of the Commission, but that, should the need arise, it may entrust the task of taking evidence and the like to another body. And indeed, in the second of the "Other points discussed by the Committee of Ministers" it is stated that the Committee "is not well equipped to take evidence, etc. and ought not normally to undertake such tasks". There the following possibilities are mentioned:

In the first place the Commission might be called in. This might be done in two ways. On the one hand a separate additional Protocol might be adopted, conferring on the Commission the power to undertake the task concerned on behalf of the Committee. On the other hand the Committee might invite the Commission to undertake this task on its behalf. The Commission would then have to be asked in each individual case whether it is prepared to do so.

Secondly, the Committee itself, possibly composed of so-called "alternate members", might undertake this task. As appears from Article 14 of the Statute of the Council of Europe, the member States are normally represented on the Committee by the Ministers for Foreign Affairs, but they may also nominate other persons ("alternates") if this is desirable in the circumstances. For the case here referred to one might consider the Ministers of Justice, or even experts specially nominated for the purpose, or the Permanent Representatives to the Council of Europe who normally act as "deputies". Point 2 also provides that the Committee may appoint a sub-committee for this purpose.

Finally, Article 17 of the Statute of the Council of Europe affords still another possibility. According to that article the Committee of Ministers may set up advisory or technical committees or commissions if it deems this desirable. The Committee might proceed to do so for the purpose of taking

---

8. Rules adopted by the Committee of Ministers for the application of Article 32 of the Convention, Council of Europe, *Collected Texts*, Strasbourg 1987, pp. 192-194. At its 409th meeting in June 1987 the Committee has again partly revised the Rules.
9. "Other points discussed by the Committee of Ministers", *ibidem*, pp. 194-196.

evidence and other tasks within the context of its function under Article 32 of the Convention.

The Committee has decided not to opt for an additional Protocol but to leave the choice open for a decision *ad hoc* should the need arise. In that case, in our opinion, the most appropriate solution would be to entrust the Commission with the task in question, since that organ appears to be best equipped for it and moreover has already performed the same task in an earlier phase of the procedure. If this construction is not chosen, it would seem best to leave the task to a committee specially nominated for the purpose. For the composition of such a committee it would then be possible to choose expert persons. Moreover, such a committee, although it would of course be directly subordinate to the Committee of Ministers, would perhaps be less focused on national interests than the members of the Committee of Ministers themselves or their "alternates".

3. When exercising its function under Article 32 of the Convention, the Committee of Ministers is composed in the same way as for the performance of the tasks resulting from the Statute of the Council of Europe.[10] This follows in so many words from the Rules adopted by the Committee in connection with the application of Article 32 of the Convention. In fact, Rule 2 provides that the representative of any member State on the Committee is fully qualified to take part in the activities of the Committee within the context of Article 32 of the Convention, even if that State has not yet ratified the Convention.

In its composition the Committee therefore has some resemblance to the Court, membership of which is also coupled - but in that case with respect to only the number of judges[11] - with membership of the Council of Europe,[12] whereas with respect to the Commission the criterion chosen for the number of the members is the number of the States which are parties to the Convention.[13]

With regard to the chairmanship of the Committee, too, in principle the normal rules apply. This means that the chairmanship rotates among the representatives of the member States in the alphabetical order of the States in the English language.[14] However, there is an exception to this rule in that, if the chairmanship of the Committee is held by the representative of a member State which is party to a dispute referred to the Committee, under Rule 7 that representative must step down from the Chair during the discussion of the Commission's report. During that period the chairmanship is then performed by the representative of the State which in the English

---

10. For this composition, see *supra* p. 30.
11. The similarity of nationality, too, exists largely in practice, although, as has been said, it is possible, and is actually the case at present, that judges may be elected in the Court who do not have the nationality of one of the member States; see *supra* p. 26.
12. See *supra* p. 2.
13. See *supra* p. 20.
14. See Rules 7 and 8 of the Rules of Procedure of the Committee of Ministers.

alphabetical order succeeds the State whose representative had to step down temporarily from the Chair.

4. Under Article 32(2), when the Committee has found that there has been a violation of the Convention, the contracting State concerned is obliged to take appropriate measures within a period to be prescribed by the Committee. It appears from Rule 5 that from this provision the Committee has derived for itself the power to give advice or make suggestions or recommendations to the State concerned, provided that these are closely related to the violation in question. It exercised this power, for instance, in the *Greek* Case.[15] Such advice, suggestions, and recommendations are not, however, to be regarded as decisions in the sense of Article 32(4) of the Convention, and do not therefore involve any obligation on the part of the governments to which they are addressed. Nevertheless they may have considerable importance, because the Committee may take them into account in deciding on whether the contracting State in question has really taken effective measures within the prescribed period under Article 32(3). Recently it has become practice that the Committee, under Rule 5, may also recommend that a certain amount of money is paid to the original applicant for expenses incurred in the proceedings before the Commission or as just satisfaction for other damages suffered.[16] According to the newly added paragraph 2 of Rule 9 the Committee may request the Commission to make proposals concerning in particular the appropriateness, nature and extent of just satisfaction for the injured party.

5. The matter of voting has already been discussed above.[17] In that context it was found that the two-third majority required by the Convention with regard to a decision on whether or not there has been a violation diverges from the line followed in the Statute of the Council of Europe, according to which resolutions of the Committee on important matters require the unanimous vote of the representatives casting a vote and of a majority of the representatives entitled to sit on the Committee. The two-third majority in the sense of Article 32 means "a majority of two-thirds of the members entitled to sit on the Committee", *i.e.* a majority of two-thirds of the total number of members. Thus, the requirements of the Convention are more liberal than those set by the Statute for important matters, but more stringent if compared with the cases for which Article 20(d) of the Statute requires a two-third majority of the representatives casting a vote and of a majority of the representatives entitled to sit on the Committee.

For the rest, Rule 10 declares that the rules laid down in Article 20 of the Statute apply. This means in particular that also any advice, suggestions

15.   See *Yearbook* XII; *The Greek Case* (1969), pp. 513-514.
16.   Resolution DH(89)1 of 18 January 1989, *Sallustio*; Resolution DH(89)5 of 2 March 1989, *Warwick*; Resolution DH(89)6 of 2 March 1989, *Veit.*
17.   See *supra* p. 31.

and recommendations referred to above, addressed to contracting States in case of a violation of the Convention, require a two-third majority of the representatives casting a vote and of a majority of the representatives entitled to sit on the Committee. The same applies in the case of the decision to discontinue the examination of the case because a friendly settlement or other arrangement has been made. Decisions concerning certain questions of procedure may be taken by a simple majority vote of the representatives entitled to sit on the Committee.

As has been said, all member States are fully entitled to take part in the activities of the Committee within the context of Article 32 of the Convention.[18] This holds good also for the respondent State. With respect to voting, this is expressly confirmed once more by Rule 10, where it is inferred from the general applicability of Article 20 of the Statute that parties to the dispute also have the right to vote in the Committee.

The same principle of full participation of all member States in the procedure under Article 32 also applies in the sense that those States which were not parties to the proceedings before the Commission are also entitled, according to Rule 3, to make submissions and deposit documents in the proceedings before the Committee via their representative on the Committee. However, the Committee has reserved its position on the possibility that they may also address to the Committee a request which has not been made before the Commission, e.g. a request for damages (point 1).

6. The position of the original individual applicant in the proceedings before the Committee of Ministers is very weak. It is hardly possible to speak of any position at all; it is much weaker still than that in the proceedings before the Court, as it was before the revision of the Rules of Court in 1982.[19]

In point 3 of the points discussed by the Committee in connection with the application of Article 32 there is a reference to the decision of the Committee not to establish a procedure permitting the communication to an individual applicant of the report of the Commission on his application, or the communication to the Committee of the applicant's observations on the report. In comparison, in consequence of Rule 33(1) of the revised Rules of Court, the report will be transmitted to the original individual applicant.[20] In the *Nielsen* Case the Commission gave as its opinion that the decision on communication of its report rests with the Committee.[21]

The Committee has adopted the view that transmission to the individual applicant of the complete text of or extracts from the Commission's report should take place only on a strictly confidential basis, and only with the consent of the State against which the application was lodged (point 3(b)). Even under these conditions it is not intended in all cases that the individual

18. See *supra* p. 194.
19. See *supra* p. 164.
20. See *Collected Texts, supra* note 8, pp. 163-164.
21. See K. Vasak, *La Convention Européenne des Droits de l'Homme,* Paris 1964, p. 207.

applicant should be notified of the content of the Commission's report; in the opinion of the Committee transmission should be confined to exceptional cases where the proceedings before the Committee render it desirable, *e.g.* when the Committee wishes to obtain the observations of the applicant (point 3(b)). Considerations based on the interest of the individual applicant do not play a part in the decision on whether the report should be transmitted. An *ad hoc* decision to transmit the report to the individual applicant was taken by the Committee, for instance, in the *Nielsen* Case for the purpose of obtaining certain information from him.[22]

Even when the individual applicant addresses the Committee in writing, such a letter is not taken into account, nor is he entitled to be heard by the Committee. The Committee bases this on the fact that in the system of the Convention he is not a party to the proceedings at this stage. This point of view is communicated to the individual applicant by the Secretary General when the latter informs him of the fact that the Commission's report on his case has been transmitted to the Committee of Ministers. If letters and documents addressed to the Committee are nevertheless received from him, the Secretary General acknowledges their receipt, explaining why they will not form part of the proceedings before the Committee and cannot be considered as documents in the case.[23]

For a long time the individual applicant could also not participate as such in proceedings before the Court. The drawbacks of this system were however met to a large extent by the manner in which the Commission functioned in those proceedings.[24] In the proceedings before the Committee of Ministers, however, this role by the Commission is not possible. In fact, the Commission, too, in principle is not involved in the consideration of the case by the Committee. The Committee has even decided not to include in its Rules any provisions concerning participation of representatives of the Commission in the proceedings (point 4), and the Rules of the Commission do not contain a separate section concerning proceedings before the Committee of Ministers, such as is the case with proceedings before the Court. If the Committee considers this desirable, it may request the Commission to supply information, but only in exceptional cases and only concerning certain specific points from its report. Consequently, even if the Commission receives such a request, its position still is not comparable to that in the proceedings before the Court, where it is able to elucidate all aspects of the case in a manner to be determined by the Commission itself.

---

22. *Ibidem*, p. 209.
23. In 1972 the Committee of Ministers made a different decision with respect to letters of individuals in the context of the supervisory function of the Committee under Art. 54 of the Convention. When it is stated therein that no compensation has been received in accordance with a decision of the Court to that effect under Art. 50 of the Convention, or any other information is furnished in connection with the execution of such a decision of the Court, the Committee deems itself competent to take cognizance of it.
24. See *supra* pp. 166-170.

7. The proceedings before the Committee of Ministers do not have a very clear-cut character. The chairman consults with the representatives of the States involved in the case to obtain their opinion about the procedure to be followed. If necessary, the Committee subsequently specifies the order in which and the time-limits within which any written submissions and other documents are to be deposited. This equally applies to inter-State disputes and to cases which originate from individual applications. However, since Rule 8 speaks of "State Party or States Parties to the dispute", it has to be assumed that, besides the State against which the original application was lodged, only the State by which the original application was submitted is considered as a State involved in the case, and not the State of which the individual applicant is a national.

8. Article 32(1) states that the proceedings before the Committee of Ministers result in a decision on whether there has been a violation of the Convention. However, just as is the case with proceedings before the Commission and before the Court,[25] proceedings before the Committee of Ministers have also sometimes been interrupted after the parties had reached some kind of settlement. In 1987, the Committee added to that end to the Rules for the application of Article 32 Rule 6bis which reads as follows:

> Prior to taking a decision under Article 32, paragraph 1, of the Convention, the Committee of Ministers may be informed of a friendly settlement, arrangement or other fact of a kind to provide a solution of the matter. In that event, it may decide to discontinue its examination of the case, after satisfying itself that the solution envisaged is based on respect for human rights as defined in the Convention.

This new rule reflects existing practice of the Committee.

In the joint Cases of *Pataki v. Austria* and *Dumshirn v. Austria*[26] the applicants had alleged violation of the right to a fair trial (Art. 6), because they were not represented in a particular phase of the criminal proceedings against them, whereas the Public Prosecutor was present. The Commission considered that the Austrian Penal Code conflicted with the Convention on this point. In the last phase of the proceedings before the Commission, Austria amended its legislation to eliminate this conflict. At the same time a temporary arrangement was made which enabled the applicants to have their case re-examined by the Austrian judicial authorities. At the suggestion of the Commission, the Committee of Ministers then expressed its satisfaction with the amendment of the law and decided that no further steps were necessary.[27] In the first Case of *Greece v. United Kingdom* the Committee also decided that no further steps were needed after Greece and the United Kingdom

---

25. See *supra* pp. 128-130 and pp. 158-161 respectively.
26. *Yearbook* VI (1963), p. 714 (738).
27. *Ibidem*, p. 730. See also Resolution DH(64)1 of 5 June 1964, concerning the *Glaser* Case.

had reached a settlement.[28]

The Committee is also inclined to stop the proceedings if no settlement between the parties has been reached but certain measures have improved the situation complained of. Thus, in the *Bramelid and Malmström* Case the applicants complained that they had been compelled to surrender their shares for a price below their real value and alleged amongst others that the arbitrators to whom their dispute was referred did not constitute a "tribunal" within the meaning of Article 6(1) of the Convention. In its report the Commission had expressed the opinion that there had been a violation of Article 6(1) of the Convention.[29] During the examination of the case, the Government of Sweden informed the Committee of Ministers that the Swedish Parliament had adopted an amendment to the legislation according to which a party not satisfied with a decision of the arbitrators could start a procedure before an ordinary court. The Committee decided that, having regard to the information supplied by the Government of Sweden, no further action was called for.[30]

There is no objection to such a procedure, in which the Committee accepts a settlement or other arrangement as a solution of the dispute, and thus as the end of the case, provided that the Committee makes sure that also the original applicant consents and that the solution is in conformity with the Convention. The Committee is a political and not a judicial organ and, in contrast with the Court, does not play a very important part in the interpretation of the Convention, so that the public interest in a declaratory decision as a preventive remedy is hardly involved here. The very fact that the Commission has not referred the case to the Court and thus leaves it to the Committee to deal with it, in general already indicates that no difficult questions of interpretation are at issue. If in such a case the respondent State takes measures by which the situation conflicting with the Convention is eliminated, and moreover the original applicant has received just satisfaction, the purpose of the proceedings before the Committee has been attained and there is no reason why the respondent State should be formally declared in default.

Strictly speaking, however, a decision of the Committee that no further steps are required is not in conformity with Article 32(1) of the Convention, since it ought formally to be preceded by a decision on whether there has been a violation of the Convention. In the above-mentioned cases the procedure followed by the Committee did not involve great problems; the first Case of *Greece v. United Kingdom* concerned an inter-State dispute, in which the Committee took its decision that no further steps were necessary

28. Resolution DH(74)2 of 26 November 1974, Council of Europe, *Collection of Resolutions adopted by the Committee of Ministers in application of Articles 32 and 54 of the European Convention for the Protection of Human Rights and Fundamental Freedoms 1959-1983*, Strasbourg 1984, p. 51.
29. Report of 12 December 1983, *D & R* 38 (1984), p. 18 (38-41).
30. Resolution DH(84)4 of 25 October 1984, *ibidem*, p. 43.

at the instance of both States involved in the dispute. In the *Pataki* Case and the *Durnshim* Case the decision of the Committee was based on a suggestion of the Commission to settle the matter with the finding that no further steps were called for. The situation was somewhat different, however, in the *Fourons* Case. This case concerned the application of the Belgian linguistic legislation in education. In its report the Commission held unanimously that Belgium had violated Article 2 of the First Protocol in conjunction with Article 14 of the Convention. After the transmission of the report, the Belgian legislation on this point was amended in such a way that the conflict with the Convention was abolished. In its resolution concerning this case the Committee took cognizance of the opinion given by the Commission in its report and also of the new Belgian legislation, and subsequently decided that no further steps were called for.[31] And in a case in which the Swiss Government had ended, by means of an amendment of the law, a situation that was contrary to the Convention, the Committee confined itself to referring to the opinion of the Commission, without itself giving any further decision.[32] In such cases, where the Commission has not been able to give its opinion on the newly arisen situation, in our view it is preferable that the Committee should adhere strictly to Article 32 of the Convention and decide that there has indeed been a violation of the Convention, but that *in its opinion* this has meanwhile been redressed by an amendment of the legislation, so that no further steps are necessary. This policy was followed, for instance, in the second *Vagrancy* Case,[33] in the *Kiss* Case[34] and in the *Hilton* Case.[35]

9. A situation which conflicts flatly with Article 32 of the Convention, and for which at present there seems to be no solution, is that which arises when in the Committee of Ministers the required two-third majority can be found neither for the view that there has been a violation nor for the view that no violation has occurred. In such a case no decision as required by Article 32 is taken, while there is no question of some kind of settlement between the parties and neither is there any guarantee that the situation conflicting with the Convention is corrected or made good with respect to the victim by the respondent State.

An example of such a case is the *Huber* Case. In its report the Commission had given as its opinion that Austria had violated Article 6(1) of the

---

31. Resolution DH(74)1 of 30 april 1974, *Inhabitants of Les Fourons*, Yearbook XVII (1974), p. 542 (614-616).
32. Resolution DH(79)7 of 19 October 1979, *Eggs*.
33. Resolution DH(72)1 of 16 October 1972, *Second Vagrancy Case*, Yearbook XV (1972), pp. 694-698.
34. Resolution DH(78)3 of 19 April 1978, *Kiss*.
35. Resolution DH(79)3 of 24 April 1979, *Hilton*. More recent examples: Resolution DH(83)8 of 22 April 1983, *B v. United Kingdom*; Resolution DH(83)9 of 23 June 1983, *Tonwerke and others*; Resolution DH(83)14 of 27 October 1983, *Orchin*; Resolution DH(84)4 of 25 October 1984, *Bramelid and Malmström*; Resolution DH(85)1 of 25 January 1985, *G, Medway and Ball*; Resolution DH(85)3 of 25 January 1985, *Zamir*; Resolution DH(85)4 of 25 February 1985, *Marijnissen*; Resolution DH(85)8 of 11 April 1985, *Neubeck*.

Convention with respect to Huber.[36] The most important passage from the resolution of the Committee of Ministers in this case reads as follows:

> Voting in accordance with the provisions of Article 32(1) of the Convention, but without attaining the majority of two thirds of the members entitled to sit. Decides therefore that no further action is called for in this case.[37]

As has been said, the Committee of Ministers has been given a task under the European Convention in order to guarantee that the supervisory procedure should result at all events in a binding decision on whether or not there has been a violation. Such a guarantee does not exist under the present system, according to which a two-third majority is required, as is evident from the *Huber* Case, and also from the *East Africans* Case[38] and from the Cases of *Dores and Silveira*.[39]

A solution for the problem mentioned here might be found by permitting the Committee to take its decision under Article 32 via a voting procedure comparable to that applying to the Court. A provision would also be conceivable according to which the Committee might decide in a second vote by a simple majority of the representatives entitled to sit on the Committee, and by a casting vote of the chairman when the votes are equal, after it has been established in the first vote that the required two-third majority cannot be obtained for either decision. The latter solution would be effective only, however, if abstentions were excluded.

However, the two-third majority requirement of Article 32 already forms an exception to the general rule according to which the Committee takes its decisions on important matters by a unanimous vote. It is not sure, therefore, that at the present moment the contracting States are prepared to allow matters which in their view affect their vital interests to be settled by a simple majority of the representatives casting a vote and te renounce the right of abstention.

10. When the Committee finds a violation of the Convention, it must prescribe, under Article 32(2), a period within which the State in question is to take the measures required in the light of the Committee's decision. So far no cases have come to our attention in which the Committee has prescribed such a period. This may be accounted for partly by the fact that hitherto the Committee of Ministers has found a violation of the Convention which in its opinion called for further action in only a few cases.

---

36. See the Report of 8 February 1973, *D & R* 2 (1975), p. 11 (29).
37. Resolution DH(75)2 of 15 April 1975, *Yearbook* XVIII (1975), p. 325 (326). On this *Huber* Case, see H. Golsong, "Die eigenartige Rolle des Ministerkomitees des Europa-rates als eine der beiden Endentscheidungsinstanzen im Rahmen der MRK", *EuGrZ* (1975), pp. 448-449, and A. Morgan, "European Convention on Human Rights, Article 32: What is Wrong?", *Human Rights Review* (1976), pp. 157-176.
38. Resolution DH(77)2 of 21 October 1977, *Yearbook* XX (1977), p. 642 (644). On this case, see A. Drzemczewski, "A 'non-decision' of the Committee of Ministers under Article 32(1) of the European Convention on Human Rights: The East African Asian Cases", *Modern Law Review* (1978), pp. 337-342.
39. Resolution DH(85)7 of 11 April 1985.

The first was the *Greek* Case, in which the Committee considered that a great many articles of the Convention had been violated.[40] However, before the Committee had found in its resolution that there had been a violation of the Convention, Greece had already withdrawn from the Council of Europe and denounced the Convention.[41] Under these circumstances the Committee observed that it was "called upon to deal with the case in conditions which are not precisely those envisaged in the Convention" and concluded "that in the present case there is no basis for further action under paragraph 2 of Article 32 of the Convention".[42]

The only other case known to us is formed by the first two Cases of *Cyprus v. Turkey*. On 21 October 1977 the Committee decided in those cases that "events which occurred in Cyprus constitute violations of the Convention". In addition the Committee requested Turkey to take measures "in order to put an end to such violations as might continue to occur and so that such events are not repeated", and urged the parties "to resume intercommunal talks".[43] To our knowledge the Committee did not prescribe a period within which these matters ought to be realized. Should this indeed be the case, the Committee has acted contrary to the explicit provision of Article 32(2).

The foregoing means that there does not yet exist any practice concerning the length of the period referred to in Article 32(2). In general this will depend on the kind of measures which the State in question has to take in connection with the resolution of the Committee of Ministers. These measures in turn will be closely related to the nature of the violation found. Thus, a violation of the Convention consisting in a faulty application of a legal regulation by a government body can be undone with less difficulty and consequently more promptly than one where the legislation itself conflicts with the Convention.

11. When the Committee prescribes a period as referred to in Article 32(2), it must also ascertain whether the State in question actually takes effective measures. If this is not the case, the Committee shall decide, again by a two-third majority of the members entitled to sit on the Committee, what further steps have to be taken, and it shall publish the report of the Commission.

The sanction on the failure to act upon the decision of the Committee of Ministers under Article 32(1) is therefore twofold. It consists on the one hand of measures the substance and the form of which may be determined by the Committee with a view to the circumstances of each individual case, and on the other hand of the publication of the Commission's report.

As has been said, in the *Greek* Case no period was prescribed, and owing to the special circumstances of that case the question as to whether or not the measures prescribed by the Committee were acted upon has not been at

40. See *Yearbook* XII; *The Greek Case* (1969), p. 512.
41. *Ibidem.*
42. *Ibidem*, p. 513.
43. Resolution DH(79)1 of 20 January 1979, *Yearbook* XXII (1979), p. 440.

issue. The Committee did decide, however, to publish the Commission's report.[44]

Also in the above-mentioned Cases of *Cyprus v. Turkey*, no period as referred to in Article 32(2) had been prescribed. By a resolution of 20 January 1979 the Committee dealt again with the matter. It regretted to find that its request that the negotiations between the Turkish and the Greek-Cypriotic community should be resumed had not been complied with by the parties, and subsequently decided

> strongly to urge the parties to resume intercommunal talks under the auspices of the Secretary General of the United Nations in order to agree upon solutions on all aspects of the dispute,

after which it stated that it considered this decision "as completing its consideration of the case Cyprus versus Turkey".[45]

This last part of the Committee's decision seems highly questionable to us. Article 32(3) provides:

> If the High Contracting Party concerned has not taken satisfactory measures within the prescribed period, the Committee of Ministers shall decide by the majority provided for in paragraph 1 above what effect shall be given to its original decision and shall publish the Report.

Even apart from the period referred to, this provision in our opinion implies that the Committee has to deal with a case in such a way that, and until the moment at which, the States concerned have taken those measures which are required with a view to the protection of human rights envisaged by the Convention. In the case under discussion Cyprus and Turkey, contrary to Article 32(4), had not given effect to the original decision of the Committee. In so far as can be ascertained, at the moment when the second decision was taken there were also no indications that they would as yet take the measures prescribed in the original decision. In such a situation the Committee should not have backed out of the case and shirked its responsibilities under the Convention by shifting the matter to the Secretary General of the United Nations.

The Committee did, however, decide also in this case, to publish the report of the Commission.[46]

From the fact that the publication of the report referred to in Article 32(3) has the character of a sanction, one might infer that the Committee does not proceed to such publication in cases in which it has come to the conclusion that there has not been a violation of the Convention. In practice, however, but for a few exceptions, all the reports of the Commission are published, regardless of whether or not the Committee considered that there had been a violation. The reason for this is presumably the interest which the respondent State may have in publication when the Committee has followed the viewpoint of the Commission in its decision and the conclusions in the

---

44. *Yearbook* XII; *The Greek Case* (1969), p. 513.
45. Resolution DH(79)1 20 January 1979, *Yearbook* XXII (1979), p. 440.
46. *Ibidem.*

Commission's report are favourable for that State. The decision to publish the report is then usually taken with the consent, or sometimes by special request, of the respondent State.

12. At its 307th meeting, in September 1979, the Ministers' Deputies adopted the rule that the individual applicant ought normally to be informed of the outcome of the examination of his case before the Committee. Surprisingly enough, the decision to give this information requires a unanimous vote. This again indicates that the Committee is more concerned with the interests of the contracting States than with those of the individual whose rights are at issue.

§ 3. COMPARISON OF THE PROCEDURE BEFORE THE COMMITTEE OF MINISTERS WITH THE ONE BEFORE THE COURT

1. The functioning of the Committee of Ministers under Article 32 of the Convention can hardly be described as perfect. Political elements sometimes have their advantages even in a procedure as provided for in the European Convention, as became clear in the discussion of the friendly settlement.[47] However, when a (quasi-)judicial function is concerned, the introduction of political elements normally involves considerable drawbacks. At all events the advantages do not appear to outweigh the distrust created among the individuals concerned when a political organ has to make judicial decisions.

The political character of the Committee of Ministers has its effects on the procedure under Article 32. This procedure is not public, not adversary, and takes place before a non-independent organ. Consequently it by no means satisfies the requirements of Article 6 of the Convention with respect to a fair trial.

2. Despite the fact that the Committee of Ministers is therefore poorly equipped for its task, in practice it still takes the final decision on whether or not there has been a violation of the Convention in almost as large a number of cases as does the Court.[48]

This is caused by the policy of the Commission and the States concerned on whether or not to bring a case before the Court. The Commission's policy of referring cases to the Court, as has already been observed above, is characterized by a certain degree of reserve, even though for the past few years a striking turn of the tide has been apparent.[49] The States still do not

---

47. See *supra* pp. 118-131.
48. P. Leuprecht, "The Protection of Human Rights by Political Bodies - The example of the Committee of Ministers of the Council of Europe", in: M. Nowak, D. Steurer & H. Tretter (eds), *Progress in the Spirit of Human Rights*, Strasbourg 1988, pp. 95-107 (101).
49. See *supra* p. 138.

show much inclination to leave the final decision to the Court. In general they prefer - certainly in the position of respondent States - to have their case dealt with by the Committee. Indeed, in that organ not only can they participate in the vote on the decision to be taken, but in other respects, too, they may greatly influence the decision via the discussions on the matter which precede the vote. Moreover, in the case of the Court four votes (in a Chamber of seven judges) are sufficient to arrive at a conviction, while in the Committee of Ministers at present sixteen votes - two-thirds of the 23 member States - are required. The proportion of votes alone makes the chances of a conviction in the last-mentioned organ considerably smaller than in the Court.

3. Even though in many cases it is the Committee of Ministers which takes the final decision on whether there has been a violation of the Convention, up to the present this organ has not played any important part at all in the interpretation of the Convention. In practically all cases the Committee follows in its decision the opinion of the Commission, without giving any further reasons. The contribution of the Committee to the further development of the legal order laid down in the Convention cannot therefore be compared to that of either the Court or the Commission - apart, of course, from the competence of the Committee, as an organ of the Council of Europe, to make recommendations to the member States to amend the Convention.

The principal reason for this appears to be the fact that the Committee as a political organ lacks a characteristic feature that is essential for the discharge of a judicial function, viz. independence. Whoever may represent the States in the Committee, Foreign Ministers, Ministers of Justice, their deputies, or even special experts, they all follow the instructions of their government.

As has been said, the fact that the Committee was endowed with a task in the procedure provided for in the Convention was the result of a compromise prompted by political reality. This same reality is still present in the sense that total elimination of the Committee from the procedure would appear to be unlikely at the moment. In fact, for this it would be necessary that the jurisdiction of the Court be made compulsory, *i.e.* that ratification of the Convention should at the same time imply recognition of the Court's jurisdiction by the contracting States for an indefinite period. Our serious doubts as to the feasibility of that idea have already been pointed out.[50]

For the time being, the legal protection of the individual and the maintenance of the legal order created by the Convention appear to be guaranteed most effectively if the Commission refers to the Court a maximum of cases declared admissible by it, at least in so far as this is made possible by the recognition of the Court's jurisdiction by the respondent State, and provided that the case is not so politically explosive that a political decision alone is able to prevent more serious detriment to the Convention and its

50.   See *supra* p. 140.

aims; which may be the case especially with inter-State disputes.

In recent years voices have been heard demanding modification of the proceedings before the Committee of Ministers in, for instance, the following ways:

- the requirement of a two-third majority could be replaced by a simple majority, to make an effective supervision possible;
- the Commission should make more use of the possibility to submit proposals to the Committee;
- the Committee should, just like the Court, be able to decide on "just satisfaction" in a binding way;
- the Committee should require more detailed measures to be taken by the States;
- the Committee should play a part in the supervision of the friendly settlements reached under Articles 28 and 30.[51]

At the first European Ministerial Conference on Human Rights, held in Vienna on 19 and 20 March 1985, in Resolution No. 1 it was, *inter alia*, recommended that the Committee of Ministers of the Council of Europe

> a) entrust the existing competent body of experts - enlarged as appropriate - with the task of examining as a matter of priority the possibility of introducing further improvements to the Convention's system of control and submitting proposals. This body should bear in mind the views expressed in the Swiss delegation's report as well as the observations made by other delegations.[52]

At the moment the Committee of Experts (DH-PR) has several proposals for improvement of the supervisory mechanism on its agenda. The position of the Committee of Ministers is, however, still a highly controversial issue in this and other governmental bodies.

---

51. See the report of the Swiss delegation at the First European Ministerial Conference on Human Rights held in Vienna on 19-20 March 1985.
52. *Information sheet* No. 17, Council of Europe, Strasbourg 1985, pp. 47-48 and p. 136.

CHAPTER V

THE SUPERVISORY FUNCTION OF THE SECRETARY GENERAL OF THE COUNCIL OF EUROPE

§ 1. INTRODUCTION

1. In addition to the complaint procedure, the European Convention provides for yet another procedure for supervising the observance by the contracting States of their obligations under the Convention. This is based on Article 57 of the Convention and is entrusted to the Secretary General of the Council of Europe. Article 57 reads as follows:

> On receipt of a request from the Secretary General of the Council of Europe any High Contracting Party shall furnish an explanation of the manner in which its internal law ensures the effective implementation of any of the provisions of this Convention.

This provision originates from the work of the United Nations. In 1947, within the context of the *travaux préparatoires* of what later developed into the Universal Declaration and the two Covenants, a text was drawn up which related to civil and political rights. This text contained a provision according to which the Secretary General of the United Nations would have the right to request the States which would become parties to the treaty then in preparation to report on the manner in which the effective implementation of the provisions of the treaty was ensured in their internal law. During the preparation of the European Convention this idea was adopted in a British proposal to the Committee of Experts and accepted by this Committee.[1]

2. Under international law there are several examples of procedures in which States have to submit reports to make possible the assessment of the observance of their obligations.[2] This system of supervision, which in general is referred to as the reporting procedure, may constitute an effective instrument of control, also and perhaps even especially in the field of the protection of human rights.

Indeed, treaties for the protection of human rights are not concerned primarily with the interests of the State, but with the interests of the individual. If such a treaty provides for an inter-State complaint procedure,

---

1. According to the original text, prepared in the United Nations, the Secretary General was to make use of his right only on the basis of a resolution of the General Assembly of the United Nations. A comparable condition was dropped in Art. 57 of the European Convention. For the history of Art. 57, see K. Vasak, *La Convention Européenne des Droits de l'Homme*, Paris 1964, pp. 221-222.
2. On this kind of procedure in general, see F. van Asbeck, "Quelques aspects du contrôle international non-judiciaire de l'application par les gouvernements des Conventions internationales", *Liber amicorum in honour of J.P.A. François*, Leyden 1959, pp. 27-41.

the contracting States will make their decision on whether to file an application dependent upon political considerations. And precisely because the interests of the State are affected to a less extent by a violation, States will proceed to file an application only in very exceptional cases. In this respect the practice with respect to Article 24 of the European Convention speaks for itself.[3]

Owing to the lack of initiative on the side of States to start a complaint procedure, a gap in the supervision of the treaty concerned may readily arise. A reporting procedure, such as is provided for in Article 57, may fill this gap, because the initiative for this may be taken by an international organ and accordingly is not dependent on a decision of a State that will be taken on political grounds.

In the case of treaties providing for an individual right of complaint the problem of the States' lack of initiative to start the complaint procedure naturally rises less frequently, because in that case this initiative may also be taken by those individuals who have a personal and direct interest in it. It should, however, be borne in mind that the individual right of complaint is optional in practically all cases, which implies that it can only be employed if a State concerned has accepted that possibility. At the moment all contracting States have accepted the right of individual complaint under Article 25 of the Convention.[4] However, situations which do conflict with the Convention but have not yet made victims in the sense of Article 25 can be complained of only by the contracting States.[5] In such cases the supervision of the observance of the obligations under the Convention, therefore, is again dependent on the lodging of a complaint by a State, with all the disadvantages and restrictions involved. Here again a reporting procedure may be useful.

But even apart from the question of whether the complaint procedure provided for functions effectively or not and whether or not the initiative has been laid also in the hands of the individual concerned, the existence of a reporting procedure side by side with a complaint procedure is of great value. A reporting procedure, precisely because its character differs from that of a complaint procedure, may enhance the effectiveness of the international supervision in some respects. Thus, via a reporting procedure all the contracting States can be controlled at the same time, while in a complaint procedure it is always the acts or omissions of only one State which are examined. The first advantage of this is that the resistance to the supervision may be less because all the States are equally subjected to examination. Further, because of the possibility of comparison a more balanced picture may be obtained of the state of affairs with respect to the implementation of the treaty in question within the whole group of contracting States, which might

3. See *supra* pp. 35-36.
4. See *supra* p. 37.
5. See *supra* pp. 39-40.

facilitate the taking of measures for the improvement of the situation. In addition, the reporting procedure makes it possible to complete the picture of implementation, because this form of supervision may comprise all the provisions of the treaty in question simultaneously, while in a complaint procedure only one, or at most a few, of the provisions at a time may be examined. Furthermore it is an advantage that the international organ concerned may assure, via the reporting procedure, a certain continuity in the supervision, because it can itself decide which aspects are to be examined and when, while in the case of a complaint procedure one must wait until a case is submitted, in which case the supervision has a more *ad hoc* character. The continuity, owing to which a comparison with the situation in the past is also possible, naturally enhances the effectiveness of the supervision. Finally the advantage may be mentioned that the reporting system will in general assume a form that is more flexible and better adapted to the particularities of States than the much more formal complaint procedure.

In view of the above-mentioned advantages it is not astonishing that many international regulations for the protection of human rights, both those concerning civil and political rights, and those concerning social, economic and cultural rights, provide for a reporting procedure.[6]

§ 2.   THE REPORTING PROCEDURE UNDER ARTICLE 57 OF THE CONVENTION

1. In comparison with most other treaties on human rights which include for the contracting States the obligation to hand in reports, the provision of Article 57 of the European Convention is very brief and leaves a great number of questions unanswered. Most of this lack of clarity, however, has been removed by practice.

2. At any rate it is clear from the text of the Article that the Secretary General has the *right* to request the contracting States to furnish an explanation of the manner in which in their internal law the effective implementation of the provisions of the Convention is ensured, and that the contracting States have the *duty* to provide him with this information.

For the rest, little can be inferred with certainty from the article. Thus, the question arises whether Article 57 confers discretionary powers upon the Secretary General or whether in the exercise of his powers he is dependent in some way on another organ of the Council of Europe. Since Article 57 is silent on this, one must assume that the Secretary General has full discretion.

---

6.   See, *e.g.*, Arts 22 and 23 of the Constitution of the International Labour Organisation, Art. 9 of the Convention on the Elimination of All Forms of Racial Discrimination, Arts 40 *et seq.* of the International Covenant on Civil and Political Rights, Arts 16 *et seq.* of the International Covenant on Economic, Social and Cultural Rights, Art. 19 of the Torture Conventie and Art. 21 of the European Social Charter.

In a statement made before the Legal Committee of the Parliamentary Assembly the then Secretary General gave as his opinion:

> The Secretary General in making a request under Article 57 is acting under his own responsibility and at his own discretion, in virtue of powers conferred upon him by the Convention independently of any powers he may have in virtue of the Statute of the Council of Europe. His power under Article 57 is not subject to control or instruction.[7]

Until now not a single contracting State has officially objected to this interpretation by the Secretary General of his supervisory powers. It may therefore be assumed that the above-mentioned statement constitutes an almost generally accepted interpretation of the Convention.[8] This is not to say, however, that the Secretary General's actions in this field are always welcomed by the contracting States. Three States have refused to furnish a reply to his fourth request: the Federal Republic of Germany, Iceland and Malta, while his fifth request has met with broad opposition so far.

3. From these discretionary powers of the Secretary General with respect to the application of Article 57, in practice a number of more specific powers which do not directly result from the text of that article have been inferred.

Thus the Secretary General may determine the date on which, and consequently the frequency with which, reports have to be submitted. Hitherto the contracting States have been invited five times to submit reports on the application of the rights laid down in the Convention, *viz.* in October 1964, in July 1970, in April 1975, in March 1983 and in July 1988.

The Secretary General, when exercising his powers under Article 57, is also free to refer to all or to a few of the provisions of the Convention, or to only one of them. In 1964 the contracting States were requested to furnish information on the question of "how their laws, their case-law and their administration practice give effect to the fundamental rights and freedoms guaranteed by the Convention and its first Protocol".[9] In that case, therefore, they had to report on all the rights set forth in the Convention and the Protocol. In 1970, on the other hand, the request of the Secretary General concerned only Article 5(5), and in 1975 information was required on the application of Articles 8, 9, 10 and 11. Moreover, on the latter occasion the Secretary General reserved to himself the right to ask for a further explanation of certain points in connection with the reports submitted by the States.[10] In 1983, the Secretary General made an enquiry into the implementation of

---

7. Statement by the Secretary General on Article 57 of the European Convention on Human Rights made before the Legal Committee of the Consultative Assembly in Oslo on 29th August 1964, Council of Europe, *Collected Texts*, Strasbourg 1987, pp. 235-236.
8. See W. Pahr, "Etude Fonctionnelle des Organes Européens de Protection Internationales des Droits de l'Homme", *R.D.H.* 2 (1969), pp. 199-207, 202-203. See also P. Mahoney, "Does Article 57 of the European Convention on Human Rights serve any useful purpose?", in: *Protecting Human Rights: The European Dimension; Studies in honour of Gérard J. Wiarda*, Cologne etc. 1988, pp. 373-393 (380-382) with reference to other authors. He also refers to the different opinion of the then governmental expert for the Federal Republic of Germany, Irene Maier.
9. See Pahr, *ibidem*, p. 203.
10. *Ibidem.*

the Convention "in respect of children and young persons placed in care or in institutions following a decision of the administrative or judicial authorities",[11] while in 1988 the request concerned Article 6(1).[12]

The question of whether a request to submit reports must be addressed to all the contracting States at the same time, or whether Article 57 may also be applied with respect to one State or some of them separately, cannot yet be answered on the basis of practice at this moment. In the five cases in which the Secretary General asserted his powers under Article 57 all the States were approached indiscriminately. In our opinion, however, the above-mentioned discretionary powers of the Secretary General might permit him to request a report from one State alone, or some of them.[13] However, it is not likely to occur very often that the Secretary General examines the acts or omissions of one State or some of them only, because this is apt to be regarded as a discriminatory and unfriendly act, and may undermine the confidence in his impartiality which is necessary for an adequate discharge of his function. Moreover, in that case a number of the above-mentioned advantages of the reporting system will no longer apply. It is only in very clear cases of massive and structural violation of the Convention, which cannot be exposed in some other way, that the Secretary General might be well-advised to make use of his powers under Article 57 with respect to a particular State. Thus, one might think of a situation like that in Greece in 1967, if at that time for some reason no complaint against this State would have been submitted. It might also have been conceivable that Turkey should have been requested to submit a report on its application of Article 15, and more generally, the situation in Turkey too, might have been reviewed via the reporting procedure as long as no complaint directed at it by a State was submitted.

4. Practice has produced some clarity concerning the question what is further to be done with the reports submitted by the contracting States and what consequences, if any, may be attached to a violation of the Convention discovered in this way. The Secretary General compiles the answers of the contracting States to his requests in a document which is subsequently brought to the notice of all the contracting States and of the Parliamentary Assembly of the Council of Europe.[14] Before this, the States is given an opportunity to intimate that they wish certain parts of the data furnished by them not to be published.[15]

As a rule therefore the answers of the contracting States are published. This in itself may already form an element of sanction for those cases in which, according to those answers, there has been a violation of the

---

11. See Mahoney, *supra* note 8, p. 375.
12. Council of Europe, *Information Sheet* No. 21, Strasbourg 1988, p. 95.
13. In that sense also Pahr, *supra* note 8, p. 205, and Mahoney, *supra* note 8, pp. 382-383.
14. The last report was also brought to the attention of the Commission and the Court.
15. Pahr, *supra* note 8, p. 203.

Convention. For that purpose some kind of (comparative) analysis with the assistance of independent experts might be desirable, as was done with the results of the third application of Article 57.[16]

In that case the defaulting State is exposed to criticism of the other States, the Parliamentary Assembly and public opinion. It is, however, doubtful whether, when serious violations have been found, this possibility will be sufficiently effective to put an end to the violation. The Secretary General has not been empowered to refer a case via a complaint procedure to the Commission, and, if necessary, later to the Court. Perhaps this could enhance the effectiveness of the supervision under Article 57, although one may ask oneself whether this power would not place the Secretary General too far outside his proper function, and whether in the public interest such a right of complaint had not better be entrusted to a separate organ, which is politically less dependent on the cooperation of the States.[17]

Under the present circumstances in many cases a violation found via the reporting procedure can be subjected to a further examination and result in a binding decision only if one of the other States is prepared - perhaps also on the ground of the information obtained by means of Article 57 - to make use of its right under Article 24. And this can be done only if the admissibility conditions of Article 26 do not eliminate that possibility. The Secretary General himself can do little else but bring the case, if there has been a very serious violation, to the notice of the Committee of Ministers, with a view to possible measures on the ground of Article 8 of the Statute of the Council of Europe. Until now, however, the Secretary General has not given any follow-up to his initiatives.

5. The procedure under Article 57 constitutes a potentially effective instrument of supervision, certainly in combination with the right of complaint under Articles 24 and 25. However, probably in particular owing to the decidedly not very strong position of the Secretary General in relation to the member States, this instrument has hardly been developed up to the present. The procedure itself to a considerable extent amounts to furnishing of information. The information furnished by the States is not, however, examined critically, *e.g.* by reference to information of third parties, such as nongovernmental organizations. Moreover, the procedure of Article 57 is still devoid of the above-mentioned advantages that may be attached to a reporting procedure, since Article 57 has not so far been applied regularly and systematically. And finally, if the obligation of the contracting States to furnish the Secretary General with the information requested is not enforced in one way or another, the procedure may even loose its function as general data-collecting device.

16.   See Mahoney, *supra* note 8, p. 375.
17.   On this, see P. van Dijk, "A European Ombudsman for Human Rights; Reopening a Discussion", *R.D.H.* 10 (1977), pp. 187-211.

CHAPTER VI

ANALYSIS OF THE RIGHTS AND FREEDOMS

§ 1. INTRODUCTION

1. As stated in the preamble to the Convention, the aim which the contracting States wished to achieve was "to take the first steps for the collective enforcement of certain of the Rights stated in the Universal Declaration". The purpose of the Convention was therefore, within the framework of the Council of Europe, to lay down certain human rights, proclaimed in 1948 by the United Nations in the Universal Declaration of Human Rights, in a binding agreement, and at the same time to provide for supervision of the observance of those human-rights provisions.

However, only certain rights were included in these "first steps". A comparison with the Universal Declaration discloses that by no means all the rights mentioned there have been laid down in the Convention. It covers mainly those rights which were to be referred to, in the later elaboration of the Universal Declaration in the two Covenants, as "civil and political rights", and not even all of those. Thus, the principle of equality before the law, the right to freedom of movement and residence, the right to seek and to enjoy asylum in other countries from prosecution, the right to a nationality, the right to own property and the right to take part in the government, which are included in the Universal Declaration,[1] are not to be found in the Convention.

Subsequent steps have been taken within the framework of the Council of Europe both in the form of additional Protocols to the Convention[2] and in the form of other conventions, among them in particular the European Social Charter of 1961,[3] while Article 60 of the Convention also opens the door to further steps outside the framework of the Council of Europe.

2. The reason for the limited scope of the Convention was stated as follows by Teitgen, the rapporteur of the Legal Committee of the Consultative Assembly of the Council of Europe, who drew up the first draft of the Convention:

---

1. Arts 7, 13, 14, 15, 17 and 21 respectively of the Universal Declaration.
2. Protocol no. 1 of 20 March 1952 entered into force on 18 May 1954; Protocols nos 2 and 3 of 6 May 1963 entered into force on 21 September 1970; Protocol no. 4 of 16 September 1963 entered into force on 2 May 1968; Protocol no. 5 of 20 January 1966 entered into force on 20 December 1971; Protocol no. 6 of 28 April 1983 entered into force on 1 March 1985; Protocol no. 7 of 22 November 1984 entered into force on 1 November 1988; Protocol no. 8 of 19 March 1985 entered into force on 1 January 1990. The Protocols nos 3, 5 and 8 are of a procedural character and have been incorporated as amendments into the text of the Convention. The texts of the Protocols can be found in *Collected Texts*, Strasbourg 1987.
3. For the text, see: *European Treaty Series* no. 35, 18 October 1961; 529 *UNTS* 89.

It [*i.e.* the Committee] considered that, for the moment, it is preferable to limit the collective guarantee to those rights and essential freedoms which are practised, after long usage and experience, in all the democratic countries. While they are the first triumph of democratic regimes, they are also the necessary condition under which they operate.

Certainly, professional freedoms and social rights, which have themselves an intrinsic value, must also, in the future, be defined and protected. Everyone will, however, understand that it is necessary to begin at the beginning and to guarantee political democracy in the European Union and then to co-ordinate our economies, before undertaking the generalization of social democracy.[4]

The drafters, therefore, concentrated on those rights which were considered essential for the integration of European democracies, which was the goal of the Council of Europe and with regard to which one might expect that an agreement could easily be reached about their formulation and about the international supervision of their implementation, since they could be deemed to have been recognized in the Member States of the Council of Europe. On the other hand, both the detailed formulation of these rights, with the possibilities of limitations and the creation of a supervisory mechanism in a binding treaty were novel and revolutionary.[5]

3. It was precisely these two points, the formulation and the supervisory mechanism, which were used as arguments for a separate regulation of, on the one hand, the civil and political rights and, on the other hand, the economic, social, and cultural rights; a solution which was ultimately also chosen within the framework of the UN. The first category of rights was considered to concern the sphere of freedom of the individual *vis-à-vis* the government. These rights and liberties and their limitations would lend themselves to a detailed regulation, while the implementation of the resulting duty on the part of the government to abstain from interference could be reviewed by a national and/or international body. The second category, on the other hand, was considered to consist not of legal rights but of programmatic rights, whose formulation necessarily is much vaguer and for whose realization the States must pursue a given policy, an obligation which does not lend itself to incidental review of government action for its lawfulness.[6]

4. Council of Europe, Cons. Ass., First Session, *Reports* (1949), p. 1144.
5. In view of the emphasis placed by the drafters on democracy it may be a matter of surprise that no provision was included on the right of participation in government and on free elections. Evidently the matter was too complex and would have delayed the signing of the Convention. The issue of free elections was covered by the First Additional Protocol soon thereafter (Art. 3).
6. See "Annotations on the text of the draft International Covenant on Human Rights, prepared by the Secretary-General", Document A/2929, pp. 7-8. See also the statement of Henri Rolin, member of the Consultative Assembly, before the Belgian Senate, quoted in H. Golsong, "Implementation of International Protection of Human Rights", *R.C.A.D.I.* 110 (1963-III), p. 58, note 21: "quelque désirable que soit la satisfaction de ces droits [sociaux], il faut reconnaître qu'ils représentent plus de conceptions morales ou politiques que juridiques; que dans l'opinion de plusieurs, ils ne reçoivent actuellement pleine satisfaction dans aucun pays et qu'à toute évidence certains pays du Conseil de l'Europe ne pourraient, dans la meilleure des hypothèses, en assurer le plein respect à l'ensemble de leurs ressortissants que dans un avenir éloigné. Il ne pouvait donc, en ce qui les concerne, être question de sauvegarde et il a fallu les écarter de la liste".

It is undeniable that there are differences, roughly speaking, between the two categories of rights with respect to their legal character and their implementation. However, such differences are also present *within* those categories. Thus, the right to a fair trial and the right to periodic elections by secret ballot, unlike, for instance, the prohibition of slavery or of torture, call not only for abstention but also for affirmative action on the part of the governments. And in the other category the right to strike has less the character of a programmatic right than has the right to work. The classic distinction therefore, certainly for some rights, is better explained by history than by essential differences in character.[7] In the modern welfare State - which typifies most of the Member States of the Council of Europe - the civil rights and liberties are being "socialized" more and more[8] and the social, economic, and cultural rights are increasingly becoming more concrete as to their content. Therefore, the question arises whether such a stringent distinction between the two categories is still justified, in particular if this entails the risk that the necessary relation between the two categories of rights is misunderstood. In fact, as the Proclamation of Teheran of 1968 states it in a striking way:

> Since human rights and fundamental freedoms are indivisible, the full realization of civil and political rights without the enjoyment of economic, social and cultural rights is impossible. The achievement of lasting progress in the implementation of human rights is dependent upon sound and effective national and international policies of economic and social development.[9]

This connection, and the limited value of the distinction between the two categories of rights, has also been recognized in the fact that the Council of Europe has embarked upon investigating whether certain economic and social rights should be added to the Convention, and, if so, which ones.[10]

4. In the present chapter the rights and freedoms laid down in the Convention and in its Protocols nos 1, 4, 5, 6 and 7 are discussed by reference to the decisions and reports of the Commission and the case-law of the Court. As indicated above, a number of provisions of the International Covenant on Civil and Political Rights may entail for those contracting States which have also ratified that Covenant[11] more far-reaching obligations than rest on them under the Convention;[12] obligations which according to Article 60 are left

---

7. For the foregoing, see in particular Th.C. van Boven, "Distinguishing Criteria of Human Rights", in: K. Vasak (ed.), *The International Dimensions of Human Rights*, Volume I, Paris 1982, pp. 43-59 (48-53).
8. On this socialization, see E.A. Alkema, *Studies over Europese Grondrechten* (Studies on European Basic Rights), Deventer 1978, pp. 31-32.
9. Text of the Proclamation in Res. 2442(XLII) of the General Assembly of the United Nations, 19 December 1968.
10. These discussions have not produced concrete results yet (May 1990).
11. These are all contracting States except Greece, Ireland, Liechtenstein, Malta, Switzerland and Turkey.
12. In Protocol no. 7 of 22 November 1984, the differences between the obligations resulting from the Covenant and those resulting from the Convention, have been partly taken away. This Protocol entered into force on 1 November 1988.

intact by the provisions of the Convention.[13] With a view to this, at the end of the discussion of each of the rights a brief comparison will be made with the corresponding provision in the International Covenant on Civil and Political Rights.[14] Wherever in that context the Covenant is referred to, always the Covenant on Civil and Political Rights will be meant. It would go beyond the scope of this book to also include references to the "general comments" and "views" of the Human Rights Committee established under the Covenant relating to the separate rights embodied therein. For that reference has to be made to the comprehensive analysis of the Covenant by Manfred Nowak.[15]

5. Article 1 of the Convention does not form part of Titel I which contains the substantive provisions concerning the rights and freedoms. It precedes Titel I and defines in a general way the obligation of the contracting States to secure these rights and freedoms, specifying in particular the personal scope of protection: "to everyone within their jurisdiction".

However, recently the Commission seems to have given a more specific meaning to Article 1 in connection with the extraterritorial scope the rights and freedoms embodied in Titel I.[16]

§ 2. ARTICLE 2: RIGHT TO LIFE

1. Everyone's right to life shall be protected by law. No one shall be deprived of his life intentionally save in the execution of a sentence of a court following his conviction of a crime for which this penalty is provided by law.
2. Deprivation of life shall not be regarded as inflicted in contravention of this Article when it results from the use of force which is no more than absolutely necessary:
(a) in defence of any person from unlawful violence;
(b) in order to effect a lawful arrest or to prevent the escape of a person lawfully detained;
(c) in action lawfully taken for the purpose of quelling a riot or insurrection.

1. Article 2 is formulated somewhat curiously. Unlike the corresponding Article 6 of the Covenant, it does not in so many words confer a right to life, but imposes upon the national authorities an obligation to protect everyone's right to life, followed by a prohibition of intentional deprivation of life.

---

13.   On this, see *supra* pp. 5-6.
14.   See "Problems arising from the co-existence of the United Nations Covenants on Human Rights and the European Convention on Human Rights; Differences as regards the Rights Guaranteed", Report of the Committee of Experts to the Committee of Ministers of the Council of Europe, September 1970, H(70)7 [hereafter: Report of the Committee of Experts]. See also the report of Mr. Sieglerschmidt to the Consultative Assembly of the Council of Europe "on the protection of human rights in the United Nations Covenant on Civil and Political Rights and its Optional Protocol and in the European Convention on Human Rights"; Council of Europe, Cons.Ass., Twenty-Eighth Ordinary Session, *Documents* 1976, Doc. 3773.
15.   M. Nowak, *Kommentar zum UNO-Pakt über bürgerliche und politische Rechte und zum Fakultativprotokoll*, Kehl am Rhein 1989. The English version will be published shortly.
16.   Appl. 10479/83, *Kirkwood v. United Kingdom, D & R* 37 (1984), p. 158 (182-183); Report of 19 January 1989, *Soering*, A.161 (1989), pp. 55-56.

As to that prohibition, it is assumed by some authors that this is addressed not only to the governments, but also to private persons.[17] Be that as it may, such a prohibition can be invoked in Strasbourg only when its violation is (also) due to a lack of protection on the part of the government, because complaints can only be directed against acts and omissions for which the government bears responsibility.[18] For the governments the prohibition of intentional deprivation of life furthermore implies the duty to abstain from acts which needlessly endanger life.[19]

The duty to protect the right to life seems to have been imposed by Article 2 in particular on the legislator: "shall be protected by law". What does this obligation imply? Is a State in default under this provision if, for instance, motorists are not subjected to speed limits, although such a measure might reduce the number of road victims? As Fawcett rightly states: "it is not life, but the right to life, which is to be protected by law".[20] The right to life does not afford a guarantee against the threats to life, but against intentional deprivation of life. The latter must be prohibited and made punishable by law except for those cases in which Article 2 permits such deprivation of life. The protection provided by the law, however, is a reality only if that law is implemented. Omission on the part of the authorities to trace and prosecute the offender in case of an unlawful deprivation of life is, therefore, in principle subjected to review by the Strasbourg organs.[21] The Commission, however, has indicated that the first sentence of the first paragraph in its opinion is not addressed exclusively to the legislator, but refers to a general obligation of the authorities to take appropriate measures for the protection

---

17. See, amongst others, E.A. Alkema, *supra* note 8, p. 32; F.G. Jacobs, *The European Convention on Human Rights*, Oxford 1975, p. 21.
18. The government's obligation to guarantee protection against the acts and omissions of individuals is implied in the first sentence of Art. 2 in conjunction with the provision of Art. 1; see Jacobs, *supra* note 17, p. 21. The content and the scope of this obligation, however, is difficult to indicate in abstracto. For the issue of *Drittwirkung* in general, see *supra* pp. 15-20.
19. See, *e.g.*, Appl. 5207/71, *X v. Federal Republic of Germany*, Yearbook XIV (1971), p. 698 (710), where a complaint based on Art. 2 on account of an order of the national court to evict a person in poor health from her house was not considered manifestly ill-founded by the Commission; Appl. 4340/69, *Simon-Herold v. Austria*, Yearbook XIV (1971), p. 352 (394-398), where the complaint based on Art. 2 concerned the medical care in a prison; Appl. 7154/75, *Association X v. United Kingdom*, D & R 14 (1979), p. 31 (32-33), where the Commission decided that in the case of a vaccination programme to which certain risks to life were attached it could not be said that the government envisaged such possible consequences; and Appl. 7317/75, *X v. Switzerland*, Yearbook XX (1977), p. 412 (436-438), where extradition to the United States was concerned and the person in question feared reprisals on the part of the CIA, but the Commission held that this fear had been made insufficiently concrete.
20. J.E.C. Fawcett, *The Application of the European Convention on Human Rights*, 2nd edition, Oxford 1987, p. 37.
21. The Committee of Experts evidently refers to this in its Report, *supra* note 14, p. 23, where it speaks of "an obligation of States to take the necessary deterrent measures with a view to preventing by law (*i.e.* by adequate legislation and its enforcement) intentional interference with life whether by a State or by individuals". Of course, a certain discretion will have to be allowed to the national authorities as regards the prosecution policy, but the fundamental character of the right to life stringently restricts that scope. As in the case of an individual complaint the applicant must be able to prove that he himself is the victim of the omission of the authorities, a complaint concerning deprivation of life will be possible only in the case of a so-called "indirect" victim; see *supra* pp. 47-48.

of life.[22] To what extent are the authorities obliged to prevent deprivation of life by individuals? They can hardly put a bodyguard at the disposal of each citizen.[23] Their task of guarding public security does involve, however, the duty to observe a certain vigilance with respect to the lives of the individual citizens, but in this duty they cannot go so far that their obligations towards other citizens are endangered. Here the national authorities will have to weigh these obligations against each other, and the way they do this can be reviewed in Strasbourg for its reasonableness.[24]

In its decision on Application 8278/78 the Commission found that Article 2 "does ... primarily provide protection against deprivation of life only". It did not wish to rule out the possibility that protection of physical integrity also comes under this provision, but if so, then exclusively protection against such injuries as involve a threat to life.[25] Other injuries to the physical - and mental - integrity may in many cases be brought under Article 3.

2. The most difficult interpretation problems concern the question about the beginning and the end of the physical life of the human person, which is protected in Article 2.

The word "everyone" does not exclude the possibility that unborn life falls under the protection of Article 2, no more than this is true of "every human being" in Article 6 of the Covenant.[26] If one takes the view that such protection is actually included, it implies that *abortus provocatus* must in principle be prohibited by the legislator and prosecuted by the authorities.

On this point, however, there is no consensus at the national and the international level.[27] This question was expressly left open by the Commission in its report in the *Brüggeman and Scheuten* Case.[28] In its later decision on

---

22. Whereas in Appl. 6839/74, *X v. Ireland*, *D & R* 7 (1977), p. 78, the Commission still left open the question of whether Art. 2 may also entail an obligation to take measures, it decided in Appl. 7154/75, *Association X v. United Kingdom*, *D & R* 14 (1979), p. 31 (32), that the State has a duty to take appropriate steps to safeguard life. See also Appl. 9348/81, *W v. United Kingdom*, *D & R* 32 (1983), p. 190 (199-200) and Appl. 9829/82, *X v. United Kingdom and Ireland*, not published, where the Commission stated that Art. 2 "may indeed give rise to positive obligations on the part of the State".
23. In Appl. 9348/81, *W v. United Kingdom*, *D & R* 32 (1983), p. 190 (200) and Appl. 9829/82, *X v. United Kingdom and Ireland*, not published, the Commission added, that from Art. 2 one cannot deduce a positive obligation to exclude any possible violence.
24. However, in Appl. 9348/81, *W v. United Kingdom*, *D & R* 32 (1983), p. 190 (200), where the applicant complained about her husband's and her brother's dead in Northern Ireland, the Commission came to the conclusion that it is not its task, when examining a complaint under Art. 2, to consider in detail the appropriateness and efficiency of the measures taken by the United Kingdom to combat terrorism in Northern Ireland.
25. Appl. 8278/78, *X v. Austria*, *D & R* 18 (1980), p. 154 (156).
26. As to the latter article this point was expressly left open: UN Doc. A/3764, para. 112.
27. See Recommendation 874 (1979) of the Parliamentary Assembly concerning a "European Charter on the Rights of the Child", Parl. Ass., *Documents*, Doc. 4376, which contains the words "the right of every child to life from the moment of conception". See also Recommendation 1046 (1986) on the use of human embryos and foetuses for diagnostic, therapeutic, scientific, industrial and commercial purposes, where the Parliamentary Assembly stresses that a definition of the biological status of the embryo is necessary and expresses its awareness of the fact that scientific progress has made the legal position of the embryo and foetus particularly precarious, and that their legal status is at present not defined by law.
28. Report of 12 July 1977, *D & R* 10 (1978), p. 100 (116).

Application 8416/79 the Commission held with respect to the word "everyone" in Article 2 that both the use of this term in the Convention in general and the context in which the term has been used in Article 2 (for this, the Commission pays attention in particular to the restrictions in Article 2, which apply exclusively to individuals already born) indicate that the term is not meant to include the unborn child.[29] The Commission did not confine itself to this, but subsequently investigated whether the term "life" in Article 2 refers only to the life of an individual already born or also includes the unborn life. In this connection it stated first of all that the views as to the question at what moment there is life tend to diverge widely, and that the term "life" may also have a different meaning according to the context in which it is used.[30] Next, the Commission distinguished the following three possibilities: (1) Article 2 is not applicable to the foetus at all; (2) Article 2 recognizes the right to life of the foetus with specific implied restrictions; or (3) Article 2 recognizes an unqualified right to life for the foetus.[31]

The third possibility was excluded by the Commission, since from the mere fact that Article 2 also protects the life of the mother certain restrictions ensue with respect to the life of the unborn child, as it cannot have been intended by the drafters that priority should be given to the latter life, particularly in view of the fact that, when the Convention was drafted, nearly all the States parties allowed abortion for the protection of the mother's life.[32] The Commission subsequently took the position that there was no need for it to pronounce an opinion in a general sense on the two other possibilities, because the case under discussion concerned an interruption of pregnancy in the early stages of pregnancy and exclusively on medical opinion. Even if one were to assume that Article 2 is applicable to the first months of pregnancy, in any case an implied restriction was concerned here, *viz.* the protection of the life and the health of the mother.[33]

The ambiguous reasoning of the Commission makes it but too evident that it felt confronted here with a complicated question, which it thought could hardly be answered in a general way.[34] The rejection of the third possibility was not very problematic. However, the Commission subsequently seems to extend the exceptional case in which abortion is necessary to spare the life of the mother rather readily to the situation where it is not the life of the mother that is at stake, but the abortion is considered desirable for some other medical reason. There is an essential difference between the protection of the life of the mother as a ground for restriction, which ensues directly

29. Appl. 8416/79, *X v. United Kingdom*, *D & R* 19 (1980), p. 244 (249-250). This argument would not seem very convincing, since, as the Commission itself mentions, Art. 4 of the American Convention, which uses the term "every person", expressly protects the unborn life.
30. *Ibidem*, pp. 250-251.
31. *Ibidem*, p. 252.
32. *Ibidem*.
33. *Ibidem*, pp. 252-253.
34. As in other difficult and highly controversial cases, here too it is astonishing that the Commission declared the complaint to be manifestly ill-founded; *ibidem*, p. 253.

from Article 2 itself and is narrowly defined, and the much wider ground "medical opinion", which Article 2 is said here to imply. Even if one assumes that a woman's right to physical and mental integrity, which may be based on Article 3,[35] may be interpreted in so wide a manner that it provides protection against any conscious injury to physical and mental health, and if on the other hand one does not rule out that Article 2 protects the unborn life, it is by no means self-evident that the former right has priority, so that the protection of that right implicitly restricts the enjoyment of the latter right by the foetus. The only point that has been decided here by the Commission is, therefore, that in the Commission's opinion in the present case, even if one assumes that Article 2 protects the unborn life, the rights and interests involved had been weighed against each other in a reasonable way. As long as the question of whether Article 2 is applicable to the unborn life has not been answered in the negative, this reasonableness will have to be reviewed in each individual case. Since a generally accepted standard seems still to be lacking, such a review is likely to be marginal only.

Who is entitled to complain in the case of abortion? Apart from the highly unlikely case of a complaint by a State, the parents will be entitled to vindicate the rights of their unborn child. However, they will proceed to do so only if abortion has been performed without their consent or the consent of one of them. If such a case concerns parents who are married or are living together in an extramarital relationship, it would seem more appropriate for them to invoke Article 8 (the right to respect for private and family life)[36] or Article 12 (the right to found a family).[37]

The question not as to the beginning, but as to the end of the life protected in Article 2, arises in connection with euthanasia. Here again a uniform regulation in the laws of the contracting States, and a uniform standard in general, is lacking. It would seem, however, that even in those situations where it must in reason be assumed that human life still exists, euthanasia does not *per se* conflict with the Convention. In fact, the value of the life to be protected can and must be weighed against other rights of the

35. Art. 2 protects the physical integrity only in so far as an injury to it constitutes a threat to life. See *supra* p. 218 and Appl. 8278/78, *X v. Austria*, *D & R* 18 (1980), p. 154 (156).
36. See Appl. 6959/75, *Brüggemann and Scheuten v. Federal Republic of Germany*, *D & R* 10 (1978), p. 100, and Appl. 8416/79, *X v. United Kingdom*, *D & R* 19 (1980), p. 244 (253). In its decision on Appl. 11045/84, *Knudsen v. Norway*, *D & R* 42 (1985), p. 247 (256), the Commission took the position that since the applicant was not a potential father, but a minister of religion within a State church, he was not affected differently by the abortion legislation than other citizens and therefore could not claim to be a victim. That he lost his office was, according to the Commission, not due to the Abortion Act but to the fact that he, because of his views on the Act, refused to perform functions that were duties of his office.
37. This holds good also for cases of sterilization and other forms of birth control against the will of the person concerned, or at least without the latter's consent. In fact, in these cases there is not yet any question of destruction of life. It is therefore curious that in connection with a man's complaint about the sterilization of his wife without his consent the Commission held that "an operation of this nature might in certain circumstances involve a breach of the Convention, in particular of Articles 2 and 3"; Appl. 1287/61, *X v. Denmark*, not published. The right to life and the right to produce life are not to be equated.

person in question, particularly his right, laid down in Article 3, to be protected from inhuman and degrading treatment. Whether the will of the person is decisive in such a case depends on whether the right to life is or is not to be regarded as inalienable. In this respect, too, a certain trend may be perceived, but not yet a *communis opinio*.[38] There is as yet hardly any standard for a strict review by the Strasbourg organs, both as to the weighing between the various rights of the person in question and as to the establishment of the dividing line between human and merely vegetative life.[39]

3. Article 2 mentions a number of cases to which the prohibition of deprivation of life does not apply. In the first paragraph, in the very formulation of the prohibition, an exception is already made for the case where a person is deprived of his life in the execution of a sentence of a court following his conviction of a crime for which the death penalty is provided by law. Consequently, execution of the death penalty or extradition to a country where the death penalty is still executed does not in itself constitute a violation of Article 2.[40] In the meantime however, Protocol no. 6 concerning the abolition of the death penalty has entered into force.[41] For those States who have not yet ratified this Protocol, it follows from other provisions of the Convention that not every death sentence pronounced by a court is permitted under the Convention: (1) the judicial decision in question must have been preceded by a fair and public hearing in the sense of Article 6; (2) the punishment must not be so disproportionate to the crime committed, and the choice of the place and manner of execution must not be such, that an inhuman and degrading treatment in the sense of Article 3 can be spoken of; (3) under Article 7 the crime must have been punishable by death at the moment it was committed; (4) under Article 14 no discrimination is permitted in the imposition and execution of the death penalty, and in the granting of pardon.[42] Therefore, the issue of whether the death penalty is still allowed under the Convention has to be considered in the context of several Convention provisions. As appears from Application 10479/83,[43] a difficult dilemma may present itself with regard to appeal proceedings, which will

---

38. See the discussion of the so-called "euthanasia declaration" in the Hubinek/Voogd Report concerning the rights of the sick and the dying, which was submitted early in 1976 in the Parliamentary Assembly of the Council of Europe; Council of Europe, Parl. Ass., Twenty-seventh Session, *Documents*, Doc. 3699.
39. The Hubinek/Voogd Report mentioned in the preceding note also only indicates the framework for a more uniform regulation. It holds that "the prolongation of life should not in itself constitute the overriding aim of medical practice, which must be concerned equally with the relief of suffering". The Report contains a recommendation to the Committee of Ministers to invite the governments of the Member States to set up committees for the drafting of ethical rules; Doc. 3699, pp. 2-3.
40. Appl. 10227/82, *X v. Spain*, *D & R* 37 (1984), p. 93.
41. This Protocol entered into force on 1 March 1985. See *infra* p. 502.
42. In the case of States which have abolished the death penalty in general, but have maintained it in respect of acts committed in time of war or imminent threat of war, the requirements under (1) and (4) apply only to the extent that derogation from them is not justified under Art. 15.
43. Appl. 10479/83, *Kirkwood v. United Kingdom*, *D & R* 37 (1984), p. 158 (181-190).

inevitably delay execution of the death sentence and during which the convicted person will be gripped with uncertainty as to the outcome of his appeal and therefore of his fate. On the one hand a prolonged appeal system generates acute anxiety over long periods owing to the uncertain, but possibly favourable outcome of each successive appeal. This anxiety could possibly constitute an inhuman or degrading treatment and punishment contrary to Article 3. On the other hand a sound appeal system serves to ensure protection of the right to life as guaranteed by Article 2 and to prevent arbitrariness. The Commission declared this aspect of the application manifestly ill-founded, because the applicant had not been tried or convicted and it could therefore not be established whether the treatment to which the applicant would be exposed, and the risk of his exposure to it, was so serious as to constitute inhuman or degrading treatment or punishment contrary to Article 3.

The British Government had taken the position that, since the second sentence of Article 2(1) of the Convention expressly provides for the imposition of the death sentence by a court, following conviction for a crime for which that penalty is provided by law, delays associated with the appeal procedure must be assumed to be compatible with both Article 2 and Article 3 of the Convention read together. The Commission rejected this argument. It acknowledged that the Convention must be read as a whole, but it stressed on the other hand that

> its respective provisions must be given appropriate weight where there may be implicit overlap, and the Convention organs must be reluctant to draw interferences from one text which would restrict the express terms of another. As both the Court and the Commission have recognized, Article 3 is not subject to any qualification. Its terms are bald and absolute. This fundamental aspect of Article 3 reflects its key position in the structure of the rights of the Convention, and is further illustrated by the terms of Article 15(2), which permit no derogation from it even in time of war or other public emergency threatening the life of the nation. In these circumstances the Commission considers that notwithstanding the terms of Article 2(1), it cannot be excluded that the circumstances surrounding the protection of one of the other rights contained in the Convention might give rise to an issue under Article 3.[44]

In the second paragraph three cases of deprivation of life are mentioned which also do not fall under the prohibition of the first paragraph. These are cases where deprivation of life results from the use of force for a given purpose. This is, however, subject to the condition that the force used "is no more than absolutely necessary". There must therefore be proportionality between the measure of force used and the purpose pursued, which moreover must be among the purposes mentioned in the second paragraph. Thus, for instance, the use of force in the case of an arrest, where the arrested person neither uses force nor attempts to flee, but only refuses to furnish certain data, will not be proportional and consequently cannot constitute a justification for a resulting deprivation of life. Moreover, the words "absolutely necessary" will have to be interpreted in such a way that there must also be

---

44. *Ibidem*, p. 184. For further details, see *infra* pp. 237-240.

some proportionality between the force used and the interest pursued. Thus, the use of force resulting in death will not be justified in the case of the escape of a prisoner, or to effect an arrest, when no serious danger is reasonably to be feared from the person concerned.[45]

When the widow of a man killed by the police during a riot complained of a breach of Article 2 by the Belgian State, the Commission declared her complaint to be "manifestly ill-founded", arguing that it was a case of lawful self-defence of a policeman who felt himself threatened, while there was no reason to assume that the latter had intended to kill the man.[46] By the latter argument the Commission obviously referred to the fact that the prohibition of deprivation of life in the first paragraph of Article 2 speaks of "intentionally". Since there was no question of this in the case under discussion, in the Commission's reasoning there was no need to examine whether the force used was absolutely necessary for one of the purposes mentioned in the second paragraph. However, in this way the Commission largely deprived the second paragraph of its meaning. In fact, in the cases mentioned the killing will seldom be intentional, but on the contrary will be the unintended result of the force used for a different purpose. This is also evident from the words "when it results from the use of force". It will therefore have to be presumed that the function of the second paragraph is not merely to impose a restriction on the prohibition in the second sentence of the first paragraph. If the latter was intended, it would have been more appropriate to add the cases, mentioned in the second paragraph, to the exception of capital punishment in the first paragraph, or to refer expressly to the second sentence of the first paragraph in the second paragraph. Instead, the second paragraph contains the words "in contravention of this Article", which imply at the same time a reference to the first sentence of the first paragraph and the general protection of the right to life contained therein. The only correct interpretation, therefore, seems to be that the second paragraph prohibits any use by the authorities of force in such a measure or form that it results in death, but for the exceptions mentioned there[47] and irrespective of the question whether the result was intended or not.

This interpretation was indeed adopted by the Commission in its decision on Application 10044/82. The case concerned the death of a boy as a consequence of an injury caused by a plastic baton, fired by a British soldier during a riot in Northern Ireland. The Commission had to examine whether the death of the boy was a consequence of the use of force contrary to Article 2. The British Government submitted that "Article 2 extends only to intentional acts and has no application to negligent or accidental acts". The Commission, however, adopted the broader view that the sphere of protection afforded by Article 2 went beyond the intentional deprivation of life. In virtue

---

45. See also F. Castberg, *The European Convention on Human Rights*, Leyden 1974, p. 82.
46. Appl. 2758/66, *X v. Belgium*, Yearbook XII (1969), p. 174 (192).
47. In the same sense F.G. Jacobs, *supra* note 17, pp. 24-25. See also Appl. 9013/80, *Farrell v. United Kingdom*, Yearbook XXV (1982), Part II, Ch. I.B, p. 124 (143).

of the object and purpose of the Convention, the Commission could not accept another interpretation. The text of Article 2, read as a whole, indicated in the Commission's opinion that paragraph 2 does not primarily define situations where it is permitted intentionally to kill an individual, but situations where the use of violence is permitted, which may then, as an unintentional consequence, result in a deprivation of life. This use of force has to be absolutely necessary for one of the purposes in sub-paragraphs (a), (b) or (c). With regard to this last condition the Commission stated, with reference, *inter alia*, to the *Sunday Times* Case, that (1) "necessary" implies a "pressing social need", (2) the "necessity test" includes an assessment as to whether the interference with the Convention right was proportionate to the legitimate aim pursued, and (3) the qualification of the word "necessary" in Article 2, paragraph 2 by the adverb "absolutely" indicates that a stricter and more compelling test of necessity must be applied. On the basis thereof the Commission concluded that Article 2, paragraph 2 permits the use of force for the purposes enumerated in (a), (b) and (c) under the condition that the employed force is strictly proportionate to the achievement of the permitted purpose. In assessing whether this condition is fulfilled, regard must be had to "the nature of the aim pursued, the dangers to life and limb inherent in the situation and the degree of risk that the force employed might result in loss of life".[48]

4. The most important complaints so far concerning Article 2 have been made by States. In Application 5310/71, *Ireland v. the United Kingdom*, the Government of Ireland alleged, *inter alia*, that a number of persons had been killed by the security forces of the United Kingdom in Northern Ireland under circumstances which could not justify an invocation of the second paragraph of Article 2. This part of the complaint, however, was declared inadmissible, because insufficient evidence had been furnished of the existence of an administrative practice, so that the local remedies rule had to be complied with.[49] In Applications 6780/74 and 6950/75 Cyprus accused the Turkish invasion forces of having murdered citizens, including women and aged people, in cold blood. These cases were declared admissible by the Commission,[50] and the Committee of Ministers has decided on the basis of the Commission's report "that events which occurred in Cyprus constitute violations of the Convention".[51]

5. Article 2 has been included in the list of articles from which under Article 15(2) no derogation is permitted in any circumstances; it belongs to the so-

---

48. Appl. 10044/82, *Stewart v. United Kingdom*, D & R 39 (1985), p. 162 (169-171). See also Appl. 9013/80, *Farrell v. United Kingdom*, Yearbook XXV (1982), part II, Ch. I.B, p. 124 (143).
49. Appl. 5310/71, Yearbook XV (1972), p. 76 (240-244).
50. Appls 6780/74 and 6950/75, *Cyprus v. Turkey*, Yearbook XVIII (1975), p. 82 (124).
51. Resolution of the Committee of Ministers, DH(79)1, Yearbook XXII (1979), p. 440. See the report of 10 July 1976, *Cyprus v. Turkey*, in particular paras 352-354, pp. 118-119.

called "non-derogable" rights.[52] Consequently, as was correctly submitted by the Irish Government in the case of *Ireland v. the United Kingdom*, the British declarations addressed to the Secretary General, announcing that with respect to Northern Ireland measures derogating from the Convention had been taken, could not be invoked against accusations of violation of Article 2.[53]

6. As to the comparison with Article 6 of the Covenant, it has already been submitted that the use of the term "every human being" does not imply any further clarification of the question about the protection of unborn life. Further, the fact that Article 6 proclaims the right to life as an "inherent right" constitutes a more elegant formulation, but would seem to be of little practical importance as to its scope.

Of greater importance is the fact that Article 6 does not use the word "intentionally" but "arbitrarily", and does not contain an enumeration of grounds of justification such as those in the second paragraph of Article 2. In the interpretation given above, *viz.* that the second paragraph of Article 2 refers not merely to cases of *intentional* deprivation of life, this provision furnishes a better protection than does the Covenant. In that interpretation, any form of force which results in the death of the victim and is not absolutely necessary for one of the purposes mentioned in the second paragraph is prohibited, regardless of whether it has to be considered arbitrary or not, while in the justifications provided for in Article 2(2) the prohibition of arbitrary use of force is implied in the stricter requirement that the force must be "absolutely necessary".[54]

The second paragraph of Article 6 of the Covenant, which deals with the death penalty, imposes a number of restrictions on the infliction of this penalty. In this respect it is much more explicit than Article 2, but it has been stated above that restrictions on the infliction and the manner of execution of the death penalty result from other provisions of the Convention.[55] All limitations mentioned in Article 6(2) of the Covenant seem to be covered by these other provisions.[56] The limitation resulting from the Convention on the Prevention and Punishment of the Crime of Genocide, to which Convention the Covenant, but not the European Convention, refers, follows for the European Convention from Articles 3 and 14, and moreover, for those contracting States which are also parties to the first-mentioned Convention, from Article 60. The same applies to the general reference to the Genocide Convention in the third paragraph of Article 6 of the Covenant; in so far as genocide could at all be justified by an invocation of Article 2 of the European Convention, such an invocation is excluded on the ground of

---

52. Article 3 of Protocol no. 6 concerning the abolition of the death penalty also prohibits any derogation from Art. 15 of the Convention.
53. Appl. 5310/71, *Yearbook* XV (1972), p. 76 (96).
54. See the decision in the *Stewart* Case, referred to *supra* note 48.
55. *Supra* p. 221.
56. Report of the Committee of Experts, *supra* note 14, p. 25.

other provisions. The fifth paragraph of Article 6 of the Covenant prohibits the imposition of the death penalty for crimes committed by persons below eighteen years of age, and its execution on pregnant women. Such provisions have not been included in the Convention, but as the Committee of Experts states in its report, the practice of the contracting States is in conformity therewith.[57] The same may be assumed to apply to the provisions in the fourth paragraph of Article 6 on amnesty, pardon and commutation of the death sentence.[58]

The words "countries which have not abolished the death penalty" in Article 6(2) might be interpreted as a prohibition to introduce the death penalty after the entry into force of or the accession to the Covenant, as the case may be.[59] Such a prohibition is not to be found in the Convention, and the same holds true for the recommendation in Article 6(6) to abolish the death penalty. This difference is now eliminated, at least for time of peace, for those contracting States which have ratified Protocol no. 6.[60]

§ 3.   ARTICLE 3: FREEDOM FROM TORTURE AND OTHER INHUMAN OR DEGRADING TREATMENT OR PUNISHMENT

No one shall be subjected to torture or to inhuman or degrading treatment or punishment.

1. The difference between the several acts prohibited in Article 3 is mainly one of gradation. As the Commission stated in its report in the *Greek* Case:

> It is plain that there may be treatment to which all these descriptions apply, for all torture must be inhuman and degrading treatment, and inhuman treatment also degrading.

The Commission itself, starting from the concept of inhuman treatment, applied the following specifications:

> The notion of inhuman treatment covers at least such treatment as deliberately causes severe suffering, mental or physical, which, in the particular situation, is unjustifiable. The word "torture" is often used to describe inhuman treatment, which has a purpose, such as the obtaining of information or confession, or the infliction of punishment, and is generally an aggravated form of inhuman treatment. Treatment or punishment of an individual may be said to be degrading if it grossly humiliates him before others or drives him to act against his will or conscience.[61]

The Commission, in that case, came to the conclusion that it had been established that in several individual cases torture or ill-treatment had been

---

57. *Ibidem.*
58. *Ibidem.*
59. The "Annotations on the text of the draft International Covenants on Human Rights", *supra* note 6, p. 30, do not create any clarity on this point. A.H. Robertson, *Human Rights in the World,* 2nd ed. Manchester 1982, p. 108, formulates it as an open question. In the Report of the Committee of Experts, *supra* note 14, p. 25, it is assumed that this was not intended.
60. For the "case-law" of the Human Rights Committee concerning Art. 6 of the Covenant reference is made to the study of Nowak, mentioned *supra* at p. 216.
61. Report of 5 November 1969, *Yearbook* XII; *The Greek Case* (1969), p. 186.

inflicted, that there had been a practice of torture and ill-treatment by the Athens Security Police and that the conditions in the cells of the Security Police building were contrary to Article 3.[62] In *Ireland v. United Kingdom* the Commission in its report based itself again on this definition. In doing so, it held unanimously that the challenged English techniques of interrogation - obliging the interrogated persons to stand for a long period on their toes against the wall, covering their heads with black hoods, subjecting them to constant intense noise, depriving them of sleep and sufficient food and drink - constituted torture and inhuman treatment in the sense of Article 3.[63]

However, the Court in its judgment in this case reached the conclusion that these techniques of interrogation did involve inhuman treatment, but not torture. It mentioned as a distinctive element between the two that torture is concerned with "deliberate inhuman treatment causing very serious and cruel suffering" and held that the particular acts complained of "did not occasion suffering of the particular intensity and cruelty implied by the word torture as so understood".[64] If this statement is placed beside the one made a good four months later in the *Tyrer* Case, where the Court held "that the suffering occasioned must attain a particular level before a punishment can be classified as "inhuman" within the meaning of Article 3",[65] one may conclude that the difference between the three kinds of treatment and punishment prohibited in Article 3 is mainly one of gradation in the suffering inflicted.

In the last-mentioned case the complaint concerned the punishment of caning for certain offences, which was provided by law and actually applied in the Isle of Man to boys between ten and seventeen. After having concluded, in conformity with the opinion of the Commission, that this did not constitute torture or inhuman punishment, the Court examined whether the punishment was to be considered degrading. Assuming that every punishment involves an element of degradation, the Court indicated as a distinctive element of degrading punishment the degree of humiliation, which must then be judged according to the circumstances of each separate case, in particular "the nature and context of the punishment itself and the manner and method of its execution".[66] Decisive for this are not the views at the moment the Convention was drawn up, but the present views, since "the Convention is a living instrument which ... must be interpreted in the light of present-day conditions".[67] Moreover, the Court is guided in this by developments and generally accepted standards in the penitentiary policy of the member States of the Council of Europe.[68] Having regard to all the circumstances, the Court concluded that the punishment concerned was degrading. The Court accorded particular weight to the fact that physical

---

62. *Ibidem*, pp. 504-505.
63. Report of 25 January 1976, B.23/I (1976-1978), p. 411.
64. Judgment of 18 January 1978, *Ireland v. United Kingdom*, A.25 (1978), pp. 66-67.
65. Judgment of 25 April 1978, A.26 (1978) p. 14.
66. *Ibidem*, p. 15.
67. *Ibidem.*
68. *Ibidem*, p. 16.

force was used by a complete stranger and in an institutionalized form.[69]

With respect to application of corporal punishment in British schools, in the Case of *Campbell and Cosans* both the Commission and the Court left the question open whether this practice in its generality was in violation of Article 3. They merely reached the conclusion that in that case it could not be said that a degrading treatment was involved, because the corporal punishment had not been actually applied to the children of the two applicants, and the gravity of the punishment and its degrading effect on the person concerned could not therefore be measured. The results of the mere exposure to the threat of corporal punishment were considered insufficient to amount to degrading treatment. On the other hand the Court emphasized that the mere fact that the treatment in question had long been in use and met with approbation among a majority of the parents was not decisive for the question of whether it had a degrading character.[70] However, recently in its report in the *Warwick* Case, the Commission held that there had been a violation of Article 3 of the Convention, since the corporal punishment inflicted on the applicant caused humiliation and attained a sufficient level of seriousness to be regarded as degrading treatment or punishment.[71] In its resolution of 2 March 1989, the Committee of Ministers noted that during the examination of the case the Committee was informed by the Government of the United Kingdom that the Education (No. 2) Act 1986 provided for the abolition of corporal punishment in State schools and that it was proposed to bring these provisions of the Act into force on 15 August 1987. The Committee did not attain the required two-thirds majority on the question whether there had been a violation of Article 3.[72]

In a number of cases the Commission held that there is question of a degrading treatment or punishment of the person concerned "if it grossly humiliates him before others or drives him to act against his will or conscience".[73] And in a more recent case the Commission refers to measures which "constitute an insult to the applicants' human dignity".[74]

Both the Commission and the Court left no doubt about the fact that Article 3 does not refer exclusively to the infliction of physical but also of mental suffering. The Commission defined the latter as covering "the infliction of mental suffering by creating a state of anguish and stress by means other than bodily assault".[75] Often there will be a combination of mental and

---

69. *Ibidem*, pp. 16-17.
70. Report of 16 May 1980, B.42 (1980-1983), pp. 43-44; judgment of 25 February 1982, A.48 (1982), pp. 12-14.
71. Report of 18 July 1986, para. 88.
72. Res. DH(89)5 of 2 March 1989.
73. Report of 5 November 1969, *Greece v. United Kingdom, Yearbook* XII (1969), p. 186; report of 25 January 1976, *Ireland v. United Kingdom*, B.23-I (1976-1978), p. 388; report of 14 December 1976, *Tyrer*, B.24 (1977-1978), p. 23; and report of 7 December 1978, *Guzzardi*, B.35 (1979-1980), p. 33.
74. Appl. 8930/80, *X, Y and C v. Belgium*, not published.
75. Report of 5 November 1969, *Yearbook* XII, *The Greek Case* (1969), p. 461. For the Court, see, *inter alia*, the judgment of 18 January 1978, *Ireland v. United Kingdom*, A.25 (1978), p. 65.

physical suffering as may be clearly seen in the application of *X and Y v. the Netherlands*, in which the Commission dealt with the question of mental suffering as a result of the sexual abuse of the victim.[76] There, the Commission stated that "mental suffering leading to acute psychiatric disturbances falls into the category of treatment prohibited by Article 3 of the Convention".[77] However, not every measure taken by a public authority that has emotional consequences of any kind for the individual falls within the scope of inhuman treatment but only such measures as "inflict severe mental or physical suffering on an individual".[78]

Does the intention of the acting person to cause physical or mental suffering, in addition to the suffering inflicted or the humiliation experienced, constitute a necessary element of the types of treatment prohibited in Article 3? It is obvious that a medically necessary operation, however painful it may be for the patient, is not to be considered as torture or inhuman treatment, provided that unnecessary suffering is avoided. But a medical experiment may have this character, although the aim is not to inflict suffering, but to advance medical science.[79] And a treatment of a detainee which in itself is inhuman does not lose this character through the mere fact that its only motive is enhancement of security. It is therefore not the intention of the acting person, but the nature of the act and its effect on the person undergoing the treatment which are decisive. Therefore, the Court used too general a phrase when it observed, in the Case of *Albert and Le Compte*, that the disciplinary measure of withdrawal of the right to practise, imposed upon a doctor, had as its object the imposition of a sanction and not the debasement of his personality; not this is decisive but the question raised next by the Court, *viz.* whether the consequences of the measure adversely affected the doctor's personality in a manner incompatible with Article 3.[80]

It cannot be said in general whether the absence of consent with the treatment on the part of the person in question constitutes a necessary element of the prohibition of Article 3, but it is a relevant factor.[81] The consent of the person concerned may deprive an act, which would be felt by another to be inhuman or degrading, of that character. However, experiments and treatments are conceivable which are so inhuman or degrade the human person to such a degree that the person in question, in spite of his previous

76. Report of 5 July 1983, A.91 (1985), pp. 22-23. In its judgment of 26 March 1985 in this case, A.91 (1985), p. 15, the Court, having found a violation of Art. 8, decided that it was not necessary to examine the case under Art. 3 as well.
77. *Ibidem*, p. 22.
78. Appl. 9191/80, *X v. Federal Republic of Germany*, not published. See also Appl. 9554/81, *X v. Ireland*, not published. Emotional stress arising from the expropriation of one's home does not meet the requirements; Appl. 9261/81, *X v. United Kingdom*, Yearbook XXV (1982), Part II, Ch. I.B, p. 200 (203).
79. See, for example, Appl. 9974/82, *X v. Denmark*, D & R 32 (1983), pp. 283-284, concerning an experiment made with a slightly different instrument, but which did not change the procedure of the operation as such. According to the Commission, the operation "cannot be considered as such a medical experiment which, if carried out without consent, could constitute a violation of Article 3 of the Convention".
80. Judgment of 10 February 1983, A.58 (1983), p. 13.
81. Appl. 9974/82, *X v. Denmark*, D & R 32 (1983), p. 282 (283-284).

229

consent, may feel himself to be the victim of a violation of Article 3. And in any case the consent of a particular victim need not bar a complaint by an indirect victim[82] or an abstract complaint by a State concerning a general practice. On the other hand the absence of consent does not in all cases give an inhuman character to a treatment affecting human integrity. Thus the Commission decided that the enforced administration of medicine to a mentally deranged detainee did not have that character, since that treatment had been declared medically necessary and this had been confirmed by a court decision.[83] However, the will of the person in question, in so far as he can be deemed capable of expressing it, must weigh heavily, since in principle he must be able himself to decide about his life and body as long as the life and the health of others are not at stake.

2. It has already been briefly pointed out that there is no absolute standard for the kinds of treatment and punishment prohibited by Article 3. The question when a treatment or punishment is inhuman or degrading must be judged by the circumstances of the case and the prevalent views of the time. Thus, in its report in the *Greek* Case the Commission considered with respect to the treatment of detainees:

> It appears from the testimony of a number of witnesses that a certain roughness of treatment of detainees by both police and military authorities is tolerated by most detainees and even taken for granted ... . This underlines the fact that the point up to which prisoners and the public may accept physical violence as being neither cruel nor excessive, varies between different societies and even between different sections of them.[84]

And in its judgment in *Ireland v. United Kingdom* the Court held:

> ill-treatment must attain a minimum level of severity if it is to fall within the scope of Article 3. The assessment of this minimum is, in the nature of things, relative; it depends on all the circumstances of the case, such as the duration of the treatment, its physical or mental effects and, in some cases, the sex, age and state of health of the victim.[85]

Thus, a certain qualification is introduced in a norm formulated in absolute terms, which is almost inevitable in the case of the application of an abstract norm, containing subjective concepts, to concrete cases.

It is, however, confusing to speak in this context of "inherent limitations", as is sometimes done.[86] In fact, there is no question of limitations with respect to the guarantee given. A detainee, for instance, has the same right to freedom from inhuman treatment as his fellow-citizens who live in freedom. However, for the question of whether in fact he has been subjected to inhuman treatment, the circumstance of his detention must be taken into consideration. This circumstance need not necessarily lead to a lowering of the standard, as may be illustrated by the additional risks which may be

---

82. On this, see *supra* pp. 47-48.
83. Appl. 8518/79, *X v. Federal Republic of Germany, D & R* 20 (1980), p. 193 (194).
84. Report of 5 November 1969, *Yearbook* XII; *The Greek Case* (1969), p. 501.
85. Judgment of 18 January 1978, A.25 (1978), p. 65. See also the report of 7 December 1978, *Guzzardi*, B.35 (1979-1980), pp. 33-35 and the report of 7 October 1981, *B v. United Kingdom, D & R* 32 (1983), p. 5 (29).
86. On this, see *infra* pp. 575-578.

incurred, especially by a person detained for a long period, in case of defective medical care.[87]

This necessity to give concrete form to the norm for each individual case makes it inevitable that a certain margin of discretion is allowed to the national authorities. The final result will, however, have to be reviewed by the Strasbourg organs for its reasonableness in the light of the aim of Article 3. In that context it is of considerable importance that in its judgment in the *Tyrer* Case the Court stressed the fact that, in reviewing the standard applied by the State in question, the Court must also be guided by the general standard adopted in the other contracting States of the Council of Europe.[88] In fact, the aim of the Convention in general - and this holds true for Article 3 as well - will be achieved only if the maintenance of the norms laid down in the Convention leads to a common European standard, at least where the most important elements are concerned. This common standard may then, via a "dynamic interpretation"[89] of the Convention, be raised further to the extent that the legal opinion in the contracting States develops.[90] For this it is indeed required that the Strasbourg organs indicate as clearly as possible what norms they apply in determining that standard. Therefore, when the Court, for instance, held in the *Markcx* Case that

> while the legal rules at issue probably present aspects which the applicants may feel to be humiliating, they do not constitute degrading treatment coming within the ambit of Article 3.[91]

this did not make for such clarity.

3. It is not surprising that in the Strasbourg procedure Article 3 has so far mainly been in issue in connection with detainees. This was the case, for instance, in the *Greek* Case and in *Ireland v. United Kingdom*, in both of which cases a conflict with Article 3 was found by the Committee of Ministers and the Court respectively. In the *Guzzardi* Case, too, the circumstances of the detention were put forward in detail and reviewed against the prohibition of Article 3. There, however, the Court, following the Commission, concluded that, however unpleasant these circumstances were, they were not as grave as is required for the applicability of Article 3.[92] The same fate hit already in the admissibility phase, the numerous complaints of IRA prisoners about the situation in the Maze prison and the treatment they received

---

87. See Appl. 7994/77, *Kotälla v. the Netherlands, Yearbook* XXI (1978), p. 522 (528), where the Commission followed the view of the Dutch court that the deterioration of the physical and mental condition of the applicant was not due to his detention. See also the report of 7 December 1978, *Guzzardi,* B.35 (1979-1980), pp. 34-35 and the report of 5 December 1979, *Bonnechaux, D & R* 18 (1980), p. 100 (148).
88. Judgment of 25 April 1978, A.26 (1978), p. 15.
89. F. Castberg, *supra* note 45, p. 83.
90. See, however, the judgment of 7 December 1976, *Handyside,* A.24 (1976), *infra* pp. 602-603, where the existence of a common European standard on morals was denied by the Court.
91. Judgment of 13 June 1979, A.31 (1979), p. 28.
92. Judgment of 6 November 1980, A.39 (1981), pp. 12-16 and p. 40. See also the report of 16 December 1982, *Kröcher and Möller, D & R* 34 (1983), p. 24 (56-57).

there,[93] but the Commission's decision does contain the important finding that the fact of the detainees carrying on a campaign against the authorities does not relieve the latter from their obligations under Article 3.[94]

In cases where the question was raised whether solitary confinement of a detainee constituted an inhuman treatment, the Commission took the position that such confinement was in principle undesirable, particularly when the prisoner concerned was in detention on remand, and might only be justified for exceptional reasons. For the question of whether an inhuman or degrading treatment is concerned, regard must be had to the surrounding circumstances, including the particular conditions, the stringency of the measure, its duration, the objective pursued and its effects on the person concerned, and also the question of whether a given minimum of possibilities for human contact has been left to the person in question.[95] In *Kröcher and Möller v. Switzerland* the Commission stated:

> The question that arises is whether the balance between the requirements of security and basic individual rights was not disrupted to the detriment of the latter.[96]

In this case the prison conditions included, *inter alia*, isolation, constant artificial lighting, permanent surveillance by closed-circuit television, denial of access to newspapers and radio and the lack of physical exercise. Although the Commission expressed "serious concern with the need for such measures, their usefulness and their compatibility with Article 3 of the Convention", it concluded that the special conditions imposed on the applicants could not be construed as inhuman or degrading treatment.[97] This conclusion was reached after it had been sufficiently shown to the Commission that these conditions were necessary to ensure security inside and outside the prison. Furthermore, the applicants were considered dangerous, they were alleged to be terrorists, and there was a risk of escape and collusion.[98] Other factors that have been accepted by the Commission to justify stringent measures are: extremely dangerous behaviour of the prisoner,[99] "ability to manipulate situations and encourage other prisoners to acts of indiscipline",[100] the safety of the applicant,[101] and the use of firearms at the time of arrest.[102] As regards the

---

93. Appl. 8317/78, *McFeeley v. United Kingdom*, D & R 20 (1980), p. 44 (77-89). See also Appl. 8231/78, *X v. United Kingdom*, D & R 28 (1982), p. 5 (27-33) concerning the obligation to wear prison clothes.
94. *Ibidem*, p. 81. See also: Appls 7572, 7586 and 7587/76, *Ennslin, Baader and Raspe v. Federal Republic of Germany*, D & R 14 (1979), p. 64 (111) and Appl. 9907/82, *M. v. United Kingdom*, D & R 35 (1984), p. 130 (133-136). In the latter case the measures taken with respect to the detainee were the result of his extremely dangerous behaviour.
95. Appl. 6038/73, *X v. Federal Republic of Germany*, Coll. 44 (1973), p. 115 (119); Appl. 6166/73, *Baader, Meins, Meinhof and Grundmann v. Federal Republic of Germany*, Yearbook XVIII (1975), p. 132 (144-146); Appls 7572, 7586, and 7587/76, *Ennslin, Baader and Raspe v. Federal Republic of Germany*, Yearbook XXI (1978), p. 418 (454-460); Report of 16 December 1982, *Kröcher and Möller v. Switzerland*, D & R 34 (1983), p. 24 (51-55).
96. Last case mentioned in the preceding note, p. 52.
97. *Ibidem*, p. 57
98. *Ibidem*, p. 52.
99. Appl. 9907/82, *M v. United Kingdom*, D & R 35 (1984), p. 13 (34).
100. Appl. 8324/78, *X v. United Kingdom*, not published.
101. Appl. 8241/78, *X v. United Kingdom*, not published.

effects on detainees, the Commission requires applicants to submit medical evidence to show that the prison conditions have had adverse effects on their mental or physical health.[103] This medical evidence must not only show that there is a direct relationship between the prison conditions complained of and the deteriorating health of the applicant,[104] but also that these conditions were such that they could "destroy the personality and cause severe mental and physical suffering" to the applicant.[105] Finally, as the degree of isolation is concerned, it has been made clear by the Commission, that absolute sensory isolation combined with complete social isolation constitutes an inhuman treatment for which no security requirements can form a justification; this in view of the absolute character of the right laid down in Article 3.[106] Moreover, the Commission has made a distinction between this absolute sensory and social isolation on the one hand, and "removal from association with other prisoners for security, disciplinary and protective reasons" on the other, and has taken the view that this form of segregation from the prison community does not amount to inhuman or degrading treatment or punishment."[107] In the latter case it is still possible to meet prison officers, medical officers, lawyers, relatives etc., and to have contact with the outside world through newspapers, radio and television.

In a series of cases, violation of Article 3 was alleged, because of the adverse effects of the mere fact of being detained as such on the health of the detainee. In such cases, reports by medical experts are of great importance.[108] According to the Commission, the question that has to be answered is whether the (mental) health of the detainee is directly affected by his detention. Furthermore, the frequency of visits by the medical staff and the medical treatment are taken into account[109] as well as the question of whether the detainee has sought medical opinion.[110] However, the latter does not take away the primary responsibility of the authorities for the medical care of the detainees.

Another major element the Commission regularly takes into account in

102. Appls 7572/76, 7586/76, 7587/76, Ensslin, Baader and Raspe v. Federal Republic of Germany, Yearbook XXI (1978), p. 418 (454).
103. See, for example, Appl. 8116/77, X v. United Kingdom, not published, and Appl. 8601/79, X v. Switzerland, not published.
104. In the applications of Ensslin, Baader and Raspe (see note 102), medical reports were presented, but they did not "make it possible to establish accurately the specific effect of this isolation in relation to their physical and mental health, as compared with other factors", Yearbook XXI (1978), p. 418 (458).
105. Appl. 8158/78, X v. United Kingdom, D & R 21 (1981), p. 99 and report of 16 December 1982, Kröcher and Möller, D & R 34 (1983), p. 24 (56).
106. Appls 7572/76, 7586/76 and 7587/76, Ensslin, Baader and Raspe v. Federal Republic of Germany, Yearbook XXI (1978), p. 418 (456).
107. Report of 25 January 1976, Ireland v. United Kingdom, B.23/I, p. 379; Appls 7572/76, 7586/76 and 7587/76, Ensslin, Baader and Raspe v. Federal Republic of Germany, Yearbook XI (1978), p. 418 (456); Appl. 8317/78, McFeeley v. United Kingdom, D & R 20 (1980), p. 44 (82); report of 16 December 1982, Kröcher and Möller, D & R 34 (1983), p. 24 (53), and Appl. 10263/83, R. v. Denmark, D & R 41 (1985), p. 149.
108. See, for example, Appl. 9554/81, X v. Ireland, not published and report of 7 October 1981, B v. United Kingdom, D & R 32 (1983), p. 5 (35).
109. See for example the report of 8 December 1982, Chartier, D & R 33 (1983), p. 41 (57-58).
110. Appl. 9813/82, X v. United Kingdom, not published.

answering the question whether a violation of Article 3 has occurred, is the behaviour of the detainee. Especially when the measures complained of are a result of the uncooperative attitude of the detainee, the Commission is very reticent in concluding that a violation has occurred.[111] However, here again, the authorities remain under the obligation to continuously review the detention arrangements.

In a number of cases the complaint concerned physical force used against a detainee by prison officers. On the one hand it is obvious that, for instance, in case of an attempt to flee or of an assault on a prison officer or fellow prisoner the use of a certain amount of force on the part of the prison officers may be inevitable. On the other hand the form as well as the intensity of the force must be proportionate to the nature and the seriousness of the threat, taking into account the possibility of excess of violence in self-defence as a ground for justification. When studying the case-law of the Commission on this point, one is struck by the difficulty confronting the Commission when it has to form an opinion on the true facts after the event, but at the same time one regrets to find no more express indications that the Commission attaches much importance to recent developments in penitentiary views.[112]

In two cases the Commission declared the applications admissible of people detained in a mental hospital who complained of violation of Article 3 on account of the treatment and living conditions in the hospitals in question. It held that at first sight these complaints were sufficiently well-founded to justify further inquiry.[113]

---

111. See, e.g., Appl. 8231/78, X v. United Kingdom, D & R 28 (1982), p. 5 (27-28), where the detainee refused to wear prison clothes, and the report of 7 October 1981, B v. United Kingdom, D & R 32 (1983), p. 5 (34-35 and 38), where the applicant had constantly refused to accept medical treatment and had refused to clean his cell himself. See also Appls 9911/82 and 9945/82, R, S, A, and C v. Portugal, D & R 36 (1984), p. 200.

112. In this connection, see the "Minimum Rules for the Treatment of Prisoners", Resolution (73)5 of the Committee of Ministers, European Yearbook XXI (1973), pp. 322-350; and more recently the "European Prison Rules", laid down in Resolution (87)3, adopted by the Committee of Ministers on 12 February 1987. In its decision on Appl. 7341/76, Eggs v. Switzerland, Yearbook XX (1977), p. 448 (460), the Commission took the position that "the conditions of detention which in certain aspects did not come up to the standard of the 'Minimum Rules' did not thereby alone amount to inhuman or degrading treatment". See also Appl. 7408/76, X v. Federal Republic of Germany, D & R 10 (1978), p. 221 (222), where on the one hand the Commission found that the punishment imposed on the applicant was not in conformity with modern views of penitentiary policy, but on the other hand came to the conclusion that the treatment in question was not inhuman or degrading. See, however, Appl. 7630/76, Reed v. United Kingdom, D & R 19 (1980), p. 113, where the complaint about ill-treatment by prison warders was declared admissible by the Commission.

113. Appl. 6840/74, X v. United Kingdom, Yearbook XXI (1978), p. 250 (282); Appl. 6870/75, B v. United Kingdom, D & R 10 (1978), p. 37 (67). In the first-mentioned case a friendly settlement was reached, by which the authorities promised a clearer regulation concerning solitary confinement of patients: D & R 20 (1980), p. 5 (8-11). In the latter case, the Commission concluded in its report of 7 October 1981 that, although the facilities in the hospital at that time were "extremely unsatisfactory", they did not amount to inhuman or degrading treatment contrary to Art. 3 of the Convention: D & R 32 (1983), p. 5 (30).

In a case which concerned the question of whether a detainee who was not mentally deranged could be detained in a closed ward of a mental hospital, a friendly settlement was reached with the respondent Austrian Government; the Minister of Justice issued a general order that was to prevent such a treatment in the future.[114] The placement of a mentally deranged person in a normal prison was considered allowable by the Commission after it had found that the person in question received adequate care there.[115]

The segregation of accused persons from convicted persons, which is expressly required in Article 10 of the Covenant, is not prescribed by the Convention, nor does it ensue *per se* from Article 3 in the Commission's opinion.[116]

Taking a prisoner through a town in handcuffs and in prison uniform was considered undesirable by the Commission but, curiously enough, was not deemed a degrading treatment in the sense of Article 3.[117]

4. Two complaints by transsexuals whose application for adaptation of the registers to their change of sex had been refused, were declared admissible by the Commission. In their complaints they had advanced, *inter alia*, violation of Article 3.[118] In the first of these cases a friendly settlement was subsequently reached. In its report in the other case, the *Van Oosterwijck* Case, the Commission did not reach the point of determining whether there was a violation of Article 3, since it had already concluded that Articles 8 and 12 had been violated.[119]

5. Via Article 3 certain rights and freedoms which are not included as such in the Convention may be brought under its protection, or at any rate the argument that they are implicitly protected by the Convention may thus be consolidated.

The clearest example is furnished by the admission and expulsion or extradition of aliens. The Convention does not contain a general right of admission to a certain country and also not a right to asylum, while Article 4 of Protocol no. 4 prohibits only *collective* expulsion of aliens and Article 1 of Protocol no. 7 only contains certain procedural guarantees against expulsion. The refusal of admission to or the expulsion from a country may, however, constitute an inhuman treatment in the sense of Article 3, for

114. Appl. 4340/69, *Simon-Herold v. Austria, Coll.* 38 (1972), p. 18.
115. Appl. 5229/71, *X v. United Kingdom, Coll.* 42 (1973), p. 140.
116. Appl. 6337/73, *X v. Belgium, D & R* 3 (1976), p. 83 (85). Article 11, para. 3 of the European Prison Rules, however, stipulates that "In principle untried prisoners shall be detained separately from convicted persons unless they consent to being accommodated or involved together in organised activities beneficial to them".
117. Appl. 2291/64, *X v. Austria, Coll.* 24 (1967), p. 31.
118. Appl. 6699/74, *X v. Federal Republic of Germany, D & R* 11 (1978), p. 16 (25); Appl. 7654/72, *Van Oosterwijck v. Belgium, Yearbook* XXI (1978), p. 476 (488-490).
119. Report of 1 March 1979, B.36 (1983), pp. 28-29. The Court did not arrive at examining the merits, since it held that the local remedies had not been exhausted: Judgment of 6 November 1980, A.40 (1981).

instance on account of the physical condition of the person concerned[120] or because it might result in the person in question being separated from a person or group of persons with whom he has a close link, even apart from the protection of family life under Article 8.[121] The violation of Article 3 may also consist in the treatment to which, on the basis of objective facts, the person in question may be expected to be subjected in the country to which he will be extradited or will have to return after expulsion or refusal of admission. In that case the State expelling or extraditing him is held indirectly responsible for the imminent treatment in that other State,[122] regardless of whether that treatment is to be expected from public authorities or from non-State actors,[123] regardless of how great the - evidently not completely successful - efforts of the government have been to prevent such treatment[124] and regardless of whether the latter State is or is not a party to the Convention.[125] The treatment must then imply a violation of any of the rights guaranteed in the Convention, and in particular of Article 3.[126] Whether the danger of such treatment is really present will have to be examined by the Commission and the Court.[127] The case-law of the Commission shows that an

---

120. Appl. 8088/77, *X v. the Netherlands*, not published. The Commission here considered it of importance in particular that medical reports showed that transportation to Ireland did not involve any special risk to the applicant's health and that he was accompanied by a doctor during the flight.
121. The Commission's decisions on Appls 7289/75 and 7349/75, *X and Y v. Switzerland*, Yearbook XX (1977), p. 372 (406-408), and on Appl. 9606/81, *X v. United Kingdom*, not published, were, therefore, incorrect to the extent that the Commission took the view that, since Art. 8 was applicable but had not been violated, no examination as to violation of Art. 3 was necessary. See also the judgment of 24 March 1988, *Olsson*, A.130 (1988), p. 38, where the applicants alleged a violation of Art. 3 mainly in two different respects. First, they contended that the taking away of the children from them without sufficient reasons was a deprivation of the children's right of growing up in their family. Secondly they put forward the frequent moving of one child from one home to another and the ill-treatment in his foster-family. In the Court's view the allegations were not substantiated to give rise to a violation of Art. 3. See, however, Appl. 10730/84, *Berrehab and Koster v. the Netherlands*, D & R 41 (1985), p. 196 (209), where the Commission stated that where an expulsion raises issues under Art. 8, a complaint under Art. 3 on the same facts should not, for that reason alone, be declared inadmissible.
122. For an extensive motivation, see Report of 19 January 1989, *Soering*, paras 94-94.
123. Appl. 10040/82, *X v. Federal Republic of Germany*, not published, where the Commission stated that "it is not necessary for the application of Article 3 that the danger emanates from the Government of the State, which requires extradition".
124. Appl. 10308/83, *Altun v. Federal Republic of Germany*, D & R 36 (1984), p. 209 (233-234).
125. See, *e.g.*, Appl. 1802/63, *X v. Federal Republic of Germany*, Yearbook VI (1963), p. 462 (480). In Appl. 9822/82, *X v. Spain*, not published, the Commission did, however, take into account as a positive factor that the case concerned an extradition to one of the State Parties to the European Convention which had accepted the right of individual petition. *Cf.* Appl. 10308/83, *Altun v. Federal Republic of Germany*, D & R 36 (1984), p. 209 (233-234), in which the fact that Turkey had not recognized the right of individual petition was taken into account as a negative factor.
126. See the first decision mentioned in the preceding note. See also Appl. 7465/76, *X v. Denmark*, D & R 7 (1977), p. 153 and Appl. 9693/82, *X v. United Kingdom*, not published. However, in Appl. 10308/83, *Altun v. Federal Republic of Germany*, D & R 36 (1984), p. 209 (231-232), the Commission held that non-compliance with the guarantees laid down in Art. 6 of the Convention, "would not in itself make extradition appear as an inhuman treatment".
127. In its decision on Appl. 7216/75, *X v. Federal Republic of Germany*, D & R 5 (1976), p. 137 (143) the Commission inferred from the conduct of the person in question that the latter himself obviously did not consider that there was any real danger. In its decision on Appl. 7465/76, *X v. Denmark*, D & R 7 (1977), p. 153 (154-155), the Commission held

(continued...)

applicant will have to advance rather strong arguments for this, and in this respect it has a great deal in common with the national case-law on the grant of asylum. On several occasions the Commission held that the fact that a deportee risks criminal prosecution in the country of destination is not itself enough to raise an issue under Article 3 of the Convention in connection with his deportation,[128] unless there is clear indication that the charges are "falsely inspired".[129] In the *Altun* Case the Commission also stated that in considering the expectations concerning the treatment after expulsion or extradition, it attaches a certain importance to the question of whether the applicant has the right of individual petition in respect of that third country.[130]

In the *Kirkwood* Case and in the *Soering* Case the Commission has developed the view that, since Article 2 of the Convention expressly permits the imposition of the death penalty, extradition of a person to a country where he risks the death penalty cannot, in itself, raise an issue either under Article 2 or Article 3 of the Convention,[131] but that this does not exclude the possibility of an issue arising under Article 3 in respect of the manner and circumstances in which the death penalty is implemented. The Commission gave as an example protracted delay in carrying out the death penalty. In the *Kirkwood* Case, which concerned a possible extradition to California, the Commission indicated as factors to be considered in assessing whether such a delay during the appeal procedure (the "death row phenomenon") amounts to inhuman treatment the following ones: the relevance of the appeal system for the protection precisely of the right to life, the delays caused by the backlog of cases before the appeal courts and the control over them, and the possibility of a commutation of sentence by the very reason of the duration

---

127.(...continued)
that the extradition of applicant to Poland, where he might be prosecuted on account of desertion from the army and the disclosure of military secrets, was not contrary to Art. 3, because the acts referred to are also punishable in most of the member States of the Council of Europe. The fact that a refugee passport had been granted to the applicant in Denmark was also considered by the Commission to be insufficient ground for the fear that an inhuman treatment would await him in Poland. In its decision on Appl. 7729/76, *Agee v. United Kingdom*, *D & R* 7 (1977), p. 164 (173), the Commission adopted the position that the deportation of applicant to the United States could not have the character of an "arbitrary, unjustified or disproportionate punishment", because the deportation had the character not of a punishment but of a measure for the protection of national security. In our view, the Commission thus dismissed the case too easily; it ought to have examined *ex officio* whether perhaps there was a question of "inhuman or degrading treatment". In its decision on Appl. 9693/82, *X v. United Kingdom*, not published, the Commission held that the applicant "has not produced *prima facie* evidence" to show that he has serious grounds for fearing treatment contrary to Art. 3. Finally, in its decision on Appl. 10308/83, *Altun v. Federal Republic of Germany*, *D & R* 36 (1984), p. 209 (233-234), the Commission had to decide about the compatibility of an extradition to Turkey with Art. 3. There the Commission held that "it cannot be absolutely ruled out that he may be regarded as someone able to provide information of such an importance that there would be a temptation to use methods of pressure incompatible with Article 3".
128. Appl. 4162/69, *X v. Federal Republic of Germany*, *Coll.* 32 (1970), p. 87; Appl. 7334/76, *X v. Federal Republic of Germany*, *D & R* 5 (1976), p. 154 and Appl. 10564/83, *L v. Federal Republic of Germany*, *D & R* 40 (1985), p. 262.
129. Appl. 10308/83, *Altun v. Federal Republic of Germany*, *D & R* 36 (1984), p. 209 (233).
130. Appl. 10308/83, *D & R* 36 (1984), p. 209 (234).
131. It does, of course, raise an issue under Protocol no. 6 for those contracting States which have ratified that Protocol.

of the detention on the "death row". The Commission reached in that case the following conclusion:

> The essential purpose of the California appeal system is to ensure protection for the right to life and to prevent arbitrariness. Although the system is subject to severe delays, these delays themselves are subject to the controlling jurisdiction of the courts. In the present case the applicant has not been tried or convicted and his risk of exposure to death row is uncertain. In the light of these reasons ... the Commission finds that it has not been established that the treatment to which the applicant will be exposed, and the risk of his exposure to it, is so serious as to constitute inhuman or degrading treatment or punishment contrary to Article 3 of the Convention.[132]

The element which the Commission adds here to its considerations, *viz.* that the applicant has not been tried or convicted and that his conviction to the death penalty is still uncertain, in our opinion is a rather strange one, since that will often be the case when the complaint concerns extradition or expulsion; what matters in those cases is that there is a real risk of the applicant's being sentenced to death.

In the *Soering* Case, which concerned a possible extradition to Virginia, the British government had contended that the applicant did not in reality risk the death penalty, pointing to the assurance that had been given by the Commonwealth Attorney that the trial judge would be informed of the wish of the British Government that the death penalty should not be imposed or carried out. The Commission observed that the sentencing judge was not obliged under Virginia law to accept the representation made to him on behalf of the British government and that it could not be assumed that he would have regard to the diplomatic considerations relating to the continuing effectiveness of the extradition relationship between the two countries; therefore the risk that the applicant would be sentenced to death was considered a serious one.[133] In its final assessment the Commission reached the conclusion - be it with only six against five votes - that there was no indication that the machinery of justice to which the applicant would be subjected was an arbitrary or unreasonable one.[134]

Unlike the Commission, the Court unanimously concluded in its judgment in the same case that the decision to extradite the applicant to the United States would give rise to a violation of Article 3 of the Convention. The Court emphasized the absolute prohibition of torture and of inhuman or degrading treatment or punishment. The question remained, however, whether the extradition of a fugitive to another State where he would be subjected or likely be subjected to torture or to inhuman treatment or punishment would engage the responsibility of a contracting State under Article 3. The Court held as follows:

> That the abhorrence of torture has such implications is recognised in Article 3 of the United Nations Convention Against Torture and Other Cruel, Inhuman or Degrading Treatment or Punishment, which provides that "no State Party shall ... extradite a person

---

132. Appl. 10479/83, *D & R* 37 (1984), p. 158 (190).
133. Report of 19 January 1989, paras 114-120. In the same sense the Court in its judgment of 7 July 1989 in this case, paras 97-99.
134. *Ibidem*, paras 151-152.

238

where there are substantial grounds for believing that he would be in danger of being subjected to torture". The fact that a specialised treaty should spell out in detail a specific obligation attaching to the prohibition of torture does not mean that an essentially similar obligation is not already inherent in the general terms of Article 3 of the European Convention. It would hardly be compatible with the underlying values of the Convention, that "common heritage of political traditions, ideals, freedom and the rule of law" to which the Preamble refers, were a Contrating State knowingly to surrender a fugitive to another State where there were substantial grounds for believing that he would be in danger of being subjected to torture, however heinous the crime allegedly committed. Extradition in such circumstances, while not explicitly referred to in the brief and general wording of Article 3, would plainly be contrary to the spirit and intendment of the Article, and in the Court's view this inherent obligation not to extradite also extends to cases in which the fugitive would be faced in the receiving State by a real risk of exposure to inhuman or degrading treatment or punishment prescribed by that Article.[135]

According to the Court, therefore, the decision by a contracting State to extradite a fugative may give rise to an issue under Article 3, and hence engage the responsibility of that State under the Convention. The Court further examined the question whether in the circumstances the risk of exposure to the "death row phenomenon" would make extradition a breach of Article 3. Although the Court indicated that capital punishment is permitted under certain conditions by Article 2(3) of the Convention, it also took account of the written comments of Amnesty International in which it was argued that the evolving standards in Western Europe regarding the existence and use of the death penalty required that the death penalty should now be considered as an inhuman and degrading punishment within the meaning of Article 3. Thus, on the one hand, the Court held that the Convention is to be read as a whole and Article 3 should therefore be construed in harmony with the provisions of Article 2.

On this basis Article 3 evidently cannot have been intended by the drafters of the Convention to include a general prohibition of the death penalty since that would nullify the clear wording of Article 2, paragraph 1.[136]

Furthermore, the Court emphasized that Protocol no. 6, as a subsequent written agreement, showed that the intention of the contracting States to adopt the normal method of amendment of the text in order to introduce a new obligation to abolish capital punishment and to do so by an optional instrument allowing each State to choose the moment when to undertake such an engagement. In these conditions Article 3 cannot be interpreted as generally prohibiting the death penalty.[137] The Court added, however, that this did not mean that the circumstances relating to a death sentence could never give rise to an issue under Article 3. Whether the treatment or punishment was to be brought under Article 3 in this case depended on the particular circumstances of the case, the length of detention prior to execution, conditions on death row and the applicant's age and mental state. The Court agreed with the Commission that the machinery of justice to which the applicant would be subject in the United States was in itself neither arbitrary

---

135. Judgment of 7 July 1989, para. 88.
136. *Ibidem*, para. 103.
137. *Ibidem.*

nor unreasonable, but, rather, respected the rule of law and afforded considerable procedural safeguards to the defendant in a capital trial. It then held as follows:

> However, in the Court's view, having regard to the very long period of time spent on death row in such extreme conditions, with the ever present and mounting anguish of awaiting execution of the death penalty, and to the personal circumstances of the applicant, especially his age and mental state at the time of the offence, the applicant's extradition to the United States would expose him to a real risk of treatment going beyond the threshold set by Article 3. A further consideration of relevance is that in the particular instance the legitimate purpose of extradition could be achieved by another means which would not involve suffering of such exceptional intensity or duration.
> Accordingly, the Secretary of State's decision to extradite the applicant to the United States would, if implemented, give rise to a breach of Article 3.[138]

Another example of a right or freedom which through Article 3 may acquire an independent status under the Convention is the prohibition of discrimination. As will be explained hereafter,[139] such a prohibition is not included in the Convention as an autonomous right, but only in connection with the enjoyment of other rights and freedoms. Discriminatory treatment on the basis of race, however, has been qualified by the Commission as degrading treatment in the sense of Article 3, which in fact converts freedom from this form of discrimination into an independent right.[140] This case-law of the Commission has implications even for those contracting States which have ratified the International Convention on the Elimination of All Forms of Racial Discrimination.[141] In the first place, for Article 3 the probability is greater than for the relevant provisions of the said Convention that it will be recognized by the national courts as directly applicable within the national legal system. And secondly, the European Convention provides for a more developed international system of review.[142] In a report in 1983 the Commission seems to imply that also "sexual and other forms of discrimination" may have such degrading aspects that Article 3 may be applicable.[143] However, if these aspects have already been dealt with in connection with Article 14, the Commission does not consider it necessary to pursue a further examination in the light of Article 3.[144]

In its report in the *Guzzardi* Case the Commission appears to have considered the possibility that also deprivation of the right of employment, which is not guaranteed in the Convention, may bring Article 3 in issue.[145]

Finally, Article 3 may serve to consolidate rights for which it is not clear

---

138. *Ibidem*, para. 111.
139. *Infra* pp. 532-533.
140. *Twenty-five complaints of Afro-Asians v. United Kingdom*, Yearbook XIII (1970), p. 928 (994). See also Appls 9214/80, 9473/81 and 9474/81, *Mmes X, Cabales and Balkandali v. United Kingdom*, Yearbook XXV (1982), Part II, Ch. 1.B, p. 159 (178-179).
141. 660 *UNTS* 195.
142. See Arts 8-16 of the Convention on Racial Discrimination.
143. Report of 12 May 1983, *Abdulaziz, Cabales and Balkandali*, A.94 (1985), pp. 56-57.
144. *Ibidem*. In its judgment of 28 May 1985 in this case, A.94 (1985), p. 42, the Court did not find a violation of Art. 3, because the difference of treatment did not denote any contempt or lack of respect for the personality of the applicants and the measures complained of were not designed to, and did not, humiliate or debase them.
145. Report of 7 December 1978, B.35 (1983), p. 35.

whether they are protected as such in the Convention. Above the example is given that the refusal of admission or the expulsion of an alien may in certain cases conflict not only with the latter's right to respect for his family life under Article 8, but may at the same time constitute an inhuman treatment in the sense of Article 3. And there is also the example of abortion or sterilization against the will of the person concerned, referred to in the preceding section, a treatment which may raise certain issues under both Article 2 and Article 12, but may also conflict with Article 3.[146]

6. Article 3 is included in the list of rights which are declared non-derogable in Article 15(2). It is therefore absolute, not only in the sense that the provision itself leaves no scope for limitations by law, as a number of other provisions do, but also in the sense that no derogation can be permitted in any public emergency. The Commission accordingly stated in its report in the *Ireland v. United Kingdom* Case:

> It follows that the prohibition under Article 3 of the Convention is an absolute one and that there can never be under the Convention, or under international law, a justification for acts in breach of that provision.[147]

7. The only difference between the first sentence of Article 7 of the Covenant and Article 3 is that in the former the word "cruel" precedes the phrase "inhuman or degrading treatment or punishment". Considering the flexibility of the concepts of "torture" and "inhuman treatment", this difference need not have any importance in practice.[148]

However, Article 7 contains a second sentence, which is lacking in Article 3 and deals with the above-mentioned requirement of consent in the case of medical or scientific experiments. In its report the Committee of Experts infers from the *travaux préparatoires* that the meaning of this provision is not intended to prohibit experiments for a genuine medical purpose, or a test such as the fluoridation of drinking-water.[149]

§ 4. ARTICLE 4: FREEDOM FROM SLAVERY, SERVITUDE AND FORCED OR COMPULSORY LABOUR

1. No one shall be held in slavery or servitude.

2. No one shall be required to perform forced or compulsory labour.

3. For the purpose of this Article the term "forced or compulsory labour" shall not include:

a) any work required to be done in the ordinary course of detention imposed according to the provisions of Article 5 of this Convention or

---

146. See *supra* p. 220.
147. Report of 25 January 1976, *Ireland v. United Kingdom*, B.23/I (1976-1978), p. 390.
148. Report of the Committee of Experts, *supra* note 14, p. 25.
149. For the "case-law" of the Human Rights Committee concerning Article 7 of the Covenant reference is made to the study of Nowak, mentioned *supra* at p. 216.

during conditional release from such detention;

b) any service of a military character or, in case of conscientious objectors in countries where they are recognised, service exacted instead of compulsory military service;

c) any service exacted in case of an emergency or calamity threatening the life or well-being of the community;

d) any work or service which forms part of normal civic obligations.

1. In Article 4 slavery and servitude are dealt with separately from forced and compulsory labour. The first two terms refer to the total status or situation of the person concerned. Slavery indicates that the person concerned is wholly in the legal ownership of another person, while servitude concerns less far-reaching forms of restraint and refers, for instance, to the total of the labour conditions and/or the obligations to work or to render services from which the person in question cannot escape and which he cannot change.[150] Forced labour and compulsory labour, on the other hand, do not refer to the total situation of the person concerned, but exclusively to the involuntary character of the work and services to be performed by him, which may, and usually will, also have a temporary or incidental character.

2. The first paragraph of Article 4 has mainly been invoked in connection with complaints of detainees against the obligation to perform work in prison. In those cases the Commission took the position that the terms "slavery" and "servitude" are not applicable to such a situation, while from the third paragraph under (a) of Article 4 it is evident that the drafters of the Convention did not wish to prohibit the imposition of such an obligation.[151]

In the *Van Droogenbroeck* Case the applicant submitted that the fact of his having been placed at the disposal of the government, as a recidivist, had reduced him to a condition of servitude, since in fact he was subject to arbitrary supervision by the administrative authorities. The Commission took the view that there was no question of servitude, because the measure was one of limited duration only, was subject to judicial review and did not affect the legal status of the person in question.[152]

The first paragraph was also invoked before the Commission by four young men who, at the age of fifteen and sixteen, had joined the Navy for a period of nine years and after some time had applied for discharge. In their complaint against the refusal of the authorities to discharge them they claimed, *inter alia*, that in view of their age their service constituted a form

---

150. See the report of 9 July 1980, *Van Droogenbroeck*, B.44 (1985), p. 30: "in addition to the obligation to provide another with certain services, the concept of servitude includes the obligation on the part of the 'serf' to live on another's property and the impossibility of changing his condition".

151. Appls 3134/67, 3172/67 and 3188-3206/67, *Twenty-one detainees v. Federal Republic of Germany*, Yearbook XI (1968), p. 528 (552). Also Appl. 7549/76, *X v. Ireland*, not published.

152. Report of 9 July 1980, B.44 (1985), p. 30.

of servitude in the sense of Article 4(1). After first having stated that military service did form an exception to the second, but not necessarily to the first paragraph, the Commission rejected the complaint as being manifestly ill-founded. The finding was based in particular on the circumstance that the relevant law prescribed for minors the consent of the parents and that in this case such consent had indeed been given.[153]

3. The second paragraph of Article 4 has played a greater part in the case-law. Hitherto the Commission and the Court have refrained from giving a definition of the term "forced or compulsory labour". Both organs, however, have made reference to conventions of the International Labour Organization, which contain far more detailed norms in this respect.[154] For the meaning of the term, the Commission referred to the five categories enumerated in Convention No. 105 of the International Labour Organisation:

> political coercion or education or as a punishment for holding or expressing political views or views ideologically opposed to the established political, social, or economic system; mobilising and using labour for purposes of economic development; labour discipline; punishment for having participated in strikes; and racial, social or religious discrimination.[155]

Elements of the concept "forced or compulsory labour" mentioned by the Commission are

> first, that the work or service is performed by the worker against his will and, secondly, that the requirement that the work or service be performed is unjust or oppressive or the work or service itself involves avoidable hardship.[156]

With respect to the first element - its involuntary nature - the Commission so far has taken the view that consent, once given, deprives the work or service of its compulsory character. And if the decision mentioned above concerning the boys who had joined the Navy, which related to the first paragraph, were followed analogously in connection with the second paragraph, the consent of the parents could presumably take the place of that of their children under age.

Such an interpretation of "forced" and "compulsory" would appear to be too restrictive.[157] Even if a person has voluntarily entered into a labour contract or has agreed to perform certain services, the circumstances may change in such a way or the objections to the work in question, especially in engagements of long duration, may become so great that holding the person

---

153. Appls 3435-3438/67, *W, X, Y and Z v. United Kingdom*, Yearbook XI (1968), p. 562 (596-598).
154. See, *e.g.*, the references to ILO Convention No. 29 by the Court in its judgment of 23 November 1983, *Van der Mussele*, A.70 (1983), pp. 16-17.
155. Appl. 7641/76, *X and Y v. Federal Republic of Germany*, D & R 10 (1978), p. 224 (230). ILO Convention No. 105 is to be found in: International Labour Office, *Conventions and Recommendations* 1919-1966 (1966), p. 891.
156. Appl. 4653/70, *X v. Federal Republic of Germany*, Yearbook XVII (1974), p. 148 (172). Likewise Appl. 8410/78, *X v. Federal Republic of Germany*, D & R 18 (1980), p. 216 (219) and Appl. 9322/81, *X v. the Netherlands*, D & R 32 (1983), p. 180 (182-183).
157. *Cf.* the judgment of 23 November 1983, *Van der Mussele*, A.70 (1983), where the Court did not attach a decisive meaning to a consent given.

unqualifiedly to his consent may indeed bring in issue Article 4(2). In our opinion this provision implies in that case that alternative possibilities should be offered to the person in question, for instance different work if the objections are directed against the nature of the work, or termination of the contract coupled with the obligation to pay a reasonable compensation.

With the second criterion, *viz.* that the obligation to perform the work must have an unjustifiable or oppressive character, or that the work itself involves avoidable hardship for the person concerned, the Commission introduces a number of elements which allow a considerable margin of discretion to the national authorities. If this second criterion were to be applied cumulatively to the first, in fact a general ground of justification would be added to the specific grounds of the third paragraph to be discussed hereafter. Even work or a service which a person has to perform against his will and which is felt by him to be oppressive would not, in that view, constitute a violation of Article 4(2), provided the national authorities can submit *prima facie* evidence that this oppressive character is not as bad as is alleged, or that the hardship was unavoidable. In our opinion the text of Article 4 would thus be strained and, therefore, the second criterion should rather be handled *alternatively* in the sense suggested above, *viz.* that even work or a service to which the person concerned has previously consented may assume a compulsory character for him if the obligations resulting therefrom involve such unjustified or avoidable hardship that they can no longer be deemed to be covered by his consent. In its Report in the *Van der Mussele* Case the Commission indeed speaks of "a subsidiary argument" in connection with the second criterion.[158]

There has been considerable dissension within the Commission about the elements of the concept of "forced" labour. This is evident from the *Iversen* Case. In that case the Norwegian legislation was brought in issue on the basis of which a dentist might be required to fill for some time a vacancy that failed to be filled after having been duly advertised. The complaint was declared by the Commission to be manifestly ill-founded. Two of the members of the Commission belonging to the majority considered the Norwegian measure justified on the basis of the ground mentioned in the third paragraph under (c), *viz.* "emergency or calamity threatening the life or well-being of the community".[159] Four members of the majority of six, however, held that there was no question of forced or compulsory labour, because the service to be rendered was exacted for a limited time, was properly remunerated and was in keeping with the profession chosen by Iversen, while the law in question had not been applied against him in an arbitrary or discriminatory manner.[160] A minority of four members of the Commission, finally, were of the opinion that the above-mentioned circumstances did not exclude the

---

158. Report of 3 March 1982, B.55 (1987), p. 33.
159. Appl. 1468/62, *Iversen v. Norway*, *Yearbook* VI (1963), p. 278 (328-330).
160. *Ibidem*, pp. 326-328.

applicability of the second paragraph, and that the possible application of the third paragraph called for a further examination.[161] In the light of this diversity of views within the Commission it is very curious indeed that the complaint was rejected as being manifestly ill-founded, which barred a thorough examination of the facts and a decision of the Court on this evidently controversial interpretation of the second paragraph.[162]

In the case of a German lawyer who complained about having to act as unpaid or insufficiently paid defence counsel, the Commission decided that the imposed obligation was not unreasonable and did not therefore fall under the prohibition of Article 4(2). The Commission did not review this form of compulsory service for its conformity with the third paragraph at all. In fact, the Commission based its decision partly on the consideration that anyone who voluntarily chooses the profession of a lawyer knows that under German law lawyers are obliged to defend clients who lack the means to pay counsel's fees in those cases where they have been nominated to do so by a judicial body. In those circumstances it could not be said that such a service had to be rendered against the will of the person in question.[163] Here the Commission seems to follow the reasoning which already appears to have been hinted at by four of its members in the *Iversen* Case, *viz.* that when certain obligations are attached to a profession, the person choosing that profession accepts those obligations implicitly. A similar decision was taken in the case of a notary public who complained about the system according to which in specific cases he was allowed to charge only reduced fees for his services. The Commission stated first of all that the applicant had not advanced that he had been forced in one way or another to give his services in specific cases, so that the question might be asked whether the first element had been satisfied. With respect to the second element the Commission found that the impugned system could not be qualified as "unjust or oppressive", since it relates to a normal part of the tasks of a notary public and ensues from his almost exclusive competence as regards the services concerned.[164] And also in the case of a Dutch football player who complained that he was, after renouncing the contract with his former football club, prevented from entering another football club in view of the prohibitive transfer sum requested by the former, the Commission took the view that the appplicant freely chose to become a professional football player, knowing that by doing so he would be

161. *Ibidem*, pp. 330-332.
162. See *supra* pp. 106-107. Jacobs, *supra* note 17, p. 40, utters the supposition that in this case the Commission had been guided by political motives under the influence of the stir which this case had caused in Norway and the decision of the Norwegian Government to renew the acceptance of the individual right of complaint for a period of only one year.
163. Appl. 4653/70, *X v. Federal Republic of Germany*, Yearbook XVII (1974), p. 148 (172). Previously, two complaints of an Austrian lawyer about free legal aid had been declared admissible by the Commission, on the ground that "these complaints raise issues of a complex nature" and could not therefore be declared manifestly ill-founded: Appls 4897/71 and 5219/71, *Gussenbauer v. Austria*, Coll. 42 (1973), p. 41 (48) and Yearbook XV (1972), p. 558 (562) respectively. These cases led to a friendly settlement, so that the merits have not been pronounced on; report of 8 October 1974.
164. Appl. 8410/78, *X v. Federal Republic of Germany*, D & R 18 (1980), p. 216 (219).

affected by the rules governing the relationships between his future employers. Moreover, the Commission was of the opinion that the system complained of, even if it could produce certain inconveniences for the applicant, could not be considered as being oppressive or constituting avoidable hardship, especially since it did not affect directly his contractual freedom.[165]

The above-mentioned argument applies only if the obligations form part of the normal exercise of a profession. The Commission, therefore, speaks of "normal professional work".[166] The obligation to lend free legal aid forms part of the normal obligations of a lawyer in the Federal Republic of Germany, as it does in most other member States of the Council of Europe, and the obligation to take for some time, if necessary, a position in the public dental service in the northern part of the country forms part of the normal obligations of a dentist in Norway after he has completed his studies.[167] This does not, however, alter the fact that it must still be ascertained for each individual case whether the concrete content of the obligation in question is not so oppressive for the person concerned that he can no longer be assumed to have consented to it by choosing his profession.

In another case, where a lawyer invoked Article 4(2) on account of his obligation to act as a free legal aid counsel, the Commission followed a somewhat different line of reasoning. It referred to Article 6(3)(c) and submitted that, since in the Convention the right to free legal aid has been recognized, the obligation for a lawyer to give legal aid in a concrete case cannot constitute forced or compulsory labour in the sense of Article 4(2).[168] The connection here established by the Commission between the two provisions seems to us not to be very logical. Indeed, the right to legal aid *per se* does not say anything about the way in which the authorities must effectuate this right and does not necessarily imply that this should be done via an obligation for lawyers to give such legal aid under conditions to be laid down by the authorities. In its later report in the *Van der Mussele* Case the Commission impliedly indicated how unsatisfactory this line of reasoning is, by stating there that the obligation of the State to provide free legal aid was not decisive in that case because legal aid was organized by the Bar Association. It, therefore, again emphasized that the obligation imposed on the applicant formed part of his normal professional work and left him so much freedom that one could not speak of forced or compulsory labour, though the Commission considered it unfortunate that pupil barristers such as the applicant were not paid at all when appointed to defend indigent persons.[169]

In the same *Van der Mussele* Case the Court took a somewhat different approach. It used as a starting point for the interpretation of "compulsory

165. Appl. 9322/81, *X v. the Netherlands,* D & R 32 (1983), p. 180 (182-183).
166. Appl. 4653/70, *X v. Federal Republic of Germany, Yearbook* XVII (1974), p. 148 (172).
167. See, however, the report of 3 March 1982, *Van der Mussele,* B.55 (1987), p. 34, where the Commission distinguishes the situation from that of the *Iversen* Case.
168. Appl. 7641/76, *X and Y v. Federal Republic of Germany,* D & R 10 (1978), p. 224 (230).
169. Report of 3 March 1982, B.55 (1987), p. 34.

labour" the definition given in Art. 2 of ILO-Convention No. 29:[170]

> all work or service which is exacted from any person under the menace of any penalty and for which the said person has not offered himself voluntarily.[171]

Although a refusal to act as a free legal aid counsel was not punishable by any sanction of a criminal law character, the Court concluded that there was a "menace of any penalty", since with such a refusal the applicant would run the risk of his name being struck off the roll of pupils or a rejection of his application for entry in the register of advocates.[172] As regards the voluntary character of the service exacted, the Court held that the argument used by the Commission that the applicant consented in advance "correctly reflects one aspect of the situation; nevertheless, the Court cannot attach decisive weight thereto".[173] The Court next observed that the applicant had to accept the requirement concerned, whether he wanted to or not, in order to become an *avocat* and his consent was determined by the normal conditions of exercise of the profession at the relevant time. Moreover, according to the Court, it should not be overlooked that the acceptance by the applicant was the acceptance of a legal regime of a general character.[174] To decide whether the service required falls within the prohibition of compulsory labour, the Court held that it should have regard to all the circumstances of the case in the light of the underlying objectives of Article 4.[175]

At first sight, the approach of the Court indeed seems quite different from that of the Commission, especially since the Court distances itself from the second criterion developed by the Commission, *viz.* that of the "unjust" or "oppressive" character of the service to be performed.[176] It is, however, striking to see that most of the circumstances of the case taken into consideration by the Court, have also been dealt with by the Commission in its report. In fact, the main difference lies in the weight, attached to the element of "consent in advance". As has been stated above,[177] the view expressed by the Commission in this respect is too restrictive. The approach of the Court, therefore, is to be welcomed. However, the Court also fails to give clear guide-lines with respect to the interpretation of "forced or compulsory labour". It restricts itself to an investigation of all the circumstances of the case, each of which, according to the Court, "provides a standard of evaluation".[178] These standards were in this case the following: the services did not fall outside the ambit of the normal activities of an *avocat*; a compensatory factor was to be found in the advantages attaching to the profession; the services contributed to the professional training of the

---

170. International Labour Office, *Conventions and Recommendations* 1919-1966 (1966), p. 155.
171. Judgment of 23 November 1983, A.70 (1983), p. 16.
172. *Ibidem*, p. 17.
173. *Ibidem*, p. 18.
174. *Ibidem*, p. 19.
175. *Ibidem*, p. 19.
176. *Ibidem*, p. 20.
177. See *supra* p. 244.
178. Judgment of 23 November 1983, *Van der Mussele*, A.70 (1983), p. 19.

applicant; the service is a means of securing the benefit, laid down in Art. 6(3)(c), and can be seen as a "normal civic obligation" as referred to in Art. 4(3)(d); and, lastly, the burden imposed was not disproportionate, since it only took about eighteen hours of the working time.[179]

Both the Commission and the Court concluded that, although the situation could be characterized as unsatisfactory because of the absence of any fee and the non-reimbursement of incurred expenditure, it did not constitute a violation of Art. 4 of the Convention.[180]

4. With respect to the exceptions mentioned in the third paragraph, the following observations may be made. The exception formulated under (a) for the work of detainees and conditionally released persons is put in quite general terms and - unlike Article 2(2)(c) of ILO Convention No. 29 - does not exclude work on behalf of private enterprises and foundations. Complaints with respect to work of such a character have therefore been declared inadmissible by the Commission.[181] The exception under (a) applies only to work "in the ordinary course of detention". In the *Vagrancy* Cases these words were interpreted by the Court to mean that it must be work directed at the rehabilitation of the prisoner.[182] Moreover the Court's judgment would seem to imply that Article 4 is violated if the detention itself in the course of which the work must be performed conflicts with the first paragraph of Article 5.[183] The view of the Commission that also in case of a conflict with the fourth paragraph of Article 5 reliance on Article 4(3)(a) by the authorities is excluded,[184] was not adopted by the Court. This is curious, since the authorities may thus refer to a situation which has been found by the Strasbourg organs to be in conformity with Article 5(1), but whose lawfulness - contrary to Article 5(4) - the applicant has not been able to have reviewed by the domestic court. Such a review could precisely have resulted in the court ordering his release, as a consequence of which the ground for the obligation to work would have ceased to exist.[185] It should finally be pointed out with respect to the exception under (a) that this does not relate exclusively to convicts - such as is the case in ILO Convention No. 29 - nor exclusively to persons whose detention is based on a judicial order - as

---

179. *Ibidem*, pp. 19-20. *Cf.* the report of 3 March 1982, *Van der Mussele*, B.55 (1987), p. 34.
180. *Ibidem*, pp. 21 and 35 respectively.
181. Appls 3134/67, 3172/67 and 3188-3206/67, *Twenty-one detainees v. Federal Republic of Germany, Yearbook* XI (1968), p. 528 (552-558), and Appl. 9449/81, *X v. Austria*, not published. In some of the contracting States, however, the courts will have to apply that restriction on the ground of the direct applicability of Convention No. 29 if ratified by those States.
182. Judgment of 18 June 1971, A.12 (1971), pp. 44-45. See also Appl. 8500/79, *X v. Switzerland*, *D & R* 18 (1980), p. 238 (248-249), where in the case of the detention of a minor the Commission examined under Art. 5(1)(d) whether the required work "was abnormally long or arduous in view of the applicant's age or was of no educational value".
183. *Ibidem*, p. 44.
184. Report of 19 July 1969, "*Vagrancy*" Cases, B.10 (1969-1970), pp. 96-97.
185. One might think here of the adage "nemo suam turpitudinem allegans audiendum est". However, the Commission followed the Court in its report of 9 July 1980, *Van Droogenbroeck*, B.44 (1985), p. 31.

Article 8 of the Covenant provides - but to all the situations of lawful deprivation of liberty mentioned in the first paragraph of Article 5.[186]

The formulation of the exception under (b), too, departs from that of Convention No. 29, where Article 2(2)(a) speaks of "any work or service exacted in virtue of compulsory military service laws for work of a purely military character". From the fact that in Article 4(3)(b) the confinement to "compulsory military service" has not been adopted the Commission concluded that "it was intended to cover also the obligation to continue a service entered into on a voluntary basis".[187] However, in view of the rationale of this exception, as it appears in particular from the reference to the service exacted instead of compulsory military service, such an application is justified only for those cases where this voluntary military service takes the place of compulsory military service. In fact, in other cases it cannot be appreciated why military service should be entitled to a special position as compared with other public service in the national interest, such as, for instance, service on the railways or for utility companies.

The fact that Article 4(3)(b) also mentions civil service exacted instead of compulsory military service in case of conscientious objectors does not in itself mean that the Convention contains a right to such alternative service for conscientious objectors; in fact, the provision contains the limitation "in countries where they are recognised". If such a right for conscientious objectors is not recognized in a given country, this situation might have to be reviewed for its conformity with Article 9.[188]

The exception mentioned under (c) speaks for itself. Here the difficulty consists of course in answering the question of when an "emergency or calamity threatening the life or well-being of the community" is involved. As has been stated above, in the opinion of some members of the Commission even a shortage of dentists could constitute such a situation.[189] It would, however, appear to be more in keeping with the terminology used not to think here of structural inconveniences like those concerned in that case, but of an acute emergency with a temporary character. Thus services are covered by this provision like aid in extinguishing a fire, urgent repairs of transport systems and dams, supply of water and food in case of a sudden shortage, transport of wounded persons or the evacuation of persons threatened by some danger, and similar incidental services which can be required of everyone in the public interest depending on everybody's capabilities and possibilities.

The exception mentioned under (d), on the contrary, refers to "normal" civic obligations, which means that no urgent and unforeseen calamity is required. It is still restricted, however, to work and services in the general

---

186. Appl. 8500/79, *X v. Switzerland*, D & R 18 (1980), p. 238 (248), which was a case under Art. 5(1)(d).
187. Appls 3435-3438/67, *W, X, Y and Z v. United Kingdom*, Yearbook XI (1968), p. 562 (594).
188. Appl. 10640/83, *A v. Switzerland*, D & R 38 (1984), p. 219 (222-223).
189. See *supra* p. 245.

interest. In our opinion, the difference with the provision under (c) is mainly one of gradation: the circumstances do not have to be as serious and urgent, but on the other hand the duties which are imposed may not be as burdensome for the person involved.[190] The formulation of the provision does not exclude special duties for particular professions in the public interest from being brought under it. In fact, the word "normal" does not necessarily refer to what may be required equally of everyone, but may also relate to what in the given circumstances may be required of the person in question according to general usage.[191] In our opinion, the rationale of this provision implies that it does not refer to the normal obligations resulting from a profession, such as the free legal aid given by lawyers, normal night duties for nurses and the like, since no compulsion in the real ense is involved there as the person concerned may quit the job. At any case the Commission would seem to have stretched the concept of "normal civic obligations" beyond any specification in a decision in which it declared this term to be applicable to the obligation of the lessor to keep the rented premises in good repair.[192]

Finally it is to be noted in this context that a practice based on any of the above-mentioned exceptions loses its permissible character if it involves discrimination. In virtue of Article 14 it then resumes the character of compulsory labour contrary to the Convention. This question played a part, for instance, in the *Grandrath* Case, where a member of the Jehova's Witnesses complained that alternative civil service had been required of him as a conscientious objector to military service, although within his religious group he held a function similar to that of ministers of other religions, who were excused from service. In the discussion of Article 14 this case will be dealt with in more detail.[193]

5. Under Article 15(2) no derogation from the first paragraph of Article 4 is permitted under any circumstances. Derogations from the second paragraph, apart from the cases mentioned in the third paragraph, are allowed only under the conditions and restrictions mentioned in Article 15.

6. As regards the prohibition of slavery and servitude, Article 8 of the Covenant differs from Article 4(1) only in that it devotes two separate paragraphs to it, and under the prohibition of slavery also mentions that of slave-trade.

The third paragraph of Article 8 prohibits forced and compulsory labour

---

190. In the Strasbourg case-law a clear distinction has not yet been made, as appears from the decision on Appl. 9686/82, *S v. Federal Republic of Germany, D & R* 39 (1985), p. 90 (91), where the obligation of a person enjoying shooting rights in a hunting district (Jagdpächter) to participate in the gassing of fox holes was considered to be justified either under (c) or under (d) in view of the public interest to control epidemics.
191. *Cf.* judgment of 23 November 1983, *Van der Mussele*, A.70 (1983), pp. 19-20.
192. Appl. 5593/72, *X v. Austria, Coll.* 45 (1974), p. 113.
193. See *infra* p. 541. See also Appl. 8500/79, *X v. Switzerland, D & R* 18 (1980), p. 238 (249), where a detainee kept under observation complained that he was compelled to perform work, whereas this did not apply to detainees under remand.

in the same terms as Article 4(2). As a general exception, however, it is added that in countries where "imprisonment with hard labour" may be imposed as a penalty the obligation to perform such hard labour in pursuance of a sentence to that effect by a competent court does not fall under the prohibition. Since this is hard labour as an additional penalty, and not the work required of the prisoner "in the ordinary course of detention",[194] it is an exception not found as such in Article 4.[195]

All the exceptions mentioned in Article 4(3) are also to be found in Article 8 of the Covenant in almost the same terms, but with the difference that Article 4(3)(a) extends the exception to any form of detention imposed under Article 5, while Article 8(3)(c)(i) merely refers to "detention in consequence of a lawful order of a court". Consequently, the exception of Article 4(3)(a) goes further, since it also covers persons who have been detained by another than a court order on any of the grounds listed under Article 5, paragraph 1.[196]

§ 5. ARTICLE 5: RIGHT TO LIBERTY AND SECURITY OF PERSON

1. Everyone has the right to liberty and security of person. No one shall be deprived of his liberty save in the following cases and in accordance with a procedure prescribed by law:

(a) the lawful detention of a person after conviction by a competent court;

(b) the lawful arrest or detention of a person for non-compliance with the lawful order of a court or in order to secure the fulfilment of any obligation prescribed by law;

(c) the lawful arrest or detention of a person effected for the purpose of bringing him before the competent legal authority on reasonable suspicion of having committed an offence or when it is reasonably considered necessary to prevent his committing an offence or fleeing after having done so;

(d) the detention of a minor by lawful order for the purpose of educational supervision or his lawful detention for the purpose of bringing him before the competent legal authority;

(e) the lawful detention of persons for the prevention of the spreading of infectious diseases, of persons of unsound mind, alcoholics or drug addicts or vagrants;

(f) the lawful arrest or detention of a person to prevent his effecting an unauthorised entry into the country or of a person against whom action

---

194. On this, see *supra* p. 248.
195. Cf. Report of the Committee of Experts, *supra* note 14, p. 27.
196. Whether in fact this leads to an extension depends on national law. According to Dutch law, for instance, other categories of detainees than those convicted cannot be compelled to work. For the "case-law" of the Human Rights Committee concerning Art. 8 of the Covenant reference is made to the study of Nowak, mentioned *supra* at p. 216.

is being taken with a view to deportation or extradition.

2. Everyone who is arrested shall be informed promptly, in a language which he understands, of the reasons for his arrest and of any charge against him.

3. Everyone arrested or detained in accordance with the provisions of paragraph 1(c) of this Article shall be brought promptly before a judge or other officer authorised by law to exercise judicial power and shall be entitled to trial within a reasonable time or to release pending trial. Release may be conditioned by guarantees to appear for trial.

4. Everyone who is deprived of his liberty by arrest or detention shall be entitled to take proceedings by which the lawfulness of his detention shall be decided speedily by a court and his release ordered if the detention is not lawful.

5. Everyone who has been the victim of arrest or detention in contravention of the provisions of this Article shall have an enforceable right to compensation.

1. In Article 5 the right to liberty of person and that to security of person are mentioned in the same breath, while in the following part of the article it is only the right to liberty of person that is developed. This difference in treatment has induced the Commission to state that the right to security of person, in contrast with the right to liberty of person, is formulated in absolute terms, which led the Commission to the conclusion that Article 18 of the Convention cannot have been violated in relation to the first-mentioned right.[197] For the rest, however, the Strasbourg case-law has always treated the two rights as one. Thus the Commission held in its decision on Applications 5573/72 and 5670/72:

> The term "liberty" and "security" must be read as a whole and, in view of its context, as referring only to physical liberty and security. "Liberty of person" in Article 5(1) thus means freedom from arrest and detention and "security of person" the protection against arbitrary interference with this liberty.[198]

And the Court held in the *Bozano* Case as follows:

> The Convention here ... also requires that any measure depriving the individual of his liberty must be compatible with the purpose of Art. 5, namely to protect the individual from arbitrariness ... What is at stake here is not only the "right to liberty", but also the "right to security of person".[199]

This case-law seems to share Fawcett's view when he says: "Liberty and security are the two sides of the same coin; if personal liberty spells actual

---

197. Report of 14 July 1974, *Kamma*, Yearbook XVIII (1975), p. 300 (316).
198. Appls 5573/72 and 5670/72, *Adler and Bivas v. Federal Republic of Germany*, Yearbook XX (1977), p. 102 (146) and Appl. 10475/83, *Dyer v. United Kingdom*, D & R 39 (1984), p. 246 (256). The words "arbitrary interference" have been elucidated by the Commission as meaning that "any decision taken within the sphere of Article 5 must, in order to safeguard the individual's right to 'security of person', conform to the procedural and substantive requirements laid down by an already existing law"; thus, *e.g.*, Appl. 7729/76, *Agee v. United Kingdom*, D & R 7 (1977), p. 164 (173).
199. Judgment of 18 December 1986, A.111 (1987), p. 23.

freedom of movement of the person, security is the condition of being protected by law in that freedom".[200]

The question arises, however, whether the purpose of the inclusion of the right to security of person is thus done justice to. After all, the obligation to give legal protection to the right to liberty of person and the prohibition of arbitrariness in the restriction of that right result from Article 5 and the system of the Convention even without the addition of "and security",[201] while the term "security" according to normal usage refers to more than mere protection against limitation of liberty. The contracting States will also have to give guarantees against other encroachments on the physical[202] security of persons and groups by the authorities as well as individuals, for instance against unnecessary threats to the physical integrity of spectators during police action or against incitement to action against a particular group of persons.[203]

2. With respect to the right to liberty of person, in the Court's opinion Article 5 affords protection exclusively against *deprivation* of liberty, not against other restrictions of the physical liberty of a person. The Court infers this from the further elaboration of Article 5, where the terms "deprived of his liberty", "arrest" and "detention" are used, and also from the fact that Article 2 of Protocol no. 4 contains a separate provision concerning the restriction of freedom of movement.[204]

The question whether there is *deprivation* of liberty depends, in the opinion of the Commission and the Court, on the individual situation of the person concerned as well as on the circumstances in which the latter has been placed as a result of the challenged act. Thus, for instance, certain restrictions of the liberty of movement of soldiers - the obligation to be present in the barracks at particular times, also during leisure - which would constitute a deprivation of liberty for civilians, may be permitted if those restrictions are not "beyond the exigencies of normal military service".[205] In the *Engel* Case, the Court distinguished as follows: it held the so-called "light arrest" and "aggravated arrest" to be not in violation of Article 5, because the soldiers concerned were not confined, but were able to perform their normal service; this in contrast with "strict arrest", which did imply confinement and therefore had to be reviewed for its justification by reference to the exceptions of Article

200. Fawcett, *supra* note 20, p. 58.
201. See the judgment of 8 June 1976, *Engel*, A.22 (1977), p. 25.
202. From the inclusion in Art. 5 it follows that "security" refers exclusively to physical security and not, *e.g.*, to mental, economic, or social security; Castberg, *supra* note 45, p. 92.
203. In its decision on Appl. 6040/73, *X v. Ireland*, Yearbook XVI (1973), p. 388 (392-394), the Commission took the view that Art. 5(1) does not involve for the contracting States the obligation to give a person individual protection in case of an alleged threat to his life.
204. Judgment of 8 June 1976, *Engel*, A.22 (1977), p. 25; judgment of 24 October 1979, *Winterwerp*, A.33 (1980), p. 16; judgment of 6 November 1980, *Guzzardi*, A.39 (1981), p. 33. In its report in the *Bozano* Case, the Commission came to the conclusion that Art. 5 of the Convention amounts to a *lex specialis* in relation to the freedom of movement; report of 7 December 1984, A.111 (1987), p. 35.
205. Report of 19 July 1974, *Engel*, B.20 (1974-1976), p. 60.

5.[206] The Commission, on its part, had concluded that the "light arrest" did not, but the "aggravated arrest" did fall under the prohibition of Article 5, because the latter sanction obliged the soldiers in question to remain within a given room during their leisure, although there was no question of confinement.[207] In the *Guzzardi* Case the Court held that in the case of enforced stay in an island, where freedom of movement was limited at night to a few buildings and in the daytime to a small area of the island, while the possibilities of social contact with other persons besides the nearest relatives was very limited, deprivation of liberty was involved.[208]

In the *Nielsen* Case the Commission and the Court also differed in opinion with respect to the question of whether a deprivation of liberty was at stake. The case concerned the hospitalization for approximately six months of a twelve-year-old boy in a psychiatric ward at a State hospital against his will, but with the consent of his mother as the sole holder of parental rights. The Commission, although acknowledging that the holders of parental rights are entitled to decide in matters concerning their children and that in the present case the applicant's mother gave her consent, having the best interests of the applicant in mind, found that consent not decisive for the question of whether there was a "deprivation" at issue. The Commission based its view on the fact that the case concerned a normally developed twelve-year-old child who was capable of understanding his situation and expressing his opinion clearly. As the protection under Article 5 also applies to minors, the will of the applicant was also relevant in these circumstances. And although the applicant had a room of his own in the ward and was allowed to make short visits to his mother's home, later on extended to weekend and holiday visits, and at the end went to school by taxi, the Commission reached the conclusion that the involuntary placement of the applicant under the conditions in which he stayed in the hospital must in principle be considered as being a deprivation of liberty.[209] The Court, however, although also accepting that the powers of the holder of parental authority cannot be unlimited, was of the opinion that the applicant was still of an age at which it would be normal for a decision to be made by the parent even against the wishes of the child. In the Court's opinion it must be possible for a child like the applicant to be admitted to hospital at the request of the holder of parental rights. Furthermore, the Court considered the restrictions to which the applicant was subjected in the ward to be normal requirements for the care of a child of twelve years of age receiving treatment in hospital. Therefore, the Court reached the opinion that Article 5 was not applicable in the case.[210] From this it appears that the dividing line between *deprivation* of liberty and other restrictions of liberty is by no means clear-cut; the distinction is one of degree or intensity rather

---

206. Judgment of 8 June 1976, A.22 (1977), pp. 25-26.
207. Report of 19 July 1974, *Engel*, B.20 (1974-1976), p. 60.
208. Judgment of 6 November 1980, A.39 (1981), p. 34.
209. Report of 12 March 1987, A.144 (1989), pp. 38-43.
210. Judgment of 28 November 1988, *ibidem*, pp. 24-26.

than one of nature or substance.[211] Moreover, the case-law shows that the Commission and the Court are prepared to oppose their own views on this to those of the government of the respondent State.

If a person who has already been deprived of his liberty is subjected to additional limitations of his liberty, by way of disciplinary penalty, in the Commission's opinion Article 5 does not apply; such a treatment might, however, be in violation of Article 3.[212]

The mere fact that a person has himself assented to this detention does not imply that the detention cannot be an unlawful deprivation of liberty. In the *Vagrancy* Cases the Court held that

the right to liberty is too important in a "democratic society" within the meaning of the Convention for a person to lose the benefit of the protection of the Convention for the single reason that he gives himself up to be taken into detention.[213]

3. *Article 5, paragraph 1* contains an enumeration of the cases in which deprivation of liberty is permitted. This is an exhaustive enumeration.[214] As appears from the words in the second sentence, *viz.* "in accordance with a procedure prescribed by law", it is required for all the cases mentioned that the procedure by means of which the deprivation of liberty has been imposed be regulated in the law of the country in question, in order that the lawfulness of the deprivation of liberty may be reviewed by reference thereto.[215] That national law itself should then also be in conformity with the Convention.[216] It does not mean that in all those cases a *judicial* procedure must have been followed, as is evident in particular from the cases under (c) and (f). Furthermore it is stipulated for each individual case that it must be "lawful", which means that the deprivation of liberty itself must be permitted by domestic law, and that this national law itself must be lawful.[217]

This does not mean that the Strasbourg organs are called upon to give their own interpretation on questions of national law, but they have to examine whether there is a legal basis for the detention, whether that legal basis is in conformity with the Convention and whether the decision of the domestic court on the question of lawfulness is not manifestly arbitrary.[218]

What follows is a brief discussion of the individual exceptions.

211. Judgment of 6 November 1980, *Guzzardi*, A.39 (1981), p. 33 and judgment of 28 May 1985, *Ashingdane*, A.93 (1985), p. 19.
212. Appl. 7754/77, *X v. Switzerland*, D & R 11 (1978), p. 216 (217).
213. Judgment of 18 June 1971, *De Wilde, Ooms and Versyp* ("*Vagrancy*" Cases), A.12 (1971), p. 36.
214. Judgment of 18 January 1978, *Ireland v. United Kingdom*, A.25 (1978), p. 74.
215. See, *e.g.*, Appl. 9920/82, *Naldi v. Italy*, D & R 37 (1984), p. 75 (82).
216. Judgment of 24 October 1979, *Winterwerp*, A.33 (1980), p. 19.
217. With reference to the legislation from the Nazi-period, see Appl. 4324/69, *X v. Federal Republic of Germany*, Yearbook XIV (1971), p. 342 (346).
218. Appl. 1169/61, *X v. Federal Republic of Germany*, Yearbook VI (1963), p. 520 (588 and 590); Appl. 9997/82, *X v. Federal Republic of Germany*, D & R 31 (1983), p. 245; report of 11 October 1983, *Zamir*, D & R 40 (1985), p. 42 (55).

4. The exception under (a) concerns a conviction by a competent *judicial* organ. A decision of the police or a public prosecutor is not sufficient,[219] no more than a decision of a military commander[220] or of an administrative organ.[221] For an organ to be a "judicial" organ, it must be "independent both of the executive and of the parties to the case".[222] It is not required that the members be jurists,[223] or that they have been nominated for an indefinite period.[224]

The requirement that the deprivation of liberty must be lawful means not only that this particular penalty must find a sufficient basis in the conviction of the court, but also - this in connection with Article 7 - that the facts to which the sentence relates constituted according to municipal law, at the time the offence was committed, a punishable act for which the imposition of imprisonment was possible. Since the interpretation and application of municipal law primarily falls under the jurisdiction of the domestic courts, the Commission and the Court will review the position adopted by these courts in the matter only marginally for manifest errors of law or arbitrariness.[225]

In addition, the sentence on which the deprivation of liberty is based must satisfy the provisions of the Convention itself. For instance, it must have been pronounced on the basis of a fair and public hearing in the sense of Article 6. Since foreign sentences may also serve as a basis for a lawful imprisonment,[226] the question arises whether the above-mentioned requirement must also be made with respect to sentences that have been passed in a country which is not a party to the Convention. The necessity of review of such a foreign sentence for its conformity with Article 6 has been left vague by the Commission in a case of an East German sentence,[227] an attitude which has

---

219. With respect to the Belgian Advocate-Fiscal, see the report of 4 March 1978, *Eggs, D & R* 15 (1979), p. 35 (62).
220. Report of 19 July 1974, *Engel*, B.20 (1974-1976), p. 63. A military commander can, however, order custody on remand, which is covered by para. 1 under (c): judgment of 22 May 1984, *De Jong, Baljet and Van den Brink*, A.77 (1984), pp. 21-22.
221. For the Austrian reservation with respect to this, see Council of Europe, *Collected Texts*, Strasbourg 1987, p. 76. If the decision of the administrative organ is based on a judicial decision, the requirement under (a) has been complied with, provided that there is a sufficiently direct link between the two: report of 1 March 1979, *Christinet, D & R* 17 (1980), p. 35 (54); report of 9 July 1980, *Van Droogenbroeck*, B.44 (1985), p. 24. See also the dissenting opinion of the Commission members Opsahl and Tenekides in the last-mentioned report.
222. Judgment of 27 June 1968, *Neumeister*, A.8 (1968), p. 44. See also the judgment of 18 June 1971, *De Wilde, Ooms and Versyp* ("*Vagrancy*" Cases), A.12 (1971), p. 41, the judgment of 16 July 1971, *Ringeisen*, A.13 (1971), p. 39, and the judgment of 8 June 1976, *Engel*, A.22 (1977), pp. 27-28.
223. Appl. 5258/71, *X v. Sweden*, *Coll.* 43 (1973), p. 71 (79).
224. The Dutch Supreme Military Court was recognized as a judicial organ in the *Engel* Case, although the four military members could be discharged from their function by the King. In the opinion of the Commission and the Court the fact that these members have taken not only the judicial, but also the military oath also did not bar their independence: judgment of 8 June 1976, A.22 (1977), pp. 27-28; report of 19 July 1974, B.20 (1974-1976), pp. 66-67.
225. See, *e.g.*, judgment of 24 October 1979, *Winterwerp*, A.33 (1980), p. 20, and Appl. 9997/82, *X v. Federal Republic of Germany*, D & R 31 (1983), p. 245 (249).
226. Appl. 1322/62, *X v. Federal Republic of Germany*, *Yearbook* VI (1963), p. 494 (516).
227. *Ibidem*, pp. 518-520.

justly been criticized.[228] The Court, on its part, in the *Wemhoff* Case appears to recognize and apply the requirement as a general rule when it speaks of the determination of guilt "in the course of a trial conducted in accordance with the requirements of Article 6".[229]

The mere fact that a judicial sentence is annulled on appeal does not deprive the imprisonment imposed in execution of that sentence of its lawful character.[230] However, the matter is different if the ground for annulment is precisely a manifest error with respect to the municipal law or a violation of one of the provisions of the Convention, in particular of Articles 6 and 7.[231]

A person detained on remand is to be considered, from his conviction by a court of first instance, as a detainee "after conviction", so that from that moment and during appeal proceedings the lawfulness of that detention must be reviewed by reference to the provision under (a) and no longer by reference to that under (c).[232] This holds true even if under domestic law the person is still considered as a remand prisoner.[233]

The words "after conviction" in Article 5(1)(a) do not, according to the Court, simply mean that "the 'detention' must follow the 'conviction' in point of time", but also that "the detention must result from, follow and depend or occur by virtue of the conviction".[234] The Commission has interpreted these words to mean that this provision also applies to judicial decisions for continued detention to prevent repeated offences (*e.g.* when the person in question is placed at the disposal of the Government), although those decisions themselves do not imply a "conviction", but have been taken on the ground of earlier convictions.[235] In the *Van Droogenbroeck* Case, the applicant was sentenced by a criminal court to two years of imprisonment, and was ordered to be "placed at the Government's disposal" for ten years. The Court had to decide whether there was sufficient connection, for the purpose of Article 5, between this sentence and order, and the subsequent deprivation of liberty on two occasions as a result of the decisions by the Minister of Justice, following applicant's disappearances. According to the Court, the

228. Jacobs, *supra* note 17, p. 48.
229. Judgment of 27 June 1968, A.7 (1968), p. 24.
230. Appl. 3245/67, *X v. Austria, Yearbook* XII (1969), p. 206 (236); report of 9 March 1978, *Krzycki, D & R* 13 (1979), p. 57 (61).
231. Thus the Commission in its decision on Appl. 6694/74, *Artico v. Italy, D & R* 8 (1977), p. 73 (88-89): the annulment of a judgment on the ground that the expiration of the term of limitation had not been observed by the lower court, rendered the imposed detention unlawful.
232. Judgment of 27 June 1968, *Wemhoff,* A.7 (1968), p. 23. See, however, *infra* pp. 279-280 for the cases in which the law does not permit execution of a judgment which is not yet final.
233. Appl. 9132/80, *N. v. Federal Republic of Germany, D & R* 31 (1983), p. 154 (173). For a somewhat different system of detention after a conviction in the first instance, see the judgment of 2 March 1987, *Monnell and Morris,* A.115 (1987), pp. 19-20.
234. Judgment of 5 November 1981, *X v. United Kingdom,* A.46 (1982), p. 17; judgment of 24 June 1982, *Van Droogenbroeck,* A.50 (1982), p. 19, and judgment of 2 March 1987, *Weeks,* A.114 (1987), p. 23. In the last-mentioned case, the Court added that "[i]n short, there must be a sufficient causal connection between the conviction and the deprivation of liberty at issue".
235. See Fawcett, *supra* note 20, pp. 69-70, and the case-law there mentioned. Fawcett considers it conceivable that the word "after" was chosen, rather than the words "as a result of", to make applications like those by the Commission possible.

sentence to imprisonment and the order to be placed at the Government's disposal constitute "an inseparable whole". The execution of this order may take several forms, which is a matter of discretion of the Minister of Justice. In this case the way in which this discretion was exercised respected the requirements of the Convention.[236]

In the *Weeks* Case, again, the "sufficient causal connection between conviction and deprivation of liberty" was at issue. Here the applicant was sentenced to life imprisonment, but released on licence some ten years later. However, the licence was revoked after 15 months by the Home Secretary. The reason for the sentence to life imprisonment was to make the applicant "subject to a continuing security measure in the interests of public safety". Since there was no medical evidence justifying an order to send him to a mental institution, this "indeterminate sentence" would enable the Home Secretary to monitor his progress. The Court concluded that there were several similarities with an order to place someone at the disposal of the Government. Therefore, the Court held as follows:

> Applying the principles stated in the *Van Droogenbroeck* judgment, the formal legal connection between Mr. Weeks' conviction in 1966 and his recall to prison some ten years later is not on its own sufficient to justify the contested detention under Article 5, para. 1(a). The causal link required by subparagraph (a) ... might eventually be broken if a position were reached in which a decision not to release or to re-detain was based on grounds that were inconsistent with the objectives of the sentencing court. In those circumstances, a detention that was lawful at the outset would be transformed into a deprivation of liberty that was arbitrary and, hence, incompatible with Article 5.[237]

However, the Court finally reached the conclusion that the sentencing judges must be taken to have known and intended that it was inherent in Mr. Weeks' life sentence that his liberty was at the discretion of the executive for the rest of his life, and that it was not for the Court, within the context of Article 5, to review the appropriateness of the original sentence.[238] Thus the Court accepted a very loose link between the original sentence and the renewed detention. However, next the Court examined whether the grounds on which the redetention was based, were sufficient. Although, here again, the Court took as a starting-point that a certain discretion has to be left to the national authorities in this matter, it conducted its own examination of the grounds in a rather detailed manner.[239]

Another aspect of the interpretation of the words "after conviction" concerns the decision of the investigating judge to arrest the person concerned. Although here there is not yet any question of a conviction, the Commission has brought this also under Article 5, para. 1(a),[240] an interpretation which would seem quite challengeable in view of the clear expression "conviction".

---

236. Judgment of 24 June 1982, A.50 (1982), pp. 20-22.
237. Judgment of 2 March 1987, A.114 (1987), pp. 25-26.
238. *Ibidem*, p. 26.
239. *Ibidem*, pp. 26-27.
240. Appl. 5973/73, *X v. Belgium*, *Coll.* 45 (1974), p. 119.

258

5. The first permissible form of deprivation of liberty mentioned under (b) - on account of non-compliance with a lawful order of a court - is clear. Here one may think, for instance, of a refusal to execute a civil sentence - in which case Article 1 of Protocol no. 4 must be observed by those countries which have ratified that Protocol[241] - to appear as a witness in a criminal case by order of the court or to submit to a blood test,[242] or of a measure to enforce an injunction concerning a statutory declaration of assets which the applicant had refused to make.[243]

The second form mentioned under (b) - deprivation of liberty in order to secure fulfilment of an obligation prescribed by law - is less clear. In fact, this wide formulation would seem to pave the way for a great many forms of deprivation of liberty without any judicial intervention, simply by the invocation of a legal norm, with the added possibility of taking preventive action even before a norm has been violated. It is true that in those cases the fourth paragraph allows appeal to a court, but this does not alter the fact that a wide interpretation of the second limb of paragraph 1(b) would erode a good many of the guarantees contained in the other provisions of Article 5.

In the *Lawless* Case the Commission submitted in its report - and the Court accepted this implicitly - that "any obligation prescribed by law" must relate to a *specific* obligation and that it is not sufficient to invoke the prevention of violations of norms in general.[244] This point also played a part in the *Engel* Case. In fact, in that case the Supreme Military Court had invoked Article 5(1)(b) in order to justify an imposed "strict arrest" as a provisional measure. The Commission and the Court rejected this viewpoint, because they considered the general obligation to comply with military discipline not sufficiently specific.[245]

In the *McVeigh, O'Neill and Evans* Case the Commission concluded that the obligation imposed on a person, when entering the United Kingdom, to submit to examination on the requirement of an examining officer is a specific and concrete obligation and that the authorities are, therefore, in principle entitled under Article 5(1)(b) to resort to detention to secure its fulfilment, even if the person in question has not refused to submit to examination. It also took the view, however, that the mere existence of an unfulfilled obligation is not of itself enough to justify the arrest or detention; there must be specific circumstances which warrant the use of detention as a means of securing the fulfilment of the obligation.[246]

---

241. See *infra* pp. 488-489.
242. Appl. 8278/78, *X v. Austria*, *D & R* 18 (1980), p. 154 (156).
243. Appl. 9546/81, *X v. Federal Republic of Germany*, not published.
244. Report of 19 December 1959, B.1 (1960-1961), p. 64; judgment of 1 July 1961, A.3 (1960-1961), p. 51 in conjunction with p. 47. See also the judgment of 6 November 1980, *Guzzardi*, A.39 (1981), pp. 37-38.
245. Report of 19 July 1974, B.20 (1974-1976), p. 64; judgment of 8 June 1976, A.22 (1977), p. 28.
246. Report of 18 March 1981, *D & R* 25 (1982), p. 15 (37-43).

In the *Ciulla* Case the applicant had been deprived of his liberty on the ground that he had failed to comply with the obligation to "change his behaviour" mentioned in Section 3 of the Italian Act 1423/56. The Commission held that this did not constitute a "specific and concrete obligation" within the meaning of Article 5(1)(b). The Commission also stressed that this provision did not contemplate arrest or detention for the prevention of offences against the public peace or public order, or against the security of the State, but for securing the execution of specific obligations imposed by law. The Commission further was of the opinion that the second ground for deprivation of his liberty, advanced by the Italian Government, *i.e.* the obligation to comply with the compulsory residence order, derived not directly from the law, but from a court decision which was still to be taken. Consequently, no obligation had yet arisen on the date when the applicant was arrested.[247]

6. The provision under (c) in Article 5, paragraph 1, like the third paragraph of that Article, refers to the detention on remand of an accused person pending a decision of the court in his case. The third paragraph requires that in case of such a measure the accused be brought *promptly* before a judicial authority and is entitled to trial *within a reasonable time* or to release pending trial. This will be discussed in connection with that provision.

The arrest or detention may be resorted to if there is a reasonable suspicion that a criminal offence has been committed, or if this measure is reasonably considered necessary to prevent a criminal offence or to prevent flight after an offence has been committed. Since these grounds have been placed side by side and have not been made cumulative, the provision lacks clarity. In fact, in its present formulation it would appear to justify detention as a measure against persons on suspicion that they will commit crimes without their having as yet committed them. This interpretation is also corroborated by the *travaux préparatoires*, *viz.* in the report of the Senior Officials, in which it is stated as follows:

> it may ... be necessary in certain circumstances to arrest an individual in order to prevent his committing a crime, even if the facts which show his intention to commit the crime do not of themselves constitute a criminal offence.[248]

But is such an arrest really aimed at bringing the accused before a competent judicial authority, as is required under (c)? Precisely because such a wide interpretation of the possibility of detention on remand might give rise to abuse, it is to be welcomed that as early as 1961, in the *Lawless* Case, the Court took the position that internment to prevent criminal offences without the accused being brought before the court, or a trial being intended, is not

---

247. Report of 8 May 1987, A.148 (1989), pp. 25-26. In the same sense the Court in its judgment of 22 February 1989, A.148 (1989), p. 16, where it held that Art. 5(1)(b) was inapplicable because the obligation arose only after the impugned decision.
248. Council of Europe, *Collected Edition of the "Travaux Préparatoires" of the European Convention on Human Rights*, Vol. IV, Strasbourg 1977, p. 260.

permitted under Article 5(1)(c).[249] The same position was taken in the *Greek Case*,[250] and in *Ireland v. United Kingdom*.[251] In the *Ciulla* Case the Italian Government argued that, when drafting the provision under (c), those preparing the Convention had in mind the fact that every legal system, in order to perform its function of maintaining social order, has to take measures to prevent criminal offences. From this the Government induced that a person constituting a danger to society may be subjected to a preventive measure imposed in the course of judicial proceedings. The Commission, however, was of the opinion that the applicant's arrest and detention were solely motivated by the fear that he might "avoid possible security measures", but had nothing to do with pending criminal proceedings against him. In these circumstances, the applicant was not detained with a view to being brought before a legal authority.[252] In the *Brogan* Case the applicants alleged that their arrest and detention was not intended to bring them before the competent legal authority. In fact they were neither charged nor brought before a court. The Court held that the existence of such a purpose must be considered independently of its achievement. There was no reason to believe that the applicants' detention was not intended to further police investigation by way of confirming or dispelling concrete suspicions which grounded their arrest.[253]

Can a person be brought before the court if there is no suspicion that he *has* in fact committed a criminal offence? Can the mere fear of *future* behaviour, *i.e.* apart from the case of an act prevented by timely intervention of the police, constitute a sufficient ground for criminal prosecution? If not, what is the use of mentioning this ground in addition to that of suspicion of having committed a criminal offence? This question applies to an even higher degree to the third ground mentioned under (c): why has the fear that the accused may flee after having committed a criminal offence been included as a separate ground, if the suspicion that such a criminal offence has been committed or will be committed is in itself already a sufficient ground for arrest? An acceptable interpretation is reached here only if it is assumed that in this provision the grounds for arrest and those for continued detention have been joined. This would then produce the following picture: arrest is permitted under the Convention in case of a reasonable suspicion that the accused has committed a criminal offence or if the arrest may reasonably be considered necessary to prevent his completing a criminal offence that he is about to commit or is committing. For continuation of the detention it is additionally required that it is likely that he will abscond or that there are reasonable grounds for assuming that after his release the arrested person will

249.   Judgment of 1 July 1961, *Lawless*, A.3 (1960-61), p. 52.
250.   Report of 5 November 1969, *Yearbook* XII; *The Greek Case* (1969), pp. 134-135.
251.   Report of 25 January 1976, B.23/I (1976-78), p. 110; judgment of 18 January 1978, A.25 (1978), pp. 74-75.
252.   Report of 8 May 1987, A.148 (1989), pp. 26-27. In the same sense the Court in its judgment of 22 February 1989, A.148 (1989), p. 18.
253.   Judgment of 29 November 1988, A.145/B (1989), pp. 28-30.

again commit a criminal offence.[254] In that case, however, it will also have to be assumed that these latter grounds of continuation do not constitute an exhaustive enumeration, since the Strasbourg organs have also recognized as such grounds the risk of suppression of evidence,[255] the danger of collusion[256] and - implicitly - the danger of subornation of witnesses.[257] However, in the case of *De Jong, Baljet and Van den Brink*, the Commission assigned an independent meaning to each of the three circumstances mentioned under (c): "The wording 'or' separating these three categories of persons clearly indicates that this enumeration is not cumulative and that it is sufficient if the arrested person falls under one of the above categories".[258] The Commission did not clarify, however, how this interpretation is to be reconciled with the *Lawless* judgment and with the rationale of the restrictive character of Article 5.

Article 5(1)(c) requires only that there be a "reasonable suspicion". At the moment the arrest is made it need not yet be firmly established that an offence has actually been committed or what the precise nature of that offence is; indeed, it is for this that the further examination is intended which the detention on remand must help to ensure.[259] Whether the mere continuation of suspicion suffices to warrant the prolongation of the detention on remand is covered not by the first but by the third paragraph of Article 5.[260]

Article 5(1)(c) also stipulates that the arrest and detention must be "lawful" and that the accused shall subsequently be brought before "a competent legal authority". In this context the very vague term "legal authority" must, in conformity with the third paragraph of Article 5, be deemed to mean: "judge or other officer authorised by law to exercise judicial power".[261] This provision does not require that the warrant of arrest itself must also originate from a judicial authority.[262] The answer to the questions of whether the arrest and detention are lawful and whether the authority bringing the arrested person before the court is competent, is determined by the law of the country

---

254. *Cf.* Castberg, *supra* note 45, pp. 94-95, and Jacobs, *supra* note 17, pp. 52-53. See also Recommendation R(80)11 of the Committee of Ministers of 27 June 1980 on detention on remand, where the grounds are indeed formulated cumulatively in Art. 3, while Art. 4 provides that detention on remand without one of the grounds of the second category presenting itself "may nevertheless exceptionally be justified in certain cases of particularly serious offences".
255. Judgment of 27 June 1968, *Wemhoff*, A.7 (1968), p. 25.
256. Report of 1 April 1966, *Wemhoff*, B.5 (1969), p. 89 and Appl. 9614/81, *G, S and M v. Austria*, *D & R* 34 (1983), p. 119 (121).
257. See the judgment of 16 July 1971, *Ringeisen*, A.13 (1971), pp. 42-43, where the Court rejects the invocation by the Austrian authorities of this ground on the basis of factual data, but seems to accept the ground itself as a possibility.
258. Report of 11 October 1982, A.77 (1984), p. 34. In its judgment of 22 May 1984, *ibidem*, pp. 21-22, the Court did not dissociate itself from this interpretation.
259. Appl. 8339/78, *Schertenleib v. Switzerland*, *D & R* 17 (1980), p. 180 (218-219) and Appl. 9627/81, *Ferrari-Bravo v. Italy*, *D & R* 37 (1984), p. 15 (37).
260. Judgment of 22 May 1984, *De Jong, Baljet and Van den Brink*, A.77 (1984), p. 22.
261. Judgment of 18 January 1978, *Ireland v. United Kingdom*, A.25 (1978), p. 75. In its judgment of 1 July 1961, *Lawless*, the Court speaks of "judicial authority" and of "judge"; A.3 (1960-61), p. 51 and p. 52 respectively. *Cf.* also the judgment of 4 December 1979, *Schiesser*, A.34 (1980), p. 13, and Appl. 9997/82, *X v. Federal Republic of Germany*, *D & R* 31 (1983), p. 245 (248-249). See also *infra* pp. 281-283.
262. Appl. 7755/77, *X v. Austria*, *D & R* 9 (1978), p. 210 (211).

concerned. The interpretation and application thereof is left to the domestic authorities, while the Strasbourg procedure provides for the marginal review of whether the national authorities have acted in good faith and reasonableness in reaching their decision.[263] That decision does not necessarily have to refer to the exact legal grounds of the arrest and/or detention, provided that these grounds are sufficiently clear by implication.[264] The mere fact that a person detained on remand is later released under a judicial decision does not yet render the arrest unlawful with retroactive effect.[265]

The word "competent" must, of course, be dealt with as a separate requirement. Rather remarkable, therefore, was the decision by the Commission on a complaint that the judge who heard the applicant after her arrest and ordered her detention on remand was not competent to do so, that the procedure followed was of a judicial nature and that "the impartiality and objectivity of the judge cannot be put in question solely by the alleged fact that he volunteered for the work"; that observation would seem to be totally beside the point.[266]

Whether there is question of "reasonable suspicion" and whether the arrest and detention could reasonably be deemed "necessary" should, in the Commission's opinion, be judged by the circumstances at the moment the decision was taken to arrest and/or detain the person in question, and not by the facts that are known at the moment the complaint is examined.[267] As will be set forth below, the necessity also has to exist subsequently, and will then have to be judged by the circumstances and facts at the moment of the judicial review in order to permit a decision on whether under Article 5(3) the person is to be provisionally released.[268]

Article 6(2) of the Convention provides that a person who is charged with an offence must be presumed innocent until proved guilty. This presumption of innocence should be respected not only during the hearing in court; out of court, too, the accused - and thus also the person detained on remand - should not be treated as if his guilt were already established. The justification of the limitations to be imposed on the person detained on remand should therefore be based on other criteria than the limitations which result from a sentence of imprisonment.[269] This might also imply that persons detained on remand must be segregated if possible from convicted persons, although,

---

263. Appl. 2621/65, *X v. the Netherlands*, Yearbook IX (1966), p. 474 (478-480) and Appl. 9860/82, *X v. France*, not published.
264. Appl. 9472/81, *X v. Austria*, not published.
265. Appl. 8083/77, *X v. United Kingdom*, D & R 19 (1980), p. 223 (225).
266. Appl. 9997/82, *X v. Federal Republic of Germany*, D & R 31 (1983), p. 245 (248-249).
267. Appl. 1602/62, *Stögmüller v. Austria*, Yearbook VII (1964), p. 168 (188), with a reference to a not published partial decision of the Commission in the *Nielsen* Case. The Commission itself must be "satisfied" that this "reasonable suspicion" and this "necessity" existed at that time: Appl. 7755/77, *X v. Austria*, D & R 9 (1978), p. 210 (211). For a review by the Commission of the national decision for its reasonableness, see Appl. 9451/81, X v. Federal Republic of Germany, not published.
268. *Infra* p. 277.
269. See Resolution (65)11 of the Committee of Ministers of the Council of Europe on detention on remand. In this Resolution it is emphasized that detention on remand should be an exceptional measure, which is applied only if "strictly necessary".

unlike in the Covenant, this is not explicitly provided for in the Convention.

7. In the first case mentioned under (d) one has to think of an order - judicial or not - to place a minor under supervision, combined with a restriction of freedom, for instance enforced stay in a reformatory institution or in a clinic.[270] Most legal systems permit such restrictions of freedom in the interest of the minor, even if the latter is not suspected of having committed any criminal offence. They then require that it may reasonably be assumed that the development or the health of the minor is seriously endangered - for instance in the case of drug addiction and/or prostitution - or that he is being ill-treated. The text speaks only of "lawful order", so that it does not appear to be required that the order emanates from a judicial organ. Under paragraph 4 of Article 5, however, these minors too - or if the law so provides, their legal representatives - are entitled to institute court proceedings in order that the lawfulness of the restriction of their freedom may be reviewed.[271]

The far-reaching powers issuing from Article 5(1)(d) have led the Court to require rather strict guarantees for the educational purpose. In the *Bouamar* Case a minor was repeatedly confined in a remand prison "for the purpose of educational supervision". Although the confinements never exceeded the statutory limit of fifteen days, the detentions (nine in total) amounted to a deprivation of liberty for 119 days in less than one year. The Court held that, in order to consider the deprivation of liberty lawful for educational supervision, the Belgian Government was under an obligation to put in place appropriate institutional facilities which meet the demands of security and educational objectives; the mere detention of a juvenile "in conditions of virtual isolation and without the assistance of staff with educational training cannot be regarded as furthering any educational aim".[272]

According to the *travaux préparatoires* the second case mentioned under (d) is concerned with the detention of minors for the purpose of bringing them before the court "to secure their removal from harmful surroundings, so that they are not covered by Article 5(1)(c)".[273] This would therefore be a measure by which the minor is protected against himself in order to prevent his sliding into criminality. It is not clear, however, what specific reason there would be to bring the person concerned before a court, if no crime has been committed. The only case known to us relating to such a measure concerned an enforced stay of eight months in an observation centre, while the

---

270. In Appl. 6753/74, *X and Y v. the Netherlands*, *D & R* 2 (1975), p. 118, applicant X, a minor who had run away from home, complained, *inter alia*, about the fact that she had been forced to spend a night at the police station before being taken home. The Commission declared this part of the complaint "manifestly ill-founded" without any further argumentation, which is very unsatisfactory in view of the serious character of the measure complained of, and the justified doubt about its legality under Art. 5.
271. See, *e.g.*, the judgment of 29 February 1988, *Bouamar*, A.129 (1988), pp. 22-25, where a breach of this provision was found to have occurred.
272. Judgment of 29 February 1988, A.129 (1988), p. 22.
273. Quotation in Fawcett, *supra* note 20, p. 82.

authorities examined whether theft and traffic offences had been committed.[274] In any case, the measure of bringing a minor before a judicial authority which decides on the prolongation of the detention, must be the purpose of the initial deprivation of liberty; consequently, there must be a sufficient ground for that measure. The organ that is competent to execute this deprivation of liberty is determined by national law ("lawful detention").

Since Article 5(1)(d) confers such far-reaching powers on the national authorities with regard to minors, the age at which a person attains majority is of the greatest importance. This age is determined by domestic law. In Resolution (72)29 the Committee of Ministers of the Council of Europe has recommended to fix this age at eighteen.[275] Domestic law also determines whether and in what cases a minor himself has the legal capacity to go to court, so that a minor who has this right in Strasbourg may be dependent on his parents or guardian for the exhaustion of the local remedies.[276]

8. The provision under (e) deals with widely divergent categories of persons as if they were all infected by a disease from which society has to be protected, but without any further differentiation as to the character and the duration of the deprivation of liberty that is considered justified. For the latter here again the word "lawful" forms the general criterion, while under the fourth paragraph of Article 5 the categories here referred to are also entitled to have the lawfulness of their detention reviewed by a court in accordance with the legal rules applying in the country concerned. The latter is important in particular for those cases where the detention can be ordered under municipal law by an administrative organ. If and in so far as, in performing this review, the court determines a civil right in the sense of Article 6, the rules for a fair trial set forth therein have to be observed.[277]

In relation to the provision under (e) - and to a certain extent also to the provision under (d) - it is of importance to stress again that complaints can only be brought before the Strasbourg organs against States. Therefore, the deprivation complained of must be or have been carried out under State responsibility. Thus, in the *Nielsen* Case, the issue arose if the hospitalization of a twelve-year-old boy in the psychiatric ward at a State hospital at the request of his mother, who was the sole holder of parental rights, involved State responsibility. The Commission took the view that, although the applicant was admitted into the State hospital at his mother's request, it was

---

274. Appl. 8500/79, *X v. Switzerland, D & R* 18 (1980), p. 238.
275. Res. (72)29 "Lowering of the age of full legal capacity" and "Explanatory Memorandum", Council of Europe, Strasbourg 1972.
276. See Stefan Trechsel, "The right to liberty and security of the person - Article 5 of the European Convention on Human Rights in the Strasbourg case-law", 1 *HRLJ* (1980), pp. 88-135 (119).
277. According to Alkema, *supra* note 8, p. 60, this is the case when a decision is made on the detention of a person of unsound mind and thus on his status as a legally incompetent person. In its *Winterwerp* report the Commission called this point "important", but did not pronounce on it, because it was of the opinion that the issue had been brought forward at too late a stage; Report of 15 December 1977, B.31 (1983), pp. 44-45.

the duty of the chief physician at that hospital to ensure that his admission was reasonable and justified in the circumstances. Therefore, the mother's consent did not relieve the chief physician of his responsibility in taking the final decision regarding the applicant's admission and regarding the conditions in which he was to be kept at the hospital.[278] In the Court's view, however, the decision on the question of hospitalization was in fact taken by the mother in her capacity as holder of parental rights. Although the chief physician's decision on admission constituted indirectly a safeguard against possible abuse of parental rights, his involvement did not alter the mother's position under Danish law as the sole person with power to decide on the hospitalization of the applicant or his removal from hospital. Consequently, the Court held Article 5 to be not applicable in so far as it is concerned with deprivation of liberty by the authorities of the State. The Court nevertheless investigated whether the circumstances of the present case, especially the restrictions imposed upon the applicant's liberty, amounted to a violation of Article 5, thus accepting that the actual treatment in the hospital could involve State responsibility notwithstanding the original consent by the applicant's mother.[279]

In the *Winterwerp* Case it was held by the Court that the requirement that the detention must be lawful means that it must have taken place in accordance with the procedural and substantive provisions of municipal law and must meet the purpose for which Article 5(1)(e) has been drafted.[280] The question of whether municipal law has been correctly interpreted and applied in the matter is not for the Strasbourg authorities to decide; they investigate only whether this law has been applied in an arbitrary way or for an improper purpose.[281] In this connection it is very important that in the *Vagrancy* Cases the Court - unlike the Commission in its report - carried out an independent investigation into the question of whether (1) the definition of the relevant category in the domestic legislation - in this case the definition of "vagrant" in Belgian law - was consistent with the common meaning of the term, and accordingly compatible with the Convention, and (2) the person in question was rightly brought under this definition by the national authorities.[282] Thus the Court, although confining itself to a marginal review of the national law and its application, takes a rather active position when it comes to a review of the conformity of that application with the wording and meaning of Article 5(1)(e). In its report in the *Winterwerp* Case the Commission adopted the same line of conduct; it also reviewed the definition of "insane person" in Dutch law for its conformity with the Convention by comparing it with the common meaning of this term, and investigated whether the person in

---

278. Report of 12 March 1987, A.144 (1989), p. 38.
279. Judgment of 22 November 1988, *ibidem*, pp. 23-24.
280. Judgment of 24 October 1979, A.33 (1980), p. 17. Also judgment of 28 May 1985, *Ashingdane*, A.93 (1985), pp. 18 and 21.
281. For such an investigation, see the judgment of 28 May 1985, A.93 (1985), pp. 21-22.
282. Judgment of 18 June 1971, *De Wilde, Ooms and Versyp*, A.12 (1971), pp. 37-38.

question had been arbitrarily brought under that definition by the Dutch authorities.[283] This case-law was confirmed by the Court in its judgment in the *Winterwerp* Case, in which the Court emphasized the fact that the term "of unsound mind" implies that three minimum conditions have to be satisfied: (1) the applicant must be "reliably shown" to be of unsound mind (which "calls for objective medical expertise"), (2) the nature or degree of the mental disorder must be such as to justify the deprivation of liberty and (3) continued confinement is only valid as long as the disorder persists.[284]

Thus a guarantee has been created against too wide a national interpretation and application of the categories mentioned under (e).[285] The necessity of a restrictive interpretation was equally emphasized by the Court in the *Guzzardi* Case, where it also held that it may not be inferred from the exception permitted under Article 5(1)(e) that the detention of persons who may constitute a greater danger than the categories mentioned in that article is permitted equally and *a fortiori*.[286]

Since paragraph 1(e) does not contain any limitation as to the duration of the detention, this in contrast with the other cases of detention regulated in the same paragraph, the question is of great importance whether paragraph 4 confers on the person concerned only the right to have the lawfulness of the deprivation of his liberty as such reviewed by a court or also the right to have recourse periodically to a court if the detention is prolonged. In the *Vagrancy* Cases the Court took the position that paragraph 4 has been complied with if the arrest or detention is based on a judicial decision as referred to in paragraph 4, but that this provision does not confer a right to submit the lawfulness of the detention periodically to the court.[287] However, in the *Winterwerp* Case,[288] and also in an earlier decision,[289] the Commission stated that this view cannot be maintained with respect to detentions *for an indefinite period*. In the Commission's opinion a person detained for an indefinite period does have the right of recourse to a court, claiming that the circumstances no longer justify his detention and applying for a release. This opinion was followed by the Court in the same case.[290]

---

283. Report of 15 December 1977, B.31 (1978-1981), pp. 36-37. See Appl. 7493/76, *X v. Federal Republic of Germany*, D & R 6 (1977), p. 82 (82-83), where the Commission decided that there is also question of "unsound mind" if a person, though not mentally defective, shows such deviating traits of personality that he is constantly inclined to violate the law, but cannot be held responsible for his acts under criminal law.
284. Judgment of 24 October 1979, A.33 (1980), pp. 16-18. Whether the detention had continued beyond the period justified by applicant's mental disorder, was investigated by the Court in great detail in the *Luberti* Case, judgment of 23 February 1984, A.75 (1984), pp. 13-15. See also the report of 7 October 1981, *B v. United Kingdom*, D & R 32 (1983), p. 5 (37-38).
285. See also the report of 16 July 1980, *X v. United Kingdom*, B.41 (1985), pp. 31-32, the report of 7 October 1981, *B v. United Kingdom*, D & R 32 (1983), p. 5 (37-38), the judgment of 23 February 1984, *Luberti*, A.75 (1984), pp. 12-13, and, finally, the judgment of 28 May 1985, *Ashingdane*, A.93 (1985), p. 18.
286. Judgment of 6 November 1980, A.39 (1981), pp. 36-37.
287. Judgment of 18 June 1971, *De Wilde, Ooms and Versyp*, A.12 (1971), p. 40.
288. Report of 15 December 1977, B.31 (1983), pp. 40-41.
289. Appl. 6859/74, *X v. Belgium*, Yearbook XIX (1976), p. 372 (374).
290. Judgment of 24 October 1979, A.33 (1980), pp. 22-23.

In the Case of *X v. United Kingdom* the question had to be answered whether placing a person of unsound mind at the disposal of the government as a measure subsequent to a criminal conviction is covered by paragraph 1(e) or rather by paragraph 1(a). In the opinion of the Commission, these two provisions are fundamentally different. The latter "refers narrowly to the conviction and sentence of a person found guilty of a criminal offence, with the attendant notions of social blame and punishment".[291] Article 5(1)(e), on the other hand, "provides for the detention of a person by virtue of the specific state of his mental health, irrespective of criminal conduct, as a person of unsound mind, by definition, cannot be held fully responsible for his acts".[292] The Court, however, came to the conclusion that, although it recognized the differences between the paragraphs 5(1)(a) and 5(1)(e), both paragraphs could be and were applicable to the applicant's deprivation of liberty, at least initially.[293] Much depends here on the factual circumstances of the case and on what the applicable domestic law provides with respect to the criminal responsibility of persons of unsound mind. It may, therefore, be assumed that the Court will adopt this view only in rather exceptional cases.[294] In the Case of *M. v. Federal Republic of Germany* the applicant was sentenced to prison for three years, which detention was to be followed by detention in a mental hospital. Here the Commission held that "in view of the fact that the detention is based on a finding of a state of unsound mind, it must in addition, and primarily, be considered under Article 5(1)(e) of the Convention".[295]

The enforced placing of an accused person in an observation clinic in most cases cannot be brought under paragraph 1(e), because as a rule it is not certain in advance that he is of unsound mind. This deprivation of liberty may perhaps find its justification in paragraph 1(b), since the measure is provided for in a judicial decision which may be enforced if it is not complied with voluntarily.

In the *Winterwerp* Case it had been argued on behalf of the applicant that Article 5(1)(e) entails for the person detained on that ground "the right to appropriate treatment in order to ensure that he is not detained longer than absolutely necessary". This submission, however, was rejected by the Court, which followed the Commission in this.[296] In the *Ashingdane* Case, both the Commission and the Court further elaborated on this. According to the Court, the lawfulness of a deprivation of liberty concerns not only the issuance of the order of the liberty-depriving measures, but also its execution. In other words,

---

291. Report of 16 July 1980, B.41 (1985), p. 30.
292. *Ibidem.* See also the report of 7 October 1981, *B v. United Kingdom*, *D & R* 32 (1983), p. 5 (36-37).
293. Judgment of 5 November 1981, *X v. United Kingdom*, A.46 (1982), p. 17.
294. See, for example, the judgment of 23 February 1984, *Luberti*, A.75 (1984), p. 12, where the Court clearly distinguished between paragraphs 1(a) and 1(e), without any further qualification.
295. Appl. 10272/82, *D & R* 38 (1984), p. 104 (111).
296. Judgment of 24 October 1979, A.33 (1980), p. 21.

the measure must not only be in conformity with the domestic law, but also with the purposes of the restrictions laid down in Article 5(1). This also follows from Article 18 of the Convention. Therefore, there must be "some relationship between the ground of permitted deprivation of liberty relied on and the place and conditions of detention". Except for this relationship, however, Article 5(1)(e) is not concerned with suitable treatment or conditions.[297]

9. The great importance of the provision under (f) consists in that, although the Convention does not grant to aliens a right of admission to or residence in the contracting States,[298] Article 5 nevertheless contains certain guarantees in case the authorities proceed to arrest or detain an alien pending the decision on his admission, deportation or extradition. These consist first of all in a guarantee that such arrest or detention must be lawful and must therefore be in conformity with the relevant regulations of domestic law,[299] coupled with the right of the person in question under paragraph 4 to have this lawfulness reviewed by a court and ultimately, if necessary, by the Strasbourg organs.[300]

The Commission distinguishes between the lawfulness of the detention and the lawfulness of the deportation or extradition itself.[301] It is obvious, however, that in reviewing the lawfulness of the detention, the lawfulness of the deportation or extradition will often also be in issue. This is especially the case when, according to national law, the lawfulness of the detention is made dependent on that of the deportation.[302] It is, *inter alia* for that reason, very important that the deportation or extradition be postponed pending the review of the legality of the detention; the outcome of this review may throw new light also on the legality of the deportation or extradition. As regards the national proceedings, the obligation of the authorities as to such postponement

---

297. Judgment of 28 May 1985, A.93 (1983), p. 21. *Cf.* the still somewhat stricter view of the Commission in its report of 12 May 1983, A.93 (1985), p. 37. See also the report of 7 October 1981, *B v. United Kingdom, D & R* 32 (1983), p. 5 (32).
298. See *infra* pp. 386-389.
299. Including directly applicable provisions of international law. See Appl. 6871/75, *Caprino v. United Kingdom, Yearbook* XXI (1978), p. 284 (290-292), where the Commission also reviewed the detention for its conformity with an EEC directive. Review for conformity with the Convention itself for the determination of the lawfulness, according to the Commission, leads to a circular reasoning. That this need not be the case is evident, *e.g.*, for a review of whether the detention has been imposed for the purpose for which the exception of Art. 5(1)(f) has been given.
300. Thus the Commission impliedly in the *Wallace* Case, Appl. 1983/63, *X v. the Netherlands, Yearbook* IX (1966), p. 286 (302). More details about the relation to Art. 5(4) in the report of 17 July 1980, *Caprino, D & R* 22 (1981), p. 5 (12).
301. In Appl. 6871/75, *Caprino v. United Kingdom*, the Commission stated that "the eventual outcome of the deportation proceedings is irrelevant for the justification of the detention provided that a lawful deportation procedure has been instituted and is being seriously pursued"; *Yearbook* XXI (1978), p. 284 (294). See also Appl. 9540/81, *X v. United Kingdom*, not published.
302. Report of 11 October 1983, *Zamir, D & R* 40 (1985), p. 42 (55). However, the fact that a domestic court has found the deportation procedure to be illegal does not deprive the applicant of his claim to be a victim of a violation of the Convention by reason of his arrest: report of 7 December 1984, *Bozano*, A.111 (1987), p. 32.

would seem to follow from the provision of Article 5(4). Indeed, how will a court be able to order the detainee's release via the proceedings under this provision if the deportation or extradition has already been carried out? This even apart from the question of whether after his deportation or extradition the person in question will still be able to institute the proceedings of Article 5(4).[303] If the detainee files an application with the Commission, after having unsuccessfully exhausted the local remedies, in our opinion the same obligation is implied in Article 25(1). The undertaking by the contracting States not to hinder by any measure the effective exercise of the individual right of complaint recognized by them, implies that they also suspend the deportation or extradition pending the Strasbourg procedure, or at least see to it that this measure is not carried out in such a way that it cannot be revoked. On the basis of Rule 41 of the Rules of Procedure of the Commission a practice of consultation between the Secretariat of the Commission and the national authorities has developed, which indeed goes somewhat in this direction, be it that this Rule does not start from the assumption that a binding obligation is involved here. If necessary, under Rule 36 of the Rules the Commission might also recommend a provisional measure for that purpose to the government in question.[304]

In addition Article 5(1)(f) implies the guarantee that the detention must have no purpose other than that of preventing the admission of the alien in question to the country or of making it possible to decide on his deportation or extradition. Article 18 of the Convention, which prohibits restrictions of the rights and freedoms for any purpose other than that for which they have been permitted, applies here as well. In the first place this means, as the Commission makes clear in the *Bozano* Case, that the deprivation of liberty is unlawful if the deportation order, and the way in which it is enforced, constitute a misuse of power.[305] In the second place it follows that the detention must not last longer and must not be attended with more restrictions for the person concerned than is required for a normal conduct of the proceedings. Thus, in its decision in the *Lynas* Case the Commission stated, after first having found that the duration of detention is only mentioned in paragraph 3 of Article 5 and that this provision refers only to detentions under paragraph 1(c) and not to cases of detention pending a decision on a request for extradition:

In this connection it may be noticed that Article 5(1)(f) clearly permits the Commission

---

303. *Cf.* the judgment of the Court of Justice of the European Communities of 8 April 1976 in Case 48/75, *Royer, Jur.* 1976, p. 497, where it was decided that, since Art. 8 of Directive no. 64/221 provides for judicial appeal against extradition measures, "the person concerned must at least be enabled to institute proceedings already before the extradition measure is put into effect and thus to have the execution of the measure suspended".
304. See the 1979 issue of Council of Europe, *Stock-Taking on the European Convention on Human Rights*, p. 75. See also Recommendation (817)1977 "on certain aspects of the right to asylum", Council of Europe, Parl.Ass., Twenty-Ninth Ordinary Session, 5-13 October 1977, *Texts Adopted.* See Appl. 15576/88, *Cruz Varas v. Sweden,* not published.
305. Report of 7 December 1984, A.111 (1987), pp. 32-34.

to decide on the lawfulness ("lawful detention/détention regulière") of a person against whom action is being taken with a view to extradition ... . The wording of both the French and English texts makes it clear that only the existence of extradition proceedings justifies deprivation of liberty in such a case. It follows that if for example the proceedings are not conducted with the requisite diligence or if the detention results from some misuse of authority it ceases to be justifiable under 5(1)(f). Within these limits the Commission might therefore have cause to consider the length of time spent in detention pending extradition from the point of view of the above cited provisions.[306]

If it has been decided to prolong the detention in the interest and at the request of the person concerned, *e.g.* in order to find a suitable country which is prepared to admit him, or in order to obtain certain guarantees from the extradition-requesting State with regard to his treatment,[307] he cannot claim afterwards that he is the victim of this prolonged detention.[308]

On several occasions, the lawfulness of the detention was challenged on the basis of an alleged lack of precision of the applicable norms.[309] So far, however, the Commission has found these complaints to be ill-founded, referring thereby to the case-law developed by the Court with regard to the expression "prescribed by law" in the second paragraph of Article 10: the law must be adequately accessible and formulated with sufficient precision.[310]

A clear example of a violation of paragraph 1(f) is offered by the *Bozano* Case. Here, the Court had to decide whether the deportation of Bozano from France to Switzerland was "lawful" and "in accordance with a procedure prescribed by law". "Lawfulness", according to the Court, also implies the absence of any arbitrariness. The circumstances of the case, *inter alia* the fact that the authorities waited about a month before serving the deportation order, prevented Bozano from making any effective use of the theoretically existing judicial remedies and contacted and only the Swiss authorities although the Spanish border was much closer to the place where Bozano was arrested, led the Court to decide that the deprivation of liberty was neither lawful nor compatible with the right to security of person. Several French courts had reached this same conclusion. The way the deportation was executed clearly indicated what the French authorities had in mind: to get round the prohibition of extradition to Italy ordered by the Limoges Court of Appeal. That was also the reason why Bozano had been delivered to the Swiss authorities: Switzerland had an extradition treaty with Italy. The Court stated therefore that the way Bozano was deprived of his liberty amounted in fact to a disguised form of extradition.[311]

10. *Article 5, paragraph 2* grants to everyone who is arrested the right to be

---

306. Appl. 7317/75, *Lynas v. Switzerland, Yearbook* XX (1977), p. 412 (440-442). See also Appl. 9706/82, *X v. Federal Republic of Germany,* not published.
307. Appl. 9706/82, *X v. Federal Republic of Germany,* not published.
308. That situation occurred in the *Wallace* Case, Appl. 1983/63, *Yearbook* IX (1966), p. 286 (304).
309. See Report of 11 October 1983, *Zamir, D & R* 40 (1985), p. 42 (55-57), and Appl. 9403/81, *X v. United Kingdom, D & R* 28 (1982), p. 235 (236-238).
310. Judgment of 26 April 1979, *Sunday Times,* A.30 (1979). See *infra* at pp. 581-583.
311. Judgment of 18 December 1986, *Bozano,* A.111 (1987), pp. 25-27. See also the report of 7 December 1984, *ibidem,* pp. 32-34.

informed promptly, in a language which he understands, of the reasons for his arrest and of any charge against him. If the national authorities fail to do so, the arrest and detention are unlawful, even if they can be brought under one of the cases mentioned in paragraph 1. The rationale of this second paragraph necessarily results from the idea underlying Article 5: the liberty of person is the rule and is guaranteed, and an encroachment on this is allowed only in the cases expressly provided for and in conformity with the law as it stands. In order for the person arrested to be able to judge, from the moment of arrest, whether these two conditions have been met and to decide whether there are reasons for recourse to court, adequate information must be available to him.[312] The second paragraph applies not only to the detentions referred to in paragraph 1 under (c), but to all cases mentioned in the first paragraph;[313] also to the case of detention of a person of unsound mind. If the person himself is unable to rightly understand the information, it should be transmitted to his representative.[314] And although the provision of the second paragraph refers in principle to the first arrest, in the case of continued detention it also applies if the ground for detention changes or new relevant facts present themselves.[315]

Article 5(2) prescribes that this information must be given "promptly" ("*dans le plus court délai*"). Since it may be assumed that the person carrying out the arrest is himself acquainted with at least the essence of the reasons, the word "promptly" will have to be interpreted to mean that the latter informs the arrested person of those reasons at the moment of the arrest or, if it is necessary to use an interpreter, as soon as provision can be made for this.[316] A precise formulation of the charges will often not be possible at once, since the person who has been instructed to carry out the arrest usually will not have the requisite data at his disposal, while the precise formulation will also frequently call for a preliminary examination and a first interrogation. In that case, however, a summary statement of the charges will have to be provided as soon as the arrested person arrives at the place of detention.[317]

The Commission takes the view that the information prescribed by Article 5(2) may be less detailed and less specific than that guaranteed by Article 6(3) in connection with the right to a fair trial.[318] The Commission requires

---

312. On this rationale, see Appl. 8098/77, *X v. Federal Republic of Germany*, *D & R* 16 (1979), p. 111 (113).
313. Report of 16 July 1980, *X v. United Kingdom*, B.41 (1985), p. 33.
314. *Ibidem*, p. 34.
315. *Ibidem*, pp. 33-34.
316. If the arresting person himself does not speak the language of the arrested person, it is sufficient under Art. 5(2) if the information is given by the public prosecutor or the magistrate, provided that the person is then brought before this officer at once: Appl. 2689/65, *Delcourt v. Belgium*, *Yearbook* X (1967), p. 238 (272).
317. Appl. 8828/79, *X v. Denmark*, *D & R* 30 (1983), p. 93 (94). See, however, Appl. 8582/79, *Skoogström v. Sweden*, not published, where the Commission accepted the fact that the arrested person was informed two days after his arrest; this, in our opinion, clearly exceeds the bounds of reasonableness.
318. Appl. 343/57, *X v. Denmark*, *Yearbook* II (1958-59), p. 412 (462). Since then this is established case-law. See, e.g., Appl. 9614/81, *X, Y and Z v. Austria*, *D & R* 34 (1983), p. 119 (121-122).

that

> the arrested person should ... be informed about the facts and the evidence which are proposed to be the foundation of a decision to detain him. In particular he should be enabled to state whether he admits or denies the alleged offence.[319]

The Commission has taken the position that the information required by Article 5(2) need not be worded in a particular form, and need not even be given in writing.[320] Nor does the Commission require that the reasons for the arrest be mentioned expressly in the decision which authorizes continued detention.[321] The rationale of paragraph 2 raises the question whether the Commission should not be a little stricter in these respects. In view of this rationale it must in any case be assumed that the request of the arrested person for a prompt written statement of the oral information will have to be complied with. In the same perspective the decision of the Commission seems disputable to us that the obligation of paragraph 2 has been complied with if the arrested person has been able to infer the reasons for that arrest and the nature of the charges clearly enough from the content and the course of any interrogations that have preceded his arrest.[322] The interests of the arrested person which paragraph 2 is designed to protect, are sufficiently guaranteed only if the prescribed information is communicated explicitly and unambiguously to him.[323] It is the authorities' duty to provide that information and they should not leave it to the arrested person to reconstruct it himself.

According to the Strasbourg case-law, Article 5(2) does not guarantee the right to contact a lawyer.[324]

The Court has so far left open the question whether Article 5(2) applies only to arrests on the ground of criminal charges, as might be deduced from the wording of that provision: "shall be informed ... of the reasons for his arrest and of any charge against him", or also to other forms of deprivations of liberty, as mentioned in Article 5(1). In the Case of *X v. United Kingdom* the Court considered that the issue under Article 5(2) was absorbed by the fact that a violation was found of Article 5(4), which also requires that the arrested person be apprised of the reasons of his arrest in order to be in a position to take proceedings with a view to having the lawfulness of his detention determined.[325] In the *Van der Leer* Case the Commission noted an important difference with the above-mentioned case in that the failure to inform the present applicant not only concerned the reasons for her

---

319. Appl. 8098/77, *X v. Federal Republic of Germany, D & R* 16 (1979), p. 111 (114). See also Appl. 10819/84, *K v. Belgium, D & R* 38 (1984), p. 230 (231).
320. Appl. 1211/61, *X v. the Netherlands, Yearbook* V (1962), p. 224 (228). Since then this is established case-law. See, *e.g.,* the first case mentioned in the preceding note, p. 113.
321. Appl. 2894/66, *X v. the Netherlands, Yearbook* IX (1966), p. 564 (566).
322. Appl. 1936/63, *Neumeister v. Austria, Yearbook* VII (1964), p. 224 (244).
323. Jacobs, *supra* note 17, p. 62, refers for this requirement to the words "in a language which he understands": not only the language, but also the wording and form chosen for the information must be such that there is a sufficient guarantee that this information is really grasped by the person concerned.
324. Appl. 8828/79, *X v. Denmark, D & R* 30 (1983), p. 93 (94).
325. Judgment of 5 November 1981, A.46 (1981), p. 28.

deprivation of liberty in the psychiatric hospital, but also the fact itself that she was deprived of her liberty. The Commission considered it to be a fundamental requirement that a person who is deprived of his liberty should be made aware of this fact, and the purpose of this requirement is not only to make it possible for the person concerned to challenge the lawfulness of the deprivation of liberty, but also, in general, to make him aware of an important change of his status. Thus, the Commission concluded that the issue under Article 5(2) was not absorbed by the issue under Article 5(4) and repeated its earlier position that paragraph 2 extends to all forms of arrest effected in accordance with any of the provisions under (a) to (f).[326]

11. *Article 5, paragraph 3* relates exclusively to the category of detainees mentioned in the first paragraph under (c): those detained on remand. However, the Commission leaves open the possibility that it reflects a general principle for all cases of detention on account of acts committed or suspicion thereof.[327] When the accused person has been provisionally released, this provision is no longer applicable.[328] The main purpose of this paragraph, in relation to Article 5(1)(c), is to "afford to individuals deprived of their liberty a special guarantee: a procedure of judicial nature designed to ensure that no one should be arbitrarily deprived of his liberty",[329] and, furthermore, to ensure that any arrest or detention will be kept as short as possible.[330] In the *Schiesser* Case the Court stated that in Article 5, para. 3 both a substantive and a procedural requirement are laid down. The procedural requirement concerns the obligation of the "officer" to hear the individual brought before him, while the substantive requirement refers to the obligation to review "the circumstances militating for or against detention", to decide "by reference to legal criteria, whether there are reasons to justify detention" and, if this is not the case, to order the release of the person.[331]

Paragraph 3 comprises first of all, in addition to the right to prompt information conferred in the second paragraph, the right to be brought "promptly" before a judicial authority. It is obvious that a person cannot always be heard by a judge immediately after being arrested. Unlike in the case of the obligation to inform him of the reasons for his arrest, for his first contact with a judge a third person is involved. The word "promptly" - the French text speaks of "*aussitôt*" - therefore must not be interpreted so literally

---

326. Report of 14 July 1988, paras 105-107. See also *supra*, p. 272.
327. Report of 25 January 1976, *Ireland v. United Kingdom*, B.23/I (1976-78), pp. 111-112. See also Appl. 10307/83, *M. v. Federal Republic of Germany*, D & R 37 (1984), p. 113 (117).
328. Appl. 8233/78, *X v. United Kingdom*, D & R 17 (1980), p. 122 (131).
329. Judgment of 4 December 1979, *Schiesser*, A.34 (1980), p. 30. See also the reports of 13 July 1983, *McGoff*, A.83 (1984), p. 30 and of 15 July 1983, *Skoogström*, A.83 (1984), pp. 13-14.
330. See the reports mentioned in the preceding note, pp. 30-31 and p. 13 respectively.
331. Judgment of 4 December 1979, A.34 (1980), pp. 13-14. See also the reports of 13 July 1983, *McGoff*, A.83 (1984), pp. 30-31 and of 15 July 1983, *Skoogström*, A.83 (1984), p. 13. For the procedural requirement see also the judgment of 22 May 1984, *Van der Sluijs, Zuiderveld and Klappe*, A.78 (1984), p. 19 and the judgment of 22 May 1984, *Duinhof and Duijf*, A.79 (1984), p. 16.

that the investigating judge must be virtually dragged out of bed to arraign the detainee or must interrupt urgent activities for this. However, adequate provisions will indeed have to be made in order that the prisoner can be heard as soon as may reasonably be required in view of his interests. Since paragraph 3 lays down an unconditional obligation upon the States to bring automatically and promptly an arrested person before a judge, it is not necessary that the arrested person first appeals against the detention order.[332]

It appears from its case-law that the Commission so far has been prepared to allow the national authorities a rather broad margin of discretion in complying with the requirement of promptness. In connection with a complaint lodged against the Netherlands it even considered a delay of four days between the arrest and the first appearance before a judge in conformity with the requirements of the Convention.[333] It is true that the Commission held that the Dutch legislation as here applied was "consistent with the general tendency of other member States of the Council of Europe",[334] but in its decision it did not furnish any further data on the legislation and the practice of those other Member States, in comparison with which the delay of four days in fact appears to be exceptionally long.[335]

The Court has also given its opinion about the interpretation of the word "promptly". In the *De Jong, Baljet and Van den Brink* Case, the Court had to answer the question whether the referral to a judicial authority seven, eleven and six days respectively after the arrest was in conformity with the requirement of promptness of Article 5(3). Although this question was answered in the negative, the Court refrained from developing a minimum standard. It only stated that "the issue of promptness must be assessed in each case according to its special features".[336] In the other cases decided by the Court on the same day, it also refrained from indicating a minimum standard.[337]

In the *Brogan* Case the Court had to deal with the question of "promptness" in case of arrest and detention, by virtue of powers granted under special legislation, of persons suspected of involvement in terrorism in Northern Ireland. The requirements under ordinary law in Northern Ireland as to bringing an accused before a court were expressly made inapplicable to such arrest and detention. None of the applicants was in fact brought before

332. Appl. 9017/80, *McGoff v. Sweden, D & R* 31 (1983), p. 72 (73).
333. Appl. 2894/66, *X v. the Netherlands, Yearbook* IX (1966), p. 564 (568).
334. *Ibidem.*
335. Fawcett, *supra* note 20, p. 93, refers to a maximum period of 48 hours as usual. In its decision on Appl. 4960/71, *X v. Belgium, Coll.* 42 (1973), p. 49, the Commission added that only in exceptional circumstances a delay of five days is acceptable. In the report of 11 October 1982, *De Jong, Baljet and Van den Brink,* B.62 (1987), p. 31 and the report of 15 July 1983, *Skoogström,* A.83 (1984), p. 18 periods of seven and eleven days were not accepted. Exceptional circumstances were deemed to be present, for instance, in Appl. 4960/71, *X v. Belgium, Coll.* 42 (1973), p. 49 (55), where after his arrest the accused was taken at his own request to a hospital and had been nursed there for four days.
336. Judgment of 22 May 1984, *De Jong, Baljet and Van den Brink,* A.77 (1984), pp. 24-25.
337. Judgments of 22 May 1984, *Van der Sluijs, Zuiderveld and Klappe,* A.78 (1984), p. 20, and *Duinhof and Duijf,* A.79 (1984), p. 18.

a judge or judicial officer during his time in custody ranging from four days and six hours to six days and sixteen and a half hours. The Commission had repeated its case-law that a period of four days in cases concerning ordinary criminal offences and of five days in exceptional cases could be considered compatible with the requirements of promptness. It had, therefore, concluded that there was a violation of Article 5(3) only in the cases where the detention had exceeded five days.[338] The Court accepted that the investigation of terrorist offences presented the authorities with special problems and that, subject to the existence of adequate safeguards, the context of terrorism in Northern Ireland had the effect of prolonging the period during which the authorities may, without violating Article 5(3), keep a person suspected of serious terrorist offences in custody before bringing him before a judge or other judicial officer. However, it also stressed that the scope for flexibility in interpreting and applying the notion of "promptness" is very limited. In the Court's view, even the shortest of the four periods of detention, namely the four days and six hours spent in police custody, fell outside the strict constraints as to time permitted by the first part of Article 5(3). The Court stated as follows:

> To attach such importance to the special features of this case as to justify so lengthy a period of detention without appearance before a judge or other judicial officer would be an unacceptably wide interpretation of the plain meaning of the word "promptly". An interpretation to this effect would import into Article 5, para. 3 a serious weakening of a procedural guarantee to the detriment of the individual and would entail consequences impairing the very essence of the right protected by this provision.[339]

12. Next, the third paragraph implies for the person detained on remand the right to be tried within a reasonable time or otherwise to be released pending trial, if necessary subject to certain guarantees for his appearance for trial. The way this provision is formulated, it seems at first sight to leave a free choice to the judicial authorities:[340] either to prolong the detention on remand, provided that it has been imposed in accordance with paragraph 1(c), up to the moment of the judgment, which must then be given within a reasonable time, or to provisionally release the detainee pending trial, which trial would then no longer be subject to a given time-limit. Such an interpretation has been resolutely rejected by the Court. In the *Neumeister* Case the Court held with regard to Article 5(3):

> that this provision cannot be understood as giving the judicial authorities a choice between either bringing the accused person to trial within a reasonable time or granting him provisional release even subject to guarantees. The reasonableness of the time spent by an accused person in detention up to the beginning of the trial must be assessed in relation to the very fact of his detention. Until conviction he must be presumed innocent, and the purpose of the provision under consideration is essentially to require his provisional release once his continuing detention ceases to be reasonable.[341]

---

338. Report of 14 May 1987, A.145/B (1989), p. 64.
339. Judgment of 29 November 1988, A.145/B (1989), pp. 33-34.
340. Literally speaking, it might even be deduced that the choice has been left to the accused himself, which, however, in view of the rationale of the provision, cannot have been intended.
341. Judgment of 27 June 1968, A.8 (1968), p. 37.

The Court does not associate the word "reasonable" with the processing of the prosecution and the trial, but with the length of the detention. The long delay of the trial may in itself be reasonable in view, for instance, of the complexity of the case or the number of witnesses to be summoned, but this does not mean that the continued detention is therefore also reasonable. The Court takes the view that Article 5(3) refers to the latter facet. This implies at the same time that the criteria for "reasonable" in Article 5(3) are different from those for the same term in Article 6(1).[342] Some delays may in fact violate Article 5(3) and still be compatible with Article 6(1).[343] This is also corroborated by the view of the Court in the *Wemhoff* Case that "an accused person in detention is entitled to have his case given priority and conducted with particular expedition".[344]

When is continued detention on remand to be considered reasonable? When the "reasonable suspicion" referred to in Article 5(1)(c)[345] ceases to exist, the continued detention becomes unlawful and accordingly the question as to the reasonableness does not arise at all;[346] the only question which remains then is whether the release has taken place promptly.[347] But even the fact that the "reasonable suspicion" continues to exist is not sufficient, in the Court's opinion, to justify, after a certain lapse of time, the prolongation of the detention.[348] It has not been indicated by the Court what further criteria have to be taken into account, but it is obvious that for each individual case and at each moment the interests of the accused will have to be weighed against the interest of the protection of society and the interest of effective prosecution and criminal proceedings, and of a fair trial.[349] In the first instance this weighing is in the hands of the national authorities, but both the Commission and the Court, here again, have clearly shown that they consider themselves competent to review for their compatibility with the Convention the grounds on which a request for release has been rejected by

---

342. See also the report of 12 July 1977, *Haase, D & R* 11 (1978), p. 78 (92): "Interpretation of 'a reasonable time' in Article 5(3) must be made with regard to the fact that a person is deprived of his liberty. The time which in such cases is permissible is shorter than the time which is permissible under Article 6(1), because the aim is to limit the length of a person's detention and not to promote a speedy trial". The relation between the two provisions is also dealt with explicitly in the judgments of 10 November 1969 in the Stögmüller Case and in the Matznetter Case, A.9 (1969), p. 40 and A.10 (1969), pp. 34-35 respectively. See also the report of 8 May 1984, *Vallon*, A.95 (1985), p. 19 and Appl. 9604/81, *X v. Federal Republic of Germany*, not published.
343. Judgment of 10 November 1969, *Matznetter*, A.10 (1969), pp. 34-35; report of 8 May 1984, *Vallon*, A.95 (1985), p. 19.
344. Judgment of 27 June 1968, A.7 (1968), p. 26.
345. On this, *supra* pp. 260-264.
346. Judgment of 10 November 1969, *Stögmüller*, A.9 (1969), p. 40: "it is clear that the persistence of such suspicion is a conditio sine qua non for the validity of the continued detention of the person concerned".
347. Judgment of 22 May 1984, *De Jong, Baljet and Van den Brink*, A.77 (1984), pp. 24-25.
348. Judgment of 10 November 1969, *Stögmüller*, A.9 (1969), p. 40.
349. See the enumeration of alternatives for (continuation of) the detention on remand in Art. 15 of Recommendation R(80)11 of the Committee of Ministers of 27 June 1980 on detention on remand.

the national authorities.[350] Thus, for example, in the *Neumeister* Case, the *Stögmüller* Case and the *Matznetter* Case the Court held that the danger of flight, even if it had initially constituted a sufficient ground for the detention on remand, afterwards had ceased to exist as a ground, specifically because of the possibility of bail.[351] The risk of a further offence, the other ground mentioned in paragraph 1(c), was held by the Court to have continued to exist in the *Matznetter* Case,[352] while it rejected that ground for prolonged detention in the *Stögmuller* Case and the *Ringeisen* Case.[353] As has already been stated above, when reviewing the lawfulness of the (prolongation of the) detention, the Court does not consider itself confined to the grounds for detention on remand expressly mentioned in paragraph 1(c), but has also accepted as such a ground the risk of subornation of witnesses and suppression of evidence.[354]

The other consequence at first sight implied in the formulation of paragraph 3, *viz.* that in case of interim release of the person detained on remand his right to a trial *within a reasonable time* ceases to exist, has also been rejected by the Court. In the *Wemhoff* Case the Court held as follows:

> It is inconceivable that they [the contracting States] should have intended to permit their judicial authorities, at the price of release of the accused, to protract proceedings beyond a reasonable time.[355]

The Court added to this:

> This would, moreover, be flatly contrary to the provision in Article 6(1).[356]

This latter addition is indispensable for the interpretation here given by the Court to Article 5(3); the word "moreover" therefore in our view might as well have been omitted by the Court. In fact, as soon as the accused has been released, Article 5(3) is no longer applicable, as it also does not apply if the deprivation of liberty is a result of the execution of a prison sen-

---

350. See the judgments of 27 June 1968, *Wemhoff and Neumeister,* A.7 (1968), pp. 24-25, and A.8 (1968), p. 37 respectively; the judgments of 10 November 1969, *Stögmüller and Matznetter,* A.9 (1969), p. 39, and A.10 (1969), p. 31 respectively; and the judgment of 16 July 1971, *Ringeisen,* A.13 (1971), p. 42. For the Commission, see especially its report of 11 December 1980, *Schertenleib, D & R* 23 (1981), p. 137 (190), where the Commission held that even if the grounds relating to the public interest are very pertinent and sufficient to justify keeping a person in detention pending trial, that does not free the authorities from their obligations under the Convention in case of an unreasonable prolongation of detention which inflicts on the acccused in the interests of public policy a greater sacrifice than would normally be demanded of a person presumed innocent. See also the report of 8 May 1984, *Vallon,* A.95 (1985), pp. 19-21, and the report of 8 July 1987, *Moudefo,* A.141/B (1989), p. 40.
351. Judgment of 27 June 1968, A.8 (1968), pp. 38-40; judgments of 10 November 1969, A.9 (1969), pp. 43-44, and A.10 (1969), p. 34. In the Wemhoff Case the Court involved in its different finding the fact that on the part of the detainee there was no evident willingness to give bail; judgment of 27 June 1968, A.7 (1968), p. 25.
352. Judgment of 10 November 1969, A.10 (1969), p. 34. See also Appl. 9451/81, *X v. Federal Republic of Germany,* not published.
353. Judgment of 10 November 1969, A.9 (1969), p. 43, and judgment of 16 July 1971, A.13 (1971), p. 43 respectively.
354. See *supra* p. 262.
355. Judgment of 27 June 1968, A.7 (1968), p. 22.
356. *Ibidem.*

278

tence.[357]

The obligation for the judicial authorities to see to it that in these cases, too, the trial takes place within a reasonable time, can be based only on Article 6(1). But precisely because Article 6(1) applies to all criminal proceedings, it is evident that Article 5(3) does not refer at all to a choice between either release or trial within a reasonable time, but to the obligation to keep a prisoner no longer in detention on remand than is reasonable and to try him within a reasonable time.

In the case-law concerning the words "within a reasonable time" no complete clarity has yet been created. With respect to the period that has to be taken into consideration for the determination of whether the trial has taken place within a reasonable time, the Court has taken the position that this is the period between the moment of arrest and that of the judgment at first instance.[358] If that judgment implies acquittal or discharge from further prosecution, at all events it will have to be followed by release, while in the case of conviction henceforth it is a matter of "detention of a person after conviction" in the sense of Article 5(1)(a), to which the provisions on detention on remand no longer apply.[359] However, afterwards the Commission has pointed out that under some legal systems the execution of a sentence is not allowed as long as an appeal against it is still pending or some other ordinary remedy is sought, so that in such a case prolongation of the detention continues to have the character of a detention on remand and therefore has to be taken into consideration for the assessment of the reasonableness of the total length of this detention. In the *Ringeisen* Case it therefore requested the Court to revise its decision in the sense that in such cases the end of the period to be assessed is the moment at which the judicial decision has become final.[360] However, the Court held that the issue did not arise in the case under consideration, because the detention after conviction at first instance coincided with the detention on remand for

---

357. Appl. 9610/81, *X v. Federal Republic of Germany*, not published. In this case the applicant, during her detention on remand, also served a prison sentence. The Commission stated that the period of the prison sentence could not be taken into account in judging the reasonableness of the total period of detention under Article 5, but was of relevance for the reasonable time under Article 6, since the investigations concerning the criminal charges could have continued during the execution of the prison sentence.
358. Judgment of 27 June 1968, *Wemhoff*, A.7 (1968), pp. 22-23. The Commission had taken the view that the commencement of the criminal proceedings should be taken as the end; B.5 (1969), p. 67. The Court bases its decision on the following two grounds: (1) It is true that the English text "entitled to trial" leaves scope for the view of the Commission, but the French text "le droit d'être jugée" points clearly in the direction of the Court's view, which is not ruled out by the English text and consequently is the only interpretation which brings the two texts into conformity with one another; (2) The Court's interpretation is most in conformity with the purpose of the provision, since it cannot be appreciated why the protection of the person detained on remand against an unjustified prolongation of his detention should be less important after the commencement of the criminal proceedings. The Commission now follows the same line of reasoning as the Court. See, *e.g.*, Appl. 9132/80, *N. v. Federal Republic of Germany*, D & R 31 (1983), p. 154 (173), and report of 8 May 1984, *Vallon*, A.95 (1985), pp. 13-14.
359. *Ibidem*, p. 23.
360. Report of 19 March 1970, B.11 (1970-71), pp. 44-45.

another criminal offence.[361] This attitude of the Court is to be regretted. Since the Court was evidently responsible for this lack of clarity in its case-law, it would have been incumbent upon it to remove this at the first opportunity, if necessary by using the tool of *obiter dictum*, from which the Court has not shrunk in other cases. As it is, the uncertainty has persisted. If the Commission's view would prevail that in the instance referred to it is not paragraph 1(a), but paragraph 1(c) that is applicable, then this form of detention on remand also has to be reviewed for its compatibility with paragraph 3. The new fact of a conviction will then have to be taken into consideration for the assessment of reasonableness. Later on, however, the Commission changed its view:

"The European Court of Human Rights and the Commission have always considered that a period spent in detention after a conviction in first instance is not to be considered as detention in the sense of Article 5(1)(c) and (3) of the Convention, even if, under national law, it is still considered as detention on remand.[362]

If a detention on remand has been preceded by a detention of another character or in relation to another criminal charge, the latter detention is not taken into consideration when determining *the period* to be considered in relation to the former one. However, that preceding detention must be taken into account in assessing the *reasonable character* of the period spent in detention on remand.[363] Two different periods of detention on remand for the same charge, interrupted by a release, have to be taken into consideration together when determining the total period and its reasonable character.[364]

As regards the assessment of reasonableness of the length of the detention, the Court takes as a starting-point the arguments which have been put forward in the national proceedings on the prolongation of the detention on remand:

It is in the light of these pointers that the Court must judge whether the reasons given by the national authorities to justify continued detention are relevant and sufficient to show that detention was not unreasonably prolonged and contrary to Article 5(3) of the Convention.[365]

However, the Court considers itself to be competent to oppose its own opinion to the view of the national authorities when examining whether the provision of Article 5(3) has been complied with.[366] Two separate questions are then at issue, *viz.* that as to the justification of the detention and its continuation - a question that must be answered by reference to Article 5(1)(c) - and the question as to the reasonableness of the length of the detention. Indeed, also a detention on remand for which the national authorities have advanced well-founded reasons may have been prolonged in

---

361. Judgment of 16 July 1971, A.13 (1971), pp. 44-45.
362. Appl. 9610/81, *X v. Federal Republic of Germany*, not published.
363. Report of 8 May 1984, *Vallon*, A.95 (1985), p. 19.
364. Appl. 9132/80, *N. v. Federal Republic of Germany*, D & R 31 (1983), p. 154 (173).
365. Judgment of 27 June 1968, *Wemhoff*, A.7 (1968), pp. 24-25. See also the judgment of 27 June 1968, *Neumeister*, A.8 (1968), p. 37 and, more recently, the judgment of 22 May 1984, *Duinhof and Duijf*, A.79 (1984), p. 18.
366. Judgment of 10 November 1969, *Stögmüller*, A.9 (1969), p. 39.

an unreasonable way, *e.g.*, when these authorities have not made sufficient efforts, precisely because the accused was detained on remand, to arrive at a decision in his case with the requisite efficiency and, if possible, with priority.[367] On the other hand it is evident that, *e.g.*, the complexity of the case or the conduct of the detainee may constitute one of the factors justifying the prolongation of a lawful detention on remand.[368] However, such factors, even if they justify a delay in the trial, can never constitute a sufficient reason for continuation of a detention on remand for which the grounds of paragraph 1(c) have ceased to exist.

The case-law shows that even in the case of detention on remand a very long duration - in the *Schertenleib* Case this was more than two and a half years - may still be deemed acceptable. It is also emphasized in that case-law that the accused, too, is largely able to expedite or delay the proceedings. In its report in the *Bonnechaux* Case the Commission observed in this connection that

> the accused is confronted with a choice between more careful preparation for the trial or more rapid procedure. Up to a certain point he must take the consequences of his choice.[369]

Finally mention may be made of the Commission's decision on Application 5078/71 to the effect that the period which the accused had spent in detention in Italy pending a decision on the request of the Federal Republic of Germany to extradite him could not be brought under the responsibility of the Federal Republic of Germany, and consequently could not be included in the assessment of the reasonableness of the detention in Germany.[370] The reasoning followed by the Commission appears incorrect to us. Although the Federal Republic of Germany is not responsible for what happens in Italy, the detention undergone in another country may quite well constitute one of the circumstances which have to be taken into consideration in assessing the reasonableness of the total length of the detention, even if that other detention does not fall under the category of paragraph 1(c) and accordingly has to be judged as a separate detention.

13. Paragraph 3 further provides that the accused should be brought before a "judge" or "other officer authorised by law to exercise judicial power". It is not yet totally clear what is the precise meaning of the latter description and

---

367. Thus the Court in the Matznetter Case, judgment of 10 November 1969, A.10 (1969), p. 35.
368. For the Court, see in particular the judgments mentioned in the two preceding notes in the Stögmuller Case and the Matznetter Case, where the complexity of the case was qualified as an attenuating circumstance (Matznetter judgment, p. 35), but not the defective manning of the judicial apparatus (Stögmuller judgment, pp. 40-41). For the Commission, reference may be made, *inter alia*, to the report of 11 December 1980, *Schertenleib, D & R* 23 (1981), p. 137 (163), where the Commission involved the complexity of the case, the handling of the case by the authorities and the conduct of the accused in its findings. See also its report of 8 May 1984, *Vallon*, A.95 (1985), pp. 19-22.
369. Report of 5 December 1979, *D & R* 18 (1980), p. 100 (147).
370. Appl. 5078/71, *X v. Federal Republic of Germany, Coll.* 46 (1974), p. 35 (40).

what guarantees it comprises. In the *Schiesser* Case, where the complaint concerned the fact that the same authority who was charged in certain cases with the prosecution also had to decide on the lawfulness of the detention, the Commission took the following position:

> Although it is certainly preferable to separate clearly the functions of the prosecutor and officer to decide on detention, Article 5(3) does not lay down such a rule expressly. Since a certain "dédoublement fonctionnel" is not uncommon for investigating and prosecuting authorities, the Convention would have been drafted differently if this should have been excluded.[371]

For its ultimate decision that Article 5(3) had not been violated in the case under discussion, the Commission deemed it essential that the functionary in question had to take his decision in full independence, according to a procedure prescribed by law and in accordance with norms laid down by law.[372] The Court endorsed this qualification by the Commission of the "District Attorney" in question as "other officer authorised by law to exercise judicial power". It held in particular that in the case under consideration there had been no blending of functions, that the functionary had been able to proceed, and had proceeded, independently, and that the procedural and substantive guarantees had been observed.[373] In the *Skoogström* Case, on the other hand, the Commission concluded that two of the three criteria (independence, procedural guarantees and substantive guarantees) were not fulfilled and that it had some doubts with regard to the third criterion. Not only was the Public Prosecutor, when deciding about the continuation of the detention, not independent because of a lack of distinction between investigating and prosecuting tasks, but she herself also did not hear the detainee. The Commission emphasized that the authorities mentioned in Article 5(3) must perform the duties, ensuing from this Article, themselves; a delegation of these powers is not permitted.[374]

Since the "judge" and the "other officer" are placed side by side, the latter, too, must perform a "judicial function", the conditions of which must be assured in all cases. The Court has put this as follows:

> [T]he "officer" is not identical with the "judge" but must nevertheless have some of the latter's attributes, that is to say he must satisfy certain conditions each of which constitutes a guarantee for the person arrested. The first of such conditions is independence of the executive and of the parties.[375]

In particular, it should be guaranteed that there is a clear separation between the functionary who in connection with his investigation may have an interest in the detention of the accused, and the functionary who has to decide on prolongation of the detention. In three cases against the Netherlands, decided by the Court on the same day, elements of the Dutch Military Code were

---

371. Report of 9 March 1978, B.32 (1983), p. 28.
372. *Ibidem.* See, however, the dissenting opinion of five members of the Commission, who did find a violation of Art. 5(3); *ibidem,* p. 30.
373. Judgment of 4 December 1979, *Schiesser,* A.34 (1980), pp. 14-16. The presence of counsel was not included by the Court among the relevant guarantees; *ibidem,* p. 16.
374. Report of 15 July 1983, A.83 (1984), pp. 15-17.
375. Judgment of 4 December 1979, *Schiesser,* A.34 (1980), pp. 13-14.

considered to be in violation of Article 5(3). The first question raised was whether the *auditeur-militair* could be considered as an "officer authorised by law to exercise judicial power". Referring to its judgment in the *Schiesser* Case, the Court answered this question in the negative, since the *auditeur-militair* was only competent to make recommendations about the applicant's detention, but he had no power to order his release himself. The Government had submitted that, in practice, these recommendations were always followed, pending a total revision of the Military Code in order to comply with the Convention. However, this practice was in the opinion of the Court an insufficient guarantee.[376] Furthermore, as the *auditeur-militair* could also be in charge of prosecuting functions in the same case, he likewise could not be considered to be independent from the parties.[377] The Court reached the same conclusion with regard to the *officier-commissaris*, especially on the ground of the lack of power to decide on the continued detention or release.[378]

In the *Pauwels* Case the investigation and prosecution functions were performed by the same *auditeur-militair* in the same case. The Court held that although the *auditeur-militair* is hierarchically subordinate to the *auditeur-generaal* and the Minister of Justice, he is completely independent in the performance of his twin duties as a member of the public prosecutor's office and as chairman of the Board of Inquiry. However, the fact that the legislation entitled the *auditeur-militair* to perform investigation and prosecution functions in one and the same case - a combination of functions which was in fact performed in the same case and in respect of the same defendant - led the Court to the conclusion that the *auditeur-militair's* impartiality was capable of appearing to be open to doubt.[379]

14. Article 5(3) expressly allows for making the release of the person detained on remand dependent on guarantees to appear for trial. The rationale of this is obvious: if and as long as prolongation of the detention would be allowed, certain guarantees may be asked for release. The express provision is important in particular because of the obligation and the limitations resulting from it for the national authorities.

Although Article 5(3) does not guarantee an absolute right to release on bail,[380] the possibility of demanding bail laid down there entails for the judicial authorities the obligation to ascertain whether by means of such a guarantee the same purpose can be achieved as is aimed at by the detention on remand. If there are sufficient indications for this, but this possibility is

376. Judgments of 22 May 1984, *De Jong, Baljet and Van den Brink*, A.77 (1984), pp. 22-24; *Van der Sluijs, Zuiderveld and Klappe*, A.78 (1984), pp. 18-19, and *Duinhof and Duijf*, A.79 (1984), pp. 15-16.
377. *Ibidem*.
378. The two last-mentioned cases at pp. 19-20 and pp. 17-18 respectively. See also the judgment of 26 May 1988, *Pauwels*, A.135 (1988), pp. 18-19.
379. Judgment of 26 May 1988, A.135 (1988), pp. 18-19.
380. Appl. 8097/77, *X v. United Kingdom*, not published.

not offered to the detainee, the detention loses its reasonable, and thus its lawful character, however much it may be justified on one of the grounds mentioned in paragraph 1(c). This will be the case in particular if the only ground for the detention is the risk of flight.[381] If the detainee declines the offer without suggesting an acceptable alternative, he has only himself to blame for the continued detention.[382]

On the other hand, the guarantee demanded for release must not impose heavier burdens on the person in question than are required for obtaining a reasonable degree of security. If, for instance, the detainee is required to give bail the amount of which he cannot possibly raise, while it may be assumed that a lower sum would also provide adequate security for his compliance with a summons to appear for trial, the prolongation of the detention is unreasonable.[383] This also means that the nature and the amount of the security demanded must be related to the grounds on which the detention on remand is based; thus, in the determination of the amount the damage caused by the accused may not be taken into account.[384] On the other hand, the financial situation of the person concerned and/or his relation to the person who stands bail for him must be taken into account.[385] The accused must provide the requisite information about this,[386] but this does not relieve the authorities from the duty of making an inquiry into it themselves, in order to be able to decide on the possibility of releasing him on bail.[387]

15. *Article 5, paragraph 4* grants to everyone who is deprived of his liberty by arrest or detention the right to take proceedings by which the lawfulness of such deprivation of liberty will be decided speedily by a court and his release ordered if the latter decides that the detention is unlawful. This is in fact the remedy of *habeas corpus*, originating from English law. It follows from the goal of Article 5(4) that this provision ceases to be applicable once a detainee has been released from detention. If he is not detained any more, Article 5(4) can only be still invoked in relation to the complaint that the decision concerning release was not taken "speedily".[388]

The fourth paragraph forms an independent provision: even if the Commission or the Court has found that the first paragraph has not been violated and that the detention, accordingly, had a lawful character, an inquiry into the possible violation of the fourth paragraph should nevertheless be

---

381. Thus also the Court in the Wemhoff Case, judgment of 27 June 1968, A.7 (1968), p. 25. See also the report of 11 December 1980, *Schertenleib*, *D & R* 23 (1981), p. 137 (195).
382. In the Court's opinion that was the case in the Wemhoff Case, *ibidem*.
383. Judgment of 27 June 1968, *Neumeister*, A.8 (1968), pp. 40-41. See the report of 12 July 1984, *Can*, A.96 (1985), p. 21.
384. *Ibidem*, p. 40.
385. *Ibidem*.
386. Report of 5 December 1979, *Bonnechaux*, *D & R* 18 (1980), p. 100 (144).
387. Report of 11 December 1980, *Schertenleib*, *D & R* 23 (1981), p. 137 (197).
388. Report of 11 October 1983, *Zamir*, *D & R* 40 (1985), p. 42 (59). More specifically, Article 5(4) has no application for the purpose of obtaining, after release, a declaration that a previous detention or arrest was unlawful: Appl. 10230/82, *X v. Sweden*, *D & R* 32 (1983), p. 303 (304-305). On the requirement of "speed", see *infra* pp. 289-290.

made.[389] This implies that even if the review by the Strasbourg organs leads to the conclusion that the detention was lawful, an assessment must be made if the detained person at the time had the possibility to have the lawfulness reviewed by domestic court. Also in case of that national review, at least in the Commission's opinion, it is not only the formal lawfulness that is at stake, but also the question of whether the substantive conditions for the detention have been met.[390] The procedure of paragraph 4 must therefore also be considered as independent of the possibility of applying for release on bail.[391]

In the "Vagrancy" Cases the Court held that the provision of the fourth paragraph does not apply to those cases of detention which are already based on a judicial decision, provided that such a decision is the outcome of proceedings which provide adequate guarantees.[392] This view is based on the assumption that in those cases the judicial review of the lawfulness of the detention, which is guaranteed by Article 5(4), has already taken place. Against the Court's interpretation militates the fact that Article 5(4) is formulated in a general way and does not contain exceptions for those cases in which the detention is based on a judicial decision. Nevertheless, a good deal is to be said for the Court's view in the cases of detention referred to in paragraph 1(a): after conviction by a court. It can hardly have been the intention of the contracting States to guarantee, in such a widely formulated provision as is the fourth paragraph, a possibility of appeal against a conviction by a court, even for cases in which the national systems of law do not provide for it. However, the case in which the Court expressed its view was not a case of detention referred to under 1(a), but rather one referred to under 1(e). Must the decision of the Court then be understood to imply for all cases that, once the lawfulness of arrest or detention has been established in judicial proceedings which provide adequate guarantees, the requirement of the fourth paragraph has been complied with?

In the discussion of paragraph 1(e) it was already mentioned that in the Commission's view this is not the case, at least not when a detention of indefinite duration is involved.[393] After the lawfulness of the detention has been established by a court, there may be good grounds for the detainee, for instance in consequence of changed circumstances, to request a court's opinion about that lawfulness again. The Commission, therefore, emphasizes in its report in the Winterwerp Case that the procedure prescribed in paragraph 4, in view of the words "to take proceedings", must be a procedure "carried out on the application of the person concerned"; the earlier judicial

---

389. See, inter alia, the judgment of 24 October 1979, Winterwerp, A.33 (1980), p. 22.
390. In detail the report of 16 July 1980, X v. United Kingdom, B.41 (1985), pp. 37-38 and the report of 17 July 1980, Caprino, D & R 22 (1981), p. 5 (12-13). In the Winterwerp Case the Court expressly left this question open; judgment of 24 October 1979, A.33 (1980), pp. 26-27. But see the judgment of 18 January 1978, Ireland v. United Kingdom, A.25 (1978), p. 77.
391. Report of 11 October 1983, Zamir, D & R 40 (1985), p. 42 (59).
392. Judgment of 18 June 1971, De Wilde, Ooms and Versyp, A.12 (1971), pp. 40-41.
393. See supra pp. 267-268.

decision is in most cases not taken upon such an application. In its opinion the national authorities must then be left the possibility to reject an application for judicial review if an earlier application of the kind is still pending or if a negative decision has been given on it shortly before.[394]

In its judgment in the *Winterwerp* Case the Court, for its part, toned down the general statement of its "*Vagrancy*" judgment. It now took the view that a case of detention like that in the *Winterwerp* Case "would appear to require a review of lawfulness to be available at reasonable intervals".[395] The Court was able to avoid an explicit decision, because it found that, unlike in the "*Vagrancy*" Cases, there had been no question of initial judicial proceedings in the sense of Article 5(4), in which a decision had been taken on the lawfulness of the detention.[396] In two more recent judgments the Court clearly distinguished between "the conviction by a competent court" in the sense of Article 5(1)(a) as "the decision depriving a person of his liberty" on the one hand, and the "ensuing period of detention in which new issues affecting the lawfulness of the detention might subsequently arise" on the other hand. It took the position that the "conviction" does not purport to deal with the latter period. In the first case the convict was committed to a mental hospital for an indefinite period. According to the Court this deprivation of liberty fell, initially at least, within the ambit of both Article 5(1)(a) and Article 5(1)(e). The Court held that

> By virtue of Article 5 para. 4, a person of unsound mind compulsorily confined in a psychiatric institution for an indefinite or lengthy period is thus in principle entitled, at any rate where there is no automatic periodic review of a judicial character, to take proceedings at reasonable intervals before a court to put in issue the "lawfulness" ... of his detention, whether that detention was ordered by a civil or criminal court or by some other authority.[397]

The other case, the *Van Droogenbroeck* Case, concerned the placing of a recidivist at the government's disposal for ten years by court order. This order was given together with a sentence to two years imprisonment. On the completion of his principal sentence, Van Droogenbroeck was placed in semi-custodial care, but he disappeared and, after his arrest, was sent to prison by a decision of the Minister of Justice. Although the Court held that the resulting deprivation of liberty occurred "after conviction" in accordance with Article 5(1)(a), it considered the fourth paragraph of Article 5 to be applicable, which required in the instant case

---

394. Report of 15 December 1977, B.31 (1983), p. 40 and pp. 43-44 respectively.
395. Judgment of 24 October 1979, A.33 (1980), p. 23. See also the judgment of 23 February 1984, *Luberti*, A.75 (1984), p. 15, and the judgment of 22 May 1984, *De Jong, Baljet and Van den Brink*, A.77 (1984), pp. 25-26.
396. *Ibidem.*
397. Judgment of 5 November 1981, *X v. United Kingdom*, A.46 (1982), p. 23. The Court, moreover, emphasized that given the scheme of Article 5, read as a whole, the notion of "lawfulness" implies that the same deprivation of liberty should have the same significance in paragraphs 1(e) and 4. See also the judgment of 28 May 1985, *Ashingdane*, A.93 (1985), pp. 22-23. In the *Weeks* Case the Commission added that Art. 5(4) not only requires the right to take proceedings at reasonable intervals, but also "at the moment of any return to detention after being in liberty"; report of 7 December 1984, A.112 (1987), p. 47.

an appropriate procedure allowing a court to determine "speedily" ... whether the Minister of Justice was entitled to hold that detention was still consistent with the object and purpose of the 1964 Act.[398]

It remains to be seen to what extent the Court will consider the fourth paragraph applicable in other cases of detention under paragraph 1(a).[399]

In the *Weeks* Case, the applicant complained about the fact that there was no periodic review of his detention. He invoked Article 5(4). The Commission reiterated its point of view that a clear borderline must be drawn between detention after conviction and detention of persons of unsound mind. Behind this distinction lies the argument that the grounds for detention can change in the latter, but not in the former case. In the present case, the applicant was convicted to a sentence of life imprisonment and therefore Article 5(1)(a) was applicable. However, as was recognized by the sentencing court, the reasons necessitating detention might cease to exist. This factor led the Commission to the conclusion that this case should be compared with those under Article 5(1)(e) and therefore required subsequent review of the lawfulness of the detention.[400]

Does the fourth paragraph also apply to the detention on remand, now that the third paragraph already prescribes that an accused person, after his arrest, shall be brought promptly before a judge or other officer authorized by law to exercise judicial power? Even in the case that the person in question has thus been brought to trial it can hardly be said that he has been able to exercise the right "to take proceedings", while moreover not in all cases is there a decision on the lawfulness of the detention by a "court" in the strict sense. It would therefore appear justifiable to hold that in certain cases Article 5(4) grants to the person detained on remand a right of recourse to a court after the (judicial) decision to detain him or to prolong the detention has been taken.[401] In the *De Jong, Baljet and Van den Brink* Case, the Court reached the same conclusion: the procedure, prescribed in Article 5(3),

> may admittedly have a certain incidence on compliance with paragraph 4. For example, where that procedure culminates in a decision by a 'court' ordering or confirming deprivation of the person's liberty, the judicial control of lawfulness required by paragraph 4 is incorporated in this initial decision. ... However, the guarantee assured by paragraph 4 is of a different order from, and additional to, that provided by paragraph 3.[402]

---

398. Judgment of 24 June 1982, A.50 (1982), p. 27.
399. See the report of the Commission of 1 March 1979, *Christinet, D & R* 17 (1980), p. 35 (56), where the Commission raises the question of whether the fourth paragraph is applicable when the renewed detention is based on an administrative decision, which, however, is to be regarded as part of the execution of a judicial decision.
400. Report of 7 December 1984, A.114 (1987), pp. 45-46.
401. See Recommendation R(80)11 of the Committee of Ministers of 27 June 1980 on detention on remand, Art. 14 of which provides: "Custody pending trial shall be reviewed at reasonably short intervals which the law or the judicial authority shall fix. In such a review, account shall be taken of all the changes in circumstances which have occurred since the person concerned was placed in custody".
402. Judgment of 22 May 1984, A.77 (1984), pp. 25-26.

In the *Bezicheri* Case the Commission indicated that in the case of detention on remand judicial review at regular intervals may even be more necessary: where relatively lengthy intervals may be appropriate for someone who is detained because of mental illness, the intervals should be relatively short for someone who is remanded in custody on suspicion of having commited an offence.[403]

Paragraph 4 entitles the accused to a decision by a "court". In the *Neumeister* Case the Court indicated as the decisive criterion for this that the competent authority "must be independent both of the executive and of the parties to the case".[404] The procedure itself was not considered decisive by the Court.[405] In the *Vagrancy* Cases, however, the Court did devote attention to the procedure and it considered the judicial features of the procedure followed in that case

> not sufficient to give the magistrate the character of a "court" within the meaning of paragraph (4) when due account is taken of the seriousness of what is at stake, namely a long deprivation of liberty attended by various shameful consequences.[406]

Consequently, of what guarantees must be attached to the procedure under the fourth paragraph of Article 5, in the Court's opinion, must be judged by the circumstances of each case, in which context in particular the consequences resulting for the person concerned from the decision to be taken in that procedure must be considered. A first requirement, however, is that the detained person be apprised of the reasons for his detention in order to be able to take proceedings with a view to determining its lawfulness.[407]

In its *Winterwerp* report the Commission set as a minimum condition for the procedure in which, for detained persons of unsound mind under paragraph 1(e), a decision is to be made about prolongation of the detention, that the arrested person is enabled to put forward his viewpoint himself or through a representative and to refute the medical and social arguments advanced for the detention. Since on the occasion of the annual decision about the prolongation of the detention neither Winterwerp nor his representative was informed of this, and since they were also not given an opportunity to put forward their viewpoint, in the Commission's opinion the procedure followed could not be considered a judicial one in the sense of Article 5(4).[408] In the same report the Commission, referring to the case-law of the Court, also held that the guarantees which the procedure of Article 5(4) must afford need not necessarily be the same as those prescribed in Article 6(1) for a "fair trial".[409] The Court, too, considered it essential for the person

---

403. Report of 10 March 1988, para. 38.
404. Judgment of 27 June 1968, A.8 (1968), p. 44. See also the report of 13 December 1984, *Sanchez-Reisse*, A.107 (1987), p. 28.
405. *Ibidem.*
406. Judgment of 18 June 1971, *De Wilde, Ooms and Versyp*, A.12 (1971), pp. 42-43.
407. Judgment of 5 November 1981, *X v. United Kingdom*, A.46 (1981), p. 28; report of 14 July 1988, *Van der Leer*, paras 112-115.
408. Report of 15 December 1977, B.31 (1983), p. 42. See also the report of 13 December 1984, *Sanchez-Reisse*, A.107 (1987), p. 29.
409. *Ibidem*, pp. 41 and 21 respectively.

concerned to have access to court and to be enabled to be heard in person or, if necessary, via a representative. According to the Court it is possible that the mental condition of the person makes specific restrictions or derogations necessary as to the exercise of this right, but this cannot in any case justify an encroachment on the right in its essence, but on the contrary calls for special procedural guarantees.[410] The Court equally concluded that in the case of Winterwerp the initial decision of detention was not taken by a "court" and that later he did not have access to a "judicial procedure".[411]

In the *Moudefo* Case the applicant complained that he did not receive effective legal assistance in appeal proceedings in connection with an application for provisional release. The Commission first stated that only Article 6(3)(c) expressly provides for the right to legal assistance and is not applicable to the proceedings at issue. However, referring to the case-law just mentioned, which implies that, although the guarantees under Article 6 cannot be relied upon in proceedings to determine the legality of detention, in such proceedings the person concerned must enjoy those procedural guarantees which are fundamental in procedures involving detention, the Commission observed that the applicant's appeal was examined by the court without any practical and effective intervention by a lawyer and that without legal assistance the applicant could not present his case properly and satisfactorily.[412] Since the purpose of the proceedings was to determine whether or not the applicant had to remain in detention and since the examination of questions of law was involved, the applicant could hardly have been expected to participate in that examination without the assistance of a lawyer. Consequently, a fundamental procedural right under Article 5(4) was not fully respected.[413] The same point of view was adopted by the Court some months later in the *Bouamar* Case, taking into consideration, *inter alia*, that the proceedings concerned a juvenile.[414]

In the *De Jong, Baljet and Van den Brink* Case the Commission concluded that the right, laid down in Article 5(4), is a *lex specialis* in relation to the right to an effective remedy, laid down in Article 13. Consequently, the two provisions cannot be relied upon cumulatively. The difference between the two articles lies in the fact that Article 5(4) requires proceedings before a "court", while Article 13 merely requires an "authority".[415]

Paragraph 4 explicitly requires that the judicial review shall take place "speedily". Compliance must be assessed in the light of the specific circumstances of the case.[416] A period of six months between the commencement of the detention and the access to court was considered contrary to this

---

410. Judgment of 24 October 1979, *Winterwerp*, A.33 (1980), p. 24.
411. *Ibidem*, p. 26.
412. The Commission referred to the judgment of 9 October 1979, *Airey*, A.32 (1979), pp. 12-14.
413. Report of 8 July 1987, A.141 (1989), pp. 42-43.
414. Judgment of 29 February 1988, A.129 (1988), pp. 23-25.
415. Report of 11 October 1982, A.77 (1984), p. 39.
416. Report of 1 March 1979, *Christinet, D & R* 17 (1980), p. 35 (57), where sixteen days was still deemed "speedily".

provision by the Commission.[417] In the *De Jong, Baljet and Van den Brink* Case the Court concluded that Article 5(4) had been violated because the right to bring proceedings to obtain a review of the lawfulness of the detention could only be exercised after seven, eleven and six days respectively. This was not in conformity with the requirement of "speediness".[418] And in the *Sanchez-Reisse* Case the time which elapsed between the lodging of two requests and the decisions thereon, thirty-one days and forty-six days respectively, equally did not satisfy the "speed"-requirement of Article 5(4). Here again, arguments like the case-load of the court and the fact that a decision on the merits of the case was pending did not justify the delay involved.[419] In assessing the speedy character required by paragraph 4 comparable factors may be taken into consideration as play a role with respect to the requirement of trial within a reasonable time under paragraph 3 and under Article 6(1), such as, for instance, the conduct of the applicant and the way the authorities have handled the case.[420]

Application 7376/76 concerned a detention in the sense of Article 5(1)(f). This detention had lasted less than two hours, after which deportation had taken place. The Commission decided that the detention

ceased within a period shorter than that which would have been necessary for the application of the procedure envisaged in Article 5(4) of the Convention.[421]

Although the fourth paragraph does not contain any provision about the length of the detention, the correctness of the Commission's view can hardly be contested. After all, the purpose of the provision of Article 5(4) is not the examination by a court of the lawfulness of the deportation, but of that of the detention, and in this case that detention had ceased sooner than could have been achieved by a judicial decision.[422] It is true that prolongation of the detention pending a judicial decision may be in the interest of the detainee, but this interest as such is not protected in the Convention. Nor will any claim for damages be possible in the case of so short a deprivation of liberty, if it was *prima facie* aimed at deportation.

In the *Sanchez-Reisse* Case, which also concerned a detention pending extradition, the Commission clearly distinguished between the lawfulness of the extradition and that of the detention itself. The latter obviously falls within the scope of Article 5(4). The Commission concluded that the procedure as a whole for dealing with requests for provisional release was not in conformity

---

417. Report of 16 July 1980, *X v. United Kingdom*, B.41 (1985), p. 39. See also the report of 11 October 1983, *Zamir, D & R* 40 (1985), p. 42 (59-60), and the report of 10 March 1988, *Bezicheri*, paras 45-48.
418. Judgment of 22 May 1984, A.77 (1984), pp. 26-27.
419. Judgment of 21 October 1986, A.107 (1987), pp. 21-22.
420. Judgment of 23 February 1984, *Luberti*, A.75 (1984), pp. 15-18.
421. Appl. 7376/76, *X and Y v. Sweden, D & R* 7 (1977), p. 123 (125).
422. See also Appl. 7447/76, *X v. the Netherlands*, not published, where the person to be extradited had been detained for a whole weekend, but the Commission held that in any case the procedure of paragraph 4 could not have been started during the weekend. Considering the practice of summary proceedings, where judges are willing to hear cases during the weekend, one may ask oneself whether this assumption was really correct.

with this provision, on the one hand because of the fact that the request had first to be considered by the Federal Police Office before the Federal Court can take a decision, on the other hand because of the fact that the detainee had not been able to comment on the advice of the Police Office. Moreover, the court did not hear the applicant.[423] The Court took a somewhat different view. It had no objections to the requirement of a previous administrative procedure, provided that this did not violate the "speed"-requirement. The Court emphasized the need of an adversary procedure. It was the lack of possibilities to submit any (written or oral) comments on the statements of the Police Office which led the Court to conclude that there was no "equality of arms". Therefore, Article 5(4) had been violated.[424]

16. *Article 5, paragraph 5* grants a right to compensation if an arrest or detention is found to be in contravention of the preceding provisions of Article 5.
At first sight this provision appears superfluous by the side of the general provision concerning just satisfaction in Article 50 of the Convention.[425] The difference, however, is that Article 50 confers a competence on the Court, while Article 5(5) grants a right *vis-à-vis* the national authorities, the violation of which right may constitute the object of a separate complaint and may subsequently lead to the Court's application of Article 50. This difference may be illustrated by the following example. If an arrest has been declared unlawful by the national court and the prisoner has subsequently been released under Article 5(4), he can still file an application with the Commission for violation of Article 5 if his claim for compensation has not been received or has been rejected. If, on the other hand, a given treatment of a detainee has been stopped after having been found by the national court to conflict with Article 3, but no damages are awarded to the injured person, there is no ground for filing an application with the Commission, since Article 3 itself does not grant a right to compensation and Article 50 can be considered applicable only after the Court has established violation of - in this case - Article 3.

In its earlier case-law the Commission took insufficient account of this distinction and held that a complaint based on Article 5(5) could only be examined after the violation of one of the other provisions of Article 5 had been established by the Court or the Committee of Ministers.[426] In its decision in the *Huber* Case, however, the Commission, after mentioning this case-law, held as follows:

On further consideration the Commission would be inclined partially to revise or develop its earlier jurisprudence and consider that where a breach of paras (1) - (4) has been

---

423. Report of 13 December 1984, A.107 (1987), pp. 29-30.
424. Judgment of 21 October 1986, A.107 (1987), p. 19. A similar approach was taken by the Commission in the *Lamy* Case; report of 8 October 1987, A.151 (1989), p. 24.
425. On Art. 50, see *supra* pp. 171-185.
426. Report of 1 April 1966, *Wemhoff*, B.5 (1969), p. 90. Thus also Appl. 4149/69, *X v. Federal Republic of Germany*, Coll. 36 (1971), p. 66 (68).

established by a national court - either directly if the said provisions form a part of the domestic law concerned, or in substance - the applicant who has been denied compensation can bring before the Commission a breach of Article 5(5) after exhaustion of domestic remedies in this respect.[427]

On the other hand, the fact that the injured person has invoked Article 5(5) neither before the national court nor before the Commission bars an award of compensation under Article 50 for damage caused by a deprivation of liberty.[428] In that respect the observation by the Commission in the *Ciulla* Case is of importance, *viz.* that, like the other rights guaranteed by the Convention, Article 5(5) guarantees a practical and effective right and that therefore it is only respected if the relevant provisions and procedures to obtain damages have been established in national law with a sufficient degree of certainty.[429]

In the *Brogan* Case the Government argued that the aim of paragraph 5 is to ensure that the victim of an "unlawful" arrest or detention should have an enforceable right to compensation. In this regard they also contended that "lawful" is to be construed as essentially referring back to domestic law and in addition as excluding any element of arbitrariness. They concluded that even in the event of a violation being found of any of the first four paragraphs, there had been no violation of paragraph 5 because the appliants' deprivation was lawful under Northern Ireland law and was not arbitrary. The Court held that such a restrictive interpretation was incompatible with the terms of paragraph 5, which refers to arrest or detention "in contravention of the provisions of this Article".[430]

The damage to be compensated under the fifth paragraph may be material as well as non-material.[431] The question of whether damage is involved concerns the merits and will have to be decided by the Court or the Committee of Ministers on the basis of the claims of the original applicant.[432] For this reason, too, the Commission ought to be very reserved in declaring an application concerning Article 5(5) inadmissible on account of manifest ill-foundedness.[433]

17. Article 5 is not included in the enumeration of Article 15(2). Under the conditions mentioned in the first paragraph of that article the member States

---

427. Appl. 6821/74, *Huber v. Austria, D & R* 6 (1977), p. 65 (69).
428. Judgment of 7 May 1974, *Neumeister*, A.17 (1974), pp. 12-14.
429. Report of 8 May 1987, A.148 (1989), p. 28.
430. Judgment of 29 November 1988, A.145/B (1989), p. 34.
431. Judgment of 22 June 1972, *Ringeisen*, A.15 (1972), pp. 9-10. See also the judgment of 2 December 1987, *Bozano*, A.124 (1988), p. 46.
432. The mere fact of violation of one or more of the first four paragraphs of Art. 5 does not in itself constitute a sufficient ground for an award of compensation; the injury must be proved: judgment of 10 March 1972, *"Vagrancy"* Cases, A.14 (1972), p. 11.
433. See *supra* pp. 106-107. In its decision on Appl. 2932/66, *X v. Federal Republic of Germany, Yearbook* XIII (1970), p. 264 (274), the Commission arrived at such a decision on the ground of the extremely curious consideration indeed that "having regard to the specific circumstances of the case, in particular to the applicant's past record and his behaviour during the rare periods when he was at liberty, there is reason to assume that the applicant did not suffer any damage".

may therefore derogate from the provision of Article 5 if, in so far as, and as long as this is necessary.

18. A comparison between Article 5 of the European Convention and Article 9 of the Covenant shows for the first paragraph of the two articles the important difference that, while Article 5 gives an exhaustive enumeration of the cases in which deprivation of liberty is permitted, Article 9 is confined to a prohibition of "arbitrary arrest or detention". On the one hand, the Convention thus affords better protection in the sense that deprivation of liberty is prohibited in all other cases than the ones there mentioned, even if such a deprivation is based on national law and although the arguments advanced for it may be reasonable. On the other hand, the text of the Covenant, through the use of the word "arbitrary", implies a guarantee for a reasonable and justified application of the possibilities for arrest and detention provided for in the law, a guarantee which is not explicitly included in Article 5(1) of the Convention outside the provision under (c). The conclusion of the Committee of Experts that "the circumstances which are set out limitatively in Article 5 of the European Convention and any action taken thereunder by European Governments could not be considered to be arbitrary"[434] is hardly convincing, since cases may be easily conceived in which the circumstances mentioned in Article 5(1) are indeed present, but where, viewed objectively and from the point of reasonableness, they do not justify deprivation of liberty in the concrete case.

The second paragraph of the two articles differs in that Article 9 of the Covenant prescribes that the accused must be informed of the reasons for the arrest *at the moment of the arrest*, while Article 5 of the Convention provides that this must be done "promptly", such as it is also prescribed - in both articles - for the information concerning charges, if any. Since the term "promptly", apart from the case of special circumstances, also implies that the person carrying out the arrest immediately states the reasons for it,[435] this difference seems not very important. The complications that may arise if the arrested person does not understand the language of the country seem not to have been foreseen in the Covenant.

The right to be brought before a judicial authority, and to a prompt trial or release pending trial if continued detention is no longer justified, appears to be granted in the third paragraph of Article 5 to a larger category of persons than in the same paragraph of Article 9. Indeed, the latter provision speaks exclusively of persons "arrested or detained on a criminal charge", and thus does not comprise those persons whose arrest or detention serves to prevent their committing a crime, which persons would seem to be covered by Article 5(3) in conjunction with Article 5(1)(c). However, as has been mentioned above with respect to the latter article, the text is not quite clear,

---

434. Report of the Committee of Experts, *supra* note 14, p. 28.
435. See *supra* p. 272.

because the grounds for arrest and those for detention are not distinguished adequately. It would therefore appear likely that this is merely a textual difference.

The provision in Article 9(3) of the Covenant that "[i]t shall not be the general rule that persons awaiting trial shall be detained in custody" is not present in the Convention. However, the idea behind it is to be found in the case-law of the Court in the form of the conditions to be fulfilled for justification of the detention and of its prolongation.[436]

As regards the text of the fourth paragraph of the two articles, it may be assumed with the Committee of Experts that in practice the difference between "speedily" and "without delay" is hardly of any importance.[437] A more important difference is that to which the Committee of Experts subsequently draws attention, viz. that it appears from the *travaux préparatoires* that the word "court" in Article 9(4) of the Covenant need not necessarily have the meaning of "court of law", which *has* been assigned to it in the case-law with respect to Article 5(4) of the Convention.[438]

The fifth paragraph of the two articles, finally, differs in that Article 9(5) grants a right to compensation to a "victim of unlawful arrest or detention" without connecting this with the preceding paragraphs of the article, whereas Article 5 does make that connection. But since an arrest or a detention which is "unlawful" also conflicts with the first paragraph of Article 9, this difference in formulation, again, does not seem to have much practical importance.[439]

§ 6. ARTICLE 6: RIGHT TO A FAIR AND PUBLIC HEARING

1. In the determination of his civil rights and obligations or of any criminal charge against him, everyone is entitled to a fair and public hearing within a reasonable time by an independent and impartial tribunal established by law. Judgment shall be pronounced publicly but the press and public may be excluded from all or part of the trial in the interest of morals, public order or national security in a democratic society, where the interests of juveniles or the protection of the private life of the parties so require, or to the extent strictly necessary in the opinion of the court in special circumstances where publicity would prejudice the interests of justice.
2. Everyone charged with a criminal offence shall be presumed innocent until proved guilty according to law.
3. Everyone charged with a criminal offence has the following minimum rights:

---

436. Thus also the Report of the Committee of Experts, *supra* note 14, pp. 29-30, with a reference to the *Neumeister* judgment.
437. *Ibidem*, p. 30.
438. *Ibidem.*
439. For the "case-law" of the Human Rights Committee concerning Article 9 of the Covenant reference is made to the study by Nowak mentioned *supra* at p. 216.

(a) to be informed promptly, in a language which he understands and in detail, of the nature and cause of the accusation against him;

(b) to have adequate time and facilities for the preparation of his defence;

(c) to defend himself in person or through legal assistance of his own choosing or, if he has not sufficient means to pay for legal assistance, to be given it free when the interests of justice so require;

(d) to examine or have examined witnesses against him and to obtain the attendance and examination of witnesses on his behalf under the same conditions as witnesses against him;

(e) to have the free assistance of an interpreter if he cannot understand or speak the language used in court.

1. For the interpretation of the first paragraph of Artice 6 the Court in its *Delcourt* judgment indicated the following guide-line:

> In a democratic society within the meaning of the Convention, the right to a fair administration of justice holds such a prominent place that a restrictive interpretation of Artice 6(1) would not correspond to the aim and the purpose of that provision.[440]

In thus rejecting a restrictive interpretation of that provision, the Court gives guidance not only for its own case-law and that of the Commission, but also to the national authorities which have to apply Article 6. Indeed, its case-law to be discussed hereafter shows that the Court considers itself competent to an in-depth examination of the way in which Article 6 has been interpreted and applied by the national authorities.

The most important questions of interpretation which the first paragraph of Article 6 evokes concern the meaning of the words "determination", "civil rights and obligations", "criminal charge" and "within a reasonable time". These issues will first be discussed.

2. Unlike the second and the third paragraph of Article 6, the first paragraph does not apply exclusively to criminal cases. In addition to the trial of criminal cases it also applies to all those proceedings in which the "determination of (...) civil rights and obligations" is (also) involved.[441]

The drafters of Article 6 have not specified what is meant by "civil rights and obligations". Even if one were to assume that rights and obligations under private law are concerned, within the legal systems of the contracting States one can arrive at widely different interpretations of these words, particularly because the demarcation between public and private law is very vague in general - and this increasingly so - but also because this line is not always drawn in accordance with the same criteria in the different legal systems. However this may be, it is by no means certain that "civil" has the restricted

---

440. Judgment of 17 January 1970, A.11 (1970), p. 15. Thus also in its judgment of 26 October 1984, *De Cubber*, A.86 (1984), p. 16.
441. Judgment of 8 June 1976, *Engel*, A.22 (1977), p. 36.

meaning of "private". The legal history of Artice 6(1), which is closely linked with that of Article 14(1) of the International Covenant on Civil and Political Rights, in our opinion indicates that such a restriction was not intended by the drafters.[442] Until now it has been left undecided by the Court "whether the concept of 'civil rights and obligations' ... extends beyond those rights which have a private nature",[443] but so far it has used the terms "civil" and "private" indiscriminately as synonyms in its legal considerations.[444]

All in all it is evident that for the effective application of the extremely important Article 6(1), and for the required uniformity and legal certainty with respect to that application, it is of the greatest importance that the Strasbourg case-law here draws the line, and in doing so keeps the necessary distance with regard to the domestic law of the contracting States. Up to a certain point this has already been done. The Court in its case-law has developed - in some cases by following the Commission, in other cases, after some hesitation, followed by the Commission - the following points of departure:

(a)   Article 6(1) not only contains procedural guarantees in relation to judicial proceedings, but also grants *a right to* a judicial procedure for the cases mentioned in this article: the right of access to court. That right is not dependent on the question of whether the domestic legal system in question provides for appeal to a court for the case concerned; indeed, if the latter is not the case, it constitutes a violation of Article 6(1).[445] As to this right of access to court the points of view within the Commission and the Court widely diverged at first,[446] but it is now generally accepted. Accordingly, Article 6(1) also applies to procedures where domestic law traditionally does not provide for judicial review, as was the case with the Crown-appeal procedure in the Netherlands.[447] With this extensive, teleological interpretation the Commission and the Court especially wanted to prevent the erosion of the guarantees of Article 6, which would otherwise be the result if in the contracting States judicial review in some fields would be restricted or even eliminated, and in other fields its introduction would be omitted.[448]

(b)   For Article 6(1) to be applicable, there must be question of a "deter-

---

442.   In detail about this P. van Dijk, "The Interpretation of 'Civil Rights and Obligations' by the European Court of Human Rights; One More Step to Take", in: F. Matscher & H. Petzhold (eds), *Protecting Human Rights: The European Dimension; Studies in honour of Gérard J. Wiarda*, Cologne etc. 1988, pp. 131-143.
443.   Judgment of 28 June 1978, *König*, A.27 (1978), p. 32; judgment of 23 June 1981, *Le Compte, Van Leuven and De Meyere*, A.43 (1981), p. 22.
444.   *Ibidem*, pp. 31-32 and p. 22 respectively. Thus also in the judgments of 23 April 1987, *Ettl and others; Erkner and Hofauer; Poiss*, A.117 (1987), pp. 16, 60 and 102 respectively.
445.   Judgment of 21 February 1975, *Golder*, A.18 (1975), pp. 13-18; judgment of 23 June 1981, *Le Compte, Van Leuven and De Meyere*, A.43 (1981), pp. 20-22.
446.   See in particular the "dissenting opinion" of Judge Fitzmaurice to the *Golder* judgment, *ibidem*, pp. 42-63.
447.   Judgment of 23 October 1985, *Benthem*, A.97 (1986), pp. 14-16.
448.   See the judgment of 21 February 1975, *Golder*, A.18 (1975), pp. 17-18.

mination" of a right or obligation. From the fact that here the French text speaks of "contestations" it may be inferred that the settlement of a dispute concerning a right or obligation must be at issue.[449] This concept of "dispute", however, must be interpreted in a broad sense: a difference of opinion between the parties concerned is sufficient,[450] provided that it is "genuine and of a serious nature".[451] And furthermore the "determination" of a "civil right" or "civil obligation" need not form the main point of the proceedings. It is sufficient that the outcome of the proceedings is also decisive for the determination and/or the exercise of the right or the determination and/or the fulfilment of the obligation, as the case may be.[452]

(c) To the words "civil rights and obligations" an autonomous meaning must be assigned. It must first be examined what is the nature of the right invoked or the obligation at issue according to the law of the respondent State. In that context the important point is the content and effect of that right or obligation rather than its legal classification. But the nature under domestic law is not decisive: what matters is whether according to general objective principles - in which context the legal systems of the other contracting States must also be taken into account - the meaning of "civil right" or "civil obligation" can be assigned to the right or obligation at issue.[453] This point of departure, too, serves to make the scope of Article 6(1) less dependent on the national legislator.

(d) Nor is it decisive for the "civil" nature of a right or obligation whether the underlying dispute is one between individuals or one between an individual and a public authority. Even if in the latter case that public authority is involved in the proceedings in a sovereign capacity, those proceedings can relate to the determination of "civil rights and obligations".[454]

---

449. Judgment of 16 July 1971, *Ringeisen*, A.13 (1971), p. 39.
450. Judgment of 23 June 1981, *Le Compte, Van Leuven and De Meyere*, A.43 (1981), pp. 20-21. In the *Baraona* Case the Court held that there was a "dispute" and contested the Government's submission that the impugned measure had no basis in Portuguese law at that time and accordingly could not give rise to liability on the part of the State. The Court held that it was not for the Court to assess either the merits of the applicant's claim under Portuguese legislation or the influence of the revolutionary situation on the application of domestic law; this belonged to the exclusive jurisdiction of the national courts. The applicant, however, could claim on arguable grounds to have a right that was recognized under Portuguese law as he understood it. Judgment of 8 July 1987, A.122 (1987), p. 17.
451. Jugment of 23 September 1982, *Sporrong and Lönnroth*, A.52 (1982), p. 30; judgment of 23 October 1985, *Benthem*, A.97 (1985), p. 15; report of 13 October 1988, *Håkansson and Sturesson*, para. 122.
452. Judgment of 16 July 1971, *Ringeisen*, A.13 (1971), p. 39; judgment of 23 June 1981, *Le Compte, Van Leuven and De Meyere*, A.43 (1981), p. 21; judgment of 22 October 1984, *Sramek*, A.84 (1984), p. 17; report mentioned in the previous note, *ibidem*.
453. Judgment of 16 July 1971, *Ringeisen*, A.13 (1971), p. 39; judgment of 28 June 1978, *König*, A.27 (1978), pp. 29-30; judgment of 23 October 1985, *Benthem*, A.97 (1985), p. 16.
454. Judgment of 28 June 1978, *König*, A.27 (1978) p. 30; judgment of 29 May 1986, *Feldbrugge*, A.99 (1986), p. 12.

(e) Finally, it is not considered decisive whether the proceedings take place before a civil court or before another body vested with jurisdiction.[455]

This case-law has as its consequence that, even if it is assumed that "civil" has to be equated with private, Article 6(1) is applicable to a great many proceedings which in themselves have a public character according to their form and subject, but the outcome of which is of direct interest for the determination and/or content of a private right or private obligation.[456]

But can "civil" in Article 6(1) be equated with "private"? Although the Court has explicitly left open this question by considering that

> [it is not] necessary in the present case to decide whether the concept of "civil rights and obligations" within the meaning of [Article 6(1)] extends beyond those rights which have a private nature,[457]

nevertheless it has hitherto started from the assumption that "civil" can be equated with "private", and it also employs these terms as synonyms.[458] Article 6(1), however, does not speak of "private rights and obligations", but of "civil rights and obligations", while the French text does not speak of "droits et obligations civils", but of "droits et obligations de caractère civil". One has to agree with the Court that for "civil rights" one must not think of the specific meaning of "basic rights" which this term has in Anglo-American legal usage (that this is not meant is abundantly clear from the French text).[459] However, that "civil rights" can be equated with "private rights" appears not to be supported by the *travaux préparatoires* of Article 6(1).

For those *travaux préparatoires* one has in fact to consult the *travaux préparatoires* of Article 14 of the Covenant, since the drafters of the Convention based themselves on this provision and there is not the slightest evidence that there was any separate discussion about the text of Article 6.[460] The only difference is that at the very last moment an alteration was made in the English text, "rights and obligations in a suit-at-law" being altered into "civil rights and obligations", but this appears to have been done solely because this was considered a better English equivalent of the French "droits et obligations de caractère civil". A change in meaning was not intended, as

---

455. Judgment of 16 July 1971, *Ringeisen*, A.13 (1971), p. 39; judgment of 28 June 1978, *König*, A.27 (1978), pp. 29-30.
456. See, *e.g.*, the judgment of 23 October 1985, *Benthem*, A.97 (1985); judgment of 29 May 1986, *Feldbrugge*, A.99 (1986).
457. Judgment of 28 June 1978, *König*, A.27 (1978), p. 32; judgment of 23 June 1981, *Le Compte, Van Leuven and De Meyere*, A.43 (1981), p. 22.
458. Thus, for instance, in the two judgments mentioned in the preceding note, *ibidem*. See also the judgments mentioned in note 444.
459. Judgment of 21 February 1975, *Golder*, A.18 (1975), p. 16. See also Ch. Rasenack, "'Civil Rights and Obligations' or 'Droits et Obligations de caractère civil' - Two crucial legal determinations in Article 6(1) of the European Convention for the Protection of Human Rights and Fundamental Freedoms", *R.D.H.* 3 (1970), pp. 51-81.
460. On this, *inter alia*, Jacques Velu, "Le problème de l'application aux juridictions administratives, des règles de la Convention européenne des droits de l'homme relatives à la publicité des audiences et des jugements", *R.D.I.D.C.* (1961), pp. 129-171 (159). See also the joint dissenting opinion to the judgments of 29 May 1986, *Feldbrugge*, A.99 (1986), pp. 26-27, and *Deumeland*, A.100 (1986), pp. 38-39.

already appears from the fact that the French text was left unamended.[461]

About these *travaux préparatoires* the position has been taken in Strasbourg, on the one hand, that they provide no clarity as to the meaning of "civil rights and obligations",[462] and on the other hand, that they point in the direction of a restrictive interpretation,[463] while an extensive interpretation was also considered by some as being in conformity therewith.[464] The Court has not yet given its opinion about the conclusions that might be drawn from the *travaux préparatoires* with regard to the interpretation of "civil rights and obligations". A study of the matter on the basis also of detailed analyses in literature[465] has induced us to conclude that it was not the intention of the drafters of Article 14 of the Covenant to restrict the application of that provision, in addition to proceedings with a criminal character, to proceedings in which private rights or obligations are at issue.[466] On the contrary, from the debates a clear opposition emerges to textual proposals which might have such a restrictive effect.[467] In our opinion too much weight has been given to the intervention of the then Danish delegate Sørensen, which is cited by the dissenters in the *Feldbrugge* and the *Deumeland* judgments from the *travaux préparatoires* in support of their argument that a restrictive meaning was presumably intended.[468] It is true that his intervention has contributed to an ultimate agreement with the American proposal to add to "rights and obligations" the words "in a suit-at-law", which curiously enough was translated in the French text by "de caractère civil". But from these ultimately chosen words and their history it is evident, in our opinion, that thus it was not intended to confine the applicability, as Sørensen had proposed, to disputes between individuals. And, as has been said above, there is no evidence that the drafters of Article 6 of the Convention have intended to introduce this restriction; it is plausible that the alteration of "in a suit-at-law" into "civil" was made exclusively because this was considered a better equivalent of the unaltered French words "de caractère civil".

A restriction which does seem to emerge from the *travaux préparatoires* is the restriction to procedures which according to the law of the State concerned have a judicial character, without an obligation to transform non-

461. Thus also the Commission in its report of 19 March 1970, *Ringeisen*, B.11 (1972), pp. 70-71. See also the Report of the Committee of Experts, *supra* note 14, p. 37.
462. Separate opinion of Judge Matscher to the judgment of 28 June 1978, *König*, A.27 (1978), p. 45.
463. Report of the Commission of 19 March 1970, *Ringeisen*, B.11 (1972), pp. 70-71; joint dissenting opinion to the judgments of 29 May 1986, *Feldbrugge*, A.99 (1986), p. 21 and pp. 26-27, and *Deumeland*, A.100 (1986), pp. 33 and 38-39.
464. Minority view of the Commission in *Benthem*, A.97 (1985), p. 37.
465. In addition to Velu, *supra* note 460, see especially: Thomas Buergenthal & Wilhelm Kewenig, "Zum Begriff der Civil Rights in Artikel 6 Absatz 1 der Europäischen Menschenrechtskonvention", *Archiv des Völkerrechts* (1966/67), pp. 393-411, and Frank C. Newman, "Natural Justice, Due Process and the New International Covenants on Human Rights: Prospectus", *Public Law* (Winter 1967), pp. 274-313.
466. In detail about this P. van Dijk, *supra* note 442, pp. 135-143.
467. See Velu, *supra* note 460, pp. 148-154. See in particular his reference at p. 150 to a statement of the Russian delegate Pavlov.
468. Joint dissenting opinion to the judgments of 29 May 1986, A.99 (1986), p. 27 and A.100 (1986), p. 39.

judicial procedures into judicial procedures. The very term "in a suit-at-law", too, seems to point in that direction.[469] But, as has been said, the Court rejected this interpretation in the *Golder* judgment, because it considered it to conflict with the text of Article 6(1) when read in the context of this provision and in the light of the object and purpose of the Convention.[470] Although from the viewpoint of legal protection this attitude is to be welcomed, on the other hand it cannot be denied that it was this very case-law which has produced far-reaching and unforeseen consequences for the domestic legal systems of a number of contracting States. It also explains why within the Court and the Commission some trends have arisen which strive to restrict these consequences again to some extent by a restrictive interpretation of "civil rights and obligations" via a presumed restriction to "private rights and obligations"; a restriction which most likely was *not* intended at the time. The present Strasbourg case-law on this point is one of lack of clarity and great uncertainty; lack of clarity because still no general definition of "civil rights and obligations" can be inferred from that case-law,[471] and uncertainty because the elements actually developed in the case-law for such a definition appear to lead within and between the Court and the Commission to entirely different views in concrete cases, while the numbers of the adherents to the various views are almost equal.[472] In our opinion this lack of clarity and this uncertainty, which constitute an undesirable situation not only for the individual seeking justice, but also for the public authorities within the contracting States, can only be eliminated when the Court breaks through its hitherto pursued casuistic approach and develops a general and readily applicable definition in the exercise of its function to give direction to the interpretation and application of the Convention. Some members of the Commission went quite a long way in the direction of a definition in their minority opinion in the *Benthem* report. On the basis, as they stated, of the case-law of the Court, they reached the following definition of "civil rights":

> all those rights which are individual rights under the national legal system and fall into the sphere of general individual freedom, be it professional or any other legally permitted activity.[473]

469. See Velu, *supra* note 460, pp. 152-156.
470. Judgment of 21 February 1975, A.18 (1975), pp. 13-18.
471. In the *Benthem* Case the Court had been invited by the Commission to give a general definition, but it confined itself to stating: "The Court does not consider that it has to give on this occasion an abstract definition of the concept of 'civil rights and obligations'"; A.97 (1986), p. 16.
472. Thus the Court decided in its judgment of 23 October 1985, *Benthem*, A.97 (1986), that Article 6(1) was applicable, by eleven to six votes, while the Commission had taken a contrary standpoint by nine votes to eight. In the judgment of 29 May 1986, *Feldbrugge*, A.99 (1986), the proportion in the Court was ten to seven, and in the Commission eight to six. In the judgment of 29 May 1986, *Deumeland*, A.100 (1986), this was nine to eight and eight to six respectively.
473. A.97 (1985), p. 36. In his presentation of the minority standpoint before the Court, Melchior amended the words "any other legally permitted activity" into "any other activity which is not absolutely prohibited by law"; *Court/Misc*(85)30, p. 10.

For this broad interpretation they referred explicitly to the *travaux prépara-toires* and to the principle of the "evolutive interpretation", according to which the social developments that have occurred since the entry into force of the Convention are to be taken into account.[474] However, by stating in their further elucidation that in cases in which on the part of the authorities - for instance for the grant of a licence - there exists an absolutely discretionary competence, there is no question of a right, and consequently also not of a "civil right",[475] they have again introduced great uncertainty. Firstly, the applicability of Article 6(1) is thus again made dependent on what the domestic law provides for, and this with regard to the very complex and controversial distinction between subjective rights and reflex rights.[476] And furthermore this implies unintentionally an invitation to the local legislator to abolish the legal restrictions to which the exercise of discretionary competence is tied down, in order thus to evade the consequences of Article 6(1). But an even stronger element of uncertainty is introduced by the very vague exception for rights which the individual does not have as a private person, but as a citizen,

> *i.e.* where a special status or specific legal relations with the public institutions of the State as such are at issue (*e.g.* public service, fiscal matters, military service, immigration matters, electoral matters).[477]

From the examples given it is quite clear how great an uncertainty would be built-in with this proposed distinction. Indeed, very broad categories are mentioned there, parts of which may be directly connected not only with "civil rights and obligations", but even with "private rights and obligations"; one need only think of the family-law aspects of the immigration policy and the labour-law aspects of the position of civil servants. This uncertainty was clearly demonstrated by the authors themselves of the definition when in the next two cases they disagreed about the application of their own definition, in consequence of which Frowein joined the majority and Melchior continued to belong to the minority.[478] Against this background one can only hope that the Court's consideration in the *Feldbrugge* and the *Deumeland* judgments that each of the applicants in these cases

> was not affected in her relations with the public authorities as such, acting in the exercise of discretionary powers, but in her personal capacity as a private individual,[479]

does not point to adoption by the Court of this new source of uncertainty.

---

474. *Ibidem*, p. 37. According to the dissenting opinion to the *Feldbrugge* and *Deumeland* judgments, however, an evolutive interpretation does not permit the introduction of perfectly new concepts, since this is a legislative function which belongs to the contracting States; A.99 (1986), pp. 27-28, and A.100 (1986), pp. 39-40.
475. *Ibidem*, p. 37.
476. A distinction which has evoked a good deal of discussion, especially among German jurists of administrative law. See P. van Dijk, *Judicial Review of Governmental Action and the Requirement of an Interest to Sue*, Alphen a/d Rijn 1980, pp. 178-190.
477. Minority standpoint of the Commission in *Benthem*, A.97 (1985), p. 37.
478. See the concurring opinion of Frowein to the reports of the Commission of 9 May 1984, *Feldbrugge*, A.99 (1986), p. 36, and *Deumeland*, A.100 (1986) p. 24.
479. Judgments of 29 May 1986, A.99 (1986), p. 15 and A.100 (1986), p. 24.

There is an urgent need of a clear and readily applicable definition by the Court, but the viewpoints within the Court diverge so widely that it must be feared that at this moment no majority can yet be found for such a definition. If that is the case, for the time being the casuistic approach by the Court will have to do, while then elements for a more general definition must be derived from the separate judgments.

Up to the present the case-law presents the picture that, in addition to the proceedings with a criminal-law character and proceedings with a civil-law character, the following cases also come within the purview of Article 6(1):

- procedures concerning a permission or another act of a public authority which forms a condition for the legality of a contract to be concluded with a private party;[480]
- procedures which may lead to the cancellation or suspension by the public authorities of the qualification for practising a particular profession or carrying on an economic activity;[481]
- those stages in expropriation and consolidation procedures which have direct consequences for the right of ownership with respect to the property involved;[482]
- procedures concerning the grant or revocation of a licence by the public authorities which is required for practising a particular profession or carrying out certain economic activities in that particular place;[483]
- procedures in which a decision is taken on claims to a sickness benefit

480. Judgment of 16 July 1971, *Ringeisen*, A.13 (1971) p. 39. See also the judgment of 22 October 1984, *Sramek*, A.84 (1986), p. 17, and the judgment of 8 July 1986, *Lithgow*, A.102 (1986), p. 70.
481. Judgment of 28 June 1978, *König*, A.27 (1978); judgment of 23 June 1981, *Le Compte, Van Leuven and De Meyere*, A.43 (1981); judgment of 10 February 1983, *Albert and Le Compte*, A.58 (1983). The case of *H v. Belgium* concerned the procedure followed by the Council of the Ordre des Avocats of Antwerp when considering applications for restoration to the roll. The Court made an analysis of the special characteristics of the profession of "avocat" in Belgium; the disputed right was indissolubly tied up with that profession. The Court held that there were clearly features of public law involved. Whilst these factors did not, in the opinion of the Court, suffice to establish that Article 6 was inapplicable, several considerations weighed in favour of the opposite conclusion: (a) the profession was traditionally treated as one of the independent professions; (b) chambers and clientele constitute property interests and as such come within the ambit of the right of property; (c) "avocats" perform numerous duties out of court often unconnected with judicial proceedings. In sum, the Court held that the asserted right was a civil one. Judgment of 30 November 1987, A.127 (1988), pp. 32-34.
482. Judgment of 23 September 1982, *Sporrong and Lönnroth*, A.52 (1982); report of 3 July 1985, *Ettl*, A.117 (1987), p. 22; judgments of 23 April 1987, *Ettl, Erkner and Poiss*, A.117 (1987), pp. 16, 60 and 102 respectively. See also report of 8 October 1987, *Jacobsson*, para. 142, where the Commission considered that a decision to issue or prolong a building prohibition on an individual's property, although of a public nature, is a decision which is "decisive" for the individual's "civil right", since such a prohibition clearly restricts the use of property rights.
483. Judgment of 22 October 1985, *Benthem*, A.97 (1986); judgments of 27 October 1987, *Pudas*, A.125 (1987) and *Bodén*, A.125 (1987). See also the report in the *Traktörer Aktiebolag* Case concerning the complaint that the applicant company had no possibility to submit to a court the revocation of a licence to serve alcoholic beverages. The Commission considered that although the company's licence to sell alcoholic beverages could not be assigned to a third party, this case could not be distinguished in law from the *Benthem* and the *Pudas* Case. It noted that the revocation had adverse effects on the goodwill and value of the business. The licence was even a condition for running the restaurant at a profit. Therefore, a civil right of the applicant was involved; report of 10 November 1987, para. 133.

on account of industrial disability;[484]
- procedures in which a decision is taken on claims to a retirement pension in virtue of a compulsory insurance against accidents.[485]

Recently the Court was confronted with several complaints concerning the procedures followed and the remedies available in connection with decisions relating to the applicants' access to their children in the care of a local authority. The Court examined these cases in the light of its effects and of the powers conferred on the local authority. In the Court's view the determination of a parental right was at issue. The existence of a power on the part of the authority to decide to allow only restricted or even no visit to a child by his parent does not, in the Court's understanding, necessarily mean that there is no longer any parental right regarding access once one of the measures in question has been taken. The Court held that the extinction of all parental rights in regard to access would scarcely be compatible with the fundamental notions of family life and the family ties which Article 8 of the Convention is designed to protect. Therefore there were arguable grounds for saying that even after the child has been taken into care, the applicant could claim a civil right to have access to him. Article 6(1) was therefore applicable.[486]

The Commission has also given its opinion in a number of cases which have not reached the Court or where the Court did not go into the issue of whether a "civil right" was at stake. Thus, already in an early stage, it took the view that procedures which concern the legal position of civil servants in their relation to the public authorities do not fall under the application of Article 6(1),[487] no more than do procedures concerning taxation.[488] So far the Commission has not considered Article 6(1) applicable to procedures concerning admission and expulsion of aliens,[489] unless respect for family life

484. Judgment of 29 May 1986, *Feldbrugge*, A.99 (1986).
485. Judgment of 29 May 1986, *Deumeland*, A.100 (1986).
486. Judgment of 8 July 1987, *O and H v. United Kingdom*, A.120 (1987), pp. 24-27 and p. 58; *W, B and R v. United Kingdom*, A.121 (1987), pp. 32-35, 76-79 and 122-124 respectively. See also the report of 14 July 1988, *Eriksson*, para. 232.
487. Appl. 423/58, *X v. Federal Republic of Germany*, Coll. 1 (1960) (pages not numbered through); Appl. 4523/70, *X v. Federal Republic of Germany*, Yearbook XIV (1971), p. 622 (630); Appl. 9248/81, *Leander v. Sweden*, D & R 34 (1983), p. 78 (83); Appl. 10582/83, *X v. Portugal*, not published; Appl. 10878/84, *Jakobsson v. Sweden*, D & R 41 (1985), p. 247 (248).
488. Appls 1904, 2029, 2094 and 2217/64, *A, B, C and D v. the Netherlands*, Yearbook IX (1966), p. 268 (284); Appl. 9908/82, *X v. France*, D & R 32 (1983), p. 266 (272); Appl. 10815/84, *X v. United Kingdom*, not published.
489. Thus still in a general sense in Appl. 9593/81, *X v. United Kingdom*, not published (admission) and in Appl. 9285/81, *X, Y and Z v. United Kingdom*, D & R 29 (1982), p. 205 (212) (expulsion). See also the decision, which in our opinion is highly disputable, in Appl. 9543/81, *X v. Federal Republic of Germany* (not published) that the proceedings in the matter of the grant of a Vertriebenenausweis do not concern a "civil right"; this in spite of the great importance of such an identity card for the economic and social activities of the bearer.

as a "civil right" was at issue,[490] while the possibility has been left open that this is also the case when expulsion constitutes a violation of the right to education.[491] In case of expropriation the procedures in which the damages are determined have been considered by the Commission as a "determination" of a "civil right",[492] as are also procedures for damages on account of unlawful acts of the public authorities, unless the damage is the consequence of the exercise - lawful or unlawful - of government power.[493] In the *Kaplan* Case, in which the Commission - following the same line as in the *König* Case - recognized that the restrictions imposed by the public authorities on conducting an insurance enterprise affected "civil rights", Article 6(1) nevertheless was deemed not to be applicable, because the applicant did not claim that the challenged decision was unlawful, so that the issue of those civil rights was not susceptible of determination by a judicial decision.[494] In the *Van Marle* Case the Commission made a distinction with the *König* Case by considering that, although the procedure complained of could lead to the conferment or denial of the right to practise as an accountant, applicants could no longer claim such a right since that right had been taken away from them by new legislation, so that they could not claim an interference with a "right";[495] a rather artificial distinction, it seems to us, since the determination of a future "right" was no doubt at stake should the domestic court find that legislation to be invalid or to have been wrongly applied. And in its decision on Appl. 10331/83 the Commission also made a distinction with the *König* Case by holding that the disciplinary procedures against the medical practitioner did not concern the latter's possible suspension, but might only result in a reprimand, so that a purely disciplinary affair was involved, which did not result in a "determination" of a "civil right".[496] With regard to patents, finally, the Commission distinguished between the procedures in which the right to the patent is at issue and the procedures which concern the question of whether the conditions for registration have been fulfilled; Article 6(1) was found to apply only to proceedings of the first type.[497]

If the protection of a basic right or of any other right *vis-à-vis* a private person is in dispute, it is of course always a matter of a "civil right". If and in so far as *Drittwirkung* is assigned to the rights guaranteed in the Convention,[498] Article 6(1) therefore is applicable to proceedings for the enforcement of those rights. Thus it was recognized by the Commission that an individual's

---

490. Appls 2991 and 2992/66, *Alam, Kahn and Singh v. United Kingdom, Yearbook* X (1967), p. 478 (500-504). See on the other hand Appl. 8244/78, *Singh v. United Kingdom, D & R* 17 (1980), p. 157.
491. Appl. 7841/77, *X v. United Kingdom,* not published.
492. Report of 8 March 1982, *Andorfer Tonwerke, D & R* 32 (1982), p. 107. See also the report of 7 March 1984, *Lithgow,* A.102 (1987), p. 117. About a right to compensation Article 6 does not, of course, provide anything; *ibidem.*
493. Report of 15 March 1985, *Adler,* para. 47.
494. Report of 17 July 1980, *Kaplan, D & R* 21 (1981), p. 5 (23).
495. Report of 8 May 1984, A.101 (1986), pp. 25-26.
496. Appl. 10331/83, *X v. United Kingdom,* not published.
497. Appl. 8000/77, *X v. Switzerland, D & R* 13 (1979), p. 82 (82).
498. For this, see *supra* pp. 15-20.

304

right to respect for his reputation by a private person is a "civil right".[499] In the Commission's opinion, however, Article 6(1) is applicable only if the person concerned tries to obtain rehabilitation via a judicial procedure with a private-law character, not if for this he chooses a procedure in order to have a penalty imposed on the culprit.[500] If such a procedure with a civil-law character is not provided for, it must be ascertained whether an alternative is available which satisfies the requirements of Article 6(1), since the lack of a possibility of access to court for the determination of a civil right in itself already conflicts with Article 6(1).

The fact that in legal relations between individuals great public interests may also be involved does not bar the applicability of Article 6(1). Thus the Court held with regard to an action contesting paternity:

> It is true that the public interest may be affected by proceedings of the kind which Mr. Rasmussen wished to institute, but, in the Court's view, this factor cannot exclude the applicability of Article 6 to litigation which, by its very nature, is "civil" in character. And an action contesting paternity is a matter of family law; on that account alone, it is "civil" in character.[501]

3. The right to appeal to a higher court is not laid down in the Convention, nor is it implied in Article 6(1).[502] However, if a given appeal is open and a decision is taken on the merits, Article 6(1) applies, provided that the court in that instance is called to determine the civil rights or obligations in dispute.[503] The latter is deemed not to be the case, for instance, when appeal is lodged with a constitutional court and this concerns exclusively the constitutionality of the previous judicial decision; that phase then does not concern a full "determination".[504] If Article 6(1) is applicable, the specific characteristics of the appeal procedure in question must be taken into account.[505] Thus, for instance, it must be examined whether the requirement of publicity of the trial in a cassation procedure still has the same fundamental importance.[506]

---

499. Appl. 808/60, *ISOP v. Austria*, *Yearbook* V (1962), p. 108 (122). If statements made in the parliament are involved, an invocation of Article 6(1) is frustrated by the principle of "parliamentary immunity": Appl. 7729/76, *Agee v. United Kingdom*, *D & R* 7 (1977), p. 164 (175). See also Appl. 9248/81, *Leander v. Sweden*, *D & R* 34 (1983), p. 78 (83): refusal to appoint someone to a post cannot, as such, be considered to be an attack on the person's good reputation.

500. Appl. 7116/75, *X v. Federal Republic of Germany*, *D & R* 7 (1977), p. 91 (92) and Appl. 8637/79, *X v. Sweden*, not published. The situation, however, is different when within the framework of criminal proceedings a civil claim can be and actually has been submitted: Appl. 8366/78, *X v. Luxembourg*, *D & R* 16 (1979), p. 196 (198).

501. Judgment of 28 November 1984, *Rasmussen*, A.87 (1984), pp. 12-13; report of 18 October 1985, *Hyatt*, para. 86; Appl. 10148/82, *Garcia v. Switzerland*, *D & R* 42 (1985), p. 98 (120).

502. Judgment of 23 July 1968, *Belgian Linguistic Cases*, A.6 (1968), p. 33; judgment of 17 January 1970, *Delcourt*, A.11 (1970), p. 14. However, see the observation above on pp. 284-287 with regard to Article 5(4).

503. Judgment of 17 January 1970, *Delcourt, ibidem*, pp. 14-15; judgment of 22 January 1984, *Sutter*, A.74 (1984), p. 13; judgment of 29 May 1986, *Deumeland*, A.100 (1986), p. 26; report of 7 October 1986, *Ekbatani*, A.134 (1988), pp. 23-24; and report of 5 May 1988, *Kamasinki*, para. 189.

504. Judgment of 22 October 1984, *Sramek*, A.84 (1984), p. 17.

505. Judgment of 17 January 1970, *Delcourt*, A.11 (1970), p. 15; judgment of 25 April 1983, *Pakelli*, A.64 (1983), p. 14; judgment of 8 December 1983, *Pretto*, A.71 (1983), p. 12.

506. Report of 14 December 1981, *Axen*, B.57 (1982-1983), p. 23.

A procedure in which exclusively a decision is taken about the question as to whether an appeal will be considered (leave of appeal), is not a procedure to which Article 6(1) is applicable.[507] The Commission took the same view with regard to the procedure in which three judges of the *Bundesverfassungsgericht* take a decision about the admission of appeals;[508] it is, however, disputable whether this is correct, since in this procedure a negative decision may also be based on the manifestly ill-founded nature of the appeal, so that there may indeed be question of a "determination".[509] A more correct view was adopted by the Commission with respect to criminal proceedings in the *Monnell* and *Morris* Case, in which Article 6(1) was deemed to be applicable on account of the close connection of the decision about admission of the appeal with the merits of the appeal procedure itself, and because this preliminary procedure as such might already lead to an extension of the detention.[510]

4. In its judgment in the *Le Compte, Van Leuven and De Meyere* Case the Court held that Article 6(1) does not prescribe the contracting States:

> to submit "contestations" (disputes) over "civil rights and obligations" to a procedure conducted at each of its stages before "tribunals" meeting the Article's various requirements. Demands of flexibility and efficiency, which are fully compatible with the protection of human rights, may justify the prior intervention of administrative or professional bodies and, *a fortiori*, of judicial bodies which do not satisfy the said requirements in every respect.[511]

In the *Albert and Le Compte* Case the Court elucidated this as follows:

> in such circumstances the Convention calls at least for one of the two following systems: either the jurisdictional organs themselves comply with the requirements of Article 6(1), or they do not so comply but are subject to subsequent control by a judicial body that has full jurisdiction and does provide the guarantees of Article 6(1).[512]

This means that, for instance, the situation in which appeal against administrative actions is open, at first instance, only to an administrative body, even if the determination of civil rights and obligations is involved, does not conflict with Article 6(1), provided that in the last resort a court can be appealed to. Precisely that last requirement had not been fulfilled in the Dutch Crown Appeal procedure, which therefore did not find favour in the eyes of the Court[513] and has been adapted to this requirement.[514]

The viewpoint that only the last resort has to fulfil all the requirements of Article 6(1) has been toned down a little to the extent that this does not

507. Appl. 6916/75, *X, Y and Z v. Sweden*, *D & R* 6 (1977), p. 101 (107); Appl. 10663/83, *X v. Denmark*, not published.
508. Appl. 9508/81, *X v. Federal Republic of Germany*, not published.
509. *Cf.* also the report of 15 March 1985, *Adler*, paras 48-50.
510. Report of 11 March 1985, A.115 (1987), p. 36. See also the judgment of 2 March 1987, *Monnell and Morris*, A.115 (1987), p. 21.
511. Judgment of 23 June 1981, A.43 (1981), p. 23.
512. Judgment of 10 February 1983, A.58 (1983), p. 16. Thus also the Commission in its reports of 8 July 1986, *Van Lierde*, para. 44, and *Houart*, para. 36.
513. Judgment of 23 October 1985, *Benthem*, A.97 (1986).
514. See P. van Dijk, "The Benthem Case and its Aftermath in the Netherlands", *Netherlands International Law Review* (1987), pp. 5-24.

apply to those procedures which have a civil character according to the domestic law concerned and in which the decision is in the hands of "courts of the classic kinds"; the requirements of Article 6(1), according to the Court, must not be reduced "in its traditional and natural sphere of application".[515] And moreover it is investigated very critically in Strasbourg whether appeal is really open in all cases to the appellate body stated by the accused State as satisfying Article 6(1), and whether this is a full appeal.[516]

If in the determination of civil rights and obligations a review of government acts is involved as, for instance, in procedures before administrative courts, the court usually has only a marginal reviewing power and a rather broad margin of appreciation is left to the administrative authorities. If the court is allowed a sufficient reviewing power to still speak of a "determination", such procedures do not conflict with Article 6(1).[517] On the other hand, however, it is then required that in the (ultimate) judicial procedure not only the application of the law but also the assessment of the relevant facts is reviewed by the court, since both are equally important for the "determination".[518]

5. The words "determination of ... any criminal charge" also raise problems of interpretation, because on this point as well there are differences between the legal systems of the contracting States, so that an autonomous meaning, independent of those national systems, had to be developed.[519] The starting-point is then, in addition to the one defined by the Court in the *Delcourt* Case and quoted at the beginning of this section, the holding by the Court in the *De Weer* Case that:

> the prominent place held in a democratic society by the right to a fair trial ... prompts the Court to prefer a "substantive", rather than a "formal", conception of the "charge" contemplated by Article 6(1).[520]

According to some legal systems, for instance, the person who has been convicted at first instance, but for whom some remedies against this sentence are still available, is no longer regarded as one against whom a charge is pending, but as a convicted person, so that in such a case, strictly speaking, Article 6 would not be applicable. However, in the *Delcourt* Case, in which

---

515. Judgment of 26 October 1984, *De Cubber*, A.86 (1984), p. 18 (impliedly for civil cases).
516. See in particular the report of 3 July 1985, *Ettl*, A.117 (1987), pp. 23-26. In its judgment of 23 April 1987, *Ettl*, A.117, the Court held that there was no question of violation of Article 6(1), since Austria had made a reservation in this respect upon ratification of the Convention.
517. Report of 17 July 1980, *Kaplan*, D & R 21 (1981), p. 5 (31-33).
518. Judgment of 23 June 1981, *Le Compte, Van Leuven and De Meyere*, A.43 (1981), p. 23; judgment of 10 February 1983, *Albert and Le Compte*, A.58 (1983), p. 18; report of 3 July 1985, *Ettl*, A.117 (1987), p. 23.
519. Judgment of 27 June 1968, *Neumeister*, A.8 (1968), p. 41: "as this word is understood within the meaning of the Convention". See also the report of 8 February 1973, *Huber*, Yearbook XVIII (1975), p. 326 (356); report of 19 July 1974, *Engel*, B.20 (1974-1976), p. 70; and judgment of 26 March 1982, *Adolf*, A.49 (1982), p. 14.
520. Judgment of 27 February 1980, A.35 (1980), p. 23; judgment of 15 July 1982, *Eckle*, A.51 (1982), p. 33; judgment of 10 December 1982, *Corigliano*, A.57 (1982), p. 13.

the Court stressed the desirability of an extensive interpretation of Article 6, it held that the charge has not yet been determined in the sense of Article 6(1) as long as the decision to convict or release the prisoner, or to dismiss the charge, is not final.[521]

This means on the one hand that, although for criminal cases, too, Article 6 does not grant a right to appeal[522] - Protocol no. 7 contains a provision about this in Article 2[523] - the hearing of the case in appeal and in cassation does form part of the "determination", and therefore must equally satisfy the minimum standard laid down in Article 6.[524] The fact that the court of cassation in its investigation is confined to the legal grounds on which the lower court has based its sentence does not alter this,[525] no more than the circumstance that in some cases appeal and cassation no longer relate to the validity of the criminal prosecution as such, but exclusively to the penalty imposed.[526] On the other hand, procedures in which a decision is taken on requests for conditional release, revision, pardon or mitigation of penalty are not covered by Article 6(1), since in that case there is a sentence which has acquired the force of *res judicata*.[527] However, in the case of a revocation of a conditional release there is question of "determination of a criminal charge" in the sense of Article 6(1), because such a procedure may result in a renewed imposition of a penalty.[528] And in the above-mentioned cases Article 6(1) *is* of course applicable again if they involve at the same time civil rights or obligations.[529]

By analogy with procedures in which "civil rights and obligations" are at issue, procedures in which a given penalty is imposed in such a way that they thus acquire a criminal character, *per se* do not have to satisfy Article 6 in every respect, provided that an appeal procedure which itself does satisfy Article 6 is open to the person in question.[530] The Court has qualified this somewhat in the *De Cubber* Case by holding that this applies only to those cases in which under the domestic law the procedure is not of a criminal, but, *e.g.*, of a disciplinary or administrative character, while moreover the bodies taking the decision within the domestic system are not considered as

---

521. Judgment of 17 January 1970, A.11 (1970), p. 14.
522. *Ibidem*.
523. See *infra* pp. 508-511.
524. Judgment of 17 January 1970, *Delcourt*, A.11 (1970), p. 14. See further *supra*, with respect to "civil rights and obligations".
525. *Ibidem*.
526. Appl. 4623/70, *X v. United Kingdom*, Yearbook XV (1972), p. 376 (394-396).
527. See Appl. 1760/63, *X v. Austria*, Yearbook IX (1966), p. 166 (174) and the case-law mentioned therein. See also Appl. 9813/82, *X v. United Kingdom*, not published, concerning a change of prison location, and Appl. 10733/84, *Asociación de Aviadores de la República, Mata et al. v. Spain*, D & R 41 (1985), p. 211 (224): a dispute concerning an amnesty after conviction does not determine a "criminal charge".
528. Appl. 4036/69, *X v. United Kingdom*, Coll. 32 (1970), p. 73 (75).
529. Thus implicitly also the Commission: Appl. 1760/63, *X v. Austria*, Yearbook IX (1966), p. 166 (174).
530. Judgment of 23 June 1981, *Le Compte, Van Leuven and De Meyere*, A.43 (1981), p. 23; judgment of 10 February 1983, *Albert and Le Compte*, A.58 (1983), p. 16; judgment of 21 February 1984, *Öztürk*, A.73 (1984), p. 22. See also the reports of 8 July 1986, *Houart*, para. 36 and *Van Lierde*, para. 44.

"courts of the classic kind". If, however, procedures are concerned which are to be classified as "criminal" both in virtue of the Convention and under domestic law, and if the body which makes the "determination" is a "proper court in both the formal and the substantive meaning of the term", Article 6 applies to this body irrespective of whether appeal is possible. The flexible standpoint with regard to disciplinary and administrative proceedings

> cannot justify reducing the requirements of Article 6(1) in its traditional and natural sphere of application. A restrictive interpretation of this kind would not be consonant with the object and purpose of Article 6(1).[531]

6. In the *De Weer* Case the Court took the position that a "criminal charge" may already be at issue in the stage in which the prosecuting authorities make a proposal for a friendly settlement which will then prevent (further) criminal prosecution.[532] On the other hand, the Commission decided on a number of occasions that the mere fact that the police are making an investigation or that witnesses are being heard, or that a judicial organ makes a preliminary inquiry, does not yet mean that there is a "criminal charge".[533]

As a general definition of the concept of "charge" in the sense of Article 6(1) the Court has given the following description:

> the official notification given to an individual by the competent authority of an allegation that he has committed a criminal offence.[534]

In its judgment in the *Foti* Case the Court added to this:

> although it may in some instances take the form of other measures which carry the implication of such an allegation and which likewise substantially affect the situation of the suspect.[535]

The mere fact that a criminal prosecution is terminated or results in dismissal of the case does not mean that in retrospect Article 6 was not applicable to the procedure concerned, in particular not when the procedure has produced certain prejudicial consequences for the person who was originally accused.[536]

Whether the procedure resulting in a criminal prosecution has been instituted by an individual or the initiative was taken by a public authority is irrelevant for the applicability of Article 6.[537] However, the individual who takes the initiative to the procedure is not himself entitled to a determination of the charge by a court; he may be entitled to the determination of his civil rights if a civil claim can be and actually has been submitted in the criminal

---

531. Judgment of 26 October 1984, *De Cubber*, A.86 (1984), p. 18.
532. Judgment of 27 February 1980, A.35 (1980), pp. 23-24.
533. Appl. 4483/70, *X v. Federal Republic of Germany*, *Coll.* 38 (1972), p. 77 (79); Appl. 4649/70, *X v. Federal Republic of Germany*, *Coll.* 46 (1974), p. 1 (18); Appl. 8089/77, *X v. Austria*, not published.
534. Judgment of 15 July 1982, *Eckle*, A.51 (1982), p. 33.
535. Judgment of 10 December 1982, A.56 (1982), p. 18; judgment of 21 february 1984, *Öztürk*, A.73 (1984), p. 21.
536. Appl. 8269/78, *X v. Austria*, *Yearbook* XXII (1979), p. 324 (340-342). See also the judgment of 26 March 1982, *Adolf*, A.49 (1982), p. 16, concerning a decision that an offence was not punishable.
537. Judgment of 25 March 1983, *Minelli*, A.62 (1983), pp. 15-17.

proceedings.[538] On the other hand, if a third person is affected in an adverse manner in his rights by measures consequential upon the prosecution of others, no criminal charge has been brought against the former, who therefore cannot invoke the guarantees of Article 6 concerning criminal proceedings.[539]

7. The question of whether Article 6 is also applicable to disciplinary procedures was originally answered in the negative by the Commission.[540] In the *Engel* Case, however, the Commission as well as the Court took the position that the character of a procedure under domestic law cannot be decisive for the question of whether Article 6(1) is applicable, since otherwise the national authorities would be able to evade the obligations of that provision by introducing disciplinary procedures with respect to offences which, in view of their nature or the character of the sanction imposed, (also) form, or at any rate should form, part of criminal law.[541] For an answer to the question of whether a disciplinary procedure also implies "a criminal charge" in the sense of Article 6(1) the Court in its judgment developed the following criteria:

(1) The classification of the allegedly violated norm under the applicable domestic legal system. Does it belong to criminal law, to disciplinary law, or to both? The Court states that this criterion affords no more than a preliminary point of departure for the ultimate assessment, since the choice made by the national legislature in this respect is of relative importance only and has to be compared with the law applying in the other contracting States. That is why the following two criteria are considered more decisive by the Court:
(2) The actual scope of the violated norm. Has a norm been violated which concerns only a very specific group, or a norm with a generally binding character?
(3) The nature and the severity of the penalty with which the violator of the norm is threatened.[542]

---

538. Appl. 8366/78, *X v. Luxembourg, D & R* 16 (1979), p. 196 (198); Appl. 9660/82, *X v. France, D & R* 29 (1982), p. 241 (244).
539. Judgment of 24 October 1986, *Agosi,* A.108 (1986), p. 22.
540. See the case-law mentioned in the report of 19 July 1974, *Engel,* B.20 (1974-1976), pp. 68-69.
541. *Ibidem,* p. 70 and the judgment of 8 June 1976, A.22 (1977), p. 34.
542. The judgment mentioned in the preceding note, p. 35. The Commission, which had mentioned other criteria in its report, adopted the criteria of the Court in its later case-law: Appl. 6224/73, *Kiss v. United Kingdom, Yearbook* XX (1977), p. 156 (172-178). In its report of 14 December 1981, *Albert and Le Compte,* B.50 (1982-1983), p. 36, the Commission proposed yet a fourth criterion: the applicable rules concerning evidence. In general, in disciplinary procedures the person concerned has no right to remain silent and no right to invoke professional secrecy. This does not, however, appear to be a correct independent criterion, since it forms a consequence of the choice made by the national legislature between a criminal and a disciplinary procedure, and moreover a consequence that is detrimental to the position of the person concerned. See also the report of 7 May 1986, *Belilos,* A.132 (1988), p. 44.

On the ground of these criteria, the Court in the *Engel* Case concluded that here indeed offences were at issue against norms regulating the functioning of the Dutch armed forces, so that they could justly form the object of disciplinary procedures, but that for some of these offences an imprisonment of considerable duration could be imposed, for which reason the conditions of Article 6(1) ought to have been observed in the disciplinary procedures in question.[543]

The penalty which, theoretically speaking, might have been imposed on the applicant Engel - two days of strict arrest - was considered insufficient by the Court for it to be regarded as a criminal penalty, but it took a different position with regard to the detention of some months to which the applicants *De Wit*, *Dona* and *Schul* could have been sentenced.[544] On the ground of this latter criterion, the Commission held in the *Eggs* Case, which also concerned a case of military discipline and in which the penalty imposed was five days of strict arrest in a civil prison:

> Although relatively harsh, this freedom-restricting penalty could not, either by its duration or by the conditions of its enforcement in Basle prison, have caused serious detriment to the applicant. It could not, therefore, in this case be classified as criminal.[545]

This case-law has therefore left a good deal of uncertainty with regard to the criterion under (3). One may ask oneself whether it would not have been more appropriate if that criterion had been interpreted in such a way that in any case where the penalty consists of a deprivation of liberty in the sense assigned to that in the case-law concerning Article 5, the guarantees of Article 6(1) should be observed in the determination of whether the substantive and formal conditions for that imposition of a penalty have to be complied with. In its report in the *Albert and Le Compte* Case the Commission indeed observed quite generally with regard to a certain disciplinary measure:

---

543. A.22 (1977), p. 36. In the second case mentioned in the preceding note, where disciplinary measures against a prisoner were concerned, the Commission arrived at a negative conclusion, because it did not consider the possible penalty, loss of the prospect of reduction of the penalty, a deprivation of liberty.
544. *Engel*, A.22 (1977), p. 36.
545. Report of 4 March 1978, *D & R* 15 (1979), p. 35 (65). See also Appl. 7754/77, *X v. Switzerland*, *D & R* 11 (1978), p. 216 (218), where by reference to the criteria developed by the Court the Commission came to the conclusion that isolated confinement of a person who is already detained, as a penalty for late return from leave of absence, is a purely disciplinary matter, for which the procedural guarantees prescribed in Article 6(1) need not be complied with. The Commission here took into account the consideration that for a person already deprived of his liberty such a confinement is not of such a "severity" as meant by the Court. In the report of 17 July 1980, *Kaplan*, the Commission held that the restrictions imposed on the company did not concern a "criminal charge", because these restrictions could not be regarded as a penalty; *D & R* 21 (1981), p. 5 (35). In the decision on Appl. 8249/78, *X v. Belgium*, *D & R* 20 (1980), p. 40 (42) concerning a disciplinary reprimand *vis-à-vis* a solicitor it is said that "the sanction imposed was intrinsically not a severe one". Finally, if a person brings disciplinary complaints against a third person, the former cannot claim any right under Article 6: Appl. 10634/83, *X v. United Kingdom*, not published.

it cannot be treated as being equivalent to a penal sanction, such as the deprivation of liberty.[546]

In a decision of 1983 the Commission also took into consideration the amount of fines which the applicant risked, in addition to the length of the detention. It concluded with the consideration that

> the sanctions which the applicant had to face in this case attained the level of severity which, according to the common standard of the Convention States, must be considered as being proper to "criminal charges" in the sense of the Convention.[547]

It is, however, this "common standard" which is not clear and has not yet been elaborated in the Strasbourg case-law.

In a case concerning IRA prisoners the Commission took the position that for the determination of the severity of the penalty imposed the cumulative effect of repeatedly imposed penalties should not be taken into account, because for the applicability of Article 6 each sentence must be considered by itself.[548] From this it would appear that the present state of the case-law leaves still too much uncertainty on this point and leads to unsatisfactory results. Indeed, although the Commission's view is formally correct, it may have the consequence that without any intervention of a court a person may be subjected to restrictions which in combination amount to a much heavier burden for him than the sanction which in a separate case would confer a criminal-law character on the procedure. The question arises whether one ought not to seek a certain analogy here with the case-law concerning Article 5(3), where, for the determination of the reasonableness of the period, also successive periods of detention for various charges are taken into account together,[549] so that it is the total situation in which the person finds himself which is taken as the starting-point, and not the separate measures taken against him.

In the *Campbell and Fell* Case the procedure could have resulted in refusal of remission of part of the imprisonment. The Court held that the practice of remission of the penalty creates for the detainee the justifiable expectation that he will be released before the end of the detention period. The procedure might therefore have such serious consequences for the person concerned as to the duration of his detention that it was to be considered of a criminal character.[550]

8. There has long been a lack of clarity as to the question of whether Article 6(1) applies to all criminal proceedings, even when offences of a less serious

---

546. Report of 14 December 1981, B.50 (1982-1983), p. 35. In its decision on Appl. 8209/78, *Sutter v. Switzerland, D & R* 16 (1979), p. 116 (173) the Commission also argues quite generally: "The applicant was charged with an offence under the Military Penal Code, punishable by imprisonment, and therefore he was undoubtedly accused of a criminal offence". Also quite generally: report of 6 May 1981, *Minelli*, B.52 (1986), p. 21.
547. Appl. 8998/80, *X v. Austria, D & R* 32 (1983), p. 150 (151-153).
548. Appl. 8317/78, *McFeeley et al. v. United Kingdom, D & R* 20 (1980), p. 44 (94).
549. Judgment of 27 June 1968, *Neumeister*, A.8 (1968), p. 37; judgment of 16 July 1971, *Ringeisen*, A.13 (1971), pp. 41-42.
550. Judgment of 28 June 1984, A.80 (1984), pp. 37-38.

nature are concerned. In fact, the Commission had included, quite super-fluously, in its decision on Appl. 8537/79 the following observation:

even assuming that Art. 6 of the Convention applies to proceedings concerning summary offences (*Ordnungswidrigkeiten*) of the kind here in question.[551]

Since Article 6 does not distinguish between a criminal charge of a serious and one of a lighter nature, and the determination of a criminal charge concerning a petty offence may be of great importance for the person in question, every procedure in which there is question of a determination of a criminal charge should fall under the guarantees of Article 6. This view has been adopted by the Court. In the *Adolf* Case, in which a petty offence was involved, which on that ground was declared non-punishable, the Court held:

non-punishable or unpunished criminal offences do exist and Article 6 of the Convention does not distinguish between them and other criminal offences; it applies whenever a person is "charged" with any criminal offence .[552]

And in the *Öztürk* Case, too, the Court held:

There is in fact nothing to suggest that the criminal offence referred to in the Convention necessarily implies a certain degree of seriousness ... . Furthermore, it would be contrary to the object and purpose of Article 6, which guarantees to "everyone charged with a criminal offence" the right to a court and to a fair trial, if the State were allowed to remove from the scope of this Article a whole category of offences merely on the ground of regarding them as petty.[553]

The Court also indicated in the *Öztürk* Case that in itself it does not conflict with the Convention to distinguish between different categories of offences, but that such a classification is not decisive for the question whether Article 6 is applicable.[554] In this case an offence was involved which was not qualified under German law as a criminal but as an administrative offence: an *Ordnungswidrigkeit*. The question whether the procedure in which a decision is taken about such an offence, and the sanction that may be imposed, no longer fell under the application of Article 6 as a result of such a "decrimi-nalization" was of great importance, since in the Federal Republic of Germany, as well as in other countries, there is a strong tendency to transfer certain petty offences from the criminal sphere to the administrative sphere. In the Netherlands, with regard to the adjudication of petty traffic offences, a kind of middle course has been taken, whereby the procedure is still regulated in the Code of Criminal Procedure, but the decriminalization finds expression in the fact that this regulation deviates on a number of points from the ordinary rules of criminal procedure. Quite in line with its case-law concerning Article 6 the Court here again is on its guard against erosion of the guarantees aimed at in that article:

if the Contracting States were able at their discretion, by classifying an offence as "regulatory" instead of criminal, to exclude the operation of the fundamental clauses of

---

551. Appl. 8537/79, *X v. Federal Republic of Germany*, not published.
552. Judgment of 26 March 1982, A.49 (1982), p. 16.
553. Judgment of 21 February 1984, A.73 (1984), p. 21. See also the report of 18 October 1985, *Lutz*, A.123 (1987), p. 33 and the judgment of 29 April 1988, *Belilos*, A.132 (1988), p. 28.
554. *Ibidem*, p. 18.

Articles 6 and 7, the application of these provisions would be subordinated to their sovereign will. A latitude extending thus far might lead to results incompatible with the object and purpose of the Convention.[555]

Consequently, it remains decisive whether the nature of the offence, and that of the sanction that may be imposed, confer a criminal character on the procedure of determination, irrespective of whether it still has that character formally under domestic law.[556]

9. Since Article 6 is applicable only to procedures which result in a determination of a criminal charge, a procedure by which a preventive detention may be imposed on the mere ground of an existing suspicion, without it being necessary to establish whether this suspicion is well-founded, is outside the scope of this provision.[557] In that case Article 5 *is* of course applicable. Equally, since the prohibition to enter a country does not amount to a criminal penalty, Article 6 cannot be applicable on that ground,[558] but may apply for other reasons, *e.g.*, since civil rights are involved, while also other provisions of the Convention, as Article 3 or Article 8, may be applicable. Finally, extradition procedures are held, thus far, not to be covered by Article 6 on the ground that "determination" involves the full process of the examination of an individual's guilt or innocence of an offence, and not the mere process of determining whether a person can be extradited to another country.[559]

10. As has already been mentioned, in the *Golder* Case the Commission and the Court developed the view that Article 6(1) not only contains certain guarantees for judicial procedures, but also grants a right to a judicial procedure for the cases mentioned there.[560] For this interpretation the Court relied on the text of Article 6(1), placed in the context of the object and the purpose of the Convention, for which it referred to the preamble of the Convention, the preamble of the Statute of the Council of Europe and Article 3 of that Statute, in which the principle of the "rule of law" is laid down. Furthermore the Court referred to a generally accepted legal principle according to which a claim must be capable of being submitted to a court,

555. Judgment of 21 February 1983, *Öztürk*, A.73 (1984), p. 18.
556. The criteria handled by the Court in such a case have been set forth at length in the *Öztürk* judgment; pp. 17-22. See also the report of 18 October 1985, *Lutz*, A.123 (1987), pp. 32-33. In its judgment of 25 August 1987 in this case, the Court repeats these criteria, indicating in this context that these criteria are alternative, and not cumulative; A.123 (1987), p. 23.
557. Report of 7 December 1978, *Guzzardi*, B.35 (1978), pp. 42-43.
558. Appl. 9593/81, *X v. Switzerland*, not published. The same holds good for the removal as an illegal entrant, since the determination of a breach of the immigration regulations is not the determination of a criminal charge, and the removal not a criminal penalty: Appl. 9174/80, *Zamir v. United Kingdom*, *D & R* 29 (1982), p. 153 (163-164).
559. Appl. 10227/85, *X v. Spain*, not published.
560. Report of 1 June 1973, B.16 (1973-1975), pp. 44-45 and judgment of 21 February 1975, A.18 (1975), pp. 16-18 respectively. Implicitly already the Commission in its report of 19 March 1970, *Ringeisen*, B.11 (1970-1971), p. 69.

and which prohibits denial of justice.[561] If Article 6(1) were to afford guarantees only for judicial procedures already provided for, these guarantees might be rendered illusory if the courts were deprived wholly or partly of their jurisdiction and these procedures were replaced, for instance, by administrative procedures.[562] As the Commission clearly states in its report in the *Kaplan* Case:

> Art. 6 thus requires that there should be a court with jurisdiction to determine the matter. The right to a court arises with the claim or dispute in question.[563]

When interpreted in this way, Article 6(1) to a considerable extent takes over the function of Article 13, which guarantees a right to an effective remedy. On the one hand Article 6 goes much further, because it implies a right of recourse to a *court* and applies to all determinations of civil rights and obligations, and not only to those which are related to one of the rights laid down in the Convention. Moreover, domestic courts may be more willing to recognize direct applicability in the case of Article 6(1) than in the case of Article 13. On the other hand Article 13 remains important for cases of violation of one of the rights which according to the Strasbourg case-law is not a "civil right" in the sense of Article 6(1).[564]

As regards the "civil rights and obligations", this implies that the person concerned not only has a right to apply for the "determination" thereof to a court and to institute the required procedure,[565] but also has a right to it that there is a competent and independent court to make this "determination":

> it may also be relied on by anyone who considers that an interference with the exercise of one of his (civil) rights is unlawful and complains that he has not had the possibility of submitting that claim to a tribunal meeting the requirements of Article 6(1).[566]

That court must then have sufficient powers to make the determination. Thus, in the cases of *W, B and R v. United Kingdom* the Court held that although the parents could apply for judicial review or institute wardship proceedings and thereby have certain aspects of the authority's access decisions examined by an English court, the latter's powers were not sufficient during the currency of the parental resolutions to satisfy fully the requirements of Article 6, para. 1, as they did not extend to the merits of the matter.[567]

For criminal cases this right of access to court does not imply the right for the victim of a criminal offence to institute himself a criminal prosecution or to have such prosecution instituted by the public prosecutor.[568] For the

---

561. A.18 (1975), pp. 16-17.
562. *Ibidem*, pp. 17-18. See in this respect also the report of 8 October 1983, *Benthem*, A.97 (1986), pp. 24-25.
563. Report of 17 July 1980, *D & R* 21 (1981), p. 5 (33).
564. Thus the Court in its judgment of 21 February 1975, *Golder*, A.18 (1975), p. 16.
565. Judgment of 9 October 1979, *Airey*, A.32, pp. 11-16.
566. Judgment of 23 June 1981, *Le Compte, Van Leuven and De Meyere*, A.43 (1981), p. 20. See also the judgment of 23 September 1982, *Sporrong and Lönroth*, A.52 (1982), p. 30 and the judgment of 28 May 1985, *Ashingdane*, A.93 (1985), p. 24.
567. Judgments of 8 July 1987, A.121 (1987), pp. 35-36, 79-80 and 125-126 respectively.
568. Appl. 6224/73, *Kiss v. United Kingdom*, Yearbook XX (1977), p. 156 (178-180); Appl. 9777/84, *T v. Belgium*, *D & R* 34 (1983), p. 158 (171-172).

accused it does not guarantee that he may demand the continuation of the prosecution and an ultimate trial by a court, but only that, when a sentence is pronounced, this is done by a court.[569] However, if the charge is dropped on the basis of a financial transaction between the accused and the prosecuting authority, without there being question of a free choice on the part of the accused, he is actually denied access to court contrary to Article 6(1).[570] And if the case is dropped under circumstances in which the odium of guilt would continue to cling to the person in question, Article 6(1) has nevertheless been violated; this also in the light of the presumption of innocence of the second paragraph.[571]

The foregoing implies that the right of access to court laid down in Article 6(1) is not an absolute right. It may be freely waived, provided that this has taken place in a clear manner.[572] Moreover, certain implicit restrictions apply in the sense that a criminal prosecution may also be terminated without intervention of a court, provided that this does not lead to a formal or factual "determination". The legislature may also lay down specific restrictive rules for access to court with regard to, for instance, minors or mentally deficient persons.[573] These restrictions, however, may not impair the right of access in its very essence for the person concerned.[574] Moreover, the limitations applied must pursue a legitimate aim, while there must be a reasonable relationship of proportionality between the means employed and the aim sought to be achieved.[575]

In the *Airey* Case it was held that the right of access to court of Article 6(1), although it does not imply an automatic right to free legal aid in civil proceedings, *does* involve the obligation for the contracting States to make access to court possible by either giving the accused a compensation for his legal costs if he is unable to pay, or reducing the costs of the suit, simplifying the proceedings or the conditions of the suit, or providing for free legal aid; all this under the condition that these costs were necessary for instituting the

569. Report of 18 October 1985, *Lutz*, A.123 (1985), p. 35.
570. Judgment of 27 February 1980, *De Weer*, A.35 (1980), pp. 25-29. In this case the person in question was subject to the threat that his shop would be closed if he did not agree to the transaction. With respect to the determination of civil rights and obligations, too, the "right to a court" can be waived, *e.g.* in an arbitration clause, but also then there must be no question of constraint: Appl. 1197/61, *X v. Federal Republic of Germany*, Yearbook V (1962), p. 88 (94-96). The same also applies to the grant of amnesty; Appl. 9005/80, *X v. Italy*, not published.
571. See judgment of 25 March 1983, *Minelli*, A.62 (1983), p. 18.
572. Judgment of 7 May 1974, *Neumeister*, A.17 (1974), p. 16; judgment of 23 June 1981, *Le Compte, Van Leuven and De Meyere*, A.43 (1981), pp. 25-26; judgment of 10 february 1983, *Albert and Le Compte*, A.58 (1983), p. 19; and the judgments of 12 February 1985, *Colozza and Rubinat*, A.89 (1985), p. 14.
573. Judgment of 21 February 1975, *Golder*, A.18 (1975), p. 19.
574. Judgment of 24 October 1979, *Winterwerp*, A.33 (1980), p. 29.
575. Judgment of 28 May 1985, *Ashingdane*, A.93 (1985), pp. 24-25; judgment of 8 July 1986, *Lithgow*, A.102 (1986), p. 71.

proceedings and/or for an adequate presentation of the case or the defence.[576] Against the background of this case-law the Commission's view that the fact of excessive costs being involved for the accused in taking evidence does not imply a violation of Article 6 also had to be modified.[577] So it did in an unpublished decision of 1984, where the Commission said that in certain circumstances the high costs could raise a problem under Article 6(1).[578] In an unpublished decision of 1982, the Commission concluded that, although it was recognized that the intended action would require the assistance of a lawyer, the refusal of legal aid did not constitute a denial of access to court, since the argument given by the Swedish authorities for the refusal, *viz.* that the applicant did not have a justified interest in having her case examined, was not arbitrary.[579] This would put the decision on the interests involved in the hands of an authority other than the court, while the right of access to court precisely requires the opposite. In our opinion, if such a practice were accepted in cases where access to court is only possible through counsel, the very essence of the right of access to court might be impaired, to use the phrase from the judgments in the *Ashingdane* and *Lithgow* Cases.[580]

In the *Golder* Case the Court attached to its view that Article 6 implies a right of access to court and that "hindering the effective exercise of a right may amount to a breach of that right, even if the hindrance is of a temporary character", the consequence that a refusal to permit detainees to correspond with persons providing legal aid or their counsel is contrary to this provision.[581] Moreover, the detainee has a right to contact with counsel or a person giving legal aid without the presence of a prison authority.[582] However, the applicant must have taken the measures reasonably to be expected from him to conduct his defence.[583]

In the *Klass* Case, to be discussed more fully below,[584] a drastic restriction was imposed on the right of access to court as developed in the Strasbourg case-law. Article 6(1) was invoked by the applicants, because the challenged legislation, which permitted interference with correspondence and wire-tapping for security reasons without the knowledge of the person concerned, had excluded the normal recourse to a court and replaced it by supervision by a parliamentary committee. Apart from the question of whether this case

---

576. Report of 9 March 1978, B.30 (1982), p. 32; judgment of 9 October 1979, A.32 (1980), pp. 11-16. See also Appl. 8158/78, *X v. United Kingdom, D & R* 21 (1981), p. 95 (101) and Appl. 9353/81, *Webb v. United Kingdom, D & R* 33 (1983), p. 133 (138-141), where the Commission made an independent investigation in the complexity of the case, the applicable rules of evidence, *etc.*
577. Appl. 1982/63, *X v. Austria,* not published.
578. Appl. 9379/81, *X v. Switzerland,* not published.
579. Appl. 9649/82, *X v. Sweden,* not published.
580. See *supra* note 575.
581. Judgment of 21 February 1975, A.18, pp. 12-20. See also the report of 11 October 1980, *Silver,* B.51 (1981-1983), pp. 100-101, the judgment of 28 June 1984, *Campbell and Fell,* A.80 (1984), pp. 46-47, and the report of 3 December 1985, *Byrne, McFadden, McCluskey and McLarnon,* paras 148-149.
582. Judgment of 28 June 1984, *Campbell and Fell,* A.80 (1984), p. 49.
583. Appl. 9503/81, *X v. United Kingdom,* not published.
584. See *infra* pp. 528-530.

concerned civil rights or a criminal charge, the Court held that a distinction should be made between the phase in which the measures could be taken without informing the person concerned and the phase in which there was no longer any ground for secrecy:

> As long as it [the security control exercised] remains validly secret, the decision placing someone under surveillance is thereby incapable of judicial control on the initiative of the person concerned, within the meaning of Article 6; as a consequence, it of necessity escapes the requirements of that Article.[585]

The Court was faced here with the difficult choice between, on the one hand, unlimited application of the principle of "access to court", a principle which it had itself developed, and, on the other hand, the necessity for the national authorities to be able to carry out an effective security control for the protection of the democratic values underlying the Convention. The Court has opted for the latter, imposing restrictions on the first-mentioned principle via what might be called a systematic interpretation of Article 6(1) in relation to Article 8(2). But the Court also emphasized, just as the German *Bundesverfassungsgericht* had done, that the secrecy *vis-à-vis* the person concerned must not last any longer than is required for the protection of the interest envisaged by the measures, after which period access to court is fully open again for the person in question.[586] The said parliamentary committee will then have to take particular care that the person in question is indeed informed as soon as the situation permits, since otherwise the national judicial review as well as the Strasbourg review might be rendered completely illusory.

11. Article 6 demands a "fair hearing". When is a hearing fair? The Commission and the Court have taken the position that *in abstracto* no enumeration of criteria can be given for this, but that in each individual case the course of the proceedings has to be assessed. What counts is the picture which the proceedings as a whole present,[587] although certain aspects *per se* may already conflict with the principle of a fair hearing in such a way that an opinion can be given about this irrespective of the further course of the proceedings,[588] *e.g.*, the way in which the evidence is collected during a preliminary hearing.

For civil proceedings the Commission has defined the term "fair hearing" to imply the guarantee

> that everyone who is a party to civil proceedings shall have a reasonable opportunity of presenting his case to the Court under conditions which do not place him under a substantial disadvantage *vis-à-vis* his opponent.[589]

585. Judgment of 6 September 1978, *Klass*, A.28 (1979), pp. 32-33.
586. *Ibidem*, pp. 32-33 in conjunction with p. 31.
587. Report of 15 March 1961, *Nielsen*, Yearbook IV (1961), p. 494 (568). This is standing case-law; see, *e.g.*, Appl. 9000/80, *X v. Switzerland*, D & R 28 (1982), p. 127 (133-135); judgment of 20 November 1989, *Kostovski*, A.166 (1990), p. 19; judgment of 6 December 1988, *Barberá, Messegué and Jabardo*, A.146 (1988), p. 31.
588. Appls 8603, 8722, 8723 and 8729/79, *Crociani et al. v. Italy*, Yearbook XXIV (1981), p. 222 (254).
589. Appl. 434/58, *X v. Sweden*, Yearbook II (1958-1959), p. 354 (370-372); Appl. 7450/76, *X v. Belgium*, D & R 9 (1978), p. 108 (110).

Thus, in the *Bricmont* Case the applicants complained that their opponent, Prince Charles of Belgium, was in a privileged position throughout the proceedings. They adduced as evidence of this the manner in which Prince Charles was heard, the lack of confrontation on all of the charges and at all events on the charges of intellectual forgery, and the fact that apart from Prince Charles and the applicants themselves, the person best informed about the accusations against them was not heard as a witness during the proceedings. After a detailed examination the Commission came to the conclusion that the applicants were in a less favourable situation than Prince Charles.[590]

For criminal cases, where the character of the proceedings already involves a fundamental inequality of the parties, this principle of "equality of arms" is even more important, and the same applies, though to a lesser degree, to administrative procedures.[591] This emphasis placed by the Commission on the principle of the "equality of arms" has been adopted by the Court.[592]

Certain aspects of a "fair hearing" are expressly stated for criminal cases in paragraphs 2 and 3 of Article 6, but the guarantees implied in the requirement of a "fair hearing" in paragraph 1 fully apply to criminal proceedings as well, and this - as the Commission also observes - *a fortiori*;[593] the content of the term "fair hearing" therefore is not confined, not even for criminal cases, to the provisions of paragraphs 2 and 3 of Article 6.[594]

The principle of "equality of arms" implies in particular that no elements of the examination of the case may be settled when one party is present or represented, but the other is not.[595] Phases in the examination during which neither of the parties was present are not considered contrary to Article 6 by the Commission on that ground alone.[596] The fact that in Belgium the Public Prosecutor participates in the deliberations of the court of cassation does not conflict in the Court's opinion with the principle of the "equality of arms", because of his independent position in relation to the Minister of Justice and of the fact that he cannot give orders or instructions to the Public Prosecutor in concrete cases.[597] The same view was adopted by the Commission with regard to the Dutch cassation procedure.[598] However, the fact that such an independent organ participates in the proceedings and gives an opinion to the

---

590. Report of 15 October 1987, paras 131-144.
591. See the judgment of 29 May 1986, *Feldbrugge*, A.99 (1986), p. 17.
592. Judgment of 27 June 1968, *Neumeister*, A.8 (1968), p. 43. See also the judgment of 17 January 1970, *Delcourt*, A.11 (1970), p. 15 and the judgment of 6 May 1985, *Bönisch*, A.92 (1985), pp. 14-16.
593. Appl. 1169/61, *X v. Federal Republic of Germany, Yearbook* VI (1963), p. 520 (572). See also Appl. 7413/76, *X v. United Kingdom, D & R* 9 (1978), p. 100 (101).
594. See the report of 15 March 1961, *Nielsen, Yearbook* IV (1961), p. 494 (548-550). See also Appl. 8289/78, *X v. Austria, D & R* 18 (1980), p. 160 (166-167).
595. See, *inter alia*, the judgment of 27 June 1968, *Neumeister*, A.8 (1968), p. 43.
596. Appl. 1793/62, *X v. Austria, Yearbook* VI (1963), p. 458 (460); Appl. 7413/76, *X v. United Kingdom, D & R* 9 (1978), p. 100 (101); Appl. 11129/84, *Brown v. United Kingdom, D & R* 42 (1985), p. 269 (272).
597. Judgment of 17 January 1970, *Delcourt*, A.11 (1970), pp. 16-19. The Court did, however, give expression to its doubts concerning "the satisfactory nature of the system in dispute".
598. Appl. 3692/68, *X v. the Netherlands, Yearbook* XIII (1970), p. 516 (522).

court does not make it less necessary for the accused to be given legal aid.[599] In the *Bönisch* Case the Court found that the expert involved in the proceedings and the powers given to that expert insufficiently guaranteed the latter's neutrality, so that he had to be considered as a witness for the prosecution rather than as an expert. Since the accused had not been given the same opportunity to call such an "expert", the principle of the "equality of arms" had been violated.[600]

Furthermore, the principle of "equality of arms" entails that the parties must have the same access to the records and other documents in the case, at least in so far as these play a part in the formation of the court's opinion.[601] A particular way in which this information must be given or be available does not follow from this, provided that no insuperable obstacles are created which in fact amount to withholding information.[602] The one party must also be given the opportunity to oppose the arguments advanced by the other party.[603] In addition, the principle entails that the two parties are afforded the same possibility to summon witnesses and experts, and that the latter in turn receive the same treatment.[604]

That the precept of a "fair hearing" in principle entails the right of the parties to be present in person at the trial is implied in the term "fair hearing" itself. Indeed, in the *Monnell and Morris* Case, the Commission took as a starting point for criminal proceedings that

> Article 6 of the Convention requires that the accused person must normally be present and be able to be heard.[605]

And in the *Colloza* Case the Court stated that

> although this is not expressly mentioned in para. 1 of Article 6, the object and the purpose of the Article as a whole show that a person "charged with a criminal offence" is entitled to take part in the hearing.[606]

In the *Ekbatani* Case the Court had to deal with a complaint concerning a conviction at first instance which was upheld by the court of cassation without a hearing. The Court stated in the first place that the notion of "fair trial" implies that persons charged with a criminal offence, as a principle, are entitled to be present at the first instance trial. It thereupon rejected the

---

599. Report of 12 December 1981, *Pakelli*, B.53 (1982-1983), p. 28.
600. Judgment of 6 May 1985, A.92 (1985), pp. 14-16.
601. Appl. 7317/75, *Lynas v. Switzerland, Yearbook* XX (1977), p. 412 (445-446); Appl. 9433/81, *Menten v. the Netherlands, D & R* 28 (1982), p. 233.
602. Appl. 8289/78, *X v. Austria, D & R* 18 (1980), p. 160 (167-168).
603. Appl. 8209/78, *Sutter v. Switzerland, D & R* 16 (1979), p. 166 (175). See also the judgment of 29 May 1986, *Feldbrugge*, A.99 (1986), pp. 17-18. There the Court came to the conclusion that Art. 6(1) had been violated, since applicant had not been given the opportunity to give her comment upon the report of a medical expert, which was of decisive importance for the outcome of the proceedings.
604. Judgment of 6 May 1985, *Bönisch*, A.92 (1985), p. 15.
605. Report of 11 March 1985, A.115 (1987), p. 39. Also the Court in its judgment of 2 March 1987 in the same case, *ibidem*, p. 23.
606. Judgment of 12 February 1985, A.89 (1985), p. 14. Report of 5 May 1983, *ibidem*, pp. 30-31. See also the report of 2 March 1988, *Brozicek*, paras 82-83; judgment of 2 March 1987, *Monnell and Morris*, A.115 (1987), p. 25, and judgment of 6 December 1988, *Barberá, Messegué and Jabardo*, A.146 (1989), pp. 33-34.

Government's argument, based on Article 2 of Protocol no. 7, that only the fundamental guarantees of Article 6 applied in the appeal proceedings and that these did not include further oral hearings before courts of second instance. The Court held that the manner of application of Article 6 to proceedings before courts of appeal depends on the special features of the domestic proceedings viewed as a whole. In the circumstances of the case, the applicant's guilt or innocence, the main question also before the court of appeal, could not have been properly determined without a direct assessment, at a full rehearing, of the evidence given in person by the applicant.[607] In the Case of *Barberá, Messegué and Jabardo* the Court held it to be in violation of a fair hearing if the accused is treated in a way which lowers his physical and mental resistance during the hearing.[608]

It may be important for the accused to be admitted in person to the court room, for instance to be able to answer questions directly, to know what defence is put forward on his behalf, and to be able to contradict any testimony of witnesses himself or via his counsel. If it is to be assumed that his presence in person may for one reason or another be important for the formation of the court's opinion and/or that of the jury, no "fair hearing" can be spoken of in the absence of the person concerned unless there are very urgent reasons.[609]

The importance of the presence in person also depends on the nature of the hearing and its meaning in the context of the proceedings as a whole, on the competence of the organ before which the hearing takes place and on the interests which are at stake for the person in question.[610] In its assessment of the fair character of a hearing at which the person himself has not been present, the Commission also involves the question whether his interests have been put forward adequately and have found protection,[611] but it is of course difficult to ascertain whether his personal contribution would not have made a difference after all.

The foregoing of course does not bar judgment by default, provided that the person in question has been summoned by the prescribed procedure and sufficient guarantees are attached to this procedure, also considering the provisions applying in other contracting States in this respect.[612] If the person in question explicitly intimates that he waives the possibility of being heard

607. Judgment of 26 May 1988, A.134 (1988), pp. 12-14.
608. Judgment of 6 December 1988, A.146 (1989), p. 31.
609. Appl. 434/58, *X v. Sweden*, Yearbook II (1958-1959), p. 354 (370-372); Appl. 8289/78, *X v. Austria*, D & R 18 (1980), p. 160 (166-167); Appl. 9315/81, *J v. Austria*, D & R 34 (1983), p. 96 (97-99); Appl. 9818/82, *M v. United Kingdom*, D & R 35 (1984), p. 117 (121-122).
610. Report of 11 March 1985, *Monnell and Morris*, A.115 (1987), pp. 39-40. In cassation proceedings, where the emphasis is on legal questions, the presence in person will in general be less important: Appl. 1169/61, *X v. Federal Republic of Germany*, Yearbook VI (1963), p. 520 (572).
611. Report of 11 March 1985, *Monnell and Morris*, A.115 (1987), pp. 39-40.
612. See Resolution (75)11 of the Committee of Ministers "on the criteria governing proceedings held in the absence of the accused"; Council of Europe, *Resolutions by the Committee of Ministers relating to crime problems*, Vol. III (1977).

in person, the matter is simple, but if it is not certain whether he is really aware that proceedings are taking place against him and that he has been summoned for a hearing, the Court examines the carefulness of the procedure by means of which contact has been sought with him.[613] In any case the fact that the accused is detained is, of course, no reason for his not being heard.[614]

A fair trial may imply the right to have the assistance of a lawyer, also during the phase preceding the trial. This aspect will be discussed under paragraph 3(c). Is it also possible to infer a right to free legal aid from the principle of fair hearing? From paragraph 3(c) it might be concluded *a contrario* that this is not the case.[615] In fact, paragraph 3(c) only mentions this right for criminal proceedings, and even then only "when the interests of justice so require". However, if one party does have the means to secure legal aid and the other does not, it is hardly possible to speak of "equality of arms" if the latter does not obtain the assistance of a lawyer as well. Above, the view of the Commission and the Court has already been mentioned that the mere right of "access to court" which is implied in Article 6(1) entails the obligation for the contracting States to make legal aid available, or at least financially possible, if otherwise the person in question would be faced with an insuperable barrier to defend himself adequately.[616] In that context the Strasbourg organs make an independent examination of the complexity of the case and other relevant factors such as the applicable rules of evidence and the emotional involvement of the applicant in the outcome of the proceedings.[617] Other expenses, too, for instance for a translator or an interpreter, may be so onerous that the principle of "fair trial" is at stake.[618]

The same applies to the question of whether under Article 6(1) the parties are entitled to have witnesses and experts summoned and examined. From the fact that Article 6(3)(d) contains explicit rules about this for criminal cases it might be inferred *a contrario* that such a right does not hold good for the parties to civil proceedings. However, here again the case-law recognizes the possibility that the court's refusal to have a particular witness summoned by a party to a dispute, or to hear him, constitutes an encroachment on the right to a "fair hearing".[619]

The principle of "fair hearing" also entails specific requirements with respect to evidence. Apart from the fact that each party must have equal opportunities for refuting the evidence brought forward by the other party, and consequently must have access to the relevant information, the evidence

---

613. Judgment of 12 February 1985, *Colozza*, A.89 (1985), p. 12.
614. Report of 11 March 1986, *Colozza*, A.115 (1987), p. 41. See also the judgment of 2 March 1987, *ibidem*, pp. 22-24.
615. Thus the standing case-law of the Commission; see, *e.g.*, Appl. 6202/73, *X and Y v. the Netherlands*, D & R 1 (1975), p. 66 (71).
616. *Supra* pp. 316-317.
617. Appl. 9353/81, *Webb v. United Kingdom*, D & R 33 (1983), p. 133 (138-141).
618. Report of 18 May 1977, *Luedicke, Belkacem and Koç*, B.27 (1982), p. 26.
619. See, *e.g.*, Appl. 5362/72, *X v. Austria*, Coll. 42 (1973), p. 145; Appl. 9000/80, *X v. Switzerland*, D & R 28 (1982), p. 127 (133-135).

produced must also be sufficiently "direct" if it is to admit actually refutation during the public hearing.[620]

In this context the *Unterpertinger* Case is of great importance. In that case the complaint concerned the fact that a criminal conviction was based exclusively on testimony of witnesses before the police and an investigating judge, while the same persons had refused to bear witness at the trial, invoking their right to refuse to answer questions because they were relatives of the accused. The fact that their testimony had been read out at the trial was not considered in itself by the Court as contrary to a fair hearing. But then in the further use of this evidence the rights of the defence must be respected, in particular if the accused has not previously been afforded the opportunity to question those who have made this testimony or have them questioned. Since the applicant had been given the opportunity by the court to comment at the trial on the testimony read out, but his request to be permitted to give counter-evidence via witnesses and an expert had been refused, his rights as an accused had been curtailed to such an extent that there was no question of a fair trial. Although the testimony in question did not constitute the sole evidence, the conviction of the accused had mainly been based thereon, so that Article 6(1) and 6(3)(d) had been violated.[621] In the *Kostovski* Case the Commission first referred to its case-law concerning caes where the hearsay evidence was corroborated by further evidence or a confession of the accused himself. In the present case, however, the evidence consisted exclusively in the declaration of two anonymous witnesses. Both the Commission and the Court concluded therefore that there had been a violation of paragraph 1 read in conjunction with paragraph 3 (d) of Article 6 of the Convention.[622] From this case-law it may be concluded that a court decision which is exclusively or almost exclusively based upon this kind of indirect evidence, has not been taken in accordance with the fair-trial requirement, unless in some way or another an adequate possibility for contradiction and counter-evidence has been afforded. The same holds good with respect to other evidence, such as tape recordings; defence against its contents must be allowed and still be practicable. According to the Court Article 6(1) does not require access to the tape itself. Its relevance for the fairness of the trial depends *inter alia* on the vital character of the contents of the tape for the evidence, while it is also relevant whether the transcript of the tape has been verified by an independent person.[623] And the evidence

---

620. See in this context Appl. 8414/78, *X v. Federal Republic of Germany, D & R* 17 (1980), p. 231 (233-234) and Appl. 8417/78, *X v. Belgium, D & R* 16 (1979), p. 200 (207-208). In the *Kamasinski* Case the Commission held it to be in violation of Article 6(1) that no note had been given to the applicant or his representative of the contents of the information which the judge, acting as rapporteur, had obtained by telephone from the judge of the regional court who had presided over the trial, report of 5 May 1988, paras 188-195.
621. Judgment of 24 November 1986, A.110 (1986), pp. 14-15. See also the judgment of 6 December 1988, *Barberá, Messegué and Jabardo,* A.146 (1989), pp. 25-26.
622. Report of 12 May 1988, paras 48-52; judgment of 20 November 1989, A.166 (1990), p. 21.
623. Judgment of 24 November 1986, *Gillow,* A.109 (1987), p. 28. See also the judgment of 12 July 1988, *Schenk,* A.140 (1988), pp. 29-30.

must have been collected by legal means.[624] Evidence that has been obtained contrary to the norms laid down in the Convention itself, such as statements via torture or other inhuman treatments, contrary to Article 3, or evidence that has been collected by means of encroachment on privacy, contrary to Article 8, conflicts on that ground alone with the Convention. As to the admissibility according to domestic law, the Strasbourg organs will be guided in the first place by the opinion of the national court. However, if the latter has taken the position that it may involve the evidence, though unlawfully obtained, in the formation of its opinion, a Strasbourg review of the way in which use is made of this evidence is very urgently needed if the principle of "fair trial" is not to be frustrated.[625]

Finally, another element of "fair hearing" that should be mentioned is the requirement that the judicial decision must state the reasons on which it is based, if these reasons do not already ensue from the content of the judgment as such in combination with the charge. The accused has a right to know what are the considerations on which the court bases its decision. Moreover, when a motivation is lacking, the remedies provided for threaten to become illusory. The detail into which the statement of the reasons must go is therefore determined by what an effective remedy against the decision requires in each particular case.[626] The practice existing in some countries to provide certain criminal judgments with a motivation only if an appeal has been instituted, is at odds with this point of departure, since the decision to institute an appeal or not may precisely be determined also by the motivation of the judgment. If, however, a court of appeal agrees with the reasons of the lower court, it does not have to explain this by restating the reasons.[627]

A number of aspects of fair civil (and administrative) proceedings, which have wholly or partly been connected, in the case-law, with the requirement of a fair hearing, such as free legal aid and the right to summon witnesses, will be discussed separately hereafter in connection with the explicitly granted guarantees for criminal cases. In this context it should be noted that this explicit provision of these guarantees for criminal cases does not mean that the finding that the proceedings are in conformity therewith make a review for their conformity with the "fair-hearing" principle superfluous in all cases. Thus the proceedings as a whole may, for instance, create the picture that the accused has had insufficient possibilities to conduct an optimal defence, although none of the explicitly granted minimum guarantees has been violated. As the Commisson stated in the *Adolf* Case:

Art. 6(3) merely exemplifies the minimum guarantees which must be accorded to the

---

624. The Commission was rather too laconic in this respect in Appl. 7450/76, *X v. Belgium*, *D & R* 9 (1978), p. 108 (110).
625. The Strasbourg organs consider themselves competent to do so: Appl. 8876/80, *X v. Belgium*, *D & R* 23 (1981), p. 233 (235).
626. Appl. 5460/72, *The Firestone Tire and Rubber Co. v. United Kingdom*, *Yearbook* XVI (1973), p. 152 (168); Appl. 8769/79, *X v. Federal Republic of Germany*, *D & R* 25 (1982), p. 240 (241).
627. Appl. 10773/84, *X v. Italy*, not published.

accused in the context of the "fair trial" referred to in Art. 6(1).[628]

This implies, on the one hand, that a negative answer to the question whether the first paragraph has been violated renders an investigation of an alleged infringement of the third paragraph superfluous,[629] on the other hand, that the investigation of violation of the fair-trial principle laid down in the first paragraph must not be confined to an examination of the third paragraph. Finally, once a violation of one of the parts of the third paragraph has been found, the Commission and the Court tend not to examine the alleged violation of the first paragraph any more.[630]

12. Article 6(1) further requires that the hearing shall be public. In its report in the *Axen* Case the Commission describes the rationale of this requirement as follows:

the public nature of the proceedings helps to ensure a fair trial by protecting the litigant against arbitrary decisions and enabling society to control the administration of justice ....
Combined with the public pronouncement of the judgment, the public nature of the hearings serves to ensure that the public is duly informed, notably by the press, and that the legal process is publicly observable. It should consequently contribute to ensuring confidence in the administration of justice.[631]

In addition to the interest which the parties to the dispute may have in a public hearing, it serves therefore a public interest as well: verifiability of and information about, and thus confidence in the administration of justice ("justice must not only be done, but must also be seen to be done"). Consequently the question arises whether the parties can waive their right to a public hearing to an unlimited degree or whether the court may only comply with a request to that effect if one of the grounds explicitly mentioned for this in Article 6 presents itself. In the *Le Compte, Van Leuven and De Meyere* Case the Court appears to have taken the first position by considering quite generally that a hearing *in camera* does not conflict with the Convention if it takes place with the consent of the parties concerned.[632] And the Court would seem to imply the same in the Case of *H. v. Belgium*, where it only observed that the evidence did not establish that H. had intended to waive his right to a public hearing and that he could not be blamed for not having demanded to exercise a right which was not afforded him by the practice of the Belgian Bar and which he had little prospect of securing.[633]

628. Report of 8 October 1980, B.43 (1985), p. 29.
629. *Ibidem*. See also the judgment of 27 February 1980, *De Weer*, A.35 (1980), pp. 30-31.
630. Report of 12 December 1981, *Pakelli*, B.53 (1982-1983), p. 29. Implicitly the judgment of 13 May 1980, *Artico*, A.37 (1980), pp. 15 and 18-19.
631. Report of 14 December 1981, B.57 (1982-1983), p. 24. See also the judgment of 22 February 1984 in this case, A.72 (1983), p. 12; judgment of 8 December 1983, *Pretto*, A.71 (1983), pp. 11-12; judgment of 22 February 1984, *Sutter*, A.74 (1983), pp. 12-13; judgment of 28 June 1984, *Campbell and Fell*, A.80 (1984), p. 43; report of 12 March 1985, *Adler*, para. 51.
632. Judgment of 23 June 1981, A.43 (1981), pp. 25-26.
633. Judgment of 30 November 1987, A.127 (1988), p. 36. See also the report of 13 October 1988, *Håkansson and Sturesson*, paras 144-149, where the Commission held that it was possible to waive the right to a public hearing either expressly or tacitly. However, where
(continued...)

With a view to the public interest which is served by publicity, in particular in criminal cases, it will, however, have to be assumed that there is merely a possibility of "waiver" of the right to a public hearing, not a right to a hearing *in camera*, and that, if a request for a hearing *in camera* is made, the court may refuse this on the ground of the weighing of the interest of the party concerned against the public interest. The court then will of course also have to involve in its considerations the protection of the private life of the party, as one of the explicitly mentioned grounds of restriction, and also the danger which publicity may constitute for the principle of *praesumptio innocentiae* protected in the second paragraph.

The requirement of publicity in principle applies to all the successive phases of the proceedings.[634] However, here again it is decisive whether a phase in the proceedings is concerned which in itself affects the "determination".[635] Moreover, the Commission has decided several times that in a particular phase a written procedure may suffice if exclusively legal questions of a technical and abstract character are at issue and this phase can no longer detract from the "fairness" with which the main points have been examined in one or more earlier phases.[636] Although this interpretation appears to be at odds with the text of Article 6(1), in so far as such a more technical and abstract phase may also lead to an ultimate "determination", in our opinion it will have to be accepted from pragmatic reasons, because indeed there is little sense in a public hearing in such a phase and the requirement of public verifiability has been complied with if the legal considerations are included in the judgment and the latter is published. However, in the preceding phase, in which an examination has been made about the factual as well as the legal questions, the requirement of publicity must have been complied with in every respect.[637]

Similar pragmatic reasons justify the standpoint that the requirement of a public judgment has been complied with if during a public session this is confined to the reading of the dictum,[638] and that even this may be omitted if the dictum contains no more than the determination that the appeal has been rejected or the case is referred back.[639] In that case the parties must

---

633. (...continued)
   the law and practice do not indicate that it is even likely that a hearing would have been held, the fact that no request was made cannot be interpreted as a tacit approval of the appeal being examined by the court without a hearing.
634. Report of 14 December 1979, *Le Compte, Van Leuven and De Meyere*, B.38 (1984), p. 44. See, however, the report of 15 March 1985, *Adler*, para. 51: "the principle of publicity must be fully respected at least in one instance dealing with the merits of a case unless one of the reasons enumerated in art. 6 para 1 ... is present".
635. Judgment of 22 February 1984, *Axen*, A.72 (1984), pp. 12-13; judgment of 22 February 1984, *Sutter*, A.74 (1984), p. 13. See also the report of 14 December 1981, *X v. Federal Republic of Germany*, B.57 (1987), p. 25.
636. See the report mentioned in note 635, pp. 24-26 and the case-law referred to there.
637. Report of 14 December 1981, *Albert and Le Compte*, B.50 (1986), pp. 40-41, and the judgment in this case, A.71 (1984), pp. 12-13.
638. Appls 8603, 8722, 8723 and 8729/79, *Crociani et al. v. Italy*, D & R 22 (1981), p. 147 (228); judgment of 8 December 1983, *Pretto*, A.71 (1983), pp. 12-13.
639. The two reports mentioned in note 634, p. 24 and para. 85 respectively.

receive a copy of the text of the judgment as soon as possible, while also the publication of at any rate those judgments in which legal questions of a more public interest are at issue, is of special importance for the verifiability.[640]

As to the grounds of restriction, it is striking that Article 6 permits restrictions exclusively with respect to the public nature of the proceedings, not with respect to the judgment. With respect to the possibilities of restriction a few observations must suffice here:

- On the one hand, the Strasbourg organs appear to be willing to leave the national authorities, and specifically the national courts, a certain "margin of appreciation" in the assessment of the question whether there is any reason for application of one of the restrictions, such as this is also the case with respect to the grounds of restriction included in other provisions of the Convention.[641] On the other hand, they appear also to make an independent examination themselves of the reasons of the restriction,[642] in which context they are not willing to accept simply a developed practice, but require that it be stated concretely for each case which ground of restriction is invoked.[643]

- When the protection of public order is at issue, one is inclined to think of the prevention of disorder. When Article 14 of the Covenant was drafted, this interpretation was indeed advocated, on the part of Great Britain, and on that ground objections were raised - in vain - to the addition of the French term "ordre public" in the English text.[644] Now that the text of Article 6 (and of Article 14) in its present form has been adopted, a comparison with Articles 10(2) and 11(2), where for the protection of public order the English text has "the prevention of disorder" and the French text "la défense de l'ordre", renders it difficult to maintain this interpretation, although on the other hand the English and the French text of Article 9(2) show that the drafters have not been very consistent in this matter. However this may be, the prevention of disorder in the court room may in any case be brought under the ground "the interests of justice". What then means "public order" in this context? In the Le Compte, Van Leuven and De Meyere Case the Belgian Government invoked this ground, alleging that publicity of the medical disciplinary cases might lead to violation of the medical professional secrecy. The Commission subsequently indeed examined this aspect under that denominator.[645] This seems to point in the direction of public order in the sense of "ordre public".

- The interest of national security so far has hardly played a part, if at all,

---

640. See *ibidem*, p. 24 and para. 86 respectively.
641. See *infra* pp. 585-606.
642. See, *e.g.*, the report of the Commission and the judgment of the Court in the *Le Compte, Van Leuven and De Meyere* Case, B.38 (1984), pp. 43-44 and A.43 (1981), p. 25 respectively; and the report of the Commission and the judgment of the Court in the *Albert and Le Compte* Case, B.50 (1986), pp. 40-41 and A.58 (1983), p. 18 respectively.
643. Judgment of 8 June 1976, *Engel*, A.22 (1977), p. 37.
644. See E/CN.4/SR.318, p. 10: "the proper conception was that closed hearings could be held with a view to preventing disorder".
645. See the report of 14 December 1979, B.38 (1984), pp. 43-44. See also the report of 14 December 1981, *Albert and Le Compte*, B.50 (1983), pp. 40-41.

in the Strasbourg case-law with respect to the public nature of the trial, but it is easy to conceive of situations in which in proceedings State secrets are involved, or other information that is security-sensitive. The court, however, will then have to form an independent opinion about this. Everything that the authorities prefer to be kept secret does not for that reason alone concern national security.

- Cases involving the protection of the private life of the parties, except for cases in which the interests of minors are involved, seem to require that a decision to consider the matter *in camera* can only be taken if the parties indeed appear to appreciate such protection.[646]

- The last ground of restriction - the interests of justice - is explicitly left to the opinion of the court. Here again, however, an ultimate supervision by the Strasbourg organs is fitting, although this is likely to be marginal.[647] And here again the Commission and the Court will not accept a mere reference to an existing practice. In its decision on Appl. 8016/77 the Commission seems to suggest that witnesses whose testimony may constitute a danger for them may rely on Article 6(1) in complaining that the court has omitted to hear them *in camera*.[648] It may indeed be accepted that the interests of justice entail that witnesses are granted adequate protection; they, too, can claim a "fair trial". The interests of justice may also require that the space available for the public does not become overcrowded and that agitators are excluded. But on the other hand the interest of publicity requires that the administration of justice takes place at locations where a reasonable accommodation for the public is present.

13. Subsequently, Article 6 stipulates in its first paragraph that the hearing of the case by the court must take place "within a reasonable time" (*dans un délai raisonnable*). Just as with regard to these same words in Article 5(3)[649] this raises the difficult question as to what criteria have to be applied for the assessment of what is reasonable, and also what period should be taken into account in this respect.

In the case of Article 5(3) it is at all events clear what should be considered as the beginning of the relevant period: this is the moment of the arrest. The rationale of that provision is that the detention on remand does not last longer than is strictly necessary. The purpose of the reasonable-time requirement of Article 6(1), however, is to guarantee that within a reasonable

---

646. Thus evidently also the Commission in its report in the *Albert and Le Compte* Case, B.50 (1986), pp. 40-41. In its decision on Appl. 7366/76, *X v. United Kingdom*, not published, consideration *in camera* was deemed justified by the Commission on this ground against the wishes of the applicant, but this concerned divorce proceedings, so that the private life of the spouse and possibly the interests of one or more minor children were also involved.
647. See the report of 14 December 1981, *Axen*, B.57 (1982-1983), pp. 24-25, in which reference of the government to the necessity to reduce the workload of the judiciary was not accepted without further argument by the Commission as an excuse for the elimination of the requirement of a "public hearing" in cassation-proceedings.
648. Appl. 8016/77, *X v. United Kingdom*, not published.
649. On this, see *supra* pp. 276-281.

time and by means of a judicial decision, an end is put to the insecurity into which a person finds himself as to his civil-law position or on account of a criminal charge against him; this in the interest of the person in question as well as of legal certainty. This rationale entails that in the case of criminal charges the starting-point may be before the moment of the arrest, while this provision also applies in cases where there is no question of detention on remand.[650]

With respect to criminal cases, the Court has held that as the beginning of the relevant period must be taken the moment at which a "criminal charge" is brought, since it is only from that moment that the "determination of ... any criminal charge" can be involved.[651] However, the rationale mentioned above implies that the period may not in all cases begin at the moment at which the person in question is officially indicted. Even before that he may have realized that he is suspected of a criminal offence, so that from that moment he has an interest in that a decision about this suspicion be made by the court. This is quite evident in those cases where an arrest precedes the moment of the formal charge.[652] It is, therefore, important here as well that in the Strasbourg case-law an autonomous meaning is assigned to the concept of "charge", the starting-point being that a substantive and not a formal concept of "charge" must be used because of the great importance that the principle of a fair trial has for a democratic society.[653] Already in an early stage the Commission took the position that

> the relevant stage is that at which the situation of the person concerned has been substantially affected as a result of a suspicion against him.[654]

On the basis of this point of departure, in the *Neumeister* Case the Commission took the view that as the date on which the period began must be taken 21 January 1960, the day on which Neumeister had first been heard as an accused.[655] However, the Court in its judgment in this case determined 23 February 1961 as the day on which Neumeister had been indicted, without even going into the criterion mentioned by the Commission.[656] But in its judgment of three years later, in the *Ringeisen* Case, the Court also took into consideration the period between the first examination and the moment at which Ringeisen was indicted, without making any reference to the formal

---

650. For the relation between the two provisions, see the judgment of 10 November 1969, *Stögmüller*, A.9 (1969), p. 40 and the report of 12 July 1977, *Haase*, *D & R* 11 (1978), p. 78 (92), where it is also stated that with respect to the reasonableness of the duration more stringent requirements must be made in the case of Article 5(3).
651. Judgment of 27 June 1968, *Neumeister*, A.8 (1968), p. 41; judgment of 27 February 1980, *De Weer*, A.35 (1980), p. 22.
652. In its judgment of 27 June 1968, *Wemhoff*, A.7 (1968), p. 26, the Court assumed that the two moments coincided.
653. See *supra* pp. 307-309.
654. Report of 27 May 1966, *Neumeister*, B.6 (1966-1969), p. 81. See the decision of the Commission on Appl. 9433/81, *Menten v. the Netherlands*, *D & R* 27 (1982), p. 233 (237), where the period between 1950 and 1976 was not calculated for the duration, because in that time, in consequence of the declaration of the Minister of Justice that he would not be prosecuted, Menten was not "affected".
655. *Ibidem.*
656. Judgment of 27 June 1968, A.8 (1968), p. 41.

criterion of the *Neumeister* judgment.[657] In its judgment in the *De Weer* Case the Court gave as a rather formal definition again:

> the official notification given to an individual by the competent authority of an allegation that he has committed a criminal offence,[658]

but in its later judgment in the *Eckle* Case the Court stated that this definition

> also corresponds to the test whether "the situation of the [suspect] has been substantially affected".[659]

Thus the Court appears now to share the view of the Commission.[660]

With respect to the determination of civil rights and obligations, as the beginning of the period may in general be taken the moment at which the proceedings concerned are instituted or at which, within the framework of other proceedings, such a right or obligation is put forward in a defence. If prior to the judicial proceedings another action - for instance an administrative appeal - must have been brought, the beginning is shifted to the moment of that action.[661] A negotiation phase preceding the proceedings, however, is not counted as part of the relevant period.[662] Legislation or a judicial practice placing obstacles in the way of a plaintiff for a prompt institution of proceedings, as well as legislation enabling him to leave the other party for a long time in uncertainty as to whether or not an action will be brought, without a reasonably short term of limitation preventing this, does not satisfy Article 6(1).[663]

The above-mentioned rationale of this part of Article 6 entails that the end of the period taken into consideration is the moment at which the court has put an end to the uncertainty concerning the legal position of the person in question. That is not, therefore, the moment at which the hearing in court starts, but the moment at which the decision in civil proceedings is taken, or conviction, acquittal or dismissal of the charge is pronounced in criminal proceedings. As the Court held in its *Wemhoff* judgment:

> there is ... no reason why the protection given to the persons concerned against the delays of the courts should end at the first hearing in a trial: unwarranted adjournments or excessive delays on the part of trial courts are also to be feared.[664]

The uncertainty comes finally to an end only when a decision on the charge against the accused has been made, or the determination of the civil rights and/or obligations at issue has taken place, at highest instance or has become

---

657. Judgment of 16 July 1971, A.13 (1971), p. 45.
658. Judgment of 27 February 1980, A.35 (1980), p. 24.
659. Judgment of 15 July 1982, A.51, p. 33.
660. See also the judgment of 10 December 1982, *Foti*, A.56 (1982), p. 18, and the judgment of 21 February 1984, *Öztürk*, A.75 (1984), p. 21.
661. Judgment of 28 June 1978, *König*, A.27 (1978), p. 33; report of 8 March 1982, *Andorfer Tonwerke*, D & R 32 (1983), p. 94 (108).
662. Report of 7 March 1984 and judgment of 8 July 1986, *Lithgow*, A.102 (1987), pp. 120 and 72 respectively.
663. In that sense also Jacobs, *supra* note 17, p. 109.
664. Judgment of 27 June 1968, A.7 (1968), p. 26.

final through the expiration of the time-limit for appeal, or when further prosecution is refrained from.[665] Moreover, it is not through the mere conviction, but only through the determination of the penalty that certainty is afforded to the accused,[666] and then only at the moment at which he can in reason be assumed to have been informed of the final verdict and its motivation.[667] The possibility of extraordinary remedies must be left out of consideration, while for other remedies - for instance an appeal in cassation - it will be decisive whether the uncertainty concerning the final "determination" actually persists as long as no decision has been taken about the appeal or the period for the lodging of such an appeal has not yet expired.[668]

In the determination of the relevant period, the *competentio ratione temporis* must be taken into account. Thus, in the case of an individual complaint concerning proceedings which were already in progress at the moment the State concerned recognized the individual's right of complaint under Article 25, only the length of the period from that moment can be taken into account, although for the assessment of the reasonableness of that period the stage in which the proceedings were at that moment is indeed taken into consideration.[669]

When in this way the length of the relevant period has been established, it must subsequently be determined whether this period is to be regarded as reasonable. For each individual case the interests of the person concerned in as prompt a decision as possible will have to be weighed against the demands of a careful examination and a proper conduct of the proceedings.

An attitude or behaviour of the person in question which has led to delay weakens his complaint about that delay.[670] However, an accused person may not be required to co-operate actively in expediting the proceedings which lead to his own conviction.[671] This is different for parties to civil pro-

---

665. Report of 8 February 1973, *Huber, Yearbook* XVIII (1975), p. 324 (360). In its judgment of 16 July 1971, *Ringeisen*, A.13 (1971), p. 45, the Court also speaks of a "final decision".
666. Judgment of 15 July 1982, *Eckle*, A.51 (1982), p. 35. In the same way, for civil proceedings, a judgment in which the right to compensation has been established but not its amount, does not mean the end of the proceedings; judgment of 10 July 1984, *Guincho*, A.81 (1984), p. 10. In the case of cumulative impositions of penalties the moment at which the last penalty became final constitutes the endpoint: *Eckle*, A.51 (1982), pp. 34-35.
667. Report of 8 May 1984, *Vallon*, A.95 (1985), pp. 22-23.
668. See the judgment of 28 June 1978, *König*, A.27 (1978), pp. 33-34, and the judgment of 6 May 1981, *Buchholz*, A.42 (1981), p. 15.
669. Report of 15 October 1980, *Foti*, B.48 (1986), p. 31; report of 15 December 1980, *Ventura*, D & R 23 (1981), p. 5 (84); report of 16 March 1981, *Corigliano*, B.49 (1986), pp. 20-21; report of 14 December 1981, *Pretto*, B.69 (1982-1983), p. 21; judgment of 26 October 1988, *Martins Moreira*, A.143 (1989), p. 16.
670. See, *e.g.*, the judgment of 16 July 1971, *Ringeisen*, A.13 (1971), p. 45; judgment of 28 June 1978, *König*, A.27 (1978), pp. 35-36; judgment of 6 May 1981, *Buchholz*, A.42 (1981), p. 19; judgment of 15 July 1982, *Eckle*, A.51 (1982), p. 362; judgment of 10 July 1984, *Guincho*, A.81 (1984), pp. 21-22; judgment of 8 December 1983, *Pretto*, A.71 (1984), p. 15; report of 15 October 1985, *Capuano*, A.119 (1987), p. 19, and judgment of 29 May 1986, *Deumeland*, A.100 (1986), p. 27.
671. Judgment of 15 July 1982, *Eckle*, A.51 (1982), p. 36; report of 12 December 1983, *Neubeck*, D & R 41 (1985), p. 13 (30-31).

ceedings.[672] A party to proceedings can alo not be blamed for making use of his right to bring an appeal.[673] It is evident that this prolongs the proceedings, but this prolongation, too, must stand the test of reasonableness.[674]

The Commission has also taken into account the conduct of the other party in its considerations concerning the reasonableness.[675] In the Strasbourg supervision, since complaints must be directed against States, this can only play a part if that other party is a public authority, or if at least that conduct can partly be imputed to the authorities.[676] If in a criminal case with two accused persons one of them retards the case, the prosecutor must separate the cases if possible, in order that the other accused does not become the victim of the delay.[677]

Furthermore, the complicated character of the case and the efforts the judicial authorities have made to expedite the proceedings as much as possible play an important part.[678] In this respect a special duty rests upon the court concerned to see to it that all those who play a role in the proceedings do their utmost to avoid any unnecessary delay. In the *Capuano* Case the Italian Government drew attention to the fact that the delays in the proceedings in first instance, which lasted for more than six years, were attributable to the experts, who filed their opinions too late. The Court held the court concerned responsible for the delays in preparing expert opinions.[679]

Overburdening of the judiciary in general is not recognized as an excuse, since the contracting States have the general duty to organize the administration of justice in such a way that the various courts can satisfy the requirements of Article 6.[680] In the *Buchholz* Case the Court indeed decided that a temporary accumulation of cases may be regarded as a justification of some delay, provided that the authorities do everything in their power to cope with this situation as quickly as possible.[681] If the situation threatens to become structural, measures must be taken to avoid a permanent situation of violation of the Convention.[682] The measures are assessed as to their effective-

672. Appl. 1794/63, *X v. Federal Republic of Germany*, Yearbook IX (1966), p. 179 (212).
673. Judgment of 15 July 1982, *Eckle*, A.51 (1982), p. 36.
674. Judgment of 23 April 1987, *Lechner and Hess*, A.118 (1987), p. 19.
675. Report of 14 May 1980, *Buchholz*, B.37 (1983), p. 27.
676. Judgment of 6 May 1981, *Buchholz*, A.42 (1982), p. 16; judgment of 8 July 1987, *Baraona*, A.122 (1987), p. 21; judgment of 26 October 1988, *Martins Moreira*, A.143 (1989), p. 17.
677. Appl. 6541/74, *Bonnechaux v. Federal Republic of Germany*, D & R 3 (1976), p. 86 (87).
678. Judgment of 27 June 1968, *Wemhoff*, A.7 (1968), p. 27; judgment of 27 June 1968, *Neumeister*, A.8 (1968), pp. 41-43; judgment of 16 July 1971, *Ringeisen*, A.13 (1971), p. 45; judgment of 28 June 1978, *König*, A.27 (1979), pp. 34-40; and judgment of 6 May 1981, *Buchholz*, A.42 (1981), pp. 15-21. See also the report of 12 December 1983, *Neubeck*, D & R 41 (1985), p. 13 (33).
679. Judgment of 25 June 1987, A.119 (1987), p. 13.
680. Judgment of 10 November 1969, *Stögmüller*, A.9 (1969), pp. 40-41; report of 8 March 1982, *Andorfer Tonwerke*, D & R 32 (1983), p. 94 (108-109); and judgment of 26 October 1984, *De Cubber*, A.86 (1984), p. 20.
681. Judgment of 6 May 1981, *Buchholz*, A.42 (1982), p. 16. See also the judgment of 10 July 1984, *Guincho*, A.81, p. 16 and the judgment of 13 July 1983, *Zimmermann and Steiner*, A.66 (1983), p. 12.
682. Judgment of 13 July 1983, *Zimmermann and Steiner*, A.66 (1983), pp. 11-13; report of 12 March 1984, *Marijnissen*, D & R 40 (1985), p. 83 (90); judgment of 26 October 1988, *Martins Moreira*, A.143 (1989), p. 20.

ness,[683] and it is also ascertained whether they have been taken in good time; measures taken afterwards cannot make up for the fact that the reasonable period has been exceeded.[684] The *Baggetta* Case dealt with the length of criminal proceedings, which lasted thirteen years and four months. The Court held according to its constant case-law that contracting States are non-liable in the event of a temporary backlog of business in their courts, provided that they take, with the requisite promptness, remedial action to deal with an exceptional situation of this kind. In the instant case, the Italian Government's efforts were not made until seven years after the proceedings began. The Court therefore found a violation of Article 6(1).[685] In the Case of *Neves e Silva* the Commission criticized the Portuguese authorities for not having taken, with the requisite promptness, effective remedial action to cope with the structural increase in cases. The situation required exceptional measures designed in particular to relieve the backlog progressively. While aware of the serious difficulties encountered by the respondent Government, the Commission considered that in the particular circumstances of the case the measures taken were inadequate and belated.[686]

From the case-law the general picture emerges that the Strasbourg authorities tend to apply fairly broad standards with respect to the above-mentioned criteria. Thus, even periods of seven and eight years were still considered "reasonable" by the Commission in certain cases,[687] and a period of nearly five years by the Court.[688] In the *Eckle* Case, however, where the duration of the proceedings was more than seventeen and ten years, the Commission and the Court considered that the permissible limit had been amply exceeded.[689]

It is important that the Strasbourg organs appear to be prepared to pay attention to special interests which may be involved for the applicant. Thus in the Case of *H. v. United Kingdom*, which concerned the length of the proceedings instituted by the applicant regarding her access to her child, which had been committed to the care of a local authority, the Court put special emphasis on the importance of what was at stake for the applicant in

---

683. Report of 12 December 1983, *Neubeck, D & R* 41 (1985), p. 13 (32-33).
684. Report of 12 March 1984, *Marijnissen, D & R* 40 (1985), p. 83 (90).
685. Judgment of 25 June 1987, A.119 (1987), p. 33. See also the judgment of 25 June 1987, *Milasi*, A.119 (1987), p. 47, where the Court held that even taking into consideration the political and social background formed by the disturbances in the region concerned, which allegedly obliged the Italian authorities to take special precautions, this could not justify a delay which continued well beyond cessation of the disturbances.
686. Report of 17 December 1987, A.153-A (1989), p. 24.
687. Report of 12 July 1977, *Haase, D & R* 11 (1978), p. 78 (88-91), and report of 15 December 1980, *Ventura, D & R* 23 (1981), p. 5 (92-97).
688. Judgment of 6 May 1981, *Buchholz*, A.42 (1981), pp. 21-22. Here a violation had been concluded at by the Commission, B.37 (1983), p. 31. Now that the Court itself admitted that "the second set of proceedings was extremely slow" and that the court in appeal "had ... on several occasions deferred its hearings for somewhat long periods", the question arises if not too important a role has been assigned to the applicant's conduct. See also the decision by the Commission on Appl. 8427/78, *X v. the Netherlands, D & R* 18 (1980), p. 225 (231).
689. Report of 11 December 1980, B.45 (1986), pp. 43-56; judgment of 15 July 1982, A.51 (1982), pp. 35-40.

the proceedings in question. Not only were these decisive for her future relations with her child, but they had a particular quality of irreversibility, involving as they did what the High Court graphically described as the "statutory guillotine" of adoption. In these circumstances the Court expected an exceptional diligence on the part of the authorities.[690] And in the Case of *B v. Federal Republic of Germany* the Commission was of the opinion that the divorce proceedings which lasted more than nine years exceeded the reasonable time. The Commission found this time excessive in the circumstances, especially having regard to the necessity to deal with divorce and related family matters speedily.[691]

If it is argued against the person who complains about an unreasonable delay of the proceedings that, contrary to Article 26, he has not waited for the end of the national proceedings, the decision about that reasonableness will partly also be decisive for the question whether he is required still to do so, which indeed will lead to an even greater delay. If at first sight the complaint does not appear ill-founded, the Commission would be well-advised to request the national authorities to suspend the domestic proceedings pending the decision in Strasbourg, unless the possibilities for a later continuation of the proceedings would be prejudiced disproportionately as a result of such a suspension. The applicant, for his part, must be able to demonstrate that in the domestic proceedings he has used any possible remedies which might have expedited the matter.

If the proceedings concern war crimes, in the Commission's opinion the "criteria determining the reasonableness of the length of ordinary criminal proceedings" are not automatically applicable, but the length of the proceedings has to be assessed in the light of the exceptional character of such an action.[692] For this view the Commission does not advance any further arguments. Since Article 1 accords the protection of the Convention to "everyone", while, if the normal criteria are applied, it is possible to take the special complexity of the case, in particular the difficulty to collect evidence, sufficiently into account, it is hard to understand why special criteria should apply. In the *Menten* Case this view was not repeated.[693]

The requirement of a trial within a reasonable time equally entails that this time may not be unreasonably short, in consequence of which it is not possible for the parties to prepare the case properly. What is expressly provided in paragraph 3(b) for criminal proceedings, in virtue of the general requirement of a fair hearing in the first paragraph applies to civil proceedings as well.

---

690. Judgment of 8 July 1987, A.120 (1987), pp. 62-63.
691. Report of 13 November 1987, para. 113.
692. Appl. 6946/75, *X v. Federal Republic of Germany*, D & R 6 (1977), p. 114 (115-116). This does not imply that the requirement of a reasonable time in those cases would not apply, but only that other criteria would apply for that reasonableness.
693. Appl. 9433/81, *Menten v. the Netherlands*, D & R 27 (1982), p. 233 (237).

Article 6(1) does not stipulate what the consequences for the proceedings are, if the reasonable-time requirement has not been met. It would seem to ensue from this provision that, if the reasonable time has been exceeded and, consequently, the determination can no longer be made within a reasonable time, the proceedings would have to be stopped and the civil action or criminal charge to be declared inadmissible. However, the Strasbourg organs have adopted a more flexible view, and indicated that

> an excessive length of criminal proceedings can in principle be compensated for by measures of the domestic authorities, including in particular a reduction of the sentence on account of the length of procedure.[694]

This point of view, which seems difficult to be reconciled with the text of Article 6(1), offers the most appropriate solution in certain cases. In civil proceedings the applicant should not become the victim of an unreasonable delay for which the public authorities are to be blamed; both parties can be victims of the delay and be entitled to some form of just satisfaction. And in criminal procedures the public interest in the prosecution and conviction of the criminal may be so great that the prosecution should not be stopped for the sole reason that the reasonable time has been transgressed; another, more appropriate compensation should be awarded to the victim of that transgression.

14. Finally, the first paragraph of Article 6 provides that the determination there referred to be in the hands of an independent and impartial tribunal, established by law. Of these qualifications of the court the first and the third have an objective, the second has a subjective character.

For the independence of the court it is required that it can base its decision on its own free opinion about facts and legal grounds, without any commitment to the parties or the public authorities and without its decision being subject to review by any other but an authority that is independent in the same sense.[695] Even a semblance of dependence must be avoided. Thus the Court held in the *Sramek* Case, where a member of the court was hierarchically subordinate to one of the parties to the suit:

> Litigants may entertain a legitimate doubt about his independence. Such a situation seriously affects the confidence which the courts must inspire in a democratic society.[696]

From the case-law discussed before it follows that Article 6(1) does not

---

694. Report of 12 December 1983, *Neubeck, D & R* 41 (1983), p. 13 (34); Appl. 10884/84, *H. v. Federal Republic of Germany, D & R* 41 (1985), p. 252 (254).
695. See the judgment of 16 July 1971, *Ringeisen*, A.13 (1971), p. 39 and the judgment of 23 June 1981, *Le Compte, Van Leuven and De Meyere*, A.43 (1981), p. 24. See also the judgment of 23 October 1985, *Benthem*, A.97 (1986), p. 18, where with regard to the Dutch procedure of Crown Appeal the Court came to the conclusion that the Administrative Litigation Division of the Council of State, which advises the Crown in this procedure, indeed satisfies the requirements of independence, but that the ultimate decision of the Crown in actual fact is in the hands of a member of the Cabinet, who is responsible for it to Parliament. It was considered insufficient that in the great majority of cases the advice is followed by the Crown, since this practice does not yet make the advice formally binding.
696. Judgment of 22 October 1984, A.84 (1984), pp. 19-20.

stipulate that every authority which has to pronounce in a particular phase of the proceedings on civil rights and obligations or a criminal charge is independent in this sense, but that the highest instance of appeal has this independence, while the requirement of independence always applies in the traditional civil or criminal proceedings, where the tribunal provided for under domestic law has the characteristics of a "court of the classic kind".[697]

For the independence it is not required that the judges have been appointed for life, provided that they cannot be discharged at will or on improper grounds by the authorities.[698] The party concerned will, however, have to be free to prove that a judge, with a view to his reappointment, was guided by other considerations than by his personal opinion. However, the latter aspect no longer refers to the independence, but to the impartiality of the court.

For the impartiality it is required that the court is not biassed with regard to the decision to be taken, does not allow itself to be influenced by information from outside the court room, by popular feeling, or by any pressure whatever, but bases its opinion on objective arguments on the ground of what has been put forward at the trial. Even when the reasons are included in a judicial decision, it is extremely difficult to ascertain by what motives a court has been led. It will therefore only be possible to conclude that a judge is biassed when this becomes quite clear from his attitude during the proceedings or from the content of the judgment. Although a judge of course also has personal emotions, also during the proceedings, he must not allow himself to be led by them during the hearing of the case and in the formation of his opinion.[699] And although judges may also have a political preference and will adhere to a specific philosophy of life, and although it is of course right that the various political streams and philosophies of life are also "represented" within the judiciary, it must not make an essential difference for the person involved whether he is tried by a judge with one or another preference.[700]

Publicity surrounding a criminal case, where the difference between "suspected of" and "guilty of" is not always taken into account, may constitute a threat to the right to a fair and impartial trial, in particular also when this publicity proceeds from the authorities, *e.g.* from the public prosecutor charged with the examination.[701] The judge should duly take this risk into account when forming his opinion, this also in connection with the presump-

---

697. See *supra* pp. 306-307 and 308-309.
698. Implicitly in the judgment of 13 July 1971, *Ringeisen*, A.13 (1971). Explicitly in the report of 12 October 1978, *Zand*, D & R 15 (1979), p. 70 (81-82), and in the report of 14 December 1979, *Le Compte, Van Leuven and De Meyere*, B.38 (1979), p. 40. With regard to military tribunals, see the judgment of 8 June 1976, *Engel*, A.22 (1977), pp. 27-28.
699. See Appl. 1727/72, *Boeckmans v. Belgium*, *Yearbook* VI (1963), p. 370 (416-420), where the complaint concerned a judge who in his indignation about a specific defence uttered a warning that its upholding might lead to an increase of the penalty. Later this case was settled: report of the subcommittee of 17 February 1965.
700. Appls 8603, 8722, 8723 and 8729/79, *Crociani et al. v. Italy*, D & R 22 (1981), p. 147 (222).
701. Appl. 8403/78, *Jespers v. Belgium*, D & R 22 (1981), p. 100 (127).

tion of innocence as guaranteed in the second paragraph.[702] In cases with a markedly political background the said risk and the necessity for the court to be on the alert against improper influences may even apply to a higher degree.[703] In the Strasbourg case-law it is assumed, however, that a professional judge will in general be very well aware of these external factors and will not readily allow himself to be influenced thereby, while moreover on appeal the higher court, in this respect, too, may correct the attitude of the lower court.[704] Thus, in the *Menten* Case the Commission held that the great publicity and the utterance of hostile feelings in this case could not be avoided, but that the Supreme Court had accurately ascertained on what testimony the lower courts had based their considerations.[705]

In cases of trial by jury the risk of the jury being influenced by public opinion or by biassed statements of witnesses or experts is more obvious.[706] Here again, however, it will be difficult to prove this, the more so because a decision of the jury does not include a written statement of reasons. In its case-law the Commission evidently assumes that if a verdict of a jury has been appealed from to a court and the latter has not found any partiality, there is no longer any reason for the Commission to review the jury's verdict in this respect,[707] and that also during the proceedings themselves in which the jury reaches its decision the court, via its attitude and statements, may have a neutralizing effect on undue influences.[708]

The requirement in Article 10(2) that the freedom of expression may be restricted "for maintaining the authority and impartiality of the judiciary" is most closely connected with the point of publicity surrounding a trial. This restriction, which relates to the prohibition of "contempt of court" embedded in Anglo-American law, was discussed at length in Strasbourg in the *Sunday Times* Case. The complaint there concerned the prohibition, imposed by the English court up to the highest instance, to publish during a given time an article about the so-called "thalidomide children", children who had been born with serious physical deformities in consequence of the use of the sedative thalidomide by their mothers during pregnancy. The prohibition had been imposed because at that moment various proceedings against the manufacturer of thalidomide were pending and the publication might lead to a "contempt of court". The Commission and the Court, though with a narrow majority,

---

702. Thus the Commission in, *e.g.*, the *Pfunders* Case (*Austria v. Italy*), *Yearbook* VI (1963), p. 740 (782-784). See also Appl. 7542/76, *X v. United Kingdom*, not published, where in a case which attracted much publicity the Commission attached great importance to the fact that the judge had drawn the jury's attention to the risk of prejudice.
703. See the Appls mentioned in note 700, pp. 222-223 and 227.
704. Appl. 3444/67, *X v. Norway*, *Yearbook* XIII (1970), p. 302 (324); Appl. 3860/68, *X v. United Kingdom*, *Coll.* 30 (1970), p. 70 (74-75).
705. Appl. 9433/81, *Menten v. the Netherlands*, *D & R* 27 (1982), p. 233 (238).
706. This risk was emphasized several times by the Commission: Appl. 1476/62, *X v. Austria*, *Coll.* 11 (1963), p. 31 (43); Appl. 3444/67, *X v. Norway*, *Yearbook* XIII (1970), p. 302 (324).
707. Appl. 3444/67, *ibidem*, pp. 324-326; Appl. 3860/68, *X v. United Kingdom*, *Coll.* 30 (1970), p. 70 (74-75).
708. Report in the *Nielsen* Case, *Yearbook* IV (1961), p. 490 (568), where the complaint concerned the fact that the jury had been influenced by a witness-expert.

came to the conclusion that in this case the prohibition was not justified. They took into account, *inter alia*, that a court is not readily influenced by publications of this kind.[709]

The mere fact that non-jurists also sit on a tribunal, as is frequently the case in disciplinary tribunals, does not mean on this ground alone that they are not impartial. But if persons are concerned who are closely allied to one of the parties, which is often the case in an arbitration tribunal, their impartiality may be open to some doubt.[710] An issue under Article 6(1) will then rise only when not all the parties or their interests are equally represented in the tribunal in question. Thus in the *Le Compte, Van Leuven and De Meyere* Case, where three medical practitioners had been summoned before a disciplinary tribunal on account of their opposition to the obligatory membership of a professional association of medical practitioners, the Commission reached the conclusion that there was no question of an impartial course of proceedings, since the tribunal judging at first instance, the Provincial Council, was composed largely of persons who had been elected by members of the professional association, while the Appeal Council consisted of medical practitioners and judges on a fifty-fifty basis. The fact that appeal to the Court of Cassation was also possible did not, in the Commission's opinion, eliminate this defect, because review was possible only on the ground of procedural errors or misapplication of the law.[711] The Court, however, did not follow the Commission. Since an appeal had been lodged with the Appeal Council, in the Court's view the impartiality of the Provincial Council did not require examination. With regard to the Appeal Council the Court held that the impartiality of such a tribunal must be presumed, unless the contrary can be proved, which had not been done in the present case in the Court's opinion.[712] In the later *Albert and Le Compte* Case the Commission maintained its original view, although it held that, in a case like this, complaints about partiality ought to refer not to the tribunal as such, but to individual members.[713]

In the *Piersack* Case the Court made a distinction between a subjective and an objective approach to impartiality. The subjective approach refers to the personal impartiality of the members of the tribunal involved; this is presumed as long as the contrary has not been proved. The objective approach refers to the question whether the way in which the tribunal is composed and organized, or whether a certain coincidence or succession of

---

709. Report of 18 May 1977, B.28 (1982), pp. 71-74; judgment of 26 April 1979, A.30 (1979), pp. 28-42.
710. See the report of 12 December 1983, *Bramelid and Malmström*, D & R 38 (1984), pp. 40-41.
711. Report of 14 December 1979, B.38 (1984), pp. 40-42.
712. Judgment of 23 June 1981, A.43 (1981), p. 25; judgment of 10 February 1983, *Albert and Le Compte*, A.58 (1983), pp. 17-18; judgment of 28 June 1984, *Campbell and Fell*, A.80 (1984), p. 41.
713. Report of 14 December 1981, B.50 (1986), pp. 39-40. See also the judgment of 10 February 1983 in this case, A.58 (1983), pp. 17-18, where the Court also maintained its previous opinion by stating: "In principle, the personal impartiality of the members of a 'tribunal' must be presumed until there is proof of the contrary".

functions of one of its members, may give rise to doubt as to the impartiality of the tribunal or that member. If there is ground for such doubt, even if subjectively there is no concrete indication of partiality of the person in question, this already leads to an inadmissible jeopardy of the confidence which the court must inspire in a democratic society. A fairly marginal subjective review is therefore followed by a very strict objective one.[714] The *Piersack* Case concerned the president of the tribunal, who had been involved in an earlier phase of the case as a public prosecutor. In the *De Cubber* Case and the *Yaacoub* Case a judge was involved who had previously in the same case acted as an investigating judge and as a president of a chamber respectively. In all those cases it was held that these facts created too much doubt about his impartiality in an objective sense.[715] In the *Hauschildt* Case, where the complaint was that the judge who had presided over the applicant's trial had, before the trial, taken several decisions on the prolongation of the applicant's detention on remand, the Commission distinguished that case from the *Piersack* and *De Cubber* Cases. In the latter cases, according to the Commission, there was an incompatibility of functions, while in the *Hauschildt* Case the different functions exercised by the judge concerned had all been attributed to the court under the institutional framework of the legal system concerned. The decision to detain on remand and the decision to convict or acquit and to determine punishment are both of a judicial character. Furthermore, the Commission found a distinction with the *Yaacoub* Case in that there the judge had taken initiatives himself during the investigations, while here the judge acted only at the request of the public prosecutor or the applicant's counsel; he did not have an investigating judge's task of eliciting and assembling the necessary information. This led the Commission to the conclusion that, in the instant case, the impartiality was not subject to doubt in an objective way.[716] This rather artificial and inconvincing reasoning was not followed by the Court. The Court held that, since a judge who decides on detention on remand has to take the indications of guilt into account, his impartiality is in doubt when later on the same judge has to determine the issue of guilt. Therefore, according to the Court, one might come to the conclusion that the impartiality of the judge concerned was at stake.[717]

The prescription that the tribunal must be "established by law" implies the guarantee that the organization of the judiciary in a democratic society is not left to the discretion of the executive, but constitutes the subject of a legal regulation by Parliament. In the Commission's view this does not, however, rule out the possibility that parts of this organization, *e.g.*, the institution of

---

714. Judgment of 1 October 1982, *Piersack*, A.53 (1982), pp. 14-16. See also the judgment of 22 October 1984, *Sramek*, A.84 (1984), pp. 19-20; judgment of 28 June 1984, *Campbell and Fell*, A.80 (1984), pp. 39-41; and judgment of 26 October 1984, *De Cubber*, A.86 (1984), pp. 13-16.
715. Judgment of 26 October 1984, *De Cubber*, A.86 (1984), pp. 15-16; report of 7 May 1985, *Yaacoub*, A.127 (1988), pp. 11-13; judgment of 29 April 1988, *Belilos*, A.132 (1988), p. 30.
716. Report of 16 July 1987, paras 102-114.
717. Judgment of 24 May 1989, paras 43-53.

specific judicial bodies, may be left by law to the executive by virtue of delegation, provided that sufficient guarantees are built in to counteract arbitrariness.[718] And in any case no right to be tried by the ordinary court can be inferred from the provision, provided that a legal basis is present for the special court as well.[719] In its report in the *Piersack* Case the Commission evidently takes the view that not only the establishment, but also the organization and the functioning of the tribunal in question must have a legal basis, but for the question of whether this tribunal has applied these legal rules in the right way it apparently relies on the opinion of the (higher) national court.[720] In that case the Court did not deal with this point after it had held the complaint concerning the violation of the requirement of impartiality to be well-founded.[721]

The tribunal required by Article 6 need not be "a court of law of the classic kind, integrated within the standard judicial machinery of the country".[722] The word "tribunal" already indicates this. It must be "an authority with power to decide legal disputes with binding effect for the parties".[723]

15. *Article 6, paragraph 2* prescribes that the person who is charged with a criminal offence shall be presumed innocent until proved guilty according to law. As in the case of the third paragraph, this paragraph concerns a special aspect of the general concept of "fair trial" in criminal cases. For that reason no further inquiry is made as to a possible violation of this provision when a violation of the first paragraph has already been found.[724] From the case-law concerning the autonomous meaning of the concept of "criminal charge" in the first paragraph it follows that the second and third paragraphs are also applicable to other than criminal proceedings - *e.g.*, disciplinary proceedings - which are to be equated with criminal proceedings by means of the criteria developed in the *Engel* Case.[725]

In the *Minelli* Case the second paragraph was defined by the Court in the sense that this provision has been violated if

> without the accused's having previously been proved guilty according to law and, notably, without his having had the opportunity of exercising his rights of defence, a judicial decision concerning him reflects an opinion that he is guilty.[726]

A reasoning by which it is only suggested that the person in question is guilty

---

718. Report of 12 October 1978, *Zand, D & R* 15 (1979), p. 70 (79-81); report of 14 December 1979, *Le Compte, Van Leuven and De Meyere,* B.38 (1984), pp. 39-40; Appls 8603, 8722, 8723 and 8729/79, *Crociani et al. v. Italy, D & R* 22 (1981), p. 147 (219).
719. Appl. 8299/78, *X and Y v. Ireland, D & R* 22 (1981), p. 51 (73).
720. Report of 13 May 1981, B.47 (1986), p. 23.
721. Judgment of 1 October 1982, A.53 (1982), p. 16.
722. Judgment of 28 June 1984, *Campbell and Fell,* A.80 (1984), p. 29; judgment of 22 October 1984, *Sramek,* A.84 (1984), p. 17.
723. *Ibidem.*
724. Judgment of 27 February 1980, *De Weer,* A.35 (1980), pp. 30-31; thus also the Commission in its report of 5 October 1978 in this case, B.33 (1983), pp. 29-30.
725. Judgment of 10 February 1983, *Albert and Le Compte,* A.58 (1983), pp. 19-20.
726. Judgment of 25 March 1983, A.62 (1983), p. 18. See also the judgments of 25 August 1987, *Lutz, Englert, Nölkenbockhoff,* A.123 (1987), pp. 25, 55 and 81 respectively.

is already sufficient for such a violation.

The most important aspect of the presumption of innocence concerns the foundation of the conviction. This aspect is very closely connected with the requirement of the court's impartiality discussed above. The court has to presume the innocence of the accused without any prejudice and may sentence him only on the basis of evidence put forward during the trial, which moreover has to belong to the "lawful" evidence recognized as such by law. This evidence has to be put forward by the prosecution and not by the court itself, while the accused must be given full opportunity to disprove this evidence.[727] The Court formulated the essence clearly as follows:

> Paragraph 2 embodies the principle of the presumption of innocence. It requires, *inter alia*, that when carrying out their duties, the members of a court should not start with the preconceived idea that the accused has committed the offence charged; the burden of proof is on the prosecution, and any doubt should benefit the accused. It also follows that it is for the prosecution to inform the accused of the case that will be made against him, so that he may prepare and present his defence accordingly, and to adduce evidence sufficient to convict him.[728]

The evidence put forward at the trial may refer back to statements previously made by the accused or testimony by witnesses, provided that the latter can be revoked or refuted during the trial.[729] If a witness wishes to remain anonymous or for other reasons does not wish to act as a witness during the trial and can advance a legitimate reason for it, there is no objection to a reading of previously borne testimony, provided that the right of the defence to question witnesses is sufficiently satisfied, *e.g.* by having provided the opportunity to interrogate and contradict that witness in an earlier phase of the proceedings. If this condition has not been satisfied, the verdict must not be based exclusively or largely on such testimony.[730]

Every case giving rise to the least doubt with regard to the evidence has to be construed in favour of the accused.[731] This does not necessarily mean that the evidence put forward must be absolutely conclusive - in several legal systems ultimately the conviction on the part of the court is the point that matters[732] - but it does mean that the court must base its conviction exclusively on the evidence put forward during the trial.[733] A sentence may of course also be based on a confession of guilt of the accused. In that case, however, the court will have to ascertain thoroughly that this confession has

---

727. See, *e.g.*, the report of 31 March 1963, *Pfunders (Austria v. Italy)*, Yearbook VI (1963), p. 740 (782-784).
728. Judgment of 6 December 1988, *Barberá, Messegué and Jabardo*, A.146 (1989), p. 33.
729. Appl. 8414/78, *X v. Federal Republic of Germany*, D & R 17 (1980), p. 231 (233-234); Appl. 8417/78, *X v. Belgium*, D & R 16 (1979), p. 200 (233-234).
730. Judgment of 24 November 1986, *Unterpertinger*, A.110 (1987), pp. 14-15. On the issue of anonymous witnesses, see also *supra* pp. 322-324.
731. Report of 31 May 1963, *Pfunders (Austria v. Italy)*, Yearbook VI (1963), pp. 782-784; judgment of 6 December 1988, *Barberá, Messegué and Jabardo*, A.146 (1989), p. 33.
732. See, *e.g.*, for the Netherlands Article 338 of the Code of Criminal Procedure.
733. The Commission does not consider itself competent to pronounce on the value of that conviction: Appl. 7628/76, *X v. Belgium*, D & R 9 (1978), p. 169.

been made in complete freedom,[734] while from a statement of the accused which is not intended to be a confession of guilt no such confession may be inferred.[735]

If during the trial statements are made or produced by the prosecutor, witnesses or experts from which bias on their part is evident, the court has to make a stand against those statements if it is to avoid the semblance of being biassed as well. If the court does this, the accused can no longer complain of such bias on the part of the first-mentioned persons.[736] The same holds good if a sentence which the accused alleges to have been dictated by bias has been upheld on appeal, while the court of appeal has made an inquiry into this very matter. In that case the accused will be able to complain only of bias on the part of this court of appeal or of the fact that the injury caused by the bias of the lower court has not been redressed by the higher court.[737]

If there has been publicity around the proceedings in which publicity the guilt of the accused is assumed, the latter will have to prove to some extent that his ultimate conviction was also influenced by that publicity. This will not be easy.[738] With respect to the practice where during the trial the criminal record, if any, of the accused is brought to the notice of the court, the Commission has given as its opinion that this practice does not constitute a conflict with Article 6(2).[739] It is obvious, however, that such information may promote a presumption of guilt on the part of the court or the jury, so that the person in question has at least to be given an opportunity to advance evidence that the criminal record has unduly influenced the court.

In addition to the establishment of guilt, Article 6(2) also has consequences for the treatment of the accused; in this respect, too, his innocence must be presumed. This applies to the treatment of the accused during the

---

734. Appl. 5076/71, *X v. United Kingdom, Coll.* 40 (1972), p. 64 (66-67). In so far as the confession has been extorted by illegal means, such as physical or mental torture, this follows already from the words "according to law"; report in the *Pfunders* Case, *supra* (note 731), p. 784.

735. In this context, see the disputed decision of the Commission on Appl. 4483/70, *X v. Federal Republic of Germany, Coll.* 38 (1972), p. 77 (79), where the Commission appears not to have examined the complaint at all for this aspect. See also Appl. 2645/65, *Scheichelbauer v. Austria, Yearbook* XII (1969), p. 156 (170-172).

736. Report of 31 March 1963, *Pfunders (Austria v. Italy), Yearbook* VI (1963), p. 740 (784); report of 15 March 1961, *Nielsen, Yearbook* IV (1961), p. 490 (568). For a case in which the accused, on the contrary, complained that the court had influenced the jury to his detriment by using the word "killing": Appl. 5881/72, *X v. United Kingdom*, not published. The Commission's consideration that the court had not used this word with that intention seems to cut no ice.

737. Report in the *Pfunders* Case, *ibidem*.

738. See, *e.g.*, Appls 7572, 7586 and 7587/76, *Ensslin, Baader and Raspe v. Federal Republic of Germany, Yearbook* XXI (1978), p. 418 (462). Applicants alleged violation of Article 6(2) on account of the press campaign against them, in which they were called criminals and murderers, and on account of the exceptional security measures around the suit, which could not but create an impression of guilt. The Commission took the position that the challenged publications and measures were a reaction to their own declarations and behaviour and were not aimed at creating an atmosphere unfavourable for the accused, and that a professional judge is sufficiently immune to any influence that might result from this. See also *supra* p. 337 and the *Menten* Case there mentioned.

739. Appl. 2742/66, *X v. Austria, Yearbook* IX (1966), p. 550 (554).

preliminary examination and the trial, as well as to the treatment of a person detained on remand: that treatment may not have a punitive character. If the conditions of Article 5(1)(c) have been fulfilled, the restrictions imposed on the detainee have to bear a relation to the purpose of the detention on remand.[740]

In a few cases the practice has been at issue according to which the accused himself, in case of discontinuance of the proceedings instituted against him, nevertheless has to pay the costs of the suit, on account of presumed guilt or because he has given rise to the proceedings.[741] In the *Minelli* Case, where the court had concluded that the plaintiffs in an action for insult could not sue since the period of limitation had expired, but still had condemned the defendant to pay two thirds of the trial costs and to pay compensation in respect of the prosecutor's expenses, because in the court's opinion he would in all probability have been found guilty if the limitation had not barred the continuance of the proceedings, the Court held that the fact that the accused is made to pay some of the costs of the suit if he is discharged need not yet in itself conflict with Article 6(2), but this *is* the case if the presumable guilt of the accused is used as the criterion for it, without the guarantees of Article 6 being observed.[742] In the *Adolf* Case, in which the court had discharged the accused, but owing to the formulation of the relevant decision had nevertheless created the impression that the accused had committed the crime with which he had been charged, although the evidence for this had not been furnished, the Commission concluded that Article 6(2) had been violated.[743] The Court largely followed the Commission in its argumentation, but not in its conclusion, because in the opinion of the Court the judicial decision concerned could not be viewed independently of the subsequent decision of the Austrian Supreme Court, ruling expressly that the dismissal of the case did not imply any pronouncement on the guilt.[744] In the *Lutz, Englert and Nölkenbockhoff* Cases the Court held that the decision to refuse reimbursement to a person "charged with a criminal offence" in the event of discontinuance of the proceedings against him, may raise an issue under Article 6(2) if the supporting reasons amount in substance to a

---

740. See Recommendation R(80)1 of the Committee of Ministers in the matter of custody on remand of 27 June 1980, Article 1 of which states: "Being presumed innocent until proved guilty, no person charged with an offence shall be placed in custody pending trial unless the circumstances make it strictly necessary. Custody pending trial shall therefore be regarded as an exceptional measure and it shall never be compulsory nor be used for punitive reasons". See also Art. 10(2)(a) of the Covenant in the matter of the special treatment of detainees on remand.
741. See Appl. 6650/74, *Liebig v. Federal Republic of Germany, Yearbook* XIX (1976), p. 330 (342) and Appl. 7640/76, *Geerk v. Switzerland, Yearbook* XXI (1978), p. 470 (476). In both cases a friendly settlement was reached. See also Appl. 9688/82, *C. Family v. Switzerland, D & R* 35 (1984), p. 98 (102). The Commission declared the complaint inadmissible, since the decision that the applicants had to pay the costs of the proceedings was based on the fact that the applicants had prompted the opening of the criminal proceedings by their own negligent behaviour.
742. Judgment of 25 March 1983, A.62 (1983), pp. 15-18.
743. Report of 8 October 1980, B.43 (1985), pp. 25-28.
744. Judgment of 26 March 1982, A.49 (1982), pp. 18-19.

343

determination of the accused's guilt without his having previously been proved guilty according to the law, in particular without having had an opportunity to exercise the right of defence.[745]

The principle embodied in paragraph 2 also applies in those criminal cases where the issue of guilt is not a central issue. In the *Salabiaku* Case the Court stated that the contracting States are in principle free, subject to certain conditions, to establish an offence on the basis of an objective fact as such, irrespective of whether it results from criminal intent or from negligence. The applicant was convicted not for the mere possession of unlawfully imported prohibited goods, but for smuggling such goods, while the legal presumption of accountability was inferred from their possession and led to the conviction. The Court stressed the relative nature of the distinction between presumption of accountability and presumption of guilt. Presumptions of fact or of law operate in every legal system; this is not contrary to the Convention. The contracting States are, however, under the obligation to remain within reasonable limits in this respect as regards their criminal law provisions, taking into account the importance of what is at stake, and to maintain the rights of the defence, because Article 6, para. 2 does not merely lay down a guarantee to be respected by courts in the conduct of legal proceedings but equally by the legislature, and the words "according to law" are not to be construed exclusively with reference to domestic law but contain a reference to the fundamental principle of the rule of law.[746]

16. *Article 6, paragraph 3* contains an enumeration of the minimum rights to which everyone charged with a criminal offence is entitled. This provision, unlike the first paragraph, does not also relate to proceedings concerning the determination of civil rights and obligations. On the one hand, however, if a party to civil proceedings is denied the rights mentioned in paragraph 3, under certain circumstances this may entail that there is no question of a "fair hearing" in the sense of the first paragraph.[747] On the other hand, the fact that "civil rights and obligations" are at issue does not exclude that the proceedings have a criminal character.[748]

The specific enumeration in the third paragraph for criminal proceedings does not imply that an examination for compatibility with the third paragraph makes an examination for compatibility with the first paragraph superfluous. As the Commission held in its *Adolf* report:

> Art. 6(3) merely exemplifies the minimum guarantees which must be accorded to the accused in the context of the "fair trial" referred to in Art. 6(1).[749]

---

745. Judgments of 25 August 1987, A.123 (1987), pp. 25-26, 54-55 and 78-81 respectively.
746. Judgment of 7 October 1988, A.141 (1989), pp. 15-17.
747. The lack of free legal aid may, for instance, bar the exercise of the right of "access to court"; see *supra* p. 317.
748. Judgment of 25 March 1983, *Minelli*, A.62 (1983), p. 15.
749. Report of 8 October 1980, B.43 (1985), p. 29. See also the judgment of 12 February 1985, *Colozza*, A.89 (1985), p. 14.

The enumeration of the third paragraph is not limitative in that respect, and it is therefore possible that, although the guarantees mentioned there have been satisfied, the trial as a whole still does not satisfy the requirements of a fair trial. As a result of an extensive and functional interpretation of the third paragraph in the Strasbourg case-law, however, examination for compatibility with the third and with the first paragraph is in fact likely to more or less coincide. With respect to the interpretation of the guarantees of the third paragraph the Commission has taken the following position:

> They exemplify the notion of fair trial ... but their intrinsic aim is always to ensure, or contribute to ensuring, the fairness of the criminal proceedings as a whole. The guarantees enshrined in Art. 6(3) are therefore not an aim in themselves, and they must accordingly be interpreted in the light of the function which they have in the overall context of the proceedings.[750]

At all events, in the case of a positive outcome of the examination for compatibility with the first paragraph an examination with regard to the third paragraph is deemed superfluous.[751] This is to be regretted, since it restricts the development of specific case-law concerning the third paragraph.

17. Under 3(a) the accused is granted the right to be informed promptly, in a language which he understands and in detail, of the nature and cause of the accusation against him. This right is very closely related to the right granted under 3(b) that he must have adequate time and facilities for the preparation of the defence.[752] Indeed, for the latter it is required that the accused be informed of the charge promptly and in a way which he can understand and which is sufficiently specified. In this context not only the nature of the charge must be specified, but also the factual and legal grounds on which the charge is based.[753] However, in this phase it is not yet necessary to furnish any evidence in support of the charge.[754]

As has been stated above with respect to Article 5(2),[755] here again it will have to be assessed in each individual case, on the basis of the specific circumstances, whether the required information has been furnished promptly (*dans le plus court délai*). Precisely in order to enable the accused to prepare his defence, the prosecutor will have to inform him as soon as it has been decided to institute criminal proceedings and, if necessary, provisions have been made for a translation or for the presence of an interpreter. On that occasion he will have to mention the relevant data available at that moment, which afterwards are to be supplemented, if need be, in particular when the

---

750. Report of 12 July 1984, *Can*, A.96 (1985), p. 15.
751. See, *e.g.*, the judgment of 27 February 1980, *De Weer*, A.35 (1980), pp. 30-31.
752. This has repeatedly been emphasized by the Commission. See, *inter alia*, Appl. 524/59, *Ofner v. Austria*, Yearbook III (1960), p. 322 (344); Appl. 8490/79, *X v. Austria*, D & R 22 (1981), p. 140 (142); report of 2 March 1988, *Brozicek*, para. 65.
753. See the cases mentioned in the preceding note, *ibidem*. An alternative charge satisfies this requirement of specificity: Appl. 3894/68, *X v. the Netherlands*, Coll. 32 (1970), p. 47 (50).
754. Appl. 7628/76, *X v. Belgium*, D & R 9 (1978), p. 169 (173); report of 5 May 1983, *Collozza and Rubinat*, A.89 (1985), p. 28.
755. See *supra* p. 272.

summons is issued. However, the defence may be of great importance already in the phase preceding the ultimate decision as to whether or not to institute proceedings, and may affect this decision, so that it results from the rationale of paragraphs 3(a) and 3(b) that even before this formal decision the accused must be kept informed as fully as possible of the suspicion against him.

Paragraph 3(a) requires that the information must be furnished "in detail". In its decision on Appl. 1169/61 the Commission stated rather cryptically that this does not imply that information "in minute detail" is required.[756]

From the words "in a language which he understands" it follows in our opinion that if the accused is insufficiently master of the vernacular, the information must be translated for him. For this no particular form is prescribed, but an oral elucidation by the person who serves the writ of summons upon him or by an interpreter would seem to be an insufficient basis for the preparation of his defence.[757] It also seems dubious to us that paragraph 3(a) has been satisfied if the information has been sent to counsel who is master of the vernacular and may find ways to inform his client, since in this way the authorities shift an obligation resting upon them on to counsel while it is important for the accused that he himself is also able to follow the defence put forward on his behalf as adequately as possible. In the *Brozicek* Case the Commission considered it contrary to the spirit and the letter of Article 6, para. 3(a) to presume that an accused who is resident in his own country can understand the content of an official communication in the language of a foreign country which has instituted proceedings against him. In such a case, it is for the judicial authority sending the communication to ascertain, by any appropriate means, that the person concerned is objectively capable of understanding its content.[758]

18. Under 3(b) the accused is guaranteed the right to have adequate time and facilities for the preparation of his defence. Besides the above-mentioned relation with paragraph 3(a), there is also a close connection with paragraph 3(c), regulating legal aid. In that context the Commission has emphasized that here not only the rights of the accused are concerned, but equally the rights of counsel, so that for the assessment of the total situation the position of both of them has to be taken into account.[759]

The question of whether the accused has been allowed adequate time for the preparation of his defence will have to be decided afterwards, according to the circumstances in which both the accused and his counsel found

---

756. Appl. 1169/61, *X v. Federal Republic of Germany*, *Yearbook* VI (1963), p. 520 (584).
757. That the Convention does not expressly prescribe that the information required by Article 6, para. 3(a) be given in writing, as was observed by the Commission in its report of 5 May 1988, *Kamasinski*, para. 138, does not exclude that this requirement may be implied in the rationale of especially para. 3(b).
758. Report of 2 March 1988, para. 75.
759. Appl. 524/59, *Ofner v. Austria*, *Yearbook* III (1960), p. 322 (352).

themselves,[760] and on the basis of the nature of the case.[761] If the accused has great confidence in a particular lawyer, who is very occupied at that moment, the judicial authorities will have to take this into account as much as possible. On the other hand, in that case the accused cannot advance the resulting delay as a ground for violation of the first paragraph of Article 6. If for one reason or another the accused has to change counsel, the new lawyer will have to be given adequate time to become acquainted with the case.[762] If there is a right to free legal aid, a lawyer has to be assigned in good time.[763] The accused, however, cannot complain if through his own fault he has created a situation in which a lawyer has to be appointed shortly before the hearing is to be held.[764]

If appeal is open, the time-limit has to be such that a thorough study of the judgment can be made to enable a decision as to whether an appeal is to be brought,[765] while the moment of the hearing of the appeal in turn will have to leave adequate time for the preparation of the hearing. The words "preparation of his defence", therefore, may not be interpreted to mean that the provision sub (b) is not applicable to the appeal proceedings when the accused has been convicted at first instance and consequently acts not as defendant but as plaintiff in these proceedings.

In the *Bricmont* Case the Commission stated that sub-paragraph (b) recognizes the right of the accused to have at his disposal, for the purposes of exonerating himself or of obtaining a reduction of his sentence, all relevant elements that can be collected by the competent authorities.[766]

---

760. *Ibidem* and Appl. 4042/69, *X v. United Kingdom*, *Yearbook* XIII (1970), p. 690 (696). See also Appl. 5523/72, *Huber v. Austria*, *Yearbook* XVII (1974), p. 314 (332), where the complaint about the very short period indeed of 14 days was declared ill-founded with a view to the nevertheless voluminous commentary which the defence had produced. This, however, is not indicative of the period granted for defence but rather of the special efforts of counsel.
761. Appl. 7909/74, *X and Y v. Austria*, *D & R* 15 (1979), p. 160 (162-163), where the Commission investigated whether the time of ten working days available to counsel was adequate, considering the complexity of the case and the fact that he could communicate with his client only with difficulty because of her poor psychological and physical condition.
762. Although it is not quite clear from the decision, the Commission accepted this perhaps implicitly in its decision on Appl. 1850/63, *Köplinger v. Austria*, *Yearbook* IX (1966), p. 240 (262). See also Appl. 4319/69, *Samer v. Federal Republic of Germany*, *Yearbook* XIV (1971), p. 322 (340).
763. Appl. 7909/74, *X and Y v. Austria*, *D & R* 15 (1979), p. 160 (162), where the Commission stated that here again the question what period is adequate for this cannot be answered in abstracto.
764. Appl. 8251/78, *X v. Austria*, *D & R* 17 (1980), p. 166 (169-170).
765. See Appl. 441/58, *X v. Federal Republic of Germany*, *Yearbook* II (1958-1959), p. 391 (395), where the Commission considered a period for appeal of two weeks sufficient, since for the institution of the appeal a summary indication of the grounds for appeal could suffice. In its decision on Appl. 5523/72, *Huber v. Austria*, *Yearbook* XVII (1974), p. 314 (332), where the period for appeal was equally short, while here it was required that the grounds were already accurately indicated in the appeal, the Commission held that such a determination "could in some circumstances raise a problem under Article 6(3)(b)".
766. Report of 15 October 1987, para. 158. Also report of 14 December 1981, *Jespers, D & R* 27 (1982), p. 61 (88), where the Commission held that the adjective "adequate" implies that the facilities which must be granted to the accused are restricted to those which assist or may assist him in the preparation of his defence. The accused cannot complain about lack of facilities if he does not cooperate in producing elements to his defence; *Bricmont* report, para. 164.

The "facilities" referred to do not include the possibility to choose counsel or have one assigned, since the right to legal aid is provided for under (c). However, in so far as this latter provision does not at the same time involve the right to have an adequate possibility to communicate and consult with counsel, this in any case forms part of the necessary "facilities". This is very important in particular for detained persons: they must also be able to prepare themselves adequately for their trial and for any appeal they may have instituted, and must be enabled to have the necessary contacts with counsel. Those contacts must in principle be permitted to be private, since the confidential relation between counsel and his client and the professional secrecy of the former, which are essential for an effective defence, require this.[767] It must, however, be recognized that security problems may be at issue in that case. In the *Can* Case the Commission took the view that restrictions constitute a violation of Article 6(3)(b) only if they are of such a nature that they affect the position of the defence during the proceedings, and thus also the outcome.[768] Such a criterion, however, would in practice appear difficult to apply, since such an impact can only be established afterwards, and even then not with certainty. If the starting-point that the confidential relation calls for a private conversation is to be maintained, an adverse influence of restrictions of this private character on the defence will have to be assumed, and the burden of proof for the necessity of the restriction will have to rest on the authorities. Searching of counsel and inspection of the correspondence of counsel with his detained client by the prison authorities are in principle also incompatible with the position of counsel. Measures of this kind are justified only in very exceptional circumstances, where the authorities have sound reasons to assume that counsel himself is abusing his position or is allowing it to be abused.[769] And even then there will have to be complete openness, so that those concerned are aware of the control.[770]

Finally, the possibility of inspection of the files must also be mentioned as an important element of the "facilities".[771] The Commission took the position

---

767. Report of 12 May 1982, *Campbell and Fell*, A.80 (1984), pp. 78-79; judgment of 28 June 1984 in the same case, A.80 (1984), p. 49.
768. Report of 12 July 1984, A.96 (1985), pp. 16-17; see also report of 8 October 1987, *Lamy*, A.151 (1989), p. 26.
769. In its decision on Appl. 2375/64, *X v. Federal Republic of Germany*, *Coll.* 22 (1967), p. 45 (47), the Commission deemed inspection of the correspondence inherent to the detention on remand. The Commission here wrongly applied only Article 8 and not Article 6, although the applicant had stated that the challenged control had also led to great delay in the correspondence. Since the restriction grounds of Article 8(2) do not necessarily also apply in the context of Article 6(3)(b), the conformity of the measure with the latter provision should also have been reviewed.
770. See the judgment of 28 June 1984, *Campbell and Fell*, A.80, p. 49. The Dutch Supreme Court had declared the practice of wire-tapping in the Menten Case unlawful, even though this was done by order of the investigating judge: Supreme Court, 10 April 1979, *NJ* 1979, no. 374. This induced the Commission to declare a complaint manifestly ill-founded which Menten nevertheless raised on this point; Appl. 9433/81, *Menten v. the Netherlands*, *D & R* 27 (1982), p. 133 (138).
771. At least from the moment of the charge: Appl. 4622/70, *X v. Austria*, *Coll.* 40 (1972), p. 15 (18).

that a right of access to the files as such is not guaranteed in Article 6(3)(b), but that this provision may imply "that under certain circumstances the person concerned or his lawyer must have reasonable access to the file".[772] However, it is difficult to understand why a "reasonable access" does not belong under all circumstances to the minimum facilities for the defence and to the elements of the "equality of arms", although of course a certain protection of files may be necessary on the basis of considerations of security or the protection of other persons.[773]

19. Paragraph 3(c) guarantees the right of the accused to defend himself in person or through legal assistance of his own choosing or (and), if he has not sufficient means to pay for legal assistance, to be given it free when the interests of justice so require. In the *Pakelli* Case the Court, referring to "the object and purpose of this paragraph, which is designed to ensure effective protection of the rights of the defence", opted for the "*et*" in the French text, and not for the "or" in the English text, which would seem to link the right to free legal aid with the first two rights. This resulted in the following interpretation by the Court:

> a "person charged with a criminal offence" who does not wish to defend himself in person must be able to have recourse to legal assistance of his own choosing; if he does not have sufficient means to pay for such assistance, he is entitled under the Convention to be given it free when the interests of justice so require.[774]

There are therefore three juxtaposed rights included in this provision.

Contrary to what the text of paragraph 3(c) seems to suggest, this provision does not imply the right of the accused to defend himself in person. At any rate the Commission took the view that the question whether the accused is entitled to do so is determined by the national law and the judicial authorities concerned.[775] And the Court accepted in the *Gillow* Case the requirement of representation by a lawyer to lodge an appeal as "a common feature of the legal systems in several Member States of the Council of Europe".[776] From paragraph 3(c) it then results that, if the national law stipulates or the judicial authorities decide that the accused must be assisted by a lawyer, he must be able himself to choose this lawyer and, in case of inability to pay for such legal aid, must have a lawyer assigned to him;

---

772. Appl. 7138/75, *X v. Austria*, *D & R* 9 (1978), p. 50 (52) and report of 14 December 1981, *Jespers*, *D & R* 27 (1982), p. 61 (86-92). See also the report of 5 May 1988, *Kamasinski*, para. 148: the accused must not be granted personal access to the file if his defence counsel has been given access and sufficient facilities to discuss the case with him.
773. See the report of 12 July 1977, *Haase*, *D & R* 11 (1978), p. 78 (91-92). This case concerned a charge of espionage for the intelligence service of the German Democratic Republic.
774. Judgment of 25 April 1983, A.64 (1983), p. 15.
775. Appl. 2676/65, *X v. Austria*, *Coll.* 23 (1967), p. 31 (35); Appl. 5923/72, *X v. Norway*, *D & R* 3 (1976), p. 43 (44). For the reverse case, but then in the sphere of a civil suit, for which paragraph 3 does not apply, see Appl. 1013/61, *X and Y v. Federal Republic of Germany*, *Yearbook* V (1962), p. 158: the court need not recognize a representative nominated by a party if the character of the case is not such that the principle of a "fair hearing" as laid down in Article 6(1) makes such a representation necessary.
776. Judgment of 24 November 1986, A.109 (1986), p. 27.

indeed, in that case such legal aid is evidently considered necessary by the national law or the judicial authorities in the interests of justice.

Does the obligation to grant free legal aid to an accused person who is unable to pay for such aid automatically cease to exist if the latter is enabled to defend himself in person? If it were assumed that in paragraph 3(c) the choice is left to the national authorities, this question would have to be answered in the affirmative. Above, however, it has been stated with regard to the first paragraph of Article 6 that a case may be so complicated that legal aid is indispensable for the accused to ensure him a "fair hearing". It may then conflict with Article 6(1) to deny him that legal aid if he is unable to pay for it.[777] In the above-mentioned *Pakelli* Case the Court indeed took the position that this is not an alternative to be chosen by the authorities, but that the right to free legal aid is an independent right, the entitlement to which has to be judged according to its own merits.[778] If on the ground of the requirements of a fair hearing or of an adequate defence an accused is entitled to free legal aid, that aid will also have to be considered to be required by the interests of justice. However, this does not imply that the term "interests of justice" is exhausted by the interests protected in paragraph 1 and paragraph 3(b),[779] but only that the latter will be the principal criterion for it. If the case is simple, Article 6(3)(c) is satisfied if the accused is given the opportunity to defend himself in person and is given sufficient possibility to prepare this defence.[780] If, on the contrary, a case is involved in which for an adequate defence a certain expertise is necessary, the accused may not be forced to defend himself without adequate legal aid.[781] If it has been recognized with regard to the written phase of the proceedings that the interests of justice require the assignment of legal aid, as a rule, and even *a fortiori*, this will also have to apply for the subsequent oral phase.[782] If a lawyer has been assigned to an accused, but the behaviour of the latter has induced counsel to withdraw, the refusal of the court to assign a new lawyer may be in conformity with the "interests of justice", provided that from that moment the accused himself is given sufficient opportunity to defend himself in person.[783]

According to the Strasbourg case-law the right of the accused to choose his own lawyer is not an absolute right; he is bound by the provisions applying in the relevant legal system with regard to the question as to who may act as counsel in court.[784] If there the court is given the power to

777. *Supra* p. 317. See also the last of the decisions mentioned in note 775.
778. Judgment of 25 April 1983, A.64 (1983), p. 15.
779. The general interest of the case exceeding the interests of the accused may also call for legal assistance.
780. Appl. 8202/78, *X v. Norway*, not published.
781. Appl. 834/60, *Glaser v. Austria*, *Coll.* 10 (1963), p. 64 (70). In detail also the judgment of 13 May 1980, *Artico*, A.39 (1980), pp. 16-18.
782. Judgment of 25 April 1983, *Pakelli*, A.64 (1983), pp. 16-18.
783. Appl. 8386/78, *X v. United Kingdom*, *D & R* 21 (1981), p. 126 (130-132).
784. Appl. 722/60, *X v. Federal Republic of Germany*, *Yearbook* V (1962), p. 104 (106); Appls 7572, 7586 and 7587/76, *Ensslin, Baader and Raspe v. Federal Republic of Germany*, *Yearbook* XXI (1978), p. 418 (464).

exclude a specific lawyer or group of lawyers from the defence, for specific accused persons this might constitute an acute problem for an optimal defence, since in certain cases it may be very difficult to find a suitable lawyer. It is therefore important that in the *Goddi* Case the Commission took the view that:

> In most cases a lawyer chosen by the accused himself is better equipped to undertake the defence. It follows that as a general rule an accused must not be deprived, against his will or without his knowledge, of the assistance of the defence counsel he has appointed.[785]

In the past the Commission has taken the view that in the case of free legal aid the accused does not have the right to make his own choice or to be consulted as to the assignment.[786] Since, however, in the *Pakelli* Case a juxtaposition of the two rights was opted for through the word *"et"* in the French text,[787] this case-law may well have to be revised. And in any case the right to an adequate defence entails that, if it should be found that there exists or arises such an unsatisfactory relationship between the accused and the lawyer assigned to him that an adequate defence is impossible, or if the qualifications of the assigned lawyer are found to be inadequate considering the nature and/or complexity of the case, paragraph 1 and paragraph 3(b) may imply that another lawyer must be assigned to the accused at the latter's request.[788] In the *Kamasinski* Case the Commission emphasized, however, that the responsibility rests in the first place on the applicant.

> The question of how counsel defends his client is primarily a matter between them. Therefore it is in the first place for the accused to ensure that his representative fulfils his duties.[789]

Only if these attempts by the accused should fail may the State authorities be called upon to take steps. In this context the Court emphasized in the *Artico* Case that the authorities have not complied with their obligation by the mere assignment of a lawyer, since Article (3)(c) speaks of "assistance" and not of "nomination", so that it must be sufficiently ensured that real assistance is provided.[790] Here again, however, the accused can forfeit his right by personally creating the situation in which at the very last moment before the hearing another lawyer must be nominated.[791]

As regards the contact with counsel, the Court has attached to the right of access to court, implied in Article 6(1), the consequence that this right has been violated if a detainee is not permitted to correspond with a lawyer or another person giving legal assistance. The Court held that:

---

785. Report of 14 July 1982, B.61 (1987), p. 25.
786. See, *e.g.*, Appl. 6946/75, *X v. Federal Republic of Germany, D & R* 6 (1977), p. 114 (116-117).
787. Judgment of 25 April 1983, A.64 (1983), p. 15. See *supra* p. 349.
788. *Ibidem.*
789. Report of 5 May 1988, paras 154-155.
790. Judgment of 13 May 1980, A.37 (1980), pp. 15-16.
791. Appl. 8251/78, *X v. Austria, D & R* 17 (1980), p. 166 (169-170).

hindering the effective exercise of a right may amount to a breach of that right, even if the hindrance is of a temporary character.[792]

Consequently, as soon as a detainee wants to institute an action or wishes to prepare his defence against a criminal charge, such contact must be possible. That contact must not even be refused to him during an internal preliminary inquiry.[793] And an *incommunicado* confinement, too, even if it should in itself be compatible with the Convention,[794] in any case does not constitute an excuse for not permitting contact with the lawyer. For the protection of the confidential character of the contacts between the accused and his counsel reference is made here to what has been observed about this with respect to paragraph 3(b).

If the accused is not assisted by a lawyer during the pre-trial phase, the question arises as to the propriety of the evidence collected there in view of the requirements of a fair trial. In that context it is considered to be highly relevant that the evidence is evaluated by the court during the trial in the presence of the accused and his counsel, who then have the opportunity to contradict the evidence, and that any confession is proved by the prosecution to have been made voluntarily.[795]

Apart from the cases in which the accused is allowed to make his defence in person and opts for that possibility, he does not derive from paragraph 3(c) the right to be present in person in court. On this point the Convention would seem to go less far in its minimum guarantees than the Covenant, which expressly mentions such a right in Article 14(3)(d). Even in the Seventh Protocol, the purpose of which was to supplement the Convention on a number of points and which was modelled after the Covenant, such a right ultimately was not included, although it *figured* in an earlier draft. However, the Commission has left open the possibility that this right may be implied in the right to a "fair hearing" if the presence in person of the accused appears to be of particular importance for the formation of the court's opinion.[796] Moreover, the Commission has recognized that the refusal to admit the accused to the hearing may constitute discrimination in the sense of Article 14.[797] The right to be present in person in court is indeed very closely linked with that to a fair trial and has been discussed in that context above.

20. Paragraph 3(d) grants to the accused the right to examine or have examined witnesses against him, and to obtain the attendance and examination

---

792. Judgment of 21 February 1975, *Golder*, A.18 (1975), pp. 12-20. Thus also the Commission in its report of 11 October 1980, *Silver*, B.51 (1987), pp. 100-101.
793. Appl. 7878/77, *Fell v. United Kingdom*, D & R 23 (1981), p. 102 (113). See also the report of 12 May 1982, *Campbell and Fell*, A.80 (1984), pp. 76-77.
794. About this, *inter alia*, Appl. 6166/73, *Baader, Meins, Meinhof and Grundman v. Federal Republic of Germany*, Yearbook XVIII (1975), p. 132 (144-146); Appls 7572, 7586 and 7587/76, *Ensslin, Baader and Raspe v. Federal Republic of Germany*, Yearbook XXI (1978), p. 418 (454-460). See also *supra* pp. 232-233.
795. Appl. 9370/81, *X v. United Kingdom*, not published.
796. Appl. 8289/78, *X v. Austria*, D & R 18 (1980), p. 160 (166-167). See *supra* p. 320-322.
797. *Ibidem*, p. 167.

of witnesses on his behalf under the same conditions as witnesses against him. This provision is closely related to the principle of the "equality of arms" as an element of a "fair hearing" in the sense of the first paragraph. Consequently, although the provision is included among the guarantees applying specifically to criminal proceedings, in the case-law the possibility has been recognized that the refusal by the court to permit a party to civil proceedings to have a particular witness summoned or examined constitutes a violation of the right to a fair hearing.[798]

The first limb of the provision, which does not contain any restriction, has been deprived of a great deal of its effect in the case-law of the Commission because the Commission leaves very wide discretion to the national court with respect to whether the questions which the accused wants to ask the witnesses against him "are likely to assist in, and thus necessary for, ascertaining the truth".[799] If in this respect the court gives evidence of bias, the right to a fair hearing has been violated,[800] but this can hardly be proved. In our opinion, the rationale of paragraph 3(d) is satisfied only if the court affords the accused or counsel ample opportunity for the examination and only makes restrictions in case of manifest abuse or improper use of the right to examination. The examination of witnesses should normally take place in the presence of the accused, unless the interests of the witnesses do not allow for that.[801]

The second limb of paragraph 3(d) clearly allows for the discretion of the national court because its only requirement is that the prosecution and the accused receive equal treatment in this respect. With regard to the summoning of witnesses for the defence and their examination, domestic law and the courts may therefore set conditions and impose restrictions, provided that these equally apply in respect of the witnesses for the prosecution.[802] Moreover, some initiative on the part of the accused is required as to the calling of witnesses, as well as, of course, during the examination; the court need not call witnesses of its own accord.[803] However, here again the fact that paragraph 3(d) has not been violated does not yet mean that the requirements of the first paragraph have been satisfied. Moreover, the Commission

---

798. See, e.g., Appl. 5362/72, X v. Austria, Coll. 42 (1973), p. 145.
799. Appl. 4428/70, X v. Austria, Yearbook XV (1972), p. 264 (282). Thus also Appl. 8417/78, X v. Belgium, D & R 16 (1979), p. 200 (207); report of 15 October 1987, Bricmont, para. 146.
800. This possibility was recognized by the Commission in its decision on Appl. 4428/70, X v. Austria, Yearbook XV (1972), p. 264 (284-286).
801. See, however, Appl. 11219/84, X v. Denmark, D & R 42 (1985), p. 287 (292), where the Commission stressed that, after the applicant was ordered to leave the court-room, the defence counsel had every opportunity, in accordance with Article 6(3)(d), to examine the two anonymous witnesses who appeared before the court.
802. Appl. 4428/70, X v. Austria, Yearbook XV (1972), p. 264 (282). Thus also Appl. 9433/81, Menten v. the Netherlands, D & R 27 (1982), p. 233 (234-238).
803. See Appl. 5881/72, X v. United Kingdom, not published, where the Commission stated that the calling of witnesses "was a matter which was within the discretion of the applicant's solicitor and counsel and the fact that they apparently chose to call only one medical witness does not suggest in any way that the applicant's rights under this provision [i.e. Article 6(3)(d)] were not respected". See also Appl. 5282/71, X v. United Kingdom, Coll. 42 (1973), p. 99 (102).

has restricted the discretion of the courts somewhat by stating that

> the right guaranteed by Article 6 para. 3(d) is a specific right and that a court must give the reasons for which it decides not to summon those witnesses whose examination has been expressly requested.[804]

In the *Unterpertinger* Case the Court took the position that a witness need not necessarily appear in person in court, but that his previously made depositions can also be read in court without this conflicting *per se* with the paragraphs 1 and 3(d) of Article 6. However, the rights of the defence may not be affected by this, specifically not the right of the accused to examine or have examined witnesses for the prosecution. If the opportunity for this is not, or not sufficiently, offered - *e.g.* at an earlier stage of the proceedings - a conviction mainly based on this testimony conflicts with paragraphs 1 and 3(d) of Article 6.[805] The position taken in this case by the Commission that there was no question of violation of Article 6(3)(d) because the prosecution, too, had not had the opportunity to examine the persons concerned,[806] fortunately was not adopted by the Court. Here the Commission transposed the equality principle, which is of decisive importance for the second limb of paragraph 3(d), *viz.* the right to summon witnesses for the defence, to the right to examine witnesses for the prosecution. That position is untenable already from a systematical and grammatical point of view.[807] But moreover there is already question of inequality if the prosecution puts forward a testimony made in a previous phase; in actual fact, in that previous phase the prosecution has had the opportunity to examine the person in question, albeit perhaps only via the police, while the accused has not. With regard to the question of the admissibility of testimony by anonymous witnesses it can be inferred from the judgment of the Court that here, too, a mere reliance on the equality principle as a justification will not do, but that guarantees and conditions must have been created under which an adequate examination by the defence or some other comparable verification remains possible. In the *Kostovski* Case the Court expressly held that, although the Convention does not preclude reliance, at the investigation stage of criminal proceeding, on sources such as anonymous informants, the subsequent use of anonymous statements as sufficient evidence to found a conviction involves limitations on the rights of the defence which are irreconcilable with the guarantees contained in Article 6. The Government's reliance on the interests of the witnesses were not considered decisive.[808]

Experts summoned in court in many cases cannot be classified as being for the prosecution or the defence. Still with regard to them, too, the right of the accused to examine them, or have them examined, and to have them

---

804. Report of 15 October 1987, *Bricmont*, para. 152.
805. Judgment of 24 November 1986, A.110 (1987), pp. 14-15. See also the report of 12 May 1988, *Kostovski*, para. 45 and the judgment of 20 November 1989 in the same case, A.166 (1990), p. 21.
806. Report of 11 October 1984, A.110 (1987), pp. 19-20.
807. See the dissenting opinion of Trechsel, *ibidem*, p. 25.
808. Judgment of 20 November 1989, A.166 (1990), p. 21; report of 12 May 1988, paras. 49-51.

summoned on an equal footing with the prosecution, applies. The Commission reaches this conclusion via an autonomous interpretation of "witness" in paragraph 3(d),[809] while the Court prefers to include this right among the elements of a fair hearing in the first paragraph.[810]

21. Paragraph 3(e), finally, grants to the accused the right to have the free assistance of an interpreter if he cannot understand or speak the language used in court. This right, too, is linked so closely with the principle of a "fair hearing" of the first paragraph that also in cases of determination of civil rights and obligations the necessary costs for a translator or an interpreter may be so burdensome for a party to the proceedings that the non-reimbursement may conflict with the first paragraph.[811]

From paragraph 3(e) it follows that the accused cannot claim that the trial or the examination is conducted in a language other than the official vernacular. The fact that counsel of the accused understands the language used in court does not, however, do away with the latter's right to an interpreter, because he himself must also be able to follow, and form an opinion on, the proceedings. However, some personal initiative may be required of the accused as to the nomination of an interpreter.[812]

The words "language used in court" have been interpreted strictly by the Commission in the sense that they cover only the contacts between the accused and the court, and not those between the accused and his counsel.[813] The first part of this interpretation - the Commission speaks of "only" - at all events would appear to be too narrow. Indeed, the provision speaks not of "language used by the court" but of "language used in court". The rationale of the provision, therefore, entails that in any case the accused must also be able to follow via an interpreter what the prosecution, witnesses and experts say. The contacts with the lawyer during the trial are indeed on a somewhat different plane, because these are not public and, therefore, cannot be said to be "language used in court". However, if as a result of the lack of opportunity for communication during the trial an adequate defence is not possible, paragraph 3(b) will apply. However this may be, in the *Luedicke, Belkacem and Koç* Case the Court appears to have taken a broader view than the Commission by holding that Article 6(3)(e) relates to:

all those documents or statements in the proceedings instituted against him which it is necessary for him to understand in order to have the benefit of a fair trial.[814]

809. Report of 12 March 1984, *Bönisch*, A92 (1985), p. 20; report of 11 October 1984, *Underpertinger*, A.110 (1987), p. 18.
810. Judgment of 6 May 1985, *Bönisch*, A.92 (1985), p. 15.
811. Report of 18 May 1977, *Luedicke, Belkacem and Koç*, B.27 (1977-78), p. 26, and report of 9 March 1977, *Airey*, B.30 (1982), p. 32.
812. Appl. 2689/65, *X v. Belgium, Yearbook* X (1967), p. 282 (318).
813. Appl. 6185/73, *X v. Austria, D & R* 2 (1975), p. 68 (70).
814. Judgment of 28 November 1978, A.29 (1978), p. 20. This may be held to also include the investigations by the police, the prosecutor and the investigating judge preceding the trial. See also the report of 5 May 1988, *Kamasinski*, para. 169, where the Commission explicitly stated that the right to interpretation was not limited to the trial, but was also of
(continued...)

In German legal practice paragraph 3(e) was applied in such a way that an interpreter was indeed freely made available to begin with, but the expense involved was ultimately made to fall under the general regulation concerning the costs of the suit. This was justly considered by the Commission and the Court to be contrary to the word "free".[815] Moreover, the Court indicated that paragraph 3(e) refers not only to the expenses of an interpreter, but also to translation expenses, and then not only to the expenses relating to the hearing itself, but also to those concerning the translation of the charge brought against the accused, as referred to in Article 6(3)(a), and of the reasons for the arrest and the charges against him, mentioned in Article 5(2).[816] Even when the accused is discharged on account of the little importance of the case, or because the period of limitation has expired, the services of an interpreter during the trial should be paid by the authorities.[817]

22. Article 6 does not occur in the enumeration of Article 15(2) and accordingly is not non-derogable.

23. A comparison between Article 6 of the Convention and the corresponding Article 14 of the Covenant briefly shows the following differences.

Article 14 expressly stresses the principle that "All persons shall be equal before the courts and tribunals". The lack of such a provision in Article 6 is made up for to a considerable extent by the conjunction of Article 14 of the Convention with Article 6 as well as by the interpretation of Article 6 itself in the case-law. Nevertheless it remains conceivable that certain differences in treatment which do not conflict with the Convention, because they do not amount to discrimination in the sense of Article 14 or relate to a right which is not regulated in the Convention, do conflict with the equality principle of Article 14 of the Covenant.[818]

Article 14 speaks of "rights and obligations in a suit at law", while Article 6 contains the term "civil rights and obligations". The French text of the two treaties, however, uses an identical terminology, so that it may be assumed that the same thing is also meant by the English text of the two provisions.[819]

814.(...continued)
   significance in the pre-trial proceedings. Already at this stage a person charged with a criminal offence is entitled to receive the free assistance of an interpreter to the extent that such assistance is necessary to provide him with an opportunity to prepare his defence and thereby to ensure that the trial will be fair.
815. Report of 18 May 1977, *Luedicke, Belkacem and Koç*, B.27 (1977-78), p. 26, and judgment of 28 November 1978 in the same case, A.29 (1979), p. 19.
816. *Ibidem.*
817. This follows from the judgment of 26 March 1982, *Adolf*, A.49 (1982), pp. 14-17, and the reports of 12 May 1982, *Öztürk*, B.58 (1987), pp. 24-32 and of 6 May 1981, *Minelli*, B.52 (1986), pp. 21-22.
818. One may think, for instance, of a regulation which, for civil proceedings, offers wider possibilities for legal assistance for nationals than for aliens, also in situations in which the principle of "fair hearing" is not at issue. The "Report of the Committee of Experts", *supra* note 14, pp. 36-37, on this point would appear somewhat over-simplified. The principle of "equality of arms", to which this Report refers, concerns the equality between parties, not equal treatment in general.
819. See *supra* p. 299.

Article 14(1) stipulates that the court has to be not only independent and impartial, but also "competent". This guarantee is lacking in Article 6. It would not appear to be correct to say simply that the same guarantee is implied there in the words "established by law" as the Committee of Experts holds in its report;[820] a judgment may have been pronounced by an authority which is established by law, but manifestly lacked jurisdiction in the case in question. Apart from the case of Article 5(1)(a), the Convention appears not to afford any protection against this.

Whereas Article 6(1) prohibits unreasonable delay for civil as well as criminal cases, Article 14(3)(c) contains such a prohibition only for criminal cases.

While Article 6 mentions the interests of minors as one of the grounds for dealing with a case in camera, Article 14(4) provides quite generally that, in proceedings concerning juveniles, their age must be taken into account.

The publicity of the judgment is prescribed in an absolute sense in Article 6, while according to Article 14 exceptions are possible, viz. in the interest of juveniles or if the proceedings concern matrimonial disputes or the guardianship of children.

Article 14(3), in which the minimum guarantees for the accused are enumerated, again mentions in the first place the principle of equality. To the extent that these guarantees are also included in Article 6(3), the same holds good under the Convention in virtue of Article 14 of the latter. On some points, however, the guarantees in the Covenant go furter, or at least they are laid down more explicitly in it. These cases concern in particular the right to communicate with counsel, the right to be present in person at the trial, the right to be informed about the right to legal aid, and the right not to be compelled to testify against oneself or to confess guilt.

Article 14(5) grants the right of appeal to the person who has been convicted of a crime. The Committee of Experts justly points out that this provision has far-reaching consequences, in particular if it were to imply that an accused person who has been acquitted at first instance, but convicted on appeal, afterwards still has a right to appeal proceedings during which both the factual and the legal grounds are assessed once again.[821] Protocol no. 7 to the Convention contains in Article 2 the following supplementary provision:

> 1. Everyone convicted of a criminal offence by a tribunal shall have the right to have his conviction or sentence reviewed by a higher tribunal. The exercise of this right, including the grounds on which it may be exercised, shall be governed by law.
> 2. This right may be subject to exceptions in regard to offences of a minor character, as prescribed by law, or in cases in which the person concerned was tried in the first instance by the highest tribunal or was convicted following an appeal against acquittal.

Consequently, on this point the Convention has been supplemented, be it with some express limitations which are lacking in the Covenant.

---

820. "Report of the Committee of Experts", *supra* note 14, p. 37.
821. *Ibidem*, pp. 40-41.

Furthermore the provision in Article 14(6), according to which a person who has been convicted of a criminal offence by a final decision, but has afterwards been awarded reversal of the verdict, or has been pardoned, on the ground of a miscarriage of justice, shall be compensated for this, is lacking in the Convention (Article 5(5) grants such a right only in case of illegal arrest or detention), but is now provided in Protocol no. 7, *viz.* in Article 3, which reads:

> When a person has by a final decision been convicted of a criminal offence and when subsequently his conviction has been reversed, or he has been pardoned, on the ground that a new or newly discovered fact shows conclusively that there has been a miscarriage of justice, the person who has suffered punishment as a result of such conviction shall be compensated according to the law or the practice of the State concerned, unless it is proved that the non-disclosure of the unknown fact in time is wholly or partly attributable to him.

Finally the Convention also does not contain a provision such as Article 14(7), in which the *ne bis in idem* principle has been laid down for criminal cases.[822] On this point, too, Protocol no. 7 *qua* text also brings the Convention closer to the Covenant. Article 4 of the Protocol provides as follows:

> 1. No one shall be liable to be tried or punished again in criminal proceedings under the jurisdiction of the same State for an offence for which he has already been finally acquitted or convicted in accordance with the law and penal procedure of that State.
> 2. The provisions of the preceding paragraph shall not prevent the reopening of the case in accordance with the law and penal procedure of the State concerned, if there is evidence of new or newly discovered facts, or if there has been a fundamental defect in the previous proceeding, which could affect the outcome of the case.
> 3. No derogation from this Article shall be made under Article 15 of the Convention.

Thus, even a "non-derogable" element is introduced into the matter regulated by Article 6.[823]

§ 7. ARTICLE 7: FREEDOM FROM RETROSPECTIVE EFFECT OF PENAL LEGISLATION

1. No one shall be held guilty of any criminal offence on account of any act or omission which did not constitute a criminal offence under national or international law at the time when it was committed. Nor shall a heavier penalty be imposed than the one that was applicable at the time the criminal offence was committed.

2. This Article shall not prejudice the trial and punishment of any person

---

822. That the "ne bis in idem" rule does not form part of the original European Convention has repeatedly been stated by the Commission. See, *e.g.*, Appl. 7680/76, *X v. Federal Republic of Germany, D & R* 9 (1978), p. 190 (193). In its decision on Appl. 9433/81, *Menten v. the Netherlands, D & R* 27 (1982), p. 233 (234-238), however, the Commission stated: "Even assuming that a violation of this principle could under specific circumstances interfere with the right to 'fair trial' enshrined in Art. 6 of the Convention", and subsequently went in detail into the question whether this principle had been violated in this case.

823. For Protocol no. 7, see *infra* pp. 503-517. For the "case-law" of the Human Rights Committee concerning Article 14 of the covenant reference is made to the study by Nowak, mentioned *supra* at p. 216.

for any act or omission which, at the time when it was committed, was criminal according to the general principles of law recognised by civilised nations.

1. The first paragraph of Article 7 contains the following two separate principles: (1) A criminal conviction can only be based on a norm which existed at the time of the incriminating act or omission (*nullum crimen sine lege*). (2) On account of the infringement of that norm no heavier[824] penalty may be imposed than the one that was applicable at the time the offence was committed (*nulla poena sine lege*).

That these are two separate principles means, *inter alia*, that even a purely declaratory judgment in which a norm of criminal law is applied with retrospective effect and is declared to have been infringed, but in which no punishment or other measure is imposed on the offender, constitutes a violation of Article 7. This is not without importance, because such a declaratory judgment, when registered, may still have prejudicial consequences for the person in question, even apart from the social repercussions that it may also entail.

2. The rationale of the *nullum crimen, nulla poena* principle necessarily entails that it is also prohibited to apply an existing norm of criminal law *by analogy* to acts for which this norm is not intended, unless such an analogous application operates in favour of the person concerned. This is also the established case-law of the Commission.[825] Moreover, the legal certainty aimed at by the principle requires that the legislature shall formulate the norms of criminal law clearly and unambiguously, and that the authority applying the law shall interpret those norms restrictively.[826] This requirement serves to avoid that a criminal conviction is based on a legal norm of which the person concerned could not, or at least need not, have been aware beforehand. This last implication, too, has been recognized by the Commission. In this context it deems itself competent to review the interpretation and application of municipal law by the national court:

> Whereas, although it is not normally for the Commission to ascertain the proper interpretation of municipal law by national courts ..., the case is otherwise in matters where the Convention expressly refers to municipal law, as it does in Article 7; whereas under Article 7 the application of a provision of municipal penal law to an act not covered by the provision in question directly results in a conflict with the Convention, so that the Commission can and must take cognisance of allegations of such false

---

824. The word "heavier" seems to refer merely to the measure of the punishment, but the rationale of Art. 7(1) entails that also a punishment of a different kind than the one formerly provided for, which may be felt as more burdensome by the person in question, shall not be applied with retrospective effect.

825. For the first time in its decision on Appl. 1852/63, *X v. Austria, Yearbook* VII (1965), p. 190 (198). See also, *e.g.*, Appl. 6683/74, *X v. United Kingdom, D & R* 3 (1976), p. 95 (96), and Appl. 7721/76, *X v. the Netherlands, D & R* 11 (1978), p. 209 (211).

826. In the assessment of whether these requirements have been fulfilled, account should be taken of any specific expertise on the part of the party addressed by the norm: Appl. 8141/78, *X v. Austria, D & R* 16 (1979), p. 141 (142). See also Appl. 10980/84, *G v. Liechtenstein, D & R* 38 (1984), p. 234 (238).

interpretation of municipal law.[827]

The Commission, however, adds that it

exercises in this respect a purely supervisory function and must carry out its task with caution.[828]

The case-law of the Commission shows that the national authorities hardly have to fear an autonomous interpretation of that municipal law by the Commission.

As an example may serve the decision on Appl. 4161/69. In that case a person who had been convicted for homosexual practices invoked Article 7, alleging that the relevant criminal provision referred to "unnatural indecency" and that the behaviour for which he had been convicted - reciprocal masturbation - could only be deemed to fall thereunder if those words were interpreted in a very extensive sense. There is no evidence at all of an independent opinion of the Commission on whether the behaviour referred to could be deemed to be covered by the term "unnatural indecency" in a restrictive interpretation. It confined itself to considering that the interpretation here followed by the highest Austrian court was generally accepted at the time the acts were committed and at the time of the conviction.[829] The Commission was evidently of the opinion that for that reason the person in question knew, or could have known, that his behaviour was considered punishable, and that it was not for the Commission to review the correctness of this established case-law.[830]

It may indeed be argued that such a case-law itself has become part of the law as it stands at the time in question, and that the correctness of the conviction in such a case ought not to be tested against Article 7, but - in the example given above - against Article 8. In that situation the legality to be guaranteed by Article 7 is not in issue. But then it is advisable that the Commission clearly points to the existence of a constant case-law and bases its decision on the latter, and that it should not argue, as it did on a few occasions, that it is not its duty to review, as a kind of court of appeal, the correctness of the interpretation followed by the national court.[831] After all, the nature of the provision of Article 7 entails that the Strasbourg organs are called upon to test the matter themselves, in order that they may be able to judge whether a wider application, or a different application, has been given to the norm of criminal law than one could reasonably expect at the decisive

827. Appl. 1852/63, *X v. Austria*, Yearbook VIII (1965), p. 190 (198).
828. *Ibidem*, pp. 198-200.
829. Appl. 4161/69, *X v. Austria*, Yearbook XIII (1970), p. 798 (804-806).
830. See also Appls 6782-6784/74, *X, Y and Z v. Belgium*, D & R 9 (1978), p. 13 (22 in conjunction with 20), where with regard to the applicants' allegation that the act for which they had been convicted (including distribution of the journal "Sekstant") did not constitute a violation "according to the principles of European morality", the Commission referred to the Court's judgment in the *Handyside* Case, to the effect that a uniform European conception of morals does not exist.
831. See, *e.g.*, Appl. 4080/69, *X v. Austria*, *Coll.* 38 (1972), p. 4 (7), and Appl. 7721/76, *X v. the Netherlands*, D & R 11 (1978), p. 209 (210).

moments. When the national court has relied on previous case-law, the Strasbourg authorities have to be on the alert that this case-law does not imply in fact an aggravation of the norm since the time the act was committed.[832]

Not only written statutes, but also rules of common law or customary law may provide a sufficient legal basis for a criminal conviction, provided that the law is adequately accessible and is formulated with sufficient precision to enable the citizen to regulate his conduct.[833] While common law is by definition law developed by the courts, Article 7(1) excludes that any acts not previously punishable should be held by the courts to entail criminal liability, or that existing offences should be extended to cover facts which previously clearly did not constitute criminal offences. This implies, according to the Commission, that constituent elements of an offence, such as, *e.g.*, the particular form of culpability required for its completion, may not be essentially changed, at least not to the detriment of the accused, but that it is not objectionable that the existing elements of the offence are clarified and adapted to new circumstances which can reasonably be brought under the original concept of the offence.[834] In Appl. 10038/82 the applicant complained about an unforeseeable conviction for contempt of court. She maintained that until then it was not considered to be an offence when documents were shown to a journalist after they had been read out in court. The government submitted that the court had applied generally accepted principles of law to a factual situation which it had not previously had to consider. The Commission declared the application admissible[835] and meanwhile a friendly settlement has been reached.

In principle the national legislature is free to decide what act or omission is to be qualified as an offence and has to be penalized. Article 7 is not in issue there. The European review in that case is confined to the question of whether any of the other provisions of the Convention has been violated by that legislation.[836]

3. The *nulla poena* principle in its requirement of legal certainty does not go to such lengths that the exact measure of the penalty, or an exhaustive enumeration of alternatives, must be laid down in the criminal law provision. If, as is customary in several legal systems, only the maxima are indicated, the

---

832. See Appl. 6683/74, *X v. United Kingdom, D & R* 3 (1976), p. 95 (96), where the English court invoked a precedent which dated from the period subsequent to the moment the fact had been committed, and even subsequent to the commencement of the proceedings. For a rather thorough review by the Commission, see Appl. 8710/79, *X Ltd. and Y v. United Kingdom, D & R* 28 (1982), p. 77 (81-82).
833. Appl. 8710/79, *X Ltd. and Y v. United Kingdom, D & R* 28 (1982), p. 77 (80-81). For these conditions, cf. the judgment of 26 April 1979, *Sunday Times*, A.30 (1979), p. 31.
834. *Ibidem.*
835. Appl. 10038/82, *Harman v. United Kingdom, D & R* 38 (1984), p. 53 (63).
836. Thus the Commission in its decision on Appl. 7705/76, *X v. Federal Republic of Germany, D & R* 9 (1978), p. 196 (204), in connection with the applicant's allegation that refusal to perform military service does not cause anyone an injury and therefore cannot constitute a criminal offence in the sense of Art. 7.

legal subjects know what is the maximum penalty they may expect upon violation of the norm. If violation of the norm is penalized without a maximum being laid down, in the literal sense there can be no question of "a heavier penalty ... than the one that was applicable at the time the criminal offence was committed", unless at the latter time a different penalty was threatened. In that case, however, the second sentence of Article 7(1) will have to be interpreted to mean that the "applicable penalty" is the penalty which is usually inflicted for that particular offence within the legal system concerned, or which at all events was reasonably to be expected for the offender.

4. The use of the term "retrospective effect" in the title of this section is misleading in so far that under Article 7(1) it is of course equally prohibited to continue to apply in the old form any norms of criminal law or sanctions which had already been repealed or modified before the time of the offence.[837] Accordingly, it also forms part of the review by the Strasbourg organs to investigate whether and to what extent the norm of criminal law applied still had effect at the relevant time. Since this is essentially a question of national (constitutional) law, they will be guided to a high degree by the opinion of the national court in the matter.[838] Nevertheless, it is ultimately incumbent upon them to decide whether Article 7 has been correctly applied.

If it is evident from the legal practice in the country concerned that a particular norm of criminal law has fallen completely into desuetude, so that the offender could not reasonably presume that acting contrary to this norm would result in prosecution, it conflicts with Article 7 if that norm is applied in his case. It is, however, obvious that in such a case a heavy burden of proof rests on the person concerned.[839]

What is the situation if after the time the offence was committed, but before the trial, the norm of criminal law or the measure of the penalty has been modified in a sense which is more favourable for the accused? Do the courts then have to apply that modified provision? With respect to the measure of the penalty, Article 15 of the Covenant provides expressly:

> If, subsequent to the commission of the offence, provision is made by law for the imposition of a lighter penalty, the offender shall benefit thereby.

Such a provision is lacking in Article 7 of the Convention. The words "at the time the criminal offence was committed" suggest that this provision does not confer a right to application of the norm as subsequently alleviated, or of the

---

837. Appl. 1169/61, *X v. Federal Republic of Germany*, Yearbook VI (1963), p. 520 (588); Appl. 7721/76, *X v. the Netherlands*, *D & R* 11 (1978), p. 209 (211).
838. *Ibidem.*
839. The possibility seems to have been recognized in principle by the Commission in its decision on Appl. 7721/76, *X v. the Netherlands*, *D & R* 11 (1978), p. 209 (211), where, however, applicant's reference to one single example was deemed insufficient. See also Appl. 4161/69, *X v. Austria*, Yearbook XIII (1970), p. 798 (804-806), where the applicant alleged that the case-law had changed, but the Commission found that this change dated from prior to the moment the fact was committed.

lowered measure of the penalty.[840] However, Article 7 does not *prohibit* such an application either. It may even be prescribed by domestic law, as is the case in Article 1 of the Dutch Criminal Code. The lack of a provision of this import in Article 7 is to be regretted in our opinion. It can only be hoped that every court, apart from special circumstances,[841] will exercise this clemency if its domestic law leaves any scope for doing so.

5. Article 7 speaks of "a criminal offence under national or international law". With respect to the word "national" the question arises as to whether exclusively the national law of the State in question is meant or whether this State may also attach certain criminal law consequences to the violation within another State, of a provision of the criminal law of the latter State which does not form part of the criminal law of the first-mentioned State. On the basis of the rationale of Article 7, and also by reference to the European Convention on the International Validity of Criminal Judgments of 1970[842] and the European Convention on Extradition of 1957,[843] Jacobs arrives at a negative answer to that question.[844] He therefore adds a critical note to the decision of the Commission on Appl. 448/59, in which the Commission did not consider it contrary to Article 7 when the authorities of a State include in a person's police record a foreign conviction for an offence that is not punishable in that State itself.[845] One may, however, ask oneself whether such a registration, as well as, for instance, the execution of a criminal judgment pronounced abroad, really falls under the prohibition of Article 7. The English text "be held guilty" could have a wider scope than the French text "être condamné", which points to the pronouncement of the judgment itself and not to later consequences to be attached to that judgment. The words "national ... law" in our view must be understood to mean that a criminal judgment can be based only on the national law of the State in question, and not on the law of another State; but the wording of Article 7 would not appear to exclude the possibility that certain consequences are attached in State A to a judgment pronounced in State B on the basis of the criminal law applying in State B at that time, even in the case of a fact that is not punishable according to the law of State A. This does not alter the fact, however, that this practice is hard to be reconciled with the idea of the rule of law underlying Article 7, and such a practice in our opinion is objectionable on that ground.

840. Appl. 3777/68, *X v. United Kingdom, Coll.* 31 (1970), p. 120 (122); Appl. 7900/77, *X v. Federal Republic of Germany, D & R* 13 (1979), p. 70 (71-72).
841. As an example may serve the circumstance that the fact was committed in a special situation which no longer was present at the moment of the adjudication - one might think of special emergency legislation - which rendered the fact specially deserving of punishment.
842. *European Treaty Series*, no. 70.
843. *European Treaty Series*, no. 24.
844. Jacobs, *supra* note 17, pp. 123-124.
845. Appl. 448/59, *X v. Federal Republic of Germany, Yearbook* III (1960), p. 254 (270).

The reference to international law in the first paragraph of Article 7 raises the question of the internal effect of international law within the national legal order. Above, in Chapter I, we have already mentioned that, according to the prevalent opinion, international law as it stands does not oblige States to give internal effect to provisions of international law without their prior "transformation" into domestic law. Neither does such an obligation ensue from the Convention.[846] The effect of international law within the national legal order is regulated by national constitutional law.[847] In those contracting States where international law has no internal effect, this effect cannot be given in incidental cases to an international criminal law provision. Here again compliance with Article 7 depends on whether the person in question could reasonably know that the offence committed by him was prohibited and punishable within the relevant legal system at that time, either in virtue of a national legal provision or in virtue of a directly applicable international legal provision with internal effect.

6. At an early stage the Commission has taken the view that Article 7 relates only to criminal prosecutions as contemplated in Article 6(1) and *for that reason* is not applicable to disciplinary procedures.[848] While it is unclear why such a relation between the two provisions should be imperative, at all events the above distinction has lost its foundation as a result of the case-law described above, which established that the mere fact that a particular matter has been brought under disciplinary law and not under criminal law within a national legal system does not yet mean that Article 6 is not applicable.[849] With respect to Article 7, too, it seems appropriate to argue that those disciplinary convictions and sanctions, which as to their nature and their consequences greatly resemble a criminal conviction and the imposition of a penalty, fall within the scope of this provision. Preventive measures, however, are not covered by it,[850] no more than decisions concerning extradition[851] as far as the applicable extradition law - apart from the criminal law elements involved - is concerned.

7. The words "be held guilty" and "be imposed" at first sight point in the direction that Article 7 can only be held to have been violated if a norm of criminal law has actually been applied with retrospective effect, not merely on the basis of the fact that such a retrospective effect has been made possible

846. *Supra* pp. 11-15.
847. For the domestic status of the Convention in the individual contracting States, see A.Z. Drzemczewski, *European Human Rights Convention in Domestic Law; A Comparative Study*, Oxford 1983, pp. 59-191.
848. Appl. 4519/70, *X v. Luxembourg*, Yearbook XIV (1971), p. 616 (622).
849. *Supra* pp. 310-312.
850. Judgment of 14 November 1960, *Lawless*, A.1 (1961), p. 54.
851. Appl. 7512/76, *X v. the Netherlands*, D & R 6 (1977), p. 184 (186).

by the legislature.[852] However, one should not overlook the fact that the Convention is addressed to the contracting States, and accordingly to all the organs of these States, including the legislature. If the legislature gives retrospective effect to a provision of criminal law, Article 7 of the Convention has been violated. It is true that such a violation in general cannot be the object of an individual complaint, because it is not yet possible to speak of a victim.[853] It is, however, one of the characteristic features of the equally provided possibility of State complaints that legislation may be submitted *in abstracto* to review for its compatibility with the Convention without it being necessary to allege that there are (already) individual victims of the application of that law.[854]

8. The second paragraph of Article 7 contains an exception to the first paragraph for the case of the trial and punishment of an act or omission which, at the time when it was committed or omitted, was a criminal offence according to general principles of law. Although this provision is formulated in a general way, it has evidently been incorporated in particular to enable the application of the national and international legislation, enacted during and after World War II in respect of war crimes, collaboration with the enemy and treason, to facts committed during the war.[855] In that sense it forms a codification of the principles laid down by the tribunals of Nuremberg and Tokyo.[856] As such the provision is still important for those contracting States where the limitation in respect of war crimes has been suspended.[857] As Alkema rightly observes,[858] this effect of the provision does not fit in well with the system of the Convention, since Article 15(2) guarantees that the *nullum crimen-nulla poena* principle also applies to war situations.

However, the second paragraph may also have effect with respect to other cases than those mentioned above. In fact, it does not relate exclusively to war crimes, but to all acts and omissions which are criminal "according to the general principles of law recognised by civilised nations". The words from Article 7(2) here quoted have been taken from Article 38 of the Statute of

852. This view seems to be implied in the report in the *Greek* Case, *Yearbook* XII; *The Greek Case* (1969), p. 185: "It is not disputed that the penalties provided ... have not been imposed in any actual case".
853. In specific cases, however, the mere existence of a criminal law provision, even when it has not yet been applied in a concrete case, may hinder a person so much in his freedom of action that he can already be regarded as a victim. On this, *supra* pp. 41-42.
854. See *supra* p. 33.
855. Thus also the Commission in its decision on, *e.g.*, Appl. 1038/61, *X v. Belgium*, *Yearbook* IV (1961), p. 324 (336).
856. See Principle II of the Nuremberg Principles as formulated in 1950 by the International Law Commission, *Yearbook I.L.C.* 1950, vol. II, p. 379: "The fact that international law does not impose a penalty for an act which constitutes a crime under international law does not relieve the person who committed the act from responsibility under international law".
857. See also the Convention on the Non-Applicability of Statutory Limitations to War Crimes and Crimes against Humanity, drafted in 1968 within the framework of the UN, *International Legal Materials* 8 (1969), p. 68.
858. Alkema, *supra* note 8, p. 69.

the International Court of Justice.[859] Even the term "civilised nations", which is virtually meaningless, was copied; this in contrast with Article 15(2) of the Covenant, which speaks of "the community of States". The principal source of these general principles of law is constituted by the national systems of law. In that context, the general principles of law are those which have been recognized in (practically) all States *in foro domestico*. Since Article 7(2) does not refer to "the principles of law common to the contracting States", but to "the general principles of law recognised by civilised nations", the contracting States may not be treated as an isolated group in this respect. The legal rule concerned will also have to be recognized outside this circle by a "representative" group of States, if the principle of law is to be regarded as a general one. In addition, or frequently also in correlation therewith, general principles of law may emerge from the developing international law, usually on the basis of a pattern of treaties which have been concluded and/or of an international practice which has been or is in the process of being formed. They can then hardly be distinguished from customary international law.[860] Be this as it may, in our opinion the concept of general principles of law as here referred to requires that the facts concerned are not only made punishable in the legal systems of nearly all countries and/or under international law, but that their punishable character ensues from a fundamental legal principle.[861] Indeed, otherwise the guarantee of the first paragraph would be seriously jeopardized in all those cases where the legislature deliberately derogates from the criminal law as it applies in most countries in a way which is more favourable for the accused.

All this makes it difficult to establish with any accuracy what offences are meant by Article 7(2). This is particularly the case because, with respect to the international principles of law, it is here not the responsibility of the State but the responsibility of individuals which is at issue, a matter which usually is not regulated by international law. In addition to the above-mentioned war crimes one will have to think in particular of the so-called crimes against peace and crimes against humanity. A definition is contained in the Charter of the International Military Tribunal,[862] but in later documents the category of crimes against humanity has also been placed outside the war context.[863] More in general, it seems logical to also link the general principles of law of Article 7(2) with fundamental principles in the field of human rights. Those principles have been defined by Van Boven as "elementary rights or supra-

---

859. On this provision, see G.J.H. van Hoof, *Rethinking the Sources of International Law*, Deventer 1983, pp. 131-151.
860. *Ibidem*, p. 145.
861. On this, see P. van Dijk, "International Law and the Promotion and Protection of Human Rights", *Wayne Law Review* (1978), pp. 1529-1553 (1545-1546).
862. See Art. 6 of the Charter of the International Military Tribunal, *A.J.I.L.* 39 (1945), Supplement, p. 257.
863. Art. I(b) of the Convention on the Non-Applicability of Statutory Limitations to War Crimes and Crimes against Humanity *(supra* note 857), speaks of "crimes against humanity, whether committed in time of war or in time of peace", and mentions as examples "inhuman acts resulting from the policy of apartheid and the crime of genocide".

positive rights, *i.e.* rights whose validity is not dependent on their acceptance by the subjects of law but which are at the foundation of the international community".[864] We may mention here, for instance, the right to life and to the physical and psychological integrity of the person, the prohibition of slavery and torture, and the prohibition of racial discrimination.[865] For the applicability of Article 7(2) it is required that the violation of these principles by individuals is punishable according to the national law of (practically) all countries, or that under international law not only the State but also the offender individually is responsible for it. Only then is it possible to speak of a "criminal act or omission".[866] Violation of the above-mentioned fundamental rights will be punishable in one form or another in most national systems, so that the problem of *Drittwirkung* will not bar their application as general principles of law. However, to the extent that general principles of international law have not been incorporated in one way or another in domestic law, they can serve as a basis for the conviction of individuals only in those cases where the violation of these principles can be qualified as a "crime against humanity".[867] In other cases, in our opinion, the individual responsibility is not yet established clearly enough under international law as it stands at present.

9. According to Article 15(2) the guarantee implied in Article 7(1) is non-derogable. As has been said, however, the consequence of the second paragraph of Article 7 is that with respect to certain offences this guarantee is not an absolute one, neither in the situations referred to in Article 15(1) nor in other cases.[868]

10. A comparison between the text of Article 7(1) and that of the corresponding first paragraph of Article 15 of the Covenant shows that the latter provision contains the following addition: "If, subsequent to the commission of the offence, provision is made by law for the imposition of a lighter penalty, the offender shall benefit thereby". The Committee of Experts assumes in its report that the words "subsequent to the commission of the offence" do not imply that a person already convicted might also derive rights from a mitigation of punishment introduced after his conviction.[869] Considering the use of the word "imposition", this appears indeed not to have been intended.

The differences between Article 7(2) and Article 15(2) are only of a textual nature. In particular the Covenant more correctly mentions of "the community of nations", while the Convention still uses the phrase of "civilised

864. Van Boven, *supra* note 7, p. 43.
865. See the enumeration by Van Boven, *ibidem*, pp. 44-48.
866. For war crimes and crimes against humanity this individual responsibility has been laid down in the above-mentioned documents. See also Art. I of the Convention on the Prevention and Punishment of the Crime of Genocide and Art. 1(2) of the International Convention on the Suppression and Punishment of the Crime of Apartheid.
867. "Crimes against humanity" used in the sense of also including war crimes, genocide and apartheid. See the preceding note.
868. See *supra* pp. 365-366.
869. Report of the Committee of Experts, *supra* note 14, p. 41.

nations".[870]

§ 8. ARTICLE 8: RIGHT TO RESPECT FOR PRIVACY

1. Everyone has the right to respect for his private and family life, his home and his correspondence.

2. There shall be no interference by a public authority with the exercise of this right except such as is in accordance with the law and is necessary in a democratic society in the interests of national security, public safety or the economic well-being of the country, for the prevention of disorder or crime, for the protection of health or morals, or for the protection of the rights and freedoms of others.

1. Since any further definition is lacking, the rights laid down in this provision cannot be clearly distinguished from each other. This is true in particular for the right to respect for private life on the one hand, and the other three rights belonging to the private sphere on the other hand. In fact, a clear delimitation is not necessary, since a complaint concerning violation of the private sphere can be based on the provision as a whole. As Jacobs rightly observes: "the fact that they are grouped together in the same Article strengthens the protection given by that Article, since each right is reinforced by its context".[871] Thus, it was held by the Commission in the case of a stepmother:

> It is here not necessary to decide whether, in the absence of any legal relationship, the ties between the applicant and the child amounted to "family life" ... . Bearing in mind that the applicant has cared for the child for many years and is deeply attached to him, the separation ordered by the court undoubtedly affects her "private life".[872]

As a collective noun designating the rights involved in Article 8, the "right to privacy" is often used nowadays. However, this term also comprises other rights than those expressly mentioned in Article 8. In Resolution 428(1970) of the Consultative (Parliamentary) Assembly of the Council of Europe, which contains the Declaration concerning the Mass Media and Human Rights, this right has been defined as follows:

> The right to privacy consists essentially in the right to live one's own life with a minimum of interference. It concerns private, family and home life, physical and moral integrity, honour and reputation, avoidance of being placed in a false light, non-revelation of irrelevant and embarrassing facts, unauthorised publication of private photographs, protection from disclosure of information given or received by the individual confidentially.[873]

---

870. For the "case-law" of the Human Rights Committee concerning Article 15 of the Covenant reference is made to the study by Nowak, mentioned *supra* at p. 216.
871. Jacobs, *supra* note 17, p. 126.
872. Appl. 8257/78, *X v. Switzerland*, *D & R* 13 (1979), p. 248 (252). See also Appls 7289/75 and 7349/76, *X and Y v. Switzerland*, *Yearbook XX* (1977), p. 372 (408-410).
873. Council of Europe, Cons. Ass., Twenty-First Ordinary Session (Third Part), *Texts Adopted* (1970); Council of Europe, *Collected Texts*, Strasbourg 1979, p. 908 (911).

And in the final conclusions of the Nordic Conference of Jurists on the Right to Respect for Privacy of 1967 the following additional elements of the right to privacy are listed: the prohibition to use a person's name, identity or photograph without his consent, the prohibition to spy on a person, respect for correspondence and the prohibition to disclose official information.[874] The Commission has connected the right to privacy of Article 8 also with the right to freedom of expression of Article 10 by stating that "the concept of privacy in Article 8 also includes, to a certain extent, the right to establish and maintain relations with other human beings for the fulfilment of one's personality".[875]

Two elements of the right to privacy as defined above which are not mentioned in Article 8 are referred to expressly in Article 10(2) as grounds for restriction of the freedom of expression: the protection of a person's reputation and the prevention of disclosure of information received in confidence. In order to rely on such grounds, however, an express legal basis is required; the restrictions must be such "as are prescribed by law". Moreover, it has been recognized by the Commission that the right to protection of one's reputation constitutes a "civil right" in the sense of Article 6(1).[876] Whether these and other, comparable interests also find protection in Article 8 depends on the content given in the national and European case-law to the rights expressly mentioned therein. In this context it is noteworthy that, although the *travaux préparatoires* appear to point in a different direction,[877] the Commission seems to have implicitly recognized the possibility that attacks on a person's reputation may constitute a breach of Article 8.[878]

2. As to the respect for private life, the question of the registration of persons attracts the greatest amount of attention at present. Strasbourg case-law so far exists only with respect to the registration by the police and the judiciary. In the Commission's opinion this does not conflict with Article 8, not even when the registration concerns persons who do not have any criminal record.[879] In this form, without any further qualifications, such a viewpoint would appear to be hardly tenable. It must be examined explicitly whether one of the two grounds of restriction mentioned in the second paragraph is applicable. Moreover, a review of the collection and use of the data for its compatibility with the *détournement de pouvoir* provision of Article 18 would seem to be required. Such a review actually took place in a more

---

874. See J. Velu, "The European Convention on Human Rights and the Right to Respect for Private Life, the Home and Communications", in: A.H. Robertson (ed.), *Privacy and Human Rights, Third International Colloquy*, Brussels 1970, Manchester 1973, p. 12 (33).
875. Appl. 8962/80, *X and Y v. Belgium, D & R* 28 (1982), p. 112 (124).
876. Appl. 808/60, *ISOP v. Austria, Yearbook* V (1962), p. 108 (122).
877. For this, see Velu, *supra* note 874, pp. 15-16.
878. Appl. 2413/65, *X v. Federal Republic of Germany, Coll.* 23 (1967), p. 1 (7).
879. See Appl. 5877/72, *X v. United Kingdom, Yearbook* XVI (1973), p. 328 (388), where the complaint concerned the taking, and storing in a file, of photographs of applicant by the police for possible future identification purposes. The Commission evidently considered it decisive here that the photographs had not been released for publication or used for purposes other than police ends.

recent case, which concerned the transmission of personal data by the police to the criminal court. The Commission considered this act justified in the interest of the prevention of crime, although this case concerned the prosecution of a crime and not its prevention. The Commission left open the question of whether the act in this case conflicted at all with the first paragraph.[880]

In the *Leander* Case the complaint concerned the fact that information derived from the secret police register had prevented the applicant from obtaining permanent employment and had led to his dismissal from provisional employment, while the authorities had refused to disclose that information to him. In that case review on the basis of the second paragraph was performed after the Commission had reached the conclusion that the facts disclosed an interference with the applicant's right to respect for his private life. The Commission agreed with the Government that the issue depended on the contents of the register concerned. A register which only contains, for instance, the name and address of an individual does not normally involve any interference with Article 8. In the case of Mr. Leander, however, the secret information was of great importance, and its handing out had seriously affected Mr. Leander, since it was the basis for the decision that from a security point of view he could not be employed. After a detailed discussion of the intelligence system concerned the Commission stated as its conclusion that, "having regard to the area of discretion which must be left to the State in respect of the defence of the national security", that system contained sufficient and effective safeguards, which justified the conclusion that the interference with Mr. Leander's right to respect for his private life was "necessary in a democratic society in the interests of national security" in the sense of the second paragraph of Article 8.[881]

The *Gaskin* Case concerned a complaint about refusal of access to a file. Mr. Gaskin wished to have access to the whole file relating to his period in care. The applicant was taken into care at a very young age, after the death of his mother, and had remained in care until he attained his majority. The complaint was presented against the background of his severe phsychological problems, which he ascribed to the way in which he was treated while in care. The Government contended that since the applicant's majority the file served no operational or practical purpose. It was retained only as a result of the proceedings pending before the Commission, and in normal circumstances would have been destroyed some three years after the applicant's majority. This case differed from the *Leander* Case as far as the character of the data is concerned but also in that in the latter case the personal information on file was the basis of decisions which Mr. Leander complained were detrimental to him, while in the *Gaskin* Case no use at all

---

880. Appl. 8170/78, *X v. Austria, Yearbook* XXII (1979), p. 308 (320-322).
881. Report of 17 May 1985, A.116 (1987), p. 39 and pp. 47-48. In its judgment in this case the Court came to the same conclusion as the Commission; judgment of 26 March 1987, *ibidem*, pp. 26-27.

was currently made of the file in relation to the applicant or any other person. In its report the Commission concentrated on the question whether the interference was necessary in a democratic society. According to the Commission the interference attributed to a legitimate aim as the confidentiality served to protect the contributors to the file from unwarranted criticism and attack in the light of their contributions. The interests of confidentiality must be weighed against the interests of the applicant. The contributors to the file had been asked whether they consented to the applicant having access to the file. Several of them had consented, but others had not. The contributors who had declined to permit access had not been asked for their reasons. Some of them had nevertheless given reasons, relating mainly to the confidential nature of the material, when it was originally contributed and the protection of contributors, *inter alia* from possible involvement in litigation. None of these reasons suggested that it might not be in the applicant's interests to have access to any particular contribution. The Commission came to the conclusion that under English law the responsible authority appeared not to be in the position to weigh the applicant's interest in access to the file against the various refusals and found

> that the absence of any procedure to balance the applicant's interest in access to the file against the claim to confidentiality by certain contributors, and the consequential automatic preference given to the contributors' interests over those of the applicant, is disproportionate to the aim pursued and cannot be said to be necessary in a democratic society.

The Commission concluded by six votes to six with a casting-vote by the Acting President that there had been a violation of Article 8.[882]

In Application 9702/82 the obligation to complete a census form was challenged. The Commission took the view that a compulsory public census, including questions relating to the sex, marital status, place of birth and other personal details may constitute a *prima facie* interference with the right to respect for private and family life which fails to be justified under the terms of the second paragraph of Article 8. Here again, however, but with a much shorter and less convincing reasoning than in the *Leander* Case, the Commission found that the interference was justified as being necessary in a democratic society - in this case "in the interest of the economic well-being of the country".[883]

In addition to the registration by the police and the judiciary, and public census, all of which have a long tradition, registration of all sorts of personal data by the public authorities and private institutions is taking place to an increasing degree, in particular as a result of the development of techniques making possible the automatic storage and processing of data. In most cases the use that is made of these data cannot be checked by the person concerned, so that, even if he has furnished the data of his own free will,

---

882. Report of 13 November 1987, para. 103. Meanwhile the case has been referred to the Court.
883. Appl. 9702/82, *X v. United Kingdom, D & R* 30 (1983), p. 239 (240-241).

that use may still imply an interference with his private life. In this respect the public authorities are bound by Article 8. As regards private institutions, the issue of the *Drittwirkung* of Article 8 arises.[884] The second paragraph of Article 8 expressly mentions "interference by a public authority". It might be inferred from this that the whole article refers only to acts by the authorities. However, the interpretation equally appears tenable that the first paragraph generally prohibits interference with privacy and the second paragraph permits such interference on particular grounds and exclusively by the public authorities. Yet, within the framework of the Council of Europe, in a resolution of the Committee of Ministers, the issue of the protection of privacy has been raised precisely with respect to the registration of persons in the private sector,[885] from which it might be concluded that this organ of the Council of Europe does not assume the *Drittwirkung* of Article 8. The case-law, too, points in that direction, since both the Court and the Commission have found with regard to Article 8 that:

> its object is essentially that of protecting the individual against arbitrary interference by the public authorities in his private or family life.[886]

Be that as it may, since neither the text of Article 8 nor the character of the right protected therein is opposed to this, and this right deserves to be protected equally against encroachment by private individuals, it would appear, in the light of the development of legal opinion in that field,[887] that a good deal is to be said in favour of assigning *Drittwirkung* to Article 8. Of course this does not mean that in Strasbourg a complaint against a private individual could be submitted,[888] but it would imply that the article could be invoked before the national courts against a private individual in those systems in which the Convention has internal effect. Moreover, Article 8 then would imply the obligation for the contracting States to assure respect for privacy by individuals to the best of their ability *via* the legislature, the administration and the courts.[889]

Another example of interference with private life is the compulsory subjection to a medical or psychological examination. As the Commission states:

---

884. See *supra* pp. 15-20.
885. Resolution (73)22 of 26 September 1973 "on the protection of the privacy of individuals *vis-à-vis* electronic data banks in the private sector", *European Yearbook* XXI (1973), p. 361.
886. Judgment of 23 July 1968, *Belgian Linguistic Case*, A.6 (1968), pp. 24-25; report of 1 March 1979, *Van Oosterwijck*, B.36 (1983), p. 24.
887. See Report of the Committee of Experts, *supra* note 14, p. 15, where it is emphasized that the problem of *Drittwirkung* is greatly determined by new developments in the matter, since the text of the Convention does not give any definite answer.
888. *Ibidem* and *supra* p. 77.
889. In its report of 1 March 1979, *Van Oosterwijck*, B.36 (1983), p. 24, the Commission held that "Article 8 does not expressly guarantee the right to be protected by the law against interferences with private life", but in the construction here defended not a legal right but a reflex effect would be in issue.

A compulsory medical intervention, even if it is of minor importance, must be considered as an interference with this right.[890]

So far only complaints of persons who had to undergo such an examination as suspects have been submitted to the Commission. The applicants generally did not invoke Article 8, but Articles 3, 5, and 6, and they were told by the Commission that such examinations constitute a normal and frequently also desirable element of the investigation of a case.[891] If the Commission had reviewed, *ex officio*, such examinations for their compatibility with Article 8, it should have ascertained whether they were authorized by law and whether subjection thereto could be justified on the basis of one of the grounds of limitation of the second paragraph. In a case where the applicant did invoke Article 8, it was indeed recognized by the Commission that a compulsory psychiatric examination constitutes a breach of the first paragraph of this provision, and the measure was reviewed for its justification under the second paragraph.[892] A similar review should take place - and in a number of cases was actually performed by the Commission - in connection with other encroachments on the private life of suspects, such as searching of the person, luggage and cars,[893] the taking and circulation of photographs, the taking of fingerprints and blood tests,[894] and the making of tape-recordings which are later used during the trial as evidence against the suspect.[895]

Another aspect of private life with regard to which far-reaching restrictions are laid down in the legislation of most of the contracting States is that of sexuality: prohibition of sexual intercourse with minors, prohibition of homosexual practices, prohibition of the use (or the sale) of contraceptives, and the like. The Strasbourg case-law has expressly recognized that sexual life forms an important part of a person's private life.[896]

A general prohibition of homosexual practices was accepted as justified by the Commission in an early decision on the basis of the protection of health and morals relied upon by the respondent State.[897] The Commission did not

890. Appl. 8278/78, *X v. Austria, D & R* 18 (1980), p. 155 (156).
891. Appl. 986/61, *X v. Federal Republic Germany, Yearbook* V (1962), p. 192 (198).
892. Appl. 8355/78, *X v. Federal Republic of Germany*, not published. The Commission held that such an examination was justified in this case "for the prevention of disorder or crime and for the protection of health".
893. See, *e.g.*, Appl. 5488/72, *X v. Belgium, Yearbook* XVII (1974), p. 222 (226).
894. For the blood test aimed at the determination of the alcohol content of the bloodstream in connection with the traffic legislation, see: Appl. 8239/78, *X v. the Netherlands, D & R* 16 (1979), p. 184 (189), where the Commission considered the test justified "for the protection of the rights of others". For a blood test aimed at the determination of paternity, see Appl. 8278/78, *X v. Austria, D & R* 18 (1980), p. 155 (157), where the Commission considered the test permissible on the same ground.
895. The justification of the latter by the Commission without an ex officio review for its justification under Art. 8, second paragraph, would therefore appear to be incorrect: Appl. 2645/65, *Scheichelbauer v. Austria, Yearbook* XII (1969), p. 156 (172). The problem of wire-tapping and the opening of correspondence between the accused and his counsel has been discussed *supra* p. 348; see also *infra* pp. 392-396.
896. For the Commission, see, *e.g.*, its decision on Appl. 5935/72, *X v. Federal Republic of Germany, Yearbook* XIX (1976), p. 277 (284-286). For the Court, see the judgment of 22 October 1981, *Dudgeon*, A.45 (1982), pp. 18-19; judgment of 26 October 1988, *Norris*, A.142 (1989), p. 17.
897. Appl. 104/55, *X v. Federal Republic of Germany, Yearbook* I (1955-57), p. 228 (229).

provide any arguments for this. In particular it does not appear from the decision whether the Commission has undertaken an independent inquiry into the necessity and proportionality of the restriction in relation to the interests to be protected, or whether, if it has done so, it has taken into account the developments in the opinions on the subject within the country concerned and also within the total area in which the Convention applies. The importance of such an inquiry became evident when the legislation in that same country was modified some time afterwards to the effect that exclusively homosexual intercourse with persons under eighteen years of age remained punishable; from this it could be deduced that opinions had indeed changed about the necessity in a democratic society of the absolute and general prohibition.[898] The issue of the scope of the inquiry to be made by the Strasbourg organs will be discussed below.[899] Here we confine ourselves to mentioning that on a later occasion, with a similar complaint of a person prosecuted for homosexual acts, the Commission clearly showed that it considered to have the power to undertake an inquiry into the justification of the restriction concerned and was prepared to take into account new developments within the country in question and elsewhere.[900] In a later stage a couple of complaints of homosexuals against the United Kingdom, in which a breach of Article 8 was alleged, were declared admissible[901] and examined as to their merits.[902] The first of these cases resulted in a resolution of the Committee of Ministers,[903] the second in a judgment of the Court.[904] The first case concerned a complaint against application of the English Sexual Offences Act, in which homosexual intercourse with male persons under 21 years of age was declared punishable. Here the Commission - followed in this by the Committee of Ministers - found that the prosecution and the punishment were justified on the ground of "the protection of the rights and freedoms of others".[905] The second case concerned a complaint against the legislation in Northern Ireland, prohibiting homosexual intercourse even between consenting male persons over 21 years of age. In this case both the Commission and the Court concluded that this penalization could not be deemed necessary for the protection of morals in a democratic society, whereas the justification of the prohibition with regard to male persons under 21 years of age, here again,

898. See Appl. 5935/72, *X v. Federal Republic of Germany*, Yearbook XIX (1976), p. 277 (284).
899. *Infra* pp. 583-606. With regard to the discrimination aspect in this case, see also *infra* p. 538.
900. See Appl. 5935/72, *X v. Federal Republic of Germany*, Yearbook XIX (1976), p. 277 (284-286), where the Commission took into consideration in particular the modern opinions on the possible effect which a homosexual relationship has on juveniles, and on the question of what age limit would have to be laid down.
901. Appl. 7215/75, *X v. United Kingdom*, Yearbook XXI (1978), p. 354 (372), and Appl. 7525/76, *X v. United Kingdom*, Yearbook XXII (1979), p. 156 (184).
902. Report of 12 October 1978, *X v. United Kingdom*, D & R 19 (1980), p. 66 and Report of 13 March 1980, *Dudgeon*, B.40 (1984), pp. 32-42.
903. Resolution DH(79)5 of 12 June 1979, D & R 19 (1980), pp. 82-83.
904. Judgment of 22 October 1981, *Dudgeon*, A.45 (1982).
905. Report of 12 October 1978, *X v. United Kingdom*, D & R 19 (1980), p. 66 (75).

was deemed justifiable by both the Commission and the Court.[906] Another complaint about the Irish legislation penalizing certain homosexual acts in private between consenting adult males was dealt with in the *Norris* Case. The Commission and Court referred to the *Dudgeon* Case and held that there was no "pressing social need" to make such acts criminal offences.[907]

In a decision of 1983 the Commission repeated in a general sense the Strasbourg case-law that "the prohibition by criminal law of homosexual acts committed in private between consenting males amounts to an interference with the 'private life' of those concerned under Article 8(1)". Here the age of the partners, or one of them, was not at issue, but the fact that the prohibiting regulation concerned soldiers. The Commission here accepted that homosexual conduct by members of the armed forces may pose a particular risk to order within the forces, which would not arise in civilian life. It referred for that to the evidence given by the Ministry of Defence to the House of Commons Select Committee, which is quoted in the Commission's decision and which the Commission accepted as legitimate.[908] However, if one reads that "evidence", one is struck by the old-fashioned and prejudiced reasoning on which it is based and which seems to neglect that the real risk to order within the forces, if any, is not created by homosexual conduct as such, but rather by the discriminatory attitude towards it in and outside military circles, against which the Convention and its organs ought to protect the individual.

A complaint against a decision of the German *Bundesverfassungsgericht* in which provisions in the new German legislation on abortion were declared unconstitutional, and against the subsequently introduced amendments, both challenged, *inter alia*, under Article 8, was declared admissible by the Commission in so far as the two female applicants were concerned. The Commission based its decision on the following, very widely formulated ground:

> the Commission considers that pregnancy and the interruption of pregnancy are part of private life, and also in certain circumstances of family life. It further considers that respect for private life "comprises also, to a certain degree, the right to establish and to develop relationships with other human beings, especially in the emotional field, for the development and fulfilment of one's own personality" ... and that therefore sexual life is also part of private life; and in particular that legal regulation of abortion is an intervention in private life which may or may not be justified under Article 8(2).[909]

As has been observed above, this formulation would appear to leave sufficient scope for the admissibility also of complaints of men against a prohibition or restriction of voluntary abortion, but the male applicant in this case had

---

906. Report of 13 March 1980, *Dudgeon*, B.40 (1984), p. 41; judgment of 22 October 1981, A.45 (1981), pp. 23-24. See also the Voogd Report on discrimination of homosexuals, submitted to the Parliamentary Assembly of the Council of Europe; Doc. 4755, 8 July 1981.
907. Report of 12 March 1987, and judgment of 26 October 1988, A.142 (1989), p. 33 and pp. 20-21 respectively.
908. Appl. 9237/81, *B v. United Kingdom*, D & R 34 (1983), p. 68 (72).
909. Appl. 6959/74, *Brüggemann & Scheuten v. Federal Republic of Germany*, Yearbook XIX (1976), p. 382 (414).

insufficiently proved the injury sustained by him.[910] In its report on the merits of the case the Commission held that the new regulation, adopted in consequence of the decision of the *Bundesverfassungsgericht*, having regard to the weighing of interests on which it was based, did not conflict with Article 8(1),[911] and the Committee of Ministers agreed with this point of view.[912]

The right to respect for private life was also invoked in two applications by transsexuals who complained about the refusal of the national authorities to take account of the change in their status which was the result of a sexual conversion operation. Both complaints were declared admissible by the Commission.[913] In one of the cases a friendly settlement was subsequently reached, after the German authorities had proceeded to enter the change of name and the change of sex in the birth register.[914] In the *Van Oosterwijck* Case the Commission concluded that the refusal of the Belgian authorities to take account of "an essential element of his personality: his sexual identity resulting from his changed physical form, his physical make-up, and his social rôle", amounted to "a veritable failure to recognise the respect due to his private life within the meaning of Article 8(1) of the Convention".[915] The Court did not reach a judgment on the merits because of its decision that Van Oosterwijck had not exhausted the local remedies.[916]

In the more recent *Rees* Case the Commission confirmed its view that Article 8 must be understood as protecting a transsexual against the non-recognition of his/her changed sex as part of his/her personality. In the opinion of the Commission, this does not mean that this legal recognition must be extended to the period prior to the specific moment of change, but "it must be possible for the individual after the change has been effected to confirm his/her normal appearance by the necessary document". In the case of Mr. Rees this requirement was not met in the Commission's view, because it was made impossible for him to have his birth certificate altered to show his male sex, which resulted for him in being treated as an ambiguous being with all annoying consequences involved.[917] The Court joined the Commission in the view that Article 8 not only protects the individual against arbitrary interference, but may also imply positive obligations on the part of the authorities. But the Court disagreed with the Commission by holding that the positive obligations do not extend so far as to require the Government to make possible annotations to the birth register as applied for by Mr. Rees and to enact detailed legislation regulating the effects of such annotations. The Court indicates the intermediate character of its judgment by stating:

---

910. See *supra* p. 42.
911. Report of 12 July 1977, *D & R* 10 (1978), p. 100 (114-118). See, however, the dissenting opinion of Commission Member Fawcett, *ibidem*, p. 144.
912. Resolution DH(78)1 of 17 March 1978, *D & R* 10 (1978), pp. 121-122.
913. Appl. 6699/74, *X v. Federal Republic of Germany, D & R* 11 (1978), p. 16 (25) and Appl. 7654/76, *Van Oosterwijck v. Belgium, Yearbook* XXI (1978), p. 476 (490).
914. *D & R* 17 (1980), p. 21.
915. Report of 1 March 1979, B.36 (1983), p. 26.
916. Judgment of 6 November 1980, A.40 (1981), pp. 13-19.
917. Report of 12 December 1984, A.106 (1987), pp. 24-26.

376

That being so, it must for the time being be left to the respondent State to determine to what extent it can meet the remaining demands of transsexuals. However, the Court is conscious of the seriousness of the problems affecting these persons and the distress they suffer. The Convention has always to be interpreted and applied in the light of current circumstances ... . The need for appropriate legal measures should therefore be kept under review having regard particularly to scientific and societal developments.[918]

This "consciousness", on the part of the Court, of Mr. Rees' distress will hardly have comforted him. It is difficult to understand why the problems with which the government is confronted by the demands of transsexuals are given more weight by the Court than these demands themselves, which concern the formal recognition of so vital an element of their personality as their sex.

The issue of the scope of the positive obligations involved in Article 8 was also discussed in the Case of *X and Y v. the Netherlands*. There a father complained that a person who had sexually abused his mentally handicapped daughter, was not prosecuted by the Dutch authorities, on the mere ground that the victim was incapable of lodging the required complaint and the father was not legally empowered to do so as her substitute. The Court held that the positive obligations inherent in Article 8 may involve the adoption of measures designed to secure respect for private life even in the sphere of the relations of individuals between themselves. It found that neither the protection afforded by Dutch civil law nor that offered by the current Criminal Code was sufficient, and that, therefore, taking account of the nature of the wrongdoing in question, the daughter was the victim of a violation of Article 8.[919]

In view of the present discussion concerning euthanasia a decision of the Commission of 1983 seems to be of special interest where the Commission took the position that the activities for which the applicant was convicted, namely aiding and abetting suicide, cannot be described as falling in the sphere of his private life in the sense of Article 8. While these activities might be thought to touch directly on the private lifes of those who sought to commit suicide, in relation to the person who committed them they were excluded from the concept of privacy "by virtue of their trespass on the public interest of protecting life".[920]

The obligation for prisoners to wear prison clothes was recognized by the Commission as an interference with the right of respect for private life, but after a very marginal review was considered justified as necessary in the interest of public safety and for the prevention of disorder and crime.[921] This approach - leaving apart the final conclusion - would seem to be more correct than the one adopted by the Commission half a year later, when it held that a general limitation of visiting facilities to relatives and close friends of the prisoners was reasonable and constituted no interference with the

---

918. Judgment of 17 October 1986, A.106 (1987), pp. 15-19.
919. Judgment of 26 March 1985, A.91, pp. 11-14.
920. Appl. 10083/82, *R v. United Kingdom, D & R* 33 (1983), p. 270 (271-272).
921. Appl. 8231/78, *X v. United Kingdom, D & R* 28 (1982), p. 5 (29-30).

prisoners' right to respect for private life.[922] In our opinion, any limitation of visitors, no matter how reasonable, constitutes an interference with privacy and should be tested for its conformity with the second paragraph.

The *Chappell* Case, finally, concerned the search of a house in connection with suspicion that video cassettes were made in breach of copyright by a company controlled by the applicant. The premises were used for both business and residential purposes. In the Commission's view, although the search was directed against the applicant's and his company's business activities, it indirectly impinged on the applicant's private life and the private sphere of items and associations which are attributes of a home. The Commission left open the question whether some private papers of the applicant constituted correspondence within the meaning of Artice 8, as the interference therewith anyway fell within the private life sphere. The Commission reached the conclusion that the interference was necessary in a democratic society for the protection of the rights of others.[923]

3. The notion of "family life" in Article 8 is an autonomous concept, which must be interpreted independently of the national law of the contracting States.[924] Moreover, the family life to be considered is not *de jure* family life, but *de facto* family life.[925] Thus the Commission and the Court took the view that the fact of birth, *i.e.* the biological tie between mother and child, as a rule creates family life in the sense of Article 8, also in the case of a mother and an illegitimate child.[926] It was also held that extra-marital relationships may raise issues of family life, provided that the persons in question live together on a permanent basis and keep house jointly.[927] The States may, however, set up a procedure to establish the truth of the alleged family links.[928] Furthermore the traditional European conception of the countries of the Council of Europe is not considered decisive; a family composed according to a different cultural pattern - *e.g.* a polygamous family - is equally entitled to protection.[929] The same respect for different cultural patterns applies in principle to the way in which parents bring up their children. Respect for family life comprises respect for a style of education which differs from that which is common in a given society, provided that the treatment involved is not to be considered criminal and punishable under the general

922. Appl. 9054/80, *X v. United Kingdom, D & R* 30 (1983), p. 113 (115).
923. Report of 14 October 1987, A.152-A (1989), p. 29.
924. Thus also the Commission in its report of 10 December 1977, *Marckx*, B.29 (1982), p. 44.
925. Appl. 5302/71, *X and Y v. United Kingdom, Coll.* 44 (1973), p. 29 (47).
926. See the decision on Appl. 6833/74, *Marckx v. Belgium, Yearbook* XVIII (1975), p. 248 (270), and the case-law there mentioned. Thus also the judgment of 13 June 1979 in this case, A.31 (1979), p. 14, where the Court uses the argument that a different standpoint would amount to discrimination on the ground of birth, contrary to Art. 14.
927. Appls 7289/75 and 7349/76, *X and Y v. Switzerland, Yearbook* XX (1977), p. 372 (408).
928. Appl. 8378/78, *Kamal v. United Kingdom, D & R* 20 (1980), p. 168 (172).
929. Implicitly recognized by the Commission in its decision in Appl. 2991/66, *Khan v. United Kingdom, Yearbook* X (1967), p. 478. This leaves apart the question of whether a State must permit the practice of polygamy.

standards prevailing in the contracting States.[930]

In the *Berrehab* Case the Court held that cohabitation is not an indispensable element for the existence of family life between parents and their minor children. The Court held as follows:

> It follows from the concept of family on which Article 8 is based that a child born of such a union [*viz.* a lawful and genuine marriage] is *ipso jure* part of the relationship; hence, from the moment of the child's birth and by the very fact of it, there exists between him and his parents a bond amounting to "family life" even if the parents are not then living together.[931]

Subsequent events, of course, may break that tie, but this was not so in the instant case, according to the Court, and consequently Article 8 was found to be applicable. It is a little peculiar that the court here seems to give a special, stronger position to children born out of a lawful marriage precisely in a case where the subsequent divorce indicated that the marriage had ended in a failure.

Relations between an adoptive parent and an adoptive child are also covered by Article 8.[932] It has not yet been decided in the case-law whether foster parents and foster children also fall under "family life". Since protection of practically identical interests is at stake here, in our opinion this question ought to be answered in the affirmative, no matter whether the foster parent has or has not been (temporarily) entrusted with the guardianship, be it that - especially in the latter case - these interests may have to yield to those of the natural parents.[933] And in any case the private life of the foster parents and foster children may be involved here.[934]

Concerning the relationship of a homosexual couple the Commission has taken the view that "[d]espite the modern evolution of attitudes towards homosexuality", that relationship does not fall within the scope of the right to respect for family life, but that, here again, the right to respect for private life may be involved.[935] The Commission does not indicate on which criterion it based its decision. The difference with an unmarried couple is not evident, while there seems to be a clear similarity of interests.

The mere existence of a family relationship is not sufficient for the applicability of Article 8; only in the case of a sufficiently close factual tie is there a question of family life.[936] In fact, if the relationship does not imply genuine ties, an *interference* is not possible.

---

930. Appl. 9253/81, *X v. Federal Republic of Germany*, not published.
931. Judgment of 21 June 1988, A.138 (1988), p. 14.
932. Appl. 9993/82, *X v. France*, D & R 31 (1983), p. 241. But the granting of an adoption order in the face of a natural parent's opposition constitutes an interference with that parent's right to respect for his family life of a particularly serious nature; Appl. 9966/82, *X v. United Kingdom*, not published.
933. See in this connection the dissenting opinion of Schermers in the report of the Commission of 14 July 1988, *Cecilia and Lisa Erikson v. Sweden*: "Normally, there will be family life (as a fact) between foster parents and their children"; A.156 (1989), p. 56.
934. Appl. 8257/78, *X v. Switzerland*, D & R 13 (1979), p. 248 (253).
935. Appl. 9369/81, *X and Y v. United Kingdom*, D & R 32 (1983), p. 220 (221).
936. See, *e.g.*, the judgment of 13 June 1979, *Marckx*, A.31 (1979), p. 15: "with the result that a real family life existed and still exists between them". See also Appl. 7626/76, *X v. United Kingdom*, D & R 11 (1978), p. 160 (166).

Whether such genuine ties exist is determined, *inter alia*, by the nature of the family relationship invoked by the applicant; for married couples and children born out of that marriage, and for other close family relationships they are assumed unless their absence is evident or proven.[937] For other relationships the genuineness of the family ties is determined by factual circumstances, *e.g.* by the fact whether the persons concerned belong to the same household.[938] In the case of a relationship other than between a couple, consideration is also given to the age and independence of the alleged victim[939] and to the place of the family in the economic life of the community in question.[940] Thus, a parent who has been, or threatens to be, separated from her or his child under age will in general have a stronger claim to respect for family life than a person who desires to be reunited with his or her adult child or brother or sister.[941] And for an adult the fact that he or she has to live at some distance from his or her parents abroad in general will be less likely to constitute an interference with family life than for a minor.[942]

A prolonged voluntary separation creates a presumption that the persons concerned do not feel the need of a closer family tie. However, the Commission seems to take this too readily for granted in its case-law.[943] In our opinion, in such cases one must take account, *inter alia*, of the question who took the initiative for the separation in the past, of the nature of the continued ties, and of the family traditions within the religious, ethnic, and/or cultural community to which the persons in question belong. For instance, in several cultures it is a self-evident obligation for a grandchild to adopt his

---

937. Thus the Court held in the *Marckx* judgment, *ibidem*, p. 21, that "family life" in the sense of Art. 8 "includes at least the ties between near relatives, for instance those between grandparents and grandchildren, since such relatives may play a considerable part in family life". See also judgment of 21 June 1988, *Berrehab*, A.138 (1988), p. 14.
938. Thus, *e.g.*, in the case of an uncle and a nephew: Appl. 3110/67, *X v. Federal Republic of Germany*, Yearbook XI (1968), p. 449 (518). See also Appls 7289/75 and 7349/76, *X and Y v. Switzerland*, Yearbook XX (1977), p. 372 (408-410), which concerned an extra-marital relationship.
939. Thus, *e.g.*, in the case of a mother-daughter relationship the age of the latter was considered relevant in addition to the fact that she was married, lived together with her husband, and had a full-time job: Appl. 5269/71, *X and Y v. United Kingdom*, Yearbook XV (1972), p. 564 (574). On the criterion of the "financial (in)dependency" see Appl. 8157/78, *X v. United Kingdom*, not published.
940. For this, see Fawcett, *supra* note 20, p. 188.
941. In Appl. 1380/62 (not published), where the complaint concerned the refusal of a visitor's visa for a brother living in Hungary, the Commission did not refer at all to Art. 8. Here the fact that this concerned a family visit, and the persons in question therefore evidently did not intend to live together in future, was an argument against an interference with family life still being concerned. In the parent-child relationship, however, there may actually still be question of a family tie, even if the intention to live together permanently is not (no longer) present. This very possibility of regular contacts via visits is advanced in many cases by the Commission as an argument that the family tie has not been affected; Appls 7289/75 and 7349/76, *X and Y v. Switzerland*, Yearbook XX (1977), p. 372 (410). See also the following note.
942. See Appl. 1855/63, *X v. Denmark*, Yearbook VIII (1965), p. 200 (204), where a refusal to grant a visitor's permit was deemed not to conflict with Art. 8, since the case concerned a 41-year-old son, who had lived abroad already for twenty years and had an opportunity to visit his parents and other relatives regularly for a reasonable time.
943. Thus, *e.g.*, Appl. 2992/66, *Singh v. United Kingdom*, Yearbook X (1967), p. 478 (500) and Appl. 5532/72, *X v. United Kingdom*, Coll. 43 (1973), p. 119 (121).

grandparent into his household after his parents have died, even if he and his grandparent may have been separated for many years. Furthermore, the degree of dependence of the applicant on his parents or other relatives, in material or in immaterial respects, must be considered.[944] And in any case the mere fact that a person has grown up does not mean that he is no longer entitled to any form of protection of the family unit of which he formed part as a child, not even when he himself has married meanwhile.[945]

The right to protection of family life implies the right to recognition of a legal relationship between members of a family. On that ground the Belgian law was found contrary to Article 8 in so far as, in addition to the production of the birth certificate of an illegitimate child, it set other conditions for the coming into existence of a legal relationship between mother and child, such as recognition by the mother or a procedure of legitimization of the child.[946] And the same view was taken with respect to the denial to an illegitimate child, "adopted by the mother", of legal relations with the parents of the mother,[947] and the denial to an illegitimate child, of rights equal to those of a legitimate child.[948] And with respect to these legal relationships it has also been recognized that Article 8 does not merely compel the State to abstain from interferences, but may also require certain positive measures. Thus, in the *Rasmussen* Case the Commission and the Court gave as their opinion that effective respect for family life obliges the contracting States to make available for the alleged father of a child an effective and accessible remedy by which he can establish whether he is the biological father of the child.[949] In its judgment the Court did not reach the conclusion that in this case there was a violation of Article 8. It concentrated its examination on the fact that Mr. Rasmussen alleged that his right to contest his paternity of a child born during marriage was subject to time-limits, whereas his former wife was entitled to institute paternity proceedings at any time. The Court did not go into the issue of Article 8 separately, although it declared that the facts of the case fell within the ambit of that Article,[950] but directly dealt with the issue of Article 14. It concluded that the difference in treatment was not discriminatory.[951]

944. See on the one hand Appl. 5532/72, mentioned in the preceding note, and on the other hand Appl. 5269/71, *X and Y v. United Kingdom*, Yearbook XV (1972), p. 564 (574).
945. The possibility of violation of Art. 8 in such a case was examined by the Commission in the case of Appl. 5269/71, mentioned in the preceding note.
946. Report of 10 December 1977, *Marckx*, B.29 (1982), pp. 44-45; judgment of 13 June 1979 in this case, A.31 (1979), pp. 16-17. The Commission refers to Art. 2 of the Draft General Principles on Equality and Non-Discrimination in respect of Persons born out of Wedlock of the Sub-Committee for the Prevention of Discrimination and for the Protection of Minorities of the UN Commission for Human Rights, *Study of Discrimination against Persons born out of Wedlock*, United Nations, New York 1967, pp. 225-227.
947. *Ibidem*, p. 47 and p. 21 respectively. Here, too, the Commission refers to the Draft General Principles, *viz.* to Art. 7.
948. *Ibidem*, pp. 48-49.
949. Report of 5 July 1983, *Rasmussen*, A.87 (1985), pp. 20-21; judgment of 28 November 1984, *ibidem*, p. 13.
950. Judgment of 28 November 1984, A.87 (1984), p. 13.
951. *Ibidem*, p. 16.

The *Johnston* Case concerned the absence of the possibility under Irish law of divorce, and of recognition of the family life of persons living in a family relationship outside marriage after the breakdown of the marriage of one of those persons and a third person. The Commission and the Court took the position that, while respect for private and family life may require provision relieving parties from the obligation to live together, it must, in principle, be left to the State to decide what form the remedy should take.[952] More or less as a logical consequence of this position the Commission and the Court held the view that, although a genuine family relationship may exist between two persons living together outside marriage and their child, one could not derive from Article 8 an obligation on the part of Ireland to establish for unmarried couples a status analogous to that of married couples.[953] There is, however, at the very least the obligation of non-interference in the family life between them and the children born out of that new relationship.[954] With respect to the legal status of the child born out of a relationship outside marriage the Commission, followed by the Court, concluded that here the Irish law was in violation of Article 8, because it did not recognize family-law relationships between the child and her parents. As a consequence the father was not regarded, as of right, as the legal guardian of his daughter, which involved far-reaching consequences for both of them. In addition the child could never be legitimated, not even after the death of her father's wife. And further the succession rights of the child could under certain circumstances be inferior to those of legitimate children. In the Commission's view, all this constituted a failure by the State to provide a framework for the proper ordering of relations between the child and her parents, and the appropriate legal regime for the proper development of their family lives. The Commission found no justification for this failure which met the requirements of the second paragraph of Article 8.[955]

Article 8 does not contain a specific regulation concerning the question to which parent will be awarded the custody of the children if the family unit is disrupted by divorce or judicial separation; in principle this is left to the national authorities, on the basis of the relevant national law.[956] From Article 8, therefore, no priority for one of the two parents may be derived.[957] Every decision about this implies by definition an encroachment on the right to respect of family life of one or both of the parents, but in addition of course has consequences for the exercise of the right to respect of family life of the child in question and of any other children forming part of the family unit.

---

952. Report of 5 March 1985, *Johnston*, A.112 (1987), p. 43; judgment of 18 December 1986, *ibidem*, pp. 26-28.
953. *Ibidem*, pp. 48-49 and p. 28 respectively.
954. *Ibidem*, pp. 48-49 and pp. 25 and 30 respectively.
955. *Ibidem*, pp. 49-51; in about the same wording the Court came to the same conclusion, *ibidem*, p. 31.
956. Appl. 1449/62, *X v. the Netherlands*, Yearbook VI (1963), p. 262 (266); Appl. 5486/72, *X v. Sweden*, Coll. 44 (1973), p. 128 (129).
957. Thus the Commission in the first case mentioned in the preceding note and in its decision on Appl. 7770/77, *X v. Federal Republic of Germany*, D & R 14 (1979), p. 175 (176).

The fact that after the divorce not all the members of the family live together under one and the same roof anymore, does not put an end to their family life nor necessarily to the genuineness of their family ties.[958] If the parents cannot reach agreement on this point or if their proposal is ignored, reliance by the national authorities on the restriction ground "protection of health and morals" or "protection of the rights and freedoms of others" in the second paragraph will usually find favour with the Commission, apart from cases of manifest unreasonableness.[959] However, for the parent who still has genuine ties with his child but to whom the custody of the child has not been awarded, a right of access follows from Article 8,[960] unless the authorities can invoke one of the grounds of the second paragraph for its denial.[961] As Opsahl rightly observes, the justification for the award of the custody to one parent rather than to the other cannot be automatically relied upon as a ground for the denial of the right of access to the latter; very serious arguments have to be put forward for the justification of the complete cutting of of the ties between parent and child.[962] All this applies in principle equally in the case of the termination of the relationship between a parent and his or her illegitimate child.[963] And the same holds good for the deprivation of parental rights, since that also constitutes a problem directly affecting the right to protection of family life of the persons concerned, because the family ties do not end by the fact that the child is taken into public care.[964] Such a measure will in general meet with few objections in Strasbourg if "the protection of the rights and freedoms of others", mentioned in the second paragraph, is invoked, because of the very marginal inquiry into the reasonableness of such a justification.[965]

In the Case of *O v. United Kingdom* the applicant alleged a violation of Article 8 because of the procedures followed in reaching a decision on terminating the applicant's access to his children and because of the absence of a remedy against that decision. The Commission found no violation of Article 8 since it interpreted the complaint as being apparently confined to the absence of an effective remedy against the decision to deprive him of access. Consequently, the Commission concluded that in the circumstances of the case there had been no violation of Article 8 of the Convention as a

---

958. Judgment of 21 June 1988, *Berrehab*, A.138 (1988), p. 14.
959. See, *e.g.*, the very marginal review in this respect in the case of Appl. 2699/65, *X v. Federal Republic of Germany*, Yearbook XI (1968), p. 366 (376), and of Appl. 5486/72, *X v. Sweden*, Coll. 44 (1973), p. 128 (129).
960. Appl. 172/56, *X v. Sweden*, Yearbook I (1955-57), p. 211 (217); Appl. 7911/77, *X v. Sweden*, D & R 12 (1978), p. 192 (193); report of 8 March 1982, *Hendriks*, D & R (1982), p. 5 (14-16).
961. See, *e.g.*, Appl. 5608/72, *X v. United Kingdom*, Coll. 44 (1973), p. 66 (68-69); Appl. 7911/77, *X v. Sweden*, D & R 12 (1978), p. 192 (193); report mentioned in the preceding note, pp. 37-40.
962. T. Opsahl, "The Convention and the Right to Respect for Family Life", in: A.H. Robertson (ed.), *Privacy and Human Rights*, Manchester 1973, p. 215.
963. See Appl. 7658/76, *X v. Denmark*, D & R 15 (1979), p. 128.
964. Judgments of 8 July 1987, *W, B and R v. United Kingdom*, A.121 (1987), pp. 27, 71 and 117 respectively. Judgment of 24 March 1988, *Olsson*, A.130 (1988), p. 29.
965. See, *e.g.*, Appl. 5132/71, *X v. Denmark*, Coll. 43 (1973), p. 57 (60-61).

result of the alleged lack of a right to a hearing before a court and of an effective legal remedy in respect of his claim for access to his children.[966] The Court held with respect to the first part of the complaint that the information provided about the procedures followed was insufficient to establish a violation of Article 8. With respect to the second part the Court had already found a violation of Article 6(1) and did not find it necessary to examine the complaint under Article 8.[967] The Case of *H v. United Kingdom* concerned proceedings instituted by the applicant regarding her access to her child. Here the Court held that, in view of the delays, the proceedings had failed to show respect for the applicant's family life since the proceedings related to a fundamental element of family life and the procedural delay led to a *de facto* determination of the matter at issue. The Court therefore considered that the duration of the proceedings was a factor that could properly be taken into account in the present context.[968]

In the Cases of *W, B and R v. United Kingdom* the complaints concerned the applicants' access to their children in the care of a local authority. According to the Commission the procedures which led to the determination of issues relating to family life had to be such as to show respect for family life. In particular parents normally should have a right to be heard and to be fully informed in this connection. The Court took the view that Article 8 contains no explicit procedural requirements, but that this was not conclusive of the matter. The relevant considerations to be weighed by a local authority in reaching decisions on children in its care must perforce include the views and interests of the natural parents. The decision-making process must therefore be such as to secure that their views and interests are made known to and duly taken into account by the local authority and that they are able to exercise in due time any remedies available to them. In the Court's view

> what therefore has to be determined is whether, having regard to the particular circumstances of the case and notably the serious nature of the decisions to be taken, the parents have been involved in the decision-making process, seen as a whole, to a degree sufficient to provide them with the requisite protection of their interests. If they have not, there will have been a failure to respect their family life and the interference resulting from the decision will not be capable of being regarded as "necessary" within the meaning of Article 8.[969]

The Court found a violation of Article 8 after examining the procedure relating to the authority's decisions to place the children with long-term foster parents with a view to adoption, and to terminate access by the applicants; in the Court's view, it revealed insufficient involvement of the applicants.

In the *Olsson* Case, the applicants asserted that the decision to take their children into care, the manner in which it had been implemented and the refusals to terminate care had given rise to violations of Article 8. As regards the question of the taking into, and the refusals to terminate care the Court

966. Report of 3 December 1985, A.120 (1987), pp. 35-36.
967. Judgment of 8 July 1987, A.120 (1987), pp. 28-29.
968. Judgment of 8 July 1987, A.120 (1987), pp. 63-64.
969. Judgments of 8 July 1987, A.121 (1987), pp. 28, 73-74 and 119 respectively.

was of the view that the applicants had been involved in the decision-making process, seen as a whole, to a degree sufficient to provide requisite protection of their interests. As to the taking into care the Court held that it is not enough justification that the child will be better off if placed in care.

> In order to determine whether the foregoing reasons can be considered "sufficient" for the purposes of Article 8, the Court must have regard to the case as a whole and notably to the circumstances in which the decision was taken.[970]

The decisions were based on social reports supported by statements from persons well acquainted with the case and the decisions were confirmed by courts which were able to form their own impression of the case and whose judgments were not reversed on appeal. Therefore, the Swedish authorities, having regard to their margin of appreciation, were in the Court's view entitled to think that the taking into care was necessary. However, the implementation of the care decision was held by the Court to be in violation of Article 8. It was not the quality of the care given that was at issue, but the separation of the children and the placement of two of them at a long distance from the applicants' home and the restrictions on their visits, which impeded easy and regular access by the members of the family to each other and thus ran counter to the ultimate aim of its reunification. In these respects, and despite the applicants' un-cooperative attitude, the measures of implementation of the care decision were not supported by sufficient reasons justifying them as proportionate to the legitimate aim.[971]

In the *Cecilia and Lisa Erikson* Case the Commission was confronted with the question whether the prohibition for the mother to remove her daughter from the foster home and the restrictions on the right of access constituted a violation of Article 8. The child was taken in care one month after she was born. When the child was five years old the care order was lifted, but in the same decision it was decided to prohibit the mother from removing the daughter from the foster home until further notice. Its effect was that the mother, although there were no longer any reproaches against her for inability to care for her daughter, was still deprived of the factual care. Another effect of the prohibition on removal was that the mother could not secure a formal decision on her right of access to her daughter. The Commission considered that

> once a decision to return a child to its natural parents has been taken it must be in the interests of all parties involved that such a decision is implemented as quickly as possible. A prohibition on removal temporarily suspends the removal of the child and is therefore, although it may be justified during a transitional period, a measure which by its very nature is likely to increase the tension between those involved in the transfer of the child. If such a situation prevails for a long time there is a great risk that, as time goes by, the conflicts will increase and that it gradually will become more difficult to establish the close relationship between the child and his or her natural parent which is a necessary condition for the transfer.[972]

---

970. Judgment of 24 March 1988, A.130 (1988), pp. 33-34.
971. *Ibidem*, pp. 33-37.
972. Report of 14 July 1988, para. 211.

The Commission came to the conclusion that the interference with the mother's right to respect for her family life was not necessary in the interest of the child. It put heavy weight on the fact that the Supreme Administrative Court had ordered that the child should return to the mother while the measures taken since that judgment could not be considered adequate to promote this aim. In particular, the regulations and arrangements concerning access to the child were inadequate to promote the aim of reunification of the applicants.

In Appl. 8416/79 it was submitted that the legislation permitting abortion without the father's consent constituted an interference with the latter's right to respect for his family life. The Commission found that, in so far as abortion constitutes an interference with the right of the father, the interference was justified here for the protection of the rights of another person, since the decision to apply abortion had been taken at the request of the mother in order to protect her physical and mental health. The Commission took also the view that the father's right to respect for his family life could not be interpreted so broadly that a right to be consulted beforehand in case of an abortion could be derived from it.[973] The Commission arrived at this latter conclusion "having regard to the right of the pregnant woman". It is not evident, however, that the woman's right to respect for her private life should rule out that the man might in principle derive from his right to respect for his family life a right to be consulted. After all, the second paragraph of Article 8 would seem to offer sufficient possibility to give priority to the woman's right, should the man refuse his consent.

4. The right of a foreigner to enter or reside in a particular country has not been laid down in the Convention, but the immigration policy of the contracting States has, of course, to be in conformity with their obligations under the Convention. Thus, the exclusion of a person from a country in which his close relatives reside may raise an issue under Article 8.[974]

Refusal of admittance or the expulsion of a husband or wife has for a long time constantly been held by the Commission not to conflict with Article 8 if the other partner has the opportunity to follow the person concerned abroad and this can reasonably be required of him or her.[975] Obviously the Commission does not wish to thwart the national policy in this respect too much, in particular when that policy is apparently intended to restrict pseudo-marriages or marriages which were contracted at a moment when the partners were fully aware of the risk that one of them would not be admitted or

973. Appl. 8416/79, *X v. United Kingdom*, *D & R* 19 (1980), p. 244 (253-254).
974. See, among several others, Appl. 9492/81, *Family X v. United Kingdom*, *D & R* 30 (1983), p. 232 (234).
975. See the case-law mentioned in: Council of Europe, *Case Law Topics* No. 2, "Family Life" (1972), pp. 6-13. See also Appl. 7729/76, *Agee v. United Kingdom*, *D & R* 7 (1977), p. 164 (174).

would be expelled.[976] If persons are involved who have already resided in the country for a considerable time and have founded a family there, the Commission appears to be inclined more readily to accept that the partner and children have good reasons for not wishing to go abroad themselves.[977] The mere opportunity to do so is not therefore decisive as to whether expulsion violates Article 8.[978]

In the *Abdulaziz, Cabales and Balkandali* Case the applications were lodged by three women who were lawfully and permanently settled in the United Kingdom, but whose husbands or prospective husbands were refused permission to remain in the United Kingdom. As to the applicability of Article 8, the Court confirmed the Commission's established case-law by stating that "although some aspects of the right to enter a country are governed by Protocol No. 4 as regards States bound by that instrument, it is not to be excluded that measures taken in the field of immigration may affect the right to respect for family life under Article 8".[979] The Court also stated that, although by guaranteeing the right to respect for family life Article 8 presupposes the existence of a family, this does not mean that all *intended* family life falls entirely outside its ambit. Therefore, even if the family life was not yet fully established for all the applicants at the moment when the request was made for permission for the men to enter or remain in the United Kingdom, this did not exclude the applicability of Article 8. In this case the Court found sufficient ground for this applicability in the fact that the couples, at least in their own opinion, were married and had lived together or wished to live together.[980] Next, confirming its case-law that there may be positive obligations inherent in an effective "respect" for the rights protected in Article 8, but that a wide margin of appreciation has to be left to the contracting States in determining the steps to be taken with due regard to the needs and resources of the community and of individuals, the Court held:

> In particular, in the area now under consideration, the extent of a State's obligation to admit to its territory relatives of settled immigrants will vary according to the particular circumstances of the persons involved. Moreover, the Court cannot ignore that the present case is concerned not only with family life but also with immigration and that, as a matter of well-established international law and subject to its treaty obligations, a State has the right to control the entry of non-nationals into its territory.[981]

The Court also observed:

> The duty imposed by Article 8 cannot be considered as extending to a general obligation on the part of a Contracting State to respect the choice by married couples of the country of their matrimonial residence and to accept the non-national spouses for

---

976. See Appl. 2535/65, *X v. Federal Republic of Germany, Coll.* 17 (1966), p. 28 (30). See also Appl. 9285/81, *X, Y and Z v. United Kingdom, D & R* 29 (1982), p. 205 (209).
977. Appl. 6357/73, *X v. Federal Republic of Germany, D & R* 1 (1975), p. 77 (77-78). See also Appl. 8244/78, *Uppal v. United Kingdom, D & R* 17 (1980), p. 149 (156), where the grandparents and the children were allowed to stay in the country, but the parents were threatened to be expelled. In this case, which had been declared admissible by the Commission on account of its complexity, a friendly settlement was reached.
978. Expressly Appl. 8061/77, *X v. Switzerland*, not published.
979. Judgment of 28 May 1985, A.94 (1985), p. 31.
980. *Ibidem*, pp. 32-33.
981. *Ibidem*, p. 34.

Since the Court found that the applicants had not shown that there were obstacles to establishing family life in their own or their husbands' home countries, or that there were special reasons why that could not be expected of them, and that all three applicants, at the time of their marriage, were aware of the risk that their husbands would not get a permanent residence permit for the United Kingdom, it concluded that there was no lack of respect for family life and, hence, no breach of Article 8 taken alone.[983] However, the Court found that the applicants were victims of discrimination on the ground of sex, in violation of Article 14 in conjunction with Article 8, because of the difference made in the 1980 Statement of Changes in Immigration Rules as to the possibility for male and female immigrants settled in the United Kingdom to obtain permission for their non-national spouses or fiancé(e)s to enter or remain in the country. The assumed difference between the respective impact of men and women on the domestic labour market was considered to be not sufficiently important to justify this difference in treatment.[984]

In order to determine whether it can reasonably be required that the family unit be continued or restored abroad, the disadvantages involved for the persons concerned have to be weighed against the interests of the respondent State served by its immigration policy. First of all, reunion abroad must be possible. If the State where the member of the family resides or to which he or she has been expelled is not prepared to admit the other member or members of the family, the expulsion or the refusal of admission - if a family relationship is indeed involved - constitutes a breach of Article 8.[985] The same holds true if an inhuman treatment in the sense of Article 3 were to await a member of the family when required to settle abroad.[986] If reunion of the family abroad is possible but the applicant for admission is a minor, the Commission generally assumes that the latter has the right to be reunited with his parents or guardians in the country of their residence, and that the latter cannot reasonably be expected to move abroad in order to join him.[987] Other aspects which the Commission involves in its weighing of the interests are, *inter alia*: the links with the other country;[988] the prospect of joint residence in the respondent State at the time when the

---

982. *Ibidem.*
983. *Ibidem.*
984. *Ibidem*, p. 37.
985. See Appl. 8061/77, *X v. Switzerland*, not published, where the woman alleged that for that reason she could not follow her husband to Yugoslavia.
986. See *supra* pp. 235-240.
987. See Council of Europe, *Case Law Topics* No. 2 "Family Life" (1972), pp. 40-41. See also Appl. 2991/66, *Kahn v. United Kingdom*, Yearbook X (1967), p. 478 (502), and Appl. 7816/77, *X and Y v. Federal Republic of Germany*, D & R 9 (1978), p. 219 (221).
988. Appl. 5301/71, *X v. United Kingdom*, Coll. 43 (1973), p. 82 (84).

family was founded;[989] the existence of ties with other relatives outside the family,[990] and the economic consequences of a removal to another country.[991] If this weighing of interests results in the conclusion that the other members of the family cannot reasonably be required to follow the person in question abroad, and that therefore non-admittance or expulsion would violate the latter's family life, the respondent State can still rely on one of the restriction grounds of the second paragraph.[992]

As has been mentioned above, in the *Abdulaziz, Cabales and Balkandali* Case the Court held that although Article 8 presupposes the existence of a family, this does not mean that all *intended* family life falls entirely outside its ambit. There, the Court declared Article 8 also applicable to a situation where admission was applied for in order to get married.[993] The applicants could also have relied on Article 12 in that case.

In the case of a divorce, the parent who is entrusted with the custody over the children can of course not reasonably be required to follow the other parent abroad in order to maintain the family ties between the latter and the children. In the *Berrehab* Case the applicant, a Moroccan national, was divorced from his Dutch wife and was appointed as co-guardian of the child born after the divorce. Because of his divorce he was refused prolongation of his residence permit. This resulted in an expulsion order. The Court took into consideration that until his expulsion from the Netherlands, Mr. Berrehab saw his daughter four times a week for several hours at a time. The fact that there were frequent and regular contacts with his daughter led to the conclusion that it could not be maintained that the ties of "family life" between them had been broken. Although the Court made allowance for the margin of appreciation that is left to the contracting States and accepted that the Convention does not in principle prohibit contracting States from regulating the entry and length of stay of aliens, it found a violation of Article 8, having regard to the particular circumstances, since there was a disproportion between the means employed and the legitimate aim pursued.[994]

5. With regard to detainees the Commission starts its considerations from the point of view that the separation between a detainee and his family, and the

---

989. Appls 5445-5446/72, *X and Y v. United Kingdom, Coll.* 42 (1973), p. 146. See also Appl. 7048/75, *X v. United Kingdom, D & R* 9 (1978), p. 42 (43), where the Commission decided that Art. 8 does not per se guarantee the right for a married couple to move their residence to a specific country, where one of the two has a visitor's permit.
990. Appl. 5269/71, *X and Y v. United Kingdom, Yearbook* XV (1972), p. 564 (574).
991. *Ibidem.* See also Appl. 9492/81, *Family X v. United Kingdom, D & R* 30 (1983), p. 232 (234-235), where the Commission found that the fact that the expulsion would prevent the son from continuing his study in the U.K. did not constitute an interference with the right of respect for family life.
992. See Appl. 312/57, *X v. Belgium, Yearbook* II (1958-59), p. 352 (353-354), and Appl. 8061/77, *X v. Switzerland*, not published, where for that reason the Commission did not inquire the question of whether the woman could really obtain the required permission of the Yugoslav authorities to join her husband.
993. Judgment of 28 May 1985, A.94 (1985), p. 31. See, however, Appl. 7229/75, *X and Y v. United Kingdom, D & R* 12 (1978), p. 32 (34).
994. Judgment of 21 June 1988, A.138 (1988), pp. 14-16.

distress resulting from it, are inherent in detention.[995] The touchstone is then whether the interference with the right of family life, to which the detainee is also entitled, "goes beyond what would normally be accepted in the case of an ordinary detainee".[996] If the restrictions cannot stand this test, the Commission appears to be inclined still to allow the national authorities a very wide margin of appreciation in the limitation of family contacts on one of the grounds of the second paragraph.[997] Thus the Commission accepted the Austrian practice according to which those who are serving a sentence of imprisonment of more than one year, are on that ground alone denied visits from their children under age, for the protection of the morals of these minors.[998] It also concluded in the case of a refusal of the English authorities to permit a detainee to attend his daughter's wedding, and in another case his mother's funeral, that there was no evidence that the authorities in question did not have sufficient reason to believe that this refusal was necessary on one of the grounds mentioned in the second paragraph.[999] In addition to an examination as to whether the justification of the restrictions by the national authorities on one of the grounds of paragraph 2 was indeed reasonable in the particular case, the Strasbourg organs will have to see to it that the restriction is not imposed on the prisoner as a disguised sanction on his behaviour, which would indeed constitute a conflict with Article 18. But even in those cases where the restriction is not intended as an additional punishment, it will nevertheless, as a result of the detention, in many cases actually have the same effect. As an example one may think of the refusal of (regular) conjugal intercourse for detainees, which still is the rule in most countries.[1000] In those and similar cases, both the national authorities and the reviewing organs in Strasbourg should take to heart the view formulated as follows by Jacobs:

> Quite apart from purely legal considerations, it would be contrary to modern penological standards to restrict unnecessarily the family life of prisoners. If they are to be able to take their place again in society, they should have the greatest contact with the outside world that is consistent with the fact of their detention. Progressing standards of penal policy may even be legally relevant, since it is sometimes legitimate to interpret the Convention in the light of the practice of the Contracting Parties. Thus, restrictions which would at one time have been justified may cease to be permitted as standards are

---

995. See, e.g., Appl. 2676/65, X v. Austria, Coll. 23 (1967), p. 31 (37). See also the report of 18 March 1981, McVeigh, O'Neill and Evans, D & R 25 (1982), p. 5 (51-52).
996. Appl. 5712/72, X v. United Kingdom, Coll. 46 (1974), p. 112 (116).
997. See, e.g., Appls 1420/62, 1477/62 and 1478/62, X and Y v. Belgium, Yearbook VI (1963), p. 590 (628), and the case mentioned in the preceding note.
998. Appl. 2306/64, X v. Austria, Coll. 21 (1967), p. 23 (33); see also Appl. 6564/74, X v. United Kingdom, D & R 2 (1975), p. 105 (106).
999. Appl. 4623/70, X v. United Kingdom, Yearbook XV (1972), p. 370 (374), and Appl. 5229/71, X v. United Kingdom, Coll. 42 (1973), p. 140 (141).
1000. See Appl. 3603/68, X v. Federal Republic of Germany, Yearbook XIII (1970), p. 332 (338) and the comparative study evidently made there by the Commission. Thus also in Appl. 8166/78, X and Y v. Switzerland, D & R 13 (1979), p. 241 (243), where the Commission also refers to the Standard Minimum Rules for the Treatment of Prisoners, recommended by the Committee of Ministers in Resolution (73)5. If in a specific case it is possible for a detainee to reside together with his family in the place of detention, the Commission deems it possible that Art. 8 has been violated if the authorities make the living conditions for the family unbearable; report of 7 December 1978, Guzzardi, B.35 (1983), pp. 35-36.

raised.[1001]

6. In view of the Strasbourg practice of marginal review of the justification of restrictions, the right to respect for the home affords only limited guarantees in most situations, since in many cases of interference with that right the national authorities will be able to invoke successfully one of the grounds of the second paragraph. In fact, as long as the national legislation in question makes this possible, the national authorities can search the home of the accused in case of any concrete, but also any vague suspicion of a criminal offence, and also all those other homes where clues might possibly be found.[1002] However, in so serious a case of interference with the right to respect for the home as the case of Cypriotic citizens being expelled from their homes by the Turkish occupying forces and the latter making return to these homes impossible, the Commission concluded that none of the grounds mentioned in the second paragraph could be advanced for its justification.[1003]

The concept of "home" was discussed in the *Gillow* Case. Mr. and Mrs. Gillow owned the house "Whiteknights" in Guernsey, which they had occupied with their family until they left the country to take employment with the FAO in 1960. During their absence they rented the house to various tenants, but they continued the ownership and retained their furniture in the house. When they returned to Guernsey to live there in 1979, they were not granted the required licence, since they did not fulfil all the requirements, some of which were introduced by legislation during the period of their absence. The Commission considered that ownership of a house is not in itself sufficient to establish it as one's home, when one has never in fact lived in the house. However, where continued ownership follows occupation of a house as one's home, such ownership is evidence of a strong continuing link with the house. In the case of the Gillows this link was further illustrated by the fact that they had left their furniture in the house. The Commission gave as its opinion that the question whether the house was still the applicants' "home" at the time of their return to it in 1979, was in part dependent on their intentions and attitude towards the house prior to and on their return, of which the key element was their actual return in 1979 to live in the house. The Commission concluded that this return was a return to their "home" within the meaning of Article 8. The fact that they were not granted the licence to live in that home and that proceedings were taken against them for unlawful occupation of the house constituted an interference with their right to respect for their home. This interference was considered by the Commission to be disproportionate in relation to the aim pursued by the authorities in making the residence requirements, and not corresponding with any pressing social need. Consequently, it was held not to have been necessary in a democratic society

---

1001. Jacobs, *supra* note 17, p. 137.
1002. See, *e.g.*, Appl. 530/59, *X v. Federal Republic of Germany*, Yearbook III (1960), p. 184 (190).
1003. Report of 10 July 1976, *Cyprus v. Turkey*, paras 209 and 210.

within the meaning of Article 8(2).[1004] The Court also found a violation of Article 8 in this case. According to the Court it was not the contested legislation which gave rise to the violation, but the manner in which the Housing Authority had exercised its discretion in the case. The Housing Authority had given insufficient weight to the applicants' particular circumstances. They had built "Whiteknights" as a residence for themselves and their family. At that time they possessed "residence qualifications" and continued to do so until the entry into force of the Housing Law 1969. By letting it over a period of eighteen years to persons approved by the Housing Authority, they had contributed to the Guernsey housing stock. On their return in 1979, they had no other "home" in the United Kingdom or elsewhere; "Whiteknights" was vacant and there were no prospective tenants. Therefore, the refusals as well as the conviction and fining of the applicants constituted interferences which were disproportionate to the legitimate aim pursued.[1005]

The guarantee of the right to respect for the home would gain considerably in practical importance if it would be recognized that Article 8 also applies to relations between individuals and that the contracting States are under the obligation to effectuate this *Drittwirkung*. Another point that is very important for the scope of Article 8 is the question of whether the right to respect for the home also implies a right to a (decent) home.[1006] Recognition of such a right would amount to a considerable socialization of Article 8 but would have mainly political relevance, because in all probability the national courts would not be prepared to declare Article 8 directly applicable if interpreted in that way.

A form of indirect interference with the right to respect for the home which, if recognized, would also substantially enlarge the scope of Article 8 and which, in our opinion, would not stand in the way of direct applicability, are deteriorations of living conditions by certain measures or circumstances. Thus, in Appl. 7889/77, which was declared admissible by the Commission because of its complexity, the applicant complained about violation of Article 8 by the British authorities on account of the great nuisance which she experienced in her home near Gatwick Airport from the descending and ascending aircraft, and from the traffic on the motor road.[1007]

7. With regard to the right to respect for correspondence, too, it may be said that, when public authorities proceed to open and censor letters and to interfere with other means of communication, in most cases they will be able to invoke the second paragraph successfully. At first the Commission even

---

1004. Report of 3 October 1984, A.109 (1987), pp. 32-41. See also Appl. 6202/73, *X and Y v. the Netherlands*, D & R 1 (1975), p. 66 (70): the right to live in the house which one owns.
1005. Judgment of 24 November 1986, A.109 (1987), pp. 22-23.
1006. This was denied by the Commission in the case of Appl. 159/56, *X v. Federal Republic of Germany*, Yearbook I (1955-57), p. 202 (203).
1007. Appl. 7889/77, *Arrondelle v. United Kingdom*, D & R 19 (1980), p. 186 (198). In this case a friendly settlement has been reached; D & R 26 (1982), p. 5.

took the view that such an invocation of the second paragraph was not necessary if the censorship or the restriction on correspondence concerned detainees, since such restrictions were considered inherent in detention. The Commission did not even deem a reference to paragraph 2 necessary for such serious cases as restriction or delay of the correspondence with defence counsel.[1008] However, in the *Vagrancy* Cases, and later more clearly in the *Golder* Case, the Court rejected this so-called "inherent features" theory for provisions like Article 8, where restrictions are expressly provided for, and held that every restriction has to be reviewed for its justification on one of the grounds mentioned explicitly in the second paragraph.[1009] At the same time, however, the Court recognized in the *Golder* Case that, when this is done, the special position of the prisoner may be taken into account.[1010] The Commission afterwards followed the Court in this reasoning.

This change in the case-law, however, is hardly of avail to the prisoner, if a very wide discretion is still allowed to the prison authorities and the prosecuting authorities in censoring incoming and outgoing letters and in other interferences with the correspondence of prisoners.[1011]

The more recent case-law, however, suggests that the Commission is inclined to conduct a more independent inquiry into the reasonableness of interference with the correspondence of prisoners by the authorities, and for this reason has desisted from declaring the complaints concerned manifestly ill-founded.[1012] A number of those cases were joined by the Commission and led to a detailed inquiry resulting in its report in the *Silver* Case.[1013] There the Commission categorically rejected the doctrine of the implied restrictions, and on that ground took the view that restrictions imposed on detainees can find their justification only in one of the grounds mentioned in the second paragraph. At the same time it rejected the thesis of the British Government that the contents of letters destined for publication are not covered by the term "correspondence".[1014] With regard to the requirement, laid down in paragraph 2, that the restriction must be necessary in a democratic society, the Commission held in its report:

> In the context of present-day conditions of imprisonment, the requirements of a democratic society involve the striking of a balance between the legitimate interests of public order and security and that of the rehabilitation of prisoners.[1015]

1008. See, *e.g.*, Appl. 2375/64, *X v. Federal Republic of Germany, Coll.* 22 (1967), p. 45 (47).
1009. Judgment of 18 June 1971, A.12 (1971), p. 45; judgment of 21 February 1975, A.18 (1975), p. 21. See also the report of 12 December 1980, *Schönenberger and Durmaz*, A.137 (1988), p. 18.
1010. *Ibidem*. See also judgment of 25 March 1983, *Silver*, A.61 (1983), pp. 37-38.
1011. See Council of Europe, *Case Law Topics* No. 1, "Human Rights in Prison" (1971), pp. 24-30. See also Appl. 6166/73, *Baader, Meins, Meinhof, and Grundman v. Federal Republic of Germany, Yearbook* XVIII (1975), p. 132 (146).
1012. In its decision on Appl. 5613/72, *Hilton v. United Kingdom, Yearbook* XIX (1976), p. 257 (276), a complaint of a detainee on interference with his correspondence was declared admissible by the Commission on account of "a conflict in the parties' statements which the Commission is unable to reconcile at this stage". The report in this case has not been published. See also Resolution DH(79)3, *Yearbook* XXII (1979), p. 442.
1013. Report of 11 October 1980, B.51 (1987), p. 72.
1014. *Ibidem*, p. 72.
1015. *Ibidem*, pp. 75-76.

In its judgment in this case the Court noted that since the Commission's report the practice in England and Wales on the control of prisoners' correspondence had undergone substantial modification, but it held that it was not empowered to review the control regime introduced after the events giving rise to the case.[1016] Both the Commission and the Court reached the conclusion that, with the exception of the censorship of those letters in which violence was threatened or crimes were discussed, the grounds on which letters of the detained applicants had been held back could find no justification in the second paragraph, at least not if one considered the way in which the relevant rules had been applied in these cases.[1017]

In the *Boyle and Rice* Case, the Court found that the stopping by the Prison Governor of a letter to a "media personality" was in breach of Article 8. The Government had acknowledged before both the Commission and the Court that the rules had been wrongly applied since the letter was a purely personal one and should have been allowed to pass.[1018]

In the *Schönenberger and Durmaz* Case the Court had to deal with the stopping of a letter addressed by a lawyer to a person held on remand. The Government relied in the first place on the contents of the letter in issue: according to the Government, it gave Mr. Durmaz advice relating to pending criminal proceedings which was of such a nature as to jeopardize their proper conduct. The Court took the view that Mr. Schönenberger sought to inform the second applicant of his right "to refuse to make any statement", advising him that to exercise it would be to his "advantage".

> In that way, he was recommending that Mr. Durmaz adopt a certain tactic, lawful in itself since, under Swiss Federal Court's case-law - whose equivalent may be found in other Contracting States - it is open to an accused person to remain silent.

The fact that the lawyer was not instructed by Mr. Durmaz was of little importance, since Mr. Schönenberger was acting on the instructions of Mr. Durmaz' wife. The contested interference was deemed not justifiable as necessary in a democratic society.[1019]

A case which led to an extensive investigation by the Commission as well as the Court into the scope of the possibilities of restriction under the second paragraph with respect to the freedom of correspondence and other forms of communication, is the *Klass* Case. This case concerned German legislation authorizing letter-opening and wire-tapping for the protection of the free democratic system or national security, without notification of the person in question and with exclusion of the normal legal remedies. After an extensive inquiry into the substance and application of the challenged legislation, which application by its very nature calls for secrecy, the Commission as well as the Court concluded that the German legislature could in reasonableness take the

---

1016. Judgment of 25 March 1983, A.61 (1983), pp. 30-31.
1017. *Ibidem*, pp. 76-98 and pp. 34-40 respectively. See also Appl. 7630/76, *Reed v. United Kingdom*, D & R 19 (1980), p. 113 (141).
1018. Judgment of 27 April 1988, A.131 (1988), p. 22.
1019. Judgment of 20 June 1988, A.137 (1988), pp. 13-14.

view that the measures in question were necessary for the protection of the above-mentioned interests.[1020] This matter will be discussed in detail later.[1021]

Another case directed against the Federal Republic of Germany concerned wire-tapping of a solicitors' office, a measure which the authorities had carried out on the ground of suspicion that the office played a part in the exchange of information between prisoners who were suspected of or convicted for terrorist activities. A number of persons whose conversations with the office had been tape-recorded, complained that, contrary to the decision of the investigating judge, those conversations, which apparently were not incriminating, were not erased immediately after recording. Although the Commission considered it regrettable that the instructions of the investigating judge had not been complied with, it held that this did not constitute a conflict with Article 8. For this it advanced the argument that the measure, as carried out, had been found by the German court to be in conformity with German law, and that this same court had decided that it could not be determined which recordings were and which were not relevant until the end of the proceedings.[1022] Here the Commission goes very far indeed in sheltering behind the point of view of the national court, without making an independent inquiry into the restrictions of the second paragraph relied upon.

More thorough, again, was the Strasbourg review of interception of telephone calls by or at the request of the police in the *Malone* Case. Mr. Malone was charged with dishonest handling of stolen goods. The police officer in charge of the investigation had ordered interception of a telephone conversation on the authority of a warrant issued by the Secretary of State for the Home Department. Moreover, Mr. Malone's telephone had been "metered" on behalf of the police by a device which automatically recorded all numbers dialled. The Court agreed with the Commission that the laws and practices existing in England and Wales which permit secret surveillance of communications, amounted to an interference with the applicant's rights under Article 8. Although this interference was lawful under the relevant law of England and Wales, both the Commission and the Court reached the conclusion that it was not "in accordance with the law" in the sense of the second paragraph of Article 8, since the relevant law did not lay down with reasonable clarity the essential elements of the authorities' powers in this domain.[1023] As to the "metering", the Court disagreed with the Government that, since the Post Office only recorded signals sent to itself as the provider of the telephone service and did not intercept conversations, it did not entail interference with any right guaranteed by Article 8. Release of that information without the consent of the subscriber did, in the Court's opinion, amount to such an

1020. Report of 9 March 1977, B.26 (1982), pp. 37-39; judgment of 6 September 1978, A.28 (1979), pp. 20-22.
1021. *Infra* pp. 597-600. See also *infra* pp. 528-530.
1022. Appl. 8290/78, *A, B, C and D v. Federal Republic of Germany, D & R* 18 (1980), p. 176 (180).
1023. Judgment of 2 August 1984, A.82 (1984), pp. 31-36.

interference. And since there appeared to be no legal rules concerning the scope and manner of exercise of the discretion enjoyed by the public authorities, this practice also was not "in accordance with the law" within the meaning of Article 8(2).[1024]

The freedom of correspondence with the Secretariat of the Commission forms a separate problem, because the prohibition against interfering with it ensues from Article 25 for the authorities of those contracting States which have recognized the individual right of complaint,[1025] and the restrictions of Article 8(2) therefore cannot be invoked. Moreover, this matter has been elaborated in a special convention.[1026] If it is alleged by an applicant that in his contacts with the Strasbourg organs he has been hindered contrary to Article 25, the point is not dealt with by the Commission as a separate complaint, but in combination with the main complaint, if consultation between the Secretary of the Commission and the authorities concerned has not resulted in abolition of the obstacles.[1027]

8. Article 8 does not pertain to the rights that are non-derogable in virtue of Article 15(2). This means that the contracting States can take measures in derogation of Article 8 in the circumstances referred to in Article 15 and under the conditions laid down therein.

9. Article 17 of the Covenant differs on a number of points from Article 8 of the Convention. First of all, in Article 17 respect for one's honour and reputation is mentioned expressly as an element of the protection of privacy. As has been indicated above, however, this does not lead to a substantive difference.[1028] Further, Article 17 prohibits not only "unlawful", but all "arbitrary" interferences with privacy, so that, when the national legislature permits particular interferences, the authorities will still have to account for the way in which they have used their powers. This principle ought always to apply in a Rule-of-Law State. As regards the European Convention, this principle is implied to some degree in Articles 17 and 18. However, owing to the marginal review by the Commission and the Court it is not always brought out sufficiently.

On the other hand, the second paragraph of Article 8 gives an exhaustive enumeration of the grounds of restriction, while Article 17 of the Covenant prescribes only that the interference or attacks must not be contrary to the law as it stands and not arbitrary, and that the law must afford protection against it.[1029] In this respect, therefore, the Convention, in spite of the wide formulation of Article 8(2), affords better protection, provided that the

---

1024. *Ibidem*, pp. 37-38.
1025. See *supra* pp. 50-51.
1026. See *supra* p. 51.
1027. See *supra* pp. 50-51.
1028. For a different view, see Report of the Committee of Experts, *supra* note 14, p. 42.
1029. On the very vague second paragraph of Art. 17 of the Covenant, see the Report of the Committee of Experts, *supra* note 14, p. 43.

application of that provision by the national authorities is effectively reviewed for its reasonableness in Strasbourg.[1030]

§ 9.   ARTICLE 9: FREEDOM OF THOUGHT, CONSCIENCE AND RELIGION

1. Everyone has the right to freedom of thought, conscience and religion; this right includes freedom to change his religion or belief and freedom, either alone or in community with others and in public or private, to manifest his religion or belief, in worship, teaching, practice and observance.
2. Freedom to manifest one's religion or beliefs shall be subject only to such limitations as are prescribed by law and are necessary in a democratic society in the interests of public safety, for the protection of public order, health or morals, or for the protection of the rights and freedoms of others.

1. The right to freedom of thought, conscience and religion is guaranteed in the Convention without qualification. Restrictions are possible only with respect to the *expression* of thought, conscience and religion, *viz.* in pursuance of the second paragraph of Article 9 with respect to the manifestation of religious and other beliefs, and in pursuance of the second paragraph of Article 10 with respect to the expression of one's opinion in general.

This absolute freedom to entertain any thoughts and views[1031] is not without practical importance. It is true that thoughts, as long as they have not been expressed, are intangible and that convictions are really valuable for the person concerned only if he can express them, but the freedom of thought also implies that one cannot be subjected to a treatment intended to change the process of thinking,[1032] that any form of compulsion to express thoughts, to change an opinion, or to divulge a religious conviction is prohibited,[1033] and that no sanction may be imposed either on the holding of any view whatever or on the change of a religion or conviction. The prohibition to practise a certain profession ("Berufsverbot") on the mere ground of one's political or philosophical conviction, for instance, falls under this provision. But in our opinion even the obligation to reveal one's religion in a census or

---

1030. For the "case-law" of the Human Rights Committee concerning Article 17 reference is made to the study by Nowak, mentioned *supra* p. 216.
1031. In our opinion, Art. 9 actually concerns any ideas and views whatever. In the Arrowsmith Case the Commission created a different impression by explicitly examining whether pacifism can really be brought under this provision: report of 12 October 1978, *D & R* 19 (1980), p. 5 (19).
1032. Such a treatment, in our opinion, will always also constitute an inhuman or degrading treatment in the sense of Art. 3.
1033. Here again there will usually also be a violation of Art. 3. One might think, for instance, of the exercise of physical or mental pressure on an accused person to extort a confession from him, or on a witness to obtain a declaration from him, or of the use of lie-detectors or hypnosis.

other registration conflicts with Article 9,[1034] as does also a practice, supported or tolerated by the authorities, according to which persons wishing to work in an Arab country or their employers must hand in a statement that they are not Jewish. Compulsory voting has not been considered contrary to Article 9, because this is only a duty to attend, and not a duty actually to register one's vote.[1035]

2. Article 9 speaks of the right "to manifest his religion or belief". It does not refer to the freedom of expression in general, a right which finds regulation in Article 10. However, the Commission appears to be prepared to put a broad interpretation on the words "religion or belief" in the sense that any conviction can be brought under it.[1036]

On the other hand, with regard to the term "manifestation" the Commission has followed a more restrictive interpretation: not every manifestation which is motivated or influenced by a conviction is protected in Article 9, but only those manifestations which "actually express the belief concerned".[1037] Thanks to the supplementary character of Article 10 in that respect, this restrictive interpretation does not create serious problems. Of greater importance are the restrictions to which manifestations may be subject under the second paragraph, since these may find also justification under the second paragraph of Article 10.

3. With respect to the exercise of the freedom of conscience, both in the national and in the Strasbourg case-law the issue of conscientious objections of a religious or other nature against military service takes an important place. Hitherto the Commission has taken the position that the Convention contains no obligation for the contracting States to exempt conscientious objectors from compulsory military service. For its position the Commission refers to the words in Article 4(3)(b) "conscientious objectors *in countries where they are recognized*" (emphasis added).[1038] The argument is evidently that, since the drafters of the Convention meant to leave the States free to recognize or not to recognize conscientious objections to military service, they

---

1034. See Appl. 2854/66, *X and Y v. Austria, Coll.* 26 (1968), p. 46, where, however, no decision was reached on this point on account of non-exhaustion of the local remedies. In Appl. 2835/66, *X v. Belgium,* not published, a detainee complained about the fact that he had wrongly been registered as a Catholic. The Commission held, without further motivation, that Art. 9 had not been violated; a decision which in our opinion is highly disputable.
1035. Appl. 1718/62, *X v. Austria, Yearbook* VIII (1965), p. 168 (172); Appl. 4982/71, *X v. Austria, Yearbook* XV (1972), p. 468 (472-474).
1036. Report of 12 October 1978, *Arrowsmith, D & R* 19 (1980), p. 5 (19). With regard to commercial advertisements by a church body, see Appl. 7805/77, *Pastor X and the Church of Scientology v. Sweden, Yearbook* XXII (1979), p. 244 (246-248). In this case the Commission did not exclude that advertisements can fall within the scope of Article 9, provided that the text of the advertisement primarily has an informative instead of an commercial character.
1037. *Arrowsmith, ibidem,* pp. 19-20.
1038. See the report of 29 June 1967, *Grandrath, Yearbook* X (1967), p. 626 (672-674). See also Appl. 5591/72, *X v. Austria, Coll.* 43 (1973), p. 161, and Appl. 7705/76, *X v. Federal Republic of Germany, D & R* 9 (1978), p. 196.

cannot have intended to deprive them of this same freedom in another provision of the same Convention. But since military service has not been included as such among the restrictions of Article 9(2), some doubt seems justified as to whether an absolute freedom for the State on this point may really be inferred from Article 4(3)(b). The formulation of the latter provision takes into account the possibility that conscientious objections may be recognized in some of the contracting States, but not in others; this does not exclude that a State, when it does not recognize this exercise of the freedom of conscience, needs to justify this by reference to one of the restriction grounds in the second paragraph of Article 9. One may think, for instance, of a reference to "the interests of public safety" in a situation where the number of persons to be recruited for military service leaves insufficient scope for the recognition of conscientious objections. The position of the Commission in fact amounts to the recognition of an "inherent limitation" in a provision containing explicit restrictions, a construction which was rejected by the Court in another context.[1039]

In Resolution 337(1967) on conscientious objections the Parliamentary Assembly of the Council of Europe inferred from Article 9, *inter alia*, the following principle:

> 1. Persons liable to conscription for military service who, for reasons of conscience or profound conviction arising from religious, ethical, moral, humanitarian, philosophical or similar motives, refuse to perform armed service shall enjoy a personal right to be released from the obligation to perform such service.
> 2. This right shall be regarded as deriving logically from the fundamental rights of the individual in democratic Rule of Law States which are guaranteed in Article 9 of the European Convention on Human Rights.[1040]

On 9 April 1987, the Committee of Ministers adopted Recommendation No. R(87)8 on the same subject. There, the following "basic principle" is laid down:

> Anyone liable to conscription for military service who, for compelling reasons of conscience, refuses to be involved in the use of arms, shall have the right to be released from the obligation to perform such service, on the conditions set out hereafter. Such persons may be liable to perform alternative service.

As far as procedure is concerned the Recommendation states:

> 2. States may lay down a suitable procedure for the examination of applications for conscientious objector status or accept a declaration giving reasons by the person concerned;
> 3. With a view to the effective application of the principles and rules of this recommendation, persons liable to conscription shall be informed in advance of their rights. For this purpose, the state shall provide them with all relevant information directly or allow private organisations concerned to furnish that information;
> 4. Applications for conscientious objector status shall be made in ways and within time-limits to be determined having due regard to the requirement that the procedure for the examination of an application should, as a rule, be completed before the individual concerned is actually enlisted in the forces;
> 5. The examination of applications shall include all the necessary guarantees for a fair

---

1039. For this, see *supra* pp. 390-391, and *infra* pp. 575-578.
1040. Council of Europe, Cons. Ass., Eighteenth Ordinary Session (Third Part), *Texts Adopted* (1967), reiterated by the Parliamentary Assembly in its Res. 816(1977), adopted on 7 October 1977; *Collected Texts, supra* note 2, pp. 222-223.

procedure;

6. An applicant shall have the right to appeal against the decision at first instance;

7. The appeal authority shall be separate from the military administration and composed so as to ensure its independence;

8. The law may also provide for the possibility of applying for and obtaining conscientious objector status in cases where the requisite conditions for conscientious objection appear during military service or periods of military training after initial service.

Finally, concerning alternative service the Recommendation provides as follows:

9. Alternative service, if any, shall be in principle civilian and in the public interest. Nevertheless, in addition to civilian service, the state may also provide for unarmed military service, assigning to it only those conscientious objectors whose objections are restricted to the personal use of arms;

10. Alternative service shall not be of a punitive nature. Its duration shall, in comparison to that of military service, remain within reasonable limits;

11. Conscientious objectors performing alternative service shall not have less social and financial rights than persons performing military service. Legislative provisions or regulations which relate to the taking into account of military service for employment, career or pension purposes shall apply to alternative service.[1041]

It is true that this Recommendation has no binding force, but still it can be considered as an authoritative interpretation, which cannot simply be ignored by the national authorities and the Strasbourg institutions. The fact that the Recommendation differs from the Resolution of the Parliamentary Assembly in that it does not expressly refer to Article 9, would seem not to be of great importance.

The possibility of imposing alternative civilian service in case of recognition of conscientious objections is expressly mentioned in Article 4(3)(b). This practice does not conflict with Article 9, provided that no service is exacted against which the person in question may likewise raise conscientious objections, and provided that in comparison with the military service the alternative service is not disproportionately onerous as to length, remuneration, arduousness of the work, *etcetera*, since this would in fact amount to a sanction being imposed on the holding of a particular opinion, in violation of paragraph 10 of the Recommendation and against the spirit of Article 9.

The Commission has dealt with some complaints in which conscientious objections to legal obligations other than compulsory military service were raised: compulsory affiliation for dairy farmers with a service for preventing and combating cattle disease,[1042] an obligation to pay social security premiums,[1043] and a compulsory motorcar insurance.[1044] Furthermore, an assistant of the "Sosjale Joenit", an organization assisting runaway children, relied on Article 9, submitting that the prohibition under Dutch law to deprive parents of their parental authority over minors by keeping those minors concealed,

1041. Council of Europe, *Information Sheet* No. 21, H/INF(87)1, p. 160. See also Resolution 1987/46 of 10 March 1987 of the United Nations Commission on Human Rights on conscientious objection to military service, where the Commission, *inter alia*, "appeals to States to recognize that conscientious objection to military service be considered a legitimate exercise of the right to freedom of thought, conscience and religion recognized by the Universal Declaration of Human Rights and the International Covenant on Civil and Political Rights".
1042. Appl. 1068/61, *X v. the Netherlands, Yearbook* V (1962), p. 278.
1043. Appl. 1497/62, *Reformed Church of X v. the Netherlands, Yearbook* V (1962), p. 286.
1044. Appl. 2988/66, *X v the Netherlands, Yearbook* X (1967), p. 472.

burdened his conscience.[1045] These cases disclose the Commission's view that Article 9 has not been violated if the challenged obligation can reasonably be justified by reference to one of the limitation grounds mentioned in the second paragraph, or if an alternative arrangement has been made for the conscientious objectors.[1046] This requires, however, that the Commission makes an independent inquiry into that reasonableness and ascertains whether the alternative arrangement really meets the conscientious objections and is not disproportionately burdensome.

In case of conscientious objections to medical treatment one has to differentiate between, on the one hand, those compulsory treatments which are intended to prevent or combat diseases which may endanger the health of other people (*e.g.* vaccination against contagious diseases) and, on the other hand, those which concern "only" the health or the life of the person in question (*e.g.* compulsory blood transfusion or artificial prolongation of life). In the first case it will always be possible to rely, as against the freedom of religion and conscience of the person concerned or of the latter's parent or guardian, as the case may be, on the "protection of public ... health" or the "protection of the rights and freedoms of others" as a justification,[1047] while in the second case it is much more dubious whether these grounds of restriction can be invoked. In that context the question also arises whether the right to life as laid down in Article 2 is an unalienable right, and for that reason the protection of this life by the public authorities, even against the will and the conscience of the person in question, in principle is indeed in conformity with the Convention.[1048]

4. The right to perform religious services in public, as laid down in Article 9, does not afford very strong guarantees, because a prohibition of such public religious services or their subjection to a system of permits will be considered justified in practically all cases on the ground of the "protection of public order" in the sense of suppression and prevention of disorders. In a case in which the Dutch Supreme Court had to decide on the compatibility of the prohibition of processions under the Dutch Constitution with Article 9 of the Convention, the Supreme Court held that a court will only be able to answer that question in the negative if it must be deemed altogether inconceivable that a legislator, when faced with the necessity to enact a regulation with a view to the protection of public order, could reasonably enact or maintain such a regulation.[1049] Since the question of whether a religious manifestation entails the risk of disorders is predominantly determined by the local situation, so that it is hardly possible to review the

---

1045. Appl. 6753/74, *X and Y v. the Netherlands*, *D & R* 2 (1975), p. 118.
1046. In none of the four cases mentioned here the Commission found a violation of Art. 9 of the Convention.
1047. This does not, however, rule out the possibility of violation of Art. 3, which does not expressly allow for such limitations; see *supra* pp. 229-230.
1048. On this, see *supra* p. 221.
1049. Netherlands Supreme Court, 19 January 1962, *NJ* 1962, no. 107.

measures taken against a "European" norm, it does not appear very likely that measures based on the law will be found by the Strasbourg organs to conflict with Article 9.

Freedom of religion also comprises the freedom not to take part in religious services. An obligation to that effect, for instance for children in schools or in boarding-schools, soldiers in barracks, patients in nursing-homes, and prisoners, conflicts with Article 9. Justification on the ground of "protection of public ... morals" would not seem possible, since this would result in the imposition of a particular conception of morals, which would manifestly be contrary to the purport of Article 9. In this respect the judgment of the Court in the *Johnston* Case is worth mentioning. Here, the applicants complained about the prohibition of divorce in Ireland. One of the applicants invoked Article 9 of the Convention, submitting that the impossibility to live together with one of the other applicants in a marital relationship, because he had already been married with a woman with which he did not live together anymore, conflicted with his conscience. Both the Commission and the Court concluded that in this case there was no violation of Article 9. According to the Court, Article 9, "in its ordinary meaning", was not involved.[1050] Judge De Meyer, however, in a partly dissenting opinion, concluded that the Convention had been violated here:

> the absence of any possibility of seeking ... the civil dissolution of the marriage constitutes, firstly and of itself, a violation, as regards each of the spouses, of the rights guaranteed in Articles 8, 9 and 12 of the Convention.

Furthermore, De Meyer referred to a report of an Irish Parliamentary Commission, which already in 1967 concluded that the prohibition of divorce was

> coercive in relation to all persons, Catholics and non-Catholics, whose religious rules do not absolutely prohibit divorce in all circumstances.[1051]

Indeed, in our opinion, too, the prohibition concerned amounts to the imposition of a certain moral point of view, also on those individuals who do not share that point of view. This clearly is not in conformity with the meaning of Article 9. With reference to the judgment of the Court in the *Young, James and Webster* Case,[1052] De Meyer concluded:

> For so draconian a system to be legitimate, it does not suffice that it corresponds to the desire or will of a substantial majority of the population ... democracy does not simply mean that the views of a majority must always prevail: a balance must be achieved which ensures the fair and proper treatment of minorities and avoids any abuse of a dominant position.[1053]

It is to be hoped that ultimately this sound view will prevail in the Strasbourg case-law.

1050. Judgment of 18 December 1986, A.112 (1987), p. 27. See for the Commission's report of 5 March 1985: *ibidem*, pp. 51-52.
1051. *Ibidem*, pp. 36-37.
1052. Judgment of 13 August 1981, A.44 (1981), p. 25.
1053. A.112 (1987), p. 37.

Special rights can be derived from the profession of a particular religion only if these rights are indispensable for free profession.[1054] The Commission, therefore, rightly declared ill-founded a complaint that the non-recognition by the public authorities of a marriage concluded exclusively in accordance with a religious ritual was contrary to Article 9.[1055] For this, the Commission relied on Article 12, which leaves the regulation of marriage to the national law. In our opinion, however, it might have confined itself to submitting that, as long as the religious celebration of the marriage is not prohibited, the legal requirement of a supplementary non-religious procedure if the marriage is to be legally valid, does not imply an encroachment on the freedom of religion.

A matter closely related to that of conscientious objections discussed above is that of the exemption from military service for certain ministers of religious communities. Unlike in the case of recognized conscientious objectors, as a rule no alternative civilian service is imposed on these ministers. A right to such an exemption exists automatically in some contracting States, but in others it exists only if such an exemption is necessary for the practice of the religion by the person himself and by the community for which he has been appointed. If an arrangement for the exemption of ministers has been made, the arrangement itself and its application must not lead to discrimination. The case-law relating to this issue will be discussed below with reference to Article 14.[1056]

When considering the Commission's case-law with respect to prisoners one cannot avoid the impression, here again, that the Commission tends to assume rather lightly that restrictions imposed on prisoners in the manifestation of their religion or conviction are inherent in detention and as such are not contrary to Article 9,[1057] or are justified by one of the restrictions of paragraph 2. It makes sense to assume that Article 9 does not imply an obligation on the authorities to provide prisoners at public expense with the books which they request for the practice of their religion and the development of their philosophy of life,[1058] or to make a minister available to prisoners who profess a religion which is not current in the country of their detention.[1059] In that situation, however, they should admit such books sent by others, and a minister of that religion who presents himself, although some

---

1054. The existence of the religion and its profession by the applicant will then have to be proved: Appl. 7291/75, *X v. United Kingdom*, *D & R* 11 (1978), p. 55 (56).
1055. Appl. 6167/73, *X v. Federal Republic of Germany*, *D & R* 1 (1975), p. 64 (65).
1056. See *infra* p. 541.
1057. For that tenor, formulated in very general terms indeed, see the decision on Appl. 4517/70, *Huber v. Austria*, *Yearbook* XIV (1971), p. 548 (566-568).
1058. Appl. 1753/63, *X v. Austria*, *Yearbook* VIII (1965), p. 174 (184). From the decision it is not clear whether the books desired were already present in the prison library, or would have to be purchased as yet. If the former was the case, the decision would be incorrect. In its decision on Appl. 6886/75, *X v. United Kingdom*, *D & R* 5 (1976), p. 100 (101), the fact that a book was kept back which had indeed a philosophical character, but contained a chapter on techniques of self-defence, was considered as a restriction of the freedom of religion by the Commission, but it was deemed justified on the basis of the restriction "protection of the rights and freedoms of others".
1059. Appl. 2413/65, *X v. Federal Republic of Germany*, *Coll.* 23 (1967), p. 1 (8).

supervision may be permitted for security reasons.[1060] But what are we to think of the Commission's acceptance of the justification of the prohibition for a Buddhist prisoner to grow a beard[1061] and of the refusal to take religious precepts into account in providing food,[1062] both on the ground of "protection of public order"? It may be called an understatement when Castberg observes with reference to the former decision: "It may be open to question how necessary it can be in a prison in a democratic State to forbid a prisoner to grow a beard for religious reasons".[1063] And although it sounds reasonable that, if prisoners are required to clean their own cells, all prisoners have to do this, as soon as it is recognized that a particular prisoner's religion does not allow cleaning floors, it is too easy to conclude that this interference with Article 9 is justified "as necessary in a democratic society for the protection of the applicant's and other prisoners' health".[1064] It cannot be maintained that this protection requires cleaning by the prisoners themselves. In more or less the same laconic way the Commission dealt with the arguments by a Sikh prisoner that his religious principles required him to wear his own clothes rather than prison clothes.[1065]

That the church imposes specific restrictions on its ministers and others employed by it, in order to preserve the purity of the doctrine and to guarantee unity in religious profession, has been considered in conformity with Article 9 by the Commission. It stated as follows:

> Through the rights granted to its members under Art. 9, the church itself is protected in its right to manifest its religion, to organise and carry out worship, teaching practice and observance, and it is free to act out and enforce uniformity in these matters. Further, in a State church system its servants are employed for the purpose of applying and teaching a specific religion. Their individual freedom of thought, conscience or religion is exercised at the moment they accept or refuse employment as clergymen, and their right to leave the church guarantees their freedom of religion in case they oppose its teachings. In other words, the church is not obliged to provide religious freedom to its servants and members, as is the State as such for everyone within its jurisdiction.[1066]

This reasoning demonstrates, in our opinion, a sound balancing of rights and interests.

5. With reference to two complaints by churches on violation of Article 9 the Commission held that a church, "being a legal and not a natural person, is incapable of having or exercising the rights mentioned in Article 9, paragraph (1) of the Convention", and on that ground cannot claim to be itself the

---

1060. It strikes us as incorrect when the Commission, without any further motivation, takes the view that writings published by Catholics do not form religious reading for a Buddhist: Appl. 1753/63, *X v. Austria, Yearbook* VIII (1965), p. 174 (184).
1061. Appl. 1753/63, *X v. Austria, Yearbook* VIII (1965), p. 174 (184).
1062. Mentioned in: Council of Europe, *Case-Law Topics* No. 1, "Human Rights in Prison" (1971), p. 31. Cf. Appl. 5947/72, *X v. United Kingdom, D & R* 5 (1976), p. 8 (8-9).
1063. Castberg, *supra* note 45, p. 147.
1064. Appl. 8231/78, *X v. United Kingdom, D & R* 28 (1982), p. 5 (38).
1065. *Ibidem*, pp. 26-27.
1066. Appl. 7374/76, *X v. Denmark, D & R* 5 (1976), p. 157 (158).

victim of the alleged violation of Article 9.[1067] This position of the Commission has been criticized. The right to freedom of religion has not only an individual but also a collective character,[1068] and the entire functioning of churches depends on respect for this right. They appear therefore to be eminently indicated to stand up for that respect, the more so as Article 25 expressly provides for the possibility of complaints by non-governmental organizations and groups.[1069]

In a decision of 1979 the Commission revised its position, and called the distinction made between a church body and its members artificial. In this context it held:

> When a Church body lodges an application under the Convention, it does so in reality on behalf of its members. It should therefore be accepted that a church body is capable of possessing and exercising the rights contained in Art. 9(1) in its own capacity as a representative of its members.[1070]

But even that reasoning seems to us to be too narrow, as was in fact recognized by the Commission in its earlier decision, referred to above, that a church has *its own right* to manifest its religion.[1071]

6. Article 9 is not included among the provisions included in the second paragraph of Article 15 as non-derogable. On this point the Convention differs from the Covenant, where in Article 4(2) the freedom of thought, conscience, and religion laid down in Article 18 is declared non-derogable. For those contracting States, which are also parties to the Covenant, the prohibition to derogate from the obligation that is incumbent on them under Article 18 of the Covenant also applies under the Convention. In fact, Article 15(1) of the Convention provides that the measures taken by a State must not be "inconsistent with its other obligations under international law", while Article 60 excludes any reference to the Convention which would have the effect of limiting or derogating from any obligation incumbent on the contracting States under other conventions in the field of human rights.

At the beginning of the present section a distinction was made between the right to freedom of thought, conscience and religion on the one hand and the freedom to express one's thoughts, conscience and religion on the other hand.[1072] With respect to the former right Jacobs submits: "It is doubtful whether even the derogations permitted under Article 15 could have any

---

1067. Appl. 3798/68, *Church of X v. United Kingdom*, Yearbook XII (1969), p. 306 (314); Appl. 4733/71, *X v. Sweden*, Yearbook XIV (1971), p. 664 (674).
1068. See P. van Dijk, *Judicial Review of Governmental Action and the Requirement of an Interest to Sue*, Alphen a/d Rijn 1980, pp. 348-350, and the reference made there to the decision of the Bundesverfassungsgericht of 4 October 1965, E 19, p. 129, in which it was expressly recognized that churches and other juridical persons may have the right to freedom of religion.
1069. See *supra* p. 39.
1070. Appl. 7805/77, *Pastor X and the Church of Scientology v. Sweden*, Yearbook XXII (1979), p. 244 (246).
1071. Appl. 7374/76, *X v. Denmark*, D & R 5 (1976), p. 157 (158).
1072. *Supra* pp. 397-398.

application here".[1073] On the one hand, a provision of the Convention cannot be brought under the special protection of the second paragraph of Article 15 if it is not expressly mentioned there, however desirable the incorporation of Article 9 into that provision *de lege ferenda* may be. On the other hand, even for those States which are not parties to the Covenant it will be extremely difficult, if not impossible, to make it plausible that any interference with the freedom of thought, conscience, and religion *per se* is "strictly required by the exigencies of the situation" in the sense of Article 15(1). Precisely on a point where the European norm is lower than the universally accepted one, a very critical examination of that necessity by the national and Strasbourg organs would seem appropriate.

7. An important difference between the Convention and the Covenant with respect to the protection of the freedom of thought, conscience and religion has been pointed out above: the fact that this freedom is non-derogable under the Covenant.

The principal difference between the two provisions themselves is that the fourth paragraph of Article 18 of the Covenant regulates the right of parents freely to ensure the religious and moral education of their children in conformity with their own conviction. This right is provided for in the Convention - as in the Covenant on Economic, Social and Cultural Rights - in the provision concerning the freedom of education, and will therefore be dealt with in the discussion of Article 2 of the First Protocol.[1074]

For the rest, the differences between Article 9 of the Convention and Article 18 of the Covenant are largely differences in formulation. The freedom "to change his religion" is formulated in Article 18 as the freedom "to have or to adopt a religion". As the Committee of Experts states in its report, this has been done to take account of communities which do not admit that their members may change their religious faith".[1075] It is submitted here, however, that in a situation where obligations continue to be attached to membership of a church, even after one has intimated that one no longer wishes to be considered as a member or where in some other way the freedom to change one's religion is restricted, there is no question of "freedom to have ... a religion ... of his choice". In our opinion, therefore, this difference in formulation ought not to have any consequences in practice.[1076]

The second paragraph of Article 18 of the Covenant prohibits the exercise of coercion impairing one's freedom to have or adopt a religion or a belief

---

1073. Jacobs, *supra* note 17, p. 144.
1074. *Infra* pp. 471-476.
1075. Report of the Committee of Experts, *supra* note 14, p. 43.
1076. In the Declaration on the Elimination of All Forms of Intolerance and of Discrimination Based on Religion and Belief, adopted by Resolution 36/55 of the General Assembly of the United Nations on 25 November 1981, the words "to adopt", which appeared in an earlier draft, were expressly omitted. This involves the risk of a restrictive interpretation of Art. 18 of the Covenant in this respect, although the Declaration stipulates in Art. 8 that nothing therein "shall be construed as restricting or derogating from any right defined in the ... International Covenants on Human Rights".

406

of one's choice. As the Committee of Experts states, this prohibition is inherent in the freedom guaranteed in the first paragraph, so that no legal significance can be attributed to the lack of such a provision in the Convention.[1077]

Paragraph 3 of Article 18 of the Covenant is practically identical with the second paragraph of Article 9 of the Convention, although the words "in a democratic society" are lacking in the former provision and this speaks - more correctly - of "order" instead of "public order".[1078]

§ 10. ARTICLE 10: FREEDOM OF EXPRESSION

1. Everyone has the right to freedom of expression. This right shall include freedom to hold opinions and to receive and impart information and ideas without interference by public authority and regardless of frontiers. This Article shall not prevent States from requiring the licensing of broadcasting, television or cinema enterprises.

2. The exercise of these freedoms, since it carries with it duties and responsibilities, may be subject to such formalities, conditions, restrictions or penalties as are prescribed by law and are necessary in a democratic society, in the interests of national security, territorial integrity or public safety, for the prevention of disorder or crime, for the protection of health or morals, for the protection of the reputation or rights of others, for preventing the disclosure of information received in confidence, or for maintaining the authority and impartiality of the judiciary.

1. The freedom of expression is closely related to the freedom of thought, conscience and religion discussed above. This is the more so as in the case of the freedom of expression emphasis is laid upon the *content* of the opinion expressed; the *means* by which a particular opinion is expressed are protected only in so far as they are means which have an independent significance for the expression of the opinion.

This does not alter the fact that Article 10 has a wider scope than Article 9. While for the applicability of Article 9 it is required that the opinion which is expressed reflects the conviction of the person who puts this opinion forward,[1079] Article 10 envisages the protection of every expression of an opinion, be it that the measure of expression may vary according to the nature of the opinion expressed.[1080] Thus, in the *Müller* Case the Court held

---

1077. Report of the Committee of Experts, *supra* note 14, p. 44.
1078. The French text speaks in both provisions of "ordre". For the "case-law" of the Human Rights Committee concerning Article 18, reference is made to the study by Nowak, *supra* p. 216.
1079. Report of 12 October 1978, *Arrowsmith*, *D & R* 19 (1980), p. 5 (19-20).
1080. Thus the Commission held that the degree of protection may vary according as political views are concerned or not: Appl. 7805/77, *Pastor X and the Church of Scientology v. Sweden*, *Yearbook* XXII (1979), p. 244 (252).

that the freedom of artistic expression of a painter is part of the freedom of expression as protected by Article 10.[1081] The fact that Article 10 protects the free expression of opinions implies that a rather strong emphasis is also laid on the protection of the specific means by which the opinion is expressed. Even if the person who provides the means is not the holder of the opinion, he is protected by Article 10.[1082]

This emphasis on the means of expression delimits the applicability of Article 10 *vis-à-vis* other freedoms, which are related to the possibility to express specific opinions, but cannot be considered as means which have an independent significance apart from other means available to the person concerned. Thus in the *Belgian Linguistic* Case the Commission rightly took the position that freedom of expression does not comprise the right to be offered the opportunity to express one's opinion in a language of one's choice, the consequence of which would be the right to being taught that language.[1083] Here Article 2 of the First Protocol is at issue, not Article 10. This would only be otherwise if, for instance, an alien were denied access to being taught the vernacular or if the required facilities for this were not provided, since he would then be deprived of an independent means of expression: expression in a locally understood language. However, in such a case, too, it would seem to make more sense to invoke Article 2 of the First Protocol. The Commission has taken the position that Article 10 does not prohibit authorities from making legal regulations for access to certain professions, not even when the exercise of those professions consists mainly in the expression of opinions.[1084] For the person in question access to such a profession as a rule does not in itself form a means which has an independent significance for expressing a specific opinion; the normal channels for doing this are not cut off or restricted if he is not admitted to that profession. Only if a person wishes to exercise a profession or start an enterprise precisely in order to be able to express his opinion in a certain way or by certain means - one might think of a publisher publishing manuscripts which may be assumed not to be accepted elsewhere or of a publisher who wishes to start a periodical of a specific character - is Article 10 at issue and can the person concerned be considered a direct or indirect victim of the violation of that article in case of a prohibition to exercise the profession or start the enterprise. It is in this light that the exception expressly included in the first paragraph with regard to broadcasting, television and cinema enterprises will have to be viewed, since they are to be

---

1081. Judgment of 24 May 1988, A.133 (1988), p. 19.
1082. *Ibidem*: the organizers of the exhibition of Mr. Müller's paintings were considered to also exercise their freedom of expression.
1083. Appl. 1474/62, *23 Inhabitants of Alsemberg and Beersel v. Belgium*, Yearbook VI (1963), p. 332 (342); Appl. 1769/62, *X v. Belgium*, Yearbook VI (1963), p. 444 (454-456). See, however, the decision of the Belgian court mentioned by Fawcett, *supra* note 20, p. 213, in which a legal obligation for enterprises to frase specific documents in a given language was considered contrary to Art. 10.
1084. See the decision mentioned in Fawcett, *supra* note 20, p. 211, concerning the profession of a solicitor.

considered as independent means of expression. In the *De Becker* Case, in which the Commission concluded that Article 10 had been violated, the penal sanctions imposed on De Becker also comprised the prohibition to exercise the profession of publisher. However, it cannot be clearly inferred from the words of the Commission with reference to these sanctions, *viz.* "in so far as they affect freedom of expression",[1085] whether the Commission considered this part of the prohibition also as such a violation.

If the legal requirements for appointment on a certain post themselves concern the freedom of opinion or expression, Article 10 would also seem to be applicable. Thus the Commission took the view that the provision of the German Civil Servants Act, prescribing that every civil servant owed an obligation of loyalty and allegiance to the Constitution as a condition for appointment and for continued employment in the civil service, directly circumscribed and impinged upon the right guaranteed by Article 10(1).[1086] In the two cases brought before the Commission, it reached the conclusion in the one case that the interference was justified as necessary in a democratic society for the protection of the rights of others and in the interests of national security,[1087] whereas in the second case it found that the interference was not necessary for any of the purposes referred to in Article 10(2).[1088] Both cases concerned teaching jobs. Mr. Kosiek was an active member of the National Democratic Party of Germany (NPD) and Mrs. Glasenapp was alleged to support the policies of the Communist Party of Germany (KPD). It was evidently the difference in closeness of the political ties and in the character of the personal activities performed and opinions expressed by the two persons which made the difference here.

Both cases were referred to the Court, which first considered the Government's argument that the cases concerned the right - not guaranteed under the Convention - of access to a post in the civil service, and not Article 10 of the Convention. With respect to Mrs. Glasenapp, the Court noted that under the Land Civil Servants Act the applicant could only become a secondary school teacher with the status of probationary civil servant, if she afforded a guarantee that she would consistently uphold the free democratic constitutional system within the meaning of the Basic Law. This requirement, according to the Court,

> applies to recruitment to the civil service, a matter that was deliberately omitted from the Convention, and it cannot in itself be considered incompatible with the Convention.[1089]

In relation to Mr. Kosiek the Court adopted a comparable reasoning.[1090] In both cases the Court came to the conclusion that in the light of the facts of

---

1085. Report of 8 January 1960, B.2 (1962), p. 11 (128). The Court struck the case out of the list on account of an interim adaptation of the Belgian legislation: A.4 (1962), pp. 23-27.
1086. Report of 11 May 1984, *Kosiek*, A.105 (1986), p. 32; Report of 11 May 1984, *Glasenapp*, A.104 (1986), p. 39.
1087. Report of 11 May 1984, *Kosiek*, A.105 (1986), p. 45.
1088. Report of 11 May 1984, *Glasenapp*, A.104 (1986), pp. 53-54.
1089. Judgment of 28 August 1986, A.104 (1986), pp. 26-27.
1090. Judgment of 28 August 1986, A.105 (1986), p. 21.

each case access to the civil service lay at the heart of the issue submitted to it. In refusing such access, the authority took account of the applicants' opinions and attitude merely in order to satisfy itself as to whether they possessed one of the necessary personal qualifications for the post in question. There was, therefore, in the Court's view no interference with the exercise of the right protected in paragraph 1 of Article 10.[1091] And in the *Leander* Case the Court, again, took the view that the personnel control procedure to which the applicant was subjected did not amount to an interference with the exercise of freedom of expression, since it appeared clearly that the purpose of this procedure was to ensure that persons holding posts of importance for national security have the necessary personal qualifications.[1092] In our opinion the Court has taken the wrong approach in these cases and should have followed the Commission. Not the purpose of a certain regulation and its application, but their effects on the freedom of opinion and expression of the person concerned are decisive for the question whether Article 10 is applicable. In the present cases it was evident that the applicants could have access to the desired posts only by accepting certain restrictions on their freedom of expression. Consequently, the Court should have examined whether these resulting restrictions were justified under paragraph 2 of Article 10.

That the right to vote is not protected in Article 10 is established case-law of the Commission.[1093] No arguments are given for this. It can hardly be denied that taking part in elections is a form of expression of an opinion. Article 3 of the First Protocol speaks of "the free expression of the opinion of the people". Nor can it be subject to doubt that it forms a means for the expression of that opinion which has an independent character. On the other hand it seems logical to assume that the drafters of Article 10 did not intend to include the right to vote. This may first of all be inferred from the incorporation of a specific provision concerning elections into the First Protocol. As an additional argument it may be stated that Article 10 refers exclusively to individual forms of expression, and to collective forms where those who wish to express a specific opinion can be individualized. This is not the case with elections by secret ballot, so that there is no question of expression of an opinion in the proper sense for the person taking part in them. The duty to vote is not in violation of Article 10 - nor of Article 9 - as long as the secret character is guaranteed; in that case the person concerned is free to express any opinion or no opinion at all.

The situation is different in the case of group demonstrations or of declarations made by an association or other organization on behalf of its members. For that reason it is understandable that a connection has been made between compulsory membership of a trade union and Article 10: as a result of that compulsory membership the employee in question is no longer

---

1091. *Ibidem*, pp. 27 and 21 respectively.
1092. Judgment of 26 March 1987, A.116 (1987), p. 28.
1093. See, *e.g.*, Appl. 6573/74, *X v. the Netherlands, D & R* 1 (1975), p. 87 (89), and Appl. 6850/74, *X, Y and Z v. Federal Republic of Germany, D & R* 5 (1976), p. 90 (93).

free to dissent from a view propagated by the trade union. This connection has in fact been recognized by the Commission and the Court.[1094]

When a parliamentarian complained about the fact that a motion proposed by him had not been placed on the agenda, and invoked Article 10 for this, his complaint was declared inadmissible by the Commission.[1095] Here again the Commission gave no further motivation for its decision. In our opinion that motivation might have been that the procedural decision about which the parliamentarian complained formed part of the very means which he wished to use for the expression of his opinion: Parliament.

In Appl. 7729/76, former CIA agent *Agee* claimed that his expulsion from England was contrary, *inter alia*, to Article 10, because his opportunity to exercise the right conferred therein was restricted by the expulsion. The Commission rightly took the position that the right to stay in a country and the right to freedom of expression have to be distinguished.[1096] Abode in a country does not constitute an independent means or independent condition for the expression of one's opinion, unless it were to be firmly established that no other country is to be found in which that particular opinion may be put forward. In the latter case, the expelling country is responsible for that situation abroad; it may then only proceed to expel the person concerned on grounds mentioned in the second paragraph. Agee's claim that his expulsion was to be regarded as a sanction on opinions expressed by him was considered ill-founded by the Commission. In fact, this argument would not have been of much avail to him, because the reason for the expulsion - national security - at the same time constitutes one of the grounds of restriction of the second paragraph.

A remarkable decision of the Commission is the one in which an invocation of Article 10 by a prisoner convicted for homosexual practices was declared admissible. The applicant had claimed, *inter alia*, that his right to express feelings of love for other men was interfered with by his detention. The Commission held with respect to this

> that there may be an issue under Article 10 regarding his ... claim that the fact of imprisonment denied him his right to express feelings of love for other men.[1097]

While in the *Brüggemann and Scheuten* Case sexual intercourse had been brought under Article 8,[1098] in Appl. 7215/75 thus the possibility of a connection with Article 10 was left open. In its report on the merits of the latter case, however, the Commission took the position, on the ground of the text of paragraph 2, that

> the concept of "expression" in Art. 10 concerns mainly the expression of opinion and receiving and imparting information and ideas ... . It does not encompass any notion of

---

1094. Report of 14 December 1979, *Young, James and Webster*, B.39 (1984), p. 48; judgment of 13 August 1981, A.44 (1981), pp. 23-24.
1095. Appl. 7758/77, *X v. Switzerland*, *D & R* 9 (1978), p. 214 (218).
1096. Appl. 7729/76, *Agee v. United Kingdom*, *D & R* 7 (1977), p. 164 (174).
1097. Appl. 7215/75, *X v. United Kingdom*, *Yearbook* XXI (1978), p. 354 (374).
1098. See *supra* pp. 373-376.

the physical expression of feelings in the sense submitted by the applicant.[1099]

2. Since correspondence, telephone and similar means of communication, protected in Article 8, also constitute means for the expression of an opinion, there is a close connection between that article and Article 10. This connection was put forward in the *Silver* Case, which was concerned with the right to respect for the correspondence of detainees. Here Commission and Court took the view that in the examination of the complaints with respect to Article 8 the freedom of expression of an opinion via correspondence had already been dealt with at such length that a separate examination with regard to Article 10 was not necessary.[1100] In an admissibility decision of one year earlier, where in a complaint against the defective functioning of the postal service a person invoked his right to information via correspondence, basing his argument on Article 8 as well as Article 10, the Commission took the position that

> the right to receive any kind of information by way of correspondence is regulated in Article 8 of the Convention, which in this respect is a special provision in relation to Article 10.[1101]

This appears to us too general a statement, since the aim of the two articles is not identical: in Article 8 the main point is the protection of the private character of the means of communication referred to, while in Article 10 its character as a means of expressing an opinion and of providing and receiving information is at issue.

3. Article 10 also shows certain overlaps with the right to freedom of assembly of Article 11, *viz.* in those situations where several persons jointly express a given opinion. Thus, a demonstration always constitutes an expression of opinion, even if it has the character of a silent procession; but there is at the same time question of an assembly. This overlap will not, however, give rise to problems in practice, since the restrictions on the two rights partly coincide, while the specific restrictions of Article 10 clearly refer to the opinion expressed, and not to the question of whether it has been expressed by one person or by several persons jointly.

4. The question of whether freedom of expression implies the right of replication or rectification still has not been clarified.[1102] Such an interpretation seems to have been suggested by the Commission, but in the relevant case it did not reach a decision on this point, because in the Commission's opinion the arguments advanced constituted an insufficient ground for a

---

1099. Report of 12 October 1978, *D & R* 19 (1980), p. 66 (80). The conclusions of the report were adopted by the Committee of Ministers in Resolution DH(79)5 of 12 June 1979.
1100. Report of 11 October 1980, B.51 (1987), p. 99; judgment of 25 March 1983, A.61 (1983), p. 41. See also the judgment of 20 June 1988, *Schönenberger and Durmaz*, A.137 (1988), p. 23.
1101. Appl. 8383/78, *X v. Federal Republic of Germany, D & R* 17 (1980), p. 227 (228-229).
1102. Within the framework of the UN a special convention was concluded on this in 1953: the Convention on the International Right of Correction, 435 *U.N.T.S.*, p. 191.

decision that the accused State was responsible for the impugned publication by the daily papers.[1103] A complicating issue here is that of the *Drittwirkung* of Article 10[1104] and also that of the liability of the State - which is the only party to be accused in Strasbourg - for violation of Article 10 by private parties.[1105] Indeed, the publications involved will usually be due to a private party, and the publication of the replication or the rectification will have to be effected in most cases by a private party as well. From Article 10 might then be derived an obligation on the part of the State to create a legal obligation to publish the replication or rectification and to ensure its enforcement by the courts, either on the ground of a civil claim to that effect or in combination with a criminal conviction for insult. Such an obligation of publication would not constitute an unlawful interference with the freedom of expression laid down in Article 10 for the person on whom it would be imposed, since the justification might be found in the restriction "protection of the reputation or rights of others".

5. The "freedom to hold opinions", mentioned separately in Article 10, can hardly be distinguished from the "freedom of thought" provided for in Article 9. It is therefore obvious that in connection with a complaint relating thereto both provisions will be involved in the examination.[1106]

As has been stated with regard to Article 9, here again it is submitted that the restrictions mentioned in the second paragraph should not be applied to this "freedom to hold opinions".[1107]

6. A more important addition is the "freedom ... to receive and impart information and ideas", also mentioned separately. While imparting information can still be regarded as an expression of an opinion - of the informant himself or of a third person -, the seeking of information precedes the formation of an opinion by the person who seeks the information, and consequently also its expression.

In the *De Geïllustreerde Pers* Case a publisher claimed that Article 22 of the Dutch Broadcasting Act, which prohibited publication of radio and television programmes in any other way than on behalf or by the authorization of the NOS - the Netherlands Broadcasting Foundation - was contrary to Article 10 of the Convention. In its report in this case the Commission

---

1103. Appl. 1906/63, *X v. Belgium*, not published.
1104. On *Drittwirkung*, see *supra* pp. 15-20.
1105. In the case of Appl. 4515/70, *X & Association of Z. v. United Kingdom, Coll.* 38 (1972), p. 86 (88), which concerned complaints about the BBC, the Commission expressly left the question of State liability open. See, however, Appl. 6586/74, *X v. Ireland*, not published, where the Commission took the view that the restraint upon staff expressing their views is a common feature of many working situations arising from the relationships of the people concerned and not from written regulations for which the State could be held responsible.
1106. Thus, *e.g.*, Appl. 1747/62, *X v. Austria*, *Yearbook* VI (1963), p. 424.
1107. Thus also the Report of the Committee of Experts, *supra* note 14, p. 45, with the argument that "any restrictions on this right would be inconsistent with the nature of a democratic society".

distinguished between "information" and "ideas". In the case of information, according to the Commission, the only one who has the right of free distribution of that information is the party who is "the author, the originator or otherwise the intellectual owner" of the information in question.[1108] The publisher, therefore, did have a protected right to publish the programmes if he himself had drawn up a survey of them by means of information which he himself had sought from the individual broadcasting licensees, but not to copy the survey coordinated by the NOS. The Commission did not elaborate the issue what rule applies with respect to the distribution of ideas. Its reasoning seems to imply, however, freedom of such distribution irrespective of the source from which those ideas are borrowed, subject to such limitations as are prescribed by law in conformity with the second paragraph. This distinction would seem rather far-fetched to us and is not corroborated by the text of Article 10. In fact, the Commission seems to disregard altogether the words "to receive ... information". These words indicate that the collection of information from any source whatever should in principle be free, although restrictions can be made under paragraph 2. In our view, therefore, the Commission should have found that the restriction imposed upon the publisher was contrary to the first paragraph of Article 10, and subsequently should have ascertained whether this restriction was justified on the basis of one or more of the restrictions of the second paragraph, in particular the one of "protection of the ... rights of others".

As the Commission submitted in the same report, a second distinction between "information" and "ideas" in Article 10 was that the rationale of the freedom of distribution of information is the safeguarding of the public's right to information, and not, for instance, the commercial interests of publishers. Therefore, restrictions imposed upon one or more publishers do not conflict with Article 10 as long as sufficient channels for the information remain available to the public.[1109] This reasoning again does not appear to be very convincing. In fact, the right to freedom of expression serves, if not in the first place, at least partly also the protection of the freedom to *impart* information. As has been said above, this freedom primarily concerns the content of the information, not the means by which it is imparted. However, the publisher of a newspaper in that capacity has only one means, and this is publication in that newspaper. For him this means therefore has an independent significance. Consequently, the argument is valid that, when prohibiting that publication, *his* right to freedom of expression has not been violated, because the public can also obtain the information from another source. The latter is, on the other hand, of relevance when assessing the justification of the prohibition by reference to the second paragraph, a review

---

1108. Report of 6 July 1976, *D & R* 8 (1977), p. 5 (13).
1109. *Ibidem*, pp. 13-14.

which the Commission has failed to undertake in this case.[1110]

In its report in the *Lingens* Case the Commission made a more meaningful distinction between "information" and "ideas" emphasizing the special scope of protection the latter deserve. The case concerned criminal proceedings instigated by the former Austrian Chancellor, Mr. Kreisky, in which the applicant, a journalist, was convicted for public defamation. Since Mr. Kreisky in his action had not alleged that Mr. Lingens had misrepresented his statements or the circumstances in which they had been made, the Commission took the position that there had been no interference with the applicant's right to impart information. Mr. Lingens was punished because he had expressed a certain opinion or certain ideas on Mr. Kreisky's behaviour and, therefore, exclusively his right to impart ideas was interfered with.[1111] Thereupon the Commission emphasized the special function which the press holds by imparting ideas or opinions. In a democratic society this function is of particular importance, especially if the matter discussed relates to political issues and other matters of public interest. With respect to the risk of defamation of public figures by the press the Commission stated as follows:

> The democratic system requires that those who hold public power are subject to close control not only by their political adversaries in the institutions of the State or other organisations, but also by the public opinion which is to a large extent formed and expressed in the media. To exercise such control is not only a right, but may even be considered as a "duty and responsibility" of the press in a democratic State.[1112]

This does not mean that politicians are not protected against defamation in the press at all; the limitation ground "the protection of the reputation", which is recognized in Article 10(2), of course also applies to them. It does mean, however, that regulations restricting the freedom of the press in this respect must meet strict requirements of proportionality.[1113] In the opinion of the Commission a politician must be prepared to accept even harsh criticism of his public activities and statements, and such criticism may not be understood as defamatory unless it throws a considerable degree of doubt on his personal character and good reputation. In that respect the Commission does not consider it decisive whether the criticism involved a discussion of certain aspects of the "private" morality of the politician concerned, as this could also be of public relevance, while on the other hand a discussion of the "public" morality of certain of his acts may reach the level of defamation. The requirement that the truth of the criticism can be proved is not accepted by the Commission, since "value judgments are an essential element of the freedom of the press and the impossibility of proof is inherent in value judgments".[1114] Finally, the Commission made the following important statement in its report:

1110. See, however, the report of 18 May 1977, *Sunday Times*, B.28 (1982), p. 212, where indeed the public interest in the information being imparted was taken into account in reviewing the matter against paragraph 2.
1111. Report of 11 October 1984, A.103 (1986), p. 34.
1112. *Ibidem*, p. 36.
1113. *Ibidem*.
1114. *Ibidem*, pp. 36-37.

415

> In the Commission's opinion it is essential in a democratic society that a pluralism of opinions including those which shock or offend is in principle recognized. In order to secure effectively the freedom of expression, any restrictions must be applied in a spirit of pluralism, tolerance and broadmindedness, in particular where freedom of expression in political matters is involved.[1115]

This assigns an independent meaning to "democratic society" in the assessment of the necessity and proportionality of the restriction.

The Court followed the Commission in stressing the special importance of freedom of ideas and freedom of the press in a democratic society. According to the Court, the penalty imposed on Mr. Lingens amounted to a kind of censure, which would be likely to discourage him from making criticism of that kind again in the future. In the political field such a sanction was liable to hamper the press in performing its task as purveyor of information and as public watchdog. The Court subsequently examined the judicial decisions at issue. The passages held against Mr. Lingens were value-judgments, so that his freedom of opinion and his right to impart ideas had been at issue. As regards value-judgments, the requirement to prove the truth of the statements in order to escape conviction is an impossible one, according to the Court.

> In the Court's view, a careful distinction needs to be made between facts and value-judgments. The existence of facts can be demonstrated, whereas the truth of value-judgments is not susceptible of proof. The Court notes in this connection that the facts on which Mr. Lingens founded his value-judgments were undisputed, as was also his good faith.

The Court concluded that the interference on Lingens' freedom of expression was not necessary for the protection of the reputation of others.[1116]

The *Barfod* Case also concerned the complaint of a journalist who had been convicted for writing an article of an allegedly defaming character. In his article he criticized a judgment in a case in which two lay judges had participated, who were both employed as civil servants in the local government, which was the defendant party in that case. The applicant's conviction was based on the fact that he suggested that the two lay judges cast their votes rather as employees of the local government than as independent and impartial judges. In the opinion of the Commission this statement concerned matters of public interest involving the functioning of the public administration, including the judiciary. According to the Commission, in such a case the test of necessity of the interference must be a particularly strict one.

> It follows that even if the article in question could be interpreted as an attack on the integrity or reputation of the two lay judges, the general interest in allowing a public debate about the functioning of the judiciary weighs more heavily than the interest of the two judges in being protected against criticism of the kind expressed in the applicant's article.[1117]

The Commission furthermore indicated that the aim mentioned in Article 10(2) to maintain the authority of the judiciary cannot be used as a basis for restraining criticism of the composition of a court which is improperly

1115. *Ibidem*, p. 37.
1116. Judgment of 8 July 1986, A.103 (1986), p. 28.
1117. Report of 16 July 1987, A.149 (1989), p. 21.

constituted under the applicable rules for the judiciary. Unlike the Commission, the Court held that the interference with the applicant's freedom of expression did not aim at restricting his right under the Convention to criticize publicly the composition of the court in question. It was quite possible to question the composition of that court without at the same time attacking the two lay judges personally. The State's legitimate interest in protecting the reputation of the two lay judges was accordingly not in conflict with the applicant's interest in being able to participate in free public debate on the question of the structural impartiality of the High Court.[1118] In our opinion, it is difficult to understand the essential difference between this "personal attack" on the two judges concerning their public performance and the criticism concerning the Austrian Chancellor in the *Lingens* Case.

In the Commission's opinion the right to impart and distribute information does not include a general and unfettered right to have access to broadcasting time on radio or TV.[1119] This stands to reason, just as it does not imply a right to have one's information inserted in a daily or weekly paper. However, the Commission rightly adds that certain circumstances may occur in which the barring of a specific person or group may result in a violation of Article 10, either in combination with Article 14 or by itself.[1120] A conviction for having used a transceiver for private purposes without the required authorization was found by the Commission to be an interference with the right to receive and impart information and ideas.[1121]

A remarkable example of imparting information was involved in a case where two persons complained that during a forty-five hour detention they had been prevented from contacting their wives. The Commission declared the total of the complaints admissible, on account of their complexity.[1122] In its report the Commission dealt with this complaint in conjunction with Article 8. After having found a breach of Article 8, it considered it unnecessary to decide on the issue of Article 10.[1123]

It is still not clear whether - and if so, to what extent - the freedom to receive information entails an obligation on the part of the authorities to impart information.[1124] An interpretation to that effect is laid down in Resolution 428(1970) of the Consultative (Parliamentary) Assembly of the Council of Europe, a document which in itself is not legally binding, but which may indeed be taken to indicate a trend in the legal opinion within the contracting States or some of them. This Resolution states with respect to the right to freedom of expression:

1118. Judgment of 22 February 1989, paras 32-33.
1119. Appl. 4515/70, *X and Association of Z v. United Kingdom*, *Coll.* 38 (1972), p. 86 (88).
1120. *Ibidem.*
1121. Appl. 8962/80, *X and Y v. Belgium*, *D & R* 28 (1982) p. 112 (124).
1122. Appls 8022, 8025 and 8027/77, *X, Y and Z v. United Kingdom*, *D & R* 18 (1980), p. 66 (76).
1123. Report of 18 March 1981, *McVeigh, O'Neill and Evans*, *D & R* 25 (1982), p. 15 (53).
1124. On this, see H.P. Furrer, "La pratique des Etats-membres du Conseil de l'Europe", in: *La Circulation des informations et le droit international*, Colloque de Strasbourg, Paris 1978, p. 65 (68).

> This right shall include freedom to seek, receive, impart, publish and distribute information and ideas. There shall be a corresponding duty for the public authorities to make available information on matters of public interest within reasonable limits and a duty for mass communication media to give complete and general information on public affairs.[1125]

However, as Alkema rightly observes, if one looks at the wording of paragraph 1, where the freedom to receive information is followed by the phrase "without interference by public authority", the drafters would seem to have had in mind an authority which refrains from interfering rather than an authority which actively imparts information.[1126] Furthermore, in Article 10 the words "to seek" in addition to "to receive and impart" have been omitted, while they are present in Article 19 of the Universal Declaration and have been taken over in Article 19 of the Covenant. If *Drittwirkung* of Article 10 is recognized, an even more problematic point is the construction of a duty on the part of the authorities to impose on individuals an obligation to impart information, and to enforce that obligation.[1127] At any rate, if and to the extent that developments in the legal opinion in contracting States appear to provide for an adequate foundation, the two constructions here discussed may be accepted as interpretations of Article 10 without there being any need to amend the text.

A comparable matter concerns the question of whether the right to receive information calls for pluriformity in imparting information, which then has to be guaranteed by the authorities, for instance by making grants to persons and institutions imparting information, where this is necessary for such pluriformity.[1128] Alkema's textual argument cited above would also seem to militate against this, but here again it is true that the text leaves sufficient scope for developments in legal thinking on this matter. In its report in the *De Geïllustreerde Pers* Case the Commission seemed to go a long way in that direction by suggesting the possibility of violation of Article 10 "by censorship or otherwise by reason of any undue State monopoly on news".[1129] In its *Handyside* report it stated as the purpose of Article 10 "to have a pluralistic, open, tolerant society".[1130] And in its *Lingens* report, as quoted above, the Commission deems a pluralism of opinions essential in a democratic society.[1131] In its judgment in that case the Court held that pluralism is of

---

1125. Council of Europe, Cons. Ass., Twenty-first Ordinary Session (Third Part), 22-30 January 1970, *Texts Adopted.*
1126. Alkema, *supra* note 8, p. 79.
1127. Subject, of course, to the restrictions of the second paragraph, in which context one may think specifically of that of the "protection of the reputation or rights of others" in connection with the protection of privacy.
1128. In its decision on Appl. 6452/74, *Sacchi v. Italy, D & R* 5 (1976), p. 43 (50), the Commission held as regards its previously given opinion that Art. 10(1) does not rule out a government monopoly for TV broadcasts: "the Commission would not now be prepared purely and simply to maintain this point of view without further consideration". However, it did not answer the question.
1129. Report of 6 July 1976, *D & R* 8 (1977), p. 5 (13).
1130. Report of 30 September 1975, B.22 (1976), p. 45. See also the judgment of 7 December 1976 in this case, A.24 (1976), p. 23, where the Court speaks of "the demands of that pluralism, tolerance and broadmindedness without which there is no 'democratic society'".
1131. Report of 11 October 1984, A.103 (1986), p. 37.

particular importance as far as the press is concerned. It further indicated that the freedom of the press is one of the best means for the public of discovering and forming an opinion on the ideas and attitudes of political leaders. The limits of acceptable criticism are wider as regards a politician than as regards a private individual. The requirements of protection of a politician's reputation have to be weighed against the interests of an open discussion of political issues.[1132] In any case it is clear that the authorities, once they proceed to subsidize persons and institutions imparting information, have the duty, under Articles 14 and 13 respectively, to do so without discrimination and to afford a remedy in case of refusal of applications.[1133]

The words "regardless of frontiers" indicate that the authorities must also admit information from beyond the frontiers of the country and allow the imparting of information from across those frontiers, subject, of course, to the possibilities laid down in the second paragraph. This does not, of course, offer a guarantee that such information is not held back outside the frontiers, since the State bears no responsibility for measures taken to that effect abroad.[1134]

7. For the most important media besides written publications, *viz.* broadcasting, television and cinema, Article 10 provides that they may be subjected to a licensing system. This provision is contained in the first, not in the second paragraph, so that it must be assumed that, when refusing a licence, the authorities are not confined to the restriction grounds mentioned in the second paragraph, although the refusal will have to meet the requirements of reasonableness and non-discrimination.[1135] The Commission even considered a system leading to a broadcasting monopoly for the State as being in conformity with Article 10, but later on revised that point of view.[1136] One may indeed wonder whether such an "interference by public authority", by which the receipt of information from independent sources is cut off completely or substantially with respect to a given medium, although it does not seem to conflict with the text of Article 10 ("This Article shall not prevent States"), does not in fact greatly conflict with the spirit of this article.[1137]

1132. Judgment of 8 July 1987, A.103 (1986), p. 26.
1133. For these provisions, see *infra* pp. 520-548.
1134. Appl. 7597/76, *Bertrand Russell Peace Foundation Ltd. v. United Kingdom, D & R* 14 (1979), p. 117 (124).
1135. See, *e.g.*, Appl. 4515/70, *X and Association of Z. v. United Kingdom, Coll.* 38 (1972), p. 86 (88-89), where a statutory prohibition for TV companies to broadcast advertising of a political nature was not deemed contrary to the first paragraph by the Commission.
1136. See on the one hand Appl. 3071/67, *X v. Sweden, Yearbook* XI (1968), p. 456 (462-464), and Appl. 4750/71, *X v. United Kingdom, Coll.* 40 (1972), p. 29 (29-30), and on the other hand Appl. 6452/74, *Sacchi v. Italy, D & R* 5 (1976), p. 43 (50).
1137. In this connection it is also illustrative that France, in ratifying the Convention, thought it necessary to declare expressly that the French Government considered the French legislation on the ORTF as being in conformity with Art. 10. The Italian Corte Constituzionale declared a presidential decree unconstitutional in so far as the installation and exploitation of local networks of cable TV were reserved to the State; see *D & R* 5 (1976), p. 49.

Under Article 14 no discrimination is permitted in the granting of licences and, in case of a State monopoly, the broadcasting time granted to a political party, trade union or other institution of a specific political, religious, philosophical or ethical character may not be disproportionate. For the assessment whether there is question of discrimination or disproportionality, all facets of the political, religious and social climate of the community concerned will have to be taken into account. Thus, departure from the arithmetical proportionality on the ground that otherwise a small political party would not be entitled to any broadcasting time at all, or to a uselessly short time only, does not constitute discrimination.

In its decision on Appl. 8266/78 the Commission took the view that, since the first paragraph envisages legislation requiring the licensing of broadcasting organizations, a State is also allowed to take measures against those who seek to promote or encourage unlicensed "pirate" stations by advertising them or making them known in some other way.[1138]

For those contracting States which are also member States of the European Communities, the power to regulate the broadcasting of foreign radio and television programmes is also governed by the Community-law provisions concerning free services. Especially after a "common broadcasting market" will be established in 1992, based upon Article 59 of the EEC-Treaty, this will have a great impact on the margin of discretion of national policies.[1139]

8. Besides restrictions, the second paragraph of Article 10 also mentions formalities, conditions and penalties as measures to which the freedoms of the first paragraph may be subjected. At first sight it is remarkable that precisely with respect to the right to freedom of expression, to which the Western democracies attach such great value, the restrictions are formulated more broadly than with respect to other rights and freedoms. However, in practice this broad formulation is of little impact. The imposition of conditions or formalities in fact also amounts to restrictions, while on the other hand the failure to observe a restriction prescribed by law will also be subject to a sanction in most cases. It does not matter much, therefore, whether the complaint is directed against the application of the legal norm restricting the exercise of the freedom or against the penalty imposed because of the violation of that norm. Indeed, the restriction implied in the imposition of a penalty may also not serve the mere purpose of a retaliation, but should be intended to protect the interests enumerated in paragraph 2.

On that account, in its report in the *De Becker* Case the Commission held that, in view of the circumstances and having regard to the nature of the crime for which the person in question had been convicted, the prohibition

---

1138. Appl. 8266/78, *X v. United Kingdom, D & R* 16 (1979), p. 190 (192).
1139. See Com(84)300, 14 June 1984, pp. 127-137; Com(85)310, 14 June 1985, pp. 30-31 and Com(87)290, 26 November 1987, pp. 86-89 and 145-149.

of journalistic or editorial activities imposed by the court on the journalist De Becker conflicted with Article 10. The judicial decision was considered to be justifiable in so far as it referred to the dissemination of his political views and in so far as the prohibition applied to that post-war period in which public order had not yet been completely restored, because to that extent it might have served the protection of public order. But the Commission was of the opinion that a complete prohibition, applying to the subsequent period as well, could no longer be considered necessary in a democratic society for the protection of one of the values mentioned in the second paragraph.[1140]

Another feature of the second paragraph of Article 10 is the explicit reference to the "duties and responsibilities" of those who exercise the right defined in the first paragraph. According to the case-law those words imply the possibility to differentiate, for the assessment of the necessity of restricting the freedom of expression, in accordance with

the particular situation of the person exercising freedom of expression and the duties and responsibilities attaching to that situation.[1141]

For the person concerned, that special responsibility may then lead to a broader as well as a narrower interpretation of the possibilities of restricting his freedom of expression.

In the *Engel* Case, for instance, the Dutch position that the prohibition imposed on soldiers to publish in and distribute a stencilled sheet was necessary in a democratic society found favour with the Commission as well as the Court on the basis of the special duties and responsibilities of members of the armed forces.[1142] And in the *Handyside* Case[1143] and the *Sunday Times* Case[1144] attention was drawn to the special responsibility of publishers. In the former case this constituted an additional argument for the justification of the ban on publication; in the latter case, it led to the contrary.[1145] As other possible groups having special duties and responsibilities concerning the distribution of information and ideas are mentioned in that case: civil servants, police officers, journalists and politicians.[1146] In the *Müller*

1140. Report of 8 January 1960, B.2 (1962), pp. 127-129.
1141. Report of 30 September 1975, *Handyside*, B.22 (1976), p. 44. See also the judgment of 7 December 1976 in this case, A.24 (1976), p. 23 and the report of 11 May 1984, *Kosiek*, A.105 (1986), p. 44.
1142. Report of 19 July 1974, B.20 (1974-76), p. 80, and judgment of 8 July 1976, A.22 (1977), p. 41.
1143. *Supra* note 1141, pp. 44 and 23 respectively.
1144. Report of 18 May 1977, B.28 (1982), p. 73; judgment of 26 April 1979, A.30 (1979), p. 38.
1145. The latter was also the case in the *Lingens* Case, *supra* at p. 415, where the Commission took the view that it is a "duty and responsibility" of the press in a democratic society to control politicians.
1146. *Ibidem.* The authors are not mentioned here by the Commission. It would appear quite tenable that this category, too, has a special responsibility which makes it precisely more difficult to justify a restriction of their freedom of expression. In a case declared admissible by the Commission, which concerned the complaint of the German poet, Geerk, residing in Switzerland, against the obligation to pay the costs of a criminal prosecution instituted against him on account of two published poems (Appl. 7640/76, *Geerk v. Switzerland*), a friendly settlement has been reached: *Yearbook* XXI (1978), p. 470. The enumeration of the Commission also does not contain the category of teachers. It is, however, obvious that
(continued...)

Case the Court stated with respect to artists that

> Artists and those who promote their work are certainly not immune from the possibility of limitations as provided for in paragraph 2 of Article 10. Whoever exercises his freedom of expression undertakes, in accordance with the express terms of that paragraph, "duties and responsibilities".[1147]

The mere belonging of a person to any of these categories, however, does not yet provide a sufficient reason for a special treatment. It is not justified, for instance, to impose greater restrictions on the freedom of expression of a civil servant or a soldier than on other citizens for this reason alone. In our opinion, therefore, the above-mentioned observations in the *Engel* Case are formulated too widely. There should be a relation between the special status of the person in question, the content of the opinion expressed or to be expressed, and/or the medium chosen for it. This relation is quite evident in the case of the distribution of information which is available to a person by virtue of his function. And if, for instance, a person chooses a medium for expressing his opinion which is directed particularly at children, this imposes a special responsibility on him, in particular if because of his function he enjoys specific authority among children. Equally, a doorman who inhabits an apartment in a government building and expresses his political preference via a poster in his window, or a police officer who takes part in a demonstration in uniform, has the special duty to ensure that it is clear that the opinion thus propagated is his private opinion.

The special status of civil servants was at issue in the Cases of *Glasenapp and Kosiek*. In its reports the Commission pointed to the fact that the rule contained in Article 11(2) permitting certain restrictions on the exercise of freedom of assembly and association on members of the armed forces, of the police or of the administration of the State, is not expressly included in Article 10(2). However, in the opinion of the Commission, this is no sufficient ground for arguing that the drafters of the Convention did not intend to impose specific restrictions of the kind included in Article 11(2) also on the freedom of opinion, since the effect of this provision in Article 11(2) may be to limit some forms of expression of opinion, such as membership of political organizations by certain categories of public employees. However, that connection between the two provisions can only be made if the restriction imposed is necessary in a democratic society in the light of the actual duties and responsibilities which the exercise of freedom of expression and opinion by the person concerned carries with it; its necessity must flow from the applicant's circumstances. On this basis the Commission adopted the view that

---

1146.(...continued)
they, too, have a special responsibility, both with regard to the children and with regard to the parents; the latter also in connection with the right of parents, given in Art. 2 of the First Protocol, to their children being taught in conformity with their own religious and philosophical conviction: Appl. 8010/77, *X v. United Kingdom, D & R* 16 (1979), p. 101 (102-103). For a case in which also lawyers were included in the list, see the decision of 5 October 1982 on admissibility of Appl. 9417/81, not published.
1147. Judgment of 28 May 1988, A.133 (1988), p. 22.

the requirement that a schoolteacher dissociated herself completely from the KPD, could not be considered a necessary condition and restriction on her freedom of opinion and expression,[1148] whereas the dismissal of a lecturer on the basis of his personal and public identification with the extreme policies of the NPD, in which he was a leading figure, was considered justified, because the dismissal could be deemed necessary and proportionate.[1149]

The wide formulation of the restriction "for preventing the disclosure of information received in confidence", which also is not mentioned among the grounds of restriction in the other articles, overlaps with other grounds. In so far as it refers to the power of the authorities to take measures against the leakage of State secrets, the ground "in the interests of national security, territorial integrity or public safety" would appear to sufficiently serve that purpose. And in so far as it refers to the possibility of exemption from a legal duty to impart information when information received in confidence is involved, for instance as a witness in judicial proceedings, what is involved is not a restriction, but on the contrary a confirmation of the freedom of expression, unless the first paragraph is also taken to contain a right to seek information and accordingly a duty of the authorities to enforce the obligation to impart information.[1150] And if the protection of a person's privacy is concerned, the restriction "protection of the reputation or rights of others" will suffice. All the same, cases may occur in which information received in confidence is revealed without one of the above-mentioned interests being involved, for instance when a civil servant reveals or intends to reveal on his own initiative an official secret which does not affect either national security or the rights of others.[1151]

A fourth feature of the second paragraph of Article 10 in comparison with the restrictions in other articles of the Convention is the restriction "for maintaining the authority and impartiality of the judiciary". This restriction would seem to have been included mainly with a view to the prohibition, familiar from Anglo-Saxon law, of "contempt of court", which is intended to prevent that the authority and the independence of the court and the rights of the parties to the proceedings are impaired by publications and other acts.[1152] This restriction was discussed at length in Strasbourg in the *Sunday Times* Case. In this case the publisher, the editorial staff and the general editor of the Sunday Times complained about the ban for a given period, imposed by an English court, on the publication of an article concerning the so-called "thalidomide children", *i.e.* children born with serious malformations of limbs, because their mothers had used the sedative thalidomide during

---

1148. Report of 11 May 1984, *Glasenapp*, A.104 (1986), pp. 45 and 53-54.
1149. Report of 11 May 1984, *Kosiek*, A.105 (1986), pp. 37-38 and 44-45.
1150. On this, see *supra* p. 418.
1151. See, *e.g.*, Appl. 4274/69, *X v. Federal Republic of Germany*, *Yearbook* XIII (1970), p. 888 (892).
1152. See para. 4 of the dissenting opinion of the Commission members Sperduti, Daver, Mangan, Polak and Frowein in the *Sunday Times* Case; report of 18 May 1977, B.28 (1982), p. 78.

pregnancy. The reason given for the prohibition was the prevention of "contempt of court", because at that time claims for damages were pending before the English court. In order to be able to answer the question of whether the ban on publication could be justified on this ground, the Commission undertook an independent inquiry into the circumstances under which the prohibition had been imposed. Ultimately it concluded that the nature of the prohibited publication did not tend to affect the impartiality of the court, since the article contained only information with which the court had already become familiar from another source. Nor could the authority of the court be impaired by the publication. In fact, at the moment of the prohibition, in the majority of these cases the parties were negotiating in order to reach a friendly settlement, while the role of the court consisted only in approving such a settlement and protecting the interests of the minors concerned. Moreover, the proposed publication was precisely also meant to protect the interests of those minors. In this particular situation the court, therefore, was not called upon to pronounce on the liability of the producer of the medicine, the issue which the publication dealt with. And as to the few cases in which the parents were quite averse to reaching a settlement, the proceedings, in the opinion of the majority of the Commission, were still in so early a stage that the influence of the publication on the ultimate outcome was negligible. Moreover, the Commission took into consideration the circumstance that, although this was a civil action, a public interest was involved in the case as well. Since that public interest had not been brought out, either in a criminal prosecution or in an inquiry instituted by the authorities, only very compelling reasons could justify a prevention of information being imparted by private persons. The Commission considered that no such compelling reasons existed.[1153] The Court basically concurred - though with the bare majority of 11 votes to 9 - with the opinion of the majority of the Commission.[1154]

If one compares this case with the *Handyside* Case, it is evident that in the *Sunday Times* Case the Commission and the Court placed their own opinion more explicitly beside that of the national authorities, quite similar to the approach of the Commission in the *Greek* Case.[1155] The *Handyside* Case concerned a complaint about the conviction of a publisher for having in his possession copies of the "Little Red School Book", and about their destruction as pornography. In that case the Commission practically confined itself to quoting the main points from the decision of the national court and holding on that basis as follows:

1153. Report of 18 May 1977, B.28 (1982), pp. 71-74.
1154. Judgment of 26 April 1970, A.30 (1979), pp. 28-42. The issue of "contempt of court" also arose in Appl. 10038/82, *X v. United Kingdom*, where a lawyer had given access to a journalist to documents which were exclusively meant for purposes of the trial; *Stock-taking on the European Convention on Human Rights*, Supplement 1984, pp. 122-123.
1155. Report of 18 November 1969, *Yearbook* XII; The Greek Case (1969), p. 1 (156-164), where the Commission took the view that the general possibility of censorship, introduced by ministerial order, for the prevention of criticism of the government, could not be regarded as a restriction which was "necessary in a democratic society".

the Commission is satisfied that the interference with the publication of the book of which the applicant complains was necessary for the protection of morals of young persons in a democratic society.[1156]

The Commission hardly discussed the special circumstances put forward by the applicant, in particular the fact that the same book was freely for sale in most other countries of the Council of Europe, and even in other parts of the United Kingdom, so that there its prohibition was evidently not considered necessary in a democratic society.[1157] Although the Court appeared to disagree to some extent with the viewpoint of the majority of the Commission that the Strasbourg organs ought not to give their own opinion on the content of the book and on the necessity of the ban on its publication, but had to confine themselves to reviewing the reasonableness of the opinion of the national authorities, still the Court also left such a wide margin of appreciation to the national authorities that an independent inquiry in fact did not take place.[1158] In the *Sunday Times* Case, therefore, a minority of the Commission, which disagreed with the "new", more independent approach of the majority, referred to the Court's *Handyside* judgment.[1159] They were put in the wrong, however, by the Court in its *Sunday Times* judgment.

The *Müller* Case concerned the convictions and sentences to fines for obscene paintings and the confiscation of the paintings at the occasion of an exhibition. Both the Commission and the Court took into account the circumstances of the case, including factors such as the social, religious and cultural composition of the population of the canton where the exhibition took place (Freibourg), and the fact that the exhibition was accessible to an every-age group, and concluded that the Swiss authorities, in convicting the applicants for obscene publications, had not exceeded the margin of appreciation which Article 10(2) left to them.[1160]

A fifth special feature, finally, of paragraph 2 as interpreted in the Strasbourg case-law concerns the variations of strictness of the necessity test. In its decision on the admissibility of Appl. 7805/77, *X and Church of Scientology v. Sweden* the Commission adopted the view that commercial "speech" as such is not outside the protection conferred by Article 10(1), but that the level of protection must be less than that accorded to the expression of "political" ideas, in the broadest sense, with which the values underpinning the concept of freedom of expression in the Convention are mainly concerned. The Commission also took into consideration the fact that most European countries that have ratified the Convention have legislation which restricts the free flow of commercial "ideas" in the interest of protecting consumers from

---

1156. Report of 30 September 1975, B.22 (1976), pp. 47-48.
1157. On p. 46 of its report the Commission holds that "it is impossible to impose uniform standards of morality on the Member States".
1158. Judgment of 7 December 1976, A.24 (1976), pp. 21-28. For more details on this "margin of appreciation", see *infra* pp. 583-606.
1159. See para. 7 of the dissenting opinion of the Commission members Sperduti, Daver, Mangan, Polak and Frowein.
1160. Report of 8 October 1986, A.133 (1988), pp. 40-44; judgment of 24 May 1988, *ibidem*, pp. 22-23.

misleading or deceptive practices. These observations led the Commission to the position that the test of "necessity" in the second paragraph of Article 10 should be a less strict one when applied to restraints imposed on commercial "ideas".[1161]

That the Strasbourg organs are not inclined to accept easily that the ideas expressed are of a commercial character, became clear in two cases in which the question was at issue whether the interference with the applicants' publications under unfair-competition law amounted to unjustified interference with their right to freedom of expression. The *Barthold* Case concerned an interview given by the applicant, in which he stated that his veterinary clinic provided a night service on a voluntary basis. He had further expressed the view that a regular night service should be established with the participation of private veterinary surgeons. The interview, which subsequently appeared in the newspaper, was accompanied by the applicant's photo and mentioned his name and the name of his clinic. A court action claiming unfair competition led to an injunction against the applicant, prohibiting him, under a penalty of a fine or imprisonment, from repeating specified statements in the general press. Both the Commission and the Court held that the restricted publication was a normal press interview and not an advertisement in the sense in which this term is generally understood. It was considered that it was not necessary in a democratic society to restrict the freedom of expression of members of a liberal profession by forbidding them to disclose their identity and function when expressing an opinion in matters of public concern, even if they relate to their sphere of professional activity.[1162]

The Case of *Markt Intern Verlag and Klaus Beermann* concerned the question of freedom of the press in business matters. The applicants, a publishing company and its editor, had reported on a dissatisfied client of a mail-order firm. The mail-order firm obtained an injunction, prohibiting publication of the report. The Commission adopted the view that, although the reported information concerned specific business practices of interest to specialized retail traders, its business and economic content did not deprive it of the protection of Article 10(1) of the Convention. The Commission noted the editorial nature of the applicants' publication. The report in question was not a commercial advertisement, which might justify a less strict application of the necessity test. The Commission was of the opinion that the approach of the domestic courts failed to distinguish between the freedom of the business-oriented press to impart specialist information on the one hand and a competitor's advertising interests on the other. This failure rendered the injunction disproportionate.[1163]

We have to confine ourselves here to the above few observations about special elements in the restrictions of Article 10(2) and about important case-

1161. *Yearbook* XXII (1979), p. 244 (252-254).
1162. Report of 13 July 1983, A.90 (1985), pp. 38-40; judgment of 25 March 1985, *ibidem*, pp. 25-26.
1163. Report of 18 December 1987, paras 224-252.

law concerning this provision. For the remainder, this second paragraph will be discussed in the general section on restrictions.[1164]

9. With regard to Article 10, too, prisoners stand out as a special group in the case-law of the Commission, and this not in connection with the above-mentioned special duties and responsibilities which may be incumbent on a person in a given capacity, but on the basis of the special requirements assumed to be involved in detention. While here again in some cases the Commission took the view that certain restrictions on the freedom to receive and impart information and ideas are inherent in detention and consequently are not contrary to the right laid down in the first paragraph,[1165] such restrictions have been considered justified in other cases on the basis of the second paragraph, in particular on the basis of a very broad interpretation of the restriction "prevention of disorder".

On that ground, for instance, the Commission considered justifiable the refusal of the prison authorities to make available, at the prisoner's request, a copy of the provisional regulations on the execution of penalties; this because he wanted to use the information in a discussion with the press.[1166] The prohibition for a Buddhist prisoner to send an article to a Buddhist journal was also permissible in the eyes of the Commission,[1167] as was the prison rule that in principle no journals from outside the United Kingdom were admitted.[1168] It is clear, in our opinion, that this case-law needs some qualification on the basis of a stricter necessity test.

10. Article 10 is not mentioned in the enumeration of Article 15(2), and the right to freedom of expression therefore is not a non-derogable right. In the *Greek* Case accordingly a violation of the Convention on account of a breach of Article 10 could only be established after the Commission had investigated whether the Greek Government had rightly invoked Article 15, and after it had reached a negative conclusion in that respect.[1169]

Just as has been submitted with regard to Article 9, here again it may be submitted that in fact the exceptions provided for in Article 15 can never be applicable to the "freedom to hold opinions" contained in Article 10, since an exception to that right can never be "strictly required" in the sense of Article 15(1).[1170]

1164. *Infra* pp. 573-606.
1165. Thus, *e.g.* in Appl. 2795/66, *X v. Federal Republic of Germany, Yearbook* XII (1969), p. 192 (204), where the applicant alleged that he had been given insufficient opportunity to consult an annotated text of the German Criminal Code for the preparation of his request for a new hearing of his case. See also Appl. 4517/70, *Huber v. Austria, Yearbook* XIV (1971), p. 548 (568).
1166. Appl. 1860/63, *X v. Federal Republic of Germany, Yearbook* VIII (1965), p. 204 (216).
1167. Appl. 5442/72, *X v. United Kingdom, D & R* 1 (1975), p. 41 (42).
1168. Appl. 5270/72, *X v. United Kingdom, Coll.* 46 (1974), p. 54 (59-60).
1169. Report of 18 November 1969, *Yearbook* XII; *The Greek Case*, p. 1 (75-76 and 100).
1170. See *supra* p. 406.

11. Article 19 of the Covenant is formulated more appropriately than Article 10 of the Convention in so far as the right to hold opinions without interference is worded in Article 19 in a separate first paragraph and it is clearly stated that the restrictions of the third paragraph are not applicable to it. The same must be deemed to apply to the Convention, although the drafters have omitted to formulate this clearly.[1171] On the other hand it is rather curious that Article 4(2) of the Covenant does declare Article 18, but not the first paragraph of Article 19, to be an obligation that is non-derogable for the States.

Of the remaining differences between Article 10 of the Convention and Article 19 of the Covenant the following are the most important: (1) Article 19 mentions expressly also the right "to *seek* information", thus constituting a stronger basis for an obligation on the part of the authorities to provide information.[1172] (2) The phrase "without interference by public authority" is lacking in Article 19, and this eliminates the strongest argument against the view that this provision may also have some *Drittwirkung*. (3) The possibility of subjecting broadcasting, television and cinema to a licensing system is not mentioned expressly in Article 19 and will therefore have to be judged by reference to the restrictions in the third paragraph. (4) The same applies to those restrictions of Article 10(2) which are not mentioned in Article 19(3): in particular the prevention of disorder and crime and of the disclosure of information received in confidence, and the maintenance of the authority and the impartiality of the judiciary. These may play a part only to the extent that they are covered by the restrictions which *are* mentioned.[1173]

§ 11.   ARTICLE 11: FREEDOM OF ASSOCIATION AND ASSEMBLY

1. Everyone has the right to freedom of peaceful assembly and to freedom of association with others, including the right to form and to join trade-unions for the protection of his interests.

2. No restrictions shall be placed on the exercise of these rights other than such as are prescribed by law and are necessary in a democratic society in the interests of national security or public safety, for the prevention of disorder or crime, for the protection of health or morals or for the protection of the rights and freedoms of others. This Article shall not prevent the imposition of lawful restrictions on the exercise of these rights by members of the armed forces, of the police or of the administration of the State.

1171. Thus also the Committee of Experts, *supra* note 14, p. 45.
1172. In the Report of the Committee of Experts, *supra* note 14, p. 45, it is submitted that such a duty is not implied therein, but it is not stated what then is the content of this additional obligation.
1173. For the "case-law" of the Human Rights Committee concerning Article 19 of the Covenant, reference is made to the study by Nowak mentioned *supra* p. 216.

1. Unlike the Covenant, in the Convention the freedom of association and that of peaceful assembly are treated in one and the same provision. The freedom of association in fact presupposes freedom of assembly, since without regular meetings of its members an association cannot lead an effective existence. Freedom of assembly is also important, however, outside the framework of associations, for instance in connection with the right to freedom of expression of the preceding article and in connection with the periodical free elections by secret ballot guaranteed in Article 3 of the First Protocol.[1174]

Both the freedom of association and the freedom of assembly are closely connected with the freedom of thought, conscience and religion provided for in Article 9 and with the freedom of expression of Article 10. In fact, the exercise of the right to freedom of association and of the right to freedom of assembly will generally involve the holding and propagation of specific opinions. This was indicated by the Commission and the Court expressly in the case of *Young, James and Webster*. In this case the Commission regarded Article 11 as a *lex specialis* in relation to the two other provisions, and on that account left the latter provisions out of consideration after having concluded that Article 11 had been violated.[1175] The Court treated the freedoms set forth in Articles 9 and 10 as elements of Article 11 and considered their violation as constituting an additional argument for the finding of a violation of Article 11.[1176]

2. Although, as the Commission held, the right to freedom of peaceful assembly, like the right to freedom of expression, "is a fundamental right in a democratic society and ... is one of the foundations of such a society",[1177] freedom of assembly still has not played an important part in the Strasbourg case-law. The adjective "peaceful" has restricted the scope of the protection offered by the first paragraph to a very large extent. If the authorities concerned could reasonably have believed that a planned assembly would not have a peaceful character or if this has become apparent during the assembly, its prohibition or restriction, as the case may be, in the Commission's opinion does not conflict with the first paragraph of Article 11. Consequently, the second paragraph need not be relied upon in that case and it is not therefore required that the prohibition or restriction be "prescribed by law". However, again according to the Commission, the fact that a peacefully organized demonstration will run the risk of resulting in disorder by developments outside the control of the organizing association, for example through a

---

1174. See the report of 5 November 1969, *Yearbook* XII; *The Greek Case* (1969), p. 1 (170-171).
1175. Report of 14 December 1979, B.39 (1984), p. 48. Thus also in Appl. 8191/78, *Rassemblement jurassien et Unité jurassienne v. Switzerland*, D & R 17 (1980), p. 93 (118), and Appl. 8440/78, *Christians against Racism and Fascism v. United Kingdom*, D & R 21 (1981), p. 138 (147-148).
1176. Judgment of 13 August 1981, A.44 (1981), pp. 23-24.
1177. Appl. 8191/78, *Rassemblement jurassien et Unité jurassienne v. Switzerland*, D & R 17 (1980), p. 93 (119).

violent counter-demonstration, does not for that reason fall outside the scope of Article 11 (1) of the Convention.[1178]

Specifically for assemblies of a public character this means that they can be subjected to a system of permits. In that case, the adjective "peaceful" allows for the use of a standard which need not be covered by the restrictions of the second paragraph. Such a system of permits and its application, however, may then only relate to that peaceful character and must not affect the right of assembly as such. The latter, for instance, is the case if the prohibition has a general character or concerns a very wide category of assemblies.[1179] The prohibition may also not be of such a nature that an independent means of expression is thus in fact excluded altogether for one or more groups. Such cases must therefore be reviewed against the second paragraph. In its report in the *Greek* Case, therefore, the Commission reviewed the restrictions applying in Greece at that time with regard to both public and private assemblies, and assemblies of a political as well as of a non-political character, for their conformity with the second paragraph of Article 11 and, on the basis of the very wide discretion which the law left to the authorities, concluded that they could not find a sufficient justification in any of the grounds of restriction mentioned therein.[1180]

In its decision on the application of *Plattform "Ärzte für das Leben"* the Commission rejected the claim of the Austrian Government that Article 11 does not include a right to protection of demonstrations against interference by private persons. It referred to the Court's case-law, where it was held that the Convention does not merely oblige the authorities of the contracting States to respect for their own part the rights and freedoms embodied in it, but in addition requires them to secure the enjoyment of these rights and freedoms by preventing and remedying any breach thereof, and that therefore the obligation to secure the effective exercise of Convention rights may involve positive obligations on the State, even involving the adoption of measures in the sphere of the relations between individuals. On that basis the Commission took the view that the right to freedom of assembly must include the right to protection against counter-demonstrators, because it is only in this way that its effective exercise can be secured to social groups wishing to demonstrate for certain principles in highly controversial issues. If the protection provided by the authorities proves to be insufficient to enable a free exercise of the right to freedom of assembly, this amounts to a restriction which has to be tested for its justification under the second paragraph. Thus, in the present case, the Commission tested the restraint of the police *vis-à-vis* the counter-

---

1178. Appl. 8440/78, *Christians against Racism and Fascism v. United Kingdom*, D & R 21 (1981), p. 138 (148); Appl. 10126/82, *Plattform "Ärzte für das Leben" v. Austria*, D & R 44 (1985), p. 65 (72).
1179. See the first case mentioned in the preceding note and the case mentioned in note 1177.
1180. Report of 5 November 1969, Yearbook XII; *The Greek Case* (1969), p. 1 (171). In the case of Appl. 8440/78, *Christians against Racism and Fascism v. United Kingdom*, D & R 21 (1981), p. 138 (150), however, a general prohibition of demonstrations for the prevention of disorder was deemed justified because there was "a real danger" of such disorder.

demonstrators for its reasonableness and proportionality with a view to the prevention of disorder on a larger scale than actually occurred, and the protection of the rights of others, *viz.* the counter-demonstrators.[1181] In its judgment, the Court gave an interpretation of Article 11, which was virtually the same as that of the Commission. It stated that the participants of a demonstration must

> be able to hold the demonstration without having to fear that they will be subjected to physical violence by their opponents; such a fear would be liable to deter associations or other groups supporting common ideas or interests from openly expressing their opinions on highly controversial issues affecting the community. In a democracy the right to counter-demonstrate cannot extend to inhibiting the exercise of the right to demonstrate.

It concluded that

> Genuine, effective freedom of peaceful assembly cannot, therefore, be reduced to a mere duty on the part of the State not to interfere: a purely negative conception would not be compatible with the object and purposes of Article 11. Like Article 8, Article 11 sometimes requires positive measures to be taken, even in the sphere of relations between individuals, if need be.[1182]

With respect to the content of these measures, the Court held that the contracting States have a wide discretion in the choice of the means to be used.[1183]

3. An autonomous meaning should be assigned to the word "association". The legal form chosen and the legal consequences attached thereto by national law cannot be decisive here, since otherwise the guarantee of Article 11 might be rendered illusory by the national legislature, and there might exist great differences in scope of that guarantee between the legal systems of the various contracting States.

By expressly mentioning the trade-unions in Article 11, the drafters obviously wanted to put it beyond doubt that the important right to trade-union freedom falls under the protection of this provision, no matter whether according to national law a trade-union can be considered an association. That political parties also fall under the term "association" was implicitly assumed by the Commission in its *KPD* decision.[1184]

In the *Young, James and Webster* Case, in respect of one of the allegations of the British Government, the Commission took the position that the term "association" presupposes a voluntary organization for a common purpose, and that there was no such organization in the case of the mere relationship between employees of the same employer, since that relationship is based on the contractual connection between the employee and the employer.[1185] In its

---

1181. Appl. 10126/82, *Plattform "Ärzte für das Leben"* v. *Austria, D & R* 44 (1985), p. 65 (72-74).
1182. Judgment of 21 June 1988, *Plattform "Ärzte für das Leben"*, A.139 (1988), p. 12. The Court refers here to its judgment of 26 March 1985, *X and Y* v. *the Netherlands*, A.91 (1985), p. 11.
1183. *Ibidem.*
1184. Appl. 250/57, *Kommunistische Partei Deutschland* v. *Federal Republic of Germany*, *Yearbook* I (1955-1957), p. 222.
1185. Report of 14 December 1979, B.39 (1984), p. 47.

decision on Appl. 6094/73 the Commission gave the following definition of "freedom of association":

a general capacity for the citizens to join without interference by the State in associations in order to attain various ends.[1186]

It may therefore be assumed that this freedom includes any voluntary association by several natural and/or legal persons for a considerable time with a given institutional structure and for common ends.[1187]

A professional organization established by the government and governed by public law, which as a rule is intended not only to protect the interests of the members, but also certain public interests, is not an "association" in the sense of Article 11. The Commission and the Court adopted this opinion in the *Le Compte, Van Leuven and De Meyere* Case with regard to the Belgian "Ordre des médecins". On the other hand, Article 11 was considered to be involved if the existence of such a public law institution ruled out the voluntary association of the colleagues in question in private professional organizations.[1188] In an earlier case the Commission had already decided that Article 11 relates exclusively to "private associations and trade-unions".[1189] From its report in the *Le Compte, Van Leuven and De Meyere* Case the criteria for this "private" character may be inferred to some extent on the basis of the characteristics there indicated for a "public-law association".

Curiously enough, this distinction between private and public associations seems not to have received any attention in a number of other cases in which compulsory membership[1190] was at issue. Thus, in a case involving the compulsory membership of the *Landbouwschap*, a Dutch public agricultural organization, the Commission confined itself to the general observation that this organization formed part of "an elaborate system for organizing effectively the economic life of the country", and that the challenged system of organization was not contrary to the Convention.[1191] And for dairy farmers the compulsory membership of a health service was considered allowable without any further argument.[1192]

In *Association X v. Sweden* the Commission considered it to be characteristic of a professional organization that it "upholds ethics and discipline within the profession or defends its members' interests in outside disputes", and of

---

1186. Appl. 6094/73, *Association v. Sweden, D & R* 9 (1978), p. 5 (7).
1187. In Appl. 7729/76, *Agee v. United Kingdom, D & R* 7 (1977), p. 164 (174), this former CIA agent invoked for his complaint against his expulsion, inter alia, Article 11, referring to his regular contacts in England with foreign intelligence agents. The Commission here left open the question of whether such a loose relation could still be considered as an association. In its decision on Appl. 8317/78, *McFeely v. United Kingdom, D & R* 20 (1980), p. 44 (97-98), however, the Commission submitted that freedom of association "does not concern the right of prisoners to share the company of other prisoners or to 'associate' with other prisoners in this sense".
1188. Report of 14 December 1979, B.39 (1984), p. 23, and judgment of 23 June 1981, A.43 (1981), pp. 26-27, respectively. See also the judgment of 10 February 1983, *Albert and Le Compte*, A.58 (1983), p. 21.
1189. Appl. 6094/73, *Association X v. Sweden, D & R* 9 (1978), p. 5 (8).
1190. For compulsory association in connection with freedom of association, see *infra* pp. 434-435.
1191. Appl. 2290/64, *X v. the Netherlands, Coll.* 22 (1967), p. 28 (32).
1192. Appl. 1068/61, *X v. the Netherlands, Yearbook* V (1962), p. 278 (284).

a trade-union that it "shall represent (its members) in a labour conflict situation against an employer".[1193] This served to show that a students' association belongs to neither of the two categories. With respect to a complaint that membership of a particular students' association was required for admission to a certain university, the Commission adopted the view that this association was to be regarded as part of the university, a State institution, so that Article 11 was not applicable.[1194] This is a curious decision. Moreover, an analogy with a political party would have been more appropriate than that with a professional association or trade-union, particularly since the Commission itself recognized that *via* the students' association participation by students in the administration of the university was regulated, and that there was the possibility that the association may adopt political positions.

4. It is remarkable that only with respect to the trade-unions does Article 11 mention the right to *form* an association. However, one must assume that this is implied in the freedom of association as such. Indeed, if people want to associate in an as yet non-existent association, the right to set up an association forms a necessary condition for the exercise of the freedom of association. That seems to be also the Commission's view,[1195] although the Commission has differentiated in that respect between membership on the one hand and participation in the board of an association on the other hand and, curiously enough, considered that the latter was not protected by Article 11.[1196]

Since Article 11 refers to "the right ... to join trade-unions", the question arises whether this implies at the same time protection against compulsory membership. This is important in particular with regard to the practice of compulsory trade-union membership, the so-called "closed shop". From the *travaux préparatoires* of Article 11 one might conclude that the drafters did not mean to prohibit such a practice.[1197] The Commission, however, stated as early as in its decision on Appl. 4072/69:

> the very concept of freedom of association with others also implies freedom not to associate with others or not to join unions.[1198]

Yet, the Commission held the complaint on this point to be manifestly ill-

1193. Appl. 6094/73, *Association X v. Sweden*, D & R 9 (1978), p. 5 (8).
1194. *Ibidem.*
1195. See Appl. 1038/61, *X v. Belgium*, Yearbook IV (1961), p. 324 (336), where the Commission speaks of "the right to set up an association or a trade-union". In its report in the *Young, James and Webster* Case it was emphasized by the Commission that trade-union freedom is not a separate right, but an element of the right to freedom of association; report of 14 December 1979, B.39 (1984), p. 44. Thus also the judgment of 13 August 1981 in that case, A.44 (1981), p. 21.
1196. Appl. 1038/61, *X v. Belgium*, Yearbook IV (1961), p. 324 (336-338). See, however, *infra* p. 435 and note 1210.
1197. See the quotation in the judgment of 13 August 1981, *Young, James and Webster*, A.44 (1981), p. 21.
1198. Appl. 4072/69, *X v. Belgium*, Yearbook XIII (1970), p. 708 (718). See also Appl. 9926/82, *X v. the Netherlands*, D & R 32 (1983), p. 274 (280).

founded, so that no decision was taken on this interpretation of Article 11. In some later cases the Commission characterized this problem as very complex and accepted complaints concerning compulsory membership of a professional organization or a trade-union.[1199]

In the first two of these cases the question was not examined any further, because the Commission and the Court held that the professional association in question was not an association in the sense of Article 11.[1200] In the *Young, James and Webster* Case, however, the question of compulsory membership was discussed at length. There the complaint concerned the discharge of the plaintiffs on account of their refusal to join a trade-union. Both the Commission and the Court considered the *travaux préparatoires* just referred to as not decisive for answering the question of whether the closed-shop system is contrary to Article 11.[1201] Both organs, however, avoided making a general pronouncement on the compatibility of the closed-shop system with Article 11, but restricted themselves to holding that Article 11 had been violated in this particular case. For this the Commission referred to the fact that the closed-shop agreement between the unions and the enterprise in question did not yet exist when the applicants entered the employment of the firm, but was concluded only afterwards. In the Commission's opinion that situation in any case constituted a breach of the applicants' freedom to decide for themselves which union they wished to join and whether they wished perhaps to set up their own union, while the discharge amounted to a sanction on their use of that freedom.[1202] The Court left open the question of whether compulsory membership of a trade-union is always contrary to Article 11, but regarded the threat of discharge for those who did not wish to join a given union as a form of coercion which affects the essence of the freedom guaranteed in Article 11. The Court, too, took into account that the compulsory membership had been introduced after the persons in question had entered the employment of the firm, while it also referred to the fact that the number of unions from which they could choose was extremely limited.[1203] Finally, the Court expressed as its opinion that the compulsion imposed on the applicants could not be deemed to be "necessary in a democratic society" in the sense of the second paragraph.[1204] On the basis of this judgment the Commission later on achieved a friendly settlement in two applications against the United Kingdom.[1205]

In the *Young, James and Webster* Case the Commission and the Court

---

1199. Appl. 6878/75, *Le Compte v. Belgium*, Yearbook XX (1977), p. 254 (276); Appl. 7238/75, *Van Leuven and De Meyere v. Belgium*, Yearbook XX (1977), p. 348 (368); and Appl. 7601/76, *Young and James v. United Kingdom*, Yearbook XX (1977), p. 520 (564).
1200. See *supra* pp. 431-432.
1201. Report of 14 December 1979, B.39 (1984), p. 46; judgment of 13 August 1981, A.44 (1981), pp. 21-22.
1202. B.39 (1984), p. 46.
1203. A.44 (1981), pp. 22-23.
1204. *Ibidem*, pp. 24-26.
1205. Appl. 9520/81, *Reed v. United Kingdom*, D & R 34 (1983), p. 107 and Appls 8476/79-8481/79, *Eaton et al. v. United Kingdom*, D & R 39 (1984), p. 11.

also assigned to this aspect of Article 11 a certain *Drittwirkung*[1206] by recognizing the liability of the British authorities for a violation by an enterprise of Article 11 such as was at issue here. For this the Court put forward the following argument:

> it was the domestic law in force at the relevant time that made lawful the treatment of which the applicants complained.[1207]

Practices like those complained of in this case are therefore prohibited under Article 11, regardless of whether they are imposed by the authorities or not, and can be put forward in Strasbourg whenever the national legislation of the respondent State allows such practices.

In conclusion it may be said that the Strasbourg case-law has not (yet) got to the point that Article 11 generally protects the freedom not to join an association or trade-union.[1208] An important move in that direction, however, has already been made, which brings Article 11 into closer agreement with Article 20 of the Universal Declaration, in which the prohibition of compulsory membership is expressly included, with Article 8 of the International Covenant on Economic, Social and Cultural Rights, which speaks of the right "to ... join the trade-union of his choice", and with Article 5 of the European Social Charter, which speaks of "freedom ... to join those organizations".

5. The case-law of the Commission and the Court has gradually refined the right to freedom of association - and in particular that of trade-union freedom - in the sense that this right also includes those rights and freedoms which are important for the enjoyment of the first-mentioned right.

Above the example has been given of the right to *form* an association,[1209] which was apparently deemed by the Commission to be implied in Article 11. And in its decision on Appl. 4125/69 the Commission, referring to Convention No. 87 of the International Labour Organisation, held that the freedom of association concerns not only an unobstructed membership, but that intimidation of an employee to make him relinquish his function within the trade-union may likewise constitute an encroachment on that freedom.[1210] In its decision on Appl. 11002/84 the Commission gave as its opinion that a court decision terminating an employee's contract because of his activity in a political party constitutes an interference with the exercise of the right guaranteed by this provision. In this case the Commission concluded that the interference was necessary in a democratic society for the protection of the rights of others, as the political party in question was known to have

---

1206. For this, see *supra* pp. 15-20.
1207. A.44 (1981), p. 20. See also the report of the Commission, B.39 (1984), p. 47.
1208. In Appl. 11518/85, not published, the applicant had also been dismissed from his employment because of his non-membership of a union. However, in this case the union membership agreement already existed before he accepted employment. It will be interesting to see what will be the opinion of the Commission in that case, which it has declared admissible.
1209. See *supra* p. 433 and note 1195.
1210. Appl. 4125/69, *X v. Ireland, Yearbook* XIV (1971), p. 198 (222).

objectives opposed to those of the employer, a foundation concerned with the welfare of immigrants.[1211]

On the other hand the State must protect the individual against the abuse by associations of their dominant position. Expulsion from a trade-union in breach of the union's rules or decided pursuant to arbitrary rules, or entailing exceptional hardship for the individual concerned, may constitute such an abuse.[1212]

In principle the right to form trade-unions involves, for example, the right of trade-unions to draw up their own rules, to administer their own affairs and to establish and join trade-union federations. Such trade-union rights are explicitly recognized in Articles 3 and 5 of ILO Convention No. 87, which must be taken into account in the present context. Accordingly, in principle trade-union decisions in these domains must not be subject to restrictions and control by the State except on the basis of Article 11, para. 2.[1213]

In three judgments concerning trade-union freedom, on the basis of the words "for the protection of his interests", the Court took the position that this freedom entitles the union members to a union that is able to serve their interests as workers. It is therefore incumbent on the authorities to allow the unions sufficient scope for this. This implies, for instance, that the trade-union must be heard by the authorities in order that it may be able to stand up for those interests, although the Court held that this obligation does not necessarily take the specific form that the authorities have to consult the unions before taking certain decisions,[1214] or that as employers they are obliged to conclude a collective agreement with a particular union.[1215] With regard to other employers, too, Article 11 does not cover a *right* for trade-unions to conclude collective agreements, which the authorities are then obliged to uphold, but only the *freedom* to conclude them, which the authorities must help to make possible.[1216] If one were to assume a *right*, to be upheld by the authorities, a more far-reaching obligation would be construed than the contracting States have undertaken under Article 6(2) of the European Social Charter, *viz.*

> to promote, where necessary and appropriate, machinery for voluntary negotiations between employers and employers' organizations and workers' organizations, with a view to the regulation of terms and conditions of employment by means of collective agreements.[1217]

Strikes are considered by the Strasbourg organs as a very important, but not the only means for union members to protect their interests. Referring to

---

1211. Appl. 11002/84, *Van der Heijden v. the Netherlands*, D & R 41 (1985), p. 264 (271).
1212. Appl. 10550/83, *Cheall v. United Kingdom*, D & R 42 (1985), p. 178 (186).
1213. *Ibidem*, p. 185.
1214. Judgment of 27 October 1975, *National Union of Belgian Police*, A.19 (1975), p. 18.
1215. Judgment of 6 February 1976, *Swedish Engine Drivers' Union*, A.20 (1976), pp. 15-16. The same applies to the collective bargaining as such: Appl. 7361/76, *Trade Union X v. Belgium*, D & R 14 (1979), p. 40 (47).
1216. See, for example, Appl. 9792/82, *Association A. v. Federal Republic of Germany*, D & R 34 (1983), p. 173 (174).
1217. Thus the Court in its *Swedish Engine Drivers' Union* judgment, A.20 (1976), p. 15.

the European Social Charter, the Court held that a right to strike, assuming that it is protected by Article 11, may in any case be subjected to restrictions by the national legislature.[1218] The authorities have to leave the trade-unions sufficient scope to stand up for the interests of the affiliated employees, since trade-union freedom would otherwise be illusory, but it is largely for the authorities to decide what means to this end they allow the unions.

It is remarkable that the Strasbourg organs, when elaborating the various elements contained in the trade-union freedom, repeatedly refer to other international instruments, such as the above-mentioned Convention No. 87 of the International Labour Organisation, the International Covenant on Economic, Social and Cultural Rights, the International Covenant on Civil and Political Rights, the European Social Charter and the Universal Declaration of Human Rights.[1219]

In Article 11(1) the words "for the protection of his interests" are grammatically related exclusively to the trade-union freedom, not to the freedom of association in general. However, associations other than trade-unions are also set up precisely for the promotion and protection of common interests, and it may therefore be said with regard also to those associations that, if the freedom of association is not to be illusory, once they have been set up, the authorities have the obligation to leave them sufficient scope to function as associations. It is self-evident that Article 11 does not guarantee that the objectives of an association are also actually realized,[1220] but efforts to that end must not be interfered with, except on the basis of any of the restrictions mentioned in the second paragraph.[1221]

From this obligation of the authorities ensues the *Drittwirkung* referred to above. The Court has at first expressly left undecided the question as to "the applicability, whether direct or indirect, of Article 11 to relations between individuals *strictu sensu*".[1222] However, the Court's position that "the Convention requires ... that under national law trade-unions should be enabled, in conditions not at variance with Article 11, to strive for the protection of their

1218. Judgment of 6 February 1976, *Schmidt and Dahlström*, A.21 (1976), p. 16. Referred to by the Commission in Appl. 10365/83, *S. v. Federal Republic of Germany*, D & R 39 (1984), p. 237 (240).
1219. See in particular the Commission's reports in the *National Union of Belgian Police* Case, B.17 (1973-1975), pp. 49-52; *Swedish Engine Drivers' Union Case*, B.18 (1974-1975), pp. 42-45 and 48; and *Schmidt and Dahlström Case*, B.19 (1974-1975), pp. 35-38. See also the judgment in this latter case, A.21 (1976), p. 16.
1220. Appl. 6094/73, *Association X v. Sweden*, D & R 9 (1978), p. 5 (7). See also Appl. 7990/77, *X v. United Kingdom*, D & R 24 (1981), p. 57 (63), where the Commission states that the authorities are not required to actively support a union or an individual union member in a particular case.
1221. In its decision on Appl. 9234/81, *X v. Federal Republic of Germany*, the Commission states that "private associations should be able to pursue their statutory aims by all lawful means, but this does not imply the right to have locus standi on all matters falling within the ambit of the statutory activities".
1222. Judgment of 6 February 1976, *Swedish Engine Drivers' Union*, A.20 (1976), p. 14; judgment of 6 February 1976, *Schmidt and Dahlström*, A.21 (1976), p. 15.

members' interests"[1223] in fact implies that Article 11 has an indirect *Drittwirkung* in the form of an obligation for the legislature to enable the (trade) unions, also *vis-à-vis* third parties, to enjoy the rights and freedoms set forth in that article. The Commission had already clearly formulated this indirect *Drittwirkung* in its report in the *National Union of Belgian Police* Case:

> It is true that the Convention fundamentally guarantees traditional freedoms in relation to the State as the holder of public power. This does not, however, imply that the State may not be obliged to protect individuals through appropriate measures taken against some forms of interference by other individuals, groups, or organizations. While they themselves, under the Convention, may not be held responsible for any such acts which are in breach of the Convention, the State may, under certain circumstances, be responsible for them.[1224]

And in its report in the *Schmidt and Dahlström* Case it held:

> It follows that freedom of association and the right to form and to join trade unions are concepts which apply also in the relationship between trade unions and employers. In other words, the State might be bound to suppress certain measures taken by employers against unions and their members.[1225]

This view was expressly confirmed by the Commission and the Court in the Case of *Young, James and Webster*.[1226]

The obligation of the authorities likewise implies that national law must assign legal personality to associations, or at least sufficient legal status for them to be able to stand up effectively for the interests of their members. A consequence on the international plane ought to be that associations must also be able to file on their own account an application under Article 25, not only in the case of a violation of Article 11, but in all those cases where they allegedly have been prejudiced by a violation of one of their own rights or of rights of their members which they have the function to protect.[1227]

6. Besides the "usual" restrictions, which are discussed separately hereafter,[1228] the second paragraph of Article 11 provides for the possibility that, with regard to members of the armed forces, the police and the administration, lawful restrictions may be imposed on the exercise of the rights laid down in Article 11. Although most complaints of violation of Article 11 hitherto examined by the Court concerned police officers, civil servants or members of the armed forces, this provision was not applied there.[1229] The Commission did apply it once, *viz.* in an unpublished decision, in which the Commission

---

1223. Judgment of 27 October 1975, *National Union of Belgian Police*, A.19 (1975), p. 18. In its report in the *Swedish Engine Drivers' Union* Case the Commission speaks of "to promote their members' economic and social interests against interference by the State and by employers", B.18 (1974-75), p. 49.
1224. Report of 27 May 1974, B.17 (1973-75), p. 48. See also *ibidem*, p. 52, and the reference to the *travaux préparatoires* of the Convention and of Article 22(1) of the Covenant.
1225. Report of 17 July 1974, B.19 (1974-75), p. 37.
1226. See *supra* pp. 434-435.
1227. See *supra* pp. 404-406.
1228. See *infra* pp. 573-606.
1229. The Court referred to the provision in its judgment of 8 June 1976, *Engel*, A.22 (1977), p. 23.

438

considered the prohibition to set up a trade-union, imposed on a Belgian police officer, to be justified on that ground.[1230] This decision would appear to be wrong, because by such a prohibition the person concerned and others belonging to the same category would be completely deprived of trade-union freedom, whereas it will no doubt be intended that restrictions can be imposed on them only with regard to particular ways of exercising this freedom, since a restriction must never affect a right in its essence.

It is not prescribed with regard to the restriction in question that it must be "necessary in a democratic society". However, the purposes of the Convention and the legal order established by it implicate that for any restriction of the rights and freedoms laid down in the Convention such a necessity must be a *conditio sine qua non*, at least as far as the requirements of reasonableness and proportionality, implied therein, are concerned.

7. Article 11 is not mentioned in the enumeration in Article 15(2) of provisions which are *non-derogable*. It has to be taken into account, however, that the right to trade-union freedom has developed, in particular in the International Labour Organisation, into a right which has to be respected by the States regardless of whether they have undertaken to do so in a treaty.[1231] Consequently, on that ground an obligation is incumbent on the contracting States which they cannot evade simply by referring to Article 15 of the Convention.

8. The Covenant devotes two separate provisions to the freedom of assembly and the freedom of association: Article 21 and Article 22 respectively. The formulation of the freedoms themselves differs in so far as for the freedom of assembly in the Covenant the formulation "The right to peaceful assembly shall be recognized" has been chosen instead of the more stringent formulation "Everyone shall have the right...", which has been employed for the freedom of association and has also been used in the Convention. However, in view of the rest of Article 21, in which also with regard to the exercise of the right to freedom of assembly the restrictions are enumerated exhaustively, this difference in formulation has no practical consequences.

More important are the differences in the formulation of the restrictions. The formulation in two separate articles makes it clear that the possibility of the imposition of restrictions on particular categories of persons under the Covenant exists only with respect to the freedom of association and not also

---

1230. Mentioned by Castberg, *supra* note 45, p. 152. See also Appl. 10365/83, *S. v. Federal Republic of Germany*, *D & R* 39 (1984), p. 237 (240), where the Commission held that a disciplinary penalty imposed on a civil servant who was a committee member of a union, and who called on civil servants to strike, did not constitute a violation of the right to exercise freedom of association, since in this case the right to strike was prohibited by law for civil servants and that prohibition as such was not inconsistent with the right of freedom of association.
1231. See P. van Dijk, "International Law and the Promotion and Protection of Human Rights", *Wayne Law Review* 1978, pp. 1529-1553 (1545-1546).

with regard to the freedom of assembly, whereas the Convention does not differentiate between the two freedoms on this point. Moreover, the Covenant here mentions exclusively the members of the armed forces and the police and not the members of the administration of the State, who are included in Article 11(2) of the Convention. Consequently, under the Covenant restrictions for these categories with regard to the freedom of assembly - and for the members of the administration with regard to the freedom of association as well - have to be based on one of the expressly mentioned grounds. In this respect, therefore, more stringent obligations apply for those contracting States which are also parties to the Covenant. Another difference in the formulation of the restrictions consists in that in both articles the Covenant speaks of "the interest of ... public order (*ordre public*)", whereas the Convention mentions as a ground of restriction "prevention of disorder or crime". This difference would seem to be of little importance. In whatever way the concept of "*ordre public*" may be interpreted, on the whole the Covenant appears to leave no less scope for the national authorities to restrict the freedoms than the Convention, so that the difference in formulation has no consequences for the contracting States parties to the Covenant.[1232]

Article 22 of the Covenant contains in a third paragraph the provision that for those contracting States, which are also parties to Convention No. 87 of the International Labour Organisation concerning Freedom of Association and Protection of the Right to Organize, the provisions of that Convention will continue to apply unabridged, regardless of the provision of Article 22. For the Convention the same applies by virtue of Article 60. Above it was mentioned that this ILO Convention has already served as a directive in the Strasbourg case-law.[1233] What was said above in sub-section 7 may be repeated here, *viz.* that trade-union freedom has developed into a right which has to be respected regardless of the existence of a treaty obligation on this point.[1234]

§ 12. ARTICLE 12: RIGHT TO MARRY AND TO FOUND A FAMILY

Men and women of marriageable age have the right to marry and to found a family, according to the national laws governing the exercise of this right.

1. Article 12 is not provided with a second paragraph formulating possibilities for restrictions. However, considering the inclusion in Article 12 of the formula "according to the national laws governing the exercise of this right", it would not be very realistic to conclude that it guarantees an absolute right. On the contrary, the national legislature has been allowed considerable scope

---

1232. *Cf.* Report of the Committee of Experts, *supra* note 14, pp. 48-49.
1233. *Supra* p. 437.
1234. For the "case-law" of the Human Rights Committee concerning Articles 21 and 22 of the Covenant reference is made to the study of Nowak, mentioned *supra* at p. 216.

for subjecting the exercise of the right to marry to certain conditions, for regulating the legal consequences of the marriage, and for laying down provisions concerning the family and the resulting family ties. Far-reaching limitations as to the exercise of the right laid down in Article 12 may result therefrom.

While Article 12 thus does not imply an absolute obligation on the part of the authorities to refrain from interference with regard to the exercise of the right to marry, it is even more difficult to interpret the provision as entailing a duty for the authorities in concrete cases to provide the material means which must enable the persons concerned to marry and to found a family. However, if they proceed to do so, they are not allowed to discriminate. And more generally their policy has to be of such a nature that the exercise of the right to marry is not unnecessarily interfered with.

2. Article 12 refers to the national laws and thus accepts the possibility that the legal systems may vary among the contracting States. In some contracting States, for instance, the law attaches to the religious marriage ceremony the legal consequences of matrimony, whereas in other contracting States this is not the case.[1235] And the question of when a person has reached marriageable age also needs not be answered the same way in all contracting States. However, this does not mean that there are no common norms which the national law and its application have to respect and against which they can be reviewed in Strasbourg. In the first place the restrictions imposed by the national legislature or by the authorities applying the law must not constitute a conflict with one of the other provisions of the Convention. But moreover the very fact that Article 12 puts the *right* first and foremost implies that domestic regulations concerning the exercise of that right must not be of such a nature that the right itself would be affected in its essence. As the Commission stated in its report in the *Hamer* Case:

> Whilst this is expressed as a "right to marry ... according to the national laws governing the exercise of this right", this does not mean that the scope afforded to national law is unlimited. If it were, Art. 12 would be redundant. The role of national law, as the wording of the Article indicates, is *to govern the exercise* of the right.[1236]

If the right to marry is denied to a person who is already married, it may be said that the legislation prohibiting bigamy is so firmly anchored in the national legal order of most of the contracting States that it may be assumed that the Convention was not intended to change this. After all, for a person who is already married the essence of the right to marry is not affected by

---

1235. With regard to this, the Commission took the position that the refusal to register a marriage which has not been concluded according to the procedure legally prescribed does not constitute a violation of Art. 12: Appl. 6167/73, *X v. Federal Republic of Germany, D & R* 1 (1975), p. 64 (65).
1236. Report of 13 December 1979, *D & R* 24 (1981), p. 5 (14). See also the report of 10 July 1980, *Draper, D & R* 24 (1981), p. 72 (78). In the same sense already the report of 1 March 1979, *Van Oosterwijck,* B.36 (1980), p. 27. In all three reports the Commission refers to the case-law of the Court to the effect that measures concerning the exercise of a right "must never injure the substance of the right".

this prohibition. Similar reasoning applies with regard to the legislation in which the right to marry is denied to persons below a given age. As long as there is a reasonable relation between that age limit and the concept of "marriageable age", the essence of the right is not affected. But if the right to marry is denied to a person because of his limited mental faculties, his state of health, or his financial situation, the relevant national law cannot be justified as against the express assignment of a right in Article 12, assuming of course that such persons can be deemed capable of determining their free will to consent to the marriage. That Article 12 does not include the right to marry a deceased person posthumously, can hardly have come as a surprise.[1237]

A more difficult point is the question of how to regard the national legislation which only allows two persons of the opposite sex to marry. Can homosexuals of marriageable age claim a right to marry a person of the same sex, submitting that marriage with a person of the opposite sex does not present a genuine marriage for them? When the text of Article 12 was drawn up, the term "marriage" no doubt alluded exclusively to an institutionalized relationship between two persons of the opposite sex. And indeed in its report in the *Van Oosterwijck* Case the Commission emphasizes that "a marriage requires the existence of a relationship between two persons of the opposite sex".[1238] However, the question would seem justified whether a dynamic interpretation is not called for in this respect under the influence of changing views.

In the *Van Oosterwijck* Case the complaint concerned the fact that Belgian law prohibited Van Oosterwijck, who had been entered in the birth registry as a woman, from marrying a woman. That case was different from the question raised above in so far as Van Oosterwijck submitted that he was mentally as well as physically a man, so that according to that submission this would not be a marriage between partners of the same sex. In this case the Commission held that

> by raising in advance to any application to marry an indirect objection based merely on the statements in the birth certificate and the general theory of the rectification of civil status certificates without examining the matter more thoroughly, the government has in fact failed in the instant case to recognise the applicant's right to marry and found a family within the meaning of Article 12 of the Convention.[1239]

It is perhaps the words "without examining the matter more thoroughly" which leave a loophole as regards the question raised above.[1240] The applicant's complaint was based on Articles 8 and 12. According to the Commission the Belgian State had violated both Articles. In a similar case in 1984 the

1237. Appl. 10995/84, *M. v. Federal Republic of Germany*, D & R 41 (1985), p. 259 (261).
1238. Report of 1 March 1979, B.36 (1980), pp. 27-28. See also the opinion of the Commission members Fawcett, Tenekides, Gözübüyük, Soyer and Batliner in the report of 12 December 1984, *Rees*, A.106 (1987), pp. 28-29, and the Court's judgment of 17 October 1986, *Rees*, *ibidem*, p. 19.
1239. *Ibidem*, B.36 (1980), p. 27.
1240. See, however, the dissenting opinion of the Commission members Sperduti and Kiernan, annexed to the report.

Commission changed its position. In the Commission's unanimous opinion Article 12 had not been violated, but the Commission was divided as to the reasons for this conclusion. There were two lines of reasoning.[1241] Five members of the Commission were of the opinion that the complaint under Article 12 was a necessary consequence of the violation of Article 8.

> There is no reason to believe that once this obstacle [the applicant is not recognized as a "man"] has been removed the applicant is still not able to marry.[1242]

The other five members of the Commission wanted to separate the application of Article 8 from the application of Article 12:

> The protection of private life includes ... the recognition ... of a person's civil status as a man or a woman ..., but the national law can clearly require men and women protected by Article 8 ... to satisfy specific requirements in order to marry and found a family with respect to the formalities required for contracting a marriage ..., and may also exclude certain specified categories of men and women.[1243]

In the instant case these five members based their view that Article 12 was not violated on the, in our opinion highly debatable, interpretation that the "social purpose" of Article 12 includes the physical capacity to procreate since the "references to marriageable age and to the different sex of the spouses are obviously intended to refer to the physical capacity to procreate". This led them to the following conclusion:

> It follows that a Contracting State must be permitted to exclude from marriage persons whose sexual category itself implies a physical incapacity to procreate either absolutely (in the case of a transsexual) or in relation to the sexual category of the other spouse (in the case of individuals of the same sex).[1244]

The question whether, even if their interpretation was correct for the moment the Convention was drafted, this social purpose may have lost that exclusive orientation in the years in which the Convention has been in existence as a "living instrument", has not been addressed by these five members. Their view was in clear contradiction with the earlier statement of the Commission in the *Van Oosterwijck* Case that

> there is nothing to support the conclusion that the capacity to procreate is an essential condition of marriage or even that procreation is an essential purpose of marriage.[1245]

However, the opinion of the five members seems to have received some support from the judgment of the Court, where it was held without much argument that

> the right to marry guaranteed by Article 12 refers to the traditional marriage between persons of the opposite biological sex. This appears also from the wording of the Article which makes it clear that Article 12 is mainly concerned to protect marriage as the basis of the family.[1246]

The Court was of the opinion that a legal impediment to the marriage of

---

1241. Report of 12 December 1984, *Rees*, A.106 (1987), p. 27.
1242. *Ibidem*, opinion of Frowein, Busuttil, Trechsel, Carrilo and Schermers, p. 27.
1243. *Ibidem*, opinion of Fawcett, Tenekides, Gözübüyük, Soyer and Batliner, pp. 28-29.
1244. *Ibidem*.
1245. Report of 1 March 1979, B.36 (1980), p. 28.
1246. Judgment of 17 October 1986, A.106 (1987), p. 19.

persons who are not of the opposite biological sex cannot be said to restrict or reduce the right in such a way or to such an extent that the very essence of the right is impaired. This may be true in general, but is it also true for the person concerned? What essence of the right to marry is left for him or her? And what is the essential difference in this respect between partners of the same sex on the one hand, and partners of the opposite sex who cannot or do not wish to have children on the other hand? Does one speak also of an "improper marriage" in the latter case?

As to the possibility that restrictions imposed by the legislature or the administration are contrary to the other provisions of the Convention, reference should be made first of all to Article 14, which prohibits the national authorities from discriminating in regulating the enjoyment of the rights and freedoms. But another instance to be thought of is the prohibition of inhuman treatment in Article 3; preventing a person from marrying or founding a family - one may think, for instance, of laws permitting compulsory sterilization in certain cases - may assume the character of an inhuman treatment,[1247] while Article 8 may also be involved.[1248]

3. Article 12 does not provide a solution for cases in which the conclusion of a marriage involves links with various legal systems. The general reference to national law implies that this is left to the rules of private international law (conflicts of law) applying in the country where the marriage is to take place. This means, for instance, that a person whose national law permits polygamy cannot rely on this law under Article 12 in a country where polygamy is prohibited by law and this norm is applied as being one of public policy. Here again, of course, application of a certain rule of private international law must not lead to discrimination.

4. Article 12 does not relate to the (possibility of) dissolution of the marriage and the legal consequences attached to this, unless the dissolution is imposed by the authorities. Article 8 may apply here.[1249] Since the exercise of the right to marry always depends on the free consent of the partners, the right to marry cannot be invoked against a law which makes divorce at the request of the other partner possible.

In Ireland divorce is not permitted. In the *Johnston* Case both the Commission and the Court held that Article 12 does not oblige Member

---

1247. See *supra* p. 241. The prohibition imposed on a detainee to marry during his detention was not considered by the Commission as an inhuman or degrading treatment: Appl. 6564/74, *X v. United Kingdom, D & R* 2 (1975), p. 105. See, however, *infra* pp. 450-453.

1248. Precisely because Art. 12 does not provide for the restrictions which are enumerated in Art. 8(2), it would not seem correct that the Commission, when it concludes that a violation of the first paragraph of Art. 8 finds its justification in the second paragraph, does not review the matter independently for its conformity with Art. 12. See, *e.g.*, Appl. 8041/77, *X v. Federal Republic of Germany*, not published, in which the applicant submitted that his deportation to the United States would destroy his marriage, because his wife would not be admitted to the United States.

1249. With regard to the right to respect for family life guaranteed in Art. 8, see *supra* pp. 382-383.

States to provide legal possibilities to dissolve a marriage. They refer for this to Article 16 of the Universal Declaration of Human Rights which stipulates "... equal rights as to marriage, during marriage and its dissolution", which was deliberately left out of the Convention. They conclude that the *travaux préparatoires* disclose no intention to include in Article 12 any guarantee of a right to have the ties of marriage dissolved by divorce.[1250] The applicants had referred to the judgment of the Court in the *Marckx* Case, where it was stated that the Convention is a living instrument which ought to be interpreted in the light of the present-day conditions. To this the Court responds as follows:

> However, the Court cannot, by means of an evolutive interpretation, derive from these instruments a right that was not included therein at the outset. This is particularly so here, where the omission was deliberate.[1251]

The Court furthermore points out that the right to divorce is not included in Protocol no. 7 to the Convention. The opportunity was not taken to deal with this question in Article 5 of the Protocol, which guarantees certain additional rights to spouses, notably in the event of dissolution of marriage. Indeed, paragraph 39 of the explanatory report to the Protocol states that the words "in the event of its dissolution" found in Article 5 "do not imply any obligation on a State to provide for dissolution of marriage or to provide any special forms of dissolution".[1252] Finally the Court holds with respect to the applicant's view that the prohibition of divorce is to be seen as a restriction on the capacity to marry that, even if this is the case, such a restriction cannot be regarded as injuring the substance of the right to marry "in a society adhering to the principle of monogamy".[1253]

In the Case of *F. v. Switzerland* the complaint concerned Article 150 of the Swiss Civil Code, which provided for a prohibition of remarriage for a period ranging from one to three years to be imposed by the court on the party at fault in the event of divorce granted on the ground of adultery. This provision had been applied to the applicant for the maximum period. The Government's argument that the system of temporarily prohibiting remarriage served to protect the institution of marriage and the rights of others was rejected by the Court. It doubted whether the system was an appropriate means for protecting the stability of marriage and it found that the interests of the future spouse were not protected by it and that the interests of the child born out of the relationship could be harmed. Next, the Court distinguished the present case from the *Johnston* Case by holding that:

> If national legislation allows divorce, which is not a requirement of the Convention, Article 12 secures for divorced persons the right to remarry without unreasonable

---

1250. Report of 5 March 1985 and judgment of 18 December 1986, A.112 (1987), pp. 43 and 24 respectively.
1251. *Ibidem*, p. 25.
1252. *Ibidem*.
1253. *Ibidem*, p. 18. We find the phrase between quotation marks difficult to understand since the possibility of divorce would precisely serve to avoid situations of factual bigamy.

restrictions.[1254]

The Court reached the conclusion that the disputed measure, which affected the very essence of the right to marry, was disproportionate to the legitimate aim pursued. Thus the Court took an approach, both concerning the question of in which case the right to marry is affected in its essence and by introducing the criterion of proportionality, which seems to differ from its *Rees* judgment, referred to above.

5. The right to marry entails for the authorities the prohibition to put a sanction on the married state. Thus the government as an employer - and private employers as well, via the *Drittwirkung* of Article 12? - is not allowed to discharge an employee - in most cases this will be a female employee - on the mere ground that the person has married. However, loss of, *e.g.*, disability benefits because of marriage is not a sanction and does not constitute an interference with the exercise of the right to marry.[1255]

The situation is different, however, when a person has promised *in full freedom* not to marry, or at least has accepted the consequence that marriage will constitute a ground for discharge. That situation occurs, for instance, when a Roman Catholic priest is relieved from his priestly and directly related functions after having given up his celibatarian state. Toleration of this by the authorities does not then conflict with Article 12.

6. With respect to the right *to found a family*, too, Article 12 does not guarantee a socio-economic right to, for instance, sufficient living accommodation and sufficient means of subsistence to keep a family. Article 12 merely implies a prohibition for the authorities to interfere with the founding of a family, for instance by prescribing the compulsory use of contraceptives, ordering a non-voluntary sterilization or abortion, or tolerating the performance thereof. Here again, it will have to be assumed that "the national laws governing the exercise of this right" may regulate the enjoyment of this right, but may not exclude it altogether or affect it in its essence. As has been said before, the victim of such a measure is also entitled to invoke Article 3, and in case of abortion perhaps also Article 2.[1256] Whether such an interference against the will of the person concerned is permitted in case of medical necessity depends on the question of whether the right to life has or has not to be considered an inalienable right, for which ultimately the authorities bear responsibility.[1257]

If the directly concerned person consents to the medical treatment leading to sterilization or abortion, but the husband does not, the question arises whether the interests of the latter are also protected by Article 12, assuming

---

1254. Judgment of 18 December 1987, A.128 (1988), p. 18.
1255. Appl. 10503/83, *Kleine Staarman v. the Netherlands*, D & R 42 (1985), p. 162 (165).
1256. *Supra* pp. 220 and 241.
1257. On this, see *supra* p. 221.

that the treatment in question is permitted by law. Since Article 12 refers to both partners, in principle the answer has to be in the affirmative. However, a conflict then arises between the rights and interests of woman and man, while in the case of abortion the issue of possible rights and interests of the foetus may also play a part.[1258] The national authorities have to resolve this conflict in their law and its application by weighing all the interests involved. The result of this may then ultimately be submitted to the Strasbourg organs for review of its conformity with, *inter alia*, Article 12. Although no concrete solution can be worked out here, we are of the opinion that at all events the law has to prescribe that before the treatment in question takes place a reasonable effort should be made to obtain the consent of both partners.[1259] If no agreement is reached, in our opinion in case of sterilization the right of the most directly affected person to control her or his own body will have to be decisive. Indeed, just as in the case of a marriage, it may be said for the foundation of a family that the agreement of both partners is required. If the consent of one of the two is lacking, it can no longer be said that the right of the other to found a family is affected in relation to the former. In the case of abortion the situation is different in so far as there the two partners have already taken a first step - whether intentional or not - to found or increase a family. If they do not agree on the question of whether the pregnancy is to continue, here again consultation of both partners should be prescribed, but ultimately in our opinion the rights and interests of the woman must have priority over those of the man. Indeed, her body is most directly concerned, and possibly her health and even her life may be at stake. In general, therefore, the consequences for the woman of the performance or non-performance of abortion will be greater than for the man. This leaves open the question of whether and, if so, how the rights and interests of the woman have to be weighed against any possible rights and interests of the foetus.[1260]

The question of whether the right to found a family also implies the right to increase the family, or on the contrary has been realized with the birth or adoption of the first child, has so far been expressly left open by the Commission.[1261] In our opinion the question has to be answered in the former sense. After the birth of their first child some parents will take the view that they have thus founded the family they wanted, but for others this is the case only after two or more children. Since the Convention does not provide any indication in this respect and could not very well do so, it must be assumed that in national law, too, no limit may be set, since such a limitation would affect the right in its essence for some people, even apart from the possible conflict with Article 9. In our view, family planning can therefore at most be

---

1258. On this, *supra* pp. 218-220.
1259. For the different view of the Commission, see *supra* p. 386.
1260. *Supra* pp. 218-220.
1261. Appl. 6564/74, *X v. United Kingdom*, D & R 2 (1975), p. 105 (106).

stimulated on a voluntary basis.[1262]

7. Must the right to found a family be deemed to be coupled with the right to marry, also mentioned in Article 12, in the sense that exclusively married couples have the former right? This was almost certainly the original intention, considering the fact that the two rights are combined into one right in Article 12 in the words "the exercise of this right", while the words "of marriageable age" also point in that direction.[1263] And indeed the Court held in the *Rees* Case that "Article 12 is mainly concerned to protect marriage as the basis of the family".[1264]

However, just as has been said above with regard to the concept of "family life" in Article 8, here again it may be submitted that since the drafting of the Convention the views with respect to the monopoly of marriage have been subject to great changes, while other forms of cohabitation, with family relations adapted thereto, are finding increasing recognition, also juridically.[1265] The text of Article 12 would seem to leave sufficient scope for an interpretation of the concept of "founding a family" in which these developments are taken into account. In Appl. 6482/74 a bachelor invoked Article 12 in a complaint against the application of Articles 227 and 228 of the Dutch Civil Code, which made adoption possible only for married couples. In its decision the Commission left open the question of whether "the right to found a family may be considered irrespective of marriage", although according to the formulation chosen it appears to be inclined to answer this question in the negative. It did, however, infer from the text of Article 12 that for the exercise of that right "[t]he existence of a couple is fundamental".[1266]

As regards adoption itself, the Commission has taken the position that a family may also be founded by means of adoption of children,[1267] but that it is not possible to infer from Article 12 a *right* to adopt children who are not the natural children of the person concerned or to integrate them in some other way into a family.[1268] The two views would seem to contradict one another. In fact, if it is recognized that there are different ways of founding a family, why should only one of those ways form part of the right conferred in Article 12, even in those cases where for the person(s) in question the other way is in fact the only possible way to found a family? Of course the

---

1262. *Cf.* Art. 16 of the Proclamation of Teheran of 1968; United Nations, *Human Rights; a Compilation of International Instruments*, New York 1988, p. 45: "Parents have a basic human right to determine freely and responsibly the number and the spacing of their children".
1263. Thus also the Commission in its decision on Appl. 6482/74, *X v. Belgium and the Netherlands*, D & R 7 (1977), p. 75 (77). See also the report of the Commission of 12 December 1984, *Rees*, A.106 (1987), opinion of Fawcett, Tenekides, Gözübüyük, Soyer and Batliner, pp. 28-29.
1264. Judgment of 17 October 1986, A.106 (1987), p. 19.
1265. See *supra* pp. 378-379.
1266. Appl. 6482/74, *X v. Belgium and the Netherlands*, D & R 7 (1977), p. 75 (77).
1267. Appl. 7229/75, *X and Y v. United Kingdom*, D & R 12 (1978), p. 32 (34). See also the report of 1 March 1979, *Van Oosterwijck*, B.36 (1980), p. 28.
1268. *Ibidem*, pp. 34-35.

national authorities will have to be allowed ample scope for regulating the conditions for adoption, in which context the rights of the persons concerned will have to be weighed carefully against those of others, while the rights and interests of the child must have priority. However, this need not bar the recognition of the right as such.

In the *Marckx* Case, Article 12 had been put forward because Belgian law linked the granting to an illegitimate child of the same status as a legitimate child enjoys, with his or her legitimization, which could only take place through a marriage of the natural parents. The Court was of the opinion that there was no need for it to pronounce on the question of whether the Convention also protects the right not to marry, since in the Court's view the freedom to marry or not was not involved, and the discrimination against a child born out of wedlock falls outside the scope of Article 12.[1269]

In the *Johnston* Case the Commission stated that it is clear that the concept of "family life" under Article 8 is not limited to the marriage-based family, but refers to people actually living together as a genuine family.[1270] However, Article 8 does not

> oblige the State to grant a right to custody and care to a natural father of a child born out of wedlock where the parents were free to marry but had chosen not to do so.[1271]

That "family" in the meaning of Article 8 is a broader concept than the marriage-based family has also been recognized by the Court, *e.g.* in the *Berrehab* Case, although there again the members of a family based on a "lawful and genuine marriage" were still given a certain preferential treatment.[1272] This case-law has not yet resulted in the adoption of an equally broad interpretation of "family" in Article 12.

8. It is recognized in the case-law that from Article 12, too, restrictions may ensue for the authorities of the contracting States as to their power of deportation or extradition and their power to refuse aliens access to the territory of the State. As regards the right to marry, however, Article 12 can be invoked successfully only against an (imminent) measure of deportation or extradition, or against a refusal of access, if the person in question can make it sufficiently plausible that he has concrete plans to marry and that both partners cannot reasonably be expected to realize those plans outside the country concerned.[1273] And with regard to the right to found a family, just as with respect to Article 8,[1274] the Commission has usually taken the view that deportation, extradition and refusal of access to the territory of the State do

---

1269. Judgment of 13 June 1979, A.31 (1979), pp. 28-29. Thus also the report of 10 December 1977, B.29 (1979), p. 55.
1270. Report of 5 March 1985, A.112 (1987), p. 46.
1271. *Ibidem*, p. 46.
1272. Judgment of 21 June 1988, A.138 (1988), p. 14.
1273. Appl. 7175/75, *X v. Federal Republic of Germany, D & R* 6 (1977), p. 138 (140).
1274. On this, *supra* pp. 386-389.

not constitute a violation of Article 12, if the partner is in a position to follow the person concerned to the country of deportation or extradition, or to the country of the latter's residence or any other country, and if this may reasonably be required of the former.[1275]

In the Case of *Abdulaziz, Cabales and Balkandali* the Court held that the expression "family life" in the case of a married couple normally comprises cohabitation. In the Court's view the latter proposition is reinforced by the existence of Article 12, for it is scarcely conceivable that the right to found a family should not encompass the right to live together.[1276]

9. With regard to Article 12, too, in the case-law the question has arisen whether from detention ensue inherent limitations for the exercise of the rights provided in that article.[1277]

When a person detained on remand complained about the refusal of the German authorities to give their consent to his marrying during his detention, the complaint was dismissed by the Commission as manifestly ill-founded. The Commission did not advance its own reasons for this, but mentioned in its decision the grounds of the *Landgericht, viz.* that it was expected that the person in question would be detained for a long time, so that he would not be able to cohabit with his future wife for a long time to come, which would be required to give a sound basis to a marriage; that in view of his personality and the unusually long engagement period it could not be assumed that he seriously intended to marry; and that marriages of prisoners inevitably tended to affect the maintenance of order in a prison.[1278] The first ground would appear absolutely objectionable to us, since, even apart from the violation of the presumption of innocence, it is not for the authorities to prescribe to a married couple a given type of conjugal life, and this certainly must not be made a condition. Many years later, in the report in the *Hamer* Case, this was fortunately recognized by the Commission. In fact, in that report it submitted:

> In considering whether the imposition of such a delay [in consequence of the detention] breached the applicant's right to marry, the Commission does not regard it as relevant that he could not have cohabited with his wife or consummated his marriage whilst serving his sentence. The essence of the right to marry, in the Commission's opinion, is the formation of a legally binding association between a man and a woman. It is for them to decide whether or not they wish to enter such an association in circumstances where they cannot cohabit.[1279]

For the second ground given in the decision referred to above insufficient arguments were advanced, at least judging from the decision as it was

---

1275. See, *e.g.*, Appl. 2535/65, *X v. Federal Republic of Germany, Coll.* 17 (1966), p. 28 (30), where the Commission furthermore took into account that the applicant, when she married, knew that her husband did not have a residence permit. For a case of refusal of admission, see Appl. 5301/71, *X v. United Kingdom, Coll.* 43 (1973), p. 82 (84).
1276. Judgment of 28 May 1985, A.94 (1985), p. 32.
1277. For a detailed discussion of the inherent limitations, see *infra* pp. 575-578.
1278. Appl. 892/60, *X v. Federal Republic of Germany, Yearbook* IV (1961), p. 240 (256).
1279. Report of 13 December 1979, *D & R* 24 (1981), p. 5 (16).

published. In cases where persons who are not detained wish to get married, their possible intention to conclude a fictitious marriage is not examined and frustrated, and rightly so; at most, certain legal consequences are denied to what is obviously a fictitious marriage, for instance the acquisition of a nationality. The argument of the fictitious marriage therefore can be used against a prisoner only if it is likely that the marriage ceremony is intended in reality, for example, to enable his escape, in which case there is indeed an abuse of right. It is only in the case of the third ground that we have to do with an inherent limitation, albeit a very broad and vague one, which is related to the purpose and the execution of the detention.

As has previously been observed, the doctrine of inherent limitations has been rejected by the Court, at least for those provisions of the Convention in which the restrictions are enumerated expressly, and then also exhaustively.[1280] Such an enumeration does not occur in Article 12; the only restriction mentioned there is the general one "according to the national laws governing the exercise of this right". Can that national law contain special restrictions for prisoners? The Commission was faced with this question in the above-mentioned *Hamer* Case, where the complaint concerned the refusal of a request by a prisoner for temporary leave with a view to the conclusion of a marriage. Here the Commission departed from its earlier - almost automatic - decisions concerning inherent limitations and decided that prisoners who have the requisite age and further satisfy the legal conditions have the right to marry. If on the basis of national law restrictions may be imposed with respect to this right at all, according to the Commission - which referred, *inter alia*, to the *Golder* judgment[1281] - these restrictions must not be of such a nature as to affect the *essence* of that right. The Commission subsequently concluded that when a person is obliged by the authorities to defer the marriage for a considerable time (in this case, for two years), in general this affects the right to marry in its essence, regardless of whether the delay is due to legislation which is only intended to regulate the exercise of that right, to an administrative act, or to a combination of the two. In the Commission's opinion the mere fact of the detention does not provide a justification for thus affecting the said right, since "no particular difficulties are involved in allowing the marriage of prisoners".[1282]

When a prisoner complained that he was not allowed conjugal life and thus also could not increase his family, the Commission - leaving open the question of whether a person who already has children can still invoke Article 12[1283] - held that Article 12 indeed contains an absolute right, but does not imply for that reason that a person must at all times be given the actual possibility to beget offspring, and that the applicant had to blame himself for

---

1280. See *supra* pp. 392-393, and *infra* pp. 575-577.
1281. Judgment of 21 February 1975, A.18 (1975), pp. 18-19.
1282. Report of 13 December 1979, *D & R* 24 (1981), p. 5 (15).
1283. On this, *supra* p. 447-448.

this temporary impossibility.[1284] If we ignore the additional remark about the blameworthiness, which would seem open to discussion according to modern doctrines of criminology and forensic psychiatry, and which at all events cannot be used as an argument for the justification of restrictions which are not justified otherwise, the Commission would appear to differentiate here between the possibility of founding a family in general and that possibility at a given moment. In the Commission's opinion measures in consequence of which a person is temporarily unable to found a family or increase his family do not constitute a violation of Article 12, since considering the preceding and the subsequent possibilities, on the whole the person in question has not been deprived of that right. It does not appear from its decision whether the Commission took into account the length of the detention, but it is obvious that this point is of great importance for the legitimacy of the reasoning followed by the Commission.

In a later decision the Commission apparently followed a different line of reasoning. This decision concerned a complaint of a husband and wife, both of whom were detained in the same prison for pre-trial investigations and who had been refused detention in the same cell. In this case the Commission assumed a relation between the right to protection of privacy and family life in Article 8 and the right to found a family in Article 12. After first having concluded that the restrictions imposed upon the married couple with respect to their right to privacy and to respect for their family life could find their justification in the second paragraph of Article 8, the Commission subsequently held that restrictions which are not contrary to Article 8 on that ground cannot constitute a conflict with the right granted in Article 12 either.[1285] In its general formulation this argument would seem to be incorrect. Article 12 occupies an independent position in the Convention beside Article 8, also as regards the second element: the right to found a family. Considering the indeed notable fact that the drafters of the Convention have not included an enumeration of restrictions in Article 12, this provision must not be subjected to the regime of the second paragraph of Article 8. However, in our opinion the argumentation of the Commission *is* correct in so far as it amounts to declaring in fact Article 8, and not Article 12, applicable to a measure by which the partners to a marriage or to a comparable relationship are temporarily deprived of the opportunity for sexual intercourse. Even if the desired sexual intercourse would actually be aimed at the foundation or increase of a family, it cannot be said that their right to do so is restricted by such a temporary measure. The same applies, for instance, with regard to conscript soldiers who during a given period are unable to lead a normal conjugal life. The situation will, however, have to be judged separately for

---

1284. Appl. 6564/74, *X v. United Kingdom*, *D & R* 2 (1975), p. 105 (106). The Commission quotes that passage in its report of 13 December 1979, *Hamer*, *D & R* 24 (1981), p. 5 (14).
1285. Appl. 8166/78, *X and Y v. Switzerland*, *D & R* 13 (1979), p. 241 (242-244). The same reasoning was also followed in Appls 5260 and 5277/71, *X and Y v. Austria*, not published.

each individual case, because in the case of a measure applied for a longer period Article 12 may indeed come into issue. In this context it is noteworthy that the Commission has opened the door for a dynamic development by referring expressly and with approval to

> the reformative movement in several European countries as regards an improvement of the conditions of imprisonment and the possibilities for detained persons of continuing their conjugal life to a limited extent.[1286]

10. Article 12 does not belong to the category of the rights which are non-derogable in virtue of Article 15(2).

11. Article 23 of the Covenant states in an introductory paragraph that the family is the natural and fundamental group unit of society and is entitled to protection by society and the State. Such an express provision is lacking in the Convention, but family life finds protection there in Article 8. Since the term family is not defined any further in Article 23, this provision is to be considered rather as a general point of departure for national policy, without any concrete obligations for the contracting States ensuing from this *per se*.[1287]

The second paragraph of Article 23, in which the right to marry and to found a family has been laid down, does not contain any reference to national law, so that there the only restriction would appear to be that one must be of marriageable age. For the interpretation of this concept, however, the national law will have to be consulted, and it is not likely that in other respects the contracting States meant to set aside their numerous national provisions concerning marriage and family. An indication for this may perhaps also be found in the formulation: "The right ... shall be recognized", which is less stringent than that of Article 12 of the Convention. Probably there will not be any great difference in the application of the two treaty provisions.[1288]

The third paragraph of Article 23 of the Covenant provides expressly that no marriage shall be entered into without the free and full consent of the intending spouses. For the parties to the Convention this requirement will already be implied in their national legislation, to which Article 12 refers.[1289]

This is different for the principle of equality of rights and responsibilities of spouses as to marriage, during marriage and at its dissolution, with respect to which the fourth paragraph of Article 23 provides that the contracting States must ensure that principle by means of appropriate measures. Such equality does not exist in all respects in the contracting States and is guaranteed only partly by Article 14 of the Convention, so that the requirements of the Covenant on this point are more stringent. The provision at the end of the fourth paragraph that in the case of dissolution of the marriage

---

1286. *Ibidem*, p. 243. Thus also earlier in Appl. 3603/68, X v. Federal Republic of Germany, *Coll.* 31 (1970), p. 48 (50).
1287. In that sense also the Report of the Committee of Experts, *supra* note 14, p. 50, where attention is also drawn to Art. 16 of the European Social Charter, in which the States undertake to promote the economic, legal and social protection of family life.
1288. See *ibidem*.
1289. *Ibidem*, p. 51.

provisions must be made for the necessary protection of any children, is also not to be found in Article 12, which - as has been said - does not refer to the dissolution of marriages. Up to a point the interests of the children are protected in Article 8 of the Convention, which prescribes respect for family life.[1290]

§ 13. ARTICLE 1 OF PROTOCOL NO. 1: RIGHT TO THE PEACEFUL ENJOYMENT OF ONE'S POSSESSIONS

Every natural or legal person is entitled to the peaceful enjoyment of his possessions. No one shall be deprived of his possessions except in the public interest and subject to the conditions provided for by law and by the general principles of international law.

The preceding provisions shall not, however, in any way impair the right of a State to enforce such laws as it deems necessary to control the use of property in accordance with the general interest or to secure the payment of taxes or other contributions or penalties.

1. The classification of the right to the enjoyment of one's possessions - at least in an unqualified form - among the human rights is not unchallenged.[1291] And indeed it has not been adopted in the Covenant from Article 17 of the Universal Declaration. That the drafters of the Convention also hesitated about the status and exact formulation of this right may appear from the fact that it was not included among the original rights and freedoms of the Convention, but was added later in the First Protocol. The right of property has actually lost a good deal of its inviolability, also in the member States of the Council of Europe, under the influence of modern social policy (*Sozialstaat*). This fact is recognized in the very far-reaching limitations which Article 1 allows the national authorities to impose upon this right.

Article 1 comprises three distinct rules. First, it states the principle of peaceful enjoyment of property. Second, it regulates the conditions to which the deprivation of possessions is subjected. And third, it contains the recognition that States are entitled to control the use of property in accordance with the general interest.[1292]

1290. For the "case-law" of the Human Rights Committee concerning Article 23 of the Covenant reference is made to the study of Nowak, mentioned *supra* at p. 216.

1291. For interesting observations on the order which the right of property occupies among human rights and the differentiations which may be made within that right, see Ch. Bay, "A Human Rights Approach to Transnational Politics", *Universal Human Rights* (1979), pp. 19-42 (29-38).

1292. Judgment of 23 September 1982, *Sporrong and Lönnroth*, A.53 (1982), p. 24; judgment of 26 June 1985, *James and others*, A.98 (1985), p. 29; judgment of 8 July 1986, *Lithgow and others*, A.102 (1986), p. 46; judgment of 24 October 1986, *Agosi*, A.108 (1986), p. 17; judgment of 23 April 1987, *Erkner and Hofauer*, A.117 (1987), p. 65; judgment of 23 April 1987, *Poiss*, A.117 (1987), p. 107.

2. The concept of "possessions" in the first sentence of Article 1 must not be understood in the technical-juridical meaning of the word; it is wider, as also appears from the French word "biens". Yet, the object of the possessions must be adequately definable in relation to the claims based thereupon.

Thus, with regard to pension schemes and social security systems, the Commission has differentiated between on the one hand systems according to which, by the payment of contributions, an individual share in a fund is created, the amount of which can be determined at each particular moment, and on the other hand systems according to which the relation between the contributions now being paid and the later benefit is much looser, which makes the object of the possessions less adequately definable. The first is a property-creating system and claims to benefits form possessions in the sense of Article 1, while the second system "is based on the principle of solidarity which reflects the responsibility of the community as a whole" and does not create for the participant any claim for an identifiable share, but only an expectation the amount of which depends on the conditions prevailing at the time the pension is paid.[1293] The latter pensions are based on the principle of collective security and are not funded by prior contributions in any individualizable way.[1294] Also in the latter case there may be a right to certain benefits as long as the system is in force and the participant fulfils the prevalent conditions of the benefit.[1295] However, in that case the right guaranteed by Article 1 is not a right to a particular amount, since this may be subject to fluctuations, *inter alia* due to legal regulations. Fluctuations in the amount of the benefit may only amount to a violation of Article 1 if a very substantial reduction of the benefit is concerned.[1296] And even if the right guaranteed extends, in principle, to periodic increases, it may be subjected to restrictions if the pension is to be paid abroad, since many countries apply specific restrictions to the payment of benefits to foreign countries.[1297]

In the *Feldbrugge* Case and the *Deumeland* Case the minority of the Commission put forward that even under a social security scheme the insurance of risks is financed by methods based on classical insurance techniques. In their view it is incorrect to argue that a property right is involved in old age insurance only if it is financed by a funding system and

---

1293. See in particular Appl. 4130/69, *X v. the Netherlands, Yearbook* XIV (1971), p. 224 (244). See also Appl. 5763/72, *X v. the Netherlands, Yearbook* XVI (1973), p. 274 (290-292) concerning amounts deducted from a Dutch social security pension in respect of pension payments received under a Norwegian pension scheme.
1294. Appl. 10094/82, *G v. Austria, D & R* 38 (1984), p. 84 (85-86) concerning a claim of entitlement to a survivor's pension for civil servants.
1295. See Appl. 7624/76, *X v. Austria, D & R* 19 (1980), p. 100 (104-105), where the reduction of an old age pension was due to the fact that the person in question did not satisfy the conditions for a full pension due to the amount of his monthly contributions. See also Appl. 7995/77, *National Federation of Self-employed v. United Kingdom, D & R* 15 (1979), p. 198 (201), where the Commission brought an increase of contributions, without a proportional increase of pension claims in return, under the justification of the second paragraph of Art. 1 "in the general interest".
1296. Report of 1 October 1975, *Müller, Yearbook* XIX (1976), p. 996 (1018-1020).
1297. Appl. 9776/82, *X v. United Kingdom, D & R* 34 (1983), p. 153 (154).

that this is not the case if the insurance is based on the pay-as-you-go system. In the minority's view the important point, in fact, is that, particularly in sickness and accident insurance, the benefits are financed by contributions directly or indirectly deducted from the worker's remuneration. In their view

The part borne directly by the worker is of course a deduction from the income earned by his work. But the contribution borne by the employer is in fact, indirectly, a similar deduction. If there was no compulsory insurance ... this contribution would be added to the worker's net remuneration ... The fact that in certain cases the scheme is also funded by State contributions in addition to those of the employers does not alter the nature of the scheme involved which remains an insurance scheme.[1298]

In the *Mellacher* Case, the Commission took as a starting point its earlier case-law according to which certain contractual rights of economic value may be assimilated to property rights within the meaning of Article 1. In the instant case, however, the applicants claimed a contractual right (to receive a monthly rent) as the owners of the real property concerned. The Commission was of the opinion that the right to use property by concluding tenancy contracts must be considered as an aspect of the possession of the real property at issue. The applicant's contractual rights to rent are therefore not a separate property and cannot be considered in isolation. Therefore, measures directed against these contractual rights must be examined as to their effect on the real property.[1299]

There is no question of possessions until the moment at which one can lay claim to the property concerned. A claim as such may constitute a "possession" in the sense of Article 1,[1300] but it should then be a concrete, adequately specified claim. Thus, the Commission decided that the claim of a notary to payment for his services does not find protection in Article 1 until it is an actual claim based on services rendered; his expectation that the applicable provisions about notarial fees were not going to be modified does not find protection in Article 1.[1301] Nor do claims which a person has as an heir during the testator's lifetime fall under the protection of Article 1, because this provision protects existing property and not the right to acquire property. It does of course protect the right of the testator to dispose of his patrimonial rights and the rights which have already been acquired by inheritance even before distribution of assets.[1302] In the *Sequaris* Case, which ended in a friendly settlement, the Commission would seem to have impliedly taken the view that a claim against a State, confirmed by an enforceable court decision applying the principles of State liability *vis-à-vis* individuals, was a

---

1298. Reports of 9 May 1984, A.99 (1986), pp. 41-43, and A.100 (1986), pp. 55-57, respectively.
1299. Report of 11 July 1988, paras 184-186.
1300. Appl. 7742/76, *A, B and Company A.S. v. Federal Republic of Germany*, *D & R* 14 (1979), p. 146 (168).
1301. Appl. 8410/78, *X v. Federal Republic of Germany*, *D & R* 18 (1980), p. 216 (219-220). See also Appl. 10426/83, *Pudas v. Sweden*, *D & R* 40, p. 234 (241) and Appl. 10438/83, *Batelaan and Huiges v. the Netherlands*, *D & R* 41 (1985), p.170 (173): expectations for future earnings can only be considered to constitute a "possession", if an enforceable claim exists.
1302. Judgment of 13 June 1979, *Marckx*, A.31 (1979), p. 23 and pp. 27-28 respectively; judgment of 28 October 1987, *Inze*, A.126 (1987), p. 19.

"possession".[1303]

In Appl. 7641/76 a counsel assigned to an accused person complained of the fact that the German court had refused to grant him an advance on his fee, notwithstanding the large amount of work that he had already had to perform for his client. He alleged, *inter alia*, that Article 1 had been violated. Without further argumentation the Commission held in this case that the applicant was entitled to a fee but that the refusal of the authorities to pay an advance did not constitute a violation of Article 1.[1304] It is not clear if the Commission examined at all whether the case submitted to it could be deemed to belong to those exceptional cases in which, according to the statement of the German Government, such advances are paid in Germany to counsels assigned to accused persons. If the case did not differ from those cases on essential points, Article 1 might have been violated by the refusal, in connection with Article 14 of the Convention.

Two complaints of an Austrian lawyer that his obligation to render *pro-deo* services as counsel was contrary to Article 1, were declared admissible by the Commission.[1305] In these cases, however, a friendly settlement was reached.[1306] In the *Van der Mussele* Case the Court held that the absence of remuneration of expenses made by the applicant for public services was unrelated to the "peaceful enjoyment" of applicant's existing possessions. The Court held that since the expenses were relatively small and resulted from obligations to accomplish work compatible with Article 4 of the Convention, there was no breach of Article 1.[1307]

In its decision on the admissibility of *Pudas v. Sweden* the Commission had to answer the question whether a licence to conduct certain economic activities gives the licence-holder a right protected by Article 1. The Commission considered that

the answer will depend *inter alia* on the question whether the licence can be considered to create for the licence-holder a reasonable and legitimate expectation as to the lasting nature of the licence and as to the possibility to continue to draw benefits from the exercise of licenced activity.[1308]

And indeed in the *Tre Traktörer Aktiebolag* Case, where the complaint concerned the decision to revoke the applicant's licence to serve beer, wine and other alcoholic beverages, the Commission held that the economic interests connected with the applicant company's restaurant business were "possessions" within the meaning of Article 1. Since that licence was an

1303. Appl. 9676/82, *Sequaris v. Belgium, D & R* 29 (1982), p. 245 (249).
1304. Appl. 7641/76, *X and Y v. Federal Republic of Germany, D & R* 10 (1978), p. 224 (230).
1305. Appls 4897/71 and 5219/71, *Gussenbauer v. Austria, Coll.* 42 (1973), pp. 41 and 94 respectively.
1306. Report of 8 October 1974.
1307. Judgment of 23 November 1983, A.70 (1983), p. 23. See also Appl. 8682/79, *X v. Federal Republic of Germany, D & R* 26 (1982), pp. 97 (99-100) where the Commission held that Art. 1 is not violated when an officially appointed defence counsel is obliged to repay an advance on his fees for not having assured the accused's defence up to the end of the proceedings.
1308. Appl. 10426/83, *Pudas v. Sweden, D & R* 40 (1985), p. 234 (241).

important element in the running of the restaurant and the applicant company could legitimately expect to keep the licence as long as it did not infringe the conditions thereof, the revocation of the licence was an interference with the company's rights under Article 1.[1309] A licence is often granted under certain conditions. If a licence-holder no longer fulfils the conditions, he cannot be considered to have a legitimate expectation to continue his activities.[1310]

The Court has held that "Article 1 is in substance guaranteeing the right of property".[1311] This "property" does not have to be very concrete and fixed. In the *Van Marle* Case the Court stated that it agreed with the Commission that the "goodwill" relied upon by the applicants may be

likened to the right of property embodied in Article 1: by dint of their own work, the applicants had built up a clientéle; this had in many respects the nature of a private right and constituted an asset and, hence, a possession within the meaning of Article 1.[1312]

Measures which are taken in order to establish who is entitled to a certain property - for instance seizure[1313] - and conditions with regard to the evidence of that entitlement in themselves do not constitute violations of Article 1, unless such conditions impose an unreasonably heavy burden of proof on the person laying claim to the property.[1314]

3. Article 1 speaks of "peaceful enjoyment". That implies that this provision may also have been violated when a person has not been affected as to his property or possessions *per se*, but is not accorded an opportunity to use that property, for instance because a necessary permit is refused to him,[1315] or because in some other way such restrictions ensue from the legislation or from government measures to the extent that there is no longer any question of a "peaceful enjoyment".[1316] This is also clear from the second paragraph, which use the words of "to control the use of property" and, consequently, does also not concern the property as such but the possibilities of using it. However, the distinction between "deprivation of possessions" and "control of the use of property" is a fluid one in certain situations.

1309. Report of 10 November 1987, para. 111.
1310. Appl. 10438/83, *Batelaan and Huiges v. the Netherlands*, D & R 41 (1985), p. 170 (173).
1311. Judgment of 13 June 1979, *Marckx*, A.31 (1979), p. 27. In the same sense the Commission in its decision on Appls 8588/79 and 8589/79, *Bramelid and Malmström v. Sweden*, D & R 29 (1982), p. 64 (81).
1312. Judgment of 26 June 1986, A.101 (1986), p. 13. See however the decision of the Commission on Appl. 10438/83, *Batelaan and Huiges v. the Netherlands*, D & R 41 (1985), p. 170 (173): the goodwill of a professional practice is an element in its valuation but does not constitute a "possession" to the extent that it is not necessarily linked with the profession in question.
1313. Appl. 7256/75, *X v. Belgium*, D & R 8 (1977), p. 161 (165-166).
1314. See Appl. 7775/77, *Pacheco v. Belgium*, D & R 15 (1979), p. 143, which was declared inadmissible by the Commission.
1315. See, e.g., Appl. 7456/76, *Wiggins v. United Kingdom*, D & R 13 (1979), p. 40 (46-47), concerning the refusal of a housing licence to the applicant to live in his own house.
1316. Report of 8 October 1980, *Sporrong and Lönnroth*, B.46 (1986), pp. 47-48, concerning, inter alia, restrictions on the possibility to build on land held in freehold. See also Appl. 7889/77, *Arrondelle v. United Kingdom*, D & R 19 (1980), p. 186, where the complaint concerned the nuisance caused to the owner of a house by the neighbouring airfield. In this case a friendly settlement has been reached; report of 13 May 1982, D & R 26 (1982), p. 5.

In the *Sporrong and Lönnroth* Case, although the expropriations left intact in law the owners' right to use and dispose of their possessions, they nevertheless in practice significantly reduced the possibility of its exercise. They also affected the very substance of ownership in that they recognized before the event that any expropriation would be lawful and authorized the City of Stockholm to expropriate whenever it found it expedient to do so. In the Court's view the applicants' right of property thus became precarious and defeasible.[1317]

In the *Erkner and Hofauer* Case and in the *Poiss* Case the applicants submitted that the provisional transfer of their land to other landowners, who were partners to a consolidation scheme, interfered with their right to property. The Court noted that the Austrian authorities did not effect either a formal expropriation or a *de-facto* expropriation (Art. 1, para. 1, second sentence). The transfer carried out was a provisional one; only the entry into force of the consolidation plan would make it irrevocable. The applicants would therefore recover their land if the final plan could not confirm the distribution made at an earlier stage of the proceedings. Nor was the provisional transfer essentially designed to restrict or control the "use" of the land (Art. 1, para. 2), but to achieve an early restructuring of the consolidation area with a view to improved, rational farming by the "provisional owners".[1318] Impliedly the Court recognised here that apart from formal expropriations the second sentence of the first paragraph of Article 1 might also extend to *de-facto* expropriations which "can be assimilated to a deprivation of possessions".[1319]

The *James* Case concerned transactions under the British Leasehold Reform Act of 1967. This legislation gives long term tenants of certain residential property the right, and in certain circumstances compels them, to purchase the landlord's interest in the property on specified compensation terms. The applicants were owners of properties, a number of which had been purchased by tenants exercising their rights under this legislation. The Court held that is was necessary to examine both the terms of the contested legislation and the consequences of its application. After it had reached the conclusion that each of the requirements of the second sentence of paragraph 1 was satisfied, it conducted no independent investigation in relation to the first sentence.[1320]

In the *Mellacher* Case the essence of the complaints was directed against the terms and conditions of the 1981 Rent Act which in the view of the applicants interfered with rent agreements which the applicants had validly concluded with their tenants on the basis of earlier legislation. After entry

---

1317. Judgment of 23 September 1982, A.53 (1982), p. 23. See also the report of 8 October 1987, *Jacobsson*, paras 129-30, where the Commission considered that the continued building prohibition on the applicant's property constituted an interference with his right to the peaceful enjoyment of possessions.
1318. Judgments of 23 April 1987, A.117 (1987), pp. 65-66 and p. 108 respectively.
1319. *Ibidem.*
1320. Judgment of 21 February 1986, A.98 (1986), p. 29.

into force of the 1981 Act the monthly rent was compulsorily reduced by the competent courts to the amounts of rent permissible under this Act. In the Commission's view, although the application of the Act affected the applicants' real property and in particular their possibilities to use it, it did not deprive them of the substance of their real property and, therefore, it could not be said that the measures complained of amounted to a *de-facto* expropriation or "deprivation of possessions". Therefore, not the first but the second paragraph was applicable.[1321]

The *Gillow* Case concerned the question whether the refusal of permission to occupy a house of which one of the applicants was the owner, constituted a violation of Article 1. This was a clear case not of deprivation of possessions but of control of use of property. The Commission concluded unanimously that there was a breach of the second paragraph of Article 1.[1322]

4. The most important restriction to be imposed by the authorities on the peaceful enjoyment of one's possessions is regulated explicitly in the first paragraph itself: expropriation in the public interest. Whether a particular expropriation has indeed been performed in the public interest will be subjected by the Strasbourg organs to a very marginal review only, the main objective being to detect cases of *détournement de pouvoir*[1323] or of manifest arbitrariness.[1324] As the Commission sets forth in its report in the *Handyside* Case in connection with the fact that the first paragraph speaks of "in the public interest" and not of "necessary in a democratic society":

> Clearly the public or general interest encompasses measures which would be preferable or advisable, and not only essential, in a democratic society.[1325]

In the *James* Case the Court held with respect to the margin of appreciation on the part of the States that

> Furthermore, the notion of "public interest" is necessarily extensive. ... The Court, finding it natural that the margin of appreciation available to the legislature in implementing social and economic policies should be a wide one, will respect the legislature's judgment as to what is "in the public interest" unless that judgment be manifestly without reasonable foundation.[1326]

In a case which concerned an expropriation of national property, the Commission expressly left open the question of whether the first paragraph

---

1321. Report of 11 July 1988, para. 199. The Commission concluded unanimously that there had been a violation of the second paragraph of Article 1.
1322. Report of 3 October 1984, A.109 (1987), p. 47. The Court could not deal with this question, since it lacked jurisdiction on the ground that the United Kingdom had not made an express declaration under Article 4 of Protocol no. 1 extending the provisions of this Protocol to Guernsey.
1323. See Appl. 3039/67, *A, B, C and D v. United Kingdom*, Yearbook X (1967), p. 506 (516-518), where the Commission uses the doctrine of the margin of appreciation also with respect to this.
1324. Report of 30 September 1975, *Handyside*, B.22 (1976), p.50; judgment of 21 February 1986, *James and others*, A.98 (1986), p. 32.
1325. *Ibidem.*
1326. Judgment of 21 February 1986, *James and others*, A.98 (1986), p. 32. See also judgment of 8 July 1986, *Lithgow and others*, A.102 (1986), p. 51.

of Article 1 presupposes a right to compensation, but subsequently did go into the issue of the amount of such compensation. By analogy with the case-law concerning old-age pension payments it submitted that a substantial reduction of the compensation may affect the very substance of the right to compensation, but that a right to compensation does not imply a claim to a particular amount.[1327]

In the *Sporrong and Lönnroth* Case the Court adopted the view that it had to determine whether a fair balance was struck between the demands of the general interest of the community and the requirements of the protection of the individual's fundamental rights. In the Court's opinion, the search for this balance is inherent in the whole of the Convention and is also reflected in the structure of Article 1. To determine whether there was such a "fair balance" in this case the Court examined the possibilities for the applicants to seek a reduction of the time limits within which the expropriation of their properties might be effected or to claim compensation for the damages suffered during the extremely long period during which the enjoyment of their property right had been impeded. Because remedies to that effect were not available, the Court decided that Article 1 had been violated.[1328] In two later cases the Commission summarized this latter reasoning as follows:

> The Court thus treated a right to compensation for interference with property rights as being an inherent feature of the right of property set forth in Article 1 in so far as it might form a necessary ingredient in a fair balance between public and private rights.[1329]

The Commission stressed that Article 1 was not intended to guarantee theoretical rights, but rights that are practical and effective.[1330] The deprivation of property, even if it has a legitimate aim in the public interest, is a violation of Article 1 when there is no reasonable proportionality between interference with the individual's rights and the objectives of public interest.[1331] For the same reason the Court examined whether a disproportionate or excessive burden had been imposed on the individual.[1332] If there is a substantial disproportion between the burden imposed on the individual and the public-interest objectives, Article 1 is violated. And although the States have a large margin of appreciation to determine the terms and conditions on which an individual can be deprived of his possessions, Article 1 encompasses the right to compensation in so far as it

> may be necessary to preserve the appropriate relationship of proportionality between the interference with the individual's rights and the "public interest".[1333]

According to both the Court and the Commission, the "deprivation rules"

1327. Appl. 7987/77, *Company X v. Austria, D & R* 18 (1980), p. 31 (47-48).
1328. Judgment of 23 September 1982, A.52 (1982), pp. 26-28.
1329. Report of 7 March 1984, *Lithgow and others,* A.102 (1987), p. 103; report of 11 May 1984, *James and others,* A.98 (1986), p. 63.
1330. *Ibidem,* p. 89 and pp. 63-64 respectively.
1331. *Ibidem,* p. 95 and pp. 66-67 respectively.
1332. Judgment of 21 February 1986, *James and others,* A.98 (1986) p. 34.
1333. Report of 7 March 1984, *Lithgow and others,* A.102 (1987), p. 96; judgment of 21 February 1986, *James and others,* A.98 (1986), p. 36.

developed in their case-law are not contrary to the *travaux préparatoires*. Article 1 does not give an absolute right to claim compensation. But to hold that property could be taken without compensation in absence of any consideration justifying such a course in the public interest, would undermine the protection afforded by Article 1.[1334] Regarding the meaning of "the public interest" the Court stated:

> a deprivation of property effected for no reason other than to confer a private benefit on a private party cannot be "in the public interest". Nonetheless, the compulsory transfer of property from one individual to another may, depending upon the circumstances, constitute a legitimate aim for promoting the public interest.[1335]

The Court also held that

> a taking of property affected in pursuance of legitimate, social, economic or other policies may be "in the public interest", even if the community at large has no direct use or enjoyment of the property taken.[1336]

The obligation to pay compensation may derive from an implicit condition in Article 1 read as a whole rather than from the "public interest" requirement. A claim that the compensation paid is unfair should, therefore, not be related to that requirement nor to the phrase "subject to the conditions provided for by law", which requires in the first place the existence of and compliance with adequately accessible and sufficiently precise domestic legal provisions.[1337] In the *James* Case and in the *Lithgow* Case both the Commission and Court adopted the view that the taking of property without payment of an amount reasonably related to its value would normally constitute a disproportionate interference. Legitimate objectives of "public interest", such as pursued in measures of economic reform or measures designed to achieve a greater social justice, may however call for less than reimbursement of the full market value.[1338] And also here the Court emphasised that its power is limited to ascertaining whether the choice of compensation terms falls outside the State's margin of appreciation in this domain.[1339]

Expropriations are permissible only if the conditions provided for by law and by the general principles of international law have been observed. As regards the fulfilment of the national legal conditions, here again the Commission and the Court do not examine whether national law has been applied correctly. They take the position that in this matter they have to refer to the judgment of the national court in the case concerned and that they must not function as a "fourth instance".

With respect to the reference to international legal principles, one is

---

1334. Judgment of 21 February 1986, *James and others*, A.98 (1986), p. 36; judgment of 8 July 1986, *Lithgow and others*, A.102 (1986), p. 50. See also the report of 11 May 1986, *James and others*, A.98 (1986), pp. 66-67 and the report of 7 March 1984, *Lithgow and others*, A.102 (1987), pp. 96-97.
1335. Judgment of 21 February 1986, *James and others*, A.81 (1986), p. 30.
1336. *Ibidem*, pp. 31-32.
1337. Judgment of 8 July 1986, *Lithgow and others*, A.102 (1987), p. 47.
1338. Judgment of 21 February 1986, A.98 (1986), p. 36; judgment of 8 July 1986, A.102 (1987), p. 51.
1339. See also the report of 13 October 1988, *Håkansson and Sturesson*, para. 103.

inclined to think first of all of the obligation to pay damages, as this obligation exists under international law or at all events existed according to the prevalent view at the moment when the First Protocol was drafted.[1340] In fact, the Commission has taken that general principle of international law into consideration. It came, however, with reference to the genesis of Article 1 to the conclusion that this principle relates exclusively to the nationalization of foreign property and cannot be invoked against the national State of the owner.[1341] On several occasions this led the Commission to conclude that in the case of expropriation in the public interest of property owned by the State's own subjects, the State is under no obligation to pay damages if this is not provided for in national law.[1342]

According to this interpretation, Article 1 of the First Protocol permits a difference in treatment between the State's own nationals and aliens, this contrary to the purpose of the Convention to secure to everyone, the same enjoyment of the rights and freedoms, as laid down in Articles 1 and 14. This result is all the more curious as the derogation from that purpose is an implied one and this even to the detriment of the State's own nationals, while other derogations are laid down expressly, viz. in Article 16 of the Convention and Article 3 of the Fourth Protocol, and are to the detriment of aliens. However, in the case of Article 1 of the First Protocol this does not create a fundamental difference between nationals and aliens, but one which exists only in so far and as long as general principles of international law actually prescribe a specific treatment of foreign property and these principles are different from those applying according to the law of the State in question to the treatment of the property of its own nationals. If any differences on this point still exist at present, developments within international law take the direction of a minimization of those differences.[1343]

In the James Case and in the Lithgow Case the Court, too, held that the reference to the general principles of international law in Article 1 means that those principles are incorporated into that Article, but only as regards those acts to which they are normally applicable, that is to say acts of a State in relation to non-nationals. For this interpretation the Court referred to Article 31 of the Vienna Convention on the Law of Treaties: the words of a treaty should be understood to have their ordinary meaning.[1344] On that

---

1340. This conclusion was also reached at that time within the Committee of Ministers: K.J. Partsch, Die Rechte und Freiheiten der Europäischen Menschenrechtskonvention, Berlin 1966, p. 224. On this point a discussion has been going on in recent years within the international forum whereby the obligation to pay compensation is related to the sovereignty of the State over its natural resources and over the economic activities on its territory: see Art. 2 of the Charter of Economic Rights and Duties of States adopted by Resolution 3281 (XXIX) of the General Assembly of the UN on 12 December 1974, International Legal Materials (1975), p. 251.
1341. An interpretation in that sense has been included in the minutes of a discussion devoted to it by the Committee of Ministers at that time: Partsch, supra note 1340, p. 225.
1342. See, e.g., Appl. 511/59, Gudmundson v. Iceland, Yearbook III (1960), p. 394 (422-424).
1343. See the Charter mentioned in note 1340.
1344. Judgment of 21 February 1986, A.98 (1986), p. 38; judgment of 8 July 1986, A.102 (1987), p. 48.

ground it rejected the grammatical argument of the applicants, based upon Article 1, that all elements of that article applied to everyone. The Court also rejected the argument of the applicants that the interpretation according to which the principle in question only applied to non-nationals, would make the reference in Article 1 to the general principles redundant since non-nationals already enjoyed the protection thereof. In the Court's view the inclusion of the reference could be seen to serve at least two purposes:

> Firstly, it enables non-nationals to resort directly to the machinery of the Convention to enforce their rights on the basis of the relevant principles of international law, whereas otherwise they would have to seek recourse to diplomatic channels or to other available means of dispute settlement to do so. Secondly, the reference ensures that the position of non-nationals is safeguarded, in that it excludes any possible argument that the entry into force of Protocol No. I has led to a diminution of their rights.[1345]

The Court also indicated that the difference in treatment did not constitute discrimination, since the differences in treatment had an "objective and reasonable justification":

> Especially as regards a taking of property effected in the context of a social reform, there may well be good grounds for drawing a distinction between nationals and non-nationals as far as compensation is concerned.[1346]

In the Court's view non-nationals are more vulnerable to domestic legislation since, unlike nationals, they will generally have played no part in the elections. Secondly, although the taking of property must always be effected in the public interest, different considerations may apply to nationals and non-nationals and there may well be a legitimate reason for requiring nationals to bear a greater burden in the public interest than non-nationals. Finally the Court pointed to the fact that also the *travaux préparatoires* and Resolution (52)1 of 19 March 1952 approving the text of the Protocol revealed that the reference to the general principles of international law was not intended to extend to nationals.[1347] In both cases the Court found that no violation of Article 1 had been established, since in the exercise of its margin of appreciation the United Kingdom was entitled to adopt the compensation provisions as applied to the applicants and these provisions and their application was deemed by the Court not to be unreasonable.

5. The second paragraph of Article 1 allows the national authorities an almost unlimited power to impose restrictions on the use of property in accordance with the general interest. Here it is not the deprivation of property itself that is concerned, but restriction of its use. In this context it is curious that with regard to this restriction it is, but with respect to the expropriation itself it is not provided that it must be necessary.[1348]

1345. *Ibidem*, p. 39 and p. 49 respectively.
1346. *Ibidem*.
1347. *Ibidem*, pp. 39-40 and pp. 48-49 respectively.
1348. The submission by an applicant that in his case the deprivation of property could not be deemed to have been necessary was not, therefore, examined by the Commission: Appl. 3039/67, *A, B, C and D v. United Kingdom*, Yearbook X (1967), p. 506 (516).

The judgment as to what is necessary in the general interest is expressly left to the State: "as it deems necessary". Consequently, the relevant national legislation and its application can be reviewed only for their conformity with the prohibition of discrimination of Article 14, with the prohibition of *détournement de pouvoir* laid down in Article 18, and possibly with Article 17.[1349] This was expressly stated by the Court in the *Handyside* Case:

> this paragraph sets the Contracting States up as sole judges of the "necessity" for an interference. Consequently, the Court must restrict itself to supervising the lawfulness and the purposes of the restriction in question.[1350]

In its report in the *Sporrong and Lönnroth* Case, however, the Commission concluded from the slightly modified wording used by the Court in the *Marckx* judgment[1351] that the Court only recognizes the States as the "sole judges" with respect to the law on which the restrictions are based, but not in relation to the necessity of the measures themselves. As regards the latter, in the Commission's opinion the possibility of review by the Strasbourg organs goes further and includes, for instance, the proportionality between those measures and the purpose of the law on which they are based.[1352]

A broad margin of discretion also applies in the case of the second restriction in the second paragraph - securing the payment of taxes or other contributions and penalties -, for which it does not even seem to be required that the national measure is "in accordance with the general interest".[1353] Thus, the power of the national authorities to levy taxes, to impose penalties (with due observance of Article 7), to make social security contributions compulsory and to impose other levies[1354] is left intact as long as there exists a legal basis for them, no discrimination is involved, and the power is not used for a purpose other than that for which it has been conferred.

A curious example of securing a certain payment was brought before the Commission in Appl. 4338/69. There a person detained on remand complained about the seizure of the money in his possession, allowed by Austrian law, as security for the payment of expenses that would ensue from his criminal

---

1349. In Appl. 4984/71, *X v. Federal Republic of Germany, Coll.* 43 (1973), p. 28 (35-36), the Commission nevertheless seems to have reviewed the measure by which a prisoner was prohibited from spending his money, be it in a very marginal way, for its necessity in the public interest.
1350. Judgment of 7 December 1976, A.24 (1976), p. 29.
1351. Judgment of 13 June 1979, A.31 (1979), p. 28.
1352. Report of 8 October 1980, B.46 (1986), pp. 48-49. From its decision on Appl. 8003/77, *X v. Austria, D & R* 17 (1979), p. 80 (84), it appears further that the Commission is prepared to go rather far in an independent review, also in respect to the legislation itself (in this case a law on rent control). Its report of 3 October 1984, *Gillow*, A.109 (1987), p. 42, shows that the Commission performs a limited review of the legitimacy of the aim of the legislation concerned and a fuller review of the proportionality of the interference with the applicant's rights.
1353. In its report in the *Greek* Cases, therefore, the Commission held with regard to this latter provision that it does not prescribe any limitation, either of form or of size; *Yearbook* XII; *The Greek Case* (1969), p. 185.
1354. E.g. a levy for the construction of a road: Appl. 7489/76, *X v. Federal Republic of Germany, D & R* 9 (1978), p. 114. See also Appl. 7669/76, *Company X v. the Netherlands, D & R* 15 (1979), p. 133 (134): contribution to a professional organization, required in virtue of a collective agreement declared generally binding by the government.

prosecution. Since he alleged that in consequence thereof he was unable to pay his counsel's fee, Article 6(3)(c) was brought into issue as well. However, in the Commission's opinion this provision had not been violated, since, if owing to the seizure he had indeed insufficient means to pay a counsel's fee, he was entitled to free legal aid.[1355] One may wonder whether the importance of being able to choose and pay one's own counsel should not have weighed more heavily in this case than the security of payment sought by the authorities.

The *AGOSI* Case concerned a forfeiture, by court order, of smuggled gold coins belonging to a third party and the subsequent refusal by the customs authorities to restore the goods. The Commission observed that AGOSI complained not of the seizure of the coins, but of their forfeiture and the denial of their return. It was not for the Commission to decide upon AGOSI's innocence or complicity in smuggling, but to examine whether the decision not to restore the coins to the applicant and the procedure which had led to that decision satisfied the procedural requirement inherent in Article 1. The Commission first recalled its case-law that forfeiture constitutes a control of the use of property, not a deprivation. In this case, since the smuggling of the coins was intended to circumvent customs legislation, the forfeiture found its justification in the security which the authorities sought to obtain for the payment of customs duties and penalties. The forfeiture presupposes that the smuggler owns the property. If he does not and if the lawful owner is unaware of the smuggling and suffers loss, the specific justification for forfeiture may be absent and it may amount to confiscation without any specific justification *vis-à-vis* the owner. In the opinion of the Commission the rule of proportionality requires that the innocent owner be given an opportunity to assert his property right and show that he is an innocent owner, this being a necessary balancing factor to the State's forfeiture powers. The Commission concluded that this proportionality requirement was not fulfilled by the legislation and the procedures concerned.[1356] Contrary to the Commission, the Court concluded that it was not established that the British system failed either to ensure that reasonable account be taken of the behaviour of the applicant company or to afford it a reasonable opportunity to put its case.[1357]

6. Since Article 5 of the First Protocol provides on the one hand that "all the provisions of the Convention shall apply accordingly", while on the other hand no separate mention is made of Article 15 (2), it follows from this that none of the rights mentioned in the First Protocol is non-derogable.

1355. Appl. 4338/69, *X v. Austria, Coll.* 36 (1971), p. 79 (81-82).
1356. Report of 11 October 1984, A.108 (1987), pp. 35-37.
1357. Judgment of 24 October 1986, *ibidem*, pp. 20-21.

7. As already mentioned in the first paragraph of the present section, the right to the peaceful enjoyment of one's possessions is not regulated in the Covenant.

§ 14. ARTICLE 2 OF PROTOCOL NO. 1: RIGHT TO EDUCATION

No person shall be denied the right to education. In the exercise of any functions which it assumes in relation to education and to teaching, the State shall respect the right of parents to ensure such education and teaching in conformity with their own religious and philosophical convictions.

1. The negative formulation of the first sentence of this provision seems to emphasize that the right to *freedom* of education is involved here rather than the social and cultural right to education. And indeed, in the *Belgian Linguistic* Cases the Court held that Article 2 does not require that the contracting States ensure at their own expense, or subsidize, education of a particular type, but implies for those who are under the jurisdiction of one of the contracting States the right "to avail themselves of the means of instruction existing at a given time".[1358] However, the exercise of the right to education, even if understood in this way, requires by implication the existence and the maintenance of a minimum of education provided by the State, since otherwise that right would be illusory, in particular for those who have insufficient means. In addition, according to the Court, it obliges the State to give official recognition in one form or another to those who have completed a given type of studies with good results, since otherwise the exercise of the right would not be very effective.[1359] The Commission has left open the question of whether this also applies to studies pursued abroad; in any case the person in question may be required to submit to an examination in the country where recognition of those studies abroad is requested.[1360]

The words from the Court's judgment quoted above, *viz.* "means of instruction existing at a given time", imply that the scope of the right to education as guaranteed in Article 2 may vary from one country to another and is also subject to developments. If in a given country a new branch or a new type of education is introduced, persons in that country have a right of access to it, provided that they satisfy the conditions of entry. The position taken by the Commission without further motivation, *viz.* that the "right to education envisaged in Article 2 is concerned primarily with elementary education",[1361] is corroborated neither by the text of Article 2 nor by the

---

1358. Judgment of 23 July 1968, A.6 (1968), p. 31.
1359. *Ibidem.*
1360. Appl. 7864/77, *X v. Belgium, D & R* 16 (1979), p. 82 (83-84).
1361. Appl. 5962/72, *X v. United Kingdom, D & R* 2 (1975), p. 50; Appl. 7010/75, *X v. Belgium, D & R* 3 (1976), p. 162 (164).

Court's interpretation, to which the Commission refers. According to the Court's interpretation Article 2 does not require from the States a particular level of education - in the member States of the Council of Europe elementary education must be assumed to be the absolute minimum -, but it does oblige them to give access to everyone to the existing education in accordance with the relevant rules.

The position of the Commission that the contracting States are not obliged to provide for a particular type of adult education[1362] or to guarantee the availability of schools which are in accordance with a certain religious conviction of the parents[1363] is therefore correct, but the complaint of a prisoner that he was not enabled to complete particular technological studies should in our opinion not have been dismissed with the argument that Article 2 does not refer to such types of adult education.[1364] The other argument advanced by the Commission in the latter case, viz. that no facilities were available in the prison for the desired education, is also unsound. If outside the prison a type of education is available which the prisoner can follow without unacceptable consequences for the execution of the penalty - for instance a correspondence course -, it is difficult to understand why prisoners should not have the right "to avail themselves of the means of instruction existing at a given time".

Although therefore in our opinion Article 2 in principle confers a right to access to any type and any level of education existing in the country concerned,[1365] this does not mean that everyone should have access to any institution for which he applies and be permitted to study there as long as he likes.[1366] It is an inherent feature of education that one can complete one's studies successfully only when one has reached the level required for it; otherwise there can be no question of education. Conditions of entry referring to an objective assessment of this level are not therefore contrary to the freedom of education.[1367] And any restrictions resulting from placement committees, fixed number of entries, maxima as regards the length of the studies, and the like are caused by the limited availability of places at a given moment in relation to the demand. Since from Article 2 there does not ensue

---

1362. The second case mentioned in the preceding note, *ibidem*.
1363. Appl. 7527/76, *X and Y v. United Kingdom*, *D & R* 11 (1978), p. 147 (150).
1364. The first case mentioned in note 1361, *ibidem*.
1365. In its decision on Appl. 5492/72, *X v. Austria*, *Coll.* 44 (1973), p. 63 (64), the Commission, too, seems to assume that in principle Art. 2 is also applicable to higher education, although in later decisions it holds that this provision primarily relates to elementary education; see *supra* note 1361. See also Appl. 6094/73, *Association X v. Sweden*, *D & R* 9 (1978), p. 5 (8): "Even assuming that Art. 2 of Protocol No. I is applicable in cases of education at university level".
1366. See the first case mentioned in the preceding note: the prohibition to take an examination after having failed twice does not conflict with Art. 2.
1367. Appl. 6598/74, *X v. Federal Republic of Germany*, not published. Art. 13(2)(c) of the International Covenant on Economic, Social and Cultural Rights speaks expressly of "on the basis of capacity". See also Appl. 8844/80, *X v. United Kingdom*, *D & R* 23 (1981), p. 228 (229), in which it was found compatible with Art. 2 of Protocol no. 1 that a person was not readmitted to the university because of the fact that he failed the first-year examination and had a poor attendance record.

the obligation to increase this availability, here again there is no question of violation of the Convention as long as no discrimination takes place in the admission.[1368] However, in our view things are different with respect to primary education. Denying a person the ability to receive primary education has such far-reaching consequences for the development of the person and for his chances to enjoy the rights and freedoms of the Convention to the full that such a treatment is contrary, if not to the letter of Article 2, at all events to the whole system of the Convention, in the light of which Article 2 has to be interpreted.

Although the right to education by its nature calls for regulation by the government, here again the general rule applies that this regulation may never be of such a nature and scope that the essence of the right[1369] is affected or one of the other rights and freedoms guaranteed by the Convention is violated as a result. This was confirmed by the Court in its judgment in the *Campbell and Cosans* Case. In this case the parents complained, *inter alia*, that their children were actually denied the right to education because they did not receive the guarantee that at the Scotch school in question no corporal punishment would be applied, while there was no alternative for them. Since the refusal of Jeffrey Cosans to accept that he should receive corporal punishment in a concrete case had resulted in suspension, and the requirement itself to submit to that kind of punishment conflicted with the parents' right laid down in the second sentence of Article 2, in the Court's opinion there was no longer any question of a reasonable regulation of access to education and the right to education had been violated.[1370]

2. Does the freedom of education also imply the freedom not to receive education? In other words: is a system of compulsory education contrary to Article 2? Article 2 relates to free access to and a certain degree of free choice of education, but does not seem to prohibit compulsory education in which sufficient scope is left to that freedom. And indeed, the Commission has adopted the view that

> it is clear that Article 2 of Protocol no. 1 implies a right for the State to establish compulsory schooling, be it in State schools or private tuition of a satisfactory standard, and that verification and enforcement of educational standards is an integral part of that right.

Therefore, the Commission concluded

> that to require the applicant parents to cooperate in the assessment of their children's educational standards by an education authority in order to ensure a certain level of literacy and numeracy, whilst, nevertheless, allowing them to educate their children at home, cannot be said to constitute a lack of respect for the applicant's rights under Article 2 of Protocol no. 1.[1371]

1368. *Cf.* the provision mentioned in the preceding note, in which a programme is laid down for general accessibility to secondary and higher education as well.
1369. For the question as to what this "essence" is, in our opinion the difference between elementary and other education has to be taken into consideration.
1370. Judgment of 25 February 1982, A.48 (1982), p. 19.
1371. Appl. 10233/83, *Family H. v. United Kingdom*, D & R 37 (1984), p. 105 (106).

It is interesting to see that here the Commission does not attach so much weight to the form of the (primary) education, but rather to the responsibility of the State for its result; a certain level of literacy and numeracy, leaving the rights of the parents unimpaired as much as possible. After all, even though compulsory education is not contrary to Article 2, it is limited by certain rights of the children and their parents, in particular the right to respect for their private lives.

3. The question has sometimes been raised whether the right to education only comprises the right to receive or also the right to provide for education; does it, for instance, include the right to provide for private education besides the existing public education?

Since the first sentence of Article 2 only refers to education, while the second sentence distinguishes between education and teaching, the above interpretation does not seem to have originally been intended. In its report in the *Kjeldsen, Busk Madsen and Pedersen* Case, however, the Commission took the view that also the right to "the establishment of and access to private schools or other means of education outside the public school system" fell under the provision of Article 2.[1372] And in its judgment in this case the Court, too, by reference to the *travaux préparatoires*, seems to have recognized that the freedom to provide for private education, though not expressly set forth in the formulation of Article 2, had been present to the minds of the drafters in the different phases of the drafting process, so that an interpretation which also covers this right is not excluded.[1373] Since in this case, however, it was not this right itself that was involved, but the question of whether the State has fulfilled its obligations under Article 2 if it respects this right, the Court could still remain vague on this point. The later Strasbourg case-law has not yet decided on the issue.[1374]

In any case the above-mentioned right does not follow from the second sentence of Article 2, because this provision refers to involvement of the government in education and does not necessarily assume the right to offer private education.

As no claim can be laid to State aid for education of any type under Article 2,[1375] this also applies to private education. However, if a certain type of education is subsidized, under Article 14 the government may not discriminate between public and private education. Whether discrimination in

---

1372. Report of 21 March 1975, B.21 (1975-76), p. 44. Alkema, *supra* note 8, p. 89, rightly submits that the Commission then also ought to revise its standpoint that legal persons cannot complain on their own account about violation of Art. 2, as it decided in the case of Appl. 3798/68, *Church of X v. United Kingdom*, Yearbook XII (1969), p. 306 (314). For this, see also *supra* pp. 404-405.
1373. Judgment of 7 December 1976, A.23 (1976), pp. 24-25.
1374. In the case of Appl. 3798/68, *supra* note 1372, it was not clear whether the individual applicants also included teachers.
1375. Judgment of 23 July 1968, *Belgian Linguistic Cases*, A.6 (1968), p. 31; followed by the Commission: Appl. 6853/74, *40 Mothers v. Sweden*, Yearbook XX (1977), p. 214 (238); Appl. 7527/76, *X and Y v. United Kingdom*, D & R 11 (1978), p. 147 (150) and Appl. 9461/81, *X and Y v. United Kingdom*, D & R 31 (1983), p. 210 (211).

the sense of Article 14 is involved in a case of difference in treatment is determined, *inter alia*, by the reasonableness of the motives for such a difference.[1376] Thus, in a situation where public education was subsidized 100 per cent and private education only 85 per cent, the Commission held that there was no question of discrimination because

> it is reasonable for the State, in relation to bodies that seek ownership and decisive control over management policy in voluntary schools, to require some degree of financial contribution.[1377]

4. The second sentence of Article 2 departs from the situation that those receiving education are minors. In fact, this provision does not concern the freedom of education of those receiving education, but the right of parents to ensure education for their children in conformity with their own religious and philosophical convictions.[1378]

What obligation does this right entail for the government? It creates obligations only if and in so far as the government is involved in education. As has already been stated above, an effective enjoyment of the freedom of education presupposes a certain amount of government activity in this field. Does the government have to create possibilities within the system of State-organized education for the religious and philosophical instruction desired by the parents, which then has to be organized in such a way that the other pupils of the school need not take part in it contrary to the wishes of their parents? Or has the government fulfilled its obligation if it leaves sufficient scope for this instruction on the initiative of private persons?

The latter was contended by the Danish Government before the Court in the *Kjeldsen, Busk Madsen and Pedersen* Case. In that case the Danish legislation was challenged which made sex education obligatory at public schools, as integrated with the teaching of other subjects, so that the parents could avoid such education for their children only by sending them to a private school. In general, the argument of the Danish Government was rejected by the Court. The second sentence of Article 2 refers to all activities of the government and consequently also implies an obligation concerning the organization of public education.[1379] At the same time, however, the Court stated that the fact that the State makes an essential contribution to the defrayment of the costs of private education must be taken into consideration when deciding whether the obligation ensuing from Article 2 has been fulfilled.[1380] It has not become clear in this case how much weight the Court is prepared to give to this aspect in a concrete case, since the Court here

---

1376. On this, *infra* pp. 541-547.
1377. Appl. 7782/77, *X v. United Kingdom*, D & R 14 (1979), p. 179 (182).
1378. The question as to who are to be considered in a concrete case as the parents of a minor is determined by national law; in this context awards of guardianship, adoptions and the like also have to be taken into account; see Appl. 7626/76, *X v. United Kingdom*, D & R 11 (1978), p. 160 (167-168).
1379. Judgment of 7 December 1976, A.23 (1976), p. 25. This point of view was followed by the Commission in its decision on Appl. 6853/74, *40 Mothers v. Sweden*, Yearbook XX (1977), p. 214 (238).
1380. *Ibidem.* See also Appl. 7782/77, *X v. United Kingdom*, D & R 14 (1979), p. 179 (181).

reached the conclusion that the obligatory sex education was of such a nature as not to conflict with the interests of the parents protected in Article 2.

In its report in the *Campbell and Cosans* Case, in regard to the argument advanced by the British Government that there existed private schools where the challenged punishment was not applied, the Commission took the position that this did not absolve the government from the obligation to respect at public schools the religious and philosophical conviction of the parents, while the fact that private schools asked a high financial contribution from the parents or such schools were situated at a great distance could render the alternative unrealistic.[1381] In contradiction with this opinion, in a later decision the Commission did away without any argument with the factor that the parents could not afford private education as an alternative.[1382]

The above-mentioned judgment in the *Kjeldsen, Busk Madsen and Pedersen* Case has produced two more clarifications as to the second sentence of Article 2. In the first place the Court rejected the submission of the Danish Government that this provision referred exclusively to specific religious instruction. According to the Court, in all education activities with which the government is concerned the right for the parents ensured in Article 2 has to be respected.[1383] Secondly, the Court clearly stated that the parents' views are not decisive for the question of whether the content of the instruction is in conformity with their religious and philosophical convictions, but that this question should be examined by reference to objective criteria. In this context the Court held first of all that the government is responsible for the curriculum and that, therefore, it is entitled to include in the teaching also the transmission of information of a directly or indirectly religious or philosophical kind, integrated with other subjects, since they will inevitably be implied in the subject-matter to be taught. Article 2 has been violated only if the transmission of ideas does not take place in an objective, critical and pluralistic way, but on the contrary assumes the character of indoctrination. The question of whether the latter was the case here, was examined independently by the Court; it took into account particularly the purpose of sex education, the content of the instruction to be given in that respect, the scope it leaves to supplementary advice to the parents in education and the possibility of taking action against abuse at a particular school or by a particular teacher.[1384]

The Court further held that the second sentence of Article 2 "aims in

---

1381. Report of 16 May 1980, B.42 (1985), pp. 38-39.
1382. Appls 10228/82 and 10229/82, *W & D.M. and M & H.I. v. United Kingdom*, D & R 37 (1984), p. 96 (100). See also its decision on Appl. 7527/76, *X and Y v. United Kingdom*, D & R 11 (1978), p. 147 (151), where the Commission took into consideration that the parents had been offered a place for their son at a Roman Catholic school in a neighbouring municipality.
1383. Judgment of 7 December 1976, A.23 (1976), p. 25.
1384. *Ibidem*, pp. 26-28. See also the Commission's decision on Appl. 6853/74, *40 Mothers v. Sweden*, Yearbook XX (1977), p. 214 (238-240), and on Appl. 7527/76, *X and Y v. United Kingdom*, D & R 11 (1978), p. 147 (151). Furthermore, see Appl. 8811/79, *Seven individuals v. Sweden*, D & R 29 (1982), p. 104 (116): reference to policy statements of a general character in official publications cannot be held to be indoctrination.

short at safeguarding the possibility of pluralism in education, which possibility is essential for the preservation of the 'democratic society' as conceived by the Convention" and that "in view of the power of the modern State, it is above all through State teaching that this aim must be realized".[1385] From the formulation of this aim itself ("essential") and from the general wording of the second sentence it follows that the pluralism referred to must also be ensured in private education, at least in so far as the government is concerned with it in one way or another via subsidies, inspection of schools, instructions with regard to the curriculum and the like. This does not mean that, for instance, religious instruction based on a particular religious conviction may not be provided at a private school, no more than that instruction in the State religion at a public school is contrary to Article 2. In such a case, however, the parents have the right to keep their children away from this instruction, and this instruction will therefore have to be organized in a way that makes this possible. In the case of integrated instruction, however, the requirement of pluralism always applies. Furthermore it follows from the relation between the first and the second sentence, as well as from the prohibition of discrimination in Article 14, that for the children concerned there must be an alternative which receives the same State aid.[1386] If at a reasonable distance schools are available where the religious instruction - or its absence - is more in conformity with the parents' convictions, they are nevertheless entitled to pluriformity in integrated education, but they cannot lay claim to separate instruction as an alternative for religious instruction at school.

Since Article 2 in principle also refers to secondary and higher education in so far as available, it will have to be assumed that the obligation on the part of the government to ensure pluriformity in religious and philosophical respects in providing for education applies also to adults asking for education. For this they may rely on the first sentence of Article 2, interpreted in the light of the whole of Article 2.

The meaning and tenor of the second sentence have been elucidated further in the *Campbell and Cosans* Case. First of all the Court, following the Commission, gave a wide interpretation to the words "philosophical convictions":

> Having regard to the Convention as a whole, including Article 17, the expression "philosophical convictions" in the present context denotes, in the Court's opinion, such convictions as are worthy of respect in a "democratic society" ... and are not incompatible with human dignity; in addition, they must not conflict with the fundamental right of a child to education, the whole of Article 2 being dominated by its first sentence.[1387]

1385. *Ibidem*, p. 25.
1386. See Appl. 4733/71, *X v. Sweden*, Yearbook XIV (1971), p. 664 (676), where a complaint about this was declared admissible, but was subsequently settled amicably.
1387. Judgment of 25 February 1982, A.48 (1982), p. 16. See also Appl. 8566/79, *X, Y and Z v. United Kingdom*, D & R 31 (1983), p. 50 (53). Cf. the definition of the Commission in its report of 16 May 1980, B.42 (1985), p. 37: "those ideas based on human knowledge and reasoning concerning the world, life, society, etc., which a person adopts and professes according to the dictates of his or her conscience. These ideas can more briefly be characterised as a person's outlook on life including, in particular, a concept of human
(continued...)

In that context and with respect to the objections submitted to corporal punishment, the Court held:

> The applicant's views relate to a weighty and substantial aspect of human life and behaviour, namely the integrity of the person, the propriety or otherwise of the infliction of corporal punishment and the exclusion of the distress which risk of such punishment entails. They are views which satisfy each of the various criteria listed above; it is this that distinguishes them from opinions that might be held on other methods of discipline or on discipline in general.[1388]

The Court also gave a definition of the words "education" and "teaching":

> the education of children is the whole process whereby, in any society, adults endeavour to transmit their beliefs, culture and other values to the young, whereas teaching or instruction refers in particular to the transmission of knowledge and to intellectual development.[1389]

On the basis of these definitions the submission of the British Government that discipline at school does not form a part of these concepts was rejected:

> it is ... an integral part of the process whereby a school seeks to achieve the object for which it was established, including the development and moulding of the character and mental powers of its pupils.[1390]

Further it was clearly established that, once the government has assumed responsibility for education, no distinction can be made between aspects of education falling under that responsibility and aspects not falling under it; certainly not where education at public schools is concerned. That responsibility therefore extends beyond the curriculum and also embraces the way in which discipline is maintained at the school, even though the government does not concern itself with such maintenance day by day.[1391]

Finally, the Court rejected the defence of the British Government that it fulfilled the obligation of Article 2, since it pursued a policy of gradual abolition of corporal punishment at schools. Referring to the *travaux préparatoires*, the Court held:

> As is confirmed by the fact that, in the course of the drafting of Article 2, the words "have regard to" were replaced by the word "respect" ..., the latter word means more than "acknowledge" or "take into account"; in addition to a primarily negative undertaking, it implies some positive obligation on the part of the State.[1392]

5. The broad definition of the word "education" by the Court in the *Campbell and Cosans* Case implies that the second sentence also applies to situations outside the framework of teaching institutions.

In the *Olsson* Case parents complained of a violation of that provision

---

1387.(...continued)
    behaviour in society". See also p. 36, where the Commission abandoned its much narrower interpretation in the *Belgian Linguistic* Cases that "philosophical opinions were added in order to cover agnostic opinions".
1388. *Ibidem*, p. 16. In order to be respected, those philosophical convictions must of course first have been brought to the attention of the authorities: See Appl. 8566/79, *X, Y and Z v. United Kingdom*, *D & R* 31 (1983), p. 50 (53).
1389. *Ibidem*, p. 14.
1390. *Ibidem*.
1391. *Ibidem*, p. 15.
1392. *Ibidem*, p. 17.

because their son Thomas had been placed in a foster family that belonged to a religious denomination and attended church with him, whereas they did not wish their children to receive a religious upbringing. The Commission first referred to its earlier case-law that in case of adoption or when the courts have removed a parent's right to custody, that parent no longer has the right to determine the child's education, since this is an integral part of the right to custody (and *a fortiori* of the rights of the adoptive parents). Whether Article 2 of Protocol no. 1 imposes on the public authorities an obligation not to transfer parental authority over a child to persons who do not share the convictions of the natural parents in matters of education, was expressly left open by the Commission.[1393] Next it held that a decision to take a child into care was of a different character and did not mean that the right to custody was removed from the parents. However, since a care order temporarily transfers certain parental rights to the public authorities, it is inevitable, according to the Commission, that the contents of the parent's rights in Article 2 of Protocol no. 1 must be reduced accordingly. On the other hand, the responsible authorities must, in the exercise of their rights under a care order, have due regard to these rights. In the case under consideration the Commission, followed by the Court, concluded that there were no serious indications that the applicants had, prior to the care order, been particularly concerned with giving their children a non-religious upbringing and that, moreover, there was no reason to believe that Thomas' religious education in the foster home would be in conflict with the education previously given by the applicants.[1394]

6. A foreigner cannot, by referring to Article 2, claim admittance to a contracting State in order to receive education there at one of the existing institutions, since only those who are already under the jurisdiction of the contracting State may derive rights from Article 2. If, however, Article 2 is interpreted to include the right to give instruction, this may imply that, for instance, a religious group established in the country may claim admittance for its members to attend a congress, a course of study, and the like, or may claim the admittance of a person who is specifically qualified to teach.[1395]

Can a foreigner challenge the refusal of an extension of his stay permit by referring to Article 2? This was done by fifteen foreign students in a complaint against the United Kingdom. The Commission, however, declared this complaint ill-founded, holding that the power of the States to decide for themselves who may reside in their territory is not limited by Article 2, unless

---

1393. Appl. 7626/76, *X v. United Kingdom, D & R* 11 (1978), p. 160 (167); Appl. 7911/77, *X v. Sweden, D & R* 12 (1978), p. 192 (194).
1394. Report of 2 December 1986, A.130 (1988), pp. 63-64; judgment of 24 March 1988, *ibidem*, p. 40.
1395. The Commission, however, rejected such a construction in its decision on Appl. 3798/68, *Church of X v. United Kingdom, Yearbook* XII (1969), p. 306 (320-322), but this after it had first taken the highly disputable view that an organization cannot derive an independent right from Art. 2; see *supra* p. 470 and note 1372.

perhaps in cases where extradition might result in the person concerned being deprived of any elementary education.[1396] Here again, therefore, as with respect to Articles 3, 8 and 12 of the Convention, the line has been followed that the situation outside the country in question must also be included in the assessment of a possible violation of the Convention.

As long as a foreigner resides legally in a contracting State, of course he also has the right to education. However, this does not imply the right to receive education in his own vernacular if that is not already offered by the State concerned; at all events not in the Court's interpretation that there exists only a right of access to the existing educational facilities.[1397] In the Court's opinion the interest in receiving education in one's own language or in the language of one's choice also is not protected in the second sentence of Article 2, because an interpretation of the terms religious and philosophical in that sense "would amount to a distortion of their ordinary and usual meaning", while according to the Court it is evident from the *travaux préparatoires* that this provision was not intended "to secure respect by the State of a right for parents to have education conducted in a language other than that of the country in question".[1398] The question remains whether in virtue of the first sentence of Article 2 it is not at least incumbent on the government to create additional facilities within the existing educational institutions for the benefit of those aliens having taken up residence in the territory for a considerable time who do not yet have sufficient command of the language in which education is conducted; otherwise the right to education will remain illusory for them for a long time. At least as regards elementary education, in our opinion this question should be answered in the affirmative on the same grounds as have been given above for minimum provisions for elementary education in general.[1399] And in any case, if certain facilities are created, they must not be discriminatory.

7. With regard to prisoners the question of the inherent limitations arises here again, since Article 2 does not contain an enumeration of restrictions. As has already been observed above, prisoners, too, are in principle entitled to make use of the existing educational facilities if this is compatible with the rationale of the detention on remand or the penalty of imprisonment, taking also into consideration changing views of penitentiary policy.[1400] Thus, correspondence courses or courses via radio and T.V., subject to the necessary security measures, must as a rule be permitted, as must also the purchase of books for purposes of study. But it follows from the negative formulation of Article 2 that the government is not obliged to defray the

---

1396. Appl. 7671/76 and fourteen other complaints, *15 foreign students v. United Kingdom*, D & R 9 (1978), p. 185 (186-187).
1397. See *supra* pp. 467-468.
1398. Judgment of 23 July 1968, *Belgian Linguistic Cases*, A.6 (1968), p. 32.
1399. *Supra* pp. 468-469.
1400. See *supra* p. 468.

costs.

8. As has been stated above with regard to Article 1 of Protocol no. 1, none of the rights included in this Protocol is to be considered as non-derogable.

9. The right to education is incorporated not in the Covenant on Civil and Political Rights, but in the Covenant on Economic, Social and Cultural Rights, *viz.* in Article 13. In the first paragraph of that article the right to education is formulated in a more positive way than is the case in Article 2 of the First Protocol. This is in conformity with its character in that treaty as a social right. The second paragraph sub (e) defines what obligation this entails for the States: an active policy with respect to the development of a system of schools at all levels, the establishment of an adequate fellowship system and continuous improvement of the material conditions of the teaching staff. Furthermore the first paragraph contains an enumeration of the aims of education.

The second paragraph provides that primary education shall be compulsory and available free to all, that secondary education in its different forms shall be made generally available and accessible to all, and that higher education shall be made equally accessible to all, on the basis of capacity. Both secondary and higher education have to be made progressively free. Further it is provided that fundamental education shall be encouraged or intensified for those who have not received or completed the whole period of their primary education.

Paragraph 3, which deals with the rights of parents (and guardians) with respect to the education of the children, has a character which differs from the corresponding provision in Article 2 of Protocol no. 1. It does not make a link with the activities of the public authorities concerning education, but only requires respect for the liberty of parents to choose private education for the children and to ensure the religious and moral education of their children in conformity with their own convictions. And in a separate fourth paragraph it is laid down that no part of the preceding paragraphs shall be construed so as to interfere with the liberty of individuals and bodies to establish and direct educational institutions, provided that the principles set forth in paragraph 1 are observed and such education conforms to such minimum standards as may be laid down by the State. The two latter provisions, which unlike the two preceding paragraphs, do not have a "programmatic" character, but lend themselves to direct application, ensure explicitly the freedom to give instruction, a freedom which can at best be inferred implicitly from Article 2.

§ 15. ARTICLE 3 OF PROTOCOL NO. 1: FREE ELECTIONS BY SECRET BALLOT

The High Contracting Parties undertake to hold free elections at reasonable intervals by secret ballot, under conditions which will ensure the free expression of the opinion of the people in the choice of the legislature.

1. The importance of Article 3 does not consist in the first place in the obligation of the States to hold free elections at reasonable intervals by secret ballot, but in the connection between those elections and the composition of the legislature. In fact, this means, as has been mentioned by the Commission in its report in the *Greek* Case, that Article 3

> presupposes the existence of a representative legislature, elected at reasonable intervals, as the basis of a democratic society.[1401]

Since such an important role has been assigned to the national legislature in ensuring the enjoyment of the rights and freedoms given in the Convention as well as in subjecting certain of these rights and freedoms to rules which may restrict their enjoyment, it is of eminent importance that this legislature should consist of democratically elected representatives of the holders of those rights and freedoms. Therefore, properly speaking, this Article 3 should have preceded the provisions of Section I of the Convention as a further elaboration of the concept of "effective political democracy" in the Preamble and of "democratic society" in various provisions of the Convention.[1402] The Court, too, in its first judgment with regard to Article 3 of Protocol no. 1 emphasized that "since it enshrines a characteristic principle of democracy, Article 3 of Protocol no. 1 is accordingly of prime importance in the Convention system".[1403]

2. With respect to both its formulation and its content, Article 3 forms an exception among the rights and freedoms laid down in the Convention and its Protocols. It is formulated neither as a right or freedom nor as an obligation for the national authorities to refrain from interfering with the exercise of a right or freedom, but as an undertaking on the part of the contracting States to *do* something.

What does that obligation imply for the States? From the text of Article 3 it follows that elections must be held at regular intervals, that those elections must be free, *i.e.* without any pressure as regards the choice, and that the secrecy of the votes cast must be safeguarded. Moreover, it follows from the word "choice" in Article 3 that there must be a real choice, which implies that the States must make possible the creation and functioning of political parties and must enable the latter - apart from the possible

---

1401. Report of 5 November 1969, *Yearbook XII; The Greek Case* (1969), p. 179.
1402. In that sense also Jacobs, *supra* note 17, p. 178.
1403. Judgment of 2 March 1987, *Mathieu-Mohin and Clerfayt*, A.113 (1987), p. 22.

applicability of Article 17[1404] - to present candidates for the elections.[1405] A one-party system imposed by the State, therefore, must be considered contrary to Article 3.[1406] And although Article 3 does not contain any concrete requirement as to the form of government of the contracting States and does not, for instance, prescribe the parliamentary form of government on the English model,[1407] it follows from the tenor of Article 3 that the legislative power must rest with the body constituted as a result of those free elections, and the possibility for the Head of State or Government to rule by decree without a parliamentary basis is contrary to that tenor.

Conditions for the admission of a group of persons as a political party to the elections have been considered permissible by the Commission if these conditions serve the purpose of guaranteeing the public character of the political process and of avoiding the confusion of the electorate by groups which cannot assume political responsibility, provided that they do not essentially interfere with free choice.[1408] Thus, the requirement of the production of a given number of signatures was considered justified, since groups standing any chance at all in the elections will easily be able to satisfy such a requirement, while groups evidently unable to bear political responsibility will thereby be excluded.[1409] In a later decision the Commission pursued this line further with respect to the requirement that an appeal against the way in which the elections have been conducted must be supported by a given number of signatures. The Commission reached this view

> having regard to the principles of a democratic society that the procedural rights related to the exercise of the right to stand as a candidate or to propose candidates, reflect the character of the elections as a public political process, and that these rights are accordingly circumscribed in such a way that they cannot be exercised by an individual acting alone, but only with the support of a certain minimum number of persons holding the same views.[1410]

The system according to which political parties are subsidized by the government on the basis of the results of the elections, too, was deemed permissible as a system which protects the parties from undue outside pressure and at the same time reflects the real importance of each of them.[1411]

1404. On Art. 17, see *infra* pp. 562-567.
1405. Report of 5 November 1969, *Yearbook* XII; *The Greek Case* (1969), p. 180. See also Appl. 7140/75, *X v. United Kingdom, D & R* 7 (1977), p. 95 (96).
1406. However, a guarantee of the right freely to offer political opposition, which occurred in the draft of the European Movement, was not included in the definite text; see Partsch, *supra* note 1340, pp. 241-243.
1407. Castberg, *supra* note 45, p. 181.
1408. Appl. 6850/74, *Association X, Y and Z v. Federal Republic of Germany, D & R* 5 (1976), p. 90 (93-94). For conditions in regard to the objectives of political parties, see the discussion of Art. 17, *infra* pp. 562-567.
1409. *Ibidem.*
1410. Appl. 8227/78, *X v. Federal Republic of Germany, D & R* 16 (1979), p. 179 (180-181).
1411. Appl. 6850/74, *supra* note 1408.

Both the constituency voting system of elections within a certain district,[1412] and the system of proportional representation[1413] are compatible with Article 3. The same will apply to a system of indirect elections, since the word "direct" does not appear in Article 3 and the people are able freely to express their opinion on the ultimate constitution of the legislature via such a system as well.[1414] In the same line it was held by the Court that Article 3 of Protocol no. 1 "does not create any obligation to introduce a specific system, ... such as proportional representation or majority voting with one or two ballots".[1415]

Once the people can participate in the composition of the legislature at regular intervals, the requirements set by Article 3 regarding participation in government have been satisfied. In particular this provision does not require that the people shall be consulted via referendum about certain legislative acts.[1416]

3. On the basis of the formulation of Article 3 as a government undertaking to do something, and not as an individual right, some authors have defended the position that this provision can only be the object of a complaint by a State and not of an individual complaint.[1417] The Commission never went so far, although its statement quoted above that the right of appeal against the way elections have been conducted is a right which "cannot be exercised by an individual acting alone"[1418] seems to go somewhat in the direction of also excluding a complaint by an individual.

At first the Commission drew from the text of Article 3 the general conclusion that this provision does not imply a right of the individual citizens to vote and to be elected. Exclusion from the franchise, not only of particular persons,[1419] but also of groups of persons,[1420] was therefore considered admissible by the Commission on that ground, be it under the condition that "such exclusion does not prevent the free expression of the opinion of the

---

1412. Thus concerning a complaint of a member of the British Liberal Party: Appl. 7140/75, *X v. United Kingdom, D & R* 7 (1977), p. 95 (96-97).
1413. Appl. 8364/78, *Lindsay v. United Kingdom, D & R* 15 (1979), p. 247 (251), with regard to a complaint about the electoral system of Northern Ireland in connection with the elections for the European Parliament. Thus also Appl. 8765/79, *The Liberal Party, Mrs. R & Mr. P v. United Kingdom, D & R* 21 (1981), p. 211 (223).
1414. That it was indeed intended not to exclude the system of indirect elections, appears also from the travaux préparatoires: Partsch, *supra* note 1340, p. 243.
1415. Judgment of 2 March 1987, *Mathieu-Mohin and Clerfayt,* A.113 (1987), p. 24.
1416. Appl. 6742/74, *X v. Federal Republic of Germany, D & R* 3 (1976), p. 98 (103), concerning the conclusion of a treaty.
1417. See, *e.g.,* Partsch, *supra* note 1340, pp. 243-244.
1418. See *supra* p. 479. In that context it is rather surprising that on the other hand the Commission still left open the question of whether a political party may be the victim of a violation of Art. 3: Appl. 8765/79, *The Liberal Party, Mrs. R & Mr. P v. United Kingdom, D & R* 21 (1981), p. 211 (223).
1419. Thus, *e.g.,* of a detainee: Appl. 530/59, *X v. the Netherlands, Yearbook* III (1960), p. 184 (190), and of a collaborator: Appl. 787/60, *X v. the Netherlands, Coll.* 7 (1962), p. 75 (79), and Appl. 6573/74, *X v. the Netherlands, D & R* 1 (1975), p. 87 (89-90).
1420. *E.g.* the exclusion of Belgian residents in Belgian Congo from the elections in Belgium: Appl. 1065/61, *X v. Belgium, Yearbook* IV (1961), p. 260 (268).

people in the choice of the legislature".[1421] This view of the Commission was corroborated to some extent by the *travaux préparatoires*: in fact, from the original draft the word "universal" was cancelled,[1422] from which it might be inferred that the drafters did not wish to include a guarantee for universal suffrage. In later decisions, however, the Commission took the position that the obligation imposed in Article 3 on the contracting States does imply "the recognition of universal suffrage".[1423] It added, however, that this did not mean that the right to take part in the elections was ensured to everyone without any restriction. In a decision of May 1975 the Commission clearly expressed its view in the following words:

> it follows both from the preamble and from Article 5 of the Protocol no. 1 that the rights set out in the Protocol are protected by the same guarantees as are contained in the Convention itself. It must, therefore, be admitted that, whatever the wording of Article 3, the right it confers is in the nature of an individual right, since this quality constitutes the very foundation of the whole Convention.[1424]

Repeating thereupon its position that Article 3 recognizes universal suffrage, the Commission concluded

> that Article 3 guarantees, in principle, the right to vote and the right to stand for election to the legislature.[1425]

Here again, however, the Commission emphasized that this does not mean that it is an absolute or unlimited right. From the words "under conditions which will ensure the free expression of the opinion of the people in the choice of the legislature" it inferred that the contracting States are allowed to impose certain restrictions on the right to vote and to be elected, provided that this is not done arbitrarily and does not constitute interference with the free expression of the people's opinion as such. It is for the Strasbourg organs to judge ultimately whether this condition has been fulfilled.[1426]

The Commission's view was endorsed by the Court in 1987. The Court held that

> the inter-State colouring of the wording of Article 3 does not reflect any difference of substance from the other substantive clauses of the Convention and Protocols. The reason for it would seem to lie rather in the desire to give greater solemnity to the commitment undertaken and in the fact that the primary obligation in the field concerned is not one of abstention or non-interference, as with the majority of the civil and political rights, but one of adoption by the State of positive measures to "hold" democratic elections.[1427]

The Court approved the Commission's interpretation of the right embodied in Article 3 as a subjective right of participation, but also recognized that there are implied limitations which leave the States a wide margin of appreciation in making the rights to vote and to stand for election subject to certain conditions. The Strasbourg organs have to satisfy themselves that these

---

1421. *Ibidem.*
1422. See Partsch, *supra* note 1340, p. 243.
1423. Appl. 2728/66, *X v. Federal Republic of Germany*, Yearbook X (1967), p. 336 (338).
1424. Appls. 6745 and 6746/74, *W, X, Y and Z v. Belgium*, Yearbook XVIII (1975), p. 236 (244).
1425. *Ibidem.*
1426. *Ibidem.*
1427. Judgment of 2 March 1987, *Mathieu-Mohin and Clerfayt*, A.113 (1987), pp. 22-23.

conditions do not curtail the rights in question to such an extent as to impair their very essence and deprive them of their effectiveness; that they are imposed in pursuit of a legitimate aim; and that the means employed are not disproportionate. In particular, such conditions must not thwart "the free expression of the opinion of the people in the choice of the legislature".[1428] Moreover, the Court emphasizes that the phrase "conditions which will ensure the free expression of the opinion of the people in the choice of the legislature"

> implies essentially - apart from freedom of expression (already protected under Article 10 of the Convention) - the principle of equality of treatment of all citizens in the exercise of their right to vote and their right to stand for election.[1429]

A touchstone for the admissibility of limitations of the right to vote will therefore have to be, besides the prohibition of arbitrariness, the question of whether the right to vote and to be elected has been conferred in a sufficiently wide and representative way to make it possible to speak of a free expression of the people's opinion as such. In addition, the restrictions have to be reviewed, in virtue of Article 5 of the First Protocol, for their conformity with the whole of the Convention, in particular with the prohibition of discrimination of Article 14. It is likely that the Commission's earlier view that the exclusion of citizens not residing in the country was justified,[1430] can also stand this new test; for the requirement of residence it advanced a number of grounds which appeared not unreasonable to it, while it considered justified the resulting difference in treatment between categories of citizens on the ground of the different situations in which they found themselves.[1431] The establishment of a minimum age for the exercise of the right to vote and to be elected in principle also fulfils the criteria indicated in the case-law.[1432] But when this limit is appreciably higher than is the case in most other member States of the Council of Europe, its reasonableness and the impact on the representative character of the elections will have to receive special attention.

In the *Mathieu-Mohin and Clerfayt* Case the Belgian 1980 Special Act was at issue, which required that candidates elected for the Flemish Council should take their parliamentary oath in Dutch. The applicants complained that this requirement prevented French-speaking electors from voting for a candidate who was likewise French-speaking. The Commission agreed that the Act had as an effect that a substantial minority in the district concerned could not have its own representatives on the Flemish Council and, therefore, constituted restrictions which were not compatible with Article 3 of Protocol no. 1, taken on its own. Having reached that conclusion, the Commission

---

1428. *Ibidem*, p. 23.
1429. *Ibidem*.
1430. See *supra* note 1420.
1431. See also Appl. 7566/76, *X v. United Kingdom*, D & R 9 (1978), p. 121 (122-123), and Appl. 8987/80, *X and Association Y v. Italy*, D & R 24 (1981), p. 192 (196).
1432. Appls 6745 and 6746/74, *W, X, Y and Z v. Belgium*, Yearbook XVIII (1975), p. 236 (244-246).

found it unnecessary to give its opinion on Article 14 of the Convention.[1433] The Court, by thirteen votes to five, reached a different conclusion. It attached great importance to the fact that the Act fitted into a general institutional system of the Belgian State, based on the territoriality principle, and was designed to achieve an equilibrium between the Kingdom's various regions and cultural communities by means of a complex pattern of checks and balances, and to defuse the language disputes in the country by establishing more stable and decentralized organizational structures. Against that background and given the State's margin of appreciation, the system - which was still incomplete and provisional - was not considered unreasonable by the Court. The fact that the French-speaking electors must vote either for candidates who will take the parliamentary oath in French and will accordingly join the French-language group in the (central) House of Representatives or the Senate and sit on the (regional) French Community Council, or else for candidates who will take the oath in Dutch and so belong to the Dutch-language group in the House of Representatives or the Senate and sit on the Flemish Council, was considered by the Court not to be a disproportionate limitation such as would thwart "the free expression of the opinion of the people in the choice of the legislature". For the same reason the Court held that there was no discrimination prejudicial to the applicants in violation of Article 14.[1434]

Denying the right to vote to women is contrary to the tenor of Article 3 as well as to the prohibition of discrimination.[1435] As to the restriction of the right to vote to the State's own nationals, this question is more difficult to answer. Article 16, which allows restriction of the political activities of aliens in certain cases, has not been related to Article 3 of the First Protocol. And the above-mentioned important role which has been assigned by the Convention to the legislature in ensuring and further regulating the enjoyment of the rights and freedoms points to an equal interest of aliens in the composition of the legislature in their host country, since Article 1 of the Convention confers the enjoyment of those rights and freedoms on them as well. On the other hand, restriction of the franchise to the State's own nationals is still fairly common, and was even more so at the time Article 3 was drafted, so that it is not very likely that the drafters wished to exclude such a system for the future.[1436] If they have intended to express this by the word "people", this is at all events inadequate; it can hardly be argued that those aliens who have been residents of a given country for a long time and as such contribute to the economic, social and cultural life of that country,

---

1433. Report of 15 March 1985, A.113 (1987), pp. 36-37.
1434. Judgment of 2 March 1987, A.113 (1987), pp. 24-26.
1435. See, with a reference to the situation in Switzerland, Jacobs, *supra* note 17, pp. 179-180, and Partsch, *supra* note 1340, p. 245. Switzerland, however, has not yet ratified the First Protocol.
1436. Thus impliedly also the Commission: Appl. 7566/76, *X v. United Kingdom, D & R* 9 (1978), p. 121 (122), and Appl. 7730/76, *X v. United Kingdom, D & R* 15 (1979), p. 137 (138).

without, for whatever reason, having been naturalized, do not belong to the "people" of that country. It is therefore not a matter of course to deny the franchise to them when one takes the principle of representative democracy, as laid down in Article 3, seriously. However, the discussions of granting the right to vote to aliens, in particular in local elections, are still in full progress, and this only in a few of the contracting States, so that it may hardly be expected that the Strasbourg case-law will force a break-through on this point.[1437]

Many legislations contain the provision that nationals can take part in elections in the country in question only if they also have residence in that country. The Commission considered this restriction as being in conformity with Article 3, and advanced the following justifications for such a restriction: (1) non-residents are less directly and continuously concerned with and less well informed on the day-by-day problems in that country; (2) candidates for the elections have less easy access to non-residents to present the different electoral issues so as to secure a free expression of opinion; (3) non-residents have less influence on the selection of candidates and the formulation of their electoral programmes; and (4) the correlation between the right to vote and the involvement in acts of the bodies elected is less.[1438] The fact that, on the other hand, in some countries nationals residing abroad who are working there in the service of their country do have the right to vote, does not in the Commission's opinion constitute discrimination in the sense of Article 14, because in view of their function they still keep a closer link with their country.[1439] Precisely in the light of the justifications for the residence requirement indicated by the Commission in the same decision, this argument does not appear quite convincing to us, because most of the reasons mentioned also apply to non-residents in public service. In the case of *X v. United Kingdom* the applicant, a resident of Jersey, complained about the fact that he could not participate in elections for the United Kingdom Parliament. Although this Parliament does have legislative competence with regard to Jersey (which it exercises occasionally) and residents of Jersey are therefore British subjects, they are not considered residents of the United Kingdom. Accordingly, they cannot participate in elections for Parliament. The Commission, after considering the specific constitutional relationship between Jersey and the United Kingdom and after considering that Jersey has its own elected legislature, concluded that there was no breach of the Article involved.[1440]

With regard to the right to vote of prisoners, whose invocation of Article

---

1437. However, the Commission has already referred expressly to those new developments: Appl. 7730/76, *X v. United Kingdom, D & R* 15 (1979), p. 137 (138).
1438. Appl. 7730/76, *X v. United Kingdom, D & R* 15 (1979), p. 137 (139). See also Appl. 7566/76, *X v. United Kingdom, D & R* 9 (1978), p. 121 (122), and with regard to the elections for the European Parliament, Appl. 8612/79, *X v. Alliance de Belges de la Communauté européenne, D & R* 15 (1979), p. 259 (264).
1439. Appl. 7730/76, *X v. United Kingdom, D & R* 15 (1979), p. 137 (139).
1440. Appl. 8873/80, *D & R* 28 (1982), p. 99 (104).

3 found no hearing under the old case-law of the Commission,[1441] it would seem to us that, if the law imposes as a penalty on a particular offence the (temporary) loss of the franchise, this is a restriction which fulfils the criteria indicated in the case-law, but that this is not the case with a general prohibition for prisoners to participate in elections, not as a punitive measure, but as a measure for maintaining order, and even less so when this is left to the discretion of the prison authorities. Since special regulations for the voting of prisoners can be made without difficulty, a general exclusion would amount to an exclusion of a group of the population which is insufficiently justified by their special status.

In the case of a Dutch conscientious objector, who complained about the general rule in the Netherlands that every prison sentence of more than one year always results in a suspension of the exercise of the right to vote for three years, the Commission concluded that, taking into account the legislator's margin of appreciation, such a measure does not go beyond the restrictions justifiable in the context of Article 3 of Protocol no. 1.[1442] In our opinion, in this case the way in which the Netherlands authorities have used the margin of appreciation leads to a disproportionate limitation such as thwarts the free expression of the opinion of the people in the sense of Article 3.

The right to stand for election to the legislature is also not unlimited. Here the same conditions apply as with regard to restrictions of the right to vote. In its decision on Appl. 10316/83, the Commission concluded that the condition that to be eligible one must not be a member of another legislature was not a restriction which was inconsistent with Article 3 of the Protocol.[1443]

In the *Mathieu-Mohin and Clerfayt* Case it was emphasized by the Court that any electoral system must be assessed in the light of the political evolution of the country concerned. In the Court's opinion it does not follow from Article 3 that all votes must necessarily have equal weight as regards the outcome of the election or that all candidates must have equal chances of victory. Thus no electoral system can eliminate 'wasted votes'".[1444]

4. What is meant in Article 3 by "legislature" (French: "corps législatif")? Does Article 3 relate only to the election of the highest legislative bodies in the contracting States,[1445] or of all bodies having legislative powers?

The Commission has taken the position that what is involved is in any case

1441. Appl. 530/59, *X v. the Netherlands*, Yearbook III (1960), p. 184 (188); Appl. 2728/66, *X v. Federal Republic of Germany*, Yearbook X (1967), p. 336 (338).
1442. Appl. 9914/82, *H v. the Netherlands*, D & R 33 (1983), p. 242 (245-246).
1443. Appl. 10316/83, *M v. United Kingdom*, D & R 37 (1984), p. 129 (133-134).
1444. Judgment of 2 March 1987, A.113 (1987), pp. 23-24. See also Appl. 8765/79, *the Liberal Party and Mrs. R & Mr. P v. United Kingdom*, D & R 21 (1981), p. 211 (224), and Appl. 8941/80, *X v. Iceland*, D & R 27 (1982), p. 145 (150).
1445. In its decision on Appl. 8364/78, *Lindsay v. United Kingdom*, D & R 15 (1979), p. 247 (251), the Commission expressly left open the possibility that Art. 3 also relates to international legislative bodies. See also Appl. 8612/79, *X v. Alliance de Belges de la Communauté européenne*, D & R 15 (1979), p. 259. In both cases the European Parliament was concerned.

the election of a body vested with legislative power and that the constitutional law of the contracting State in question is decisive in this respect. A body which can only propose bills, but cannot itself enact them, does not belong to the "legislature".[1446] The Commission has added the criterium that the legislative power has to be an autonomous power. With regard to bodies which have indeed legislative powers, but only by virtue of delegation by a superior legislator, and with regard to bodies whose legislative powers only concern a limited circle of persons, the obligation to hold free elections does not apply.[1447] The body concerned must, in that opinion, be the legislative body which derives its legislative powers directly from the written or unwritten constitution. Moreover, it will have to be the body that can really be identified as the "legislature", and not, for instance, also the Head of State, even though the passing of a bill depends on the latter's assent. It can hardly be assumed that the drafters wished to exclude the existence of a monarchy with hereditary succession to the throne for the Member States of the Council of Europe! However, as said above, this Head of State must then not have the power to take legislative measures by decree.

For those States which are a federation, such as the Federal Republic of Germany, Austria and Switzerland, the highest legislative bodies of the constituent states, too, will have to be considered as belonging to the "legislature", since they do not exercise their legislative powers by virtue of delegation by the federal legislator, but derive these powers directly from the federal constitution. In the *Mathieu-Mohin and Clerfayt* Case the Court indeed took the position that the word "legislature" does not necessarily mean only the national parliament. According to the Court, its meaning has to be interpreted in the light of the constitutional structure of the State in question. On that basis the Court held that the Flemish Council in Belgium was vested with competences and powers wide enough to make it a constituent part of the Belgian "legislature" in addition to the House of Representatives and the Senate.[1448] The criterion of the autonomous power is not mentioned by the Court and might in some cases be rather inflexible. In our opinion the reasoning used by the Court leaves enough scope for the thesis that also for countries like the Netherlands, a unitary State, the same applies with regard to the legislative bodies of the provinces and municipalities, which indeed also may be said to have been vested with competences and powers wide enough to make them also constituent parts of the legislature.[1449] If one

1446. Appls 6745 and 6746/74, *W, X, Y and Z v. Belgium*, Yearbook XVIII (1975), p. 236 (240-244).
1447. Appl. 5155/71, *X v. United Kingdom*, D & R 6 (1977), p. 13, and Appl. 9926/82, *X v. the Netherlands*, D & R 32 (1983), p. 274 (281).
1448. Judgment of 2 March 1987, A.113 (1987), p. 23.
1449. The question as to whether the Municipal Councils in the Netherlands are legislative bodies in the sense of Art. 3 was at issue in Appls 8348 and 8406/78, *Glimmerveen and Hagenbeek v. the Netherlands*, D & R 18 (1980), p. 187 (197), but could be passed over in silence by the Commission, because in its opinion Art. 17 of the Convention was applicable to the applicants. See also report of 15 March 1985, *Mathieu-Mohin and Clerfayt*, A.113 (1987), p. 34.

assumes - which in our opinion one should - that there is a connection between Article 3 and the guarantee incorporated in several articles of the Convention, that restrictions to be imposed on the enjoyment of rights and freedoms have to be "prescribed by law", this broad interpretation of the word "legislature" would also seem to follow from the broad interpretation in the case-law of the word "law" in the latter articles.[1450]

5. From the fact that Article 5 of the First Protocol does not contain a reference to Article 15(2) of the Convention it follows also for Article 3 that it does not belong to the provisions which are non-derogable.[1451] On the other hand it has been stated above that the principle of democratic representation in the legislative bodies forms one of the basic conditions for the effectiveness of the Convention. In the supervision of the application of Article 15, and particularly in the assessment of the necessity of the temporary derogation from this principle, this fundamental character should be taken into account very seriously. If the derogation is of a rather long duration, the question even arises whether the country in question does not lose by this very fact the basis of its membership in the Council of Europe.

6. Article 25 of the Covenant confers on citizens the right: (a) to take part in the conduct of public affairs, directly or through freely chosen representatives; (b) to vote and to be elected at genuine periodic elections which shall be by universal and equal suffrage, and shall be held by secret ballot; and (c) to have access, on general terms of equality, to public service in their country. These rights must be conferred on them "without unreasonable restrictions". It is obvious that this provision goes further than Article 3 of the First Protocol.

The right to take part in the conduct of public affairs, mentioned under (a), is not defined more precisely as to the kind of government bodies concerned. It will have to be assumed with the Committee of Experts that this provision refers only to "those organs of government which are normally elected in democratic States, particularly the legislature".[1452] If so, this provision would go a long way in the direction of Article 3.

The provision under (b), which forms a specific elaboration of the general principle laid down under (a), expressly confers the right to vote and to stand for election on the citizens of the State. It is formulated in a more positive way than Article 3 of the First Protocol, from which, as we have seen above, such a right can be inferred only indirectly. Article 25 confers this right on "every citizen", so that it thus also recognizes universal suffrage. It must,

---

1450. On this, *infra* pp. 579-581.
1451. See *supra* p. 466.
1452. Report of the Committee of Experts, *supra* note 14, p. 53. See also: United Nations General Assembly, *Annotations on the text of the draft International Covenant of Human Rights*, Doc. A/2929, p. 60, where it is stated that a proposal for universal suffrage with regard to "all organs of authority" was rejected on the ground "that in most countries not all organs of authority were elective".

however, be borne in mind that, as appears from the opening words of Article 25, it is guaranteed only that the rights mentioned are conferred "without unreasonable restrictions". In practice therefore this provision will not differ greatly from the "modern" Strasbourg view, to the effect that universal suffrage has been granted in principle, but that in individual cases restrictions may be imposed, provided that the free expression of the opinion of the people as such is not interfered with by it and there is no question of discrimination. The examples, mentioned above, of the requirement of a given minimum age or the requirement of domicile will in all probability not be regarded as "unreasonable restrictions". That the requirement of citizenship as a restriction is not prohibited by the Covenant follows already from the word "citizen".

The provision under (c) has no equivalent in the Convention. There again, on the ground of the words "without unreasonable restrictions", limitations connected with the nature of the function and the requirements for its discharge are admissible, provided that no discrimination takes place.[1453]

§ 16. ARTICLE 1 OF PROTOCOL NO. 4: PROHIBITION OF DEPRIVATION OF LIBERTY ON THE GROUND OF INABILITY TO FULFIL A CONTRACTUAL OBLIGATION

No one shall be deprived of his liberty merely on the ground of inability to fulfil a contractual obligation.

1. This provision contains a further restriction of the powers of the authorities to deprive a person of his liberty. As such it is closely related to Article 5 of the Convention and it specifically limits the possibility of deprivation of liberty mentioned in that article *sub* (1)(b) "for non-compliance with the lawful order of a court in order to secure the fulfilment of any obligation prescribed by law". In those States which have ratified the Fourth Protocol[1454] the courts will not be allowed to give such an order merely on the ground that the person in question is unable to pay a debt or to meet some other contractual obligation.

2. Article 1 speaks of "inability". If a debtor is able to pay, but refuses to do so, Article 1 does not exclude deprivation of liberty. Moreover, there is the word "merely". If a debtor acts in a fraudulent or malicious way, Article 1 does not bar his detention on that ground, even if it is established or it

---

1453. For the "case-law" of the Human Rights Committee concerning Article 25 reference is made to the Study by Nowak, mentioned *supra* at p. 216.
1454. See the survey on p. 3, note 5.

appears afterwards that he was unable to pay his debt.[1455] A person whose detention had been ordered by the court because, contrary to the law, he had refused at the request of the creditor to make an affidavit in respect of his property, was not therefore entitled to the protection of Article 1.[1456] In its report to the Committee of Ministers, the Committee of Experts gives the following examples of cases to which Article 1 does not apply: a person orders a meal at a restaurant, knowing that he is unable to pay; through negligence a person fails to supply goods when he is under a contract to do so; a debtor is preparing to leave the country to avoid meeting his commitments.[1457] If this interpretation of the word "merely" will be followed in the case-law the prohibition of Article 1 has only a very limited scope.

3. As to the question of whether the rights and freedoms are *non-derogable*, for the Fourth Protocol the same reasoning applies as that set out above with regard to the First Protocol: since Article 6(1) of the Fourth Protocol declares that all the provisions of the Convention are applicable and does not make any provision concerning an addition to the enumeration of Article 15(2), it must be assumed that under the circumstances and conditions referred to in Article 15(1) derogations from the provisions of the Fourth Protocol are possible.

4. The comparable provision in Article 11 of the Covenant employs the words "no one shall be imprisoned" where in Article 1 of Protocol no. 4 the wider formulation "no one shall be deprived of his liberty" has been chosen in order to cover also deprivations of liberty of short duration outside a prison.[1458] In this respect therefore the Convention confers wider protection. On the other hand, in virtue of Article 4(2) of the Covenant, the prohibition of Article 11 is *non-derogable*.[1459]

§ 17. ARTICLE 2 OF PROTOCOL NO. 4: THE RIGHT TO LIBERTY OF MOVEMENT WITHIN THE TERRITORY OF A CONTRACTING STATE, TO CHOOSE ONE'S RESIDENCE THERE, AND TO LEAVE IT

1. Everyone lawfully within the territory of a State shall, within that territory, have the right to liberty of movement and freedom to choose his residence.

1455. See the *Explanatory Reports on the Second to Fifth Protocols to the European Convention for the Protection of Human Rights and Fundamental Freedoms,* submitted by the Committee of Experts to the Committee of Ministers, H(71)11 (1971), pp. 39-40.
1456. Appl. 5025/71, *X v. Federal Republic of Germany, Yearbook* XIV (1971), p. 692 (696-698).
1457. See the Explanatory Reports mentioned in note 1455, p. 40.
1458. *Ibidem,* p. 38.
1459. For further details about Article 11 of the Covenant reference is made to the study by Nowak, mentioned *supra* p. 216.

2. Everyone shall be free to leave any country, including his own.

3. No restrictions shall be placed on the exercise of these rights other than such as are in accordance with law and are necessary in a democratic society in the interests of national security or public safety, for the maintenance of ordre public, for the prevention of crime, for the protection of health or morals, or for the protection of the rights and freedoms of others.

4. The rights set forth in paragraph 1 may also be subject, in particular areas, to restrictions imposed in accordance with law and justified by the public interest in a democratic society.

1. In the discussion of some of the other rights and freedoms, it has been pointed out above that the Convention does not provide for a general right to be admitted to the territory of the contracting States.[1460] The Fourth Protocol ensures such a right only to the nationals of the contracting State in question, *viz.* in Article 3, to be discussed below. Admission of aliens has so far been left by the Convention to the national legislation and national policy, provided that the rights and freedoms which *are* ensured in the Convention are respected.

This non-interference with the admission policy of the national authorities with regard to aliens is expressed in this Article 2 in the words "lawfully within the territory of a State" in the first paragraph. Indeed, without these words the national authorities would be prohibited from expelling an alien who has managed to enter the country illegally, on grounds other than those mentioned in the third and the fourth paragraph. It is precisely with a view to keeping the discretion of the national authorities in this respect as wide as possible that the word "legally" ("légalement") from the original draft was replaced by "lawfully" ("régulièrement").[1461]

Since Article 3 of this same Protocol contains the obligation to admit the State's own nationals and prohibits their expulsion, it follows from this that a national is always lawfully within the territory of his own State. It is rather curious that this consequence of Article 3 has not been explicitly stated in Article 2.

2. He who has been admitted to a given country is there lawfully only as long as he complies with the conditions under which he has been admitted. Thus, his presence becomes unlawful after the expiration of the period for which the stay permit applies, but also, for instance, when the person admitted no longer has sufficient means of livelihood, in violation of the conditions of admission made in that respect. These conditions, however, apart from the cases mentioned in the third and the fourth paragraph, must not relate to his freedom of movement itself in the country and his freedom to

---

1460. See *supra* pp. 236, 241, 269, 387 and 475-476.
1461. Explanatory Reports, *supra* note 1455, p. 40.

choose his residence there, since the first paragraph of Article 2 then would not contain any guarantee; indeed, a right the enjoyment of which completely depends on the discretion of the authorities is not a right, but only a favour.[1462]

The restrictions of the third paragraph of course also apply to those persons who have always had residence in the country and not only to these who have been admitted under certain conditions. Thus, with respect to a woman who was convicted of running a disorderly house or brothel, the ban imposed upon her to close down her business, which according to her complaint had as a consequence that she could no longer reside with her husband, was considered justified as a measure necessary for the prevention of crime and for the protection of health and morals.[1463]

3. The right to leave a country, conferred in the second paragraph, has not a very broad scope, because practically all conceivable motives for the authorities to refuse a person this right can be brought under the restrictions of the third paragraph.

Thus, the ground of "the maintenance of *ordre public*" or of "the prevention of crime" will be invoked against a person who is serving a term of imprisonment, who is detained on remand, or whose extradition has been decided on, if he should claim the right to leave the country.[1464] Indeed, one cannot seriously argue, on the ground that it is better to be rid of the person than to keep him in the country, that the refusal to let him go is not "necessary in a democratic society". The same grounds of the third paragraph may also justify measures which are aimed at preventing a person to leave the country, such as the requirement imposed upon an accused or convicted person to surrender his passport as a condition for provisional or conditional release.[1465]

The Committee of Experts, referring to the words "any country" ("n'importe quel pays"), has assigned a certain external effect to the second paragraph. Although of course only the contracting States are bound by this provision, it may have the consequence that a court, when it has to pronounce on the question of whether a person has lawfully left the territory of a non-contracting State, should decide that reference to the law of that State is authorised only in so far as that law does not prejudice the principle of freedom to leave a country.[1466]

1462. In approximately the same sense: Jacobs, *supra* note 17, p. 184. In a different sense, however, the Committee of Experts, Explanatory Reports, *supra* note 1455, p. 41, where these conditions are mentioned as examples of possible conditions.
1463. Appl. 8901/80, *X v. Belgium*, D & R 23 (1981), p. 237 (243).
1464. See Appls 3962/69, 4256/69, 4436/70 and 7680/76, all of them directed against the Federal Republic of Germany: *Yearbook* XIII (1970), p. 688 (690); *Coll.* 37 (1971), p. 67 (68-69); *Yearbook* XIII (1970), p. 1028 (1032-1034); *D & R* 9 (1978), p. 190 (193). See also Appl. 8988/80, *X v. Belgium*, D & R 24 (1981), p. 198 (204): forbidding a bankrupt from absenting himself was considered necessary for the maintenance of "ordre public" and for the protection of the rights and freedoms of others.
1465. Appl. 10307/83, *M. v. Federal Republic of Germany*, D & R 37 (1984), p. 113 (118-119).
1466. Explanatory Reports, *supra* note 1455, p. 42.

4. Besides the grounds of restrictions in the third paragraph, which do not differ from the "usual" list and for which reference is made here to their general discussion,[1467] in the fourth paragraph a special ground for restricting the rights conferred in the first paragraph has been included: the public interest in a democratic society. Restrictions which are justified on this ground are to be imposed in particular areas.

This restriction has been the subject of a good deal of discussion within the Committee of Experts, as is evident from its report.[1468] It was intended to make possible restrictions which serve the public interest of the country in situations where it cannot be clearly established that the *ordre public* is also involved. Although the majority of the Committee was opposed to the express inclusion of "economic welfare" as a ground of restriction, the chosen formulation "in the public interest" is so wide that the economic welfare of society as a motive for the imposition of restrictions does not appear to be excluded by it. In our opinion the grant of a housing licence only to those who have an economic link with the municipality in question might be justified on that ground, and so might, for instance, the transfer of government departments, with the obligation for those employed by those departments to move, on penalty of loss of their function. The scope of application or the ground of application of the restrictive measures, however, will have to be localized, according to the text of the fourth paragraph, within particular areas - *e.g.* areas with an extraordinary dense population or with a high unemployment rate -, and consequently must not apply to the country as a whole. Furthermore, of course, here again no discrimination is permitted in the application of the restrictions.

The restriction here mentioned does not apply to the freedom to leave the country, regulated in the second paragraph. A contracting State may not therefore prohibit emigration, in the public interest, on purely economic grounds, *e.g.* in order to prevent brain drain.

5. Article 5(4) of the Fourth Protocol provides that, if a contracting State has also declared the Protocol to be applicable to any territory for whose foreign relations it is responsible, this territory and the territory of the contracting State to which the Protocol already applies by virtue of the ratification itself shall be treated as separate territories for the application of Article 2. Thus, for instance, although the Fourth Protocol has been declared applicable by the Netherlands to the Netherlands Antilles, one cannot derive from the right to stay and choose residence in the Netherlands Antilles any right to stay, to freely move and to choose residence in the Netherlands, and *vice versa*.

1467. *Infra* pp. 573-606.
1468. Explanatory Report, *supra* note 1455, pp. 43-46.

6. As has been said, none of the rights mentioned in the Fourth Protocol is *non-derogable*.[1469]

7. The formulation of the first two paragraphs of Article 12 of the Covenant is identical in the English text with that of the first two paragraphs of Article 2 of the Fourth Protocol. The first paragraph of the French text, however, uses the term "légalement" instead of "régulièrement", which, as stated above, might mean that the Covenant leaves a little less scope for discretion on the part of the national authorities.[1470]

The Covenant does not contain a provision like that laid down in Article 5(4) of the Fourth Protocol to the effect that territories which have been brought by a contracting State under the application of the Covenant are to be regarded as separate territories for the application of Article 12. The Netherlands, however, when ratifying the Covenant, made the reservation that for the application of paragraphs 2 and 4 the Netherlands and the Netherlands Antilles are to be regarded as separate countries. The United Kingdom did the same in relation to each of the territories comprising the United Kingdom and its dependencies.[1471]

The third and fourth paragraphs of Article 2 of Protocol no. 4 contain a number of restrictions which do not occur in the corresponding third paragraph of Article 12 of the Covenant. As the Committee of Experts rightly observes, this need not imply that the Covenant offers wider protection. In fact, it is quite conceivable that the words "necessary to protect ... public order (*ordre public*)" may be interpreted within the context of the Covenant in the sense that the restrictions not expressly mentioned will be deemed also to be covered thereby.[1472] It is certainly not impossible that this applies also to the restriction included in Article 2(4) of the Protocol, although this is precisely intended to provide for cases which in the opinion of the majority of the Committee of Experts could not be brought under the term "ordre public".[1473]

The Covenant speaks of "necessary" without the addition of "in a democratic society". For the Council of Europe the term democratic as a condition for membership has a very special meaning, which it does not have within the world community of States. However, considering the as yet not very autonomous role played by the condition "necessary in a democratic society" as touchstone in the Strasbourg case-law,[1474] this difference will be

---

1469. See *supra* p. 489.
1470. The Report of the Committee of Expert, *supra* note 14, p. 33, states that "this is a divergence in form, which does not represent a difference in substance". The fact that in its Explanatory Reports the Committee had attached certain consequences to this terminology with regard to Article 2 is not even mentioned there at all.
1471. See United Nations, *Human Rights; Status of International Instruments*, New York 1987, p. 41 and pp. 47-48 respectively.
1472. Report of the Committee of Experts, *supra* note 14, p. 34.
1473. *Supra* p. 492.
1474. On this, *infra* pp. 583-606.

found not to be very relevant in practice.[1475]

§ 18. ARTICLE 3 OF PROTOCOL NO. 4: PROHIBITION OF EXPULSION OF NATIONALS; THE RIGHT OF NATIONALS TO BE ADMITTED TO THEIR OWN COUNTRY

1. No one shall be expelled, by means either of an individual or of a collective measure, from the territory of the State of which he is a national.
2. No one shall be deprived of the right to enter the territory of the State of which he is a national.

1. Although the term expulsion is generally used in connection with aliens and *not* with the State's own nationals, the drafters of Article 3 preferred the word "expelled" to "exiled", because exile is a word pregnant with meaning, which might raise many interpretation problems. It is not only exile as a penalty or as a political measure which is prohibited by Article 3, but any expulsion of a national from the territory.

According to a definition given by the Commission, expulsion is involved when "a person is obliged permanently to leave the territory of the State ... without being left the possibility of returning later".[1476] The words "permanently" and "without being left the possibility of returning later" in this definition evidently serve to support the decision of the Commission that extradition does not fall under the concept of expulsion, and consequently not under the prohibition of Article 3 either.[1477] For its point of view the Commission could rely on the *travaux préparatoires*. In fact, in its report to the Committee of Ministers, the Committee of Experts had held: "It was understood that extradition was outside the scope of this paragraph".[1478] This does raise the question why the drafters did not bring out this intention somewhat more clearly in the formulation of Article 3. As this provision is now worded, from a wide interpretation of the word "expelled" one might conclude that a national enjoys protection against any measure according to which he has to leave his country under compulsion; in fact, in its report the Committee of Experts itself puts on the word "expel" the very wide interpretation of "to drive away from a place".[1479]

1475. For more details concerning Art. 12 of the Covenant reference is made to the study by Nowak, mentioned *supra* p. 216.
1476. Appl. 6189/73, *X v. Federal Republic of Germany*, *Coll.* 46 (1974), p. 214.
1477. *Ibidem*. Two weeks later, in its decision on Appl. 6242/73, *Brückmann v. Federal Republic of Germany*, *Yearbook* XVII (1974), p. 458 (478), the Commission took the same position with the following definition of the two concepts: "Expulsion is the execution of an order to leave the country, while extradition means the transfer of a person from one jurisdiction to another for the purpose of his standing trial or for the execution of a sentence imposed upon him".
1478. Explanatory Reports, *supra* note 1455, p. 47.
1479. *Ibidem*.

However this may be, one can hardly agree with Jacobs that the text of Article 3 is "clear and unambiguous" in prohibiting extradition as well, so that the *travaux préparatoires* are not longer relevant to the interpretation.[1480] On the one hand the curious use of the term expulsion with regard to nationals and on the other hand the unmistakable difference between expulsion and extradition in a juridical sense make the article anything but clear. For that reason any indications inferred from its genesis are of particularly great importance. Moreover, one may wonder whether the interpretation of Jacobs is at all desirable, now that it does not follow imperatively from the text of Article 3. In our opinion the system chosen in the European Convention on Extradition is to be preferred, according to which a State is not *prohibited* from extraditing its nationals, but it is *allowed* to refuse such extradition.[1481] Thus, under international law the difference in treatment between nationals and aliens is reduced, while it leaves open the possibility for the national authorities to consider the nature and circumstances of the concrete case before deciding on the extradition.

Here again one may recall that it has been recognized in the case-law that extradition - of aliens as well as of nationals - may constitute a violation of one of the other rights and freedoms, specifically of the prohibition of inhuman treatment and of the right to respect of family life.[1482]

2. The second paragraph of Article 3, which contains without any restriction the right to be admitted to the State of which one is a national, would confront in particular the United Kingdom with serious problems, since numerous people outside the United Kingdom, particularly in the Commonwealth countries, have acquired British nationality by birth. However, the United Kingdom has not ratified Protocol no. 4. This does not alter the fact that, if that country, in admitting people having its nationality, should discriminate with respect to a particular racial group, it could still come into conflict with its obligations under the Convention; not under Article 14, which in that case indeed could only have been violated in conjunction with Article 3 of the Fourth Protocol, but because such discrimination may constitute a degrading treatment in the sense of Article 3 of the Convention.[1483]

3. With respect to the inhabitants of colonies and other territories for whose international relations a contracting State is responsible, the Protocol itself already provides for a possibility of avoiding certain consequences in case of ratification. And this in connection with the first as well as the second paragraph of Article 3. First of all, in case of ratification States may indicate under Article 5 to what extent they also wish this Protocol to apply to these

---

1480. Jacobs, *supra* note 17, p. 185, with a reference to the rule of interpretation laid down in Art. 32 of the Vienna Convention on the Law of Treaties.
1481. *European Treaty Series* No. 24, Art. 6(1).
1482. *Supra* pp. 236-240 and 386-389.
1483. *Supra* p. 240.

territories; this, therefore, irrespective of the extent to which they have declared the Convention itself applicable. Thus, they are able to declare that some articles of the Protocol are applicable to these territories and others are not. Moreover the fourth paragraph of Article 5 provides in relation to Article 3 that where there is a reference to "the territory of a State", the territory of the contracting State itself and these territories are treated as separate territories.

4. In its Explanatory Reports the Committee of Experts states that the proposal to include the word "arbitrarily" in the second paragraph, in accordance with Article 12(4) of the Covenant, was expressly rejected, but that the members of the Committee were agreed that the right of the national to be admitted to his State does not confer on him an absolute right to stay within that State. The report gives the example of a national who, after first having been extradited to another country, takes refuge again in his own State, and of a national who, after having served in the army of another State, wishes to return to his own country.[1484]

These examples, however, seem to indicate that the Committee is raising a fictitious problem here. Indeed, in those cases the absolute character of the right of Article 3(2) is not affected, but in the first example the State has the right to decide to extradite the person again, and in the second example it has the right to impose on service in the army of another State the sanction of forfeiture of nationality and of the rights associated with it.

5. Can a State actually evade its obligations under Article 3 by depriving a person of his nationality? In principle the Convention leaves it to the States to regulate the acquisition and the loss of nationality; a right to a nationality, such as it is incorporated in Article 15 of the Universal Declaration of Human Rights, does not form part of the rights and freedoms laid down in the Convention. However, if a person can be deprived of his nationality for the sole purpose of his expulsion or refusal to admit him, the protection of Article 3 may be rendered illusory.

It appears from the Explanatory Reports that the Committee of Experts was aware of this problem, but that it rejected a proposal to include in Article 3 a provision according to which "a State would be forbidden to deprive a national of his nationality for the purpose of expelling him". Although the Committee stated that it approved of the underlying principle, the majority thought "it was inadvisable in Article 3 to touch on the delicate question of the legitimacy of measures depriving individuals of nationality".[1485]

This does not answer the above question, for even though in its generality Article 3 leaves intact the right of the State to decide to whom it will grant its nationality and whom it will deprive of it, still such a decision by the

---

1484. Explanatory Reports, *supra* note 1455, pp. 48-49.
1485. *Ibidem*, pp. 47-48.

national authorities in a given case may involve a violation of that article. Thus, with regard to a refusal of nationality combined with an order of expulsion it was expressly recognized by the Commission that the link between the two decisions could create the presumption that the refusal of nationality had the mere purpose of making the expulsion possible.[1486] Indeed, a measure of the national authorities which has as its sole object evasion of an obligation under the Convention is equivalent to a violation of that provision. A rule to that effect forms an essential requirement for an effective maintenance of the Convention and is also in conformity with the rationale underlying Article 17. However, it can be assumed only in very evident cases that the national authorities actually intended *exclusively* to evade the operation of the Convention by their measure. In the above-mentioned decision the Commission in fact adopted the view that in this case nothing justified such a conclusion.[1487]

6. To Article 3 again the above statement applies that the rights incorporated in the Fourth Protocol are not *non-derogable*.[1488]

7. The Covenant does not contain any separate provision concerning the expulsion of the State's own nationals. Article 13 deals with the expulsion of aliens and will be discussed below in comparison with Article 4 of Protocol no. 4.

The right of Article 3(2) is regulated in the Covenant in Article 12(4), with the difference that there the formulation is "to enter his own country" instead of "to enter the territory of the State of which he is a national". This is not a matter of a less accurate formulation, but the result of a specific amendment by States who found the formula used in the Convention unsatisfactory, because it excluded the right of return for persons who were not nationals but who had established their home in the country.[1489] The Committee of Experts, therefore, rightly suggests that Article 12(4) may also apply to stateless people and nationals of another State who have very close relations with the country in question.[1490]

The Covenant does not contain a provision comparable to Article 5(4) to the effect that territories which have been placed by a contracting State under the applicability of the Covenant may be regarded as separate territories for the application of Article 12(4). However, the Netherlands, when ratifying the Covenant and declaring it applicable also to the Netherlands Antilles, made the reservation that the Netherlands will apply Article 12(4) in the sense that the Netherlands and the Netherlands Antilles are to be regarded as separate

---

1486. Appl. 3745/68, *X v. Federal Republic of Germany, Coll.* 31 (1970), p. 107 (110).
1487. *Ibidem*, p. 111.
1488. See *supra* p. 489.
1489. See United Nations General Assembly, *Annotations on the text of the draft International Covenants on Human Rights,* Doc. A/2929, New York 1955, p. 39.
1490. Report of the Committee of Experts, *supra* note 14, p. 35.

countries.[1491]

Article 12(4) of the Covenant contains the word "arbitrarily", which was expressly cancelled from the draft of Article 3(2). It is evident that the latter provision thus provides a wider guarantee than its counterpart in the Covenant.[1492]

§ 19. ARTICLE 4 OF PROTOCOL NO. 4: PROHIBITION OF COLLECTIVE EXPULSION OF ALIENS

Collective expulsion of aliens is prohibited.

1. This provision prohibits only the *collective* expulsion of aliens, but this without any possibility of restriction outside the case of Article 15. Besides the general prohibition of expulsion of a State's own nationals as laid down in the above-mentioned Article 3, the Consultative Assembly had wished to make the expulsion of aliens in this article subject to stringent conditions. According to its draft, expulsion of an alien lawfully residing in a contracting State would be permitted only on the ground of danger to national security or violation of the *ordre public* or morality. However, the Committee of Experts did not adopt this part of the draft and proposed an entirely new provision, referring exclusively to collective expulsion.[1493]

The first argument advanced by the Committee was that the subject-matter brought up in the draft of the Consultative Assembly had already been regulated in the European Convention on Establishment of 1955.[1494] Against this, however, it may at once be argued that this renders regulation in the Fourth Protocol by no means superfluous, since the Establishment Convention confers protection only on the nationals of the other States parties to that Convention and not, as would be the case in the proposal of the Consultative Assembly, on *all* aliens residing in one of the contracting States. Moreover, the Establishment Convention lacks an international supervisory procedure as provided for in the Convention. And since the text of the draft of the Consultative Assembly was almost identical with that of the Establishment Convention, there was no reason to fear that those contracting States, which have also ratified the Establishment Convention, would have to confer, via the operation of Articles 14 and 60 of the Human Rights Convention, on these "other" aliens (i.e. those aliens who are not nationals of one of the other parties to the Establishment Convention) a more far-reaching protection than that which Article 4 of the Fourth Protocol itself would oblige them to

---

1491. The United Kingdom made a reservation of a more general character in regard to its dependent territories. *Supra* note 1471, *ibidem.*
1492. For more details on Article 12 of the Covenant reference is made to the study of Nowak, mentioned *supra* p. 216.
1493. Explanatory Reports, *supra* note 1455, p. 50.
1494. *Ibidem.* The Convention has been published in *European Treaty Series*, No. 19.

confer.[1495]

The second argument put forward in favour of the cancellation - and the one which was no doubt decisive - is that the majority of the Committee did not wish to restrict the grounds for expulsion and did not wish the motives which induce a State in each individual case to expel an alien, to be subjected to international supervision.[1496]

Meanwhile the Seventh Protocol has been entered into force on 1 November 1988. Article 1 provides for certain procedural guarantees in the case of expulsion of individual aliens who are lawfully resident in the territory of a contracting State. The provision will be discussed separately hereafter.

2. Even in its ultimate formulation Article 4 is not entirely devoid of importance, considering such practices, also existing within countries of the Council of Europe, as the expulsion of groups of gypsies seeking a camp or groups of migrant workers seeking employment.

The effect of Article 4 depends largely on the interpretation that is put on the word "collective". Is this to refer to expulsion of *all* aliens residing in a given State or at least of all aliens *of one particular nationality*? Or is there also question of collective expulsion if a number of people within one of those groups or any number of aliens is concerned? The first-mentioned interpretation would render Article 4 almost completely devoid of any importance. Collective expulsion of all aliens, also of those who are lawfully in a country, would, if any country should ever be able or wish to do so, only take place in very urgent and exceptional circumstances; and in those very circumstances Article 15 of the Convention would most likely deprive Article 4 of its protective effect. The same will usually apply if there are reasons for expelling all aliens of a particular nationality indiscriminately. It has therefore to be assumed that the contracting States did not mean to restrict Article 4 to these very exceptional cases of collective expulsion, but wanted to prohibit any expulsion of aliens *as a group*.

Even then, however, the question of what exactly distinguishes the expulsion of a group of aliens from the expulsion of a number of individual aliens has not yet been answered. How large must such a group be? Is the expulsion of an entire family to be considered a collective expulsion? And is this true, for instance, for the expulsion of a musical society consisting of foreigners? If so, why then do such "groups" deserve more protection than a foreigner who lives on his own or an individual foreign musician? This problem can be solved only if one uses neither the number of which the group consists nor the link knitting together the members of that group as the decisive criterion for the application of Article 4, but the *procedure* followed in the expulsion. If a person is expelled along with others without his case having received an individual treatment, his expulsion is a case of collective

---

1495. This fear is advanced as a possible argument by Jacobs, *supra* note 17, p. 187.
1496. Explanatory Reports, *supra* note 1455, pp. 50-51.

expulsion.

This seems also to be the view of the Commission. In its opinion there is no question of collective expulsion if the decision of expulsion is based on "particular circumstances relating to each of the applicants as individuals".[1497] In a later decision, moreover, the Commission made that individual treatment dependent on certain minimum conditions by giving the following definition of "collective expulsion of aliens":

> any measure of the competent authorities compelling aliens as a group to leave the country, except where such a measure is taken after and on the basis of a reasonable and objective examination of the particular cases of each individual alien of the group.[1498]

At first sight it would appear as if here the Commission has introduced a restriction to the absolutely formulated prohibition of Article 4, since Article 4 does not make any exception for cases where an examination such as that mentioned in the definition by the Commission has taken place with regard to each member of the group. However, this is not really the case. In fact, the national authorities can always evade the absolute prohibition of Article 4 by following a procedure in which there is no question of a *collective* expulsion in the proper sense. In its decision the Commission precisely indicates that a pure formality is not enough for evading Article 4, but that an objective examination must be involved, in which a reasonable weighing takes place between the interests of each individual separately and the interest envisaged by the authorities with the expulsion. The Commission therefore in fact introduces certain minimum procedural guarantees, although a proposal to that effect had been expressly rejected by the Committee of Experts.[1499]

The definition of the Commission, however much it may have to be welcomed *per se*, raises the problem that for the expulsion of an alien who forms part of a particular group certain requirements are made for the examination underlying that expulsion, which were not prescribed for the expulsion of other aliens. Therefore, the issue remains as to when there is question of a group and why a group deserves more protection than an individual. In our opinion, a satisfactory solution is reached only if it is assumed that any expulsion of an alien as an alien, without an objective examination having been made of his individual situation and interests, in fact is part of a prohibited collective expulsion, irrespective of whether his expulsion in actual fact is or is not accompanied by the expulsion of other aliens in a comparable situation. It must be admitted, however, that thus the word "collective" is interpreted in a rather improper sense which seems to be contrary to the genesis of Article 4. As was mentioned above, the Convention has now been complemented with a Seventh Protocol, stipulating in Article

---

1497. Appls 3803 and 3804/68, *X and Y v. Sweden*, not published. The Commission is not very clear in its decision on Appl. 7704/76, *Kalderas Gypsies v. Federal Republic of Germany*, not published: "although the applicants act as a group, or rather as two groups, the official processing of the matter also shows several individual variations within these groups".
1498. Appl. 7011/75, *Becker v. Denmark*, Yearbook XIX (1976), p. 416 (454) concerning the refusal of entry visas and stay permits to a group of Vietnamese children.
1499. See *supra* p. 497.

1 minimum procedural rights for aliens lawfully within a contracting State, who are confronted with expulsion. However, the Seventh Protocol has not yet been ratified by all the States which have ratified the Fourth Protocol, so that the issues raised above still remain valid for the situation in the latter States.

Here again it has to be pointed out that the expulsion of aliens may also constitute a violation of the Convention on other grounds. One may think in particular of those cases in which the consequences of the expulsion are such that it entails an inhuman treatment contrary to Article 3 or a severance of family ties contrary to Article 8.[1500]

3. As has already been alluded to above, Article 4 is not *non-derogable* on the ground of the argumentation given above for the whole of the Fourth Protocol.[1501]

4. In contrast with Article 4 of the Fourth Protocol, Article 13 of the Covenant contains general guarantees with regard to the expulsion of aliens. Unlike the proposal of the Consultative Assembly in its draft for Article 4 and also unlike the provisions in the European Convention on Establishment, these guarantees do not concern the grounds on which, but the procedure by which expulsion may be proceeded to. The decision must have been reached in accordance with law, and the person concerned must be allowed to submit the reasons against his expulsion and to have his case reviewed by the competent authority or by a person or persons especially designated by the competent authority for that purpose.

These guarantees are less far-reaching than the requirements made by the Commission for the examination of the individual cases of a group. Indeed, the assessment of whether the decision has a reasonable foundation leaves the international supervisory organ greater scope than the assessment of whether the decision is in accordance with law, in those cases where a review by a competent authority does not in itself guarantee objectivity. On the other hand, the Covenant offers these guarantees for any case of expulsion of an alien, irrespective of whether it is a case of individual or collective expulsion.

Article 1 of the Seventh Protocol contains a number of procedural guarantees for aliens lawfully in the territory of a contracting State who are threatened to be expelled. The adoption of this provision has brought the Convention more or less up to the level of the Covenant in this respect.[1502]

1500. See *supra* pp. 236-240 and 389-390 respectively.
1501. See *supra* p. 489.
1502. See *infra* pp. 503-508. For more detailed information on Art. 13 reference is made to the study by Nowak, mentioned *supra* p. 216.

§ 20. ARTICLE 1 OF PROTOCOL NO. 6: ABOLITION OF DEATH PENALTY

The death penalty shall be abolished. No one shall be condemned to such penalty or executed.

1. The abolition of the death penalty has since long been a matter of concern in- and outside the Council of Europe. As early as 1957, the European Committee on Crime Problems studied the problem of capital punishment in the States of Europe. The Parliamentary Assembly also regularly dealt with this question. In 1980 it adopted two resolutions, in which on the one hand it appealed to national parliaments to abolish capital punishment from their penal systems, if they had not already done so,[1503] and on the other hand called upon the Committee of Ministers to "amend Article 2 of the European Convention on Human Rights to bring it into line with Resolution 727".[1504] In December 1982, the Committee of Ministers adopted the text of draft Protocol no. 6, prepared by the Steering Committee for Human Rights, and opened it for signature and ratification by the Member States of the Council of Europe on 28 April 1983. The Protocol entered into force on 1 March 1985, after it had received five ratifications.[1505]

2. Article 1 of the Protocol must be read in conjunction with Article 2 of the Convention. It follows from this that a State which wants to become a party to the Protocol first has to delete the death penalty from its criminal law. The second sentence of Article 1 underlines that it contains not only an obligation, but also a right: every individual has the right not to be condemned to the death penalty or to be executed.

However, the scope of the obligation to abolish the death penalty is limited to acts committed in peace time. Protocol no. 6 does not apply to acts committed in times of war or of imminent threat of war, provided that the law lays down the instances in which the death penalty may be applied and that the relevant provisions of the law are communicated to the Secretary General. It follows from the wording of Article 2 that even after a State has ratified the Protocol, it may introduce the death penalty for those situations, as is clear from the formulation of Article 2.[1506] It may, of course, withdraw

---

1503. Resolution 727 of the Parliamentary Assembly, adopted on 22 April 1980 during its 32nd Session, *Yearbook* XXIII (1980), p. 66.
1504. Resolution 891 of the Parliamentary Assembly, adopted on 22 April 1980 during its 32nd session, *Yearbook* XXIII (1980), p. 66.
1505. At present (1 January 1990) the following contracting States have ratified the Protocol: Austria, Denmark, Federal Republic of Germany, France, Iceland, Italy, Luxembourg, the Netherlands, Norway, Portugal, San Marino, Spain, Sweden and Switzerland.
1506. Art. 2 of the Protocol reads as follows: "A State may make provisions in its law for the death penalty in respect of acts committed in time of war or of imminent threat of war; such penalty shall be applied only in the instances laid down in the law and in accordance with its provisions. The State shall communicate to the Secretary General of the Council of Europe the relevant provisions of the law." What is meant by the phrase "imminent threat of war" is not made clear in the Protocol or the Explanatory Memorandum thereto.

or modify this legislation later on and notify the Secretary General of this. The requirement that in those situations the death penalty shall be applied only in the instances laid down in the law in fact is superfluous since this also stems from Article 7 of the Convention.[1507] However, Article 2 adds to this that this penalty shall only be applied "in accordance with" the law, which also concerns the way the death penalty is executed.

3. The prohibition of the death penalty is non-derogable.[1508] When read in conjunction with Article 2 of the Protocol, this means that a death penalty can only be executed in time of war or imminent threat of war if the State has regulated this possibility in time of peace. The existing legislation cannot be changed during wartime.

Moreover, according to Article 4 of the Protocol it is not possible to make any reservation in respect of the provisions of the Protocol.

4. The Covenant does not provide for the duty to abolish the death penalty, but imposes a number of restrictions on the infliction of this penalty.[1509] Article 6, paragraph 6 of the Covenant contains a recommendation to abolish the death penalty. This, however, does not amount to a duty to do so.

The second paragraph of Article 6 starts with the words "countries which have not abolished the death penalty". This might be interpreted as a prohibition to introduce the death penalty after the entry into force of or accession to the Covenant, as the case may be.[1510] Such a prohibition is of course part of the Sixth Protocol, with the exception of acts committed in time of war or of imminent threat of war.

§ 21. ARTICLE 1 OF PROTOCOL NO. 7: EXPULSION OF ALIENS

1. An alien lawfully resident in the territory of a State shall not be expelled therefrom except in pursuance of a decision reached in accordance with law and shall be allowed:
a. to submit reasons against his expulsion,
b. to have his case reviewed, and
c. to be represented for these purposes before the competent authority or a person or persons designated by that authority.
2. An alien may be expelled before the exercise of his rights under paragraph 1(a), (b) and (c) of this Article, when such expulsion is necessary in the interests of public order or is grounded on reasons of

---

1507. See *supra*, p. 362-363.
1508. Art. 3 of the Protocol.
1509. Art. 6(2) and (5) of the Covenant, See also *supra* pp. 225-226.
1510. The "Annotations", *supra* note 1452, p. 30, do not create any clarity on this point. Robertson, *supra* note 59, p. 108, formulates it as an open question. In the Report of the Committee of Experts, *supra* note 14, p. 25, it is assumed that this was not intended.

national security.

1. The original aim of the Seventh Protocol, as recommended by the Parliamentary Assembly in 1972, was "to insert as many as possible of the substantive provisions of the Covenant on Civil and Political Rights in the Convention".[1511] However, the Committee of Experts, which prepared the draft of the Protocol, followed a more restrictive approach, keeping in mind "the need to include in the Convention only such rights as could be stated in sufficiently specific terms to be guaranteed within the framework of the system of control instituted by the Convention".[1512] Although the idea of such an extension was already born in the early seventies, it was not until 22 November 1984 that the Protocol was opened for signature. And only in 1988 sufficient States had ratified the Protocol for it to enter into force.[1513]

The enthusiasm about Protocol no. 7 appears to be quite small. This has to do with the fact that the original aim of the Protocol can hardly be said to have been achieved. In the comparative report of the Committee of Experts[1514] a series of rights have been enumerated, which are included in the Covenant but not in the Convention. Only some of these rights are now included in this Protocol. A clear clarification of the reasons for it, other than the above-mentioned general viewpoint of the Committee of Experts, is not to be found in the Explanatory Memorandum. Although it is true that some of the other rights do not fulfil the requirement of "sufficiently specific terms to be guaranteed", it is by no means clear why, for example, the right of the accused to be informed of his right to have legal assistance or the right of equality before the law, have not been included in this Protocol. Furthermore, the Protocol met with serious criticism, because the rights that have been incorporated are on the whole formulated rather narrowly.[1515] Most of the rights are framed in more restricted terms than their counterparts in the Covenant. It may be concluded, therefore, that the outcome of this lengthy exercise is rather disappointing.

States which ratify or have ratified the Protocol have to make a separate declaration under Article 25 of the Convention in order to give individuals the right to submit individual applications, and have to separately accept the jurisdiction of the Court, pursuant to Article 46 of the Convention, with respect to the rights guaranteed in the Protocol.[1516]

2. The European Convention contains in several articles implied guarantees

1511. Explanatory Memorandum, Doc. H(84)5, p. 5.
1512. *Ibidem*, p. 6.
1513. At present (1 January 1990) the following contracting States have ratified the Protocol: Austria, Denmark, the Federal Republic of Germany, France, Greece, Iceland, Luxembourg, Norway, San Marino, Sweden and Switzerland.
1514. *Supra* note 14, pp. 4-5.
1515. See Stefan Trechsel, "Das Verflixte Siebente? - Bemerkungen zum 7. Zusatzprotokoll zur EMRK", in: Nowak/Steurer/Tretter (eds), *Fortschritt im Bewusstsein der Grund- und Menschenrechte; Festschrift für Felix Ermacora*, Kehl etc. 1988, pp. 195-211.
1516. See Art. 7(2) of the Protocol.

for aliens against whom a measure of expulsion is taken. First of all, Article 4 of Protocol no. 4 contains the prohibition of collective expulsion of aliens. But also in individual cases Articles 3, 5(1)(f), and 8, in conjunction with Article 13, do provide some guarantees against measures of expulsion.[1517] Article 1 of Protocol no. 7 has been added "in order to afford minimum guarantees to such persons (aliens) in the event of expulsion from the territory of a Contracting Party".[1518] And minimal they are indeed.

As is clear from the text of the Article, and is emphasized in the Explanatory Memorandum,[1519] the guarantees only apply to certain categories of aliens, and even then not in all circumstances. Indeed, Article 1 only concerns aliens lawfully resident in the territory of the State in question. The word resident is intended to exclude any alien who has arrived at the border or (air)port, but has not yet passed through the immigration control. Aliens who have been admitted for the purpose of transit or for other non-residential purposes, or who are waiting for a decision on a request for a residence permit, are also excluded from the scope of this Article. The term "lawfully" refers to domestic law. It is up to the domestic law to determine the conditions for a person's presence in the territory to be considered "lawful". As soon as an alien does not comply any more with one or more of these conditions, his presence can no longer be considered "lawful".

According to the Explanatory Memorandum the phrase "expulsion" must be considered as an autonomous concept, independent of any domestic definition. It refers to any measure compelling the departure of an alien from the territory except extradition.[1520]

3. Expulsion may take place only "in pursuance of a decision reached in accordance with law". The word "law" refers to domestic law. It is therefore up to the domestic law to determine which authority is competent to decide about the measure of expulsion and which procedure has to be followed, provided that the requirement of an effective remedy of Article 13 of the Convention is met. A judicial authority is not required, unless in cases where Article 6 of the Convention applies. However, during the procedure, the alien concerned has some minimum rights, as mentioned under paragraph 1(a)-(c).[1521] As regards the first right: to submit reasons against his expulsion, here again it is up to domestic law to determine the conditions governing the exercise of this right. This right may, however, be exercised in the first phase of the procedure and not only at the review stage, as is clear from its formulation separately from (b).[1522]

As regards the second right: to have his case reviewed, it is emphasized

---

1517. See *supra* pp. 236-240, 269-272 and 387-390. For Art. 13 and its implications for procedural guarantees, see *infra* pp. 520-532.
1518. Explanatory Memorandum, *supra* note 1511, p. 6.
1519. *Ibidem*, p. 7.
1520. *Ibidem*.
1521. See also Art. 5 of the Convention.
1522. See Explanatory Memorandum, *supra* note 1511, p. 8.

in the Explanatory Memorandum that this does not necessarily imply "a two-stage procedure before different authorities, but only that the competent authority should review the case in the light of the reasons against expulsion submitted by the person concerned".[1523] This may be the same or a higher authority. The form of the review, again, is determined by domestic law. The minimal approach, which overshadowed the preparation of the Protocol, can be clearly inferred from the Explanatory Memorandum where it is expressly stated that Article 1 does not relate to the stage of proceedings, existing in some States, in which aliens have the possibility of lodging an appeal against the decision taken following the review of their case: "The present Article ... does not therefore require that the person concerned should be permitted to remain in the territory of the State pending the outcome of the appeal introduced against the decision taken following the review of his case".[1524]

Also for the third right: to be represented before the competent authority or a person or persons designated by that authority, it is up to the domestic legislation to determine the form of representation and the competent authority. It is not required that the representative is a lawyer or that the competent authority is a judicial organ. It is not even required that the authority be the authority who finally decides about the expulsion. In order to comply with this Article, it is sufficient that the competent judicial or administrative authority makes a recommendation to an (other) administrative authority, who then decides about the measure of expulsion.[1525] The provision does not give the alien or his representative the right to be physically present when the case is considered, nor does the procedure have to include an oral hearing; the whole procedure may be a written one.[1526]

4. As a rule, the alien concerned has the right to make use of the minimum guarantees laid down in the first paragraph of Article 1 before being expelled. The second paragraph, however, allows for exceptions to this rule "when such expulsion is necessary in the interests of public order or is grounded on reasons of national security". The words "in a democratic society", which are coupled to the necessity requirement in the several provisions of the Convention which allow for restrictions of the rights embodied therein, are lacking here for unclear reasons. However, the Strasbourg case-law has not (yet) made these words play a separate role. With reference to that case-law the Explanatory Memorandum states that the exceptions have to be applied "taking into account the principle of proportionality as defined in the case law of the European Court of Human Rights".[1527]

When a State relies on this exception in the interest of public order, it is up to that State to show why in the particular case or cases that exception

---

1523. *Ibidem.*
1524. *Ibidem.*
1525. *Ibidem.*
1526. *Ibidem.*
1527. *Ibidem.*

was necessary. If, however, a State grounds the exception on reasons of national security, according to the Explanatory Memorandum "this in itself should be accepted as sufficient justification".[1528] Since this view would imply that review by the Strasbourg organs was not possible at all, it cannot be accepted as in accordance with the purpose of the Protocol to place the rights embodied therein under the supervisory system of the Convention; especially the necessity requirement must be subject to the review of the Strasbourg organs, be it that the latter may leave a broad margin of discretion to the national authorities in that respect.

In the above-mentioned cases it is only scant comfort for the alien concerned to know that he may still exercise his rights under paragraph 1 of this Article after his expulsion.

5. Article 1 is not a non-derogable right under Article 15.

6. To a large extent the guarantees laid down in Article 1 resemble the guarantees of Article 13 of the Covenant. However, there are some differences. Thus, Article 13 of the Covenant speaks of an "alien lawfully in the territory of a State Party", while Article 1 of Protocol no. 7 requires the alien to be "lawfully resident" in the territory. According to the Explanatory Memorandum, to be resident the alien has to fulfil some strict requirements. The Strasbourg case-law will have to show whether this difference is a substantive or only a textual one. Article 13 of the Covenant also enumerates the guarantees laid down in Article 1, paragraph 1(a)-(c) of Protocol no. 7. The difference consists in the possibilities for the States to expel an alien before he has exercised the rights laid down in the articles. Article 1(2) of Protocol no. 7 provides for the possibility to expel the alien, if it is "necessary in the interests of public order or is grounded on reasons of national security", while Article 13 of the Covenant permits expulsion only if this is required by "compelling reasons of national security". Moreover, although both articles mention national security, States Parties to the Covenant do have to submit *compelling* reasons for the expulsion; reasons which can be reviewed by the Human Rights Committee. On the basis of the review, the Human Rights Committee is able to see to it that the measure is proportionate to the aim of safeguarding national security. Under the Protocol, at least according to the Explanatory Memorandum, States only have to ground the expulsion on reasons of national security. These reasons do not have to be compelling and, moreover, are not subject to any review by the Strasbourg organs. Although, as has been said above, this exclusion of the Strasbourg review is not in conformity with the purpose of the Protocol and, therefore, is not likely to be accepted by the Strasbourg organs, in this way the stage seems to have been set for a larger discretion on the part of the authorities to expel an alien before he has exercised his rights under Article 1, especially also

1528. *Ibidem*, p. 9.

because of the very broad additional ground of the "interests of public order", even though with regard to the latter phrase, control by the Strasbourg organs is not excluded in any respect.[1529]

§ 22. ARTICLE 2 OF PROTOCOL NO. 7: THE RIGHT TO REVIEW BY A HIGHER TRIBUNAL

1. Everyone convicted of a criminal offence by a tribunal shall have the right to have his conviction or sentence reviewed by a higher tribunal. The exercise of this right, including the grounds on which it may be exercised, shall be governed by law.
2. This right may be subject to exceptions in regard to offences of a minor character, as prescribed by law, or in cases in which the person concerned was tried in the first instance by the highest tribunal or was convicted following an appeal against acquittal.

1. The right to review by a higher tribunal is new in the Convention system. The present article was aimed at equating on this point the Convention with the Covenant, which provides for such a right in Article 14(5). However, here, too, there are some differences between the two provisions.

Both provisions do restrict the right to review to convictions and sentences in criminal proceedings.

2. In the first sentence of paragraph 1 of this Article it is emphasized that the conviction must have been imposed "by a tribunal". According to the Explanatory Memorandum this phrase was added to make it clear that the right laid down in this provision is not applicable to "offences which have been tried by bodies which are not tribunals within the meaning of Article 6 of the Convention".[1530] Trechsel rightly observes that this is a somewhat strange provision, since Article 6 of the Convention requires that the determination of criminal charges be made by an independent tribunal. Therefore, trial of a criminal offence by a non-judicial organ would in itself be a violation of the Convention. However, since the Strasbourg case-law has accepted the possibility that the determination of a criminal charge is made, in the first instance, by a non-judicial body provided that from that determination appeal lies to a tribunal, the drafters must be assumed to have intended to make it clear that this first appeal to a tribunal is not a review in the sense of Article 2; in that case there is a right to have that decision on appeal reviewed by a higher tribunal.[1531]

Furthermore, the first sentence of paragraph 1 provides that everyone has

---

1529. For the case-law of the Human Rights Committee concerning Article 13 of the Covenant, reference is made to the study of Nowak, mentioned *supra* at p. 216.
1530. *Supra* note 1511, p. 9.
1531. Trechsel, *supra* note 1515, pp. 201-202.

the right to have the "conviction or sentence" reviewed. The reason for using the word "or" instead of "and"[1532] is, again according to the Explanatory Memorandum, that it is not required that in every case both the conviction and the sentence should be reviewed. For example, if a person has pleaded guilty and has been convicted, the right of review may be restricted to the review of the sentence. Here, too, this line of reasoning is not very convincing. Although in most cases in which a suspect has pleaded guilty the review will in fact mainly focus on the sentence, it may be necessary to also review the way the confession was obtained, and therefore the basis of the conviction. On the other hand, a review of the conviction alone, without the sentence being also reviewed, is only possible in those cases in which the suspect has been found guilty, but no sentence has been imposed.[1533] Just as in the Covenant, it would therefore have been better if the word "and" instead of "or" had been used.

3. As is made clear in the second sentence of the first paragraph, the exercise of this right of appeal shall be governed by law. In other words, the modalities of the review are left for determination by domestic law. The Explanatory Memorandum adds to this that the review may either concern a review of findings of facts and questions of law or be limited to questions of law.[1534] In the latter case the review is a rather restricted one and one may wonder why the drafters, if they considered such a restricted review sufficient, have not expressed that more clearly in the text. In any case one may expect that the Strasbourg organs will not accept as sufficient a restricted form of review of questions of law which cannot result in an annulment or alteration of the conviction and sentence.

Some countries have a system according to which persons who wish to appeal to a higher tribunal must in certain cases first apply for leave of appeal, which may be granted or refused. According to the Explanatory Memorandum such a procedure is in itself to be regarded as a form of review within the meaning of this Article.[1535] It may, however, be doubted if this interpretation is in conformity with the text of the Article. The decision may be based upon reasons of expediency and does not necessarily imply a review of the conviction or sentence as Article 2 would seem to guarantee, but rather block such a review. Moreover, one may wonder whether such a decision can be said to always amount to a review "by a higher tribunal". In our opinion, the Strasbourg organs should be guided by the text and purpose of Article 2 rather than by the restrictive interpretation given thereto in the Explanatory Memorandum.

4. The second paragraph of Article 2 contains three exceptions to the right

---

1532. See Art. 14(5) Covenant.
1533. See Trechsel, *supra* note 1515, pp. 202-203.
1534. *Supra* note 1511, p. 9.
1535. *Ibidem.*

laid down in the first paragraph. The first exception concerns offences of a minor character. It is this part of Article 2 which differs most from the Covenant, since Article 14(5) does not provide for this exception.[1536] The guarantee of Article 2 is therefore less far-reaching than that of Article 14(5) of the Covenant.

In practice it will not always be clear where the dividing line between serious and minor offences lies. The Explanatory Memorandum proposes as a guiding criterion the question of whether the offence is punishable by imprisonment or not. Although this criterion is a clear one, it will not lead to a common or autonomous concept of "offences of a minor character". Since the question of imprisonment is entirely regulated by domestic law, major differences will occur in the contracting States. More importantly, in several States a great many minor offences, such as infringements of traffic rules, are made punishable by imprisonment, though such sentences are never imposed in practice. It is unlikely that the drafters of the Protocol wished to have the right of review by a higher tribunal also applied in such cases.

5. The second exception concerns cases in which a person has been tried in the first instance by the highest tribunal. It refers to cases in which the domestic law has assigned the highest tribunal as a court of first instance because of the status of the accused as a minister, judge or other high official, or because of the nature of the offence. It is obvious that in those cases review by a higher tribunal is not possible.

6. The third exception is more controversial. It concerns cases where the conviction has been pronounced following an appeal against acquittal. For the person concerned this exeption can be very unsatisfactory, especially when he thinks that the court of second instance has made an error of facts or of law. In most countries of the Council of Europe, however, the convicted person will normally have the right of appeal in cassation to another procedure or third instance. In that case, at least any possible error of law can be restored.

7. Article 2 does not belong to the non-derogable rights in the sense of Article 15(2) of the Convention.

8. There are some differences between Article 2 of the Protocol and Article 14(5) of the Covenant. First, there are some textual differences between the two articles, of which it is as yet not clear whether they will also have any significance in practice. Thus, the Protocol uses the words "criminal offence", while the Covenant merely refers to "crime". Furthermore, both provisions refer to national law with regard to the exercise of the right, but Article 2 adds to this that this includes "the grounds on which it may be exercised".

1536. See the General Comment of the Human Rights Committee concerning Article 14, *Report of 1984*, Annex VI, para. 17.

Next, the Protocol restricts the right to review to convictions "by a tribunal". As has been observed above, this may imply the right to a third instance, if in the first instance a penalty has been imposed by a non-judicial body. The main difference between the two provisions consists in that the Covenant does not provide for any exceptions to the right concerned, while Article 2 of the Protocol permits three exceptions, of which the first, offences of a minor character, is the most controversial one.[1537]

§ 23. ARTICLE 3 OF PROTOCOL NO. 7: COMPENSATION FOR MISCARRIAGE OF JUSTICE

When a person has by a final decision been convicted of a criminal offence and when subsequently his conviction has been reversed, or he has been pardoned, on the ground that a new or newly discovered fact shows conclusively that there has been a miscarriage of justice, the person who has suffered punishment as a result of such conviction shall be compensated according to the law or the practice of the State concerned, unless it is proved that the non-disclosure of the unknown fact in time is wholly or partly attributable to him.

1. The right laid down in this Article can only be exercised if four preconditions have been fulfilled.

First, a person must have been convicted of a criminal offence by a final decision. A decision is final

> if, according to the traditional expression, it has acquired the force of *res judicata*. This is the case when it is irrevocable, that is to say when no further ordinary remedies are available or when the parties have exhausted such remedies or have permitted the time-limit to expire without availing themselves of them.[1538]

The person concerned must, as a result of this final decision, have suffered punishment. Consequently, the Article does not apply in cases where the charge is dismissed or the accused is acquitted.[1539]

Secondly, the right laid down in this Article can only be exercised, if the conviction has been reversed or pardoned.

Thirdly, the reversal or pardon must have taken place because of new or newly discovered facts. In the latter case, it must moreover be assessed whether the circumstance that these facts were not disclosed in time is wholly or partly attributable to the person concerned. It is obvious that if a person is willingly withholding relevant information, he loses his right to compensation because the prejudice suffered is (partly) due to his own conduct. If, besides

---

1537. For the "case-law" of the Human Rights Committee concerning Art. 14(5), reference is made to the study of Nowak mentioned *supra* p. 216.
1538. *Explanatory Report of the European Convention on the International Validity of Criminal Judgments, Commentary on Article 1(a)*, Council of Europe, Strasbourg 1970, p. 22.
1539. Explanatory Memorandum, *supra* note 1511, p. 10.

the convicted person, also others are responsible for the fact that certain relevant facts were not disclosed, it may not always be fair to put the blame solely on the former by fully denying him a right to compensation. In that case a partial compensation may be more appropriate to reflect reality.

Fourthly, the new or newly discovered facts on the basis of which the person's conviction has been reversed or he has been pardoned must conclusively show that there has been a miscarriage of justice. By this phrase is meant a "serious failure in the judicial process involving grave prejudice to the convicted person".[1540] Reversal or pardon on other grounds - especially pardon may often be granted on other grounds - does not create a right to compensation. According to the Explanatory Memorandum, the intention is that compensation should be paid only in "clear cases of miscarriage of justice, in the sense that there would be acknowledgement that the person concerned was clearly innocent".[1541] In what follows the Explanatory Memorandum seems to imply that reversal on the ground that new facts have been discovered which introduce a reasonable doubt as to the guilt of the accused is not enough.[1542] In our opinion this interpretation would be too strict, especially in view of the right to be presumed innocent, laid down in Article 6(2) of the Convention, which implies that reasonable doubt and clear innocence should lead to the same result.[1543]

2. If all four preconditions have been fulfilled, Article 3 of this Protocol requires that

> the person who has suffered punishment as a result of such conviction shall be compensated according to the law or the practice of the State concerned.

What is meant by the phrase "the practice of the State concerned" is not very clear. The Explanatory Memorandum does not clarify it any further than by providing that "the State should provide for the payment of compensation in all cases to which the Article applies".[1544] In our opinion, it would have been wiser to avoid this phrase, which does not appear anywhere else in the Convention. It does not add anything to the reference that has already been made to national law and it may lead to confusion as to its meaning. Article 5(5) of the Convention, which establishes a right to compensation for victims of arrest or detention in contravention of the provisions of Article 5, uses the words "an enforceable right to compensation". This phrase should also have been adopted here.

3. Article 3 does not belong to the non-derogable rights in the sense of Article 15(2) of the Convention.

1540. *Ibidem.*
1541. *Ibidem.*
1542. *Ibidem.*
1543. See also Trechsel, *supra* note 1515, pp. 206-207.
1544. *Supra* note 1511, p. 10.

4. The text of Article 3 is almost literally the same as that of Article 14(6) of the Covenant. The only difference consists in the above-mentioned reference to "the practice of the State".[1545]

§ 24. ARTICLE 4 OF PROTOCOL NO. 7: NE BIS IN IDEM

1. No one shall be liable to be tried or punished again in criminal proceedings under the jurisdiction of the same State for an offence for which he has already been finally acquitted or convicted in accordance with the law and penal procedure of that State.
2. The provisions of the preceding paragraph shall not prevent the re-opening of the case in accordance with the law and penal procedure of the State concerned, if there is evidence of new or newly discovered facts, or if there has been a fundamental defect in the previous proceedings, which could affect the outcome of the case.
3. No derogation from this Article shall be made under Article 15 of the Convention.

1. In paragraph 1 of this Article the basic principle is laid down: nobody may be tried or punished again in the same State for an offence for which he has already been finally acquitted or convicted. This right is made subject to some limitations.

First, Article 4 only applies to criminal proceedings under the jurisdiction of one and the same State, thus limiting its scope to the national level. It, therefore, still allows that a person is punished more than once for the same act in two or more countries, depending on the rules on jurisdiction of the States involved. Thus, for example, a German citizen who deals in heroin in the Netherlands may be punished for that both in the Netherlands and in the Federal Republic of Germany. As Trechsel observes, this limitation is a necessary consequence of the fact that criminal law in the Member States of the Council of Europe has still been insufficiently harmonized.[1546] Although the Council of Europe has already, by adopting three Conventions,[1547] given a certain international scope to the *ne bis in idem* principle, this in itself was considered an insufficient ground for laying down an unconditional, internationally applied *ne bis in idem* principle.

Secondly, the principle is limited to criminal proceedings. In the Explanatory Memorandum it is expressly stated that the same act may, apart from criminal proceedings, also be made subject to action of a different

---

1545. For the "case-law" of the Human Rights Committee concerning Article 14(6) reference is made to the study of Nowak, mentioned *supra* at p. 216.
1546. Trechsel, *supra* note 1515, p. 208.
1547. These Conventions are: the European Convention on Extradition (1957), the European Convention on the International Validity of Criminal Judgments (1970) and the European Convention on the Transfer of Proceedings in Criminal Matters (1972).

character, for example disciplinary or administrative action.[1548] If this is correct at all, in our opinion the rationale of Article 4 and the Strasbourg case-law according to which, for the purpose of Article 6 of the Convention, such action may be equated with criminal proceedings depending on certain criteria,[1549] would imply that they are also to be equated for the purpose of Article 4 if the same criteria are met.

2. Paragraph 1 of Article 4 furthermore provides that this principle is only applicable if the conviction or acquittal has become final. Here again, just as in the preceding Article 3, a decision is to be considered final "if, according to the traditional expression, it has acquired the force of *res judicata*". This is the case when it is irrevocable, that is to say when "no further ordinary remedies are available or when the parties have exhausted such remedies or have permitted the time-limit to expire without availing themselves of them".[1550]

This does not, however, prevent that a case may be re-opened if there is evidence of new or newly discovered facts, irrespective of the question whether this is in favour or to the detriment of the person concerned (paragraph 2 of Art. 4). According to the Explanatory Memorandum the term "new or newly discovered facts" also "includes new means of proof relating to previously existing facts".[1551] What is exactly meant by these words is not clear, but it seems to be apt to lead to misuse. Is the meaning of this phrase that new technologies or previously forbidden forms of collecting evidence may lead to a re-opening of a case, if that technology or form has become available after the closing of a case? Especially when these "facts" may also lead to a situation detrimental to the person concerned, this might create legal uncertainty for that person. In fact, a person may, even after an acquittal, be found guilty after the re-opening of a case as a result of new technologies or a change in the case-law concerning proof. This would practically mean that an accused may only feel safe after the prosecution for a criminal offence has become barred by limitation.

Reopening of the proceedings and any other changing of the judgment, again according to the Explanatory Memorandum, may also take place on other grounds, if this is in favour of the convicted person.[1552]

3. According to the third paragraph of Article 4, the principle of *ne bis in idem* is non-derogable in the sense of Article 15(2) of the Convention.

4. A comparison between Article 4 of the Protocol and Article 14(7) of the Covenant shows that the principle is described in comparable wordings.

1548. Explanatory Memorandum, *supra* note 1511, p. 10.
1549. See *supra* pp. 310-313.
1550. See *supra* note 1538.
1551. *Supra* note 1511, p. 11.
1552. *Ibidem.*

Differences consist in that Article 4 puts more emphasis on the national character of the principle: the words "under the jurisdiction of a State" are not enshrined in Article 14(7). Furthermore, in the Covenant no mention is made of the possible exception to the principle in the form of a re-opening of cases. This does not necessarily mean, however, that the Covenant does not allow for the same exceptions. The main difference between the two Articles lies in the fact that the principle is made non-derogable under the Seventh Protocol, while Article 14(7) does not have that status. In this respect, the guarantee under the Protocol is stronger than the one under the Covenant.[1553]

§ 25. ARTICLE 5 OF PROTOCOL NO. 7: EQUALITY OF RIGHTS AND RESPONSIBILITIES BETWEEN SPOUSES DURING AND AFTER MARRIAGE

Spouses shall enjoy equality of rights and responsibilities of a private law character between them, and in their relations with their children, as to marriage, during marriage and in the event of its dissolution. This Article shall not prevent States from taking such measures as are necessary in the interests of the children.

1. The rights and obligations to which this equality principle refers are of a private-law character; the equality concerns only the relations between the spouses themselves, with respect to their personal status or their property, and their relations with their children. As the Explanatory Memorandum puts it, "the Article does not apply to other fields of law, such as administrative, fiscal, criminal, social, ecclesiastical or labour laws".[1554] Since under the system of the Convention complaints can be lodged against States only, the scope of the Strasbourg review will be rather restricted and mainly concern the obligation of the State to enact and enforce the appropriate legislation. At the national level, however, in those legal systems where the Convention and its Protocols have internal effect, the scope may be much broader, as Article 5 clearly implies *Drittwirkung*.[1555]

To a large extent the equality of spouses is already secured by Article 8, in conjunction with Article 14 of the Convention. On the basis of the case-law of the Strasbourg organs it is, however, also clear that besides the rights of each of the spouses, the interests of children have to be taken into account. In accordance therewith Article 5 provides that States are not prevented from taking such measures as are necessary in the interests of the children, even if this results in inequality between the spouses.

1553. For the "case-law" of the Human Rights Committee concerning Article 14(7) reference is made to the study of Nowak, mentioned *supra* at p. 216.
1554. *Supra* note 1511, p. 12.
1555. On this, see *supra* pp. 15-20.

2. The rights and obligations "as to marriage" relate to the legal effects connected with the conclusion of marriage. Article 5 is not applicable to the period preceding marriage. It also is not concerned with the conditions of capacity to enter into marriage. It is, therefore, left to the States to determine these conditions. It is, for instance, allowed for States to make a difference between men and women with regard to the minimum age required for marriage, since this concerns the pre-marital period, provided that this regulation is in conformity with Article 12 in conjunction with Article 14 of the Convention.

3. The words "in the event of its dissolution" in Article 5 do not imply a right to divorce. States are not obliged to provide for dissolution of marriage. In this context, it is noteworthy that the phrase referring to the dissolution of marriage in Article 23(4) of the Covenant and Article 5 of this Protocol is identical in the French version, but not in the English version. In the French version both articles speak of "lors de sa dissolution". In the English version, Article 23(4) of the Covenant uses the words "at its dissolution", while Article 5 of Protocol no. 7 states "in the event of its dissolution". Apparently this change has been introduced to take into consideration the situation in some States where the dissolution of a marriage is still prohibited.[1556]

The Explanatory Memorandum states in too broad a phrase that Article 5 "should not be understood as preventing the national authorities from taking due account of all relevant factors when reaching decisions with regard to the division of property in the event of dissolution of marriage".[1557] To the extent that these "relevant factors" are related to the interests of the children, it follows from the express provision in Article 5 itself. But if the taking into account of other factors leads to an unequality of rights and obligations between the two spouses, it will have to meet the requirement of an objective and reasonable justification and that of reasonable proportionality, which have been developed in the Strasbourg case-law with respect to Article 14.[1558]

4. Article 5 does not belong to the non-derogable rights in the sense of Article 15(2) of the Convention.

5. The main difference in formulation between Article 5 of Protocol no. 7 and Article 23(4) of the Covenant is that the latter is phrased as an obligation of the States, while the former states and individual right. For the international review this difference does not have to have any consequence, but in the case of domestic implementation and supervision the latter formulation would seem to provide a stronger case for *Drittwirkung*. A more important difference consists in the fact that Article 23(4) does not restrict

1556. Trechsel, *supra* note 1515, p. 209.
1557. *Supra* note 1511, p. 12.
1558. See *infra* pp. 541-547.

the rights and responsibilities to those of a private law character. This could mean, *e.g.*, that also an inequality of rights and obligations under fiscal law would be in violation of that provision. Finally, the interests of the children are referred to in Article 23(4) only in connection with the dissolution of marriage, while Article 5 provides in general that measures to protect these interests are allowed under the latter provision.[1559]

1559. For the "case-law" of the Human Rights Committee concerning Article 23(4) reference is made to the study of Nowak, mentioned *supra* at p. 216.

CHAPTER VII

PROVISIONS CONCERNING ENJOYMENT OF THE RIGHTS AND FREEDOMS AND CONCERNING RESTRICTION OF THESE RIGHTS AND FREEDOMS

§ 1. INTRODUCTION

1. Articles 13 to 18 of the Convention form part of Section I but, unlike the preceding provisions of this Section, do not contain independent rights and freedoms. They cannot, therefore, constitute the object of a separate complaint lodged with the Commission, but can be put forward only in conjunction with one of the preceding provisions of Section I or one of the rights and freedoms set forth in Protocols nos 1, 4, 6 and 7.

According to prevalent opinion the same is true for Article 1, which, preceding Section I, is important for ensuring the rights and freedoms laid down therein, but cannot be put forward in Strasbourg independently of one of these rights and freedoms. In the case of an individual complaint this means that Commission and Court will not undertake a separate inquiry into the violation of Article 1; the individual applicant can allege that he is a "victim" only if he is able to advance the violation of one of the rights and freedoms.[1] In the case of a complaint by a State the matter is more complicated, since according to the broad formulation of Article 24 - "any alleged breach of the provisions of the Convention" - such a complaint need not be confined to the violation of a right. In fact, a State may have violated an obligation under Article 1 even if there has been no actual violation of one of the rights and freedoms, for instance when a State has failed to take the necessary legislative and other measures so as to ensure that those rights and freedoms are respected. Since a State does not have to prove that such negligence has produced concrete victims, Article 24 would seem to leave scope for a separate examination of the alleged violation of Article 1.

In fact, a State may lodge a complaint even when it is not yet possible to identify concrete violations of any of the rights set forth in the Convention, for instance because a legal rule has not yet been applied in a concrete way. Thus, the Court held in the Case of *Ireland v. United Kingdom*:

> Article 24 enables each Contracting State to refer to the Commission "any alleged breach of any of the provisions of the Convention by another State". Such a "breach" results from the mere existence of a law which introduces, directs or authorises measures

---

1. The Commission, therefore, has so far refrained from instituting a separate inquiry into the alleged violation of Article 1 in the case of an individual complaint. See its decisions on Appl. 5493/72, *Handyside v. United Kingdom*, Yearbook XVII (1974), p. 228 (300) and Appl. 5613/72, *Hilton v. United Kingdom*, Yearbook XIX (1976), p. 256 (272).

incompatible with the rights and freedoms safeguarded.[2]

The Court stressed, however, that such an "abstract complaint" concerning the legislation must be sufficiently clear and exact to make the violation immediately manifest, since otherwise a decision on the complaint can be taken only by reference to the specific application of that legislation.[3]

It is obvious, however, that in the case of a specific complaint that a State has not fulfilled its obligations under Article 1, one or more of the other provisions will always be involved as well, in addition to Article 1. In actual fact, therefore, the question as to a violation of Article 1 has little significance independently of the question of whether the State has violated one or more of those other provisions, be it that the examination of the latter question cannot be confined to the issue of whether a concrete violation in relation to one or more persons has already taken place.

The main importance, however, of Article 1 concerns the scope of application *ratione personae* of the Convention and has already been discussed above within that context.[4]

2. Articles 13, 14, 15(2) and 18 provide an additional guarantee for the enjoyment of the rights and freedoms laid down in the Convention. These provisions, accordingly, are also only invoked before the Strasbourg organs in connection with a complaint concerning the violation of one or more of these rights or freedoms. Articles 15(1) and 16, on the other hand, authorize the contracting States to limit the enjoyment of certain rights and freedoms for particular situations or with regard to a particular group of persons. They will therefore be invoked as a defence by the State against which a complaint is addressed. Article 17 contains elements of both categories.

A discussion of each of the above-mentioned articles will be followed in this chapter by some general observations on the specific restrictions mentioned in Articles 8 to 11 inclusive of the Convention and Article 2 of Protocol no. 4 and Article 1 of Protocol no. 7. The chapter concludes with a section concerning the possibility of making reservations with respect to one or more provisions of the Convention.

§ 2. ARTICLE 13: RIGHT TO AN EFFECTIVE REMEDY BEFORE A NATIONAL AUTHORITY

Everyone whose rights and freedoms as set forth in this Convention are violated shall have an effective remedy before a national authority notwithstanding that the violation has been committed by persons acting

---

2. Judgment of 18 January 1978, A.25 (1978), p. 91. See also the separate opinion of Judge O'Donogue, *ibidem*, p. 109.
3. *Ibidem*, p. 91.
4. *Supra* p. 3.

in an official capacity.

1. According to the concept of the Rule of Law, which along with the idea of democracy forms one of the pillars of the Council of Europe,[5] a general guarantee of an effective remedy for anyone who considers that one of his rights has been violated by the authorities or by a fellow-citizen would in our opinion certainly have been in place in the Convention.

It is evident, however, from the words "whose rights and freedoms as set forth in this Convention are violated" that Article 13 does not contain such a general guarantee. It refers exclusively to cases in which the alleged violation concerns one of the rights and freedoms of the Convention.[6] It cannot therefore be invoked independently from, but only in conjunction with one or more of these rights and freedoms.

This ancillary character of Article 13 is probably one of the reasons why the case-law with regard to its application is not yet firmly established.[7] In fact, every single element of this provision has given rise to difficulties of interpretation.

2. This holds true first of all for the words "are violated" and "has been committed". These words should of course not be interpreted to imply that Article 13 may be invoked in Strasbourg only if the violation of one or more of the said rights and freedoms *has been established* in advance by a national authority. In fact, such an interpretation would be in very poor keeping with the aim of the Convention, which precisely provides for the possibility to submit an application to an international authority if the Convention has allegedly been applied incorrectly or not at all by the national authorities. Moreover, such an interpretation would largely deprive Article 13 of its meaning, because the very establishment of the alleged violation would indicate that the applicant did have an effective remedy before a national authority. It is also, and pre-eminently, in those cases where the national authority concerned declared that the Convention has not been violated, or where no decision about this could be obtained, that Article 13 can be put forward in Strasbourg. Indeed, even if ultimately, as a result of the Strasbourg procedure, there proves to have been no violation, the contracting State was

---

5. See in particular the Preamble and Art. 3 of the Statute of the Council of Europe. See also Resolution (78)8 of the Committee of Ministers, where "the right of access to justice" is called an "essential feature of any democratic society"; Council of Europe, *Information Bulletin on Legal Activities*, 1 June 1978, p. 48.
6. Thus also the case-law of the Commission. See, *inter alia*, Appl. 6753/74, *X and Y v. the Netherlands, D & R* 2 (1975), p. 118 (119), and the report of 17 July 1980 in the *Kaplan Case, D & R* 21 (1981), p. 5 (35).
7. See the concurring opinion of judges Bindschedler-Robert, Gölcüklü, Matscher and Spielmann in the *James* Case, judgment of 21 February 1986, A.98 (1986), p. 51. In the same vein judges Matscher and Pinheiro Farinha, in their partly dissenting opinion in the *Malone* Case, judgment of 2 August 1984, A.82 (1984), p. 41, uphold "that Article 13 constitutes one of the most obscure clauses in the Convention and that its application raises extremely difficult and complicated problems of interpretation. This is probably the reason why, for approximately two decades, the Convention institutions avoided analysing this provision, for the most part advancing barely convincing reasons."

nevertheless obliged to provide an effective remedy for the examination of the alleged violation. In this sense Article 13 ensures an independent right even though it can only be invoked in conjunction with one of the other rights or freedoms of the Convention.

The Commission has long taken a different position,[8] but the Court, after having left open the question in its judgments in the *Vagrancy* Case[9] and in the *Swedish Engine Drivers' Union* Case,[10] in its *Klass* judgment clearly decided in the above sense. It held with respect to Article 13:

> This provision, read literally, seems to say that a person is entitled to a national remedy only if a "violation" has occurred. However, a person cannot establish a "violation" before a national authority unless he is first able to lodge with such an authority a complaint to that effect. Consequently, as the minority of the Commission stated, it cannot be a prerequisite for the application of Article 13 that the Convention be in fact violated. In the Court's view, Article 13 requires that where an individual considers himself to have been prejudiced by a measure allegedly in breach of the Convention, he should have a remedy before a national authority in order both to have his claim decided and, if appropriate, to obtain redress. Thus, Article 13 must be interpreted as guaranteeing an "effective remedy before a national authority" to everyone who *claims* that his rights and freedoms under the Convention have been violated.[11]

In its report in the *Kaplan* Case the Commission adopted this view of the Court.[12] It maintained, however, a restriction to the effect that Article 13 does not apply if it is ultimately found that none of the substantive provisions of the Convention is applicable.[13] This position of the Commission in our opinion raises similar objections as does its initial case-law. Apart from the case where it is beforehand evident that none of the substantive provisions of the Convention invoked is applicable to the case, it would seem to follow from the rationale of Article 13 that it must also be possible to have precisely the question as to that applicability decided in an effective national procedure. Indeed, the question as to the applicability and that as to the violation cannot be viewed independently of each other in many cases. And the *Kaplan* Case concerned precisely a question as to the applicability of a substantive provision of the Convention which in its admissibility decision the Commission itself had qualified as "important and complex".[14] The definition which the Commission gave a few months later, in its report in the *Silver* Case, of the meaning of Article 13, *viz.*:

> that Article 13 requires the High Contracting Parties to provide domestic remedies whereby an individual's claim of a breach of a Convention right or freedom, at least in substance, may be determined, and redressed should the claim be established[15]

8. See its report of 9 March 1977, *Klass*, B.26 (1978), pp. 39-40 and the case-law mentioned there.
9. Judgment of 18 June 1971, A.12 (1971), p. 46.
10. Judgment of 6 February 1976, A.20 (1976), p. 18.
11. Judgment of 6 September 1978, A.28 (1979), pp. 29-30.
12. Report of 17 July 1980, *D & R* 21 (1981), p. 5 (35).
13. *Ibidem*. See also Appl. 8782/79, *X and Y Laboratory v. Belgium*, D & R 25 (1982), p. 243 (250).
14. Appl. 7598/76, *Kaplan v. United Kingdom*, Yearbook XXII (1979), p. 190 (242).
15. Report of 11 October 1980, B.51 (1987), p. 102.

would appear broad enough to also comprise the determination of the question of whether the applicant has rightly based his claim on a substantive provision of the Convention. In the *Bramelid* and *Malmström* Case the Commission adhered unequivocally to the view "that a violation of Article 13 does not presuppose violation of the rights and freedoms set forth in other Articles of the Convention".[16] At present the case-law of the Court and the Commission on this point may be summed up as follows:

> where an individual has an arguable claim to be the victim of a violation of the rights set forth in the Convention, he should have a remedy before a national authority in order both to have his claim decided and, if appropriate, to obtain redress.[17]

3. The arguability-test, thus introduced in the *Silver* Case, has hardly been elaborated in the case-law until now. In fact, the Court has refrained from giving - in its own words - "an abstract definition of the notion of arguability".[18] Rather the test is applied on a case-by-case basis.

Nevertheless, some general indications, albeit negative ones, have been provided by the Court. On the one hand, the Court does not interpret Article 13 so as to require a remedy in domestic law in respect of any supposed grievance under the Convention that an individual may have, no matter how unmeritorious his complaint may be.[19] On the other hand, non-arguability, according to the Court, is not the same thing as manifest ill-foundedness; a complaint may be manifestly ill-founded and yet arguable. At first sight, this point of view might seem remarkable. Indeed, the Court itself has conceded that according to the ordinary meaning of the words, it is difficult to conceive how a claim that is manifestly ill-founded can nevertheless be arguable, and vice versa.[20] This discrepancy may be explained by the fact that the Commission, when conducting its admissibility investigation as to manifest ill-foundedness, does not confine itself to asking whether or not the applicant has a *prima facie* case, but comes close to a fullfledged examination as to the merits.[21] Conceived in this way, manifest ill-foundedness cannot be put on the same line as arguability, meaning that a claim "only needs to raise a Convention issue which merits further examination".[22] Indeed, this would run counter to the above-mentioned point of departure that a violation of Article 13 does not presuppose violation of one of the substantive rights or freedoms.

Summing up, this case-law implies in its extreme that Article 13 secures the right to have the manifestly ill-foundedness of a claim established through an effective remedy, as long as that claim is arguable. This extreme consequence bears out the independent character of the right contained in Article

16. Report of 12 December 1983, *D & R* 38 (1984), p. 18 (41).
17. Judgment of 25 March 1983, *Silver and others*, A.61 (1983), p. 42; judgment of 26 March 1987, *Leander*, A.116 (1987), pp. 29-30.
18. Judgments of 27 April 1988, *Boyle and Rice*, A.131 (1988), p. 24 and of 21 June 1988, *Platform Ärzte für das Leben*, A.139 (1988), p. 11.
19. Judgment of 27 April 1988, *Boyle and Rice*, A.131 (1988), p. 23.
20. *Ibidem*, pp. 23-24.
21. See *supra* p. 105.
22. See the Commission's position before the Court in the case of *Boyle and Rice*, *supra* note 19, p. 23.

13. Conversely, it follows that if the Commission finds a complaint under the Convention to be admissible - and thus not manifestly ill-founded - it has to conclude that the complaint is arguable as far as Article 13 is concerned. This was confirmed by the Commission in the *Soering* Case concerning Article 3, where it was held:

> It follows from the nature of the guarantee under Article 13 that the requirements to provide an effective remedy must also extend in this domain to arguable claims made by a person whose extradition or expulsion is imminent and who may be exposed to harm which is irremediable in nature. Any other interpretation would substantially weaken the guarantee of an effective remedy under this provision.[23]

4. The troublesome character of Article 13 is also exposed by the case-law concerning the relation between this provision and other rights or freedoms contained in the Convention. Particularly Article 6 is a case in point here. In the discussion of Article 6(1) we mentioned that the Court has inferred from that provision a right of access to an independent and impartial tribunal in the cases there referred to, *i.e.* among other instances, when a "civil right" is involved.[24] When interpreted in this way, Article 6(1) strengthens and extends on a number of points the guarantee which Article 13 is intended to provide:

(1) The right to an effective national remedy consists not only in the case of an alleged violation of one of the rights and freedoms guaranteed in the Convention, but in the case of violation of any "civil right" in the sense of Article 6(1).[25] In the latter case, that right to a national remedy may actually constitute the object of an independent complaint, because it is guaranteed in Article 6 as one of the rights and freedoms. There, too, the violation of, or interference with, a "civil right" has to be proved by only *prima facie* evidence and need not have been established. The Strasbourg organs would not even be competent to establish such a violation if a "civil right" not laid down in the Convention is concerned. To what extent Article 6(1) also confers a right of access to a court against acts and omissions of the authorities depends on the question of whether in such a case a "civil right" (or a "civil obligation") may be involved.[26] In any case Article 13 remains relevant for those cases where the complaint concerns a violation of one of the rights or freedoms of the Convention without a "civil right" in the sense of Article 6(1) being at issue; it is of a subsidiary character.[27]

(2) Article 6(1) guarantees access to a court, while the term "remedy before a national authority" is so wide that it also refers to procedures other than judicial ones.[28] These too will then have to be endowed with sufficient

---

23. Report of 19 January 1989, para. 163.
24. *Supra* pp. 314-318.
25. On the meaning of "civil rights", *supra* pp. 295-306.
26. *Ibidem.*
27. This also holds true with regard to other provisions of the Convention where the right to judicial proceedings forms part of the substantive right guaranteed. See Appl. 7341/76, *Eggs v. Switzerland*, Yearbook XX (1977), p. 448 (458), where this was held concerning the relation between Art. 13 and Art. 5(4).
28. Thus also the Court in its judgment of 21 February 1975, *Golder*, A.18 (1975), p. 16, and in its judgment of 6 September 1978, *Klass*, A.28 (1979), p. 30.

guarantees; otherwise it is not possible to speak of an "effective remedy".[29]

(3) While Article 13 has been considered as a provision which does not lend itself to direct application by the national courts,[30] this direct applicability *has* been recognized for Article 6, so that this can be invoked before the national courts in those countries where the Convention has internal effect within the domestic legal order.

From the above it is evident that, if the Commission or the Court has concluded that Article 6 has not been violated, because there is no question of a "civil right", a separate inquiry into a possible violation of Article 13 may be required. If a violation of Article 6 *has* been found, a further inquiry concerning Article 13 may be superfluous, *viz.* to the extent that the guarantees of the two provisions overlap or that of Article 13 is subordinate to that of Article 6. In a number of recent cases the Court has indeed used what would seem to have become a standard formula holding that examination of the complaint under Article 13 is not necessary, because the requirements of the latter are less strict or absorbed by those ensuing from Article 6.[31] However, when a violation of Article 6 has been found, this may precisely raise the question of whether against such a violation - *e.g.* excessively long proceedings - an effective remedy was available.[32] Not surprisingly, therefore, this case-law of the Court has given rise to doubts:

> It was only with some hesitation that we concurred in the decision that it was not necessary to examine the case under Article 13 of the Convention. We are not quite sure that such examination was made superfluous by the finding of a violation ... of the entitlement to a hearing by a tribunal within the meaning of Article 6, para. 1. Are the "less strict" requirements of Article 13 truly "absorbed" by those of Article 6, para. 1? Do these provisions really "overlap"? It appears to us that the relationship between the right to be heard by a tribunal, within the meaning of Article 6, para. 1, and the right to an effective remedy before a national authority, within the meaning of Article 13, should be considered more thoroughly.[33]

The Court and the Commission follow a comparable line of reasoning with respect to the relation between Article 13 and Article 5(4). In the Case of *De Jong, Baljet and Van der Brink* both the Commission and the Court, after having found a violation of Article 5(4), decided not to examine the alleged violation of Article 13 on the basis of the argument that since Article 5(4) guarantees a right to proceedings before a "court" and not merely before an

---

29. On this, *infra* pp. 528-531.
30. See E.A. Alkema, *Studies over Europese Grondrechten* (Studies on European Human Rights), Deventer 1978, p. 67.
31. See, for instance, the judgment of 28 June 1984, *Campbell and Fell*, A.80 (1984), p. 51; judgment of 8 July 1987, *O v. United Kingdom*, A.120 (1987), p. 29; and the judgment of 27 October 1987, A.125 (1988), p. 17.
32. Appl. 7987/77, *Company X v. Austria*, D & R 18 (1980), p. 31 (46). In such a case it will have to be a judicial remedy, since appeal to a non-judicial authority against an act or omission of a judicial organ indeed would impair the independence of the court which is also guaranteed by Article 6. In this respect, see the individual opinion of Commission member Trechsel in the *Kaplan* report of 17 July 1980, *D & R* 21 (1981), p. 37.
33. Joint separate opinion of judges Pinheiro Farinha and De Meyer, judgment of 8 July 1987, *W v. United Kingdom*, A.121 (1987), pp. 40-41; see also the partly dissenting opinion of Mr. Schermers, joined by Mr. Jörundsson, annexed to the report of the Commission in this case, A.121 (1987), pp. 55-56.

authority of unspecified status, Article 5(4) must be considered as a *lex specialis* with respect to the general principle of providing an effective remedy for any victim of a violation of the Convention.[34]

Finally, the relationship between Article 13 and other rights and freedoms of the Convention has come up with respect to Article 8. The picture emerging from the case-law concerned is far from clear. In a case decided in 1984 the applicant raised complaints concerning *inter alia* the refusal to allow confidential consultation by a prisoner with his lawyer and restrictions on a prisoner's personal correspondence. Whereas with respect to the latter complaint the Court found a violation of Article 8, with respect to the former it did not.[35] These different findings did not prevent the Court from subsequently examining the alleged violation of Article 13 with respect to both complaints.[36] In our view this would seem to be the correct approach doing justice to the independent - albeit ancillary - character of Article 13 outlined above.[37]

However, in a number of more recent cases the Court strengthens the impression that, once a violation of a substantive provision of the Convention has been found, it is not much inclined to consider Article 13 as well. In the *Malone* case, where the interception of postal and telephone communications as well as the release of information obtained from the "metering" of telephones were found to be in violation of Article 8, with respect to the alleged violation of Article 13 it was held without any further argument: "Having regard to its decision on Article 8 ... the Court does not consider it necessary to rule on this issue".[38] Similarly, in the Case of *X and Y v. the Netherlands* the Court stated that it

> has already considered in the context of Article 8, whether an adequate means of obtaining a remedy was available to Miss Y. Its finding that there was no such means was one of the factors which led it to conclude that Article 8 had been violated. This being so, the Court does not have to examine the same issue under Article 13.[39]

Thus the Court goes far beyond what is required by the ancillary character of Article 13. In fact, it reduces the independent character of that provision to an extent which in our view is unwarranted.

5. From the words "notwithstanding that the violation has been committed by persons acting in an official capacity" it might be inferred that an effective legal remedy must also, and *a fortiori*, be provided for when the violation has been committed by an individual; in this interpretation an argument for *Drittwirkung* of the rights and freedoms guaranteed in the Convention might

---

34. Report of 11 October 1982, A.77 (1984), p. 39 and judgment of 22 May 1984, A.77 (1984), p. 27. See also the judgment of 29 February 1988, *Bouamar*, A.129 (1988), p. 25.
35. Judgment of 28 June 1984, *Campbell and Fell v. United Kingdom*, A.80 (1984), p. 50.
36. *Ibidem*, p. 52, where the Court concluded that there had been a violation of Article 13 on both scores.
37. See *supra* pp. 521-523.
38. Judgment of 2 August 1984, A.82 (1984), p. 39.
39. Judgment of 26 March 1985, A.91 (1985), p. 15.

be derived from Article 13.[40]

If this *Drittwirkung* is indeed recognized for those articles of the Convention which lend themselves to it, from the general obligation of Article 1 to guarantee the rights and freedoms ensues the obligation for the contracting States to effectuate this *Drittwirkung* in their national system of law. Consequently, violations by an individual in cases where the State has failed to fulfil that obligation may then become the object of a complaint against that State. In that context Article 13 may also be invoked.

As to the words "persons acting in an official capacity", the Commission has held so far that this term does not include the legislator. In its report in the *Young, James and Webster* Case it held as follows:

> It cannot be deduced from Art. 13 that there must be a remedy against legislation as such which is considered not to be in conformity with the Convention. Such a remedy would in effect amount to some sort of judicial review of legislation because any other review - generally sufficient for Art. 13 which requires only a "remedy before a national authority" - could hardly be effective concerning legislation. Without a clear indication in the text Art. 13 cannot be extended that far. This provision rather contains a textual element which supports the reading adopted here. As Art. 13 adds to the main guarantee the words "notwithstanding that the violation has been committed by persons acting in an official capacity" it indicates that the Article is concerned with individuals acting for the State. Even if these words are mainly directed to exclude any doctrine of immunity of State organs, they can be used as an element to show the scope of the Article. Art. 13 does not relate to legislation and does not guarantee a remedy by which legislation could be controlled as to its conformity with the Convention.[41]

The case-law of the Court on this issue was summed up in its recent judgment in the *Leander* Case, in which as one of the principles for the interpretation of Article 13 it was set forth that

> Article 13 does not guarantee a remedy allowing a Contracting State's laws as such to be challenged before a national authority on the ground of being contrary to the Convention or equivalent domestic norms.[42]

Since it has been recognized in the Strasbourg case-law that a legal regulation as such may impair a person's rights guaranteed in the Convention, even if this regulation has not yet been applied to him,[43] a gap arises here in the national remedies against violation of those rights, and thus in the system of Article 13.

Similarly, complicated situations may arise with respect to those contracting States where the Convention is not part of domestic law and where no constitutional procedure exists permitting the validity of laws to be challenged for non-observance of fundamental rights, as in the United Kingdom. In such situations the Court adheres to its above-mentioned point of departure that Article 13 does not go so far as to guarantee a remedy allowing a contracting State's laws to be challenged before a national authority on the ground of being contrary to the Convention or to equivalent legal norms. As far as the

---

40. On Drittwirkung and Art. 13, see *supra* pp. 17-18.
41. Report of 14 December 1979, B.39 (1984), p. 49. Thus also the report of 17 July 1980, *Kaplan, D & R* 21 (1981), p. 5 (36).
42. Judgment of 26 March 1987, A.116 (1987), pp. 29-30.
43. See *supra* pp. 42-43.

application of the laws in question to the alleged victim is concerned, the Court's judgment on the effectiveness of the available remedies seems again to depend to a large extent on the question of whether or not it finds the law concerned to be in conformity with the substantive provisions of the Convention, such as Articles 6 and 8. If this is the case, the Court seems to be inclined to conclude that no violation of Article 13 had occurred.[44] If not, the requirements which the Court derives from Article 13 seem to turn out more strict.[45]

6. If it comes to the examination of an alleged violation of Article 13, when can a given remedy be said to be "effective"? A number of general principles elaborated by the Court for the interpretation of Article 13, and recently summed up in its judgment in the *Leander* Case, are relevant in this respect. According to the Court, the authority referred to in Article 13 need not be a judicial authority but, if it is not, the powers and the guarantees which it affords are relevant in determining whether the remedy before it is effective.[46] In addition the Court takes the position that, even if no single remedy may in itself entirely satisfy the requirement of Article 13, the aggregate of remedies provided for under domestic law may do so.[47]

Not listed among these principles, but in fact underlying them, is the systematic approach towards Article 13 as employed by the Court. In the *Leander* judgment this approach was explained as follows:

> The Convention is to be read as a whole and therefore ... any interpretation of Article 13 must be in harmony with the logic of the Convention.[48]

From the *Klass* Case it had already become clear that this in fact means that the Court is not prepared to interpret or apply Article 13 in a way which amounts to nullifying its conclusions derived from the (preceding) interpretation of one or more of the (other) rights and freedoms set forth in the Convention.[49]

In the *Klass* Case a judge, a public prosecutor and three lawyers complained about the German legislation which allows interception of correspondence and wire-tapping in certain cases without the person concerned having to be informed of it. Besides violation of Article 8, they also alleged violation of Articles 6(1)[50] and 13. As to Article 13, it was argued that the challenged legislation did not provide for an "effective remedy", because the normal judicial remedies had been replaced by supervision by a committee of parliamentarians which was regularly informed

---

44. See the judgment of 21 February 1986, *James and others*, A.98 (1986), pp. 47-48, and the judgment of 8 July 1986, *Lithgow and others*, A.102 (1987), pp. 74-75.
45. See the judgment of 28 May 1985, *Abdulaziz, Cabales and Balkandali*, A.94 (1985), pp. 42-43.
46. Judgment of 26 March 1987, A.116 (1987), pp. 29-30.
47. *Ibidem.*
48. *Ibidem*, p. 30.
49. Judgment of 6 September 1978, A.28 (1979), pp. 30-31.
50. On this, see *supra* pp. 392-396 and 318 respectively.

by the authorities about the cases in which the legal provision here challenged had been applied. Moreover, those who had been affected by that application were not in a position to challenge this personally, since it was not certain whether and when they would be informed of that application. The Court formulated in the first place the principle mentioned above, *viz.* that:

> the authority referred to in Article 13 may not necessarily in all circumstances be a judicial authority in the strict sense ... . Nevertheless, the powers and procedural guarantees an authority possesses are relevant in determining whether the remedy before it is effective.[51]

Next the Court examined the existing remedies *in concreto*. It noted that a person having an interest in the matter may request the *Bundesverfassungsgericht* to review the legislation in question for its conformity with the German Constitution. It is true that it is not the conformity of the legislation with the Convention that is reviewed, but conformity with provisions in the German Constitution. However, the relevant provisions in this case greatly resemble the relevant Article 8 of the Convention.[52] Furthermore, a person who suspects that the legal provision has been applied to him may approach the above-mentioned parliamentary committee, and thereafter may again appeal to the *Bundesverfassungsgericht*, which may then request the authorities to supply all the information desired. With respect to this, the Court held:

> Admittedly, the effectiveness of these remedies is limited and they will in principle apply only in exceptional cases. However, in the circumstances of the present proceedings, it is hard to conceive of more effective remedies being possible.[53]

And as to the complaint that the factual victim cannot defend himself because he does not know whether the provision has been applied to him, the Court, following the Commission, adopted the position - "albeit to its regret" - that secret control may after all be necessary, and that

> the Court cannot interpret or apply Article 13 so as to arrive at a result tantamount in fact to nullifying its conclusion that the absence of notification to the persons concerned is compatible with Article 8 in order to ensure the efficacy of surveillance measures.[54]

Thus the Court to a high degree stripped Article 13 of its autonomous character recognized in this same judgment. The issue whether it is still possible to speak of a "remedy" and whether the latter is "effective" was turned by the Court into a relative question, which has to be judged in accordance with the circumstances of each case. If those circumstances are such that they do not constitute a violation of one of the rights or freedoms of the Convention, no further requirements for legal protection than those circumstances allow can ensue from Article 13.

The Court thus actually created the same vicious circle which it wished to break in the first place. It is precisely the question whether these circumstances are in conformity with the Convention which the person concerned wants

---

51. Judgment of 6 September 1978, A.28 (1979), p. 30.
52. *Ibidem*, pp. 30 and 31 in conjunction with p. 13.
53. *Ibidem*, p. 31.
54. *Ibidem*, pp. 30-31.

to have established in a national procedure. This right is conferred on him by Article 13, but then the national procedure must provide an actual possibility for it. As has been observed above with respect to the application of Article 6(1) in this case,[55] the Court was confronted with the choice between, on the one hand, the interest of the person in question in an effective remedy and, on the other hand, the general interest of an effective surveillance for the protection of the democratic values underlying the Convention. The Court in fact gives priority to the latter interest via a systematic interpretation of Article 13 in conjunction with Article 8(2). However, an argument evidently weighing heavily with the Court is the fact that, in accordance with a decision of the German *Bundesverfassungsgericht*, the authorities are obliged to inform the person involved of the measures "as soon as the surveillance measures are discontinued and notification can be made without jeopardising the purpose of the restriction".[56] From that moment the normal remedy is open again to the person involved. Previously, the remedy against unlawful acts of the authorities is in the hands of the above-mentioned parliamentary committee and, if appealed to, the *Bundesverfassungsgericht*. In this phase, too, there is a certain amount of supervision of the way in which interests of national security and the rights and freedoms of individuals have been weighed against each other by the authorities, although this supervision cannot be called very effective, because the person concerned must rely on presumptions as to the application of the security measures against him.

The impact of the systematic approach as employed by the Court with respect to Article 13 can also be noticed in its judgment in the *Silver* Case concerning the effectiveness of the various remedies that were available in the case of a breach of the right of a detainee to respect for his correspondence. With respect to the relevant British legislation the Court made the following distinction:

> in those instances where the norms in question were incompatible with the Convention and where the Court has found a violation of Article 8 to have occurred there was no effective remedy and Article 13 has therefore also been violated. In the remaining case, there is no reason to assume that the applicants' complaints could not have been duly examined by the Home Secretary and/or the English courts and Article 13 has therefore not been violated."[57]

Here, too, the Court seems to be inclined to apply stricter standards if it first has found a violation of one of the rights laid down in the Convention.

That the systematic approach may entail very far-reaching consequences became clear in the *Leander* Case. This case concerned the use of information kept in a secret police-register when assessing a person's suitability for employment on a post of importance for national security. As far as Article 13 was concerned Mr. Leander complained that neither he nor his lawyer had

---

55. See *supra* p. 318.
56. *Supra* note 51, p. 31.
57. Judgment of 25 March 1983, A.61 (1983), p. 44.

been given the right to receive and comment upon the complete material upon which the appointing authority had based its decision not to employ him and that he had not had any right to appeal to an independent authority with power to render a binding decision as to the correctness and release of information kept on him.

Consequently, the Court had to review the effectiveness of the remedies which the Swedish legal system provides in cases like this. According to the Court the Chancellor of Justice and the Parliamentary Ombudsman, to both of whom complaints may be addressed, are independent of the Government, but lack the power to render a legally binding decision.[58] The other remedy, to which Mr. Leander actually had recourse, consisted in fact of a complaint to the Government. The Court observes that there can be no question about the power of the Government to deliver a binding decision in this respect. On that basis it concludes that "the aggregate of the remedies set out above ... satisfies the conditions of Article 13 in the particular circumstances of the instant case."[59] What the Court omits to refer to, however, is the obvious fact that Government officials are not independent of the Government.

The odd result in the *Leander* Case is premised on the systematic approach set forth by the Court:

> the requirements of Article 13 will be satisfied if there exists domestic machinery whereby, *subject to the inherent limitations of the context*, the individual can secure compliance with the relevant laws.[60]

In the instant case this context dictated that

> an effective remedy under Article 13 must mean a remedy that is as effective as it can be, having regard to the restricted scope for recourse inherent in any system for the protection of national security.[61]

In sum, the systematic approach permeates the Strasbourg interpretation to the point where the meaning of Article 13 is virtually nullified. This approach requires the Convention to be interpreted in harmony with its logic. The present authors cannot discern any illogicality in asking the question of whether a meaningful interpretation of Article 13 should not - in certain instances - have a bearing upon the interpretation of other Convention provisions instead of the other way round. This question, as far as we can see, is not raised in the Strasbourg case-law despite the pivotal role of the guarantee of an effective remedy within the framework of the concept of the Rule of Law.[62]

7. The provision in the Covenant that is comparable with Article 13 of the Convention is included as paragraph 3 of Article 2, immediately succeeding the obligation of the contracting States to guarantee the rights laid down in

---

58. Judgment of 26 March 1987, A.116 (1987), p. 31.
59. *Ibidem*, p. 32.
60. *Ibidem*, p. 30 (emphasis added).
61. *Ibidem*, p. 32.
62. See supra p. 521.

the Covenant and the obligation - not occurring in the Convention - to take the necessary legislative and other measures for the implementation of the Covenant.

This third paragraph of Article 2 consists of three clauses, the first of which is similar to Article 13, although it does not contain the words "before a national authority". To the latter, the whole of the second clause of paragraph 2 is devoted; it contains the words of "by competent judicial, administrative or legislative authorities, or by any other competent authority provided for by the legal system of the State". This definition brings out more clearly than Article 13 of the Convention does, that the authority need not be a judicial organ, although it states at the same time that the States undertake "to develop the possibilities of judicial remedy". A third clause provides that in case a remedy has been granted, it shall be enforced. As the Committee of Experts rightly observes in its report, the latter is implied in the word "effective" in Article 13.[63]

§ 3. ARTICLE 14: PROHIBITION OF DISCRIMINATION

The enjoyment of the rights and freedoms set forth in this Convention shall be secured without discrimination on any ground such as sex, race, colour, language, religion, political or other opinion, national or social origin, association with a national minority, property, birth or other status.

1. Like the previously discussed Article 13, Article 14 according to its formulation does not grant any independent right, in this case the right to freedom from discrimination. Here again it may be said that such a right ought not to be lacking in the Convention. At the drafting stage of Protocol no. 4 the Consultative Assembly in its proposal had advocated the inclusion of a general provision to the effect that "all persons are equal before the law". However, this proposal was deleted from the draft by the Committee of Experts on the ground of arguments which, as compared with the importance of the elimination of discrimination, cannot be considered very convincing,[64] and which are contradicted more or less by the later case-law.

The Convention thus lags behind the developments in the United Nations, where the elimination of discrimination has received and still receives a good deal of attention, as has been expressed in a number of conventions: the UN Convention of 1952 on the Political Rights of Women, the Conventions of the International Labour Organisation of 1951 and 1958 on Equal Remuneration

---

63. "Problems arising from the Co-existence of the United Nations Covenants on Human Rights and the European Convention on Human Rights; Differences as regards the Rights Guaranteed", Report of the Committee of Experts on Human Rights to the Committee of Ministers, Strasbourg 1970, H(70)7, p. 18.

64. See Council of Europe, *Explanatory Reports on the Second to Fifth Protocols to the European Convention for the Protection of Human Rights and Fundamental Freedoms*, H(71)11, pp. 52-53.

and on Discrimination in Employment and Occupation respectively, the UNESCO Convention of 1960 against Discrimination in Education, the UN Convention of 1965 on the Elimination of All Forms of Racial Discrimination, the UN Convention of 1979 on the Elimination of All Forms of Discrimination against Women, and last but not least: Article 26 of the Covenant on Civil and Political Rights. These as well as other conventions drafted within the framework of the United Nations organizations constitute an important addition to the, on this point defective, guarantees in the Convention in so far as the contracting States are parties to them.[65]

2. Since an addition to the Convention in this respect has not been realized thus far, the developments that have taken place in the case-law with respect to Article 14 are of all the greater importance. That case-law of the Commission and the Court presents a rather complex picture and is moreover not characterized by very great consistency.

Two closely connected questions concerning the relationship between Article 14 and the rights and freedoms of Section I are more or less interwoven in the case-law. On the one hand, the question of whether Article 14 has its own significance independently of the rights and freedoms protected in the Convention. On the other hand, the question of whether in relation to those rights and freedoms Article 14 grants an autonomous or only an accessory protection, that is whether or not it can only be applied when any of those rights or freedoms has been violated. Both questions have been summarily answered as follows by the Commission, with a reference to the Court's judgment in the *Belgian Linguistic* Case,[66] to be discussed below:

> the guarantee of Article 14 of the Convention "has no independent existence in the sense that, under the terms of Article 14, it relates solely to rights and freedoms set forth in the Convention"; nevertheless "a measure which in itself is in conformity with the requirements of the Article enshrining the right or freedom in question, may however infringe this Article when read in conjunction with Article 14 for the reason that it is of a discriminatory nature".[67]

The starting point with regard to the first-mentioned question is, therefore, that Article 14 has no significance, independently of the rights and freedoms ensured in Section I. In a later case the Commission once again expressed this as follows:

> Article 14 is not directed against discrimination in general but only against discrimination in relation to the rights and freedoms guaranteed by the Convention.[68]

As will become apparent below, this starting-point is qualified to a certain extent in connection with the second above-mentioned question concerning the relationship between Article 14 and the rights and freedoms protected by the

---

65. For that, see: United Nations, *Human Rights, A Compilation of International Instruments*, New York 1988.
66. See *infra* p. 536.
67. Appl. 4045/69, *X v. Federal Republic of Germany, Yearbook* XIII (1970), p. 698 (704-706). See also: Report of 3 March 1982, *Van der Mussele*, B.55 (1987), p. 37.
68. Appl. 8410/78, *X v. Federal Republic of Germany, D & R* 18 (1980), p. 216 (220).

Convention.

As regards this second question, the earlier case-law of the Commission seems to point in the direction that the dependent character of Article 14 entails that this provision can be brought up only if there is *prima facie* evidence that one of the rights or freedoms of the Convention has been violated.[69] This accessory character then implies at the same time that the restrictions of the "main" article may be advanced for the justification of what in itself constitutes discrimination.[70]

However, unlike Article 13, Article 14 does not refer solely to cases involving alleged *violations*, but to *every* discriminatory restriction on the enjoyment of the rights and freedoms. Even if a restriction in itself finds support in the relevant provision of the Convention, the restriction must not be applied in a discriminatory way. This interpretation has also found increasing support in the case-law of the Commission, contrary to its above-mentioned position. An example is its decision on Appl. 2065/63, where an elder of the Reformed Church, in his complaint against the Netherlands concerning the General Old Age Insurance Act, alleged among other things that this Act implied a discrimination between two categories of conscientious objectors. After having rejected the invocation of Article 1 of the First Protocol as manifestly ill-founded on the basis of the justification "in the public interest" mentioned there, the Commission nevertheless instituted a separate inquiry into the complaint concerning Article 14.[71]

The Commission clearly set forth its argument for this approach in its report in the *Belgian Linguistic* Case:

the applicability of Article 14 is not limited to cases in which there is an accompanying violation of another Article. Such a restricted application would deprive Article 14 of any practical value. The sole effect of the discrimination would be to aggravate the violation of another provision of the Convention. Such an interpretation would hardly be

69. See *e.g.* Appl. 808/60, *ISOP v. Austria, Yearbook* V (1962), p. 108 (124): since the right to a fair hearing of Art. 6(1) has not been violated, Art. 14 cannot be applicable. See also Appl. 6782/74, *X, Y, and Z v. Belgium, D & R* 9 (1978), p. 13 (21); Appl. 7729/76, *Agee v. United Kingdom, D & R* 7 (1977), p. 164 (176); and Appl. 7742/76, *A, B, and Company A.S. v. Federal Republic of Germany, Yearbook* XXI (1978), p. 492 (514). For other examples, see M.A. Eissen, "L'autonomie de l'article 14 de la Convention européenne des Droits de l'Homme dans la jurisprudence de la Commission", in: *Mélanges offerts à Polys Modinos*, Paris 1968, pp. 122-145 (127-132).
70. In this context see the decisions in which the Commission held that the German legislation in which homosexuality between men was penalized, but between women not, might find its justification in the protection of health and morals in the sense of Art. 8(2), and on this ground concluded that the complaint was inadmissible because it was manifestly ill-founded: *inter alia*, Appl. 104/55, *X v. Federal Republic of Germany, Yearbook* I (1955-57), p. 228 (229). See also Appl. 5935/72, *X v. Federal Republic of Germany, Yearbook* XIX (1976), p. 276 (282-288), in which a complaint about the said German legislation was considered manifestly ill-founded, because the criterion of "necessity of social protection" used by the Federal Republic of Germany was objective and reasonable in the Commission's view. Two complaints against the United Kingdom concerning discrimination between homosexuality of men on the one hand and of women on the other were, however, declared admissible by the Commission: see Appl. 7215/75, *X v. United Kingdom, Yearbook* XXI (1978), p. 354 (370-374) and Appl. 7525/76, *X v. United Kingdom, Yearbook* XXII (1979), p. 156 (184-186). For the report on Appl. 7215/75, see *D & R* 19 (1980), p. 66, and for the judgment in the *Dudgeon* Case, see *infra* pp. 543-544.
71. Appl. 2065/63, *X v. the Netherlands, Yearbook* VIII (1965), p. 266 (272). For other examples, see Eissen, *supra* note 69, pp. 132-145.

compatible with the wording of Article 14: this states that the enjoyment of the rights and liberties set forth in the Convention shall be *secured (doit être assuré)* without any discrimination. It thus places on States an obligation which is not simply negative.

...

Article 14 is of particular importance in relation to those clauses of the Convention which, while establishing a right or freedom, give States discretionary power with regard to the steps to be taken to ensure the enjoyment of that right or freedom. It is not a normative provision of the same kind as Article 8 of the Convention or Article 2 of the Protocol: it concerns the means or the extent of the enjoyment of rights and freedoms already stated elsewhere. It may happen that different measures taken by a State in respect of different parts of its territory or population entail no breach of the Article in the Convention defining the right in question, but that the differentiation entails a violation if the State's conduct is judged from the point of view of Article 14. The question would then arise of a violation not only of Article 14 but of the right in question as mentioned in the relevant Article in conjunction with Article 14: in fact, an individual who suffers prejudice as a result of a State's infringement of Article 14 does not enjoy the right or freedom in question on the conditions or to the degree laid down in the Convention viewed as a whole.[72]

In this reasoning the Commission still relates Article 14 very closely to one of the other provisions, which in itself has not, but in conjunction with Article 14 has been violated. In a number of later decisions it seems to be going further in attributing an autonomous character to Article 14. Thus, in its decision on Appl. 5763/72, the Commission first held that Article 1 of Protocol no. 1 was not applicable because social security benefits do not constitute "possessions" in the sense of that article, but nevertheless examined whether the challenged legislation was discriminatory in its application. The argument it advanced was that

the allegations which the applicant has made under Article 14 of the Convention *are related to* the right to peaceful enjoyment of possessions and therefore raise an issue under Article 1 of Protocol no. 1.[73]

In a case against the Federal Republic of Germany the Commission held that for the application of Article 14 it is sufficient "that the 'subject matter' *falls within the scope* of the Article in question".[74] In between the formulations used by the Commission in these two decisions we find that of its decision on Appl. 6573/74:

Article 14 may be taken in conjunction with another article which need not itself be violated. It is enough for the matter at issue *to be covered by* that other article.[75]

This case-law shows that the Commission has qualified its above-mentioned view that Article 14 refers only to discrimination in relation to the rights and freedoms protected in the Convention. Nevertheless, it still appears from that case-law that the matter complained of must have some connection with one of the rights and freedoms guaranteed, if there is to be question of violation

---

72. Report of 24 June 1965, B.3 (1965-67), pp. 305-306.
73. Appl. 5763/72, *X v. the Netherlands, Yearbook* XVI (1973), p. 274 (296); emphasis added.
74. Appl. 5935/72, *X v. Federal Republic of Germany, Yearbook* XIX (1976), p. 276 (288); emphasis added. See also the report of 10 December 1977, *Marckx*, B.29 (1977-1979), p. 49.
75. Appl. 6573/74, *X v. the Netherlands, D & R* 1 (1975), p. 87 (89); emphasis added.

of Article 14.[76]

The development in the case-law as just described would seem to have culminated, - at least for the time being - in a standard formula, used by the Court, according to which

> "Article 14 complements the other substantive provisions of the Convention and the Protocols. It has no independent existence, since it has effect solely in relation to 'the enjoyment of the rights and freedoms' safeguarded by those provisions. Although the application of Article 14 does not necessarily presuppose a breach of those provisions - and to this extent it is autonomous -, there can be no room for its application unless the facts at issue fall within the ambit of one or more of the latter."[77]

This formula makes it clear that Article 14 is not independent in the sense that there has to be at least some kind of relation with the rights and freedoms of the Convention; differential treatment in a field which falls outside the scope of the Convention cannot amount to a violation of Article 14.[78] At the same time the judgment referred to bears out that Article 14 is autonomous in the sense that its application does not require the simultaneous violation of one of the Convention's rights or freedoms.

This autonomous character of Article 14 had been recognized also by the Court before. Thus, in the *Belgian Linguistic* Case the Court held:

> "While it is true that this guarantee [*viz.* that laid down in Article 14] has no independent existence in the sense that under the terms of Article 14 it relates solely to 'rights and freedoms set forth in the Convention', a measure which in itself is in conformity with the requirements of the Article enshrining the right or freedom in question may however infringe this Article when read in conjunction with Article 14 for the reason that it is of a discriminatory nature".[79]

According to the Court, Article 14 forms as it were "an integral part of each of the Articles laying down rights and freedoms".[80]

In later case-law the Court took a similar view. In its judgment in the *National Union of Belgian Police* Case it held:

> "Although the Court has found no violation of Article 11(1), it has to be ascertained whether the difference in treatment complained of by the applicant union contravenes Articles 11 and 14 taken together ... A measure which in itself is in conformity with the requirements of the Article enshrining the right or freedom in question may therefore infringe this Article when read in conjunction with Article 14 for the reason that it is of

---

76. In the case mentioned in the previous note the applicant has been disenfranchised and on that basis alleged violation of Art. 14 in conjunction with Art. 10. The Commission held that the right to vote could not be brought under Art. 10, so that Art. 10 could not be invoked nor, therefore, Article 14. Compare Appl. 8701/79, *X v. Belgium, D & R* 18 (1980), p. 250 (254), where the Commission decided "that, in the present case, the matter at issue (the right to vote) is covered by Article 3 of the First Protocol and that Article 14 may be taken in conjunction with Article 3 of this Protocol".
77. Judgment of 28 May 1985, *Abdulaziz, Cabales, and Balkandali,* A.94 (1985), p. 35. See also the judgment of 28 November 1984, *Rasmussen,* A.87 (1984), p. 12, and the judgment of 23 November 1983, *Van der Mussele,* A.70 (1983), p. 22.
78. See, for instance, Appl. 8493/79, *De Meester v. Belgium, D & R* 25 (1982) p. 210 (217): "In the instant case, the discrimination complained of by the applicant relates to the freedom to apply for a position in the judiciary, a freedom which ... the Convention does not protect. Consequently, Article 14 of the Convention is not relevant to the instant case."
79. Judgment of 23 July 1968, A.6 (1968), p. 33.
80. *Ibidem,* p. 34. Also the Commission in its report of 15 July 1983, *Rasmussen,* A.87 (1985), p. 22.

a discriminatory nature".[81]

Summarizing, the case-law discussed above induces us to conclude that Article 14 contains an autonomous, though complementary guarantee in relation to the rights and freedoms protected in Section I. Even though the article in question on itself has not been violated, the facts may show a violation of that article in conjunction with Article 14.

3. Curiously enough, the Commission and the Court adopt a different attitude when a violation of one of the articles from Section I is actually found. In that case they take the position that in general it is not necessary any more to make an inquiry into the possible violation of that article in conjunction with Article 14. In other words: in such cases Article 14 is not treated as an autonomous and complementary, but only a subsidiary guarantee.

In its decision in the *Airey* Case the Court formulated this view, which has been repeated in later judgments, as follows:

> Article 14 has no independent existence; it constitutes one particular element (non-discrimination) of the rights safeguarded by the Convention ... . The Articles enshrining those rights may be violated alone and/or in conjunction with Article 14. If the Court does not find a separate breach of one of those Articles that has been invoked both on its own and together with Article 14, it must also examine the case under the latter Article. On the other hand, such an examination is not generally required when the Court finds a violation of the former Article taken alone. The position is otherwise if a clear inequality of treatment in the enjoyments of the right in question is a fundamental aspect of the case.[82]

Even apart from the fact that the meaning of the formulation "clear inequality of treatment" is left vague and therefore admits of more than one interpretation in a concrete case,[83] the line followed by the Court would appear not to be very consistent. It cannot be appreciated why Article 14 should have another character in cases where a violation of another article of the Convention has already been found than in cases where there is no question of a violation of any of these articles as such. As Judge Evrigenis rightly stated in his dissenting opinion in the *Airey* Case:

> Discrimination in the enjoyment of a right protected by the Convention contravenes Article 14 irrespective of whether such discrimination lies within or outside the area of violation of that right. The word "enjoyment", within the meaning of Article 14, must cover all situations that may arise between, at the one extreme, plain refusal of a right protected by the Convention and, at the other, full embodiment of that right in the domestic system.[84]

---

81. Judgment of 27 October 1975, A.19 (1975), p. 19. Contra Judge Fitzmaurice in his separate opinion, *ibidem*, p. 38: "No question of the discriminatory or non-discriminatory application or enjoyment of a right can arise unless that right itself exists in the first place, to be conceded whether discriminatory or not". For the Court's view, see also the judgment of 6 February 1976, *Swedish Engine Drivers' Union*, A.20 (1976), pp. 16-17, and the judgment of 13 June 1979, *Marckx*, A.31 (1979), p. 24.
82. Judgment of 9 October 1979, A.32 (1980), p. 16. See also the judgment of 22 October 1981, *Dudgeon*, A.45 (1982), p. 26.
83. See the dissenting opinions of Judge Evrigenis in the *Airey* Case *(ibidem*, p. 29) and of the Judges Evrigenis and Garcia De Entecre in the *Dudgeon* Case *(ibidem*, p. 25), who, unlike the majority of the Court, concluded that in these cases there was decidedly a question of a "clear inequality of treatment".
84. *Ibidem*, p. 29.

In the *Dudgeon* Case the Court gave the following argument for the distinction it made with regard to Article 14:

> Once it has been held that the restriction on the applicant's right to respect for his private sexual life gives rise to a breach of Article 8 by reason of its breadth and absolute character ... there is no useful legal purpose to be served in determining whether he has in addition suffered discrimination as compared with other persons who are subject to lesser limitations on the same right.[85]

From the argumentation of the Court it appears that it has in mind in particular a "useful legal purpose" from the viewpoint of the individual applicant concerned. Even leaving apart whether in the case at issue the applicant took the same view, and whether the Court's approach not to investigate all the elements of the complaint is correct from a procedural point of view,[86] in our opinion this argument ignores the fact that decisions of the Court, as the highest organ competent to interpret the Convention, have an effect far exceeding the concrete aspects of the case submitted to it, and that these decisions may therefore also have implications of a more general character.[87]

Nevertheless, the Court would seem to stick to its position that once it has found a violation of one or more of the Conventions's rights and freedoms, an investigation into the alleged violation of Article 14 becomes superfluous. In a fairly recent case it does not even adduce arguments anymore for its position. After having found a violation of Article 8 with respect to one of the applicants - an illegitimate child whose legal situation under Irish law differed considerably from that of a legitimate child - the Court simply opined:

> Since succession rights were included among the aspects of Irish law which were taken into consideration in the examination of the general complaint concerning the third applicant's legal situation ... the Court ... does not consider it necessary to give a separate ruling on this allegation [concerning discrimination contrary to Article 14].[88]

---

85. Judgment of 22 October 1981, A.45 (1982), p. 26.
86. See the position of Judge Matscher in his dissenting opinion in the *Dudgeon* Case: "In my view, when the Court is called on to rule on a breach of the Convention which has been alleged by the applicant and contested by the respondent Government, it is the Court's duty, provided that the application is admissible, to decide the point by giving an answer on the merits of the issue that has been raised. The Court cannot escape this responsibility by employing formulas that are liable to limit excessively the scope of Article 14 to the point of depriving it of all practical value" *(ibidem,* p. 36).
87. *Cf.* in this context also what has been observed *supra* pp. 158-159, with regard to the position of the Court in the *De Becker* Case.
88. Judgment of 18 December 1986, *Johnston and others,* A.112 (1987), p. 31. The Court's position on this issue would seem to constitute well-established case-law by now, judging from the fact that only one member of the Court dissented on this point; see the separate opinion, partly dissenting and partly concurring, of Judge De Meyer, *ibidem,* pp. 39-40: "I consider that in the present case the Court should, as in the *Marckx* Case, have found not only a violation of the right to respect for private and family life but also a violation, as regards that right, of the principle of non-discrimination. In my view, the latter violation arises from the very fact that, on the one hand, the legal situation of the third applicant, as a child born out of wedlock, is different from that of a child of a married couple and that, on the other hand, the legal situation of the first and second applicants [the unmarried parents of the third applicant] in their relations with or concerning the third applicant is different from that of parents of a child of a married couple in their relations with or concerning that child".

4. The concept of equality and the ensuing prohibition of discrimination constitute one of the most complex principles of law. This is not the place to extensively deal with the concept of equality.[89] The following general observations, however, would seem to be at place.

Fundamental principles, like the principle of equality, can play a prominent role in any legal order. Because of their general character and their ensuing wide scope, principles can enhance coherence of and structure within the set of rules of which a legal order is made up. Principles, in other words, can constitute an integrating factor, if they function adequately. This makes it clear that, conversely, the malfunctioning of principles can have very negative consequences for the legal order concerned. To the extent that, for instance, the concept of inequality is insufficiently developed, this may lead to unclarity and uncertainty. It is therefore of the utmost importance that the concept of equality is well elaborated at the various levels at which it is to play its integrating role, *i.e.* at that of the legislature, that of the executive branch of government, and that of the judiciary.

For our purposes particularly the latter level is most relevant and it therefore suffices to briefly outline the elements which should be taken into account if a given treatment or situation is reviewed for its conformity with the principle of equality and the prohibition of discrimination. These elements are the following. A violation of the principle of equality and non-discrimination arises if there is (a) differential treatment of (b) equal cases without there being (c) an objective and reasonable justification, or if (d) proportionality between the aim sought and the means employed is lacking.

As far as the first element is concerned, it should be observed from the outset that Article 14 - despite the French text "sans distinction aucune" - does not prohibit every difference in treatment. On the contrary, the obligation contained therein may even entail unequal treatment. For Article 14 is not only concerned with *formal* equality - equal treatment of equal cases - but also with *substantive* equality: unequal treatment of unequal cases in proportion to their inequality. In other words, a difference in treatment which is aimed at eliminating an existing inequality creates substantive equality and is consequently in conformity with Article 14.

Thus, a progressive income tax is not discriminatory, provided the progressive measure is proportional and consequently results in a fairer distribution of income than would be the case without it. Obviously, what may

---

89. For a discussion on the concept of equality, see P. Westen, "The Empty Idea of Equality", 95 *Harvard Law Review* (1982-1983), pp. 537-595; E. Chemerinsky, "In Defense of Equality: A Reply to Professor Westen", 81 *Michigan Law Review* (1983), pp. 575-595; A. D'Amato, "Is Equality a Totally Empty Idea?", 81 *Michigan Law Review* (1983), pp. 600-603; P. Westen, "The Meaning of Equality in Law, Science, Math and Morals: A Reply", 81 *Michigan Law Review* (1983), pp. 604-663; S. Burton, "Comment on "Empty Ideas": Logical Positivist Analysis of Equality and Rules", 91 *The Yale Law Journal* (1982), pp. 1136-1152; P. Westen, "On 'Confusing Ideas': Reply", 91 *The Yale Law Journal* (1982), pp. 1153-1165; A. Greenawolt, "How Empty is the Idea of Equality?", 83 *Columbia Law Journal* (1983), pp. 1167-1185; and P. Westen, "To Lure the Tarantula from Its Hole: a Response", 8 *Columbia Law Journal* (1983), pp. 1186-1208.

be called "fair" and "proportional" in such cases is to a large extent still dependent upon the national situation, so that the reasonableness of the national authorities' views on this matter can be reviewed only very marginally in Strasbourg. A complaint concerning a difference in treatment under the fiscal legislation was therefore declared "manifestly ill-founded" by the Commission on the basis of the very general argument indeed: "that it is a common incident of taxation laws that they apply in different ways or in different degrees to different persons or entities in the community".[90]

The second comparative element of the concept of equality consists of the question of whether the cases at hand are equal or unequal in the relevant respects. In order to be able to answer that question, a yardstick has to be developed, which has to be applied to both cases, and on that basis the ensuing results have to be compared. The crux of the matter is the yardstick or the criteria used for the comparison. Since two cases can be said always to be equal in some respects and unequal in others, for the comparability test to be meaningful, the criteria used have to be adequately related to the object of the provision which prescribes equal treatment. To the extent that such is the case, the comparison which is inherent in the equality test puts in focus the goals underlying the provisions concerned. Consequently, if the comparability test is skipped or merged into the third element - the justification test - the danger arises that the interests protected and/or the goals envisaged in the provisions embodying equality become under-exposed. As will be argued below, this danger materializes not infrequently in the Strasbourg case-law.

The comparability test was clearly performed by the Court in its *Van der Mussele* judgment and its judgment in the *Johnston* Case. In both cases the Court refers not to equal, but to "analogous" situations. In the first-mentioned case it was alleged, *inter alia*, that Belgian *avocats*, unlike medical practitioners, veterinary surgeons, pharmacists, and dentists, were required to provide their services free of charge to indigent persons and that such a difference in treatment constituted arbitrary inequality. The Court pointed out that between the Bar and the other professions cited there existed fundamental differences as to legal status, conditions for entry to the profession, the nature of the functions involved, the manner of exercise of those functions, etc. The Court, consequently, did not find any similarity between the disparate situations in question, because each one was characterized by a corpus of rights and obligations of which it would be artificial to isolate one specific aspect.[91]

In the *Johnston* Case the two applicants alleged violation of Article 14 on the basis of the fact that the first applicant was unable to obtain a divorce in order subsequently to marry the second applicant, whereas other persons resident in Ireland and having the necessary means could obtain abroad a

90. Appl. 511/59, *Gudmundsson v. Iceland, Yearbook* III (1960), p. 394 (424).
91. Judgment of 23 November 1983, *Van der Mussele*, A.70 (1983), pp. 22-23.

divorce which could be recognized *de jure* or *de facto* in Ireland. The Court, however, noted that under general Irish rules of private international law foreign divorces are recognized in Ireland only if they have been obtained by persons domiciled abroad and that, therefore, the situations of such persons and of the first and the second applicants could not be regarded as analogous.[92]

The category of cases just referred to in fact presents relatively few difficulties, because the comparability test is clearly performed instead of being merged into the justification test, or even skipped completely. Obviously, this is not to say that the comparability test may not be very complex. It is not always easy to decide whether the situations concerned are different or equal, or rather to select the relevant criteria on which that decision has to be based. This became apparent, for instance, in the *Grandrath* Case. There a member of the Jehova's Witnesses complained that as a leader of a bible club he did not qualify for release from compulsory military service without substitute civil service, while such a release was granted to ministers of other religious communities. After the Commission had first decided that the substitute civil service for conscientious objectors did not constitute compulsory labour in the sense of Article 4 of the Convention, it examined whether its imposition took place in a discriminatory way, contrary to Article 14. It concluded that this was not so, because the distinction made in the relevant German legislation consisted "in the function performed by different categories of ministers and is not according to the religious community to which they belong".[93] However, the Commission's interpretation may be disputed. In fact, in the German legislation the nature of the function and the scope of the religious activities formed criteria only for other ministers than those of the Reformed and the Roman Catholic religion. This legislation might, for instance, lead to the result that a person who was to become a Roman Catholic priest and was predestined to teach mathematics later on, was relieved from civil service, but a Jehova's Witness who was engaged very intensively in preaching the Bible, albeit that this was not his chief function, was not relieved. In that respect, therefore, the religious community, and not the nature of the function, was conclusive. In fact, this had not been denied by the German Government. But the latter defended the distinction by referring to arrangements which had been made between the State and the favoured religious communities.[94] In our opinion, therefore, the Commission ought to have examined whether a difference in treatment based on this ground actually made for substantive equality.

5. Nevertheless, in the above-mentioned kind of cases the discussion at least goes to the heart of the matter, *i.e.* whether the situations at hand are equal

---

92.   Judgment of 18 December 1986, *Johnston and others*, A.112 (1987), pp. 26-27.
93.   Report of 29 June 1967, *Grandrath*, Yearbook X (1967), p. 626 (682 and 684).
94.   *Ibidem*, p. 650.

or unequal. In most instances of the Strasbourg case-law, however, the comparability test is glossed over, and the emphasis is (almost) completely on the justification test. This result ensues from the approach which the Court takes with respect to Article 14. According to the Court, for the purposes of Article 14 a difference of treatment is discriminatory if it has no objective and reasonable justification, that is, if it does not pursue a legitimate aim or if there is no reasonable relationship of proportionality between the means employed and the aim sought to be realized.[95] This approach was developed in the earlier case-law of the Court in its judgment in the *Belgian Linguistic* Case[96] and subsequently outlined by the Commission. According to this scheme discrimination contrary to Article 14 occurs when in a given case the existence of the following three elements can be established:

(a) the facts found disclose a differential treatment; (b) the distinction does not have an aim, *i.e.* it has no objective and reasonable justification having regard to the aim and effects of the measure under consideration; and (c) there is no reasonable proportionality between the means employed and the aim sought to be realized.[97]

Review of an allegedly discriminatory act on the part of a contracting State by reference to the above criteria has become established case-law of the Strasbourg organs.[98]

As was already observed, this approach entails the danger that the interests or goals embodied in the comparability test are implicitly subordinated to those which are enhanced by an objective and reasonable justification which is often derived from the general interest. An example of this is to be found in the Court's judgment in the *Belgian Linguistic* Case. In that case the Belgian linguistic legislation, which differentiated on a number of points between the different linguistic entities, was found by the Court not to conflict with Article 14, except on a few points; not because that legislation served to abolish existing differences, but because in the Court's opinion the differences in treatment in this case

strike a fair balance between the protection of the interests of the community and respect for the rights and freedoms safeguarded by the Convention.[99]

---

95. See, for instance, the judgments of 21 February 1986, *James and others*, A.98 (1986), p. 44, and of 8 July 1986, *Lithgow and others*, A.102 (1987), p. 66.
96. Judgment of 23 July 1968, A.6 (1968), p. 34.
97. See the report of 6 July 1976, *Geïllustreerde Pers N.V. v. the Netherlands*, D & R 8 (1977), p. 5 (14-15).
98. As far as the Commission is concerned, see, *inter alia*, Appl. 5935/72 referred to in note 74 above; Appl. 6741/74, *X v. Italy*, D & R 5 (1976), p. 83 (85), where a complaint that an Italian law prohibiting the re-establishment of the fascist party was contrary to Article 14 in conjunction with Articles 9, 10, and 11 was rejected by the Commission on the basis of the argument that "the difference in treatment ... is justified by the fact that it pursues a legitimate aim, that of protecting democratic institutions"; Appl. 7729/76, *Agee v. United Kingdom*, D & R 7 (1977), p. 164 (176) seems to imply the view of the Commission that the status of alien in itself already constitutes an objective and reasonable justification for difference in treatment between nationals and aliens in the field of immigration legislation; and Appl. 7721/76, *X v. the Netherlands*, D & R 11 (1978), p. 209 (211), in which the Commission seems to imply that the very fact that decisions are taken by an independent court already constitutes an objective and reasonable justification for different results in more or less equal criminal cases: "it is a general principle that decisions in criminal matters are taken on the particular circumstances of each case".
99. Judgment of 23 July 1968, A.6 (1968), p. 44.

In the Court's view this was not the case only for those provisions in the challenged linguistic legislation where access to the French-language schools in some predominantly Dutch-speaking suburbs of Brussels was refused to those children who did not live in these suburbs. Since the Dutch-language schools in those same suburbs on the contrary were open to anyone irrespective of his place of residence, the majority of the Court held that there was unlawful discrimination with regard to the French-speaking parents as concerned the restriction on the right of parents to choose the education of their children in accordance with their own views.[100] It is true that in this case the Court instituted an independent inquiry - five members of the Court precisely blamed the majority for having gone too far in this[101] - but it is obvious that the question of whether an inequality in treatment results in a factual equality or inequality leaves much more scope for an independent inquiry by the organs of the Convention than does the question of whether a given measure does or does not serve the general interest of the State, especially in a politically so delicate matter as the one concerned in this case.

Another clear example is that of the *Dudgeon* Case.[102] In this case Northern-Irish legal provisions were at stake, which contained a general prohibition of certain homosexual acts irrespective of the circumstances in which these took place and of the age of the persons involved. A 35-year old man alleged, *inter alia*, violation of Article 14 because the legislation concerned prevented him from having sexual relations with young men under 21 - even in private and with their consent - whereas the minimum age for heterosexual and lesbian relations was fixed under Northern-Irish law at 17. The Court settled the issue summarily as follows: it stressed

"the legitimate necessity in a democratic society for some degree of control over homosexual conduct, notably to provide safeguards against the exploitation and corruption of those who are specially vulnerable by reason, for example, of their youth", and decided that the fixing of ages with a view to affording such safeguards falls within the competence of the national authorities.[103]

It needs no explanation that the protection of the young constitutes a legitimate aim. In fact, this point remained undisputed. The complaint, however, concerned the fact that the legislation of Northern Ireland wanted to realize this aim in very diverging ways with respect to cases which, according to Dudgeon, were comparable in all relevant respects. The Court did not go into this argument of the applicant; it skipped the comparability test and directly applied the justification test in the form of a reference to the protection of the young. This is all the more remarkable as the Court had shortly before opined that

There can be no denial that some degree of regulation of male homosexual conduct, *as indeed of other forms of sexual conduct* by means of criminal law can be justified.

---

100. *Ibidem*, pp. 69-70.
101. See the collective dissenting opinion of the Judges Holmbäck, Rodenbourg, Ross, Wiarda, and Mast, *ibidem*, p. 89 (95).
102. Judgment of 22 October 1981, A.45 (1982).
103. *Ibidem*, p. 25.

and in that context had pointed in particular to

> those who are especially vulnerable because they are young, weak in body or mind, inexperienced, or in a state of special, physical, official or economic independence.[104]

From these considerations it is difficult to draw any other conclusion than that as far as the protection of vulnerable groups - in particular the young - is concerned, homosexual, lesbian, as well as heterosexual relationships have to be put on the same line and, therefore, be treated equally.

Something similar holds good with respect to one of the elements of the complaint with which the Court had to deal in its judgment of 28 May 1985 in the Case of *Abdulaziz, Cabales, and Balkandali*.[105] In this case Mrs Balkandali, among other things, alleged discrimination on the ground of birth, because the British immigration rules distinguished between female residents who themselves, or whose parents, were born in the United Kingdom and those with whom this was not the case. It was only for the foreign spouses of women belonging to the first-mentioned group that the British legislation opened the possibility to settle in the United Kingdom. The applicant was a British resident, but she as well as her parents were born in Egypt. Consequently, her Turkish husband was not permitted to take up permanent residence in the United Kingdom.

According to the government the distinction was designed to avoid the hardship which women having close ties with the United Kingdom would encounter if, on marriage, they were obliged to move abroad in order to stay with their husbands. The Court accepted this justification without a blow. It simply stated that "there are in general persuasive social reasons for giving special treatment to those whose link with a country stems from birth within it".[106] This may be true in general, but in special cases the criterion of birth does not appear to be the most suitable one. For the existence of close ties it is not only decisive whether or not one is born in the country, but particularly also whether or not and, if so, how long one has lived there. It is likely, for instance, that Mrs Balkandali, having lived in the United Kingdom for more than ten years, had closer ties with that country than persons whose parents are born there, but who themselves have taken up residence only recently. The Court itself conceded that

> It is true that a person who, like Mrs Balkandali, has been settled in a country for several years may also have close ties with it, even if he or she was not born there.[107]

In other words, as far as the existence of close ties with the United Kingdom is concerned, Mrs. Balkandali, although not born there, could in all relevant respects be put on the same line with female residents born in that country. Nevertheless, the Court subordinated the comparability aspect without further argument to the justification aspect.

---

104. *Ibidem*, p. 20; emphasis added.
105. A.94 (1985).
106. *Ibidem*, p. 41.
107. *Ibidem*.

From the above-mentioned examples it becomes evident that an objective and reasonable justification for differences in treatment is usually based on considerations derived from the public interest. It is at least questionable, however, whether such a more or less automatic subordination of individual interests to the public interest - without there being an adequate relationship in all cases between the unequal treatment and the existing inequality which the authorities wish to redress - can find support in the text and the spirit of Article 14. After all, the individual interest of enjoyment of the rights and freedoms without discrimination is given a prominent place there, while no restrictions based on the public interest are provided for, as is the case in various other provisions of the Convention.[108]\\\\ The upshot is in our view that Article 14 has been deprived of much of its meaning, since only those inequalities for which no objective and reasonable justification can be found are considered to conflict with it.

This emphasis on the public interest has the additional consequence that the Strasbourg organs leave a wide margin of discretion to the national authorities in appreciating the weight of the public interest concerned as compared with the individual interests at stake.[109] In fact, as a result of the above-mentioned definition of the concept of equality in the case-law it is often added that

> the Contracting States enjoy a certain margin of appreciation in assessing whether and to what extent differences in otherwise similar situations justify a different treatment in law.[110]

Clearly, this approach further detracts from the importance of Article 14 in the case-law.

An example of this approach is the *Rasmussen* judgment.[111] In this case Mr Rasmussen alleged violation of Article 14, because under a Danish Act of 1960 his right to contest his paternity of a child born during marriage was subject to time-limits, whereas his former wife was entitled to institute paternity proceedings at any time. The Court started with skipping the comparability test. It felt that it did not have to deal with the question of whether or not husband and wife were placed in analogous situations, because "the positions and interests referred to are also of relevance in determining whether the difference of treatment was justified".[112] With respect to this latter question the Court subsequently relied on the margin of appreciation to be granted to the contracting States, and pointed out that one of the relevant factors in this respect might be the existence or non-existence of common ground between the laws of the contracting States on the issue

---

108. See *e.g.* Arts 4(3), 5(1), 6(1), 8(2), 9(2), 10(2), and 11(2) of the Convention; Art. 1 of Protocol no. 1; Art. 2(2) of Protocol no. 4; and Art. 1(2) of Protocol no. 7.
109. For more details on this so-called margin of appreciation, see *infra* pp. 583-606.
110. For instance, judgment of 8 July 1986 in the Case of *Lithgow and others*, A.102 (1987), p. 67, where the Court further observed that "the scope of this margin will vary according to the circumstances, the subject-matter and its background".
111. Judgment of 28 November 1984, A.87 (1985).
112. *Ibidem*, pp. 13-14.

concerned. The Court found no such common ground, as the position of the mother and that of the husband was regulated in different ways in the various legal systems and, therefore, concluded that the Danish authorities were entitled to think that the difference made was justified.[113]

In the same vein the Court finally decided that the proportionality-requirement was fulfilled:

> the competent authorities were entitled to think that as regards the husband the aim sought to be realized would be most satisfactorily achieved by the enactment of a statutory rule, whereas as regards the mother it was sufficient to leave the matter to be decided on a case-by-case basis.[114]

Our main concern here is not whether one should agree or disagree with the Court on the outcome of this case. Whatever the outcome, the point is that the approach taken by the Court waters down the significance of Article 14 to the bare minimum.

All this, of course, does not mean that the Court's approach could not result in a finding of a breach of Article 14. In the above-mentioned Case of *Abdulaziz, Cabales, and Balkandali* the Court concluded that there was a violation of Article 14 because of discrimination on the ground of sex, since the British immigration rules made it more difficult for women than for men to obtain a permit to stay with their foreign spouses. As a justification the British Government had adduced the aim of protecting the domestic labour market. In the view of the Court this was not enough reason to justify the difference in treatment, the main argument being that "the advancement of the equality of the sexes is today a major goal in the Member States of the Council of Europe".[115] In the *Marckx* Case the Court also held that the distinction, made on different points in the Belgian legislation, between legitimate and illegitimate children, was contrary to the Convention.[116]

Nevertheless, the approach taken by the Court implies a very restrictive interpretation of Article 14 as is also witnessed by the judgments of the Court in the *National Union of Belgian Police* Case and in the *Swedish Engine Drivers' Union* Case. In these cases the Court examined whether, with the difference in treatment complained of, the national authorities had a justified aim in view or whether they pursued "other and ill-intentioned designs".[117] The latter conclusion is likely to be reached only in cases of evident arbitrariness. But has this inquiry anything to do with the question of discrimination? A government may decide on grounds derived from the public interest that only children of parents having sufficient means shall be admitted to universities, in order thus to restrict the government expense in the matter of scholarships. For this, objective and perhaps even reasonable criteria may be advanced.

---

113. *Ibidem*, p. 15.
114. *Ibidem*, pp. 15-16.
115. *Ibidem*, p. 37.
116. Judgment of 13 June 1979, A.31 (1979), pp. 17-27.
117. Judgment of 27 October 1975, *National Union of Belgian Police*, A.19 (1975), p. 21, and the judgment of 6 February 1976, *Swedish Engine Drivers' Union*, A.20 (1976), p. 17 respectively.

Would this not constitute prohibited discrimination? The aim of the Convention is to provide protection not only against unreasonable, but also against reasonable authorities.

6. Alkema has rightly pointed at the socializing effect which Article 14 may have on the rights and freedoms laid down in the Convention.[118] The Convention is concerned mainly with what might broadly be called freedom rights, which by their nature do not require a specific performance on the part of the authorities, but oblige them to refrain from restrictive interference. If, however, the authorities proceed in one way or another to specific performance in a field connected with one or more of the rights in question, they are obliged to do so without discrimination. If, for instance, they proceed to subsidize a particular religious community or to promote education in a particular language, other religious communities or other linguistic communities are in principle be entitled to the same treatment. Such a right in itself is not laid down in the Convention, but derives its protection from the operation of Article 14. Here again, however, such a right does not arise when the preferential treatment by the authorities is intended precisely to remove an existing inequality or - according to the case-law developed by the Commission and the Court - may be justified on other objective and reasonable grounds.

7. As appears from the words "on any ground such as" ("*ou toute autre situation*"), the enumeration of grounds for a difference in treatment which constitute discrimination is not exhaustive.[119] No distinctive feature or distinctive situation whatsoever may constitute a ground for an unequal treatment, unless that inequality is precisely intended to remove for the person concerned the disadvantages resulting from the distinctive feature or the distinctive situation.

8. As has already been indicated, the great difference between the Convention and the Covenant consists in the fact that the Covenant, in addition to a provision comparable to Article 14 of the Convention in the form of Article 2(1), contains in Article 26 an independent right to freedom from discrimination.[120]

Article 14 of the Convention and Article 2(1) of the Covenant do not differ very much. The terminology of Article 2(1) "without distinction of any kind" seems to go further than "without discrimination on any ground" in Article 14. The French text, however, uses the word "distinction" in both cases, and in both cases the intention will be not to prohibit every difference in treatment, but only unequal treatment of cases which are otherwise

118. Alkema, *supra* note 30, pp. 116 and 121.
119. See, for instance, the judgment of 21 February 1986, *James and others*, A.98 (1986), p. 44.
120. For Articles 2(1) and 26 of the Covenant reference is made to the study by Nowak, mentioned *supra* p. 216.

equal.[121] Moreover, Article 26 of the Covenant too, like Article 14 of the Convention, speaks of "discrimination on any ground".

The enumeration of grounds for a distinction constituting discrimination is in both treaties not exhaustive. This enumeration is almost identical in the two cases. However, the said articles of the Covenant do not mention the ground "association with a national minority". In this respect the Committee of Experts points out that the Covenant contains in Article 27 a special provision about minorities,[122] but this provision refers to particular rights and freedoms. It must, however, be assumed that the words "other status" have a sufficiently wide scope to include the status of belonging to a minority.

In both treaties, discrimination on the ground of sex is prohibited. Nevertheless, the Covenant guarantees in a separate Article 3 "the equal right of men and women to the enjoyment of all civil and political rights set forth in the present Covenant". The Committee of Experts rightly finds in its report that this provision "does not add anything to the provisions of Article 2 of the U.N. Covenant".[123]

§ 4. ARTICLE 15: DEROGATION FROM THE RIGHTS AND FREEDOMS IN CASE OF A PUBLIC EMERGENCY

1. In time of war or other public emergency threatening the life of the nation any High Contracting Party may take measures derogating from its obligations under this Convention to the extent strictly required by the exigencies of the situation, provided that such measures are not inconsistent with its other obligations under international law.

2. No derogation from Article 2, except in respect of deaths resulting from lawful acts of war, or from Articles 3, 4 (paragraph 1) and 7 shall be made under this provision.

3. Any High Contracting Party availing itself of this right of derogation shall keep the Secretary General of the Council of Europe fully informed of the measures which it has taken and the reasons therefor. It shall also inform the Secretary General of the Council of Europe when such measures have ceased to operate and the provisions of the Convention are again being fully executed.

1. Article 15 contains a general authorization for temporary derogation from the rights and freedoms laid down in the Convention - in so far as they are not excepted in the second paragraph - in case of a public emergency threatening the life of the nation. As the Secretariat of the Commission observes in a publication, here "the overriding rights of the State to protect

---

121. See *supra* p. 539.
122. See the report mentioned in note 63, p. 17.
123. *Ibidem*, p. 18.

its democratic institutions" are concerned.[124] This general authorization is additional to the special restrictions to be discussed below, which are incorporated into some articles of the Convention concerning the cases there provided for and in which "national security" and "public safety" are also mentioned.[125]

In connection with the application of Article 15, just as with respect to the special restrictions, two questions arise: (1) are the values which are to be protected by means of this derogation from or restriction of rights and freedoms really threatened, and (2) are the legislation enacted, the measures taken, or the penalties imposed really "necessary" or, as Article 15 formulates it even more restrictively, "strictly required" for the safeguarding of these values?

The demarcation between on the one hand the discretion of the national authorities, and on the other hand the review thereof by the Strasbourg organs, has been defined by the Commission in its report in the first case in which Article 15 was at issue: *Greece v. United Kingdom*. In this case the Commission took the position that, on the one hand, the Strasbourg organs are competent to institute an inquiry into both the above-mentioned questions, but that, on the other hand,

the Government should be able to exercise a certain measure of discretion in assessing the extent strictly required by the exigencies of the situation.[126]

More or less the same point of view was adopted by the Court in the *Lawless* Case. In this case the Court started its observations on the applicability of Article 15 with the words:

whereas it is for the Court to determine whether the conditions laid down in Article 15 for the exercise of the exceptional right of derogation have been fulfilled in the present case.[127]

Subsequently, with regard to the first of the above-mentioned questions it concluded that

the existence at the time of a "public emergency threatening the life of the nation" was *reasonably* deduced by the Irish Government from a combination of several factors.[128]

With regard to the second question, however, the Court appeared to institute a completely independent inquiry, which then resulted in the conclusion that the condition of "strictly required" had been satisfied.[129] And in the *Greece* Case, although the Commission had included in its report a reference to the "margin of appreciation" of the Greek Government,[130] it subsequently gave a negative answer to the first question on the basis of a detailed examination

---

124. *Case-Law Topics* No. 4, "Human Rights and their limitations", Strasbourg 1973, p. 3.
125. See Arts 8(2), 9(2), 10(2) and 11(2) of the Convention, Art. 2(3) of Protocol no. 4 and Art. 1(2) of Protocol no. 7.
126. Appl. 176/56, *Greece v. United Kingdom*, *Yearbook* II (1958-59), p. 174 (176).
127. Judgment of 1 July 1961, A.3 (1960-61), p. 55.
128. *Ibidem*, p. 56; emphasis added.
129. *Ibidem*, pp. 57-59.
130. Report of 5 November 1969, *Yearbook* XII; *The Greek Case* (1969), p. 72.

of testimony, publications in the press and other information besides the views of the governments involved.[131] There is hardly any evidence in that report of a restriction to a marginal review of the reasonableness of the position of the Greek Government.

If on the basis of the preceding case-law a lack of clarity concerning the attitude of the Strasbourg organs has arisen, this seems to have been removed by the Court in *Ireland v. United Kingdom*. There the Court adopted the line of the "margin of appreciation" with respect to Article 15, which, like the Commission, it had followed with respect to the imposition of special restrictions in the *Belgian Linguistic* Case and in the *Handyside* Case.[132] The judgment of the Court contains the following observations:

> It falls in the first place to each Contracting State, with its responsibility for "the life of [its] nation", to determine whether that life is threatened by a "public emergency" and, if so, how far it is necessary to go in attempting to overcome the emergency. By reason of their direct and continuous contact with the pressing needs of the moment, the national authorities are in principle in a better position than the international judge to decide both on the presence of such an emergency and on the nature and scope of derogations necessary to avert it. In this matter Article 15 § 1 leaves those authorities a wide margin of appreciation.
> Nevertheless, the States do not enjoy an unlimited power in this respect. The Court, which, with the Commission, is responsible for ensuring the observance of the States' engagements (Article 19), is empowered to rule on whether the States have gone beyond the "extent strictly required by the exigencies" of the crisis ... . The domestic margin of appreciation is thus accompanied by a European supervision.[133]

In exercising in this case the European supervision, mentioned at the end of the quotation, the Court indeed gave evidence of instituting an independent inquiry into the necessity of the derogations, but with respect to those points where differences of opinion were possible as to the interpretation of facts and the effectiveness of measures, it confined itself to an assessment of the reasonableness of the position taken in the matter by the respondent government.[134]

Nothing at all is left of the supervision by the Strasbourg organs - which is already very marginal - of the application of Article 15 by the contracting States when a reservation, as made by France with respect to Article 15, is accepted.[135] In fact, this reservation implies, *inter alia*, that the words "to the extent strictly required by the exigencies of the situation" must not be interpreted as restrictions on the power of the President of the French Republic to take "measures required by the circumstances".[136] The consequence of this is that derogation from the rights and freedoms protected in the Convention, with the exception of those mentioned in Article 15(2), remains at the free discretion of the contracting State in question, without any real review of the use of that discretion by means of "European supervision"

---

131. *Ibidem*, pp. 73-76.
132. See *infra* pp. 586-590.
133. Judgment of 18 January 1978, A.25 (1978), pp. 78-79.
134. See, *e.g.*, paras 214 and 243 of the judgment, *ibidem*, pp. 81-82 and 92-93.
135. On the question of whether this French reservation is legitimate or not, see *infra* p. 611.
136. For the full text of the French reservation, see Council of Europe, *Collected Texts*, Strasbourg 1987, pp. 76-77.

being possible.

In some situations it may turn out to be difficult to judge the exact scope of the Strasbourg supervision over the observance of Article 15. In a case which has remained unique until now, France, Norway, Denmark, Sweden and the Netherlands alleged a violation of Article 15 on the part of Turkey, but subsequently reached a friendly settlement with the latter.[137] As far as Article 15 was concerned, the States concerned noted that Turkey had in the meantime progressively reduced the geographical scope of martial law and had declared that it would be lifted from the remaining provinces within 18 months, and that a number of decrees or other legal enactments, mentioned by the applicant governments in their applications, had been changed or amended.[138] The Commission accepted the settlement by concluding that it had been secured on the basis of respect for human rights in the sense of Article 28(8).[139] In accordance with Article 30 the Commission's report is confined to a brief statement of the facts and of the solution reached. Consequently, no arguments can be found to support the Commission's conclusion that respect for human rights had indeed been secured.[140]

2. The interpretation of the term "time of war" in the first paragraph does not raise great problems. This situation is present at any rate in case of an official declaration of war on the part of, or directed against, the State in question, or when that State is actually involved in an international armed conflict. Whether a "time of war" can also be considered to exist in case of civil war, a question that is of great importance for the applicability of humanitarian law of war,[141] is not very relevant here on account of the addition "or other public emergency threatening the life of the nation".

3. In its report in the *Lawless* Case the Commission gave the following definition of "public emergency threatening the life of the nation":

> an exceptional situation or crisis of emergency which affects the whole population and constitutes a threat to the organised life of the community of which the State is composed.[142]

This definition was adopted by the Court in its judgment in this case.[143] In that judgment the Court ruled that the Irish Government could have reasonably deduced, on the basis of a combination of the following factors, that there was a "public emergency" at a given moment: (1) the existence in

---

137. Appls 9940-9944/82, report of 7 December 1985, *D & R* 44 (1985), p. 31.
138. *Ibidem*, p. 39.
139. *Ibidem*, p. 41.
140. On 25 May 1987, the Turkish Government informed the Secretary General of the Council of Europe that martial law would be lifted in the remaining provinces from 19 July 1987; Council of Europe, *Information Sheet* No. 21 (1987), p. 14.
141. On this, F. van Hoof, "The Protection of Human Rights and the Impact of Emergency Situations under International Law with Special Reference to the Present Situation in Chile", *R.D.H.* 10 (1977), p. 213 (228-232).
142. Report of 19 December 1959, B.1 (1960-61), p. 82.
143. Judgment of 1 July 1961, A.3 (1961), p. 56.

the territory of the Republic of a secret army which was engaged in unconstitutional activities and was using violence to attain its ends; (2) the fact that this army was also operating outside the territory of the State, thus seriously jeopardizing the relation of the Republic with its neighbour; and (3) the steady and alarming increase in terrorist activities in the period preceding the decisive moment.[144]

In the *Greek* Case the above-mentioned definition was elaborated by the Commission. It pointed out beforehand that the French - authentic - text of the *Lawless* judgment, in which the Court adopted its definition, mentioned not only the word "*exceptionnel*", but also the word "*imminent*". In the opinion of the Commission an emergency must have the following characteristics if it is to be qualified as a "public emergency" in the sense of Article 15:

(1) It must be actual or imminent.
(2) Its effects must involve the whole nation.
(3) The continuance of the organized life of the community must be threatened.
(4) The crisis or danger must be exceptional, in that the normal measures or restrictions, permitted by the Convention for the maintenance of public safety, health and order, are plainly inadequate.[145]

The arguments of the Greek Government for its submission that there was a "public emergency" were summarized as follows by the Commission: (1) communist danger, (2) crisis of constitutional government and (3) crisis of public order.[146] In support of its submission the Greek Government had stated in particular that the communists were preparing an armed revolt within the State and from outside and were planning to seize power, that the other political parties were collaborating with the communists and were corrupt, that the numerous changes of government had rendered the administration of the country impossible and the constant strikes had brought the State on the verge of bankruptcy, and that the violent demonstrations had led to anarchy.[147] In the Commission's opinion, however, the Government had not thus sufficiently demonstrated that the situation in Greece showed the above-mentioned characteristics at the decisive moment.[148]

In *Ireland v. United Kingdom* both the Commission and the Court, on the basis of a very brief finding, concluded that the "public emergency" invoked by the British Government indeed appeared to exist in Northern Ireland, and observed that this fact had not been contested by Ireland.[149] Since large-scale violent actions by a paramilitary organization were concerned, which were largely directed against the British security forces, the conclusion of the Commission and the Court can indeed hardly be disputed. The brief finding

---

144. *Ibidem.* See also Appl. 493/59, *X v. Ireland, Yearbook* IV (1961), p. 302 (316), where a similar complaint, which also related to a later period, was declared manifestly ill-founded by the Commission, which invoked for this the *Lawless* judgment of the Court.
145. Report of 5 November 1969, *Yearbook* XII; *The Greek Case* (1969), p. 72.
146. *Ibidem*, p. 45.
147. *Ibidem*, pp. 46-71.
148. *Ibidem*, pp. 76 and 100.
149. Report of 25 January 1976, B.23/I (1976-78), p. 94; judgment of 18 January 1978, A.25 (1978), p. 78.

might, however, create the impression that, if the existence of a "public emergency" in the sense of Article 15 has not been disputed by the applicant State, the Commission and the Court need not institute an independent inquiry into it any more. Such an attitude would, however, be mistaken. In fact, certainly in the case of inter-State applications, the procedure has an objective character for the maintenance of the legal order as such created by the Convention, and not just for the protection of particular rights or interests of the parties.[150] Consequently, a passive attitude with respect to the parties' submissions is not fitting, certainly not in the case of derogations which lead to a partial suspension of that legal order.

4. The question of whether the derogations applied by a State are "strictly required" in order to be able to cope with the "public emergency" will logically arise only if it has first been established that a "public emergency" exists. However, in its report the Commission must anticipate the possibility that the Committee of Ministers or the Court does not share its view that there is no question of a "public emergency". That is why, in its report in the Greek Case, the Commission also went into the question of the necessity of the restrictions.[151]

In the determination of the "strictly required" character of the derogations, three elements play a part: (1) the necessity of the derogations to cope with the threat; (2) the proportionality of the measures in view of the threat; (3) the duration of the derogations.[152] In the Lawless Case the Court found that the requirement of necessity had been satisfied, because the Irish Government proved that the existing legislation and the normal procedures for the maintenance of the legal order were not sufficient. The requirement of proportionality had been satisfied in the Court's opinion, because on the one hand the Irish Government had not proceeded to take more far-reaching measures, such as the complete closure of the frontiers, while on the other hand in the internment system a number of guarantees against abuse of power by the authorities had been incorporated.[153] The issue of the duration of the measures was not examined by the Court in this case, evidently because the Court held that the situation called for the same stringent measures during the entire relevant period. It is, however, conceivable that, even if it can be established that the "public emergency" continues, the effect of the measures adopted or of certain developments has been such that from a given moment continuation of the derogations to the same extent can no longer be deemed "strictly required".

In Ireland v. United Kingdom it had been argued by the Irish Government that the English internment measures had proved ineffective and after a given point in time had not therefore been applied any longer. With respect to this

150. See supra pp. 33-34.
151. Report of 5 November 1969, Yearbook XII; The Greek Case (1969), p. 104.
152. On this, F. van Hoof, supra note 141, pp. 237-238.
153. Judgment of 1 July 1961, A.3 (1961), pp. 57-59.

the following position was taken by the Court:

> It is certainly not the Court's function to substitute for the British Government's assessment any other assessment of what might be the most prudent or most expedient policy to combat terrorism. The Court must do no more than review the lawfulness, under the Convention, of the measures adopted by that Government from 9 August 1971 onward. For this purpose the Court must arrive at its decision in the light, not of a purely retrospective examination of the efficacy of those measures, but of the conditions and circumstances reigning when they were originally taken and subsequently applied.[154]

A curious reaction to a curious argument! From the side of the applicant State the argument would be expected that the respondent State has gone to unnecessary lengths with its measures, and in doing so has exceeded the limit of proportionality, while the argument of Ireland seems to have the opposite purport, viz. that England has not gone far enough in fighting the IRA. But in itself the argument is valid: if certain measures are not adequate for checking or restricting the dangers against which they are aimed, those measures cannot be considered necessary and must be modified or abolished as soon as that inefficacy is established. It is certainly for the Court to judge whether this has been done and, if so, whether it has been done in good time, although the Court must allow the national authorities sufficient discretion to assess that efficacy themselves. In evident cases of inefficacy, however, the conditions of Article 15 have not been satisfied. By establishing this, the Strasbourg organs indeed do "no more than review the lawfulness, under the Convention, of the measures", since this is a matter of review for conformity with the condition that they must be "strictly required".

In fact, in one of the following paragraphs of the same judgment the Court did go into the obligation of the State always to ascertain, when applying derogations under Article 15, whether and to what extent the scope of these derogations can be restricted. Thus the Court found with respect to the right to judicial review, which Article 5(4) grants to everyone who has been deprived of his liberty, that it would have been preferable if this had been provided for immediately upon the introduction of the internment measures, but that the British Government *might* have been of the opinion that this was not yet possible in the initial period: "The interpretation of Article 15 must leave a place for progressive adaptations".[155]

5. The provision in Article 15 that the measures adopted must not be inconsistent with the other obligations resting on the State under international law has played little part in the case-law thus far. Both in the *Lawless* Case - *ex officio*[156] - and in *Ireland v. United Kingdom*[157] the Court held that no evidence was found of any infringement of this condition. To the extent that obligations under other international conventions concerning human rights are concerned, this condition also follows from Article 60 of the Conven-

---

154. Judgment of 18 January 1978, A.25 (1978), p. 82.
155. *Ibidem*, p. 83.
156. Judgment of 1 July 1961, A.3 (1961), p. 60.
157. Judgment of 18 January 1978, A.25 (1978), p. 84.

tion.[158] In that context it is of interest that the Covenant in Article 4 also provides for the possibility of derogations in case of a "public emergency", but that more rights are "non-derogable" there. The enumeration of Article 4(2) of the Covenant also includes Article 11 (the prohibition of imprisonment merely on the ground of inability to fulfil a contractual obligation) and Article 18 (freedom of thought, conscience and religion). A contracting State which has also ratified the Covenant therefore cannot take derogatory measures with respect to those rights either, unless, where the freedom to manifest one's religion or beliefs is concerned, the restriction is one which is supported by the third paragraph of Article 18 of the Covenant. Apart from the Covenant, other provisions that may be thought of are, for instance, those of the Geneva Conventions concerning humanitarian law, which are intended to be applied in situations such as those mentioned in Article 15. The wide formulation "other obligations under international law" also covers obligations under other - not humanitarian - conventions, under customary international law and under generally recognized legal principles. It is evident, however, that on this point the Strasbourg organs will not lightly go beyond the scope of conventional law, unless they can rely on clear international case-law or an express consensus within the community of States.

6. Besides the conditions mentioned in Article 15 itself, the exercise of the power of derogation granted in that article is also subject to conditions ensuing from a number of other articles of the Convention, viz. Articles 14, 17, 18 and, as stated above, 60.

7. The second paragraph of Article 15 contains an enumeration of the provisions of the Convention from which no derogation may be made under any circumstances, not even under those mentioned in the first paragraph: these provisions are non-derogable. In Chapter VI, in the discussion of each individual right and freedom, the issue has been addressed whether it is non-derogable, also with respect to the additional Protocols.

8. As to the information to be given to the Secretary General, as prescribed in the third paragraph, the Court held in the Lawless Case that this must take place "without delay" after the entry into force of the measures concerned. A delay of twelve days was still considered to be in conformity with this obligation.[159] The Commission, in its report, had used the words "without any avoidable delay",[160] thus evidently indicating that allowance must be made for the special difficulties with which a government may be confronted in case of a "public emergency". A delay of four months in the

---

158. On this, supra p. 5-6.
159. Judgment of 1 July 1961, A.3 (1961), p. 62.
160. Report of 19 December 1959, B.1 (1960-61), p. 73.

Greek Case, however, was considered too long by the Commission.[161] No special form is prescribed for the information, nor need it be stated expressly that it is intended as information in the sense of Article 15(3).[162] However, in the words of the Commission, the government must

> furnish sufficient information concerning them [the measures in question] to enable the other High Contracting Parties and the European Commission to appreciate the nature and extent of the derogation from the provisions of the Convention which these measures involve,[163]

while the information must also be sufficient to enable them to infer therefrom the reasons for the measures.[164] It is solely for the Strasbourg organs to judge whether the condition of the third paragraph has been fulfilled. However, as appears from the above-mentioned words "reasonable" and "avoidable", here again these organs leave some discretion to the government concerned.

What are the consequences if a contracting State makes use of the possibilities of derogation provided for in the Convention, but omits to inform the Secretary General thereof in the way prescribed in Article 15(3)? Since the Convention does not explicitly lay down such consequences, a number of variants are conceivable. Failure to inform the Secretary General might rule out reliance on Article 15 for the justification of derogation measures taken. Sanctions of a different kind are also conceivable. Finally there is the possibility that non-observance of Article 15(3) has no (legal) consequences at all. The question here referred to arose in the joined Applications 6780/74 and 6950/75, where Cyprus complained about the action of the Turkish invasion forces. In the first Case of *Greece v. United Kingdom* and in the *Lawless* Case, too, this question had already arisen, but then in a more indirect way. In these cases the Commission had "reserved its view as to whether failure to comply with the requirements of Art. 15(3) may 'attract the sanction of nullity or some other sanction'".[165] The question was raised expressly, however, in the joined Applications just mentioned. The Turkish Government had not furnished any information as referred to in Article 15(3), because, as it submitted, it had no jurisdiction over the Northern part of Cyprus occupied by the Turkish forces.[166] The Commission, on the contrary, had held in its decision on the admissibility that

> the Turkish armed forces in Cyprus brought any person or property there "within the jurisdiction" of Turkey, in the sense of Art. 1 of the Convention, "to the extent that they exercise control over such persons or property".[167]

During its examination of the merits the Commission was therefore confronted

---

161. Report of 5 November 1969, *Yearbook* XII; *The Greek Case* (1969), p. 43. See also the dissenting opinion of Commission member Delahaye, *ibidem*, pp. 43-44.
162. Report of 19 December 1959, *Lawless*, B.1 (1960-61), p. 73. See also the judgment of 1 July 1961 in this case, A.3 (1961), p. 62.
163. *Ibidem.*
164. Judgment of 1 July 1961, *Lawless*, A.3 (1961), p. 62.
165. Report of 10 July 1976, *Cyprus v. Turkey*, para. 526.
166. *Ibidem.*
167. *Ibidem*, para. 525.

with the question of the consequences of the Turkish Government's failure to provide the relevant information. Despite the fact that this question thus became prominent, the Commission, curiously enough, began its answer with the following finding:

> In the present case the Commission still does not consider itself called upon generally to determine the above question.[168]

It continued with the following words:

> It finds, however, that, in any case, Art. 15 requires some formal and public act of derogation, such as a declaration of martial law or state of emergency, and that, where no such act has been proclaimed by the High Contracting Party concerned, although it was not in the circumstances prevented from doing so, Art. 15 cannot apply.[169]

Thus, in a case of a failure on the part of the authorities to publicly declare the state of war or other public emergency, they are deprived of the right to invoke Article 15(1). This still leaves open the question of what are the consequences if a State has publicly declared such a state, but has failed to inform the Secretary General about it. It is to be regretted that the Commission has not taken the opportunity to also clarify the consequences of non-fulfilment of the information obligation laid down in Article 15.

That a strict review of this obligation by the Strasbourg organs is called for without allowing for any retrospective effect of the required communication, became clear from the attitude which the British Government permitted itself in the aftermath of the Court's judgment in the *Brogan* Case. That judgment of 29 November 1988 held that the United Kingdom had violated, *inter alia*, Article 5(3) because the applicants, after being detained, were neither brought promptly before a judicial authority nor released promptly following their arrest. As far as Article 15 is concerned, the judgment contains the following considerations:

> The Government have adverted extensively to the existence of particularly difficult circumstances in Northern Ireland, notably the threat posed by organized terrorism. ... The Government informed the Secretary General of the Council of Europe on 22 August 1984 that they were withdrawing a notice of derogation under Article 15 which had relied on an emergency situation in Northern Ireland ... . The Government indicated accordingly that in their opinion "the provisions of the Convention are being fully executed". In any event, as they pointed out, the derogation did not apply to the area of law in issue in the present case. Consequently, there is no call in the present proceedings to consider whether any derogation from the United Kingdom's obligations under the Convention might be permissible under Article 15 by reason of a terrorist campaign in Northern Ireland.[170]

On 23 December 1988, however, the U.K. Government provided the Secretary General with a set of information in order to ensure compliance with its obligations under Article 15(3). The contents of this information was at least confusing and from the perspective of the United Kingdom's obligations under the Convention even dubious. Formally the Note Verbale in which the

---

168. *Ibidem*, para. 527.
169. *Ibidem*. The proclamation of martial law in Turkey itself, which had been notified, according to the Commission could not be deemed "to cover the treatment of persons brought into Turkey from the northern area of Cyprus"; *ibidem*, para. 530.
170. Judgment of 29 November 1988, A.145/B (1989), pp. 28-29.

information was contained could be taken as a notice on the part of the U.K. Government that from 23 December 1988 it was going to make use of the possibility provided for by Article 15 to derogate from certain of the obligations ensuing from the Convention. In a technical sense there is nothing wrong with such a step. It is even fully justified, provided that the Government can convincingly argue that the circumstances prevailing in the country call for the application of Article 15. In the present case, however, that was hard to imagine. Given the above-mentioned position taken by the British Government during the *Brogan* Case, the circumstances requiring application of Article 15 should have arisen between the date of the Court's judgment and 23 December 1988. The Note Verbale did not make this clear at all. On the contrary, reference was made to "recent years" of campaigns of organized terrorism and to the year 1974, in which the Government found it necessary to introduce special measures to combat this terrorism. Since the Government did not rely on Article 15 in the *Brogan* Case, the position taken in the Note Verbale, in our view, bore witness to at least bad faith on the part of the British Government as far as the period starting from 23 December 1988 was concerned.

As far as the period between the date of the judgment up to 23 December 1988 was concerned, there was an outright violation of the Convention and the Note Verbale did not even bother to conceal it. After recalling that

> The Court held that even the shortest of the four periods of detention concerned ... fell outside the constraints as to time permitted by the first part of Article 5(3)

the Note Verbale bluntly added that

> Following this judgment ... the Government did not believe that the maximum period of detention should be reduced.

Finally it was concluded that

> Since the judgment of 29 November 1988 as well as previously, the Government have found it necessary to continue to exercise, in relation to terrorism connected with the affairs of Northern Ireland, the powers described above enabling further detention without charge, for periods of up to five days.[171]

In our view, all this leaves room for no other conclusion than that Article 15 cannot be considered to be applicable at all and that steps on the part of the Committee of Ministers under Article 54 of the Convention are called for.

9. The possibility of derogation under Article 15 has been made use of several times and by different countries. This has also resulted in a number of complaints about violation of Article 15. These complaints have been referred to above: *Greece v. United Kingdom*,[172] *Lawless v. Ireland*,[173] *Denmark, Norway, Sweden and the Netherlands v. Greece*,[174] *Ireland v. United Kingdom*,[175]

---

171. DH(89)1, pp. 10-11.
172. Appls 176/56 and 299/57; see *Yearbook* II (1958-59), pp. 182 and 186.
173. Appl. 332/57; see *ibidem*, p. 308.
174. Appls 3321-3323/67 and 3344/67; see *Yearbook* XI (1968), pp. 690 and 730.
175. Appls 5310/71 and 5451/72; see *Yearbook* XV (1972), pp. 76 and 78.

and *Cyprus v. Turkey*.[176] Turkey, which invoked Article 15 for the period from 16 June 1970 to 5 August 1975, from 26 December 1978 to 26 February 1980 and from 12 September 1980 to 19 July 1987,[177] has been confronted with complaints by Denmark, France, the Netherlands, Norway and Sweden, lodged on 1 July 1982.[178]

In the *McVeigh, O'Neill and Evans* Case the Commission held that it will take any derogations made under Article 15 into consideration only if the respondent government relies on them.[179]

It goes without saying that an effective maintenance of the rights and freedoms guaranteed in the Convention requires that derogations from the provisions of the Convention be minimized. This calls for a continuous and strict supervision of the observance of the conditions laid down in Article 15. One may wonder whether the supervision mechanism provided for in the Convention, which comes into operation only after submission of a complaint and consequently has an incidental character, is sufficient in this respect.

10. Article 4 of the Covenant, which contains a similar derogation clause, differs as to its first paragraph from Article 15(1) on a few points. First of all, in Article 4(1) no distinction is made between "time of war" and "other public emergency", which is only a textual difference, since the state of war will in any case be a "public emergency". Moreover, Article 4 requires that the existence of the public emergency "is officially proclaimed"; such a formality is in the interest of legal security and enhances legal protection. As was mentioned above,[180] the Commission has made the invocation of Article 15 subject to the same requirement. Finally, the first paragraph of Article 4 provides that the measures adopted under that paragraph must not constitute any discrimination. This provision again is lacking in Article 15, but, as said above,[181] it will have to be assumed that the general prohibition of discrimination in ensuring the enjoyment of the rights and freedoms, as laid down in Article 14, also refers to the derogations under Article 15.

As has been observed, the enumeration of the provisions which are non-derogable differs in the sense that Article 4 also includes the prohibition of imprisonment merely on the ground of inability to fulfil a contractual obligation, and also the freedom of thought, conscience and religion.

Article 4, third paragraph, which contains the obligation to notify the Secretary General, is more specific as to the content of that notification, by requiring that the provisions which have been derogated from, shall be mentioned and the reasons for the derogation shall be stated. In the case of

176. Appls 6780/74 and 6950/75; report of 10 July 1976, not published.
177. See *Yearbook* XIII (1970), p. 18; *Yearbook* XVIII (1975), p. 16; *Yearbook* XXI (1978), p. 18; *Yearbook* XXII (1979), p. 26; *Yearbook* XXIII (1980), p. 10 and Council of Europe, *Information Sheet* No. 22 (1987), p. 14.
178. Appls 9940/82-9944/82, *D & R* 35 (1984), p. 143.
179. Report of 18 March 1981, *D & R* 25 (1982), p. 5 (32-34).
180. See *supra* p. 557.
181. See *supra* p. 555.

the Convention this is not specifically required, not even in the case-law of the Commission and the Court, although there the condition has been made that the notification shall contain sufficient information to enable the other contracting States and the Commission to appreciate the nature and extent of the derogation.[182]

§ 5. ARTICLE 16: RESTRICTIONS ON THE POLITICAL ACTIVITY OF ALIENS

Nothing in Articles 10, 11 and 14 shall be regarded as preventing the High Contracting Parties from imposing restrictions on the political activity of aliens.

1. The provision now laid down in Article 16 did not occur in the draft of the Consultative Assembly; it was added thereto by the Committee of Experts.[183] It constitutes an important encroachment on the system of the Convention, which, as ensues in particular from Articles 1 and 14, guarantees the enjoyment of the rights and freedoms to everyone under the jurisdiction of one of the contracting States, irrespective of nationality. That guarantee is restricted to a considerable degree by Article 16 for those persons who are indeed under the jurisdiction of the contracting State in question, but do not possess the nationality of that State.

As to Articles 10 and 11, Article 16 implies that the freedom of expression and freedom of association and assembly guaranteed in those articles may be restricted for aliens also in cases not provided for in the second paragraph thereof, when political activities are concerned. With regard to Article 14 it means that the national authorities may discriminate to the detriment of aliens in relation to the rights guaranteed in the Convention. The latter then applies not only to the rights provided for in Articles 10 and 11, but to all rights, in so far as this discrimination aims at the limitation of the political activities of aliens. In this context one may think especially of the right to vote and to be elected, at least if one assumes that Article 3 of the First Protocol in principle confers this right on aliens as well. But one may also think of restrictions on the freedom of education in connection with political activities.

2. The term aliens (*étrangers*) refers both to persons having the nationality of one of the other contracting States (while not also having the nationality of the State in question) and of other foreigners, including stateless persons. The Convention does not therefore grant, as does the law of the European

---

182. See *supra* p. 556. For Art. 4 of the Covenant reference is made to the study by Nowak, mentioned *supra* p. 216.
183. Council of Europe, *Collected Editions of the "Travaux Préparatoires" of the European Convention on Human Rights*, Vol. III, The Hague 1976, p. 238.

Communities with respect to nationals of member States of the Communities, a privileged position to those aliens who are nationals of one of the member States of the Council of Europe.

3. The rights of Articles 10 and 11 and the protection of Article 14 are not *set aside* with respect to aliens. In so far as these rights relate to other than political activities, aliens are entitled to the same guarantees in relation to these articles as the nationals of the State in question. The scope of the restrictions that can be applied to them is therefore determined by the interpretation put upon the term "political activity" (*activité politique*).

Since Articles 10 and 11 themselves already mention as a general restriction "the interests of national security and public safety" and Article 10 adds to that "the prevention of disorder", while Article 11 speaks of "peaceful assembly", the drafters evidently wished to protect other interests of the State by Article 16. In this context one should think in particular of the interest of good relations with other States. Thus, for instance, demonstrations of South Moluccans in the Netherlands directed against Indonesia, or demonstrations or publications of Moroccan migrant workers residing in the Netherlands criticizing the regime in Morocco may be prohibited on that ground to the extent that the persons involved do not possess Dutch nationality. The fact that such activities of aliens often serve to promote and protect the very values on which the Convention is based, unfortunately does not stand in the way of the application of Article 16, since the latter does not contain any reservation in that respect. Even a plea for respect of the Convention itself, addressed to another contracting State, might fall under censorship under certain circumstances, when such a plea is not advanced by a national of the State on whose territory it is aired.

But Article 16 goes further still. It also permits restriction of the freedom of expression, association and assembly, and of the prohibition of discrimination, if the political implications thereof concern exclusively the host country itself. Thus, a State would have the right to impose on migrant workers a prohibition from advocating improvement of that State's social security measures, the granting of stay permits or other measures directly concerning them. They might even be prohibited from advocating better application by that State of the Convention with regard to them, an application to which they are entitled. And all this may be done without certain interests of the State concerned, such as national security or public order, being at stake. These examples clearly demonstrate that in its present, unqualified form Article 16 hardly fits into the system of the Convention, which is based on the idea of democracy. Or is this also a value the implications of which are confined to the State's own nationals?

4. The question of whether in a particular case a "political activity" is involved must ultimately be judged by the Strasbourg organs, since this concerns the interpretation of a part of the Convention. To the best of our

knowledge the question has not yet been raised before them thus far. In the light of the case-law concerning other possibilities to restrict the enjoyment of certain rights it is to be expected that for the answer to that question, too, they will leave a "margin of appreciation" to the national authorities. However, the latter will have to advance reasonable arguments for their qualification of an activity as "political". Thus it is self-evident that a regulation prescribing that the responsible publishers of all journals must possess the nationality of the country in which they are published, without any differentiation between journals which do and those which do not deal with political issues,[184] may find no favour with the Commission and the Court. Precisely because of the above-mentioned far-reaching consequences of Article 16, which hardly fit into the system of the Convention, it is of great importance that the term "political activity" shall be interpreted restrictively.

5. In our opinion it is high time to follow up the 1977 recommendation of the Parliamentary Assembly in which the Committee of Ministers was urged

> to instruct the competent committee of experts to make proposals for the amendment of the European Convention for the Protection of Human Rights and Fundamental Freedoms in such a way as to exclude restrictions at present authorized by Article 16 with respect to political activity on the exercise by aliens of the freedoms guaranteed by Article 10 (freedom of expression) and Article 11 (freedom of association).[185]

6. The UN Covenant on Civil and Political Rights does not contain any provision comparable to Article 16 of the Convention.

§ 6.   ARTICLE 17: PROHIBITION OF ABUSE OF THE RIGHTS AND FREEDOMS SET FORTH IN THE CONVENTION AND OF THEIR LIMITATION TO A GREATER EXTENT THAN IS PROVIDED FOR IN THE CONVENTION

Nothing in this Convention may be interpreted as implying for any State, group or person any right to engage in any activity or perform any act aimed at the destruction of any of the rights and freedoms set forth herein or at their limitation to a greater extent than is provided for in the Convention.

1. From the formulation of Article 17 it is quite clear that this provision does not have an independent character; its violation is necessarily connected with one or more of the rights and freedoms enumerated in Section I of the

---

184. The example has been taken from K.J. Partsch, *Die Rechte und Freiheiten der europäischen Menschenrechtskonvention*, Berlin 1966, p. 261.
185. Recommendation 799(1977) on the political rights and position of aliens, 25 January 1977; Council of Europe, Parliamentary Assembly, 28th Ordinary Session, Third Part, *Texts Adopted* (1977).

Convention and its First, Fourth, Sixth and Seventh Protocols.[186] This connection varies somewhat depending on whether Article 17 is invoked against an individual or against a State.

With regard to individuals and groups the aim of Article 17 is to prevent them from invoking the rights and freedoms to which they are entitled, when they use them for the purpose of destroying or limiting those rights and freedoms for others.[187] In this case Article 17 must therefore be connected both with the rights of the person against whom this article is invoked and with one or more of the rights of others. As to the first-mentioned rights, the Commission held in the *Glimmerveen and Hagenbeek* Case:

> Article 17 covers essentially those rights which, if invoked, will facilitate the attempt to derive therefrom a right to engage personally in activities aimed at the destruction of any of the rights and freedoms set forth in the Convention.[188]

In proceedings before a national court Article 17 has the function, in a dispute between two individuals, of one of the criteria for weighing the rights of one party against those of the other party. In a dispute between an individual and a governmental body and in proceedings before the Strasbourg organs Article 17 forms a possible ground of justification for the respondent State to rely on against a claim of violation of the Convention.

However, Article 17 not only implies a prohibition for persons and groups, but also for "any State". Thus it is also intended to prevent the national authorities from making use of their powers under the Convention to limit the enjoyment of the rights and freedoms in order to destroy the essence of those rights and freedoms or to limit them to a greater extent than is provided for in the Convention. In this case, therefore, Article 17 is of a dependent character in that it must be connected both with the possibilities which other provisions of the Convention allow the national authorities to limit certain rights and freedoms and with those rights and freedoms themselves. Article 17 may here be invoked by an individual against the authorities in conjunction with the complaint about violation of one of his rights protected in the Convention.

The latter characteristic of Article 17 has been very tersely summarized by the Commission in the following manner:

> Where a Government seeks to achieve the ultimate protection of the rule of law and the democratic system, the Convention itself recognises in Article 17 the precedence which such objectives take, even over the protection of the specific rights which the Convention otherwise guarantees. Nevertheless, precisely because of the cardinal importance to be attached to the preservation of the rule of law and the democratic system, the Convention requires a clearly established need for any interference with the rights it guarantees, before such interference can be justified on that basis.[189]

2. In cases where Article 17 has the function of a justification on the part

---

186. See the judgment of 8 June 1976, *Engel*, A.22 (1977), p. 43.
187. Thus also the Court in its judgment of 1 July 1961, *Lawless*, A.3 (1961), p. 45.
188. Appls 8348 and 8406/78, *D & R* 18 (1980), p. 187 (195).
189. Reports of 11 May 1984, *Glasenapp*, A.104 (1986), p. 49, and *Kosiek*, A.105 (1986), pp. 42-43. In both cases the Court did not deal with Article 17, since it held that the question complained of was not covered by the Convention. See *supra* pp. 409-410.

of the authorities, the decision that the invocation of Article 17 by the respondent State is well-founded, in fact is at the same time a decision on the merits, since it is thus established that the Convention has not been violated by this State. On this account, and also in view of the very important and complex questions to which such an invocation of Article 17 gives rise, it is highly desirable that the Commission, if it does not consider reliance on Article 17 by the State concerned to be manifestly ill-founded, should join its examination to the merits, in order that the final decision may rest not with the Commission, but with the Court or the Committee of Ministers, as the case may be.

This policy, however, has not always been followed by the Commission. When the *Kommunistische Partei Deutschland* submitted a complaint against the Federal Republic of Germany with respect to the decision of the *Bundesverfassungsgericht* in which it had been dissolved and had been declared a prohibited party, the Commission, apparently *ex officio*, instituted an inquiry into the applicability of Article 17. On the basis of depositions made by the KPD during the proceedings before the *Bundesverfassungsgericht* the Commission concluded that the aim of the KPD was to establish a socialist-communist system by means of a proletarian revolution and the dictatorship of the proletariat, and that it had intimated that it still adhered to these principles. Even if it should be found that the KPD was trying to seize power only via constitutional methods, in the Commission's opinion this did not yet mean that it had renounced these principles. On that ground the Commission deemed Article 17 to be applicable and came to the decision that the application could not be based on any of the provisions of the Convention and was therefore inadmissible as being incompatible with the Convention.[190]

In its later decision in the *Lawless* Case the Commission did join the question about the applicability of Article 17 to the merits.[191] In our view there would also have been every reason for this in the *KPD* Case. In fact, the decision taken in that case by the Commission, on the basis of exclusively written proceedings, not only was very far-reaching, but also did not as a matter of course ensue from the facts described and from the formulation of Article 17, in particular considering the words "activity" and "act"; indeed, the Commission's decision was based exclusively on the aims and not on the actual activities of the KPD.

In the *Glimmerveen and Hagenbeek* Case the Commission again declared the application inadmissible by invocation of Article 17. In this case Glimmerveen complained about his criminal conviction for having possessed, with the aim of distribution, leaflets of the "Nederlandse Volks Unie", which were found to incite to racial discrimination. In addition, both applicants

---

190. Appl. 250/57, *Yearbook* I (1955-57), p. 222 (224-226).
191. Appl. 332/57, *Yearbook* II (1958-59), p. 308 (340). In the *De Becker* Case the invocation of Art. 17 by the Belgian Government took place only after the declaration of admissibility, during the examination of the merits; see the report of 8 January 1960 in this case, B.2 (1962), p. 133.

complained of the invalidation by the Central Voting Boards of Amsterdam and The Hague of the list of candidates of the "Nederlandse Volks Unie". The Commission recognized that the challenged acts constituted a breach of the freedom of expression of Article 10, and possibly a violation of the right to be elected, laid down in Article 3 of the First Protocol. It also called to mind the finding of the Court in the *Handyside* Case, that the freedom of expression forms one of the essential foundations of a democratic society. It concluded, however, that, pursuant to Article 17, the two applicants could not invoke this provision, or these provisions, and declared the applications "incompatible with the provisions of the Convention".[192] Here again in our opinion it would have been more appropriate to join the question of the applicability of Article 17 to the merits. This would also have been desirable in view of the important implications of the Commission's decision and the not indisputable foundation thereof. Indeed, it is difficult to ignore that the Commission relied on the "softer" right of freedom from discrimination (Article 14 in conjunction with Article 3), which the Convention guarantees to a limited extent only (at least in the view thus far taken by the Commission itself), and some of the rights from the Fourth Protocol, not yet ratified by the Netherlands at that moment, whereas the applicants invoked the "hard" right of freedom of expression as laid down in Article 10 of the Convention.

3. The Commission - followed in this by the Court - has introduced a very important restriction on the respondent State's possibility of invoking Article 17 as a justification. Both in the *Lawless* Case and in the *De Becker* Case it was held that, even if it is firmly established that the applicant himself aims at the destruction or restriction of the fundamental rights of others, or belongs to a group with such an objective, this does not yet entail that he may therefore remain deprived of all the rights laid down in the Convention; Article 17 applies exclusively to those rights which he abuses directly for the said aim. In the *Lawless* Case this connection between that aim and the rights invoked was altogether absent in the opinion of the Commission and the Court; even if Lawless had been involved in IRA activities, his invocation, as a detained person, of the guarantees of Articles 5 and 6 in any case was not aimed at engaging in such activities.[193] And in the *De Becker* Case, where the complaint concerned the freedom of expression, the connection was absent, because De Becker's totalitarian views and activities dated from the past and it had not been shown that he would abuse his freedom of expression again for that purpose.[194] This case-law is important, for instance, for war criminals and terrorists detained in prison or meanwhile released; the

---

192. Appls 8348 and 8406/78, *D & R* 18 (1980), p. 187 (194-197).
193. See the report of 19 December 1959 and the judgment of 1 July 1961 in this case, B.1 (1960-61), p. 180 and A.3 (1960-61), pp. 45-46 respectively.
194. Report of 8 January 1960, B.2 (1962), pp. 137-138. The Court did not take a decision on this point, because the case was struck from the list after the Belgian legislation had been amended.

mere fact of their past does not constitute a sufficient ground for denying them certain rights and freedoms.

The question of how close the link between the right claimed and the activity prohibited under Article 17 must be is of course open to discussion. When a Swiss company claimed that the confiscation of its property in the German Federal Republic was contrary to Article 1 of Protocol no. 1, the German Government invoked Article 17, submitting that the aim of the company was to manage and protect real property of the *Kommunistische Partei Deutschland*. However, the applicants submitted that they only claimed compensation and were able to guarantee that this would not be used for anti-constitutional activities. The request, however, was declared inadmissible on account of non-exhaustion of the local remedies, so that the Commission did not reach a decision on this point.[195] Here again a highly factual examination would have been concerned, which in our opinion the Commission should not use as a basis for a declaration of inadmissibility but should join to the merits.

4. An instance of an invocation of Article 17, not by the respondent State but by the applicant against that State, is to be found in the *Dona and Schul v. the Netherlands* Cases. The applicants alleged that the penalty imposed on them for having written an article in a journal could not be justified in this particular case by the second paragraph of Article 10 and consequently constituted a violation of Article 17. The Commission declared this part of the complaint to be admissible,[196] but it was later declared ill-founded by the Court, following the Commission in that respect, after it had been found that the challenged prohibition was justified under Article 10(2).[197] From this decision the subsidiary character of this element of Article 17 becomes particularly clear: if the restriction imposed is justified under the Convention, Article 17 has not been violated, while, if it is not justified, besides Article 17 one of the rights or freedoms will also have been violated. This is different only in those cases where the disputed measure does not directly constitute a violation of one of the rights and freedoms, but because of its effect amounts to a circumvention of the guarantees contained in the Convention and thus in fact leads to a restriction not provided for.[198]

This means that in the case of those articles which themselves already contain fairly wide possibilities for restrictions, Article 17 can very seldom be invoked successfully against a State; this also in view of the wide margin of appreciation which the Strasbourg organs are willing to allow the national

---

195. Appl. 712/60, *Retimag S.A. v. Federal Republic of Germany*, Yearbook IV (1961), p. 384 (392-394).
196. Appls 5354/72 and 5370/72, Yearbook XV (1972), p. 508 (556-558).
197. Judgment of 8 June 1976, A.22 (1977), pp. 42-43.
198. See the report of 19 July 1974, *Engel*, B.20 (1974-76), p. 70, where the Commission suggested as a possibility of such a case a situation in which a State introduces or maintains a disciplinary procedure in order to evade the guarantees of Art. 6. Thus also Appl. 5916/72, *X v. United Kingdom*, Coll. 46 (1974), p. 165 (166-167).

authorities in the application of those restrictions.[199] In such cases, therefore, the Commission and the Court usually confine themselves to the statement that the restrictions imposed have been found to be in conformity with the provision in question, so that the applicability of Article 17 need not be discussed any further.[200] But in the case of a provision of the Convention which does not provide for any restrictions or in which they are defined less expressly or somewhat less broadly, Article 17 may be very important as an autonomous or a complementary criterion for the lawfulness of the restriction. Thus, in the *Sporrong and Lönnroth* Case, after having found that the restrictions imposed on the part of the authorities with regard to the peaceful enjoyment of the property by the applicants had a lawful character in virtue of Article 1 of the First Protocol, the Commission subsequently instituted an inquiry into the question of whether these restrictions did not after all go beyond what is provided for in the Convention.[201] Eventually the Commission concluded unanimously that there had been no violation of Article 17. After having noted the Commission's conclusion, the Court without any additional argument held that

> Having found that there was a breach of Article 1 of Protocol No. 1, the Court does not consider it necessary also to examine the case under Article 17 ... of the Convention.[202]

The Commission seems to have pursued the approach taken in the *Sporrong and Lönnroth* Case. In the *Lithgow* Case it first found that the nationalization measures at stake were compatible with Article 1 of the First Protocol and that the taking of the applicants' property on that basis could be considered justifiable in view of the purposes of that provision. Subsequently, it dealt with the alleged violation of Article 17, but concluded that the measures concerned were not shown to have been aimed at the destruction or excessive limitation of the applicants' rights.[203]

5. Article 17 of the Convention and the corresponding Article 5(1) of the Covenant are literally identical, with one editorial exception: the Covenant speaks of "recognized", while the Convention uses the words "set forth".[204]

---

199. On this, *infra* pp. 583-606.
200. Besides the report and judgment in the *Engel* Case mentioned *supra* in notes 198 and 197, pp. 84-85 and p. 43 respectively, reference may also be made to Appl. 1747/62, *X v. Austria, Yearbook* VI (1963), p. 424 (442-444). If, on the other hand, the restriction imposed is already contrary to that other provision, review against Art. 17 is also considered superfluous: report of 5 November 1969, *Yearbook* XII; *The Greek Case* (1969), p. 113.
201. Report of 8 October 1980, B.46 (1986), p. 53.
202. Judgment of 23 September 1982, A.52 (1982), p. 28.
203. Report of 7 March 1984, A.102 (1987), p. 115. The Court did not have to deal with this question, since the particular issue of violation of Article 17 had not been referred to it.
204. For Art. 5(1) of the Covenant reference is made to the study by Nowak, mentioned *supra* p. 216.

§ 7. ARTICLE 18: PROHIBITION OF MISUSE OF POWER IN RESTRICTING THE RIGHTS AND FREEDOMS

The restrictions permitted under this Convention to the said rights and freedoms shall not be applied for any purpose other than those for which they have been prescribed.

1. Article 18 contains for the contracting States a general prohibition to use the restrictions permitted under the Convention for any purpose other than those for which they are intended.

This prohibition cannot constitute the object of a separate complaint, but can be advanced only in conjunction with one of the rights and freedoms; it forms one of the non-independent provisions of Section I.[205] As is the case with respect to Article 14,[206] Article 18 too has nevertheless been given a fairly autonomous character in the case-law of the Commission, in the sense that this provision may be violated in conjunction with another article, even though this latter article has not itself been violated.[207] The Court, on the other hand, has so far considered a separate examination concerning Article 18 superfluous if it has concluded that the right invoked has not been violated,[208] or if in considering the restrictions it has already gone into the aims envisaged by the limitations imposed.[209] In the latter case the Court in fact incorporates Article 18 into the provision on limitations of the article in question. And also when the Court has already concluded that one of the rights has been violated, it considers discussion of Article 18 superfluous.[210]

2. It appears from its formulation that Article 18 refers to all restrictions permitted under the Convention. These include not only the special restrictions provided for in Articles 8 to 11 inclusive of the Convention, Article 2 of Protocol no. 4 and Article 1 of Protocol no. 7. Article 18 also applies to the general restrictions ensuing from Articles 15, 16 and 17. Thus the Commission relied in part on Article 18 in the *De Becker* Case to conclude that measures which were taken in accordance with Article 15 in connection with an emergency situation are no longer justified when they remain in force after the emergency has ceased to exist.[211] Indeed, in that case the objective which constituted the justification for such measures have equally ceased to exist.

---

205. Report of 14 July 1974, *Kamma*, Yearbook XVIII (1975), p. 300 (316); report of 19 July 1974, *Engel*, B.20 (1974-76), p. 86; report of 8 October 1980, *Sporrong and Lönnroth*, B.46 (1986), p. 53; Appl. 9990/82, *Bozano v. France, D & R* 39 (1984), p. 119 (141).
206. For this, see *supra* pp. 534-537.
207. See the reports mentioned in note 205, *ibidem*.
208. Judgment of 8 June 1976, *Engel*, A.22 (1977), p. 43.
209. Judgment of 7 December 1976, *Handyside*, A.24 (1976), p. 30.
210. Judgment of 8 June 1976, *Engel*, A.22 (1977), pp. 39-40.
211. Report of 8 January 1960, B.2 (1962), p. 133. In its report in the *Greek* Case the Commission did not get as far as discussing Art. 18 in conjunction with Art. 15, because it held that even the conditions of Art. 15 itself had not been fulfilled: Report of 5 November 1969, *Yearbook* XII; *The Greek Case* (1969), p. 113.

Moreover, Article 18 is applicable to restrictions which may ensue from the regulation of a specific right itself. This implies, conversely, that a right which is formulated in absolute terms and with respect to which consequently no restrictions are possible cannot, according to the Commission,[212] lead to a violation of Article 18. However, if and to the extent that the regulation of a right or freedom does leave scope for restrictions, their application has to be reviewed for its conformity with Article 18. Thus, in the *Sporrong and Lönnroth* Case, the Commission took Article 18 into consideration in connection with the question of whether the restrictions in that case were lawful measures imposed in the general interest in the sense of Article 1 of the First Protocol.[213] The question of whether Article 18 is also applicable to "inherent limitations" must be preceded by the question of whether "inherent limitations" are at all permitted under the Convention, and if so, to what extent.[214] In so far as they are considered lawful, in our opinion their application has to be reviewed for its conformity with Article 18, because they are then to be considered as "permitted under this Convention" in the sense of that article. In that case such a review is extremely important precisely because Article 18, in conjunction with Articles 14 and 17, then constitutes the sole yardstick of the Convention.[215]

3. Article 18 is a provision which is hard to apply in practice, as is the case for the prohibition of misuse of power (*détournement de pouvoir*) in general. Indeed, it requires an exact determination of the motives on the part of the authorities taking a given measure, while it must also be established that these were not in conformity with the aims envisaged when the restriction in question was incorporated into the Convention. Although bad faith does not as such constitute an element of *détournement de pouvoir*, still in most cases determination of the former is implied in that of the latter. It is thus not surprising that the Commission and the Court are not readily inclined to take Article 18 into consideration on their own motion, although on the basis of the task entrusted to them in Article 19 they are undoubtedly competent, and arguably even obliged, to do so.[216] A particularly difficult burden of proof comes to rest on the applicant party when the latter makes Article 18 a part of his complaint, unless the intention of the national authority concerned

---

212. See the reports of 14 July 1974, *Kamma*, and of 19 July 1974, *Engel*, mentioned *supra* note 205, *ibidem.*
213. Report of 8 October 1980, B.46 (1986), p. 53.
214. On this, *infra* pp. 575-578. Jacobs infers from the words "restrictions under this Convention" from Art. 18 that "inherent limitations" are not permissible; F.G. Jacobs, *The European Convention on Human Rights,* Oxford 1985, p. 203.
215. Another view, however, is taken by Alkema, *supra* note 30, p. 41, who draws from the finding of the Commission in the Kamma Case "that a violation can only arise where the right or freedom concerned is subject to 'restrictions permitted under this Convention' the conclusion that Art. 18 can be applicable exclusively to restrictions expressly provided for in the Convention.
216. Thus, *e.g.*, F. Castberg, *The European Convention on Human Rights,* Leyden 1974, p. 173, and J.E.C. Fawcett, *The Application of the European Convention on Human Rights,* Oxford 1987, p. 320.

clearly ensues from the nature of the measure or finds expression in the motivation given for it.

4. The most illustrative case so far in which Article 18 played a preponderant role was that of *Kamma v. the Netherlands*. Kamma, while in detention on remand on the suspicion of swindle and attempted robbery, had been removed for one month to the police station for interrogation in relation to another case concerning murder. He alleged that the possibility which the Convention offers the authorities to deprive a person of his liberty, *viz.* detention on remand under Article 5(1)(c), had temporarily been used for another purpose, *viz.* for a police interrogation which did not respect certain rules provided for under Dutch law and under the Convention. He submitted that as a result he had suffered an injury in that his detention on remand had thus been prolonged by one month and that he had been subjected to a more rigorous regime during that month as a result of his detention at the police station.

As a matter of fact, under Dutch law the suspicion of murder in itself would have been a sufficient ground for a separate decision to detain him on remand. If such a decision had been taken, Article 18 would not have come into play. The complication, however, was that the court, when it decided on detention for the period in question, was not informed of Kamma's detention at the police station and the inquiry into the murder, so that in fact that decision related only to the suspicion of swindling. The investigating judge, on the contrary, *was* informed of the second suspicion, but apparently had not considered it necessary to take a separate decision.

In its report the Commission found, *inter alia*, that (1) good reasons had been advanced for the temporary removal to a police station, in particular since not a single provision in the Convention prohibited a police station as a place of detention; (2) the interrogation of a person detained on remand with respect to a case other than that for which the decision to detain him on remand had been taken was, as such, neither contrary to Dutch law nor contrary to the Convention; (3) the actual interrogation at the police station took eighteen days in all, *i.e.* only two days more than would have been possible without a decision of the court, if Kamma had not already been detained on remand; (4) his detention at the police station was subject to a certain judicial supervision, though not of the court, but of the investigating judge; and (5) if the interrogation in the murder case had caused a prolongation of the detention on remand, Kamma himself was to blame for this, since he himself had spread the rumour about his involvement in that case and on the second day of the interrogation had made a confession without being compelled, while the continued examination had resulted in the charge being dropped in that case. This induced the Commission to find that Article 18 had not been violated.[217] Curiously enough, the Commission concluded its report with the following observation:

217. Report of 14 July 1974, *Kamma*, Yearbook XVIII (1975), pp. 316-322.

The Commission has, however, duly noted that the respondent Government concluded their observations on the merits with an indication that they intend to examine the question as to whether a reform of the relevant legislation is necessary in order to avoid ambiguous situations which may, as in the present case, arise under the existing provisions concerning interrogation by the police of persons already in detention on remand.[218]

From this it may be deduced that, although the Commission concluded that the challenged acts of the authorities in question were not contrary to the Convention, it considered them undesirable.

The Commission's opinion that in this case there was no violation of Article 18 seems to be based on the following train of thought: the deprivation of liberty, which as such was lawful, has been used for another purpose: interrogation in another case; however, that interrogation and the circumstances under which it took place, particularly considering the fact that Kamma was already detained, were not in themselves contrary to Dutch law or the Convention; consequently, it could not be said that the authorities pursued a (continuation of an) unlawful deprivation of liberty. Although the latter may be true, in our opinion it does not get down to the essence of Article 18. In connection with Article 18 the question is not whether the restriction of the right to liberty is or is not legitimate as such, but precisely whether that restriction, assuming that it is justified on the ground advanced for it, was really imposed on that ground and not for another purpose, for which the restriction is not permitted. The way in which the Commission has applied Article 18 in this case deprives that provision of any independent meaning in addition to the provisions in which the rights and freedoms, and any restrictions thereof, are laid down. Unfortunately, the *Kamma* Case was not referred to the Court, but was disposed of by the Committee of Ministers in conformity with the opinion of the Commission.[219]

In the *Engel* Case, Dona and Schul - two of the five conscripts who acted as applicants - had submitted, *inter alia*, that the disciplinary punishment imposed on them for writing articles in a barracks journal was based by the Court Martial on the restrictions of Article 10(2), but in fact was intended to restrict their trade-union freedom.[220] The Commission dismissed this complaint by submitting that with respect to Article 10 it had concluded that "prevention of disorder" justified the restriction of the right of Article 10 under the given circumstances, and that also no violation of Article 11 had taken place: "It is therefore clear that there has been no breach of Article 18 in this respect".[221] The Court, too, did not go into Article 18.[222]

Against the reasoning here followed, the same objection may be raised as against the way in which Article 18 was applied by the Commission in the *Kamma* Case: it seems to ignore altogether the rationale of Article 18 and

218.   *Ibidem*, p. 322.
219.   *Yearbook* XVIII (1975), p. 300.
220.   See the report of 19 July 1974, *Engel*, B.20 (1974-76), pp. 85-86.
221.   *Ibidem*, p. 86.
222.   See *supra* p. 568 and note 208.

deprives that provision of all independent meaning. Article 18 does not refer to "any purpose in violation of the said rights and freedoms", but of "any purpose other than those for which they have been prescribed". Even if the inquiry in connection with Article 10, on account of the invocation of the second paragraph of this provision, leads to the conclusion that this article in itself has not been violated, it must still be possible that the inquiry concerning Article 18 subsequently alters this conclusion. In the present case: if Dona and Schul could furnish *prima facie* evidence that the disciplinary measure had indeed been imposed on them to restrain their trade-union activities in general, and not so much out of concern for order in the barracks, Article 10 would have been violated in conjunction with Article 18, regardless of whether the result of that measure also conflicted with Article 11. Indeed, review on the basis of the second paragraph of Article 10 provides an answer only to the question of whether the authorities *could* hold that the measure was necessary for the protection of one of the values mentioned in it. The *real* motives of the authorities taking the measure concerned are not at issue at that stage; those are dealt with afterwards in connection with the review under Article 18. If one starts from the position that, if the first review has a positive result, the second need not be performed at all, Article 18 has no meaning at all, since if the first review has a negative result, the second is no longer necessary anyway.

In its report in the *Handyside* Case the Commission appears to have corrected its position. The applicant, a publisher who had been prohibited from publishing the so-called "Little Red Schoolbook", submitted that in fact the authorities had not taken action against him for the protection of morals, but for other motives, such as the desire to resist the development of modern teaching techniques at schools. The Commission in its report stated first of all that the infringement of the applicant's freedom of expression ensuing from the prohibition imposed was justified on the ground of the second paragraph of Article 10. However, it continued as follows:

> Furthermore, an examination of the case as it has been submitted does not disclose any evidence which might suggest that the authorities and courts in the United Kingdom in taking the action complained of against the publication and distribution of the *Schoolbook*, have in any way been guided by motives other than those described in Article 10(2).[223]

In our opinion the Commission thus intimates that it has carried out an independent inquiry into the violation of Article 18. In the judgment of the Court in this case, in the considerations concerning Article 10 an opinion was given on what in the view of the Court was the real aim of the measures adopted, so that the Court could indeed refer back to this in dealing with Article 18.[224]

223. Report of 30 September 1975, B.22 (1976), p. 52.
224. Judgment of 7 December 1976, A.24 (1976), pp. 25 and 30.

This line taken in the *Handyside* Case was continued in its later case-law.[225] In the fairly recent *Bozano* Case the applicant alleged that his deportation by the French authorities to Switzerland and the ensuing deprivation of his liberty were, *inter alia*, contrary to Article 5. The Commission agreed and went on to examine the question of whether the unlawfulness of the deportation affected the applicant's detention in respect of Article 18 of the Convention as well. The Commission pointed to the fact that a French administrative court had found the deportation - and hence the applicant's detention - unlawful on the ground that the executive, by proceeding in this way, had sought to circumvent the competent judicial authority's veto on extraditing the applicant, which was binding on the French Government. Consequently, it was concluded that the applicant's detention had a purpose different from detention with a view to deportation, as provided for in Article 5(1)(f).[226] The Court, similar to its approach in the *Handyside* Case, did not deem it necessary to examine the issue under Article 18, as it had already noted, in connection with Article 5(1) taken alone, that the deportation procedure was abused for objects and purposes other than its normal ones.[227] Thus, like Article 14, Article 18 has actually been made an integral part of all those provisions of the Convention in which the rights and freedoms are regulated, at least in so far as those provisions permit any restriction of the rights and freedoms laid down therein. In our view, in this way only is the meaning of Article 18 done justice to.

5. The provision of Article 18 has no equivalent in the Covenant. However, the organs which have to apply the provisions of the Covenant may reach a similar result on the basis of good faith and the prohibition of *détournement de pouvoir* as general principles of law.

§ 8. THE GROUNDS OF RESTRICTION, IN PARTICULAR THOSE REFERRED TO IN ARTICLES 8-11 OF THE CONVENTION, ARTICLE 2 OF PROTOCOL NO. 4 AND ARTICLE 1 OF PROTOCOL NO. 7

8.1. Introduction: the system of the restrictions

1. From the discussion of the individual rights and freedoms in Chapter VI the fundamental importance of the issue of restrictions has become quite clear. Indeed, in a great many cases the very question as to the possibility of

---

225. See the decisions concerning the admissibility on Appl. 6794/74, *X v. Federal Republic of Germany*, D & R 3 (1976), p. 104 (107), and on Appl. 7317/75, *Lynas v. Switzerland*, Yearbook XX (1977), p. 412 (446); see also the report of 18 May 1977, *Sunday Times*, B.28 (1982), p. 77, and the report of 8 October 1980, *Sporrong and Lönnroth*, B.46 (1986), p. 53.
226. Report of 7 December 1984, A.111 (1987), p. 54.
227. Judgment of 18 December 1986, A.111 (1987), p. 27.

restricting the enjoyment of a particular right and as to the nature and scope of that possibility was found to be decisive for the question of whether or not a violation had taken place. The possibilities of their restriction are a decisive factor as to the scope of the rights and freedoms guaranteed in the Convention.

2. The rights and freedoms of the Convention can be distinguished into absolute and non-absolute rights and freedoms. In this context it must be pointed out first of all that the "restriction" of Article 17 applies to all the rights and freedoms without exception.[228] For every notion of rights, however, the prohibition of abuse is so self-evident that the provision that the enjoyment and the exercise of the rights and freedoms laid down in the Convention may not be directed at the destruction of those rights and freedoms themselves, or at a limitation to a greater extent than is provided for in the Convention, cannot be considered to affect the absolute character of a right. It is precisely because of this self-evidence that the prohibition of abuse of right is to be considered a general principle of law.

Some rights and freedoms are non-derogable in the sense that no derogation from them is permitted even in times of war or other general emergency.[229] This applies under Article 15(2) for the right to life, except in respect of deaths resulting from lawful acts of war (Art. 2), for the prohibition of torture and inhuman or degrading treatment (Art. 3), for the prohibition of slavery or servitude (Art. 4(1)) and for the prohibition of retrospective effect of criminal law (Art. 7). It also applies for Protocol no. 6 concerning the abolition of the death penalty and for Article 4 of Protocol no. 7 concerning the prohibition to be tried in criminal proceedings for an offence which one has already been finally acquitted or convicted. With the exception of the right to life of Article 2 the said rights and freedoms moreover are formulated in absolute terms, so that no restriction is permitted in any case, neither in times of an emergency nor in a normal situation.

Outside the situation referred to in Article 15, and in addition to the above-mentioned articles, the Convention does also not permit restrictions with respect to Article 6(2) of the Convention and with respect to Articles 1, 3 and 4 of Protocol no. 4. These articles, too, are formulated in absolute terms.

With respect to the other rights and freedoms guaranteed in the Convention certain restrictions are possible. These restrictions may take different forms. A case apart in this respect is the possibility to restrict certain rights under Article 16. In fact, this refers to a specific category of activities: political activities; for a specific category of persons: aliens; and with reference to particular rights and freedoms: the freedom of expression and the freedom of association and assembly; while in addition it allows restrictions of the prohibition of discrimination of Article 14 with reference to the said

228. On this Article, see *supra* pp. 562-568.
229. On this, see *supra* p. 555.

categories.[230]

For the rest the restrictions may ensue in the first place from the way a right has been formulated, because certain limitations are inherent in the formulation of the right itself, or because it is expressly stated that particular cases are not covered by the right in question. The following articles belong to this category: Articles 2, 4 (with the exception of paragraph 1), 5, 6 (with the exception of paragraph 2) and 12 (in view of the words "according to the national law governing the exercise of this right"), as well as Articles 1, 2 and 3 of Protocol no. 1, Article 1(1) of Protocol no. 7 (except in pursuance of a decision in accordance with law), and also Articles 2, 3 and 5 of Protocol no. 7. The restrictions of this nature have been mentioned and discussed above in connection with the respective rights and freedoms.

Secondly, a number of articles, after having defined the guaranteed right in their first paragraph, contain in a second or third paragraph an enumeration of a number of possible restrictions. This applies to Articles 8-11 of the Convention, Article 2 of Protocol no. 4 and Article 1 of Protocol no. 7. These restrictions have been treated briefly in the discussion of the articles in question. For a more detailed discussion, however, reference has been made there to this separate section, because the enumerations in the various articles are broadly similar and the same observations need not be made about each individual article. The fact must, however, be taken into account that the separate paragraphs of one and the same article must be interpreted in connection with each other, so that a given ground for restriction in one article may have a somewhat different meaning than in another article. This does not alter the fact, however, that the case-law with respect to these restrictions is broadly the same for the different articles, determined as this case-law is by the "margin of appreciation" which the Commission and the Court allow to the national authorities in applying these restrictions.

8.2. "Inherent limitations"

1. Before the special restrictions are discussed individually, a short reference must be made to the doctrine of "inherent limitations".

For a long time the Commission took the position that, in addition to the expressly mentioned restrictions or in the absence of such an express reference, the scope of the rights and freedoms laid down in the Convention may be subject to implied limitations. Unlike the express restrictions, these implied ones do not have the character of a justification of a breach of these rights and freedoms; they are inherent in those rights and freedoms themselves, so that, as long as these rights and freedoms with their inherent limitations are respected, there is no breach and the question as to possible limitations does not arise. The Commission developed this doctrine specifically

230. On Art. 16, see *supra* pp. 560-562.

with respect to persons in a special legal position, such as detained persons, psychiatric patients, soldiers and civil servants. This special position was assumed to entail for persons of these categories a more limited scope of certain rights and freedoms than for those outside these categories. Thus, according to that doctrine the right to respect for family life[231] and correspondence[232] was assumed to have a more limited character for a detained person in view of the inherent limitations which the execution of imprisonment involves for the exercise of these rights.

The Court, however, rejected this doctrine of the Commission, at any rate with respect to those articles of the Convention where express restrictions are incorporated in a separate paragraph. The Court adopted the view that the enumerations given there are exhaustive, so that there is no room for "inherent limitations".[233] Admittedly, the exhaustively enumerated restrictions are worded so broadly and the national authorities are allowed so wide a discretion by the Commission and the Court that the above-mentioned examples of "inherent limitations" could in all likelyhood still be brought under them in most cases. This applies all the more as the Court has also adopted the view that in the application of those restrictions by the national authorities still the fact may be taken into account that the person in question belongs to a particular category.[234] Nevertheless, the position of the Court presents the great advantage that the limitations in question are not examined only impliedly within the context of the interpretation of the right in question, but are, as restrictions, expressly subjected to the opinion of the Strasbourg organs, which then also have to review their application for its conformity with provisions such as Article 18.[235]

With respect to those rights which have not been provided in the Convention with express possibilities of restriction, the Court too has adopted the doctrine of "inherent limitations".[236] This view of the Court - and the Commission - appears to us to be wrong. It results from Article 1 that the Convention applies equally to everyone within the jurisdiction of one of the contracting States. If the drafters should have wanted to permit special restrictions in relation to particular categories of persons, they could have stated this in each individual article, as has indeed been done, for instance,

---

231. Appl. 2676/65, *X v. Austria, Coll.* 23 (1967), p. 31.
232. Appl. 2375/64, *X v. Federal Republic of Germany, Coll.* 22 (1967), p. 45; Appl. 2749/66, *Kenneth Hugh de Courcy v. United Kingdom, Yearbook* X (1967), p. 388.
233. Judgment of 18 June 1971, *De Wilde, Ooms and Versyp ("Vagrancy" Cases)*, A.12 (1971), p. 45; judgment of 21 February 1975, *Golder*, A.18 (1975), pp. 21-22.
234. *Golder* Case, *ibidem*. In the *Schönenberger and Durmaz* Case the Court referred to its earlier case-law, where it held that in the case of a prisoner the pursuit of the objective of the prevention of disorder or crime may justify wider measures of interference than in the case of a person at liberty. The Court held that the same reasoning may be applied to a person being held on remand and against whom inquiries with a view to bringing criminal charges are being made, since in such a case there is often a risk of collusion; judgment of 20 June 1988, A.137 (1988), p. 13.
235. This becomes evident, for instance, from the observations in the report of 11 October 1980, *Silver*, B.51 (1987), p. 72.
236. *Golder* Case, A.18 (1975), pp. 18-19.

in the second paragraph of Article 11.[237] Just as from an exhaustive enumeration of the express restrictions, in our opinion it also follows from the absence of any provision to that effect that the drafters did not want to include any (other) limitations.[238] The whole system of the Convention would therefore appear to be opposed to the notion that the rights and freedoms laid down in it can be subjected to so-called "inherent limitations". Moreover, an argument against that notion can be derived from Article 18 of the Convention. That article provides that the restrictions permitted under the Convention may not be applied for any purpose other than those for which they have been prescribed. From the formulation of that article it follows that only those restrictions are allowed which have been permitted for a given purpose. Since no implicit purposes for restrictions are permissible, inherent limitations too must be deemed not to be allowed.

2. Even in the view defended here that the doctrine of "inherent limitations" should be rejected not all questions as to the scope of the rights and freedoms with respect to persons in a special legal position have been settled yet. So much is clear that as to those rights and freedoms which are formulated in an absolute way no derogations or restrictions are permitted in a normal situation under any circumstances, also not on the ground of the special legal position in which a person finds himself. With respect to the other rights and freedoms, however, certain questions as to their scope still tend to arise, which may then have a special dimension for particular categories of persons. Do, for instance, the position of a prisoner and the requirements inherent in the prison regime permit him to marry, to have regular sexual intercourse with his spouse, to keep regular contacts with the family, or to take up a study?

In our opinion, in answering these questions one should not start from the conception of "inherent limitations", but from the view that everyone, detained persons included, is entitled to these rights. Next, it has to be investigated what restrictions may be imposed on the right in question by reason of its formulation or on the basis of express grounds of restriction. To this end, all the relevant circumstances of the case must be taken into account, which may include the special legal position of the persons involved. When the imposed restrictions are tested for their conformity with the relevant provision of the Convention, account may therefore also be taken of the "ordinary and reasonable requirements"[239] which are inherent in that special legal position. This is, however, another matter than the acceptance in advance of special

---

237. See also Art. 4(3)(a) and (b).
238. Cf. also the report of 19 July 1974, Engel, B.20 (1974-76), p. 58: "From this analysis of the Convention, and the method adopted therein, it is clear that the Convention is not conceived in terms of whose rights shall be protected but in terms of what rights shall be guaranteed and to what extent".
239. Judgment of 21 February 1975, Golder, A.18 (1975), p. 21. See also the judgment of 8 June 1976, Engel, A.22 (1977), p. 25 where the Court speaks of "specific demands" and "normal restrictions"; judgment of 20 June 1988, Schönenberger and Durmaz, A.137 (1988), p. 13.

"inherent limitations" for persons in a special legal position. The question of whether the "requirements" advanced by the national authorities are indeed "ordinary and reasonable" may be assessed in each individual case by the Strasbourg organs. When confronted with the questions raised above with respect to detained persons, for instance, modern penitentiary conceptions with respect to the scope which the execution of a detention permits as to the provisions and measures required for the enjoyment of the rights in question must also be involved in the evaluation. In this matter a European standard may be gradually developed.[240]

8.3. "Prescribed by law"; "in accordance with the law"

1. In the enumerations of the specific restrictions it is stated expressly that the latter must be "prescribed by law" (Arts 9(2), 10(2) and 11(2) of the Convention) or "in accordance with the law" (Art. 8(2) of the Convention, Art. 2(3) and (4) of Protocol no. 4 and Art. 1(1) of Protocol no. 7). Thus the Convention refers to the legal system of the State involved, which must provide an adequate basis for the restrictive measure.[241]

The interpretation of municipal law is a matter for the national authorities[242] and forms in principle an established fact for the Strasbourg organs, unless a manifest error of law is concerned. Equally, the question of whether a certain law has been enacted in the prescribed manner and is also in other respects in conformity with national (constitutional) law is not for the organs of the Convention to judge. However, this does not mean that the Strasbourg organs should simply accept as a fact the position of the respondent State - which may even be based upon a judgment of the highest national court - to the effect that a given restrictive measure was based on domestic law. These "facts" may and must be tested for their conformity with the Convention. In that case it is not the interpretation and application of domestic law that is at issue, but the interpretation and application of the words "prescribed by law" and "in accordance with the law" in the Convention itself. Nevertheless, also in this case the Court appears to leave quite a broad margin of appreciation to the national authorities:

> the logic of the system of safeguard established by the Convention sets limits upon the scope of the power of review exercisable by the Court in this respect. It is in the first place for the national authorities, notably the courts, to interpret and apply the domestic law: the national authorities are, in the nature of things, particularly qualified to settle

---

240. See, e.g., the report of 13 December 1979, *Hamer, D & R* 24 (1981), p. 5, where the Commission considered a two years' delay of the possibility of marrying, imposed on a detained person, in its generality an encroachment on his right to marry.
241. This need not necessarily be the national law of that State; it may also be a provision of international law which, in virtue of the monistic system applying for that State, forms part of the national legal order, e.g. a prohibition of war propaganda or the incitement to racism, as restrictions on the freedom of expression.
242. On the other hand, the Commission has rejected the contention that justiciability is an inherent requirement of the concept of "prescribed by law" or "in accordance with the law"; Appl. 8231/78, *X v. United Kingdom, D & R* 28 (1982), p. 5 (30).

the issues arising in this connection.[243]

2. The Court has dealt with the phrases "prescribed by law" and "in accordance with the law" in a number of cases. It has pointed out, first of all that no importance is to be attached to the existence in the English text of the different formulations of the requirement of a sufficient legal basis.[244] Indeed the French text uses the words "prévue par la loi" for "prescribed by law" as well as for "in accordance with the law". Furthermore, the Court has elaborated four principles in its case-law.

It has taken as its point of departure

that the phrase "in accordance with the law" does not merely refer back to domestic law but also relates to the quality of law, requiring it to be compatible with the rule of law, which is expressly mentioned in the preamble to the Convention.[245]

On that basis the Court has stated as a first principle that the word "law/loi" is to be interpreted as covering not only written law but also unwritten law.[246] According to the Court

it would clearly be contrary to the intention of the drafters of the Convention to hold that a restriction imposed by virtue of the common law is not "prescribed by law" on the sole ground that it is not enunciated in legislation: this would deprive a common-law State which is a Party to the Convention of the protection of Article 10 para. 2 and strike at the very roots of that State's legal system.[247]

For the remainder the Strasbourg case-law has hardly defined the term "law/loi". The Commission and the Court have in fact accepted as a sufficient legal basis what had been qualified as such by the national authorities, including royal decrees, emergency decrees, and even internal regulations based on the law.[248]

In this context Alkema rightly calls this a laconic attitude towards the concept of law and deems this to be unsatisfactory, since that very concept determines to a great extent the legal security which the Convention is intended to provide. In his opinion the condition "necessary in a democratic society", to be referred to below, and the provision of Article 3 of Protocol no. 1, the great importance of which in connection with the prescribed legal basis of the restriction has been stressed above,[249] imply that such a legal basis can be taken to exist only if the relevant law has a parliamentary basis.[250] This would mean that the required legal basis can consist only of an

---

243. Judgment of 25 March 1985, *Barthold*, A.90 (1985), p. 22.
244. Judgment of 25 March 1983, *Silver and others*, A.61 (1983), pp. 32-33; judgment of 2 August 1984, *Malone*, A.82 (1984), p. 31.
245. Judgment of 2 August 1984, *Malone*, A.82 (1984), p. 32. See also the Commission in its Report of 11 October 1980, *Silver*, B.51 (1987), p. 74.
246. Judgment of 2 August 1984, *Malone*, A.82 (1984), p. 31.
247. Judgment of 26 April 1979, *Sunday Times*, A.30 (1979), p. 31.
248. See the judgment of 18 June 1971, *De Wilde, Ooms and Versyp* ("*Vagrancy*" *Cases*), A.12 (1971), p. 45. See also the decisions of the Commission on Appl. 1017/61, *X v. the Netherlands, Coll.* 8 (1962), p. 1 (4), and on Appl. 1983/63, *Wallace v. the Netherlands, Yearbook* VIII (1965), p. 228 (264 in conjunction with 246). For legislation based on delegation, see Appl. 7736/76, *X v. Switzerland, D & R* 9 (1970), p. 206 (207) and Appl. 7308/75, *X v. United Kingdom, D & R* 16 (1979), p. 32 (34-35).
249. *Supra* pp. 478 and 487.
250. Alkema, *supra* note 30, p. 42.

Act of Parliament or a regulation enacted in virtue of a delegation of legislative power by Parliament.

If, however, one accepts the thesis defended by us above that the "legislature" in the sense of Article 3 of Protocol no. 1 includes all the organs which have been vested with powers wide enough to make them constituent parts of the legislature,[251] the foregoing implies that regulations by lower representative bodies with legislative power may be regarded as "law" and the restrictions laid down therein must be deemed to possess the required legal foundation, without a conflict arising with the demands of "a democratic society".[252] Only if such legislative power, or a composition based upon free elections, is lacking the restriction in question must originate from an express delegation by Parliament. In a common-law system the unwritten law may also be said to have a firm democratic basis, since it is impliedly endorsed by Parliament.

As was already indicated this matter has not been settled yet by the Strasbourg case-law. In a case against the Federal Republic of Germany the Rules of Professional Conduct for Veterinary Surgeons were at stake. These rules emanated from the Veterinary Surgeons' Council and not directly from Parliament. The Court nevertheless considered these rules as "law" within the meaning of Article 10(2):

> The competence of the Veterinary Surgeons' Council in the sphere of professional conduct derives from the independent rule-making power that the veterinary profession ... traditionally enjoys, by parliamentary delegation.[253]

Whether and if so, to what extent the Court considers this "parliamentary delegation" to be a condition, is not clear from this judgment.

It is dubious whether the legislation of the European Communities satisfies the democratic criterion. Its internal legal effect, indeed, may be said to originate from acts of parliament ratifying the EC Treaties for the separate Member States, but, as being of a higher order, its content and effect cannot be modified by the national parliaments, while a democratic superstructure is still lacking in the Communities, even now that the European Parliament is composed of directly elected members and the Single European Act of February 1986 has somewhat widened the legislative powers of the European Parliament.

As a second principle it has been recognized that "the interference in question must have some basis in domestic law".[254] In itself this principle is

---

251. *Supra* p. 487.
252. See the definition of H.P. Furrer, "La pratique des états membres du Conseil de l'Europe", in: *La circulation des informations et le droit international*, Colloque de Strasbourg 1978, pp. 65-85 (84): "prévues par la loi, à savoir une acte émanant de l'autorité représentative de la legitimité démocratique".
253. Judgment of 25 March 1985, *Barthold*, A.90 (1985), pp. 21-22. The Court took also into account, however, that "it is a competence exercised by the Council under control of the State, which in particular satisfies itself as to observance of national legislation" and that "the Council is obliged to submit its rules of professional conduct to the Land Government for approval."
254. Judgment of 2 August 1984, *Malone*, A.82 (1984), p. 31.

rather trivial and it has, consequently, been qualified in the case-law so as to include the third and the fourth principle, encompassing respectively the accessibility requirement and the foreseeability requirement.[255]

In the *Silver* Case the Court has explained the accessibility requirement as meaning that "the law must be adequately accessible: the citizen must be able to have an indication that is adequate, in the circumstances, of the legal rules applicable to a given case". Subsequently, the Court held that the Orders and Instructions at issue in that case did not meet this criterion because they "were not published".[256] The point of view that unpublished rules do not meet the accessibility requirement at first sight would seem to square uneasily with the above-mentioned first principle according to which "law" does not only cover written but also unwritten law. However, what was at issue in the *Sunday Times* judgment was common law in general, which as such is unwritten law but which in most cases is easily accessible, often through published sources like court decisions, text books and other publications. In the *Silver* Case, on the contrary, the Court was faced with internal orders and instructions which, generally speaking, could only be made accessible by their publication (or by their communication in some other way, which was not shown to be the case). In fact, however, in the *Silver* Case the Court did not have to rely solely on the unpublished Orders and Instructions. The main prescriptions in the form of the British Prison Act and the Rules were published and, therefore, satisfied the accessibility requirement. It was with respect to the interpretation and application of these published provisions - *i.e.* in the context of the foreseeability requirement - that the Court took the unpublished rules nevertheless into account. According to the Court the (unpublished) Orders and Instructions established a practice

> which had to be followed save in exceptional circumstances ... . In these conditions, the Court considers that although those directives did not themselves have the force of law, they may - to the admittedly limited extent to which those concerned were made sufficiently aware of their contents - be taken into account in assessing whether the criterion of foreseeability was satisfied.[257]

The foreseeability requirement implies that

> a norm cannot be regarded as "law" unless it is formulated with sufficient precision to enable the citizen to regulate his conduct: he must be able - if need be with appropriate advice - to foresee, to a degree that is reasonable in the circumstances, the consequences which a given action may entail.[258]

The Court has repeatedly pointed out in this respect that it is impossible to attain absolute precision in framing laws and that many laws are couched in more or less vague terms whose interpretation and application are questions of practice.[259] In other words, many laws inevitably entail a certain degree of discretion. However, according to the Court "a law which confers a discretion

---

255. *Ibidem*, pp. 31-32.
256. Judgment of 25 March 1983, *Silver and others*, A.61 (1983), p. 33.
257. *Ibidem*, pp. 33-34; see also judgment of 26 March 1987, *Leander*, A.116 (1987), p. 23.
258. The *Silver* Case, *ibidem*, p. 33.
259. See, *e.g.*, the judgment of 25 March 1985, *Barthold*, A.90 (1985), p. 22.

must indicate the scope of that discretion".[260] In this context, the Court has held that although safeguards must particularly exist in the case where a text bestows wide discretionary powers these have not to be enshrined in that very text.[261] The Court took the latter position in connection with its point of view, referred to above,[262] that rules governing the interpretation and application of a law do not have to be embodied in the same text but may even be contained in unpublished rules.

Quite illustrative for the Court's subtle approach to the foreseeability requirement is the *Olsson* judgment concerning Swedish legislation allowing the taking of children into public care. The Court held as follows:

> The Swedish legislation applied in the present case is admittedly rather general in terms and confers a wide measure of discretion, especially as regards the implementation of care decisions. ... On the other hand, the circumstances in which it may be necessary to take a child into public care and in which a care decision may fall to be implemented are so variable that it would scarcely be possible to formulate a law to cover every eventuality. To confine the authorities' entitlement to act to cases where actual harm to the child has already occurred might well unduly reduce the effectiveness of the protection which he requires. Moreover, in interpreting and applying the legislation, the relevant preparatory work ... provides guidance as to the exercise of the discretion it confers. Again, safeguards against arbitrary interference are provided by the fact that the exercise of nearly all the statutory powers is either entrusted to or is subject to review by the administrative courts at several levels ... . The Court thus concludes that the interferences were "in accordance with the law".[263]

The Court has accepted that the requirement of foreseeability cannot be exactly the same in the case of implementation of the law through secret measures - such as the interception of communications for the purposes of police investigations and secret controls of staff in sectors affecting national security - and implementation in other comparable fields. However,

> where the implementation of the law consists of secret measures, not open to the scrutiny by the individuals concerned or by the public at large, the law itself, *as opposed to the accompanying administrative practice*, must indicate the scope of any discretion conferred on the competent authority with sufficient clarity, having regard to the legitimate aim of the measure in question, to give the individual adequate protection against arbitrary interference.[264]

On this basis the Court conluded in the *Leander* Case

> that Swedish law gives citizens an adequate indication as to the scope and the manner or exercise of the discretion conferred on the responsible authorities to collect, record and release information under the personnel control system.[265]

A main reason underlying this conclusion was that, although the first paragraph of section 2 of the Swedish Personnel Control Ordinance conferred a wide discretion on the National Policy Board, "the scope of this discretion is however limited by law in important respects through the second para-

260. Judgment of 25 March 1983, *Silver and others*, A.61 (1983), p. 22.
261. *Ibidem*, p. 34.
262. See *supra* p. 581.
263. Judgment of 24 March 1988, A.130 (1988), pp. 30-31; see also judgment of 22 June 1989, *Eriksson*, A.156 (1989), pp. 24-25.
264. Jugdment of 26 March 1987, *Leander*, A.116 (1987), p. 23; emphasis added.
265. *Ibidem*, p. 24.

graph".[266] In its earlier *Malone* judgment the Court had reached a different conclusion:

> In the opinion of the Court, the law of England and Wales does not indicate with reasonable clarity the scope and manner of exercise of the relevant discretion conferred upon the public authorities,

because

> it cannot be said with any reasonable certainty what elements of the powers to intercept [telephone communications] are incorporated in legal rules and what elements remain within the discretion of the executive.[267]

Similarly, with respect to the process of so-called "metering" - involving the use of a device which registers the numbers dialled on a particular telephone and the time and duration of each call - the Court concluded that

> apart from the simple absence of prohibition, there would appear to be no legal rules concerning the scope and exercise of the discretion enjoyed by the public authorities. Consequently, ... the interference resulting from the existence of the practice in question was not "in accordance with the law" within the meaning of paragraph 2 of Article 8.[268]

8.4. "Necessary in a democratic society in the interest of .../for the protection of ..."; the doctrine of the "margin of appreciation"

1. The condition "necessary in a democratic society" occurs in Articles 8-11 of the Convention and in Article 2 of Protocol no. 4, while Article 1 of Protocol no. 7 deletes the words "in a democratic society". Those articles subsequently list a number of interests for the promotion or protection of which the imposed restriction must be necessary in a democratic society. A restriction is in conformity with the Convention only when it is necessary in the light of the interests advanced as weighed against the requirements of a democratic society.

2. It is obvious that very wide concepts are involved here, which, if interpreted broadly, might make the guarantee aimed at by the Convention illusory. It is therefore of great importance that these concepts should be clearly defined in the Strasbourg case-law.

The review by the Strasbourg organs usually proceeds as follows. After it has been established that the right laid down in the first paragraph of the relevant article has been interfered with, it is examined whether that interference may be justified by the next paragraph of the same article. This last examination in fact consists of three parts. The first concerns the question - dealt with in the preceding section - whether the interference was "prescribed by law" or "in accordance with the law". Subsequently it is examined whether the legislation on which the interference is based aims at the protection of one of the interests listed as grounds for restrictions in the

---

266. *Ibidem.*
267. Judgment of 2 August 1984, A.82 (1984), p. 36.
268. *Ibidem*, p. 38.

relevant provision of the Convention. Finally, it must be decided whether, with a view to the interest to be protected, the interference may be considered necessary in a democratic society.

Emphasis is laid by the Strasbourg organs on the issue of the necessity of the interference. In fact, the examination of the question of whether the protection of a justifiable interest is at issue generally coincides with the examination as to the necessity. As a result, the interests listed as grounds for restrictions have received only scant independent attention in the case-law. They are defined in relation to the evaluation of what may be considered necessary in a democratic society.

An autonomous interpretation has been given with respect to the difference between, on the one hand, "the protection of public order" in Article 9(2) of the Convention and, on the other hand, "the prevention of disorder" in Articles 8(2), 10(2) and 11(2). In its judgment in the *Engel* Case the Court, following the Commission,[269] decided that "disorder" refers not only to "public order" but "also covers the order that must prevail within the confines of a special social group".[270] From this it seems to follow likewise that "public order" in the sense of Article 9(2) of the Convention - and Article 1(2) of Protocol no. 7 -, contrary to the French term "ordre public" in Article 2(3) of Protocol no. 4, does not refer to the notion of "public policy", but to "order in places accessible to everyone".[271] In general, however, the grounds of restrictions are defined *via* demarcation of the democratic necessity.[272]

The enumerations of the interests vary somewhat from one article to another, but they are largely similar. The interests mentioned are: national security[273] and public safety,[274] public order,[275] the prevention of crimes,[276] morals,[277] health,[278] the reputation and the rights and freedoms of others,[279]

269. Report of 19 July 1974, B.20 (1974-76), p. 210.
270. Judgment of 8 June 1976, A.22 (1977), p. 41.
271. See Alkema, *supra* note 30, p. 43.
272. An illustrative example of the approach followed in Strasbourg is the judgment of 22 October 1981, *Dudgeon*, A.45 (1981), pp. 18-25.
273. See, *e.g.*, the *Klass* Case to be discussed *infra* pp. 597-600.
274. See, *e.g.*, Appl. 8166/78, *X and Y v. Switzerland, D & R* 13 (1979), p. 241 (243), in which the refusal to married prisoners to continue their married life in prison was considered justified. See also the judgment of 25 March 1983, *Silver*, A.61 (1983).
275. See, *e.g.*, Appl. 8191/78, *Rassemblement Jurassien and Unité Jurassienne v. Switzerland, D & R* 17 (1980), p. 93 (120), concerning a prohibition to hold demonstrations.
276. See, *e.g.*, Appl. 8170/78, *X v. Austria, D & R* 16 (1979), p. 145 (152-153), in which the collection of personal data by the police for use in criminal proceedings was considered a justifiable violation of Art. 8.
277. On this, see *infra* the *Handyside* Case (pp. 588-589) the *Dudgeon* Case (p. 593) and the *Müller* Case (p. 594).
278. See, *e.g.*, Appl. 8209/78, *Peter Sutter v. Switzerland, D & R* 16 (1979), p. 166 (173), in which with respect to the obligation for soldiers to wear their hair cut so as not to touch the collar, the Commission considered without any further argument that "it can indeed be reasonably regarded as a measure necessary for the protection of health".
279. See, *e.g.*, Appl. 8239/78, *X v. the Netherlands, D & R* 16 (1979), p. 184 (189), in which it was held: "while compulsory blood-testing may be seen as constituting a violation of private life within the meaning of Article 8, paragraph 1, it may also be seen as necessary for the protection of the rights of others".

the economic welfare of the country,[280] the prevention of disclosure of information received in confidence[281] and the guaranteeing of the impartiality of the judiciary.[282]

3. As to the question of whether a given restriction is necessary, and consequently also with regard to the further interpretation of the values protected, the national authorities are allowed a very broad "margin of appreciation".

The "margin of appreciation" doctrine is rooted in national case-law concerning judicial review of governmental action.[283] The same doctrine also makes sense within the framework of the European Convention. There, however, the scope of its applicability should in our view be rather limited. In this respect a distinction has to be made between determination of facts on the one hand and determination of questions of law on the other hand. As far as the determination of facts is concerned, application of the "margin of appreciation" doctrine by the Strasbourg organs would seem to be justified and self-evident. It should be borne in mind that national law and its interpretation are also factual data from the point of view of the Strasbourg organs. For the determination of those facts, *i.e.* for answering the question of whether and in what way precisely the facts took place and what are the exact contents and meaning of national law, the national authorities are in a better position than international organs. The latter therefore will generally be inclined to depend to a high degree on the determination of these facts by the authorities of the respondent State, in particular if an independent court was also involved in that determination. This holds good even more if in the proceedings before the Commission the facts, as determined by the national authorites, are not disputed by the applicant.

The situation is in our opinion quite different as far as the determination of questions of law is concerned. For the latter, *viz.* the assessment whether the facts as they have ultimately been established in the Strasbourg proceedings constitute a violation of the Convention, only the Strasbourg organs are competent in the last resort. According to Article 19 of the Convention it is the Court's and the Commission's task "To ensure the observance of the engagements undertaken by the High Contracting Parties in the present Convention". In performing this task they should not refer to the opinion of the national authorities of the State concerned. On the contrary, in our view the opinion of the national authorities must be reviewed by the Strasbourg organs on the basis of an independent examination and interpretation.

---

280. See, *e.g.*, Appl. 7456/76, *Paul Henry Wiggins v. United Kingdom, D & R* 13 (1979), p. 40 (45-46), in which this restriction formed a justification for a system of housing licences which violated the right to privacy.
281. Appl. 4274/69, *X v. Federal Republic of Germany, Yearbook* XIII (1970), p. 888 (890-892).
282. On this, see *infra* the *Sunday Times* Case, pp. 590-591.
283. See Jacobs, *supra* note 214, p. 201.

In sum, application of the "margin of appreciation" doctrine should in our view be confined to the establishment of the facts, including the interpretation of domestic law. In addition, there may, of course, be questions of law which are influenced by the facts to such an extent that in that respect the doctrine should also be applied. For the rest, the review by the Strasbourg organs should be a strict one, based upon an independent examination of the case. This was indeed the attitude followed by the Commission in its very earliest case-law, which was concerned with Article 15. The further development of the case-law, however, shows a completely different picture, which has been summarized recently by one of the members of the Court in the following manner:

> The margin of appreciation is at the heart of virtually all major cases that come before the Court, whether the judgments refer to it explicitly or not.[284]

The doctrine was first applied in the Case of *Greece v. United Kingdom*. The Commission showed itself willing, in the case of derogation from the Convention under Article 15, to grant the State concerned "a certain measure of discretion in assessing the extent strictly required by the exigencies of the situation".[285] In the *Lawless* Case the Commission left the respondent State a rather wide discretion in connection with Article 15. Its President argued this as follows before the Court:

> The concept behind this doctrine is that Article 15 has to be read in the context of the rather special subject-matter with which it deals; namely the responsibilities of a government for maintaining law and order in times of war or public emergency threatening the life of the nation. The concept of the margin of appreciation is that a government's discharge of these responsibilities is essentially a delicate problem of appreciating complex factors and of balancing conflicting considerations of the public interest; and that, once the Commission or the Court is satisfied that the Government's appreciation is at least on the margin of the powers conferred by Article 15, then the interest which the public itself has in effective government and in the maintenance of order justifies and requires a decision in favour of the legality of the Government's appreciation.[286]

4. The Commission's conception of the rationale of the "margin of appreciation", as quoted above, creates the impression that application of this doctrine was considered justified by the Commission only on the ground of the special situations to which Article 15 relates. However, it has gradually also applied the doctrine in connection with other articles of the Convention.

In the development of the case-law on this point two cases may be considered as marking a kind of intermediate phase. In the *Iversen* Case as well as in the *Belgian Linguistic* Case the consistency with the Convention of an important part of government policy was at issue. In the former case the Norwegian measures were challenged, according to which dentists could be employed against their will in the cold and sparsely populated northern region

---

284. R.J. MacDonald, "The margin of appreciation in the jurisprudence of the European Court of Human Rights", in: *International law and the time of its codification; Essays in honour of Roberto Ago*, Milan 1987, pp. 187-208 (208).
285. Appl. 176/56, *Greece v. United Kingdom*, *Yearbook* II (1958-59), p. 174 (176).
286. Report of 19 December 1959, B.1 (1960-61), p. 408.

of the country. In the latter case the complaints concerned the Belgian linguistic legislation.[287] In both cases some members of the Commission concluded that the complaints had to be rejected via the application of the "margin of appreciation" doctrine. Although Article 15 was not involved in these cases, more or less on the analogy of a public emnergency these members of the Commission held that in these cases, too, there was question of an emergency situation in which the respondent State had to be allowed a certain margin of appreciation.

Within the framework of the application of the "margin of appreciation" doctrine, the development of a concept resembling something of a "quasi-emergency" situation has proved quite attractive. In our view, however, this involves the danger of undermining the Convention's structure based on the clear-cut distinction between normal situations and emergency situations. In its fairly recent *Brogan* judgment[288] the Court found Article 15 not to be applicable after the respondent Government had conceded this point of view during the proceedings. In his dissenting opinion, however, Judge Martens did not confine his analysis to the distinction between emergency situations and normal situations, but indeed subjected normal situations to a further categorization by discerning extra-ordinary situations.[289] To these extra-ordinary situations Judge Martens also holds applicable his very wide version of the "margin of appreciation" doctrine.[290]

Judge Martens did not define his concept of an extra-ordinary situation - although it is said to concern special provisions of special laws directed against terrorism - nor did he adduce arguments derived from the Convention or from the Strasbourg case-law to support his distinction between ordinary and extra-ordinary situations. In our view that is not surprising, because there are no such arguments. On the contrary, the Convention's structure strongly argues against such a distinction. The concept of the extra-ordinary situation somehow reminds one of the old doctrine of the "inherent limitations". According to that doctrine for persons in a special legal position such as detained persons, psychiatric patients, soldiers and civil servants a more limited scope of certain rights and freedoms has to be assumed than for persons outside these categories. This doctrine has expressly been rejected by the Court on the basis of the argument that, as restrictions are to be considered exhaustively enumerated in the Convention, there is no room for "inherent limitations".[291] Now Judge Martens seems to introduce a comparable doctrine implying limitations on the scope of the Strasbourg supervision which are "inherent" in extra-ordinary situations in the sense that in such situations

287. On these cases, see *supra* pp. 244-245 and pp. 542-543 respectively.
288. Judgment of 28 November 1988, A.145-B (1989).
289. See *ibidem*, pp. 54-55, where the *Brogan* Case is distinguished from an ordinary law provision, and most specifically p. 54 where it is stated that "we are not dealing with the ordinary criminal law of the United Kingdom but ... with a special provision of a special law directed against terrorism".
290. On the various versions of the doctrine, see *infra* pp. 590-592.
291. See *supra* pp. 575-578.

the Strasbourg organs should leave a wide margin of appreciation to the national authorities. This point of view should be rejected along similar lines of reasoning: as the Convention, in its Article 15, embodies a set of specific provisions dealing with emergency situations there is no room for the assumption that in addition there could be other than normal situations. In short, the concept of "extra-ordinary" situations is incompatible with the system of the Convention and cannot therefore constitute a sufficient basis for broadening the scope of application of the "margin of appreciation" doctrine.

In the meantime, long before Judge Martens' dissenting opinion in the *Brogan* Case, the Strasbourg organs had applied the doctrine to a large number of cases where no "emergency" or "extra-ordinary situation" was involved. The case-law shows examples particularly with respect to the restrictions contained in Articles 8-11. In actual fact, however, the doctrine has been applied to most of the Convention's other rights and freedoms as well, and it is in fact deemed to be susceptible of application to all the Convention's provisions. As has been observed by MacDonald:

> In theory there is no limit to the articles of the Convention to which the margin of appreciation could be applied, for the Court has never imposed a limit.[292]

5. Despite the rather long period of time during which the Court and the Commission have now been using the doctrine it is still extremely difficult to precisely define the nature of the test enshrined in the margin of appreciation doctrine as well as the conditions of its application. The present authors share the conclusion that although the doctrine is now well established in the Strasbourg case-law, "its exact ambit and role are far from being fully developed".[293] With this *caveat* in mind the following general principles may nevertheless be discerned.

The foundations of the application of the doctrine were in fact laid in the highly illustrative *Handyside* judgment, where the compatibility with Article 10(2) of the restrictions placed by the British authorities on the publication of the so-called Little Red Schoolbook were at issue. The Court put forward the following reasons for the application of the doctrine:

> By reason of their direct and continuous contact with the vital forces of their countries, State authorities are in principle in a better position than the international judge to give an opinion on the exact content of these requirements [of the protection of morals] as well as on the "necessity" of a "restriction" or "penalty" intended to meet them.[294]

After having compared the term "necessary" with the terms "indispensable", "absolutely necessary", and "strictly necessary" - which in the Court's opinion have a more absolute character - and also with the weaker terms "admissible", "ordinary", "useful", "reasonable" and "desirable", all of which also occur in the Convention, the Court subsequently held that "it is for the national authorities to make the initial assessment of the reality of the pressing social

---

292. See MacDonald's survey referred to in note 284 (p. 192).
293. *Ibidem*, p. 207.
294. Judgment of 7 December 1976, A.24 (1976), p. 22.

need implied by the notion of 'necessity' in this context", and that consequently a "margin of appreciation" must be left to the States in that respect.[295] However, it followed this up at once with the statement that the "power of appreciation" of the national authorities is not unlimited:

> The Court, which, with the Commission, is responsible for ensuring the observance of those States' engagements (Article 19), is empowered to give the final ruling on whether a "restriction" or "penalty" is reconcilable with freedom of expression as protected by Article 10. The domestic margin of appreciation thus goes hand in hand with a European supervision. Such supervision concerns both the aim of the measure challenged and its "necessity"; it covers not only the basic legislation but also the decision applying it, even one given by an independent court ... .
> The Court's supervisory functions oblige it to pay the utmost attention to the principles characterising a "democractic society".[296]

The point of departure thus formulated in the *Handyside* judgment has served as the basis upon which the demarcation between the margin of appreciation granted to the competent national authorities and the Strasbourg supervision has subsequently been elaborated. A series of judgments over the past decade bear out that the Court in using the margin of appreciation doctrine applies a kind of model test. This model was summarized in the *Silver* Case in the form of the following set of principles:

> (a) the adjective "necessary" is not synonymous with "indispensable", neither has it the flexibility of such expressions as "admissible", "ordinary", "useful", "reasonable" or "desirable" ...;
> (b) the Contracting States enjoy a certain but not unlimited margin of appreciation in the matter of the imposition of restrictions, but it is for the Court to give the final ruling on whether they are compatible with the Convention ...;
> (c) the phrase "necessary in a democratic society" means that, to be compatible with the Convention, the interference must, *inter alia*, correspond to a "pressing social need" and be "proportionate to the legitimate aim pursued" ...;
> (d) those paragraphs of Articles of the Convention which provide for an exception to a right guaranteed are to be narrowly interpreted ... .[297]

In its *Lingens* Case the Court has added a number of elements which together with the said principles seem to make up the core of the "margin of appreciation" test. In explaining its supervisory jurisdiction the Court held that it

> cannot confine itself to considering the impugned ... decisions in isolation; it must look at them in the light of the case as a whole ... . The Court must determine whether the interference at issue was "proportionate to the legitimate aim pursued" and whether the reasons adduced ... to justify it are "relevant and sufficient".[298]

The development of this model has not provided clarity in all respects as far as the application of the margin of appreciation doctrine is concerned. Particularly the additional elements set forth in the *Lingens* judgment make it clear that the exact scope of the national discretion to a large extent depends upon the particular characteristics of each case. It is, in other words, still quite hazardous to try and foretell whether in a given case the national authorities will be allowed a narrower or a wider margin of appreciation. The

---

295. *Ibidem.*
296. *Ibidem*, p. 23.
297. Judgment of 25 March 1983, A.61 (1983), pp. 37-38.
298. Judgment of 8 July 1986, A.103 (1986), pp. 25-26.

Strasbourg case-law presents a rather erratic picture on that score.

6. As far as the scope of the margin of appreciation is concerned, a number of different approaches of the doctrine can be discerned in the Strasbourg case-law. Apart from cases where no margin at all is allowed to the national authorities and the Convention organs conduct a full-fledged review themselves, basically three approaches may be discerned. For the sake of convenience these may be labeled the narrow approach, the reasonableness test, and the not-unreasonable test.

The demarcation between a full-fledged review and the narrow approach is not always clear. Despite reference to the existence of a "certain measure of appreciation" on the part of the competent national authorities it is not uncommon for the Commission and the Court to subsequently conduct a comprehensive independent inquiry into the question of whether or not the requirement of necessity has been satisfied, without apparently being guided very much by the views of the national authorities.

A good example is offered by the position taken by the Strasbourg organs in the landmark *Sunday Times* Case concerning an alleged violation of Article 10. A British court had prohibited the applicants from publishing in the Sunday Times an article dealing with so-called thalidomide children. The British Government defended the injunction by referring to the aim "maintaining the authority and impartiality of the judiciary" contained in Article 10(2) in view of the fact that a suit was pending between the parents of those children and the producer of thalidomide in the United Kingdom. The Commission concluded that "the restriction imposed on the publication of the draft article concerned was not necessary for the maintenance of the authority and impartiality of the judiciary or for any other reason stated in Article 10(2) of the Convention".[299] The Commission summarized the arguments underlying its conclusion as follows:

> that the litigation involved was civil in character, that the contents of the draft article need not necessarily be understood as passing legal judgment on the issues involved in the actions and was not aimed at directly influencing the opinion of the judge, and that at the time of the granting of the injunction the thalidomide proceedings were at the stage of settlement and no court action apart from the approval of the settlement because of the involvement of minors was likely to be forthcoming in the immediate future.[300]

The Court, too, examined the scope of the injunction, the phase in which the thalidomide case was before the national court at the moment in question, as well as the circumstances in which the affair had taken place. It concluded that the injunction of the publication could not be considered necessary in a democratic society for maintaining the authority of the judiciary.[301] The Court reached its decision on the basis of a narrowly defined concept of the margin of appreciation doctrine. Referring to its formulation of the doctrine in the

299. Report of 18 May 1977, B.28 (1982), p. 66.
300. *Ibidem*, p. 73.
301. Judgment of 26 April 1979, A.30 (1979), pp. 38-42.

Handyside Case[302] it elucidated its position by holding that the margin of appreciation does not mean

> that the Court's supervision is limited to ascertaining whether a respondent State exercised its discretion reasonably, carefully, and in good faith. Even a Contracting State so acting remains subject to the Court's control as regards the compatibility of its conduct with the engagements it has under the Convention.[303]

Nine judges of the Court, the largest possible minority, proved in favour of a more wide-ranging approach to the doctrine in that they wanted to assign a very broad discretion to the national authorities in determining the necessity.[304] The minority view is most clearly reflected in the following passage:

> This [European] supervision is concerned, in the first place, with determining whether the national authorities have acted in good faith, with due care and in a *reasonable manner.*[305]

Compared to the majority view just quoted this approach would indeed imply a very marginal review on the part of the Strasbourg organs. Even in comparison with the Court's position in the *Handyside* Case, to which the nine judges made reference, the minority view would amount to a step back, as it would reduce the margin of appreciation doctrine in so many words to a reasonableness test.

The trend of widening the national authorities' discretion is taken to the extreme in cases where the *reasonableness* test is turned into a *not-unreasonable* test. In the latter approach it is required of the national authorities not that the government acted reasonably, but that they did not act unreasonably. This is more than a mere play of words, since the not-unreasonable test would seem to imply a change with respect to the burden of proof. While the reasonableness test requires the government to prove that the national authorities have acted reasonably, the not-unreasonable test seems to burden the applicant (or the Strasbourg organs themselves?) with sustaining that they have not.

The not-unreasonable approach seems to have followed by the Court in two fairly recent cases touching upon the economic policies of the State concerned. In its judgment of 21 February 1986 in the *James* Case the Court dealt with the compulsory transfer of property under the Leasehold Reform Act of 1967, while the judgment of 8 July 1986 in the *Lithgow* Case concerned the right to and the method of compensation. In both cases the applicants alleged a violation of Article 1 of Protocol no. 1 on the part of the United Kingdom. In the first-mentioned case the Court held as follows:

> The Court finding it natural that the margin of appreciation available to the legislature in implementing social and economic policies should be a *wide* one, will respect the legislature's judgment as to what is "in the public interest" *unless that judgment be*

---

302. See *supra* pp. 588-589.
303. Judgment of 26 April 1979, A.30 (1979), pp. 35-37.
304. See the joint dissenting opinion of the nine judges, *ibidem*, pp. 47-56.
305. *Ibidem*, p. 50 (emphasis added).

manifestly without reasonable foundation.[306]

The Court concluded that

> the United Kingdom Parliament's belief in the existence of social injustice was *not* such as could be characterized as *manifestly unreasonable.*[307]

In almost identical words it was held in the *Lithgow* Case that

> The Court's power of review in the present case is limited to ascertaining whether the decisions regarding compensation fell outside the United Kingdom's wide margin of appreciation; it will respect the legislature's judgment in this connection unless that judgment was *manifestly without reasonable foundation.*[308]

The use of the not-unreasonable test, has not been kept confined to the above-mentioned matters concerning economic policy. It has also been applied to cases concerning secret surveillance measures[309] and has been advocated within the Court even with respect to the requirement of promptness contained in Article 5(3). In the *Brogan* Case the majority of the Court conducted a full-fledged review as to this latter requirement. In his dissenting opinion Judge Martens in fact proposed the use of the not-unreasonable test for answering the question of whether a seven-day period for detaining an accused before bringing him before a judicial authority was compatible with the requirement of promptness:

> the Court can find that the United Kingdom ... overstepped the margin of appreciation it is entitled to ... only if it considers that the arguments for maintaining the seven-day period are wholly unconvincing and cannot be reasonably defended.[310]

The issues at stake in the *Brogan* Case he described as "questions on which reasonable people may hold different views". According to Judge Martens

> This means that the Court should respect the United Kingdom Government's choice and cannot but hold that they did not overstep their margin of appreciation.[311]

7. As was already observed, the Strasbourg organs have not yet developed hard and fast standards for the application of the (different approaches to the) doctrine of the margin of appreciation. Nevertheless, the case-law seems to indicate that the width of the margin allotted to the national authorities may depend on two sets of questions: (1) What is the nature of the alleged violation, and (2) to what extent can a European standard be deduced from the national legal systems of Member States of the Council of Europe. The first set of questions comprises the following sub-questions: what ground of restriction did the Government invoke and what right or freedom was interfered with?

As far as the grounds of restriction are concerned the Court held in the *Sunday Times* Case that the national authorities' discretion may vary dependent on the question of what restriction exactly is at issue; some

---

306. Judgment of 21 February 1986, A.98 (1986), p. 32 (emphasis added).
307. *Ibidem*, p. 34 (emphasis added).
308. Judgment of 8 July 1986, A.102 (1987), p. 51 (emphasis added).
309. See *infra* pp. 597-600.
310. Judgment of 28 November 1988, A.145 (1989), p. 55.
311. *Ibidem*, p. 56.

grounds of restriction allow a more far-reaching Strasbourg supervision than do others. According to the Court the protection of morals, which was at issue in the *Handyside* Case, cannot be put on the same level with maintaining the authority of the judiciary, which was under discussion in the *Sunday Times* Case. The former concept cannot be objectified to the same degree as the latter. With respect to maintaining the authority of the judiciary, therefore, a more extensive European supervision corresponds to a less discretionary power of appreciation on the part of the national authorities.[312] In the same vein in the *Norris* Case the Court held that the "national authorities ... do enjoy a wide margin of appreciation in matters of morals".[313]

For the choice between a greater or smaller margin to be left to the national authorities the criterion of the degree to which the interest to be protected by the restriction can be objectified is certainly appropriate.[314] However, this criterion has hardly been further developed so far, whereas its (limited) application is rather curious. After all, the schoolbook, the prohibition of which was held to be justified in the *Handyside* Case on the ground of the protection of morals, freely circulated in the majority of contracting States.[315] On the other hand, in the *Sunday Times* Case The Court disapproved of the British publication injunction as not being necessary in a democratic society for maintaining the authority of the judiciary,[316] while the latter ground of restriction was incorporated in the Convention precisely at the instigation of the United Kingdom with a view to the concept of contempt of court applying there, while a European concept could hardly be spoken of.[317]

Similarly, the other sub-question mentioned above, the nature of the right involved, has not yet emerged from the case-law as a clear guide for leaving a larger or smaller discretion to the national authorities. Questions concerning the nature of the ground of restriction and the nature of the right are closely intertwined. The Court has brought this to the fore with respect to Article 8. The Court considers that provision to be of such a nature that it has an impact on the width of the margin of appreciation. In the *Dudgeon* Case the complaint was directed at the existence in Northern Ireland of laws which had the effect of making certain homosexual acts, also between consenting adult males, criminal offences. The Court held that

> not only the nature of the aim of the restriction but also the nature of the activities involved will affect the scope of the margin of appreciation. The present case concerns a most intimate aspect of private life. Accordingly, there must exist particularly serious reasons before interference on the part of public authorities can be legitimate for the purposes of paragraph 2 of Article 8.[318]

---

312. Judgment of 26 April 1979, *Sunday Times*, A.30 (1979), pp. 35-37.
313. Judgment of 26 October 1988, A.142 (1989), p. 20.
314. See also *infra* pp. 602-604 on the appropriateness of using the availability of a European standard as a criterion.
315. Judgment of 7 December 1976, A.24 (1976), pp. 26-28.
316. Judgment of 26 April 1979, A.30 (1979), p. 37.
317. The Court itself alludes to that; *ibidem.*
318. Judgment of 22 October 1981, A.45 (1981), p. 21. The Court reiterated this decision in the almost identical *Norris* Case of 26 October 1988, A.142 (1989), p. 20.

Another of the Convention's provisions to which the Court assigns such a prominent place that its nature is to affect the scope of the margin of appreciation, is the freedom of expression contained in Article 10. In the *Handyside* Case the Court held that freedom of expression constitutes one of the essential foundations of a democratic society.[319] Subsequent case-law has consistently reiterated this point of view. The Court summed up its approach in its fairly recent *Müller* judgment. There freedom of expression is characterized as one of the pillars

> of a democratic society, indeed one of the basic conditions for its progress and for the self-fulfilment of the individual ... it is applicable not only to "information" or "ideas" that are favourably received or regarded as inoffensive or as a matter of indifference, but also to those that offend, shock or disturb the State or any section of the population. Such are the demands of that pluralism, tolerance and broadmindedness without which there is no "democratic society".[320]

A third area in which the scope of the margin would seem to be affected by the nature of the right involved is that where the economic order of the respondent State is touched upon,[321] usually cases concerning Article 1 of Protocol no. 1. In this area, however, the nature of the right does not narrow the scope of the margin of appreciation, but rather has the effect of broadening it. In the *James* Case dealing with the long leasehold system of tenure in England and Wales the Court explicitly found it "natural that the margin of appreciation available to the legislature in implementing social and economic policies should be a wide one".[322] Similarly in the *Lithgow* Case the Court held with respect to compensation in the case of nationalization:

> Because of their direct knowledge of their society and its needs and resources, the national authorities are in principle better placed than the international judge to appreciate what measures are appropriate in this area and consequently the margin of appreciation available to them should be a wide one.[323]

Finally, the *Gillow* Case also concerned aspects of the economic policy of a contracting State. Not Article 1 of Protocol no. 1, but the applicants' right to their home was allegedly violated because they were refused a licence to occupy the house they owned and were subsequently prosecuted for unlawful occupation. The Court decided that the contested legislation as such - leaving apart its application in this particular case - did not constitute a breach of Article 8. In taking that decision the Court was guided by the consideration that "the Guernsey legislature is better placed than the international judge to assess the effects of any relaxation of the housing controls".[324] In summary this fairly recent body of case-law seems to bear out that when economic policies are involved, the Court takes an attitude of greater aloofness by granting a

---

319. Judgment of 7 December 1976, A.24 (1976), p. 23.
320. Judgment of 24 May 1988, A.133 (1988), p. 22.
321. See also *supra* pp. 591-592.
322. Judgment of 21 February 1986, A.98 (1986), p. 32.
323. Judgment of 8 July 1986, A.102 (1986), p. 51.
324. Judgment of 24 November 1986, A.109 (1987), p. 22. Subsequently, however, the Court decided that the application of the legislation in the particular circumstances of the applicants' case constituted a violation of Article 8; *ibidem*, pp. 23-24.

wider margin of discretion to the national authorities.

In comparison to the above-mentioned *Dudgeon* Case and *Norris* Case the *Gillow* Case also makes clear that the scope of the margin may vary depending on what elements of a particular provision - *in casu* Article 8 - is at issue. The right to respect for his private life of the first-mentioned cases would seem to be "stronger" than the right to respect for his home of the latter; put differently: interference in private life would seem to require a more far-reaching justification than interference in the right of respect for his home. The required justification in its turn also depends on the ground of restriction invoked, such as the protection of morals or the economic well-being of the country. All this points to the fact that the Court's case-law on this score has developed an intricate interplay between the nature of the right involved and the nature of the ground of restriction adduced to justify the Government's interference. The resulting balance is upset, however, if the interference by the authorities oversteps the limit beyond where a reasonable justification can no longer be advanced.

That situation was found to exist in the *De Becker* Case. There, very far-reaching restrictions had been imposed upon a Belgian citizen with respect to his right to freedom of expression, because he had collaborated with the enemy during the Second World War. Thus he had been prohibited for life from engaging in any form of written publication, irrespective of whether its contents did or did not have a political character. The Commission found that such a rigid restriction of the freedom of expression as a penalty did not occur in the other contracting States, and held that this exceeded what was necessary in a democratic society:

> such a lifelong and all-embracing deprivation of freedom of expression scarcely appears to be reconcilable with the ideals and traditions of the democracies of the Council of Europe.[325]

A comparable case is the *Golder* Case. There a prisoner had been refused permission to contact a lawyer. The Court held first of all that in principle it may be necessary in a democratic society to subject correspondence to control, especially where prisoners are concerned. Since in this case, however, a refusal of permission to write even a letter was involved - and moreover a letter which was intended to enable the prisoner to exercise a right which Article 6 grants to him - the Court concluded that this necessity did not exist "even having regard to the power of appreciation left to the Contracting States".[326]

8. Under the heading of the nature of the right involved and its impact on the scope of the national margin of appreciation two more, quite distinct categories of cases should be dealt with, *i.e.* those concerning so-called positive obligations and those regarding secret surveillance.

---

325. Report of 8 January 1960, B.2 (1962), p. 128.
326. Judgment of 21 February 1975, A.18 (1975), p. 26.

As far as positive obligations are concerned, the Court is again inclined to leave the national authorities a very wide margin of appreciation. Among the cases in which positive obligations were eventually assumed to exist three in particular shed light on the impact of positive obligations on the scope of the margin of appreciation: the *X and Y* Case, the *Abdulaziz, Cabales and Balkandali* Case and the *Rees* Case. In the last-mentioned case the Court observed that

> although the essential object of Article 8 is to protect the individual against arbitrary interference by the public authorities, there may in addition be positive obligations inherent in an effective respect for private life, albeit subject to the State's margin of appreciation.[327]

Rees complained about the non-recognition for legal purposes of his post-operative new sexual identity, in particular about the practice of issuing him a birth certificate on which his sex continued to be recorded as "female". The Court concluded that in order to overcome the problems raised by Rees the British Government would have been forced to replace or completely change the prevailing legal regime and that "Having regard to the wide margin of appreciation afforded to the State in this area ..., the positive obligations arising from Article 8 cannot be held to extend that far".[328] In the *Abdulaziz, Cabales and Balkandali* Case the applicants were lawfully and permanently settled in the United Kingdom, but in accordance with the immigration rules of the United Kingdom their (future) husbands were not permitted to remain with or to join them in that country. The Court did not consider this to constitute a lack of respect for family life, given the wide margin of appreciation to be left to the competent national authorities:

> The duty imposed by Article 8 cannot be considered as extending to a general obligation on the part of a Contracting State to respect the choice by married couples of the country of their matrimonial residence and to accept the non-national spouses for settlement in that country.[329]

The *X and Y* Case concerned the impossibility of having criminal proceedings instituted against the perpetrator of a sexual assault on a mentally handicaped girl, who still was a minor. The Court's point of departure was again that the steps required by the positive obligations involved fall within the States' margin of appreciation. Surprisingly, however, the Court seems to leave the respondent State hardly any margin in this case. It found that the protection afforded by the civil law of the Netherlands was insufficient for the wrong-doing of the kind inflicted on Miss Y and subsequently decided without adducing additional arguments:

> This is a case where fundamental values and essential aspects of private life are at stake. Effective deterrence is indispensable in this area and it can be achieved only by criminal-law provisions; indeed, it is by such provisions that the matter is normally regulated.[330]

---

327. Judgment of 17 October 1986, A.106 (1987), p. 14.
328. *Ibidem*, p. 17.
329. Judgment of 28 May 1984, A.94 (1985), p. 34; with regard to the alleged violation of Art. 14 in conjunction with Art. 8 the Court held that the immigration rules constituted a discrimination on the ground of sex; *ibidem*, p. 39.
330. Judgment of 26 March 1985, A.91 (1985), p. 13.

In the *Gaskin* Case, which bears some similarity with the above-mentioned *Rees* Case,[331] the Court did not refer to the margin of appreciation at all, but in determining whether or not a positive obligation existed focused on the "fair balance that has to be struck between the general interest of the community and the interests of the individual".[332] According to the Court there was a violation of Article 8 because the British system would have been balanced only if it had provided that an independent authority finally decides whether access to the files in question has to be granted in cases where a contributor withholds consent.[333]

Balancing the interests involved is also a central element in the above-mentioned category of cases concerning secret surveillance measures. Unlike the *Gaskin* Case, however, where there is not even a reference to the margin of appreciation, the secret surveillance cases led the Court to granting a wide discretion to the national authorities. Both these elements - the balancing of interests and the granting of a wide margin - come clearly to the fore in the *Leander* Case, where information used in assessing a person's suitability for employment on a post of importance for national security was kept in a secret police-register, allegedly in violation of Article 8. There the Court held as follows:

> The Court accepts that the margin of appreciation available to the respondent State in assessing the pressing social need in the present case, and in particular of choosing the means for achieving the legitimate aim of protecting national security, was a wide one. Nevertheless, in view of the risk that a system of secret surveillance for the protection of national security poses of undermining or even destroying democracy on the ground of defending it, the Court must be satisfied that there exist adequate and effective guarantees against abuse.[334]

The Swedish personnel control system did satisfy the Court:

> Having regard to the wide margin of appreciation available to it, the respondent State was entitled to consider that in the present case the interests of national security prevailed over the individual interests of the applicant ... . The interference to which Mr. Leander was subjected cannot therefore be said to have been disproportionate to the legitimate aim pursued.[335]

Two conclusions stand out from this judgment. First, in matters of secret surveillance the national authorities' margin of appreciation is extremely wide. Secondly - and consequently - in balancing the individual and the general interests, the Court in the final analysis opts for a *raison d'état* approach: in weighing the full enjoyment of the rights and freedoms on the one hand and the interests advanced by the State for their restriction on the other, the Court appears to assign an overriding importance to the latter.

The latter attitude was already implied - in a more subtle manner - in the Court's earlier *Klass* judgment. The facts of this important case were as

---

331. Gaskin alleged violation of positive obligations flowing from Art. 8 because of his lack of access to the whole of his case-file held by a social services body under the care of which he had been placed during childhood.
332. Judgment of 7 July 1989, A.160 (1989), p. 17.
333. *Ibidem*, p. 20.
334. Judgment of 26 March 1987, A.116 (1987), p. 25.
335. *Ibidem*, p. 27.

follows. A number of German lawyers, including a judge and a public prosecutor, submitted that Article 10(2) of the German Constitution and the law of 13 August 1968 enacted on the basis of it (further to be called the "G.10") conflicted with the Convention. According to the applicants the violation of the Convention consisted in that the legal provisions in question permitted control of correspondence by post, telegraph, and telephone of private persons, without the authorities being obliged in each individual case to notify the persons concerned, while the normal judicial remedies against an order to exercise such control were debarred. The central issue in the proceedings before the Court was the question of the possible conflict of the "G.10" *in the abstract* with Article 8 of the Convention. Its application to the applicants was not at issue. This would hardly have been possible in this case, because whether any measures of control had in fact been taken against the applicants was uncertain, given the secret character of these measures.[336] That secret character played a decisive part in the inquiry concerning the "G.10".

Certain questions which arose in the course of that inquiry presented no problems. It was evident for the Court that the "G.10" amounted to an "interference" as referred to in Article 8 and as such constituted in principle a breach of the Convention. The Commission had reached the same conclusion and the German Government did not even dispute it. Next, it had to be ascertained whether the "interference" was justified on one of the grounds of Article 8(2). The Court had no difficulty in establishing that the interference was "in accordance with the law" as required in Article 8(2).[337] The same applied with respect to the condition "in the interest of national security and for the prevention of disorder or crime".[338]

However, it was more difficult to answer the question of whether the measures permitted under the "G.10" could be deemed necessary in a democratic society. In this context the Court alluded to the "margin of appreciation" doctrine:

> the Court points out that the domestic legislature enjoys a certain discretion. It is certainly not for the Court to substitute for the assessment of the national authorities any other assessment of what might be the policy in this field.[339]

In fact, however, the Court gave evidence of assessing independently the policy followed in the matter by the German authorities and the arguments advanced for it, and it conducted a full and independent review of the conformity of that policy with the Convention, even though the formulation of the conclusion is somewhat confusing on a few points.[340]

The Court first of all gave a description of the "G.10", and subsequently pointed out that control of the application of this Act might be conceived at

---

336. On this, *supra* pp. 43-45.
337. Judgment of 6 September 1978, A.28 (1979), p. 22.
338. *Ibidem.*
339. *Ibidem*, p. 23.
340. *Ibidem*, p. 28: "the Court concludes that the German legislature was justified to consider ... as being necessary in a democratic society"; emphasis added.

three moments, to wit the moment at which the order is given to take the measures provided for, the moment at which they are carried out, and the period thereafter. As regards the first two moments, the Court referred to the principle of the "rule of law", which is a fundamental principle in a democratic society:

> The rule of law implies, *inter alia*, that an interference by the executive authorities with an individual's rights should be subject to an effective control which should normally be assured by the judiciary, at least in the last resort, judicial control offering the best guarantees of independence, impartiality and a proper procedure.[341]

At first sight the word "normally" in this passage is rather curious. One would think that especially with respect to the principle of the "rule of law" any exception implies the undermining of that principle itself. The Court, however, was more or less forced to utter this contradiction, for shortly before it had submitted:

> As regards the first two stages, the very nature and logic of secret surveillance dictate that not only the surveillance itself but also the accompanying review should be effected without the individual's knowledge.[342]

This induced the Court to find that

> having regard to the nature of the supervisory and other safeguards provided for by the G.10 ... the exclusion of judicial control does not exceed the limits of what may be deemed necessary in a democratic society.[343]

Although this conclusion of the Court falls foul of its earlier case-law concerning Article 6(1)[344] and implies a restrictive interpretation of Article 13,[345] its inevitability for the period in which secrecy is indispensable for the purpose for which the measures are taken has to be recognized, provided that this purpose presents an overriding interest. With respect to the latter the Court made the following observation:

> Democratic societies nowadays find themselves threatened by highly sophisticated forms of espionage and by terrorism, with the result that the State must be able, in order effectively to counter such threats, to undertake the secret surveillance of subversive elements operating within its jurisdiction.[346]

The Court's decision is based on an interpretation of the relevant provision within the total system of the Convention, at the roots of which are the values that the German legislation is designed to protect. However, that same system of the Convention - in particular Article 13 - likewise entails that an individual must be able to form an opinion about the weighing that has taken place between his rights and freedoms on the one hand, and the interests of the State which are also recognized in the Convention on the other hand. Further, he must be able to appeal against the decision which is the result of this weighing. This requires that the person whose rights and freedoms are

---

341. *Ibidem*, p. 25.
342. *Ibidem*.
343. *Ibidem*. On the non-judicial review system of the "G.10", see *ibidem*, pp. 9-14.
344. See *supra* pp. 317-318.
345. See *supra* p. 528.
346. *Supra* note 337, p. 23.

infringed by the authorities be notified. In the case under discussion this will have to be done at any rate afterwards, *i.e.* as soon as the protection of the value for which the measure was taken makes this possible. This latter point was also emphasized by the Court, which followed the German *Bundesverfassungsgericht* in that respect.[347] It is only when the person concerned ultimately has the opportunity to defend his rights against the authorities that there is really observance of the "rule of law". If this principle were to be abandoned, legislative measures could create the danger of "undermining or even destroying democracy on the ground of defending it".[348]

The Court has gone very far here in considering restrictions on the right to a legal remedy permissible, basing itself on a weighing of the encroachment upon democracy threatening from both sides. It is regrettable, however, that the Court has not expressly qualified, as contrary to the democratic principles underlying the Convention, the possibility which the German legislation seems to leave open, also in the interpretation by the *Bundesverfassungsgericht*, *viz.* that in a given case the person concerned is not notified, even after a certain time, of the surveillance carried out over him. In cases like the one under discussion it is important who decides whether and at which moment the specific situation permits the notification of the person in question. The possibility of appeal - mentioned in the *Klass* judgment - to the parliamentary committee and the *Bundesverfassungsgericht* for that purpose is not very effective, because the person concerned then has to depend on presumptions, while the secret character of the measures entails that in many cases such a presumption will not exist. Even the supervision procedure provided for in the Convention itself cannot enter into operation with respect to concrete measures as long as the secrecy has not been removed. A heavy duty thus rests on the parliamentary committee which is informed about the measures taken. It should weigh in each individual case the interest of national security, advanced by the authorities, against the rights and freedoms of the individual, and should also assess whether secrecy still is strictly necessary.

In the third judgment to be mentioned within the framework of secret surveillance cases the Court did not reach the stage of judging the balance struck by the respondent State between individual and general interests. In this *Malone* Case, as was pointed out above,[349] the Court found a breach of Article 8 on account of its conclusion that the interferences on the part of the British Government were not in accordance with the law/prescribed by law.

9. The emphasis on the striking of a balance between individual and general interests in the above-mentioned cases as well as in many other cases in which the margin of appreciation is involved, derives from the principle listed

---

347. *Ibidem*, p. 31.
348. *Ibidem*, p. 23.
349. See *supra* p. 583.

in the *Silver* Case[350] according to which the phrase "necessary in a democratic society" means that, to be compatible with the Convention, the interference must, *inter alia*, correspond to a pressing social need and be proportionate to the legitimate aim pursued. This weighing of the various interests involved is indeed characteristic for the very nature of the Convention. For this reason one cannot but agree with the following conclusion:

> That the Convention is essentially concerned with the balancing of Convention rights in the light of stipulated public interests is inherent in the language of the doctrine [of the margin of appreciation].[351]

However, the question is not so much whether a weighing of interests has to take place, but rather which authority in the final analysis is empowered to do the weighing. It is this latter question which the debate on the margin of appreciation doctrine sharply puts in perspective. Those who argue that the dcotrine should not - or only in its narrow version - be applied within the framework of the Convention in fact hold that the Strasbourg organs ultimately are the only competent bodies in this respect. Those, on the other hand, who favour application of the wider versions of the doctrine opt for a primary role of the competent authorities of the contracting States.

The former position is defended here. In our view, the arguments underlying that position were aptly summarized by the Court in the *Norris* Case. In that case the Irish Government argued with respect to the protection of morals:

> Within broad parameters the moral fibre of a democratic nation is a matter for its own institutions and the Government should be allowed a degree of tolerance in their compliance with Article 8, that is to say, a margin of appreciation that would allow the democratic legislature to deal with this problem in the manner which it sees best.[352]

In reaction the Court countered as follows:

> The Government are in effect saying that the Court is precluded from reviewing Ireland's observance of its obligation not to exceed what is necessary in a democratic society when the contested interference with an Article 8 right is in the interests of the "protection of morals". The Court cannot accept such an interpretation. To do so would run counter to the terms of Article 19, under which the Court was set up in order "to ensure the observance of the engagements undertaken by the High Contracting Parties".[353]

Indeed, also in our view Article 19, which reflects the structure of the European Convention, leaves room for no other conclusion than that in the final analysis only the Strasbourg organs are competent to conduct the weighing of interests involved in the Convention. Leaving this task to the national authorities is eventually going to undermine the Convention's entire structure. Granting the extreme latitude inherent in the above-mentioned wide version of the margin of appreciation doctrine - and exemplified by the Irish Government's claim in the *Norris* Case - would reduce the Strasbourg supervisory machinery to a mechanism for rubberstamping almost anything a

---

350. See *supra* p. 589.
351. MacDonald, *supra* note 284, p. 195.
352. Judgment of 26 October 1988, A.142 (1989), p. 19.
353. *Ibidem*, p. 20.

Government wants.

10. The task of the Strasbourg organs to ensure the observance of the engagements undertaken by the Contracting States in our view encompasses the elaboration of uniform standards in interpreting the Convention.[354] In this respect the following observation has been made:

> Commentators have noted that the interpretation of the Convention may legitimately be based on the common legal traditions and practices of the States Parties. There is no reason why this approach cannot be extended validly to govern the margin of appreciation doctrine.[355]

Indeed, as we have argued in the foregoing, the structure of the Convention provides every reason to elaborate common standards, thereby reducing the area of application of the margin of appreciation doctrine. However, the case-law up to this point shows only a modest use of common or uniform European standards and where such standards are resorted to for deciding cases, they do not seem to rest on very firm ground. One authoritative commentator has observed in this respect with reference to the *Dudgeon* Case and the *Sunday Times* Case:

> Search as one may, through both judgments, there is no reference whatsoever to the relevant legislation of all or even most Contracting States, let alone comparative analysis to establish what degree of unity may or may not have existed.[356]

In the earlier *Handyside* Case the Court formally instituted an independent inquiry into the question of whether the restrictions imposed were necessary in a democratic society. It did not, however, apply a European standard, or at least not one independent to some extent of the local situation at that moment, because - except for a very marginal review - it conformed to the views of the national court. In fact, in this case the publisher, afterwards supported by a minority of the Commission, had alleged that the seizure of the "Little Red Schoolbook" on the ground of its alleged indecent character could not be considered necessary in a democratic society, because in other parts of the United Kingdom no measure had been taken against the book, while in addition translations of the original Danish edition of the book

---

354. See in this respect the dissenting opinion of Judge Gölcüklü in the *Barford* Case, A.149 (1989), p. 17: "Finally I wish to stress that it is difficult to reconcile the Convention, whose ultimate purpose is to establish European standards, with specific national features such as those put forward by the Government".
355. T.A. O'Donnell, "The Margin of Appreciation Doctrine: Standards in the Jurisprudence of the European Court of Human Rights", in: *Human Rights Quarterly* (1982), pp. 474-496 (484).
356. MacDonald, *supra* note 284, p. 201. According to the author "In Dudgeon ..., the Court had to consider the legality of criminal sanctions against homosexual acts involving males under the age of 21 as well as acts involving those over the age of 21. ... With regard to the latter group the Court looked at the existing European consensus on the matter; but with regard to the former, the Court's judgment suggests that the Government's acts were regarded as legitimate in the absence of any such survey". With respect to the *Sunday Times* Case it is observed by him that the majority discovered a fairly substantial measure of common ground in this area, while the minority concluded that the notion of the authority of the judiciary is by no means divorced from national circumstances and cannot be determined in a uniform way. *(Ibidem*, pp. 200-201.)

circulated freely in most member States of the Council of Europe. The Court, however, took the position that this difference in attitude of the authorities in the various parts of the United Kingdom and in the individual member States of the Council of Europe was not conclusive. In the view of the Court there existed no such thing as "a uniform European conception of morals".[357] Even assuming that this was a correct conclusion it would still be up to the Court - and the Commission - to develop such a "European conception", since the term "morals" is frequently mentioned in the Convention. That this term is interpreted in each individual case by reference to the national conceptions on this point is irreconcilable with a collectively guaranteed set of internatio-nal norms like the Convention, at least in the long run.

Nevertheless, since the delivery of the *Handyside* judgment in 1976, the case-law has not changed on this point. In its 1988 *Müller* judgment the Court held that

> Today, as at the time of the Handyside judgment ..., it is not possible to find in the legal and social orders of the Contracting States a uniform European conception of morals.[358]

After having recognized that conceptions of sexual morality had changed in recent years and after having inspected the allegedly obscene paintings in question the Court concluded that

> having regard to the margin of appreciation left to them ..., the Swiss courts were entitled to consider it necessary for the protection of morals to impose a fine on the applicants for publishing obscene material.[359]

The *Müller* judgment clearly bears out that the existence or conversely the lack of common standards in the contracting States influences the width of the margin of appreciation. As indicated above, in our opinion the Commis-sion and the Court, in their case-law, should make efforts at searching for and - to the extent possible - elaborating common standards for the interpretation of the Convention.[360] In that respect the Strasbourg practice up to now offers the following picture. First, the case-law does not show a determined effort on the part of the Commission and the Court to systemati-cally search for and elaborate such common standards. Secondly, conclusions as to the existence or the lack of common standards do not appear to rest on the firm basis of comparative legal analysis. Thirdly - and maybe consequently - there is not infrequently disagreement as to the existence or lack of common standards. Fourthly, in areas where there is agreement, conclusions as to the lack or existence of common standards are not always consistently applied.[361] We, therefore, fully support the plea expressed by a member of the Court that

> In the future the Court may wish to pay more attention to reviewing the relevant laws of the Contracting States, as opposed to merely to general expresssions of law, and to

---

357. Judgment of 7 December 1976, A.24 (1977), p. 22.
358. Judgment of 24 May 1988, A.133 (1988), p. 22.
359. *Ibidem*, p. 23.
360. *Supra* at this same page.
361. See O'Donnell, *supra* note 355, pp. 479-484.

11. The preceding analysis has attempted to schematize the complex Strasbourg case-law concerning the margin of appreciation. As is the case with any scheme, this one too, at least to some degree, distorts reality. The reader, therefore, should not be led to believe that the entire body of relevant case-law neatly fits into one or more elements of the scheme, let alone that the scheme could provide a sure guide to predicting the outcome of future cases. Actual practice is often much more erratic than abstract scholarly analysis tends to suggest.

In order to illustrate this point we must briefly return to one of the principles set forth in the *Silver* Case, according to which an interference is justified only to the extent that it is proportionate to the legitimate aim pursued. If we are not mistaken, the Court (and the Commission) employs this proportionality principle as a kind of feed-back mechanism. When the case at hand cannot satisfactorily be decided according to one of the principles, elements or other established lines of reasoning developed in the case-law, the Court relies on its judgment as to the proportionality to decide the case. The Court's case-law provides more than a few of this type of decisions.[363] Judgments in this category typically contain a (sometimes extensive) listing of the factors to be taken into account, but then somewhat abruptly - without additional arguments as to the weight of the factors concerned - conclude, for instance, that "the injunctions complained of are not proportionate to the legitimate aim pursued",[364] that "a proper balance was not achieved between the interests involved and that there was therefore a disproportion between the means employed and the legitimate aim pursued",[365] or that "the political context in which the tax case was fought cannot be regarded as relevant for the question of proportionality".[366] Although this way of deciding that particular type of cases is understandable from the point of view of the Court, these judgments are unsatisfactory from the perspective of the guiding function which the Court in our view is to play.[367]

12. The preceding discussion of the margin of appreciation doctrine may be summed up as follows. In our view within the framework of the European Convention the margin of appreciation doctrine to some extent is to be compared to a spreading disease. Not only has the scope of its application gradually been broadened to the point where in principle none of the Convention's rights and freedoms is excluded, but also has the illness been intensified in that wider versions of the doctrine have been added to the

---

362. MacDonald, *supra* note 284, p. 201.
363. See, for instance, the *Dudgeon* Case, judgment of 22 October 1981, A.45 (1982), p. 24, *Young, James and Webster Case*, judgment of 13 August 1981, A.44 (1981), pp. 25-26; and *Gillow* Case, judgment of 24 November 1986, A.109 (1987), pp. 23-24.
364. Judgment of 26 March 1985, *Barthold*, A.90 (1985), p. 26.
365. Judgment of 21 June 1988, *Berrehab*, A.138 (1988), p. 16.
366. Judgment of 22 February 1989, *Barford*, A.149 (1989), p. 14.
367. See also *supra* p. 602.

original concept; this in our view to the detriment of the task of the Commission and the Court to "ensure the observance of the engagements undertaken by the High Contracting Parties".

The "margin of appreciation" doctrine has been discussed at such length here because in fact it constitutes one of the cardinal points of the Strasbourg case-law. The cases dealt with in the foregoing in our view are typical of the attitude of the Strasbourg institutions towards the restrictions of the Convention. The Commission and the Court appear to follow in many cases what might be called a *raison d'état* interpretation: when they weigh the full enjoyment of the rights and freedoms on the one hand and the interests advanced by the State for their restriction on the other hand. They appear to be inclined to pay more weight to the latter. In our opinion, however, the "object and purpose" of the European Convention would seem to dictate a different attitude, which might be referred to as the "constitutional" attitude. The latter implies that the full enjoyment of the rights and freedoms constitutes the point of departure and that the possibilities to restrict this enjoyment are exceptions which should be interpreted restrictively, while the organ examining the case should review these restrictions in an independent way for their conformity with the conditions laid down by the Convention.[368]

As has been said, a "margin of appreciation" is almost inevitable if an alleged violation of Article 15 is at issue.[369] Whether a situation exists which threatens the life of the nation depends on a complex of usually very complicated facts. In the first instance therefore this can best be assessed by the national authorities, who are more familiar with the local situation and are more directly concerned in the actual developments. Even after an inquiry on the spot the Commission and the Court can do little more than examine the plausibility of the government's view.

However, the Commission and the Court are not always at such a disadvantage as compared with the national authorities that they cannot themselves establish the facts without having to refer to the opinion of the respondent State on the matter. Even with regard to the establishment of the facts therefore the application of the "margin of appreciation" doctrine is justified only *in so far as* the national authorities are in so much better a position to judge on these facts that such an establishment cannot be made independently by the Strasbourg organs. As has been said, with respect to questions of law the point of departure should be that they are examined and answered in an autonomous way by the Strasbourg organs. However, with respect to questions of law, too, it may be necessary to grant the national authorities a certain discretion, if the aspects of expediency, which are usually of a highly factual nature, clearly predominate over the aspects of lawfulness.

The latter occurs, for instance, when the issue is whether the grant of guardianship or the grant of a visiting right to one of the divorced parents

368. See *supra* pp. 585-586.
369. On this, see *supra* p. 586.

is in the interest of the child, a question which may be important for judging whether a violation of the right to family life of Article 8 is to be considered justified on the ground of the second paragraph.[370] More or less the same applies to the question of whether the measures taken are "strictly required" in the sense of Article 15. Although this is a question of law - have the conditions of Article 15 been complied with? - still questions of expediency play a very important part as well, and the local situation will be conclusive in many cases.

In our view, however, the situation is generally different for the question of whether a restriction imposed on one of the rights and freedoms is "necessary in a democratic society in the interest of .../for the protection of ...". It is true that here too the circumstances of the individual case and the questions of expediency connected therewith play a part, but still the relevant norm, in view of the very reference to "democratic society", can be objectified and interpreted independently of the actual situation to a much greater extent, so that the review here leaves greater scope for an independent assessment by the examining international organ. Indeed, the meaning of the term "democratic society" is not determined by the situation in a particular State, but refers to a common value of the Member States of the Council of Europe. As such it forms the foundation of the Convention and its essentials should be safeguarded by the organs of the Convention via an independent assessment of the justification of an imposed restriction, advanced by the national authorities. This naturally means then that the terms "public order", "morals" and the like must also be given an autonomous meaning, independent to some extent of the national context, and this for all of these terms and not, as done by the Court, for one term, but not for another.[371]

§ 9. ARTICLE 64: THE POSSIBILITY OF MAKING RESERVATIONS

1. The inclusion of the possibility of making reservations was a controversial matter at the time the Convention was drafted. The Committee on Legal and Administrative Questions of the Consultative Assembly was opposed to giving the States unlimited power to do so: "Such a power would threaten to deprive the latter [the Convention] of its practical effect and in any case of its moral authority". The Committee therefore proposed that the validity of a reservation would at the least have to be subjected to the approval of a qualified majority of the other contracting States, and that the State in question would have to give reasons for every reservation. Moreover, it was suggested that a

---

370. See the judgment of 22 June 1989, *Eriksson*, A.156 (1989).
371. To this, Judge Zekia seems to allude in his concurring opinion in the *Sunday Times* Case when he states: "I may be repeating myself in saying that this Court should not hesitate to lay down when the occasion requires a set of principles to serve as guidelines and a common denominator in the observance of the freedoms and the permissible limitations on such freedoms within the terms and ambit of the Convention"; judgment of 26 April 1979, A.30 (1979), p. 66.

State which made a reservation should submit periodically a report in which the reasons for the maintenance of that reservation would have to be given.[372]

These suggestions were not adopted by the Committee of Ministers. The text of Article 64 was ultimately drafted as follows:

> 1. Any State may, when signing this Convention or when depositing its instrument of ratification, make a reservation in respect of any particular provision of the Convention to the extent that any law then in force in its territory is not in conformity with the provision. Reservations of a general character shall not be permitted under this Article.
> 2. Any reservation made under this Article shall contain a brief statement of the law concerned.

2. Several contracting States have made reservations in respect of the Convention.[373] Most of these reservations have a limited scope and concern substantive provisions, *i.e.* the rights and freedoms protected by the Convention and the Protocols. The specific questions to which reservations concerning procedural provisions give rise will be dealt with separately below.[374]

3. The first general question to be discussed as to the Convention's system of reservations concerns the competence to decide on the legal validity of reservations. As was said above, the Convention does not stipulate that a reservation requires acceptance by other contracting States. On the other hand, the Convention embodies a specific mechanism of supervision of its observance. It seems obvious, therefore, that the said competence lies with the Convention organs.

It was only in 1988 that the Court had the opportunity to address this issue. In the *Belilos* Case the Court succinctly asserted jurisdiction to determine the validity of a reservation under Article 64. Without much ado it was held:

> That the Court has jurisdiction is apparent from Articles 45 and 49 of the Convention ..., and from Article 19 and the Court's case-law.[375]

In our view the position adopted by the Court is the only viable option given the object and purpose of the Convention. Indeed, the task entrusted to the Court and the Commission in Article 19 "To ensure the observance of the engagements undertaken by the High Contracting Parties" can only be fulfilled if in the last instance the Strasbourg organs, and not the States, determine the contents of the obligations as well as the validity and scope of reservations pertaining thereto.[376]

The Court's straightforward assertion of jurisdiction in the *Belilos* Case should not obscure the fact that in many cases the question as to the validity of reservations remains open as long as it is not raised in proceedings in

---

372. Council of Europe, Cons. Ass., Ordinary Session 1950, Documents, Part II, Doc. 6, p. 534.
373. The reservations made by the different contracting States are included in *Collected Texts*, *supra* note 136, p. 66 *et seq.*
374. *Infra* pp. 611-613.
375. Judgment of 29 April 1988, A.132 (1988), p. 24.
376. In its report of 5 March 1983, *Temeltasch*, *D & R* 31 (1983), p. 120 (145), the Commission had taken the same position.

connection with an alleged violation of one of the rights and freedoms. This may lead to protracted uncertainty. It would therefore appear to be desirable to set up a special procedure by which the admissibility of reservations can be judged by the Court at the moment at which they are made.

4. Another issue also arose in the *Belilos* Case owing to the fact that, at the time of ratification of the Convention, in addition to two reservations Switzerland had made two interpretative declarations, one of which was at issue before the Court. As a result the Court was faced with "The question whether a declaration described as 'interpretative' must be regarded as a 'reservation'".[377] The Court's extensive analysis of this issue led it to recognize

> that it is necessary to ascertain the original intention of those who drafted the declaration[378]

and subsequently that

> In order to establish the legal character of such a declaration, one must look behind the title given to it and seek to determine the substantive content.[379]

In conclusion the Court set out to examine the validity of the interpretative declaration in question, as in the case of a reservation, in the context of Article 64.[380]

5. In general, reservations must not go beyond what is compatible with the "object and purpose" of the treaty concerned.[381] Under the European Convention, in addition, reservations of a general character are not permitted. Article 64(1) provides this in so many words. The prohibition of general reservations may also be inferred from the first sentence of the first paragraph, which provides that a reservation may only concern "any particular provision". From this it would seem to ensue that, when a reservation is made, the provision of the Convention to which it refers must be expressly mentioned, and the effect of the reservation remains confined exclusively to that provision.

Initially, the Commission did not interpret Article 64(1) restrictively on this point. Thus, in its decision on Appl. 1452/62 the Commission found:

> whereas it is true that this reservation does not make any express reference to Article 6 of the Convention; ... whereas the Commission, in interpreting the terms of the reservation, has to take into consideration the clear intention of the Government ...; whereas, accordingly, the reservation must be extended to cover not only "the measures for the deprivation of liberty" but also the proceedings leading up to a decision by which an accused person is deprived of his liberty in accordance with the Acts mentioned in the

---

377. Judgment of 29 April 1988, A.132 (1988), p. 24.
378. *Ibidem*, pp. 23-24.
379. *Ibidem*, p. 24.
380. *Ibidem*.
381. See Art. 19 of the Vienna Convention of the Law of Treaties of 1969, *International Legal Materials* 8 (1969), pp. 679 *et seq*. See also the advisory opinion of the International Court of Justice on "Reservations to the Convention on the Prevention and the Punishment of the Crime of Genocide", *I.C.J. Reports* 1951, p. 15 (24).

reservation.[382]

The second requirement of the first sentence of Article 64(1) was likewise not applied very stringently by the Commission. This requirement implies that a reservation may be made only "to the extent that any law then in force in its territory is not in conformity with the provisions". The meaning of this phrase is clear. The reservation must be restricted to specified legal measures, which must be indicated explicitly in the reservation. This appears from the second paragraph: "Any reservation made under this Article shall contain a brief statement of the law concerned". Austria had made a reservation in respect of Article 1 of the First Protocol in connection with Part IV and Part V of the State Treaty which Austria has concluded with the Western Allies and the Soviet Union in 1955. A complaint directed against Austria was concerned with a law of 1958, which had been enacted in execution of Part IV of the State Treaty, but which had not been mentioned in the reservation. The Commission nevertheless brought the law within the scope of the Austrian reservation, holding that:

in making a reservation with respect to Parts IV and V of the State Treaty, Austria must necessarily have had the intention of excluding from the scope of the First Protocol everything forming the subject matter of Parts IV and V of the said Treaty; whereas it follows that the Austrian reservation relating to Parts IV and V of the said Treaty must be interpreted as intended to cover all legislative and administrative measures directly related to the subject matter of Parts IV and V of the State Treaty.[383]

More recent case-law, however, shows a more strict approach. Thus, as to the prohibition of general reservations, the Court held in the *Belilos* Case with respect to the above-mentioned interpretative declaration on the part of the Swiss Government[384] that

By "reservation of a general character" in Article 64 is meant in particular a reservation couched in terms that are too vague or broad for it to be possible to determine their exact meaning and scope. While the preparatory work and the Government's explanations clearly show what the respondent State's concern was at the time of ratification, they cannot obscure the objective reality of the actual wording of the declaration. The words "ultimate control by the judiciary over the acts or decisions of the public authorities relating to [civil] rights or obligations or the determination of [a criminal] charge" do not make it possible for the scope of the undertaking by Switzerland to be ascertained exactly, in particular as to which categories of dispute are included and as to whether or

382. Appl. 1452/62, *X v. Austria, Yearbook* VI (1963), p. 268 (276). See also Appl. 473/59, *X v. Austria, Yearbook* II (1958-59), p. 400 (406); Appl. 2432/65, *X v. Austria, Coll.* 22 (1967), p. 124 (127); Appl. 4002/69, *X v. Austria, Yearbook* XIV (1971), p. 178 (186). In a later decision the Commission clearly showed that it wanted to reconsider the position here taken by it. In Appl. 8180/78, *X v. Austria, D & R* 20 (1980), p. 23 (27-28), it held, after an express reference to the case-law just mentioned: "The Commission has now come to the opinion that in view of the various questions which may be raised by the scope of a reservation and its compatibility with Article 64 of the Convention, its previous decisions on this matter could usefully be reconsidered". The reconsideration announced did not take place in this case because the complaint concerned was declared manifestly ill-founded.
383. Appl. 2765/66, *X v. Austria, Yearbook* X (1967), p. 412 (418). See also Appls 1821-1822/63, *Hudetz, Haiek and Von Beringe v. Austria, Yearbook* IX (1966), p. 214 (236).
384. This declaration was worded as follows: "The Swiss Federal Council considers that the guarantee of fair trial in Article 6, paragraph 1 of the Convention, in the determination of civil rights and obligations or any criminal charge against the person in question is intended solely to ensure ultimate control by the judiciary over the acts or decisions of the public authorities relating to such rights or obligations or the determination of such a charge".

not the "ultimate control by the judiciary" takes in the facts of the case. They can therefore be interpreted in different ways, whereas Article 64 § 1 requires precision and clarity. In short, they fall foul of the rule that reservations must not be of a general character.[385]

From this it may be concluded that, according to the Court, the exact sope of the reservation must be deducible from the terms of the reservation.

The requirement contained in Article 64(2) that any reservation shall contain a brief statement of the law concerned has similarly been tightened in more recent case-law. In the *Belilos* Case the Swiss Government attempted to justify its failure to comply with that formality on the basis of the very flexible state-practice in this respect and the argument that Article 64(2) does not take account of the specific and allegedly almost insuperable problems faced by federal States. As to this latter argument, according to the Government,

Switzerland would have had to mention most of the provisions in the twenty-six cantonal codes of criminal procedure and in the twenty-six cantonal codes of criminal procedure, and even hundreds of municipal laws and regulations.[386]

Neither of these arguments were honoured by the Commission or the Court. The Commission, referring to its report in the *Temeltasch* Case, had held that "the undeniable practical difficulties put forward by the Government could not justify the failure to comply with paragraph 2 of Article 64".[387] The Court agreed, adding

that the "brief statement of the law concerned" both constitutes an evidential factor and contributes to legal certainty. The purpose of Article 64 § 2 is to provide a guarantee ... that a reservation does not go beyond the provisions expressly excluded by the State concerned.[388]

Article 64(1) in addition stipulates that the legal measures concerned must already have existed at the time of the signature or ratification of the Convention by the State in question. This unambiguous provision seems to leave room for no other conclusion than that no later law may be brought within the scope of the reservation once it has been made. However, thus far the Strasbourg organs have not held on to the letter of this provision.

Thus, the Commission declared a complaint inadmissible concerning an Austrian Act of 1960 on road traffic. This Act replaced an Act of 1947 and had been enacted after the date of the Austrian reservation in question. The Commission considered that the Act of 1960 was covered by the reservation in view of the fact

that the subject matter covered by the Road Traffic Act of 1947 and the Road Traffic Act of 1960 is substantially the same; whereas, therefore, the latter Act does not have the effect of enlarging, *a posteriori*, the subject matter which is excluded from the competence of the Commission by the above reservation.[389]

---

385. Judgment of 29 April 1988, A.132 (1988), p. 26.
386. *Ibidem*, p. 27.
387. *Ibidem*.
388. *Ibidem*, pp. 27-28.
389. Appl. 2432/65, *X v. Austria, Coll.* 22 (1967), p. 124 (127). See also Appl. 3923/69, *X v. Austria, Coll.* 37 (1971), p. 10 (15).

A similar reasoning was applied by the Commission as well as the Court in the *Campbell and Cosans* Case.[390]

6. The preceding observations concerned reservations with respect to the substantive provisions of the Convention. In addition thereto, and leaving aside the Convention's concluding articles, the Convention comprises two types of provisions: provisions concerning the enjoyment and the restriction of the rights and freedoms (Arts 1 and 13-18), and provisions concerning the supervisory mechanism (Arts 19-57).

With respect to the former category of provisions reservations seem to us impermissible. It is true that the text of Article 64 speaks of "*any* particular provision", but this cannot be considered conclusive. The obligations ensuing from Articles 1 and 13-18 are of such a fundamental importance for the enjoyment of the rights and freedoms laid down in the Convention that restricting them by means of a reservation is incompatible with the "object and purpose" of the Convention, and consequently must be considered inadmissible.

In our view, therefore, the reservation which France has made with respect to Article 15 conflicts with the Convention. This reservation is to the effect that the circumstances specified in Article 16 of the French Constitution and other relevant national legislation regarding proclamation of a state of siege or emergency

> must be understood as complying with the purpose of Article 15 of the Convention, and ... secondly, for the interpretation and application of Article 16 of the Constitution of the Republic, the terms "to the extent strictly required by the exigencies of the situation" shall not restrict the power of the President of the Republic to take "the measures required by the circumstances".[391]

Article 15 in itself is already a highly exceptive clause. It confers on the contracting States the power to derogate from a number of provisions of the Convention in exceptional cases. As such, Article 15 draws the line beyond which the contracting States may not go under the Convention. It must therefore be considered out of the question that this limit could be shifted even further in favour of the States by means of a reservation. This holds true in particular also for the French reservation since its formulation is so wide that in fact the Strasbourg supervision of the implementation of Article 15 is eliminated altogether.

The category of provisions pertaining to the supervisory machinery (Arts 19-57) includes two clauses - Articles 25 and 46 - which have an optional character. The contracting States therefore can remain exempt from the

---

390. See the judgment of 25 February 1982, A.48 (1982), pp. 17-18, in which it was held that the new legislation was no more than an echo of the identical provision from the old legislation and "therefore goes no further than a law in force at a time when the reservation was made". In the Commission's report of 16 May 1980, B.42 (1985), p.39, it is held that the new law "has not the effect of enlarging a posteriori the field which the United Kingdom Government wanted to exclude from the competence of the Commission".
391. See *Collected Texts, supra* note 136, p. 77.

procedures laid down in these provisions without having to make a reservation at the time of ratification. However, from the optional character of these provisions - the competence of the Commission to receive individual applications, and the jurisdiction of the Court - it may also be inferred that the drafters of the Convention meant that for the rest the supervisory mechanism would operate unabridged with regard to each of the contracting States. In our opinion any reservations, particularly in respect of the right of states to lodge complaints (Art. 24), the binding effect of decisions of the Committee of Ministers (Art. 32) and the reporting procedure at the request of the Secretary General (Art. 57) are therefore incompatible with the "object and purpose" of the Convention. It appears from the preamble that the purpose of the Convention was "to take the first steps for the collective enforcement of certain of the Rights stated in the Universal Declaration". Any backing out of the mechanism provided for this "collective enforcement" going beyond that expressly permitted by the Convention would, with respect to the State concerned, hamper this "collective enforcement", and accordingly the purpose of the Convention.

The question of whether reservations are permissible with respect to the optional Articles 25 and 46 themselves was answered affirmatively in the previous edition of this book. The main argument to sustain that conclusion was that a State which may decide not to recognize the competence of the Commission and the Court in question altogether may also recognize it under certain conditions.

In the meantime, on 28 January 1987, the Government of Turkey has made a declaration pursuant to Article 25(1) attaching a number of conditions which boil down to reservations.[392] This declaration and the ensuing debate in litterature[393] have induced us to reconsider our original point of view.

Turkey's declaration contains five conditions. First, the Commission's competence extends only to applications concerning acts or omissions performed within the territory to which the Turkish Constitution is applicable. Secondly, the competence of the Commission does not comprise matters regarding the legal status of military personnel and the system of discipline in the armed forces. The three remaining conditions in fact prescribe the Commission a certain interpretation of the Articles 8, 9, 10 and 11 of the Convention. The first condition is most probably aimed at preventing the Commission from dealing with the situation in Northern Cyprus, to which we have referred in discussing the territorial scope of the Convention.[394] The

---

392. For the text of the declaration, see Council of Europe, *Information Sheet* No. 21, Strasbourg 1988, pp. 3-4.
393. See C. Tomushat, "Turkey's Declaration under Article 25 of The European Convention on Human Rights", in M. Nowak, D. Steuer and H. Tretter (eds), *Fortschritt im Bewusstsein der Grund- und Menschenrechte* (Progress in the Spirit of Human Rights), Festschrift für Felix Ermacora, Kehl am Rhein 1988, pp. 119-138; and J. van der Velden, "Voorbehouden ten aanzien van de ECRM" (Reservations within the framework of the European Convention), *NJCM Bulletin* (1987), pp. 353-365.
394. See *supra* p. 8, note 25.

second condition purports to unilaterally introduce a kind of inherent limitation on the right of complaint of Turkish military personnel. As was pointed out, an approach like that has been rejected in the Strasbourg case-law.[395] Furthermore, this condition conflicts with the requirement contained in Article 64(1) that a reservation must be in respect of any particular provision of the Convention.

The three remaining conditions most clearly run counter to the object and purpose of the Convention. According to its preamble the Convention, *inter alia*, aims at taking "the first steps for the collective enforcement of certain of the Rights stated in the Universal Declaration". Obviously, the machinery for collective enforcement provided for in the Convention cannot effectively function unless the Commission and the Court have the final say in interpreting the Convention. A machinery for collective enforcement is for all practical purposes non-existent if a contracting State by making a reservation to such an effect can dictate to the Commission and/or the Court a specific interpretation. For this reason the conditions contained in the Turkish declaration of 28 January 1987 must be deemed unacceptable.[396]

395. See *supra* pp. 576-577.
396. On 9 March 1990 Turkey renewed its declaration with only a few small amendments.

EPILOGUE

The first edition of this book concluded with a chapter VIII entitled "Final Observations". That chapter basically addressed three issues. First, it attempted an evaluation of the impact of the Convention. Secondly, a number of improvements were suggested with respect to the Convention's functioning in matters of procedure, both at the national and at the international level, as well as with respect to its substantive provisions. Finally, a number of possible future developments relevant to the Convention's functioning were briefly outlined.

The authors decided to delete the chapter on final observations from the present edition for the following reasons. The first reason is a very practical one. Even without an elaborate concluding chapter the size of the present edition is approaching the limits of what is still tolerable. During the eighties the Strasbourg case-law has brought about considerable changes in quantitative as well as qualitative respects. The number of cases dealt with by the Strasbourg organs has increased disproportionately, especially as far as the judgments by the Court are concerned. Furthermore, in qualitative respect - also as a consequence of the quantitative increase - new issues have come up before the Commission and the Court, as a result of which new answers had to be found and sometimes new approaches were chosen. The inclusion of these developments in the present edition has led to a considerable expansion of the preceding chapters as compared with the first edition.

This brings us to the substantive reasons for deleting such a concluding chapter. At various points in the analysis in the preceding chapters comments and suggestions were made with respect to several issues. Obviously they need not be repeated in a concluding chapter. Furthermore, while on the one hand some of our suggestions in the first edition of this book are still topical in the sense that the respective situations which they addressed have remained basically unchanged, in that problems have been left unsolved and/or that suggested improvements have not materialized, on the other hand other opinions voiced by us there, in particular those with respect to possible future developments, seem to have become obsolete. On the one hand those opinions have simply been overtaken by the factual developments, while on the other hand these developments have become so multifacetted and complicated that old projections are now extremely unsettled. Mainly because of the latter reason we now feel unable to conduct a prospective analysis as contained in the first edition. At the time of that writing - 1984 - the situation in Western Europe was stable in the sense that it permitted a more or less educated guess as to the impact of that situation on future developments relevant to the Convention's functioning. In view of the present uncertainties, a similar effort would now amount to crystal-gazing.

Future historians may well characterize the second half of the eighties - up to this very year 1990 - as a revolutionary period, particularly for Europe. Even to contemporaries it is clear that far-reaching shifts were inaugurated. It suffices in this respect to highlight two of the most eye-catching events dating from that period. In 1986 the Member States of the European Communities agreed upon the Single European Act amending the EEC Treaty. Whatever shortcomings may be attributed to this international agreement - particularly from a legal point of view - one thing is beyond doubt: the Single Act signals the unmistakable determination on the part of the Member States to speed up the process of economic integration in Western Europe and to bring it to its logical end. The train of European integration now seems on an irreversible track. Its exact route and precise time-schedule may still be subject to changes, but not so its destination: an internal market and eventually a European union. The claim for a social dimension of this internal market, next to its economic and financial dimensions, has also brought human-rights issues more to the fore.

In sharp contrast with the above are the very recent events in Eastern Europe. Although these have in no way fully crystallized yet, it seems safe to conclude already at this point that they have brought about the total collapse of the legitimacy of the former system of government in the countries concerned. At the present moment it is impossible to predict where the process now set in motion will eventually lead to. Similarly, one has presently at best the beginning of an impression of the consequences resulting from the interplay between developments in Western and Eastern Europe, also as far as the European Convention and other human-rights instruments and procedures are concerned.

In these circumstances we consider it unwarranted to deal with possible future developments with respect to issues such as the relation between the Convention and economic, social and cultural rights, the relation between the Convention and the European Communities, and the future functioning of the Convention in the light of some developments in the contracting States, in a similar fashion as was done in the first edition. The first issue would now seem to be absorbed in the above-mentioned debate on the social dimension of the Community internal market and/or attempts to revitalize the European Social Charter, while the second one is likely to become part of the broader issue of the democratic legitimacy of the European Community. Answers concerning the third issue seem premature in so far as a number of Eastern European States have announced their application for membership of the Council of Europe, thereby setting the stage for accession to the European Convention.

Despite all these uncertainties we cannot resist the temptation to indulge in some crystal-gazing with respect to the Convention's functioning itself. The

Convention's immediate future in our view does not look very bright in all respects. We find it difficult to escape the impression that there is a trend of declining acceptance. After an initial period during which the contracting States had to get accustomed to the new phenomenon of an international instrument dealing with such a vital matter as human rights on the basis of a penetrating supervisory mechanism, the Convention entered a relatively prolonged period characterized by acceptance on the part of the contracting States. There was, of course, occasional criticism from varying quarters on individual judgments of the Court, depending on whether the judgment concerned was considered as going too far or, conversely, not far enough. On the whole, however, the middle course which the Court - in the words of its former President[1] - was steering met with approval. In the first edition of this book we summarily described this situation by the catchword "loyalty", meaning that on the whole the contracting States did not systematically curtail the rights and freedoms protected by the Convention and, most important of all, did not engage in procedural obstruction, not even in cases concerning politically sensitive issues.

Since that time the tide seems to have been turning to a certain extent. In recent years one may discern - even in contracting States which traditionally could be counted among the most Convention-minded ones - a growing dissatisfaction with and sometimes even obstruction to the consequences resulting from the judicial activism which the Court is alleged to practise. Criticism of this kind is usually not manifested through formal objections on the part of governments, but in more subtle ways. Consequently, the trend discerned is not easy to document.[2] Nevertheless, on the basis of various more or less clear indications a body of opinion is emerging that the Convention's success is now starting to backfire.[3]

As was accentuated in the previous edition of this book, the Convention's success was to a considerable extent derived from its dynamic character, resulting in a protection which has been constantly growing stronger. In that context reference was made to the so-called "Strasbourg spring", indicating that both the number and the importance of the cases decided by the Strasbourg organs was increasing and that, moreover, the interpretation of at least some of the Convention's provisions evolved in a direction favouring the

1. G.J. Wiarda, *Rechterlijke voortvarendheid en rechterlijke terughoudendheid bij de toepassing van de Europese Conventie tot bescherming van de rechten van de mens* (Judicial activism and judicial restraint in the application of the European Convention on Human Rights), The Hague 1986, p. 18.
2. However, the reaction of the British Government to the Court's Brogan judgment constitutes a case in point; see G.J.H. van Hoof, "The Future of the European Convention on Human Rights", *Netherlands Quarterly of Human Rights* (1989), pp. 451-463 (453-455).
3. Thus, within the framework of a discussion of reservations to the Convention MacDonald puts forward: "It is argued that the teleological and purposive construction by the Court is imposing obligations that States never intended to accept at the time of ratification". It is added furthermore that "Indeed it is understood that some States have considered withdrawing from the Convention so that they may reratify subject to more accommodating reservations". R.J. MacDonald, "The margin of appreciation in the jurisprudence of the European Court of Human Rights", in: *International law and the time of its codification; Essays in honour of Roberto Ago*, Milan 1987, pp. 187-208 (208).

interests of individual applicants over those of respondent States.

The trend of declining acceptance may well culminate in the disapproval or even rejection of what certain circles in the contracting States regard as judicial activism on the part of the Court. In the view of at least some of them the progressive development of the protection emanating from the Convention is now approaching the limits of what is acceptable. If this trend continues, the danger of stagnation or even of a downward spiral becomes imminent. The success or failure of international instruments, including those like the European Convention, in the end depends on the political will of the States involved. Legal arguments, however cogent they may be, in the final analysis seldom override political considerations when States feel that their vital interests are at stake.

In our view, it would be a grave mistake, also from a political point of view, if the contracting States were now to try, in one way or another, to decrease the effectiveness of the Convention's supervisory machinery in reaction to the Court's alleged judicial activism. Judicial activism, if it occurs, does not arise of its own accord. It usually emerges in response to problems arising from acts or omissions of the other branches of government. In national legal systems, too, when individuals or groups are dissatisfied because certain issues in their view are insufficiently dealt with by the legislature and/or the executive, they not infrequently turn to the courts as a last resort. As a consequence of the prohibition of denial of justice the courts are usually forced to come up with some kind of decision, which in the situations as perceived here often imply a filling of the gaps left by the legislative and/or the executive authorities. In such situations, which as far as we can judge prevail in various contracting States, the courts in fact play the role of a safety net or an exhaustion valve as a kind of substitute legislature. Efforts to remove or weaken this safety net or exhaustion valve obviously do not solve the underlying problems, but rather create the danger that the underlying tensions manifest themselves in another, less peaceful, manner than through institutionalized court procedures. This holds good *mutatis mutandis* for the European Court of Human Rights.

It should be added that in the present discussion there may be more at stake than simply more or less judicial activism. The independence and the ensuing role of the judiciary are part and parcel of the concept of the democratic society based on the rule of law. That concept is reinforced every time its principles are adhered to, particularly when the consequences resulting therefrom seem troublesome.

In the meantime the Strasbourg organs may experience their position as a difficult one. They may find themselves faced with a choice between (further) giving in to the pressure of taking more account of the interests of the contracting States in interpreting the Convention (*raison d'état* approach) and sticking as much as possible to the Convention's object and purpose of protecting individual rights and freedoms. Obviously the Court and the Commission cannot completely ignore the above-mentioned signals from the governments of the contracting States. To be sure, however, the interests of States are already duly taken into account in the Strasbourg case-law - and perhaps even more than that - through a very broad application of the margin of appreciation doctrine as described above. On the other hand, it should be remembered that an important part of the "constituency" of the Strasbourg organs is to be found in the citizens of the contracting States and that the Convention's success up to now is to no small extent derived from the dynamic character of the case-law constantly improving the level of protection of human rights. In that light it would be paradoxical if in an era in which the peoples of Eastern Europe revolt because they have been denied rights and freedoms like those contained in the Convention, the level of protection of those very rights and freedoms in the democratic societies of Western Europe were to be lowered.

BIBLIOGRAPHY

Alkema, E.A., *Studies over Europese Grondrechten* (Studies on European Basic Rights), Deventer 1978.

Alkema, E.A., "The third-party applicability or "Drittwirkung" of the ECHR", *Protecting Human Rights: The European Dimension, Studies in Honour of Gérard J. Wiarda*, Köln 1988, pp. 33-45.

Amnesty International, *Turkey, Brutal and Systematic Abuse of Human Rights*, Londen 1989.

Asbeck, F. van, "Quelques aspects du contrôle international non judiciaire de l'application par les gouvernements des Conventions internationales", *Liber Amicorum in honour of J.P.A. Francois*, Leyden 1959, pp. 27-41.

Bay, Ch., "A Human Rights Approach to Transnational Politics", *Universal Human Rights*, 1(1979), pp. 19-42.

Betten, L., *The Incorporation of Fundamental Rights in the Legal Order of the European Communities*, The Hague 1985.

Boven, Th.C. van, *"Distinguishing Criteria for Human Rights"*, *The International Dimensions of Human Rights*, deel 1, Paris 1982, pp. 43-59.

Buergenthal, Th. and Kewenig, W., "Zum Begriff der Civil Rights in Artikel 6 Absatz 1 der Europäischen Menschenrechtskonvention", *Archiv des Völkerrechts*, 13 (1966/67), p. 393.

Burton, S., "Comment on 'Empty Ideas'; Logical Positivist Analysis of Equality and Rules", 91 *The Yale Law Journal* 1982, pp. 1136-1152.

Castberg, F., *The European Convention on Human Rights*, Leyden 1974.

Chemerinsky, E., "In Defense of Equality: A Reply to Professor Westen", 81 *Michigan Law Review* 1983, pp. 575-595.

Committee of Experts, *Explanatory Report on the Second to Fifth Protocols to the European Convention for the Protection of Human Rights and Fundamental Freedoms*, H(71)11, Strasbourg 1971.

Council of Europe, *Case Law Topics*, No. 1, "Human Rights in Prison", Strasbourg 1971.

Council of Europe, *Case Law Topics*, No. 2, "Family Life", Strasbourg 1972.

Council of Europe, *Case Law Topics*, No. 3, "Bringing an application before the European Commission on Human Rights", Strasbourg 1972.

Council of Europe, *Case Law Topics*, No. 4, "Human Rights and their limitations", Strasbourg 1973.

Council of Europe, *Collected Edition of the "Travaux Préparatoires" of the European Convention on Human Rights*, Vol. I-IV, The Hague 1977.

Council of Europe, *European Convention on Human Rights, Collected Texts*, Strasbourg 1987.

Council of Europe, *Human Rights Files, Outline of the position of the individual applicant before the Eurepean Court of Human Rights (1)*, DDH (78)3, Strasbourg, 28 maart 1978.

Council of Europe, *Manual of the Council of Europe*, Londen 1970.

Council of Europe, European Commission on Human Rights, *Survey of Activities and Statistics*, Strasbourg 1988.

Council of Europe, European Commission on Human Rights, *Survey of Activities and Statistics*, Strasbourg 1989.

Council of Europe, *Stock-Taking on the European Convention on Human Rights*, Strasbourg 1979.

Council of Europe, *Stock-Taking on the European Convention on Human Rights*, Strasbourg 1981.

Council of Europe, *Stock-Taking of the European Convention on Human Rights*, Strasbourg 1984.

Council of Europe, *Stock-Taking of the European Convention on Human Rights (1954-1984)*, Strasbourg 1984.

Council of Europe, *Stock-Taking of the European Convention on Human Rights*, Strasbourg 1985.

Council of Europe, *Stock-Taking of the European Convention on Human Rights*, Strasbourg 1986.

Council of Europe, *Stock-Taking of the European Convention on Human Rights*, Strasbourg 1987.

Council of Europe, *The Protection of Human Rights in Europe*, Strasbourg 1981.

D'Amato, A., "Is Equality a Totally Empty Idea?", 81 *Michigan Law Review* 1983, pp. 600-603.

Drzemczewski, A., *European Human Rights Convention in Domestic Law; A Comparative Study*, Oxford 1983.

Drzemczewski, A., "The domestic status of the European Convention on Human Rights: New dimensions", *Legal Issues of European Integration* (1977), pp. 1-85.

Drzemczewski, A., "A 'non-decision' of the Committee of Ministers under Article 32(1) of the European Convention on Human Rights: The East African-Asian Cases", *Modern Law Review* 1978, pp. 337-342.

Dijk, P. van, "International Law and the Promotion and Protection of Human Rights", *Wayne Law Review* 1978, pp. 1529-15553.

Dijk, P. van, "The Interpretation of "Civil Rights and Obligations" by the European Court of Human Rights; One more Step to take", *Protecting Human Rights; The European Dimension, Studies in honour of Gérard J. Wiarda*, Köln 1988, pp. 131-143.

Dijk, P. van, "The Benthem Case and its Aftermath in the Netherlands", *Netherlands International Law Review* 1987, pp. 5-24.

Dijk, P. van, *Judicial Review of Governmental Action and the Requirement of an Interest to Sue*, The Hague 1980.

Dijk, P. van, "A European Ombudsman for Human Rights: Reopening a Discussion", *RDH* 10 (1977), pp. 187-211.

Dijk, P. van, "Domestic Status of Human Rights Treaties and the attitude of the Judiciary; The Dutch Case", *Progress in the Spirit of Human Rights; Festschrift für Felix Ermacora*, Kehl am Rhein 1988.

Edeson, W.R. and Wooldridge, F., "European Community Law and Fundamental Human Rights; some recent decisions of the European Court and National Courts", *Legal Issues of European Integration* (1976/1), pp. 1-55.

Eissen, M.-A., "La Convention et les devoirs des Individues", *La protection des droits de l'homme dans le cadre européen*, Parijs 1961, pp. 167-194.

Eissen, M.-A., "The European Convention on Human Rights and the United Nations Covenant on Civil and Political Rights: Problems of Coexistence", *Buffalo Law Review* 1972, p. 181.

Eissen, M.A., "L'Autonomie de l'article 14 de la Convention européenne des Droits de l'Homme dans la jurisprudence de la Commission", *Mélanges offert á Polys Modinos*, Paris 1968, pp. 122-145.

Fawcett, J.E.C., *The Application of the European Convention on Human Rights*, Oxford 1969.

Fribergh, E., "The Commission Secretariat's handling of provisional files", *Protecting Human Rights: The European Dimension, Studies in Honour of Gérard J. Wiarda*, Köln 1988, pp. 181-191.

Furrer, H.P., "La pratique des Etats-Membres du Conseil de l'Europe", *La circulation des informations et le droit international*, Colloque de Strasbourg, Paris 1978, pp. 65-85.

Golsong, H., "Die eigenartige Rolle des Ministerkomitees des Europarates als eine der beiden Endentscheidungsinstanzen im Rahmen der MRK", *EuGRZ* 1975, pp. 448-449.

Golsong, H., "Implementation of International Protection of Human Rights", *RCADI* 110 (1963-111), pp. 1-151.

Graefrath, B., Menschenrechte und internationale Kooperation; *10 Jahre Praxis des Internationales Menschenrechtskomitees*, Berlin 1988.

Greenawolt, A., "How Empty is the Idea of Equality?", 83 *Columbia Law Journal* 1983, pp. 1167-1185.

Guradze, H., *Die Europäische Menschenrechtskonvention*, Berlin 1968.

Guradze, H., "Die Schutzrichtung der Grundrechtsnormen in der Europäischen Menschenrechtskonvention", *Festschrift Nipperdey*, deel II 1965, pp. 759-769.

Hahne, M.M., *Das Drittwirkungsproblem in der Europäischen Konvention zum Schutz der Menschenrechte und Grundfreiheiten*, Heidelberg 1973.

Hoof, G.J.H. van, "The Protection of Human Rights and the Impact of Emergency Situations under International Law with Special Reference to the Present Situation in Chile", *RDH* 10 (1977), pp. 228-232.

Hoof, G.J.H. van, *Rethinking the Sources of International Law*, Deventer 1983

Hoof, G.J.H. van, "The Future of the European Convention on Human Rights", *Netherlands Quarterly of Human Rights* 1989, pp. 451-463.

Jacobs, F.G., *The European Convention on Human Rights*, Oxford 1985.

Kapteyn, P.J.G. and VerLoren van Themaat, P., *Introduction to the Law of the European Communities*, Deventer (second edition) 1989.

Krüger, H., "The European Commission of Human Rights", *HRLJ* Vol. 1(1980), pp. 66-87.

Krüger, H., Nørgaard, C.A., "Reflections concerning friendly settlement under the European Convention on Human Rights", *Protecting Human Rights: The European Dimension*, Studies in Honour of Gérard J. Wiarda, Köln 1988, pp. 329-334.

Leuprecht, P., "The Protection of Human Rights by Political Bodies. The example of the Committee of Ministers of the Council of Europe", *Progress in the Spirit of Human Rights*, Strasbourg 1988, pp. 95-107.

MacDonald, R.J., "The margin of appreciation in the jurisprudence of the European Court on Human Rights", *International law and the time of its codification; Essays in honour of Roberto Ago*, Milan 1987, pp. 187-208.

Mahoney, P. "Does Article 57 of the European Convention on Human Rights serve any useful purpose?" *Protecting Human Rights: The European Dimension, Studies in Honour of Gérard J. Wiarda*, Köln 1988, pp. 373-393.

Meuwissen, D.H.M., *De Europese Conventie en het Nederlandse Recht* (The European Convention and Dutch Law, Leyden 1968.

Meyer, J. de, "International Control Machinery", *The European Convention on Human Rights in relation to other International Instruments for the Protection of Human Rights, Colloquy on Human Rights*, Athens 21-22 september 1978, Strasbourg 1978.

Mikaelson, L., *European protection of human rights*, Alphen a/d Rijn 1980.

Monconduit, F., *La Commission Européenne des Droits de l'Homme*, Leyden 1965.

Morgan, A., "European Convention on Human Rights, Article 32: What is wrong?", *Human Rights Review* 1976, pp. 157-176.

Netherlands Advisory Committee on Human Rights and Foreign Policy, *Towards a Semi Permanent European Commission of Human Rights*, Report No. 8, April 1989.

Newman, Frank C., "Natural Justice Due Process and the New International Covenants on Human Rights; Prospectus", *Public Law*, winter 1967, pp. 274-313.

Nowak, M., "The Effectiveness of the International Covenant on Civil and Political Rights - Stocktaking after the first eleven sessions of the UN-Human Rights Committee", *HRLJ* , Vol. 1 (1980), pp. 136-170.

Nowak, M., "Survey of decisions of the Human Rights Committee", *HRLJ*, parts 1-4 (1982), pp. 207-220; *HRLJ*, parts 2-4 (1984), pp. 199-219; *HRLJ*, parts 2-4 (1986), pp. 287-307.

Nowak, M., *CCPR-Kommentar zum UNO-Pakt über bürgerliche und politische Rechte und zum Fakultativprotokoll*, Kehl am Rhein 1988.

O'Donnell, T.A., "The Margin of Appreciation Doctrine: Standards in the Jurisprudence of the European Court of Human Rights", *Human Rights Quarterly* 1982, pp. 474-496.

Opsahl, T., "The Convention and the Right to Respect for Family life", A.H. Robertson (ed.), *Privacy and Human Rights*, Manchester 1973, p. 182.

Opsahl, T., "Ten years coexistence Strasbourg-Geneva", *Protecting Human Rights; The European Dimension, Studies in Honour of Gérard J. Wiarda*, Köln 1988, pp. 431-439.

Pahr, W., "Etude Fonctionelle des Organes Européens de Protection Internationales des Droits de l'Homme", *RDH* 2 (1969), pp. 199-207.

Partsch, K., *Die Rechte und Freiheiten der europäischen Menschenrechtskonvention*, Berlin 1966.

Peaslee, A.J., *Constitutions of Nations*, third revised edition, Vol. III Europe, The Hague 1968.

Pelloux, R., "L'Arrêt de la Cour Européenne des Droits de l'Homme dans l'affaire Belge (Exception Préliminaire)", *Annuaire Français de Droit International* 1967, pp. 205-216.

Polak, C.H.F., "Het Europees verdrag tot bescherming van de rechten van de mens en de fundamentele vrijheden" (The European Convention for the protection of human rights and fundamental freedoms), *Rechten van de mens in mundiaal en Europees perspectief* (Human Rights in worldwide and European perspective), 2nd ed., Utrecht 1980, pp. 58-76.

Report of the Committee of Experts to the Committee of Ministers of the Council of Europe, "Problems arising from the co-existence of the United Nations Covenants on Human Rights and the European Convention on Human Rights, Differences as regards the Rights Guaranteed", *H(70)7* september 1970.

Rasenack, Ch., "Civil Rights and Obligations or Droits et Obligations de caractère civil - Two Crucial legal determinations in Article 6(1) of the European Convention for the protection of Human Rights and Fundamental Freedoms", *RDH* 3(1970), pp. 51-81.

Rehof, L.A. and Gulman, C. (eds.), *Human Rights in Domestic Law and Development Assistance Policies of the Nordic Countries*, Dordrecht 1989.

Robertson, A.H., *Human Rights in the World*, 2nd ed., Manchester 1982.

Rosenne, S., *The Law and Practice of the International Court*, Leyden 1965.

Shaw, M.N., *International Law*, Cambridge 1986.

Sørensen, M., "Obligations of a State Party to a treaty as regards its municipal law", *Human Rights in National and International Law*, Manchester 1968, pp. 11-31.

Tomuschat, C., "Evolving Procedural Rules: The UN Human Rights Committee's First Two Years of Dealing with Individual Communications", *HRLJ*, Vol 1 (1980), pp. 249-257.

Tomuschat, C., "Turkey's Declaration under Article 25 of the European Convention on Human Rights", *Progress in the Spirit of Human Rights; Festschrift für Felix Ermacora*, Kehl am Rhein 1988, pp. 119-138.

Trechsel, S., "Das Verflixte Siebene? - Bemerkungen zum 7. Zusatzprotokoll zur EMRK", *Progress in the Spirit of Human Rights, Festschrift für Felix Ermacora*, Kehl am Rhein 1988, pp. 195-211.

Trechsel, S., "The right to liberty and security of the person - Article 5 of the European Convention on Human Rights in the Strasbourg case-law", *HRLJ* (1980), pp. 88-135.

United Nations, Centre for Human Rights, *A Compilation of International Instruments*, New York 1988.

Vasak, K., *La Convention Européenne des Droits de l'Homme*, Paris 1964.

Velde, J. van de, "Voorbehouden ten aanzien van de ECRM" (Reservations within the frame-work of the European Convention), *NJCM-Bulletin* 1987, pp. 353-365.

Velu, J., "Le problème de l'application aux jurisdictions administratives des règles de la Convention européenne des droits de l'homme relatives à la publicité des audiences et des jugements", *RDIDC* 1961, pp. 129-171.

Velu, J., "The European Convention on Human Rights and the Right to Respect for Private Life, the Home and Communications", in A.H. Robertson (ed.), *Privacy and Human Rights, Third International Colloquy*, Brussels 1970, Manchester 1973.

Verzijl, J.H.W., *International Law in Historical Perspective*, deel I, Leyden 1968.

Visscher, Ch. de, "La déni de justice en droit international", *RCADI* 52, (1935-11), pp. 364-442.

Weil, G.L., *The European Convention on Human Rights, European Aspects*, Series C, no. 12, Leyden, A.W. Sijthoff.

Westen, P., "The Empty Idea of Equality", 95 *Harvard Law Review* (1982-1983), pp. 537-595.

Westen, P., "The Meaning of Equality in Law, Science, Math and Morals: A Reply", 81 *Michigan Law Review* 1983, pp. 604-663.

Westen, P., "On 'Confusing Ideas', Reply", 91 *The Yale Law Journal* 1982, pp. 1153-1165.

Westen, P., "To Lure the Tarantula from Its Hole: A Response", 83 *Columbia Law Journal* 1983, pp. 1186-1208.

Wiarda, G.J., "Rechterlijke voortvarendheid en rechterlijke terughoudendheid bij de toepassing van de Europese Conventie tot bescherming van de rechten van de mens" (Judicial activism and judicial restraint in the application of the European Convention on Human Rights), The Hague 1986.

Zanghi, C., "The Effectiveness and Efficiency of the Guarantees of Human Rights enshrined in the European Convention on Human Rights", *Proceedings of the Fourth International Colloque about the European Convention on Human Rights*, Council of Europe, Strasbourg 1976.

APPENDIX I
TABLE OF DECISIONS OF THE COMMISSION
CONCERNING ADMISSIBILITY

631

APPENDIX II
TABLE OF REPORTS OF THE COMMISSION CONCERNING THE MERITS

635

APPENDIX III
TABLE OF JUDGMENTS OF THE COURT

= Cases exclusively referred to the Court by the respondent State
+ Cases referred to the Court by the respondent State and subsequently by the Commission
* Cases referred to the Court by the Commission and subsequently by the respondent State
# Cases exclusively referred to the Court by the Commission

638

APPENDIX IV
TABLE OF RESOLUTIONS OF THE COMMITTEE OF MINISTERS

SUBJECT INDEX